# Praise for H. G. WELLS

"Wells almost rivals Swift." —*Spectator* (U.K.)

"Wells is less a man of letters than a literature."
—**JORGE LUIS BORGES**, author of *Ficciones, Labyrinths,* and *The Aleph*

"Thinking people are in some sense Wells's own creation. . . . The minds of us all, and therefore the physical world, would be perceptibly different if Wells had never existed."
—**GEORGE ORWELL**, author of *1984* and *Animal Farm*

"I have the highest respect for Wells's imaginative genius."
—**JULES VERNE**, author of *Twenty Thousand Leagues under the Sea, From the Earth to the Moon,* and *A Journey to the Center of the Earth*

"Still fresh and enjoyable. . . . Wells's scientific romances were not youthful aberrations or escapist fantasies, but works of art with unique relevance for our times. . . . He believed—though not blindly—that men were capable of improvement and might one day build sane and peaceful societies on all the worlds that lay within their reach. We need this faith now, as never before, in the history of our species."
—**ARTHUR C. CLARKE**, honorary vice president of the H. G. WELLS SOCIETY, and author of *2001: A Space Odyssey*

"Wells contrives to give over humanity into the clutches of the Impossible and yet manages to keep it down (or up) to its humanity, to its flesh, blood, sorrow, folly."
—**JOSEPH CONRAD**, author of *Heart of Darkness*

Wells's greatest gift was his ability to range widely through this world, inventing characters whose actions mirror the enormous social anxiety and who each represent a class caught in flux. . . . Wells's efforts seem touchingly brave and might serve as a model for those who want to expand, once more, the province of the novel."
—**ANDREA BARRETT**, National Book Award-winning author of *The Voyage of the Narwhal* and *Ship Fever*

"I personally consider the greatest of English living writers to be H. G. Wells."
—**UPTON SINCLAIR**, Pulitzer Prize–winning author of *The Jungle* and *Mental Radio*

"[Wells's novels] achieve a near poetry which makes them part of the popular mythology of their age. . . . The best of his work has a vitality, a verve, an imaginative compulsion unsurpassed by any of his contemporaries."
—**N. C. NICHOLSON**, author of *H. G. Wells*

T0099257

H. G. Wells from the *Hulton-Deutsch Collection* / CORBIS

# The H. G. Wells Reader

## *A Complete Anthology from Science Fiction to Social Satire*

Edited by John Huntington

TAYLOR TRADE PUBLISHING
*Lanham • New York • Oxford*

First Taylor Trade Publishing edition 2003

This Taylor Trade Publishing paperback edition of *The H. G. Wells Reader* is an original publication. It is published by arrangement with the editor.

Published by Taylor Trade Publishing
A Member of the Rowman & Littlefield Publishing Group
4501 Forbes Boulevard, Suite 200
Lanham, Maryland 20706

Distributed by National Book Network

**Library of Congress Cataloging-in-Publication Data**

Wells, H. G. (Herbert George), 1866–1946
  The H.G. Wells reader : a complete anthology from science fiction to
social satire / edited by John Huntington.—1st Taylor Trade Pub. ed.
     p. cm.
Includes bibliographical references.
  ISBN 0-87833-306-1 (pbk. : alk. paper) ISBN: 978-0-87833-306-6
  1. Science fiction, English. 2. Satire, English. I. Huntington,
John, 1940– II. Title.
PR5772 .H865 2003
823'.912—dc21

                                                2003002119

∞ ™ The paper used in this publication meets the minimum requirements of American National Standard for Information Sciences—Permanence of Paper for Printed Library Materials, ANSI/NISO Z.39.48-1992.
Manufactured in the United States of America.

# Contents

# Introduction

For the first half of the twentieth century H. G. Wells was a tremendously popular fiction writer, an influential thinker, and a widely heeded voice of insight and rationality. George Orwell's remark that Wells was *too* sane to be of much help in the dark years of the late 1930s follows his acknowledgment that for young people at the time Wells had been the most important writer in the first twenty years of the century. The comment also implies that it is in relation to Wells that one can calibrate the crises in modern history. Wells's opinions on biology, on the novel, on politics, on sexuality startled and made people rethink their ideas.

As the works included here should amply demonstrate, Wells's fiction renders with complexity, intelligence, and flair crucial modern situations. At the most obvious, he engages increasingly serious issues of technology and the possibilities of the future. He is an important Darwinian. He may be the greatest English utopianist. He has few rivals as a comic writer. Finally—though this is a quality that is seldom acknowledged as a virtue—he brings to the level of art the experience and understanding of the lower classes. Only Dickens is his match in this respect. Put these virtues together and you have an art full of the richness we associate with the great realist novels, enlivened by an ironic intelligence of the first order, and engaged on important subjects even when most fanciful.

◆

Wells lived an extraordinarily full life whose early parts are especially important for an understanding of his angle of vision and as a measure of his accomplishment. By all rights, given his class origins, his parents' vision, and his upbringing, he should have frittered his life away as a clerk who might rise to middle-level manager. He is, in a very special sense, a "self-made man," not in the usual American sense of amassing a fortune for himself (though he did that, too), but in the sense that through intelligence and will he fashioned a poor, small, sickly boy into a figure of worldwide intellectual influence.

Sarah Wells's dream was to establish her son's secure future by apprenticing him as a draper's assistant in a department store. Sarah herself was the head domestic servant at Up Park, a large country house which, though it offered the young Wells a good library, also, especially with its tunnel from the kitchen to the main house, came to symbolize for him oppression and inefficiency. Sarah Wells soon got H. G. a place in an emporium, and when he was dismissed after a brief tenure she pulled all the strings at her disposal to get him another place. This one he endured for two years. He finally insisted against both his parents' wishes that he be allowed to go to school, and an arrangement was established with Horace Byatt, who ran a school for boys, that Wells, a very bright boy, could attend as an assistant teacher. Byatt and he developed a scheme whereby Wells would teach himself a subject by cramming from textbooks, then take a national exam on the subject, and by doing exceptionally well earn scholarship money for the school. Both parties benefited: Byatt financially, and Wells by obtaining an education, and even more, by teaching himself that he could get along by using his mind.

◆

This period of intellectual scramble paid off when Wells earned a scholarship to the Normal School of Science in South Kensington, the technical college recently established as the model for a new kind of scientific education by T. H. Huxley, from the beginning the greatest defender of Darwin's theory of evolution. During his first year Wells studied biology under Huxley himself, and much later in his *Experiment in Autobiography* he would call it "the most educational year of my life." The next two years were less exciting, and Wells's academic work declined—in part due to poorer teachers (Huxley would be a hard act to follow), and in part due to an understandable burnout. Wells managed to get a degree, but he left the college doubting that he wanted a career in science. For the next few years he made a living tutoring medical students in biology, and his very first book was a textbook on the subject.

Biology was not Wells's only interest during this period, however. He also began writing imaginative fiction for the college literary magazine, and the very first beginning draft of *The Time Machine* was published in *The Science Schools Journal* in 1888 as "The Chronic Argonauts." He also fell in love with his cousin, Isabel, and in 1891 he married her and set up a house in which they lived with her mother. In 1894, after an affair with a former student, Amy Catherine Robbins, Wells divorced Isabel and married Miss Robbins, whom he always called "Jane." The marriage lasted until Jane's death in 1928, and, despite Wells's fame and his promiscuity, she maintained a comfortable and stable household on which he much depended.

◆

During this early period Wells cobbled together a living with teaching and writing. Although in poor health and overworked, he nevertheless published a number of articles on science, especially on Darwinism, put out a steady stream of literary reviews, and developed his own comic voice in witty sketches. In the fall of 1894, at the encouragement of W. E. Henley, he again set to work on *The Time Machine*, which he published first serially and then as a book in 1895. It was greeted with great acclaim, and Wells's life changed. Writing "for dear life," he produced in the next five years the body of work that would establish the genre he called "the scientific romance": *The Island of Doctor Moreau* (1896), *The Invisible Man* (1896), *The War of the Worlds* (1898), *When the Sleeper Wakes* (1899), *The First Men in the Moon* (1901), as well as three collections of short stories, most of which are in the imaginative-scientific mode that he was inventing. He also, it should be noted, found time to write, in addition to numerous articles and reviews, three other novels: *The Wonderful Visit* (1895), about an angel who accidentally comes to earth; *The Wheels of Chance* (1896), the comic story of a draper's assistant on a cycling holiday; and the autobiographical *Love and Mr. Lewisham* (1900).

Wells's restless imagination prevented his contenting himself with the success of a genre fiction writer. In 1901, with the publication of *Anticipations of the Reaction of Mechanical and Scientific Progress upon Human Life and Thought*, he opened up a new dimension of his talent. This vision of the world 100 years later—with detailed descriptions of vastly improved transportation, the growth of suburbs, and a new generosity of mind arising from the emancipation from hard labor—earned him a second reputation as a forecaster. The book is often cited as the first such work in the forecasting genre. On the basis of this book Beatrice and Sidney Webb, the leaders of The Fabian Society, chose to pursue his acquaintance, and for the next six years he was an active and influential—and disruptive—member of the Society. The possibility of actually guiding social change led to a new direction in Wells's work. He began to write Socialist tracts, such as *Mankind in the Making* (1903), *New Worlds for Old* (1908), and the brilliant pamphlet "This Misery of Boots" (1907). In addition, he increasingly indulged his utopian proclivities, not only in *A Modern Utopia* (1905), but in novels like *The Food of the Gods* (1904) and *In the Days of the Comet* (1906), which start from a familiar scientific romance or social narrative but culminate in a wholly new world.

◆

In 1908 Wells outraged the Fabian society by engaging in a love affair with Amber Reeves, a Cambridge student and daughter of two members of the Society. The affair was, in one respect, a consequence of ideas about what used to be called "free love" that Wells had begun to preach in *A Modern Utopia* and *In the Days of the Comet*. From this time forth Wells became promiscuous, and, with the agreement of Jane, he often kept another house. When the young Rebecca West wrote a dismissive review of Wells's 1911 novel, *Marriage*, they became acquainted, fell rapturously in love, soon had a son (Anthony West, who became a novelist in his own right and wrote an admiring memoir about his father), and stayed together for ten years. The breakup, when it finally came in 1922, was acrimonious.

Wells's life was a long one: after the breakup with West he still had twenty-four productive years ahead. He lived long enough to hear of the defeat of fascism and the dropping of the atomic bomb on Hiroshima. In the 1920s and 1930s he devoted himself increasingly to a massive educational project, a "Bible of Civilization." *The Outline of History* (1920), *The Science of Life* (1930), and *The Work, Wealth and Happiness of Mankind* (1931), the last two written in collaboration, were huge encyclopedic works intended to offer the common reader insight into areas of thought that are important for thinking through the possibilities of the future. Although he continued to write fiction steadily, he was recognized in those last decades less as a novelist than as a public intellectual of worldwide reputation and many interests. As totalitarian censorship and persecution became more prevalent, Wells served as international president of the PEN club. In 1939, as discussion of the establishment of the United Nations began, he served as the first chairman of the commission that eventually, under the chairmanship of Lord Stankey, issued "The Declaration of Human Rights." In the early 1940s he wrote polemical articles about the state of Europe and the war, but by 1945 he had lost some crucial element of energy and optimism. *Mind at the End of Its Tether*, Wells's last book, despairs about the future.

Wells's poor and unpromising origins give him an ideological perspective rare in English literature. He combines a cynicism about the world that he inhabits, a social anger that expresses itself in visions of apocalypse, a strong and unself-pitying ethic of work and its rewards, and a utopian dream of a better situation. His successful escape from the drudgery that his mother had planned for him, his scientific training, and his audacious sense that a mind can solve even the most seemingly intractable problem give him a special and original repertory of devices and expectations. Finally, what is often called his "bumptiousness," a quality of cheerful aggressiveness, is both a resource for him and a handicap that he has to overcome. In class-conscious England he will always have to struggle to assure himself and the world that he is a legitimate resident of the sophisticated and generally aristocratic world of "literature." One of his greatest literary accomplishments is his ability to use style to enter that otherwise unattainable literary social space without entirely sacrificing the painful and disruptive ideological understanding that he earned via his upbringing.

A paradoxical advantage of a lower-class background is an ability to take a comic view of the poor and the oppressed without demeaning them the way a more privileged perspective might. Wells puts this comedy to intellectual use. In *The Wheels of Chance*, the novel that he wrote immediately after *The Time Machine*, he performs a magnificent comedy about class difference. Comedy permits Wells to look squarely at the outrageous irrationality of human behavior in the world and render it calmly and in detail. The spottily educated working man confronting the larger worlds of politics and wealth becomes a favorite device. Comedy even gives Wells a realistic and ironic perspective on the basis of his own deepest and most earnest political positions. Under the comic gaze, the rationality that inspires the utopian visions is itself revealed as foolishly ambitious, and humanity is displayed as inadequate to the promise of a utopian technology. From the provincial selfishness and distrust that thwart Griffen's ambitions (themselves revealed to be *ruthlessly* selfish) in *The Invisible Man*, to the ignorance and incompetence of Mr. and Mrs. Skinner, who let loose the Food of the

Gods, the complacent pretensions of human reason are subjected to a withering inspection by Wells's comic spirit.

♦

Wells is always ready to destroy the world. In stories of devastating assault, he is as much on the side of the attackers as that of besieged humanity. As he said to a friend while writing *The War of the Worlds*, "I'm doing the dearest little serial for Pearson's new magazine in which I completely wreck and sack Woking—killing my neighbours in painful and eccentric ways—then proceed via Kingston and Richmond to London, which I sack, selecting South Kensington for feats of peculiar atrocity" (Mackenzie 113). He would talk of "my Martians." If Wells humiliates the anarchist in "The Stolen Bacillus," it is not before he has depicted—in the voice of the scientist it should be noted—the terrible destruction the bacillus could cause. It is remarkable how many of his tales end with disaster even when there is the possibility of a happy ending. "The Country of the Blind," in the original version that is included here, ends with Nunez dying among the mountains.

Wells appreciated the apocalyptic implications of evolutionary theory and its devastating rebuke to the complacent and self-satisfied pride of pious middle-class Britain. Huxley, in his important series of lectures in 1893, "Evolution and Ethics," directed in part against the "social Darwinists" who found in the concept of "survival of the fittest" a justification for capitalism, had argued that evolutionary theory could not be used for ethical justifications. In the early 1890s, in some of his first publications, Wells pushed the idea that evolution was neither ethical nor necessarily progressive. Evolution does not favor the human species, and retrogression is always possible. As the Time Traveler memorably put it, "we are kept keen on the grindstone of pain and necessity," a doctrine that warns that success may jeopardize any species' long-term survival.

Huxley's sense that ethical behavior is an act of moral choice and will—independent of the biological process—led Wells to find moral positions that flew in the face of the evolutionary reality. To be human in the fullest sense would come to mean for him to exercise sympathies that bridge the divisions among competing species. Time and again, in the early work especially, one finds his protagonists put into an evolutionary conflict and at the moment of crisis generously understanding the other creature. The most stunning and paradoxical of such moments occurs in *The Island of Doctor Moreau* when Prendick confronts the leopard man who has reverted to carnivore:

> I saw the creature we were hunting. I halted. He was crouched together into the smallest possible compass, his luminous green eyes turned over his shoulder regarding me.
>
> It may seem a strange contradiction in me—I cannot explain the fact—but now, seeing the creature there in a perfectly animal attitude, with the light gleaming in its eyes, and its imperfectly human face distorted with terror, I realized again the fact of its humanity.

In another moment other of its pursuers would see it, and it would be overpowered and captured, to experience once more the horrible tortures of the enclosure. Abruptly I slipped out my revolver, aimed between his terror-struck eyes and fired.

"The fact of its humanity" strikes Prendick just when he sees its "perfectly animal attitude" and its "luminous green eyes." It is an extraordinary, terrible moment, when the bond between them is recognized across the profound gap of species difference, and yet the only "humane" act possible is to kill the beast man.

In view of the dark quality of Wells's imagination and his readiness to unleash destruction, we may be all the more struck with his seemingly optimistic resolutions to some other dire and unresolvable crises. When at the end of *The War of the Worlds* the Martians die off because of ecological factors, the author is instructing his readers about the complexity of what "the fittest" means in the Darwinian vision of nature. Then there are the many tales which envision a happier world, commonly in the form of a utopian change—the rationality of "larger" humans in *The Food of the Gods*, the global "sanity" at the end of *In the Days of the Comet*—or a pastoral escape, as in *The History of Mr. Polly*.

◆

Wells is fascinated with the pleasures of fiction, that is, of deception. The fraudulent Taxidermist in "The Triumphs of a Taxidermist" speaks of the "pure joy . . . to a real artist" that artificial creation inspires:

> "I have *created* birds," he said in a low voice. "*New* birds. Improvements. Like no birds that was ever seen before."
> He resumed his attitude during an impressive silence.
> "Enrich the universe; *rath-er*. Some of the birds I made were new kinds of humming birds, and very beautiful little things, but some of them were simply rum. The rummest, I think, was the *Anomalopteryx Jejuna. Jejunus-a-um–empty*—so called because there was really nothing in it; a thoroughly empty bird—except for stuffing. Old Javvers has the thing now, and I suppose he is almost as proud of it as I am. It is a masterpiece, Bellows. It has all the silly clumsiness of your pelican, all the solemn want of dignity of your parrot, all the gaunt ungainliness of a flamingo, with all the extravagant chromatic conflict of a mandarin duck. *Such* a bird. I made it out of the skeletons of a stork and a toucan and a job lot of feathers. Taxidermy of that kind is just pure joy, Bellows, to a real artist in the art."

The "art" of the fiction writer is like that of the taxidermist whom Wells depicts in this early story. Each creates an illusion of a new reality out of random pieces of a more familiar reality. And, like his taxidermist, the con-man writer takes pleasure in the deception with no concern for the moral implications of the lie. The name of the narrator whom the taxidermist addresses, "Bellows," contains an anagram of "Wells." And Bellows may be no more trustworthy than the taxidermist. He closes the very brief story with words that cause us further doubt: "The note about the New Zealand bird certainly appeared in a morning paper of unblemished reputation, for the Taxidermist keeps a copy and has shown it to me." Can we trust a forger's newspaper? Or even can we trust Bellows himself when he claims to have seen the clipping? We can imagine much, and we can trust nothing.

This double motion—brilliant invention coupled with deep suspicion—appears often in the early work. In "Æpornis Island" a man with the suggestive name "Butcher" tells how he killed the last representative of a now extinct species of bird and how he begrudges the fact that he does not get credit for an ornithological and archeological discovery. Early in the story, however, we are given reasons to suspect Butcher's narrative as self-serving. Sent to a remote island with two native assistants to collect fossils, Butcher exhibits classic signs of colonialist condescension towards his helpers, and when one, claiming to have been bitten by a centipede, drops and breaks a valuable fossil egg, Butcher "hit him about rather" (10). Later, when he finds the helper dead, "all puffed up and purple," he concludes off-handedly that the native had told the truth and was the victim of "some snake, scorpion, or centipede unknown" (264). The subtle language here rings of evasion: by gratuitously adding the snake and scorpion to the centipede, Butcher implies that there is something mysterious about the death, even as he reveals the plain truth that the assistant had actually been badly stung—just as he claimed. Clearly, Butcher is a man of slippery conscience.

◆

But Wells does not leave us simply with a story of racist offense. After another egg hatches and produces a huge chick, Butcher befriends it in its early stages, lives companionably with it for a couple of years, affectionately names it "Friday," and imagines "how [he] could make a living out of him by showing him about" (14). Only when as an adult Æpornis the bird becomes dangerous—he "was then about fourteen feet high to the bill of him, with a big, broad head like the end of pickaxe" (15)—does Butcher in self-defense kill him. And then a remarkable thing happens: Butcher, after begrudging the bird's power over "me a human being—heir of the ages and all that" (15), regrets his act. "I felt like a murderer" (16). Although he was unable to feel any bond with his native assistants, now "I felt exactly as if he [i.e. the Æpornis] was human. As it was, I couldn't think of eating him, so I put him in the lagoon, and the little fishes picked him clean. I didn't even save the feathers" (16). It is hard to imagine the man who thoughtlessly murders natives having such feelings or forgoing the profit that the feathers might have brought, but it is the very implausibility that may signal that Butcher is here telling the truth. But then again, we should be cautious: such an appeal to our own sensitivities may be the con-man artist's best tactic for persuading us of a tall tale's actuality. We should always remember that the narrator sees the Time Traveler as untrustworthy, and many of the men who know him consider his tale "a gaudy lie." The point is not that the Time Traveler is a liar. It is that Wells

xiii

*delights* in the undecided and the ambiguous, in the situations in which we, the readers, must stay on our toes.

One dimension of this complex style is brilliant satire that retains traces of utopian ideas and hopes. The voice that we hear in the last sections of *The First Men in the Moon*, when Cavor interviews the Grand Lunar, is fraught with satiric edge, but unlike Swift's it also plays with the possibilities of the bizarre world being juxtaposed to our own. Consider the following majestic passage toward the end of Cavor's description of the lunar society in which "every citizen knows his place. He is born to that place, and the elaborate discipline of training and education and surgery he undergoes fits him at last so completely to it that he has neither ideas nor organs for any purpose beyond it" (161):

> [Cavor reports,] "The making of these various sorts of operative must be a very curious and interesting process. I am still much in the dark about it, but quite recently I came upon a number of young Selenites, confined in jars from which only the forelimbs protruded, who were being compressed to become machine-minders of a special sort. The extended 'hand' in this highly developed system of technical education is stimulated by irritants and nourished by injection while the rest of the body is starved. Phi-oo [Cavor's informant], unless I misunderstood him, explained that in the earlier stages these queer little creatures are apt to display signs of suffering in their various cramped situations, but they easily become indurated to their lot; and he took me on to where a number of flexible-limbed messengers were being drawn out and broken in. It is quite unreasonable, I know, but these glimpses of the educational methods of these beings have affected me disagreeably. I hope, however, that may pass off and I may be able to see more of this aspect of this wonderful social order. That wretched-looking hand sticking out of its jar seemed to appeal for lost possibilities; it haunts me still, although, of course, it is really in the end a far more humane proceeding than our earthly method of leaving children to grow into human beings, and then making machines of them." (163)

Startlingly different tonalities play against each other here: the cool recitation of this "curious and interesting process," the pathos of the little Selenite's conditioning, the disturbingly incompatible languages—"being drawn out and broken in" as "educational methods"—Cavor's effort to overcome his natural revulsion and admire "this wonderful social order," and finally the wrenching refocusing at the end when this terrible conditioning is understood as benign compared to the horrors of *laissez faire* industrialism. Profound questions that will plague the twentieth century—of sociological and cultural objectivity, of intuition and reason, of controlled and free economies—are all raised in strong articulation in this amazing passage.

♦

If Wells is an author who thinks through fiction, however, he is also one attuned to the sheer pleasure that fiction can provide. He is a great descriptive artist. Again

xiv

and again in the most fanciful invention, he startles us with precise detail. Even after an idea is established, he will continue to think about it and discover new implications, as in *The Invisible Man* when we discover how vulnerable this supposedly superior man is to such elemental dangers as broken glass and cold. In natural descriptions he takes pleasure in word painting, as in the elegant and symbolic sunsets in *War of the Worlds*. Nowhere is Wells's descriptive talent put to more impressive use than in the scenes in *The Time Machine* when the Time Traveler moves farthest into the future and finds the desolate beach, the dying sun, and the last feeble (though still threatening) signs of life. Before everything else, H. G. Wells is a brilliant storyteller. If he has an eye for small details that make implausible things believable and an ear for the tricks of language that make characters real, then he has a talent for plots that have clear shape, with startling beginnings, developed middles, and meaningful ending.

Between 1924 and 1928 Wells himself published a collected edition of his work in twenty-four volumes, "The Atlantic Edition." It was limited to 1,670 copies and is generally to be found only in well-stocked libraries. In recent years scholarly editions of some of the early novels (*The Time Machine, The War of the Worlds, The Island of Doctor Moreau*) have begun to appear, and a good number of the social novels are occasionally reprinted in paperback. Unfortunately, these last tend to go out of print fairly quickly, and one must be alert to find them. The exception is *Tono-Bungay*, which has been reprinted more often than the other social novels. Wells himself described his career and the goals of his work in *An Experiment in Autobiography* (1934). Long after his death, a supplementary manuscript describing some of his love affairs was published by his son, G. P. Wells, under the title *H. G. Wells in Love* (1985). In the first decades after his death, Wells's letters to Henry James, Arnold Bennett, and George Gissing were published in separate volumes, and *The Collected Letters of H. G. Wells*, edited by David Smith, was published in 1992.

I have selected the texts for this anthology with an eye to quality and to what I see as the central issues and styles of Wells. In the case of such a prolific and varied artist, there is danger of dispersal and dilution. I have therefore confined the selection strictly to fiction. I have also narrowed this selection by limiting it to work Wells published in the first decade and a half of his writing career. Later Wells is a fascinating area, but only to readers who already have a sense of what early Wells is about. If I have emphasized the scientific romances, it is with a sense of how it leads into social novels like *Tono-Bungay* and *The History of Mr. Polly*—for which in his own time Wells was scandalously famous. Some of the volatile issues engaged in these novels have lost their urgency, but these novels continue to resonate with lively ideas and charged anger. Finally, because Wells was an important novelist and this part of his work is often hardest to find in print, I have included one complete novel, and lengthy selections of two others—all of which move beyond the scientific romance. I regret that space limits prevent giving the whole of *The Time Machine* or of *Tono-Bungay*, this last an extraordinary work that deserves much more attention than it gets.

Wells was an amazingly enlightened man, but he could not escape certain conventions and prejudices of his age. I have chosen not to bowdlerize or edit the texts to rid them of occasional moments that modern readers may find offensive. As often as not, as I argue above and in the prefaces to each piece, Wells himself would share our sense of outrage, and we underestimate the quality of his art if we too easily ascribe all the attitudes expressed by characters in these works to Wells himself.

—JOHN HUNTINGTON
MARCH 2003

Editor's note: ***** indicates text deleted for this volume.

# Chronology

Wells lived an amazingly active and full life, and it would be impossible to do it justice in a schematic chronology. In what follows, I have noted the major changes and events in his life, the publication of the novels included in this *Reader*, and a few other defining publications.

1866    Wells is born on September 21 to Sarah and Joseph Wells, she a servant in Atlas House; Bromley, he a semiprofessional cricket player and later owner of a small, not very successful shop.

1872    Wells attends Bromley Academy.

1880    Sarah Wells moves her family to Up Park, where she becomes housekeeper. Wells's first apprenticeship as a draper with Rodgers and Denyer in Windsor lasts a month.

1881    Wells apprenticed at the Southsea Drapery Emporium in Southsea.

1883    By threatening suicide and by running away, Wells convinces his mother to let him give up the apprenticeship and to work as an assistant master at Horace Byatt's Midhurst School.

1884    Wells enters the Normal School of Science in South Kensington. In the first year he studies biology under T. H. Huxley.

1888    "The Chronic Astronauts," the first version of *The Time Machine*, published in *The Science Schools Journal*.

1891    Wells marries his cousin, Isabel.

1894    Wells separates from Isabel to live with Amy Catherine Robbins, whom he always calls "Jane."

1895    Wells marries Jane. The marriage lasts until her death in 1928. They move to Woking and over the next few years Wells becomes friends with Arnold Bennett, George Gissing, Henry James, Joseph Conrad, Stephen Crane, and Ford Maddox Heuffer (later Ford). *The Time Machine; The Stolen Bacillus and Other Incidents* is published.

1896    *The Wheels of Chance; The Island of Doctor Moreau* is published.

1897    *The Invisible Man; The Plattner Story and Others* is published.

1898    Wells and Jane visit Rome. *War of the Worlds* is published.

1899    *When the Sleeper Wakes; Tales of Space and Time* is published.

1900    Wells commissions Spade House at Sandgatge in Kent. *Love and Mr. Lewisham* is published.

1901    Wells and Jane's first son, "Gip," is born. *The First Men in the Moon; Anticipations of the Reaction of Mechanical and Scientific Progress upon Human Life and Thought* is published.

1902    *The Discovery of the Future* is published.

1903    Wells and Jane's second son, Frank, is born. Wells joins Fabian Society. *Mankind in the Making* is published.

1904    *The Food of the Gods* is published.

1905    *A Modern Utopia; Kipps* is published.

1906    Wells begins fight for control of the Fabian Society. He tours the United States, where he meets with Theodore Roosevelt. *In the Days of the Comet* is published.

1908    Wells begins his affair with Amber Reeves. *The War in the Air; New Worlds for Old; First and Last Things* is published.

1909    *Tono-Bungay; Ann Veronica* is published.

1910    Wells ends the affair with Amber Reeves. *The History of Mr. Polly*

1911    *The Country of the Blind and Other Stories; The New Machiavelli*

1912    Wells meets Rebecca West after she reviews *Marriage*. They begin a ten-year affair.

1913    *The Passionate Friends* is published.

1914    Wells and Rebecca's son, Anthony West, is born.

1920    Wells meets with Lenin. *The Outline of History* is published.

1928    Jane dies.

1930    *The Science of Life: A Summary of Contemporary Knowledge about Life and Its Possibilities*, written in collaboration with Gip Wells and Julian Huxley, T. H. Huxley's grandson, is published.

        *The Work, Wealth and Happiness of Mankind* is published.

        Wells meets with Stalin. *Experiment in Autobiography: Discoveries and Conclusions of a Very Ordinary Brain–Since 1866* is published.

1940    *The Rights of Man, or What Are We Fighting For?* is published.

1941    *Mind at the End of Its Tether* is published.

1945    Wells dies on August 13.

# "The Stolen Bacillus"
# (1894)

*"The Stolen Bacillus" is the lead story of Wells's first collection of stories. At the story's center is the comic scene of the scientist chasing the anarchist, who has stolen what he thinks is a test-tube of deadly cholera bacteria, while the scientist's wife, Minnie, offended at her husband's state of undress ("running about London—in the height of the season too—in his socks") chases him. As Wells imagines a tremendous terror threatening modern civilization, he also cannot help but observe the triviality of that civilization's conventions. The story is typical of Wells for the way it unifies the strongly discrepant tonalities of comedy and tragedy, of convention and science, of triumph and defeat.*

"This again," said the Bacteriologist, slipping a glass slide under the microscope, "is a preparation of the celebrated Bacillus of cholera—the cholera germ."

The pale-faced man peered down the microscope. He was evidently not accustomed to that kind of thing, and held a limp white hand over his disengaged eye. "I see very little," he said.

"Touch this screw," said the Bacteriologist; "perhaps the microscope is out of focus for you. Eyes vary so much. Just the fraction of a turn this way or that."

"Ah! now I see," said the visitor. "Not so very much to see after all. Little streaks and shred of pink. And yet those little particles, those mere atomies, might multiply and devastate a city! Wonderful!"

He stood up, and releasing the glass slip from the microscope, held it in his hand towards the window. "Scarcely visible," he said scrutinizing the preparation. He hesitated. "Are these—alive? Are they dangerous now?"

"Those have been stained and killed," said the Bacteriologist. "I wish, for my own part, we could kill and stain every one of them in the universe."

"I suppose," the pale man said with a slight smile, "that you scarcely care to have such things about you in the living—in the active state?"

"On the contrary, we are obliged to," said the Bacteriologist. "Here, for instance—" He walked across the room and took up one of several sealed tubes. "Here is the living thing. This is a cultivation of the actual living disease bacteria." He hesitated. "Bottled cholera, so to speak."

A slight gleam of satisfaction appeared momentarily in the face of the pale man. "It's a deadly thing to have in your possession," he said, devouring the little tube with his eyes. The Bacteriologist watched the morbid pleasure in his visitor's expression. This man, who had visited him that afternoon with a note of introduction from an old friend, interested him from the very contrast of their dispositions. The lank

1

black hair and deep grey eyes, the haggard expression and nervous manner, the fitful yet keen interest of his visitor were a novel change from the phlegmatic deliberations of the ordinary scientific worker with whom the Bacteriologist chiefly associated. It was perhaps natural, with a hearer evidently so impressionable to the lethal nature of his topic, to take the most effective aspect of the matter.

He held the tube in his hand thoughtfully. "Yes, here is the pestilence imprisoned. Only break such a little tube as this into a supply of drinking-water, say to these minute particles of life that one must needs stain and examine with the highest powers of the microscope even to see, and that one can neither smell nor taste—say to them, 'Go forth, increase and multiply, and replenish the cisterns,' and death—mysterious, untraceable death, death swift and terrible, death full of pain and indignity—would be released upon this city, and go hither and thither seeking his victims. Here he would take the husband from the wife, here the child from its mother, here the statesman from his duty, and here the toiler from his trouble. He would follow the water-mains, creeping along streets, picking out and punishing a house here a house there where they did not boil their drinking-water, creeping into the wells of the mineral-water makers, getting washed into salad, and lying dormant in ices. He would wait ready to be drunk in the hose-troughs, and by unwary children in the public fountains. He would soak into the soil, to reappear in springs and wells at a thousand unexpected places. Once start him at the water supply, and before we could ring him in, and catch him again, he would have decimated the metropolis."

He stopped abruptly. He had been told rhetoric was his weakness.

"But he is quite safe here, you know—quite safe."

The pale-faced man nodded. His eyes hone. He cleared his throat. "These Anarchist—rascals," said he, "are fools, blind fools—to use bombs when this kind of thing is attainable. I think—"

A gentle rap, a mere light touch of the finger-nails was heard at the door. The Bacteriologist opened it. "Just a minute, dear" whispered his wife.

When he re-entered his laboratory his visitor was looking at his watch. "I had no idea I had wasted an hour of your time," he said. "Twelve minutes to four. I ought to have left here by half-past three. But your things were really too interesting. No, positively I cannot stop a moment longer. I have an engagement at four."

He passed out of the room reiterating his thanks, and the Bacteriologist accompanied him to the door, and then returned thoughtfully along the passage to his laboratory. He was musing on the ethnology of his visitor. Certainly the man was not a Teutonic type nor a common Latin one. "A morbid product, anyhow, I am afraid," said the Bacteriologist to himself. "How he gleamed on those cultivations of disease-germs!" A disturbing thought struck him. He turned to the bench by the vapor-bath, and then very quickly to his writing-table. Then he felt hastily in his pockets, and then rushed to the door. "I may have put it down on the hall table," he said.

"Minnie!" he shouted hoarsely in the hall.

"Yes, dear," came a remote voice.

"Had I anything in my hand when I spoke to you, dear, just now?"

Pause.

"Nothing, dear, because I remember—"

"Blue ruin!" cried the Bacteriologist, and incontinently ran to the front door and down the steps of his house to the street.

Minnie, hearing the door slam violently, ran in alarm to the window. Down the street a slender man was getting into a cab. The Bacteriologist, hatless, and in his carpet slippers, was running and gesticulating wildly towards this group. One slipper came off, but he did not wait for it. "He has gone *mad!*" said Minnie; "it's that horrid science of his"; and, opening the window, would have called after him. The slender man, suddenly glancing round, seemed struck with the same idea of mental disorder. He pointed hastily to the Bacteriologist, said something to the cabman, the apron of the cab slammed, the whip swished, the horses' feet clattered, and in a moment cab, and Bacteriologist hotly in pursuit, had receded up the vista of the roadway and disappeared round the corner.

Minnie remained straining out of the window for a minute. Then she drew her head back into the room again. She was dumbfounded. "Of course he is eccentric," she meditated. "But running about London—in the height of the season, too—in his socks!" A happy thought struck her. She hastily put her bonnet on, seized his shoes, went into the hall, took down his hat and light overcoat from the pegs, emerged upon the doorstep, and hailed a cab that opportunely crawled by. "Drive me up the road and round Havenlock Crescent, and see if we can find a gentleman running about in a velveteen coat and no hat."

"Velveteen coat, ma'am and no 'at. Very good, ma'am." And the cabman whipped up at once in the most matter-of-fact way, as if he drove to this address every day in his life.

Some few minutes later the little group of cabmen and loafers that collects round the cabmen's shelter at Haverstock Hill were startled by the passing of a cab with a ginger-colored screw of a horse, driven furiously.

They were silent as it went by, and then as it receded—"That's 'Arry 'Icks. Wot's *he* got?" said the stout gentleman known as Old Tootles.

"He's a-using his whip, he is, *to* rights," said the ostler boy.

"Hullo!" said poor old Tommy Byles; "here's another bloomin' lunatic. Blowed if there ain't."

"It's old George," said old Tootles, "and he's driving a lunatic, *as* you say. Ain't he a-clawin' out of the keb? Wonder if he's after 'Arry 'Icks?"

The ground round the cabmen's shelter became animated. Chorus: "Got it, George!" "It's a race." "You'll ketch 'em!" "Whip up!"

"She's a goer, she is!" said the ostler boy.

"Strike me giddy!" cried old Tootles. "Here! I'm a-goin' to begin in a minute. Here's another comin'. If all the kebs in Hampstead ain't gone mad this morning!"

"It's a fieldmale this time," said the ostler boy.

3

"She's a followin' *him*," said old Tootles. "Usually the other way about."

"What's she got in her 'and?'"

"Looks like a 'igh 'at."

"What a bloomin' lark it is! Three to one on old George," said the ostler boy. "Necst!"

Minnie went by in a perfect roar of applause. She did not like it but she felt that she was doing her duty, and whirled on down Haverstock Hill and Camden Town High Street with her eyes ever intent on the animated back view of old George, who was driving her vagrant husband so incomprehensively away from her.

The man in the foremost cab sat crouched in the corner, his arms tightly folded, and the little tube that contained such vast possibilities of destruction gripped in his hand. His mood was a singular mixture of fear and exultation. Chiefly he was afraid of being caught before he could accomplish his purpose, but behind this was a vaguer but larger fear of the awfulness of his crime. But his exultation far exceeded his fear. No Anarchist before him had ever approached this conception of his. Ravachole, Vaillant, all those distinguished persons whose fame he had envied dwindled into insignificance beside him. He had only to make sure of the water supply, and break the little tube into a reservoir. How brilliantly he had planned it, forged the letter of introduction and got into the laboratory, and how brilliantly he had seized his opportunity! The world should hear of him at last. All those people who had sneered at him, neglected him, preferred other people to him, found his company undesirable, should consider him at last. Death, death, death! They had always treated him as a man of no importance. All the world had been in a conspiracy to keep him under. He would teach them yet what it is to isolate a man. What was this familiar street? Great Saint Andrew's Street, of course! How fared the chase? He craned out of the cab. The Bacteriologist was scarcely fifty yards behind. That was bad. He would be caught and stopped yet. He felt in his pocket for money, and found half-a-sovereign. This he thrust up through the trap in the top of the cab into the man's face. "More," he shouted, "if only we get away."

The money was snatched out of his hand. "Right you are," said the cabman, and the trap slammed, and the lash lay along the glistening side of the horse. The cab swayed, and the Anarchist, half-standing under the trap, put the hand containing the little glass tube upon the apron to preserve his balance. He felt the brittle thing crack, and the broken half of it rang upon the floor of the cab. He fell back into the seat with a curse, and stared dismally at the two or three drops of moisture on the apron.

He shuddered.

"Well! I suppose I shall be the first. *Phew!* Anyhow, I shall be a Martyr. That's something. But it is a filthy death, nevertheless. I wonder if it hurts as much as they say."

Presently a thought occurred to him—he groped between his feet. A little drop was still in the broken end of the tube, and he drank that to make sure. It was better to make sure. At any rate, he would not fail.

4

Then it dawned upon him that there was no further need to escape the Bacteriologist. In Wellington Street he told the cabman to stop, and got out. He slipped on the step, and his head felt queer. It was rapid stuff this cholera poison. He waved his cabman out of existence, so to speak, and stood on the pavement with his arm folded upon his breast awaiting the arrival of the Bacteriologist. There was something tragic in this pose. The sense of imminent death gave him a certain dignity. He greeted his pursuer with a defiant laughter.

"Vive l'Anarchie! You are too late, my friend. I have drunk it. The cholera is abroad!"

The Bacteriologist from his cab beamed curiously at him through his spectacles. "You have drunk it! An Anarchist! I see now." He was about to say something more, and then checked himself. A smile hung in the corner of his mouth. He opened the apron of his cab as if to descend, at which the Anarchist waved him a dramatic farewell and strode off towards Waterloo Bridge, carefully jostling his infected body against as many people as possible. The Bacteriologist was so preoccupied with the vision of him that he scarcely manifested the slightest surprise at the appearance of Minnie upon the pavement with his hat and shoes and overcoat. "Very good of you to bring my things," he said, and remained lost in contemplation of the receding figure of the Anarchist.

"You had better get in," he said, still staring. Minnie felt absolutely convinced now that he was mad, and directed the cabman home on her own responsibility. "Put on my shoes? Certainly, dear," said he, as the cab began to turn and hid the strutting black figure, now small in the distance, from his eyes. Then suddenly something grotesque struck him, and he laughed. Then he remarked, "It is really very serious, though.

"You see, that man came to my house to see me, and he is an Anarchist. No—don't faint, or I cannot possibly tell you the rest. And I wanted to astonish him, not knowing he was an Anarchist, and took up a cultivation of that new species of Bacterium I was telling you of, that infest, and I like a fool, I said it was Asiatic cholera. And he ran away with it to poison the water of London, and he certainly might have made things look blue for this civilized city. And now he has swallowed it. Of course, I cannot say what will happen, but you know it turned that kitten blue, and the three puppies—in patches, and the sparrow—bright blue. But the bother is, I shall have all the trouble and expense of preparing some more.

"Put on my coat on this hot day! Why? Because we might meet Mrs. Jabber. My dear, Mrs. Jabber is not a draught. But why should I wear a coat on a hot day because of Mrs.—? Oh! Very well."

# "The Triumphs of a Taxidermist"
# (1894)

*In "The Triumphs of a Taxidermist," one of his very first published stories, Wells announces himself in simple and elegant terms: the Taxidermist, like the poor young man with a scientific degree but no profession, is a marginal and disreputable figure. He is an interloper, barely respectable in his shabby shop, his greasy clothes, and his leering, comic drunkenness. His pure joy in artistic fraud is at a deeper level a reveling in the success of his gamble about acceptance. He calls into question the legitimacy of the field he works in: "one of the genuine great auks was made by me." He also represents a frightening picture of poverty and self-delusion, a future that, while it has its secret victories, is of depressing inconsequence. As one can tell from the Taxidermist's response to untranscribed questions near the beginning, the outrageous and offensive claims about stuffing humans clearly alarm Bellows, the interviewer. Here Wells, while placing the Taxidermist outside all social decorum, at the same time intimates his own uneasiness about the morals and motives of such an art. It is a disturbing little vignette, full of dangerous possibilities and ambiguous to the very bottom.*

Here are some of the secrets of taxidermy. They were told me by the Taxidermist in a mood of elation. He told me them in the time between the first glass of whisky and the fourth, when a man is no longer cautious and yet not drunk. We sat in his den together; his library it was, his sitting and his eating-room—separated by a bead curtain, so far as the sense of sight went, from the noisome den where he plied his trade.

He sat on a deck chair, and when he was not tapping refractory bits of coal with them, he kept his feet—on which he wore, after the manner of sandals, the holy relics of a pair of carpet slippers—out of the way upon the mantelpiece, among the glass eyes. And his trousers, by-the-by—though they have nothing to do with his triumphs—were a most horrible yellow plaid, such as they made when our fathers wore side-whiskers and there were crinolines in the land. Further, his hair was black, his face rosy, and his eye a fiery brown; and his coat was chiefly of grease upon a basis of velveteen. And his pipe had a bowl of china showing the Graces, and his spectacles were always askew, the left eye glaring naked, at you, small and penetrating; the right, seen through a glass darkly, magnified and mild. Thus his discourse ran: "There never was a man who could stuff like me, Bellows, never. I have stuffed elephants and I have stuffed moths, and the things have looked all the livelier and better for it. And I have stuffed human beings—chiefly amateur ornithologists. But I stuffed a nigger once.

"No, there is no law against it. I made him with all his fingers out, and used him as a hat-rack, but that fool Homersby got up a quarrel with him late one night and

6

spoilt him. That was before your time. It is hard to get skins, or I would have another.

"Unpleasant? I don't see it. Seems to me taxidermy is a promising third course to burial or cremation. You could keep all your dear ones by you. Bric-a-brac of that sort stuck about the house would be as good as most company and much less expensive. You might have them fitted up with clockwork to do things.

"Of course they would have to be varnished, but they need not shine more than lots of people do naturally. Old Manningtree's bald head . . . Anyhow, you could talk to them without interruption. Even aunts. There is a great future before taxidermy, depend upon it. There is fossils again . . ."

He suddenly became silent.

"No, I don't think I ought to tell you that." He sucked at his pipe thoughtfully. "Thanks, yes. Not too much water.

"Of course, what I tell you now will go no further. You know I have made some dodos and a great auk? No! evidently you are an amateur at taxidermy. My dear fellow, half the great auks in the world are about as genuine as the handkerchief of Saint Veronica, as the Holy Coat of Treves. We make 'em of grebes' feathers and the like. And the great auk's eggs too!"

"Good heavens!"

"Yes, we make them out of fine porcelain. I tell you it is worth while. They fetch—one fetched £300 only the other day. That one was really genuine, I believe, but of course one is never certain. It is very fine work, and afterwards you have to get them dusty, for no one who owns one of these precious eggs has ever the temerity to clean the thing. That's the beauty of the business. Even if they suspect an egg they do not like to examine it too closely. It's such brittle capital at the best.

"You did not know that taxidermy rose to heights like that. My boy, it has risen higher. I have rivaled the hands of Nature herself. One of the *genuine* great auks"—his voice fell to a whisper—"one of the *genuine* great auks *was made by me.*"

"No. You must study ornithology, and find out which it is yourself. And what is more, I have been approached by a syndicate of dealers to stock one of the unexplored skerries to the north of Iceland with specimens. I may—some day. But I have another little thing in hand just now. Ever heard of the dinornis?

"It is one of those big birds recently extinct in New Zealand. 'Moa' is its common name, so called because extinct: there is no moa now. See? Well, they have got bones of it, and from some of the marshes even feathers and dried bits of skin. Now, I am going to—well, there is no need to make any bones about it—going to *forge* a complete stuffed moa. I know a chap out there who will pretend to make the find in a kind of antiseptic swamp, and say he stuffed it at once, as it threatened to fall to pieces. The feathers are peculiar, but I have got simply lovely way of dodging up singed bits of ostrich plume. Yes, that is the new smell you noticed. They can only discover the fraud with a microscope, and they will hardly care to pull a nice specimen to bits for that.

"In this way, you see, I give my little push in the advancement of science."

7

"But all this is merely imitating Nature. I have done more than that in my time. I have—beaten her."

He took his feet down from the mantel-board, and leant over confidentially towards me. "I have *created* birds," he said in a low voice. "*New* birds. Improvements. Like no birds that was ever seen before."

He resumed his attitude during an impressive silence.

"Enrich the universe; *rath*-er. Some of the birds I made were new kinds of humming birds, and very beautiful little things, but some of them were simply rum. The rummest, I think, was the *Anomalopteryx Jejuna. Jejenus-a-um*—empty—so called because there was really nothing in it; a thoroughly empty bird—except for stuffing. Old Javvers has the things now, and I suppose he is almost as proud of it as I am. It is a masterpiece, Bellows. It has all the silly clumsiness of your pelican, all the solemn want of dignity of your parrot, all the gaunt ungainliness of a flamingo, with all the extravagant chromatic conflict of a mandarin duck. *Such* a bird. I made it out of the skeletons of a stork and a toucan and a job lot of feathers. Taxidermy of that kind is just pure joy, Bellows, to a real artist in the art.

"How did I come to make it? Simple enough, as all great inventions are. One of those young genii who write us Science Notes in the papers got hold of a German pamphlet about the birds of New Zealand, and translated some of it by means of a dictionary and his mother-wit—he must have been one of a very large family with a small mother—and he got mixed between the living apteryx and the extinct anomalopteryx; talked about a bird five feet high, living in the jungles of the North Island, rare, shy, specimens difficult to obtain, and so on. Javvers, who even for a collector, is a miraculously ignorant man, read these paragraphs, and swore he would have the thing at an price. Raided the dealers with enquiries. It shows what a man can do by persistence—will-power. Here was a bird collector swearing he would have a specimen of a bird that did not exist, that never existed, and which for very shame of its own profane ungainliness, probably would not exist now if it could help itself. And he got it. *He got it.*

"Have some more whisky, Bellow?" said the Taxidermist, rousing himself from a transient contemplation of the mysteries of will-power and the collecting turn of mind. And, replenished, he proceeded to tell me of how he concocted a most attractive mermaid, and how an itinerant preacher, who could not get an audience because of it, smashed it because it was idolatry, or worse, at Buslem Wakes. But as the conversation of all the parties to this transaction, creator, would-be preserver, and destroyer, was uniformly unfit for publication, this cheerful incident must still remain unprinted.

The reader unacquainted with the dark ways of the collector may perhaps be incline to doubt my taxidermist, but so far as great auks' eggs, and the bogus stuffed birds are concerned, I find that he has the confirmation of distinguished ornithological writers. And the note about the New Zealand bird certainly appeared in a morning paper of unblemished reputation, for the Taxidermist keeps a copy and has shown it to me.

# "Æpyornis Island"
# (1894)

*See the introduction for an extended analysis of "Æpornis Island." Putting it next to "Triumphs of a Taxidermist," we can see further Wells's interest in the nearness of science and deception. He cannot help but admire the scam even as he teaches us to suspect it. Ornithology in particular—so important to Darwin's invention of the theory of evolution and yet so traditionally the province of amateurs—is prone to such deceptions.*

The man with the scarred face leant over the table and looked at my bundle.

"Orchids?" he asked.

"A few," I said.

"Cypripediums," he said.

"Chiefly," said I.

"Anything new? I thought not. I did these islands twenty-five–twenty-seven years ago. If you find anything new here—well, it's brand new. I didn't leave much."

"I'm not a collector," said I.

"I was young then," he went on. "Lord! How I used to fly round." He seemed to take my measure. "I was in the East Indies two years and in Brazil seven. Then I went to Madagascar."

"I know a few explorers by name," I said, anticipating a yarn. "Whom did you collect for?"

"Dawsons'. I wonder if you've heard the name of Butcher ever?"

"Butcher—Butcher?" The name seemed vaguely present in my memory; then I recalled *Butcher v. Dawson.* "Why!" said I, "you are the man who sued them for four years' salary—got cast away on a desert island. . . . "

"Your servant," said the man with the scar, bowing. "Funny case, wasn't it? Here was me, making a little fortune on that island, doing nothing for it neither, and them quite unable to give me notice. It often used to amuse me thinking over it while I was there. I did calculations of it—big—all over the blessed atoll in ornamental figuring."

"How did it happen?" said I. "I don't rightly remember the case."

"Well. . . . You've heard of the Æpyornis?"

"Rather; Andrews was telling me of a new species he was working on only a month or so ago. Just before I sailed. They've got a thigh-bone, it seems, nearly a yard long. Monster the thing must have been!"

"I believe you," said the man with the scar. "It *was* a monster. Sindbad's roc was just a legend of 'em. But when did they find these bones?"

"Three or four years ago—'91, I fancy. Why?"

"Why? Because I found them—Lord!—it's nearly twenty years ago. If Dawsons' hadn't been silly about that salary they might have made a perfect ring in 'em. . . . I couldn't help the infernal boat going adrift."

He paused. "I suppose it's the same place. A kind of swamp about ninety miles north of Antananarivo. Do you happen to know? You have to go to it along the coast by boats. You don't happen to remember, perhaps?"

"I don't. I fancy Andrews said something about a swamp."

"It must be the same. It's on the east coast. And somehow there's something in the water that keeps things from decaying. Like creosote it smells. It reminded me of Trinidad. Did they get any more eggs? Some of the eggs I found were a foot and a half long. The swamp goes circling round, you know, and cuts off this bit. It's mostly salt, too. Well . . . What a time I had of it! I found the things quite by accident. We went for eggs, me and two native chaps, in one of those rum canoes all tied together, and found the bones at the same time. We had a tent and provisions for four days, and we pitched on one of the firmer places. To think of it brings that odd tarry smell back even now. It's funny work. You go probing into the mud with iron rods, you know. Usually the egg gets smashed. I wonder how long it is since these Æpyornises really lived. The missionaries say the native have legends about when they were alive, but I never heard any such stories myself. But certainly those eggs we got were as fresh as if they had been new laid. Fresh! Carrying them down to the boat one of my nigger chaps dropped one on a rock and it smashed. How I lamed in on the beggar! But sweet it was, as if it was new laid, not even smelly, and its mother dead these four hundred years, perhaps. Said a centipede had bit him. However, I'm getting off the straight with the story. It had taken us all day to dig into the slush and get these eggs out unbroken, and we were all covered with beastly black mud, and naturally I was cross. So far as I knew they were the only eggs that have ever been got out not even cracked. I went afterwards to see the ones they have at the Natural History Museum in London; all of them were cracked and just stuck together like a mosaic, and bits missing. Mine were perfect, and I meant to blow them when I got back. Naturally I was annoyed at the silly duffer dropping three hours' work just on account of a centipede. I hit him about rather."

The man with the scar took out a clay pipe. I placed my pouch before him. He filled up absent-mindedly.

"How about the others? Did you get those home? I don't remember—"

"That's the queer part of the story. I had three others. Perfectly fresh eggs. Well, we put 'em in the boat, and then I went up to the tent to make some coffee, leaving my two heathens down by the beach—the one fooling about his sting and the other helping him. It never occurred to me that the beggar would take advantage of the peculiar position I was in to pick a quarrel. But I suppose the centipede poison and the kicking I had given him had upset the one—he was always a cantankerous sort—and he persuaded the other.

10

"I remember I was sitting and smoking and boiling up the water over a spirit-lamp business I used to take on these expeditions. Incidentally I was admiring the swamp under the sunset. All black and blood-red, it was, in streaks—a beautiful sight. And up beyond the land rose grey and hazy to the hills, and the sky behind them red, like a furnace mouth. And fifty yards behind the back of me was these blessed heathen—quite regardless of the tranquil air of things—plotting to cut off with the boat and leave me all alone with three days' provisions and a canvas tent, and nothing to drink whatsoever beyond a little keg of water. I heard a kind of yelp behind me, and there they were in this canoe affair—it wasn't properly a boat—and, perhaps, twenty yards from land. I realized what was up in a moment. My gun was in the tent, and, besides, I had no bullets—only duck shot. They knew that. But I had a little revolver in my pocket, and I pulled that out as I ran down to the beach.

"'Come back!' says I, flourishing it.

"They jabbered something at me, and the man that broke the egg jeered. I aimed at the other—because he was unwounded and had the paddle, and I missed. They laughed. However, I wasn't beat. I knew I had to keep cool, and I tried him again and made him jump with the whang of it. He didn't laugh that time. The third time I got his head, and over he went, and the paddle with him. It was a precious lucky shot for a revolver. I reckon it was fifty yards. He went right under. I don't know if he was shot, or simply stunned and drowned. Then I began to shout to the other chap to come back, but he huddled up in the canoe and refused to answer. So I fired out my revolver at him and never got hear him.

"I felt a precious fool, I can tell you. There I was on this rotten black beach, flat swamp all behind me, and the flat sea, cold after the sunset, and just this black canoe drifting steadily out to sea. I tell you I damned Dawsons' and Jamrach's and Museums and all the rest of it just to rights. I bawled to this nigger to come back, until my voice went up into a scream.

"There was nothing for it but to swim after him and take my luck with the sharks. So I opened my clasp-knife and put it in my mouth, and took off my clothes and waded in. As soon as I was in the water I lost sight of the canoe, but I aimed, as I judged, to head it off. I hoped the man in it was too bad to navigate it, and that it would keep on drifting in the same direction. Presently it came up over the horizon again to the south-westward about. The afterglow of sunset was well over now and the dim of night creeping up. The stars were coming through the blue. I swum like a champion, though my legs and arms were soon aching.

"However, I came up to him by the time the stars were fairly out. As it got darker I began to see all manner of glowing things in the water—phosphorescence, you know. At times it made me giddy. I hardly knew which was stars and which was phosphorescence, and whether I was swimming on my head or me heels. The canoe was as black as sin, and the ripple under the bows like liquid fire. I was naturally chary of clambering up into it. I was anxious to see what he was up to first. He seemed to be lying cuddled up in a lump in the bows, and the stern was all out

11

of water. The thing kept turning round slowly as it drifted—kind of waltzing, don't you know. I went to the stern and pulled it down, expecting him to wake up. Then I began to clamber in with my knife in my hand, and ready for a rush. But he never stirred. So there I sat in the stern of the little canoe, drifting away over the calm phosphorescent sea and with all the host of the stars above me, waiting for something to happen.

"After a long time I called him by name, but he never answered. I was too tired to take any risks by going along to him. So we sat there. I fancy I dozed once or twice. When the dawn came I saw he was as dead as a door-nail and all puffed up and purple. My three eggs and the bones were lying in the middle of the canoe, and the keg of water and some coffee and biscuits wrapped in a Cape *Argus* by his feet, and a tin of methylated spirit underneath him. There was no paddle, nor, in fact, anything except the spirit tin that I could use as one, so I settled to drift until I was picked up. I held an inquest on him, brought in a verdict against some snake, scorpion, or centipede unknown, and sent him overboard.

"After that I had a drink of water and a few biscuits, and took a look round. I suppose a man low down as I was don't see very far; leastways, Madagascar was clean out of sight, and any trace of land at all. I saw a sail going south-westward—looked like a schooner but her hull never came up. Presently the sun got high in the sky and began to beat down upon me. Lord! it was pretty near made my brains boil. I tried dipping my head in the sea, but after a while my eye fell on the Cape *Argus*, and I lay down flat in the canoe and spread this over me. Wonderful things these newspapers! I never read one through thoroughly before, but it's odd what you get up to when you're alone, as I was. I suppose I read that blessed old Cape *Argus* twenty times. The pitch in the canoe simply reeked with the heat and rose up into big blisters.

"I drifted ten days," said the man with the scar. "It's a little thing in the telling, isn't it? Every day was like the last. Except in the morning and the evening I never kept a lookout even—the blaze was so infernal. I didn't see a sail after the first three days, and those I saw took no notice of me. About the sixth night a ship went by scarcely half a mile away from me, with all its lights ablaze and its ports open, looking like a big firefly. There was music aboard. I stood up and shouted and screamed at it. The second day I broached one of the Æpyornis eggs, scraped the shell away at the end bit by bit, and tried it, and I was glad to find it was good enough to eat. A bit flavoury—not bad, I mean—but with something of the taste of a duck's egg. There was a kind of circular patch, about six inches across, on one side of the yolk, and with streaks of blood and a white mark like a ladder in it that I thought queer, but I did not understand what this meant at the time, and I wasn't inclined to be particular. The egg lasted me three days, with biscuits and a drink of water. I chewed coffee-berries too—invigating stuff. The second egg I opened about the eighth day, and it scared me."

The man with the scar paused. "Yes," he said, "developing."

12

"I dare say you find it hard to believe. I did, with the thing before me. There the egg had been, sunk in that cold black mud, perhaps three hundred years. But there was no mistaking it. There was the—what is it?—embryo, with its big head and curved back, and its heart beating under its throat, and the yolk shriveled up and great membranes spreading inside of the shell and all over the yolk. Here was I hatching out the eggs of the biggest of all extinct birds, in a little canoe in the midst of the Indian Ocean. If old Dawson had known that! It was worth four years' salary. What do *you* think?

"However, I had to eat that precious thing up, every bit of it, before I sighted the reef, and some of the mouthfuls were beastly unpleasant. I left the third one alone. I held it up to the light, but the shell was too thick for me to get any notion of what might be happening inside; and though I fancied I heard blood pulsing, it might have been the rustle in my own ears, like what you listen to in a seashell.

"Then came the atoll. Came out of the sunrise, as it were, suddenly, close to me. I drifted straight towards it until I was about half a mile from shore, not more, and then the current took a turn, and I had to paddle as hard as I could with my hands and bits of the Æpyornis shell to make the place. However, I got there. It was just a common atoll about four miles round, with a few trees growing and a spring in one place, and the lagoon full of parrot-fish. I took the egg ashore and put it in a good place, well above the tide lines and in the sun, to give it all the chance I could, and pulled the canoe up safe, and loafed about prospecting. It's rum how dull an atoll is. As soon as I had found a spring all the interest seemed to vanish. When I was a kid I thought nothing could be finer or more adventurous than the Robinson Crusoe business, but that place was as monotonous as a book of sermons. I went round finding eatable things and generally thinking; but I tell you I was bored to death before the first day was out. It shows my luck—the very day I landed the weather changed. A thunderstorm went by to the north and flicked its wing over the island, and in the night there came a drencher and howling wind slap over us. It wouldn't have taken much, you know, to upset that canoe.

"I was sleeping under the canoe, and the egg was luckily among the sand higher up the beach, and the first thing I remember was a sound like a hundred pebbles hitting the boat at once, and a rush of water over my body. I'd been dreaming of Antananarivo, and I sat up and halloaed to Intoshi to ask her what the devil was up, and clawed out at the chair where the matches used to be. Then I remembered where I was. There were phosphorescent waves rolling up as if they meant to eat me, and all the rest of the night as black as pitch. The air was simply yelling. The clouds seemed down on your head almost, and the rain fell as if heaven was sinking and they were baling out the waters above the firmament. One great roller came writhing at me, like a fiery serpent, and I bolted. Then I thought of the canoe, and ran down to it as the water went hissing back again; but the thing had gone. I wondered about the egg, then, and felt my way to it. It was all right and well out of reach of the maddest waves, so I sat down beside it and cuddled it for company. Lord! what a night that was!

13

"The storm was over before the morning. There wasn't a rag of cloud left in the sky when the dawn came, and all along the beach there were bits of plank scattered—which was the disarticulated skeleton, so to speak, of my canoe. However, that gave me something to do, for taking advantage of two of the trees being together, I rigged up a kind of storm-shelter with these vestiges. And that day the egg hatched.

"Hatched, sir, when my head was pillowed on it and I was asleep. I heard a whack and felt a jar and sat up, and there was the end of the egg pecked out and a rum little brown head looking out at me. 'Lord!' I said, 'You're welcome,' and with a little difficulty he came out.

"He was a nice friendly little chap at first, about the size of a small hen—very much like most other young birds, only bigger. His plumage was a dirty brown to begin with, with a sort of grey scab that fell off it very soon, and scarcely feathers—a kind of downy hair. I can hardly express how pleased I was to see him. I tell you, Robinson Crusoe don't make near enough of his loneliness. But here was interesting company. He looked at me and winked his eye from the front backward, like a hen, and gave a chirp and began to peck about at once, as though being hatched three hundred years too late was just nothing. 'Glad to see you, Man Friday!' says I, for I had naturally settled he was to be called Man Friday if ever he was hatched, as soon as ever I found the egg in the canoe had developed. I was a bit anxious about his feed, so I gave him a lump of raw parrot-fish at once. He took it, and opened his beak for more. I was glad of that, for, under the circumstances, if he'd been at all fanciful, I should have had to eat him after all.

"You'd be surprised what an interesting bird that Æpyornis chick was. He followed me about from the very beginning. He used to stand by me and watch while I fished in the lagoon, and go shares in anything I caught. And he was sensible, too. There were nasty green warty things, like pickled gherkins, used to lie about on the beach and he tried one of these and it upset him. He never even looked at any of them again.

"And he grew. You could almost see him grow. And as I was never much of a society man, his quiet friendly ways suited me to a T. For nearly two years we were as happy as we could be on that island. I had no business worries, for I knew my salary was mounting up at Dawsons'. We would see a sail now and then, but nothing ever came near us. I amused myself, too, by decorating the island with designs worked in sea-urchins and fancy shells of various kinds. I put ÆPYORNIS ISLAND all around the place very nearly, in big letters, like what you see done with colored stones at railways stations in the old country, and mathematical calculations and drawings of various sorts. And I used to lie watching the blessed bird stalking round and growing, growing; and think how I could make a living out of him by showing him about if I ever got taken off. After his first moult he began to get handsome, with a crest and a blue wattle, and a lot of green feathers at the behind of him. And then I used to puzzle whether Dawsons' had any right to claim him or not. Stormy weather and in the rainy season we lay snug under the shelter I had made

14

out of the old canoe, and I used to tell him lies about my friends at home. And after a storm we would go round the island together to see if there was any drift. It was kind of idyll, you might say. If only I had had some tobacco it would have been simply just like heaven.

"It was about the end of the second year our little paradise went wrong. Friday was then about fourteen feet high to the bill of him, with a big, broad head like the end of a pickaxe, and two huge brown eyes with yellow rims, set together like a man's—not out of sight of each other like a hen's. His plumage was fine—none of the half-mourning style of your ostrich—more like a cassowary as far as color and texture go. And then it was he began to cock his comb at me and give himself airs, and show signs of a nasty temper . . .

"At last came a time when my fishing has been rather unlucky, and he began to hang about me in a queer, meditative way. I thought he might have been eating sea-cucumbers or something but it was really just discontent on his part. I was hungry, too, and when at last I landed a fish I wanted it for myself. Tempers were short that morning on both sides. He pecked at it and grabbed it, and I gave him a whack on the head to make him leave go. And at that he went for me. Lord! . . .

"He gave me this in the face." The man indicated his scar. "Then he kicked me. It was like a cart-horse. I got up, and, seeing he hadn't finished, I started off full tilt with my arms doubled over my face. But he ran on those gawky legs of his faster than a race-horse, and kept landing out at me like a sledge-hammer kicks and bringing his pick-axe down on the back of my head. I made for the lagoon, and went in up to my neck. He stopped at the water, for he hated getting his feet wet, and began to make a shindy, something like a peacock's, only hoarser. He started strutting up and down the beach. I'll admit I felt small to see this blessed fossil lording it here. And my head and face were all bleeding, and—well, my body just one jelly of bruises.

"I decided to swim across the lagoon and leave him alone for a bit, until the affair blew over. I shinned up the tallest palm-tree, and sat there thinking of it all. I don't suppose I ever felt so hurt by anything before or since. It was the brutal ingratitude of the creature. I'd been more than a brother to him. I'd hatched him, educated him. A great gawky, out-of-date bird! And me a human being—heir of the ages and all that.

"I thought after a time he'd begin to see things in that light himself, and feel a little sorry for his behavior. I thought if I was to catch some nice little bits of fish, perhaps, and go to him presently in a casual kind of way, and offer them to him, he might do the sensible thing. It took me some time to learn how unforgiving and cantankerous an extinct bird can be. Malice!

"I won't tell you all the little devices I tried to get that bird round again. I simply can't. It makes my cheek burn with shame even now to think of the snubs and buffets I had from this infernal curiosity. I tried violence. I chucked lumps of coral at him from a safe distance, but he only swallowed them. I shied my open knife at him and almost lost it, though it was too big for him to swallow. I tried starving him

15

out and struck fishing, but he took to picking along the beach at low water after worms, and rubbed along on that. Half my time I spent up to my neck in the lagoon, and the rest up the palm-trees. One of them was scarcely high enough, and when he caught me up it he had a regular Bank Holiday with the calves of my legs. It got unbearable. I don't know if you have ever tried sleeping up a palm-tree. It gave me the most horrible nightmares. Think of the shame of it, too! Here was this extinct animal mooning about my island like a sulky duke, and me not allowed to rest the sole of my foot on the place. I used to cry with weariness and vexation. I told him straight that I didn't mean to be chased about a desert island by any damned anachronisms. I told him to go and pack a navigator of his own age. But he only snapped his beak at me. Great ugly bird, all legs and neck!

"I shouldn't like to say how long that went on altogether. I'd have killed him sooner if I'd known how. However, I hit on a way of settling him at last. It is a South American dodge. I joined all my fishing-lines together with stems of seaweed and things, and made a stoutish string, perhaps twelve yards in length or more, and I fastened two lumps of coral rock to the ends of this. It took me some time to do, because every now and then I had to go into the lagoon or up a tree as the fancy took me. This I whirled rapidly round my head, and then let it go at him. The first time I missed, but the next time the string caught his legs beautifully, and wrapped round them again and again. Over he went. I threw it standing waist-deep in the lagoon, and as soon as he went down I was out of the water and sawing at his neck with my knife . . .

"I don't like to think of that even now. I felt like a murderer while I did it, though my anger was hot against him. When I stood over him and saw him bleeding on the white sand, and his beautiful great legs and neck writhing in his last agony . . . Pah!

"With that tragedy loneliness came upon me like a curse. Good Lord! you can't imagine how I missed that bird. I sat by his corpse and sorrowed over him, and shivered as I looked round the desolate, silent reef. I thought of what a jolly little bird he had been when he was hatched, and of a thousand pleasant tricks he has played before he went wrong. I thought if I'd only wounded him I might have nursed him round into a better understanding. If I'd had any means of digging into the coral rock I'd have buried him. I felt exactly as if he was a human. As it was, I couldn't think of eating him, so I put him in the lagoon, and the little fishes picked him clean. I didn't even save the feathers. Then one day a chap cruising about in a yacht had a fancy to see if my atoll still existed.

"He didn't come a moment too soon, for I was about sick enough of the desolation of it, and only hesitating whether I should walk out into the sea and finish up the business that way, or fall back on the green things . . .

"I sold the bones to a man named Winslow—a dealer near the British Museum, and he says he sold them to old Havers. It seems Havers didn't understand they were extra large, and it was only after his death they attracted attention. They called 'em Æpyornis—what was it?"

"*Æpyornis vastus*," said I. "It's funny, the very thing was mentioned to me by a friend of mine. When they found an Æpyronis with a thigh a yard long, they thought they had reached the top of the scale and called him *Æpyronic maximus*. Then someone turned up another thigh-bone four feet six or more, and that they called *Æpyornis titan*. Then your *vastus* was found after old Havers died, in his collection, and then a *vatissimus* turned up."

"Winslow was telling me as much," said the man with the scar. "If they get any more Aepyornises, he reckons some scientific swell will go and burst a blood-vessel. But it was a queer thing to happen to a man, wasn't it—altogether?"

# from *The Time Machine*
# (1895)

*The Time Machine,* Wells's first success and by many estimates his greatest work, presents *an elegant and dark tale of decline. It is Wells's comment on the tendency to read Darwinism as an optimistic doctrine justifying human ascendancy in the struggle for survival. The great accomplishment of the novel, however, is not its pessimism but its skillful process of revelation in what is at heart an adventure story. In the novel's middle section, deleted from this selection, the Time Traveler keeps having to reinterpret the social-natural relations that he finds in 802,701 when humanity has split into two species, the child-like Eloi, who live above ground, and the sloth-like Morlocks, who live in machine-ventilated tunnels underground. The first short selection describes time travel. In the second selection the Time Traveler, having narrowly escaped a Morlock trap, roams well beyond 802,701. At first he discovers an enigmatic evolutionary development, and as he moves further on he finds a dying Earth. The powerful vision of cosmic entropy raises questions about the meaningfulness of all human attainment. The epilogue, also included here, offers different interpretations of the future's possibilities.*

### from CHAPTER IV
### TIME TRAVELLING

\* \* \* \* \*

"I drew a breath, set my teeth, gripped the starting lever with both hands, and went off with a thud. The laboratory got hazy and went dark. Mrs. Watchett came in, and walked, apparently without seeing me, towards the garden door. I suppose it took her a minute or so to traverse the place, but to me she seemed to shoot across the room like a rocket. I pressed the lever over to its extreme position. The night came like the turning out of a lamp, and in another moment came to-morrow. The laboratory grew faint and hazy, then fainter and even fainter. To-morrow night came black, then day again, night again, day again, faster and faster still. An eddying murmur filled my ears, and a strange, dumb confusedness descended on my mind.

"I am afraid I cannot convey the peculiar sensations of time traveling. They are excessively unpleasant. There is a feeling exactly like that one has upon a switchback—of a helpless headlong motion! I felt the same horrible anticipation, too, of an imminent smash. As I put on pace, night followed day like the flapping of a black wing. The dim suggestion of the laboratory seemed presently to fall away from me, and I saw the sun hopping swiftly across the sky, leaping it every minute, and ever minute marking a day. I supposed the laboratory had been destroyed, and I had come into the open air. I had a dim impression of scaffolding, but I was already going too fast to be conscious of any

18

moving things. The slowest snail that ever crawled dashed by too fast for me. The twinkling succession of darkness and light was excessively painful to the eye. Then, in the intermittent darknesses, I saw the moon spinning swiftly through her quarters from new to full, and had a faint glimpse of the circling stars. Presently, as I went on, still gaining velocity, the palpitation of night and day merged into one continuous grayness; the sky took on a wonderful deepness of blue, a splendid luminous color like that of early twilight; the jerking sun became a streak of fire, a brilliant arc, in space, the moon a fainter fluctuating band; and I could see nothing of the stars, save now and then a brighter circle flickering in the blue.

"The landscape was misty and vague. I was still on the hillside upon which this house now stands, and the shoulder rose above me gray and dim. I saw trees growing and changing like puffs of vapor, now brown, now green: they grew, spread, shivered, and passed away. I saw huge buildings rise up faint and fair, and pass like dreams. The whole surface of the earth seemed changed—melting and flowing under my eyes. The little hands upon the dials that registered my speed raced round faster and faster. Presently I noted that the sun-belt swayed up and down, from solstice to solstice, in a minute or less, and that, consequently, my pace was over a year a minute; and minute by minute the white snow flashed across the world, and vanished, and was followed by the bright, brief green of spring.

"The unpleasant sensations of the start were less poignant now. They merged at last into a kind of hysterical exhilaration. I remarked, indeed, a clumsy swaying of the machine, for which I was unable to account. But my mind was too confused to attend to it, so with a kind of madness growing upon me, I flung myself into futurity. At first I scarce thought of stopping, scarce thought of anything but these new sensations. But presently a fresh series of impressions grew up in my mind—a certain curiosity and therewith a certain dread—until at last they took complete possession of me. What strange developments of humanity, what wonderful advances upon our rudimentary civilization, I thought, might not appear when I came to look nearly into the dim elusive world that raced and fluctuated before my eyes! I saw great and splendid architecture rising about me, more massive than any building of our own time, and yet, as it seemed, built of glimmer and mist. I saw a richer green flow up the hillside, and remain there without any wintry intermission. Even through the veil of my confusion the earth seemed very fair. And so my mind came round to the business of stopping.

"The peculiar risk lay in the possibility of my finding some substance in the space which I, or the machine, occupied. So long as I traveled at a high velocity through time, this scarcely mattered: I was, so to speak, attenuated—was slipping like a vapor through the interstices of intervening substances! But to come to a stop involved the jamming of myself, molecule by molecule, into whatever lay in my way: meant bringing my atoms into such intimate contact with those of the obstacle that a profound chemical reaction—possibly a far-reaching explosion—would result, and blow myself and my apparatus out of all possible dimensions—into the Unknown. This possibility had occurred to me again and again while I was making the machine; but then

19

I had cheerfully accepted it as an unavoidable risk—one of the risks a man has got to take! Now the risk was inevitable, I no longer saw it in the same cheerful light. The fact is that, insensibly, the absolute strangeness of everything, the sickly jarring and swaying of the machine, above all, the feeling of prolonged falling, had absolutely upset my nerve. I told myself that I could never stop, and with a gust of petulance I resolved to stop forthwith. Like an impatient fool, I lugged over the lever, and incontinently the thing went reeling over, and I was flung headlong through the air.

"There was the sound of a clap of thunder in my ears. I may have been stunned for a moment. A pitiless hail was hissing round me, and I was sitting on a soft turf in front of the overset machine. Everything still seemed gray, but presently I remarked that the confusion in my ears was gone. I looked round me. I was on what seemed to be a little lawn in a garden, surrounded by rhododendron bushes, and I noticed that their mauve and purple blossoms were dropping in a shower under the beating of the hailstones. The rebounding, dancing hail hung in a cloud over the machine, and drove along the ground like smoke. In a moment I was wet to the skin. 'Fine hospitality,' said I, 'to a man who has traveled innumerable years to see you.'

"Presently I thought what a fool I was to get wet. I stood up and looked round me. A colossal figure, carved apparently in some white stone, loomed indistinctly beyond the rhododendrons through the hazy downpour. But all else of the world was invisible.

"My sensations would be hard to describe. As the columns of hail grew thinner, I saw the white figure more distinctly. It was very large, for a silver birch tree touched its shoulder. It was of white marble, in shape something like a winged sphinx, but the wings, instead of being carried vertically at the sides, were spread so that it seemed to hover. The pedestal, it appeared to me, was of bronze, and was thick with verdigris. It chanced that the face was towards me; the sightless eyes seemed to watch me; there was the faint shadow of a smile on the lips. It was greatly weather-worn, and that imparted an unpleasant suggestion of disease. I stood looking at it for a little space—half a minute, perhaps, or half an hour. It seemed to advance and to recede as the hail drove before it denser or thinner. At last I tore my eyes from it for a moment, and saw that the hail curtain had worn threadbare, and that the sky was lightening with the promise of the sun.

"I looked up again at the crouching white shape, and the full temerity of my voyage came suddenly upon me. What might appear when that hazy curtain was altogether withdrawn? What might not have happened to men? What if cruelty had grown into a common passion? What if in this interval the race had lost its manliness, and had developed into something inhuman, unsympathetic, and overwhelmingly powerful? I might seem some old-world savage animal, only the more dreadful and disgusting for our common likeness—a foul creature to be incontinently slain.

"Already I saw other vast shapes—huge buildings with intricate parapets and tall columns, with a wooded hillside dimly creeping in upon me through the lessening storm. I was seized with a panic fear. I turned frantically to the Time Machine, and strove hard to readjust it. As I did so the shafts of the sun smote through the thunderstorm. The gray downpour swept aside and vanished like the trailing garments of a ghost. Above me, in the intense blue of the summer sky, some faint brown shreds of cloud whirled into nothingness. The great buildings about me stood out clear and distinct, shining with the wet of the thunderstorm, and picked out in white by the unmelted hailstones piled along their course. I felt naked in a strange world. I felt as perhaps a bird may feel in the clear air, knowing the hawk wings above and will swoop. My fear grew to frenzy. I took a breathing space, set my teeth, and again grappled fiercely, wrist and knee, with the machine. It gave under my desperate onset and turned over. It struck my chin violently. One hand on the saddle, the other on the lever, I stood painting heavily in attitude to mount again.

"But with this recovery of a prompt retreat my courage recovered. I looked more curiously and less fearfully at this world of the remote future. In a circular opening, high up in the wall of the nearer house, I saw a group of figures clad in rich soft robes. They had seen me, and their faces were directed towards me.

"Then I heard voices approaching me. Coming through the bushes by the White Sphinx were the heads and shoulders of men running. One of these emerged in a pathway leading straight to the little lawn upon which I stood with my machine. He was a slight creature—perhaps four feet high—clad in a purple tunic, girdled at the waist with a leather belt. Sandals or buskins—I could not clearly distinguish which—were on his feet; his legs were bare to the knees, and his head was bare. Noticing that, I noticed for the first time how warm the air was.

"He struck me as being a very beautiful and graceful creature, but indescribably frail. His flushed face reminded me of the more beautiful kind of consumptive—that hectic beauty of which we used to hear so much. At the sight of him I suddenly regained confidence. I took my hands from the machine.

* * * * *

### from CHAPTER XIV
### THE FURTHER VISION

"I have already told you of the sickness and confusion that comes with time traveling. And this time I was not seated properly in the saddle, but sideways and in an unstable fashion. For an indefinite time I clung to the machine as it swayed and vibrated, quite unheeding how I went, and when I brought myself to look at the dials again I was amazed to find where I had arrived. One dial records days, another thousands of days, another million of days, and another thousands of millions. Now instead of reversing the levers I had pulled them over so as to go forward with them, and when I came to look at these indicators I found that the thousands hand was sweeping round as fast as the seconds hands of a watch—into futurity. Very cautiously, for I remembered my former headlong fall, I began to reverse my motion. Slower and slower went the circling

21

hands until the thousands one seemed motionless and the daily one was no longer a mere mist upon its scale. Still slower, until the gray haze around me became distincter and dim outlines of an undulating waste grew visible.

"I stopped. I was on a bleak moorland, covered with a sparse vegetation, and gray with a thin hoarfrost. The time was midday, the orange sun, shorn of its effulgence, brooded near the meridian in a sky of drabby gray. Only a few black bushes broke the monotony of the scene. The great buildings of the decadent men among whom, it seemed to me, I had been so recently, had vanished and left no trace: not a mound even marked their position. Hill and valley, sea and river—all, under the wear and work of the rain and frost, had melted into new forms. No doubt, too, the rain and snow had long since washed out the Morlock tunnels. A nipping breeze stung my hands and face. So far as I could see there were neither hills, nor trees, nor rivers: only an uneven stretch of cheerless plateau.

"Then suddenly a dark bulk rose out of the moor, something that gleamed like a serrated row of iron plates, and vanished almost immediately in a depression. And then I became aware of a number of faint-gray things, colored to almost the exact tint of the frost-bitten soil, which were browsing here and there upon its scant grass, and running to and fro. I saw one jump with a sudden start, and then my eye detected perhaps a score of them. At first I thought they were rabbits, or some small breed of kangaroo. Then, as one came hopping near me, I perceived that it belonged to neither of these groups. It was plantigrade, its hind legs rather the longer; it was tailless, and covered with a straight grayish hair that thickened about the head into a Skye terrier's mane. As I had understood that in the Golden Age man had killed out almost all the other animals sparing only a few of the more ornamental, I was naturally curious about the creatures. They did not seem afraid of me, but browsed on, much as rabbits would do in a place unfrequented by men; and it occurred to me that I might perhaps secure a specimen.

"I got off the machine, and picked up a big stone. I had scarcely done so when one of the little creatures came within easy range. I was so lucky as to hit it on the head, and it rolled over at once and lay motionless. I ran to it at once. It remained still, almost as if it were killed. I was surprised to see that the thing had five feeble digits to both its fore and hind feet—the fore feet, indeed, were almost as human as the fore feet of a frog. It had, moreover, a roundish head, with a projecting forehead and forward-looking eyes, obscured by its lank hair. A disagreeable apprehension flashed across my mind. As I knelt down and seized my capture, intending to examine its teeth and other anatomical points which might show human characteristics, the metallic-looking object, to which I have already alluded, reappeared above a ridge in the moor, coming towards me and making a strange clattering sound as it came. Forthwith the grey animals about me began to answer with a short, weak yelping— as if of terror—and bolted off in a direction opposite to that from which this new creature approached. They must have hidden in burrows or behind bushes and tussocks, for in a moment not one of them was visible.

"I rose to my feet, and stared at this grotesque monster. I can only describe it by comparing it to a centipede. It stood about three feet high, and had a long segmented body, perhaps thirty feet long, with curiously overlapping greenish-black plates. It seemed to crawl upon a multitude of feet, looping its body as it advanced. Its blunt round head, with a polygonal arrangement of black eye spots, carried two flexible, writhing, horn-like antennae. It was coming along, I should judge, at a pace of about eight or ten miles an hour, and it left me little time for thinking. Leaving my grey animal, or grey man, whichever it was, on the ground, I set off for the machine. Halfway I paused, regretting that abandonment, but a glance over my shoulder destroyed any such regret. When I gained the machine the monster was scarce fifty yards away. It was certainly not a vertebrated animal. It had no snout, and its mouth was fringed with jointed dark-colored plates. But I did not care for a nearer view.

"I traversed one day and stopped again, hoping to find the colossus gone and some vestige of my victim; but, I should judge, the giant centipede did not trouble itself about bones. At any rate both had vanished. The faintly human touch of these little creatures perplexed me greatly. If you come to think, there is no reason why a degenerate humanity should not come at last to differentiate into as many species as the descendants of the mud fish who fathered all the land vertebrates. I saw no more of any insect colossus, as to my thinking the segmented creature must have been. Evidently the physiological difficulty that at present keeps all the insects small had been surmounted at last, and this division of the animal kingdom had arrived at the long-awaited supremacy which its enormous energy and vitality deserve. I made several attempts to kill or capture another of the grayish vermin, but none of my missiles were so successful as my first; and, after perhaps a dozen disappointing throws, that left my arm aching, I felt a gust of irritation at my folly in coming so far into futurity without weapons or equipment. I resolved to run on for one glimpse of the still remoter future—one peep into the deeper abysm of time—and then to return to you and my own epoch. Once more I remounted the machine, and one more the world grew hazy and gray.

"As I drove on, a peculiar change crept over the appearance of things. The palpitating grayness grew darker; then—though I was still traveling with prodigious velocity— the blinking succession of day and night, which was usually indicative of a slower pace, returned, and grew more and more marked. This puzzled me very much at first. The alternations of night and day grew slower and slower, and so did the passage of the sun across the sky, until they seemed to stretch through centuries. At last a steady twilight brooded over the Earth, a twilight only broken now and then when a comet glared across the darkling sky. The band of light that had indicated the sun had long since disappeared; for the sun had ceased to set—it simply rose and fell in the west, and grew ever broader and more red. All trace of the moon had vanished. The circling of the stars, growing slower and slower, had given place to creeping points of light. At last, some time before I stopped, the sun, red and very large, halted motionless upon the horizon, a vast dome glowing with a dull heat, and now and then suffering a momentary extinction. At one time it had for a little while glowed more brilliantly again, but it speedily reverted to its sullen red-heat. I perceived by this slowing down of its rising and setting that the work of the tidal drag was done. The earth had come to rest with one face to the sun, even as in our own time the moon faces the earth. Very cautiously, for I remembered my former headlong fall, I began to reverse my motion. Slower and slower went the circling hands until the thousands one seemed motionless, and the daily one was no longer a mere mist upon its scale. Still slower, until the dim outlines of a desolate beach grew visible.

"I stopped very gently and sat upon the Time Machine, looking round. The sky was no longer blue. North-eastward it was inky black, and out of the blackness shone brightly and steadily the pale white stars. Overhead it was a deep Indian red and starless, and south-eastward it grew brighter to a glowing scarlet where, cut by the horizon, lay the huge hull of the sun, red and motionless. The rocks about me were of a harsh reddish color, and all the trace of life that I could see at first was the intensely green vegetation that covered every projecting point on their south-eastern face. It was the same rich green that one sees on forest moss or on the lichen in caves: plants which like these grow in a perpetual twilight.

"The machine was standing on a sloping beach. The sea stretched away to the south-west, to rise into a sharp bright horizon against the wan sky. There were no breakers and no waves, for not a breath of wind was stirring. Only a slight oily swell rose and fell like a gentle breathing, and showed that the eternal sea was still moving and living. And along the margin where the water sometimes broke was a thick incrustation of salt—pink under the lurid sky. There was a sense of oppression in my head, and I noticed that I was breathing very fast. The sensation reminded me of my only experience of mountaineering, and from that I judged the air to be more rarefied than it is now.

"Far away up the desolate slope I heard a harsh scream, and saw a thing like a huge white butterfly go slanting and fluttering up into the sky and, circling, disappear over some low hillocks beyond. The sound of its voice was so dismal that I shivered and seated myself more firmly upon the machine. Looking round me again, I saw that, quite near, what I had taken to be a reddish mass of rock was moving slowly towards me. Then I saw the thing was really a monstrous crab-like creature. Can you imagine a crab as large as yonder table, with its many legs moving slowly and uncertainly, its big claws swaying, its long antennae, like carters' whips, waving and feeling, and its stalked eyes gleaming at you on either side of its metallic front? Its back was corrugated and ornamented with ungainly bosses, and a greenish incrustation blotched it here and there. I could see the many palps of its complicated mouth flickering and feeling as it moved.

"As I stared at this sinister apparition crawling towards me, I felt a tickling on my cheek as though a fly had lighted there. I tried to brush it away with my hand, but in a moment it returned, and almost immediately came another by my ear. I struck at this, and caught something thread-like. It was drawn swiftly out of my hand. With a

24

frightful qualm, I turned, and saw that I had grasped the antenna of another monster crab that stood just behind me. Its evil eyes were wriggling on their stalks, its mouth was all alive with appetite, and its vast ungainly claws, smeared with an algal slime, were descending upon me. In a moment my hand was on the lever, and I had placed a month between myself and these monsters. But I was till on the same beach, and I saw them distinctly now as soon as I stopped. Dozens of them seemed to be crawling here and there, in the somber light, among the foliated sheets of intense green.

"I cannot convey the sense of abominable desolation that hung over the world. The red eastern sky, the northward blackness, the salt Dead Sea, the stony beach crawling with these foul, slow-stirring monsters, the uniform poisonous-looking green of the lichenous plants, the thin air that hurts one's lungs: all contributed to an appalling effect. I moved on a hundred years, and there was the same red sun—a little larger, a little duller—the same dying sea, the same chill air, and the same crowd of earthy crustacea creeping in and out among the green weed and the red rocks. And in the westward sky I saw a curved pale line like a vast new moon.

"So I traveled, stopping ever and again, in great strides of a thousand years or more, drawn on by the mystery of the earth's fate, watching with a strange fascination the sun grow larger and duller in the westward sky and the life of the old earth ebb away. At last, more than thirty million years hence, the huge red-hot dome of the sun had come to obscure nearly a tenth part of the darkling heavens. Then I stopped once more for the crawling multitude of crabs had disappeared, and the red beach save for its livid green liverworts and lichens, seemed lifeless. And now it was flecked with white. A bitter cold assailed me. Rare white flakes ever and again came eddying down. To the north-eastward, the glare of snow lay under the starlight of the stable sky, and I could see an undulating crest of hillock pinkish-white. There were fringes of ice along the south margin, with drifting masses further out; but the main expanse of that south ocean, all bloody under the eternal sunset was still unfrozen.

"I looked about me to see if any trace of animal-life remained. A certain indefinable apprehension still kept me in the saddle of the time machine. But I saw nothing moving, in earth or sky or sea. The great slime on the rocks alone testified that life was not extinct. A shallow sandbank had appeared in the sea and the water had receded from the beach. I fancied I saw some black object flopping about upon this bank but it became motionless as I looked at it, and I judged that my eye had been deceived, and that the black object was merely a rock. The stars in the sky were intensely bright and seemed to me to twinkle very little.

"Suddenly I noticed that the circular westward outline of the sun had changed; that a concavity, a bay, had appeared in the curve. I saw this grow larger. For a minute perhaps I stared aghast at this blackness that was creeping over the day, and then I realized that an eclipse was beginning. Either the moon or the planet Mercury was passing across the sun's disk. Naturally, at first I took it to be the moon, but there is much to incline me to believe that what I really saw was the transit of an inner planet passing very near to the earth.

25

"The darkness grew apace; a cold wind began to blow in freshening gusts from the east, and the showering white flakes in the air increased in number. From the edge of the sea came a ripple and whisper. Beyond these lifeless sounds the world was silent. Silent? It would be hard to convey the stillness of it. All the sounds of man, the bleating of sheep, the cries of birds, the hum on insects, the stir that makes the background of our lives—all that was over. As the darkness thickened, the eddying flakes grew more abundant, dancing before my eyes; and the cold of the air more intense. At last, one by one, swiftly, one after the other, the white peaks of the distant hills vanished into blackness. The breeze rose to a moaning wind. I saw the black central shadow of the eclipse sweeping towards me. In another moment the pale stars alone were visible. All else was rayless obscurity. The sky was absolutely black.

"A horror of this great darkness came on me. The cold, that smote to my marrow, and the pain I felt in breathing overcame me. I shivered, and a deadly nausea seized me. Then like a red-hot bow in the sky appeared the edge of the sun. I got off the machine to recover myself. I felt giddy and incapable of facing the return journey. As I stood sick and confused I saw again the moving thing upon the shoal—there was no mistake now that it was a moving thing—against the red water of sea. It was a round thing, the size of football perhaps, or, it may be, bigger, and tentacles trailed down from it; it seemed black against the weltering blood-red water, and it was hopping fitfully about. Then I felt I was fainting. But a terrible dread of lying helpless in that remote and awful twilight sustained me while I clambered upon the saddle.

### from CHAPTER XV
### THE TIME TRAVELLER'S RETURN

"So I came back. For a long time I must have been insensible upon the machine. The blinking succession of the days and nights was resumed, the sun got golden again, the sky blue. I breathed with greater freedom. The fluctuating contours of the land ebbed and flowed. The hands spun backward upon the dials. At last I saw again the dim shadows of houses, the evidences of decadent humanity. These, too, changed and passed, and others came. Presently, when the million dial was at zero, I slackened speed. I began to recognize our own petty and familiar architecture, the thousands hand ran back to the starting-point, the night and day flapped slower and slower. Then the old walls of the laboratory came round me. Very gently, now, I slowed the mechanism down.

* * * * *

### EPILOGUE

One cannot choose but wonder. Will he ever return? It may be that he swept back into the past, and fell among the blood-drinking, hairy savages of the Age of Unspoiled Stone; into the abysses of the Cretaceous Sea; or among the grotesque saurians, the huge

26

reptilian brutes of the Jurassic times. He may even now—if I may use the phrase—be wandering on some plesiosaurus-haunted Oolitic coral reef or beside the lonely saline lakes of the Triassic Age. Or did he go forward, into one of the nearer ages, in which men are still men, but with the riddles of our own time answered and its wearisome problems solved? Into the manhood of the race: for I, for my own part, cannot think that these latter days of weak experiment, fragmentary theory, and mutual discord are indeed man's culminating time! I say, for my own part. He, I know—for the question had been discussed among us long before the Time Machine was made—thought but cheerlessly of the Advancement of Mankind, and saw in the growing pile of civilization only a foolish heaping that must inevitably fall back upon and destroy its makers in the end. If that is so, it remains for us to live as though it were not so. But to me the future is still black and blank—is a vast ignorance, lit at a few casual place by the memory of his story. And I have by me, for my comfort, two strange white flowers—shriveled now, and brown and flat and brittle—to witness that even when mind and strength had gone, gratitude and a mutual tenderness still lived on in the heart of a man.

# from *The Wheels of Chance*
# (1895)

*In the cheerful comedy,* The Wheels of Chance, *written immediately after* The Time Machine, *Wells gives a realistic and contemporary reading of the class differences that so much structure the middle part of the earlier novel. The naive and optimistic drapers assistant, Mr. Hoopdriver, represents a version of the man Wells would have become had his mother had her way. In the course of a bicycling holiday (Wells himself loved to tour the countryside on the newly invented bicycle) our hero meets an upper class young woman, Jessie Milton. She has become entangled with a scoundrel, Bechamel, who pretending to help her run away from her hated stepmother, actually intends to seduce her. Mr. Hoopdriver, infatuated with Jessie and acutely conscious of their social difference, tries to rescue her. Much of the comedy comes from the good-natured misunderstandings that these two young people have of each other. Jessie declares, "I am resolved to Live my Own Life," and Mr. Hoopdriver, who from his youth has worked for a living, has no idea what she is talking about, though he admires her assurance. Jessie, on her side, misinterprets the fawning and deferential manners of a store clerk, which Mr. Hoopdriver cannot shake, as those of "a colonial." The selection comes from the middle of the novel after Mr. Hoopdriver has ridden off with Jessie. They are traveling incognito as brother and sister. Mr. Hoopdriver, ashamed of his name, has given Jessie a false one, but he has also forgotten it.*

## Chapter XXVIII
### The Departure from Chichester

He caused his 'sister' to be called repeatedly, and when she came down, explained with a humorous smile his legal relationship to the bicycle in the yard. 'Might be disagreeable, y' know.' His anxiety was obvious enough. 'Very well,' she said (quite friendly); 'hurry breakfast, and we'll ride out. I want to talk things over with you.' The girl seemed more beautiful than ever after the night's sleep; her hair in comely dark waves from her forehead, her ungauntleted finger-tips pink and cool. And how decided she was! Breakfast was a nervous ceremony, conversation fraternal but thin; the waiter overawed him, and he was cowed by a multiplicity of forks. But she called him 'Chris.' They discussed their route over his six-penny county map for the sake of talking, but avoided a decision in the presence of the attendant. The five-pound note was changed for the bill, and through Hoopdriver's determination to be quite the gentleman, the waiter and chambermaid got half a crown each, and the ostler a florin. "Olidays,' said the ostler to himself, without gratitude. The public mounting of the bicycles in the street was a moment of trepidation. A policeman actually stopped and watched them from the opposite kerb. Suppose him to come across and ask: 'Is that your bicycle, sir?' Fight? Or drop and run?

It was time of bewildering apprehension, too, going through the streets of the town, so that a milk-cart barely escaped destruction under Mr. Hoopdriver's chancy wheel. That recalled him to a sense of erratic steering, and he pulled himself together. In the lanes he breathed freer, and a less formal conversation presently began.

'You've ridden out of Chichester in a great hurry,' said Jessie.

'Well, the fact of it is, I'm worried, just a little bit, about this machine.'

'Of course,' she said. 'I had forgotten that. But where are we going?'

'Jest a turning or two more, if you don't mind,' said Hoopdriver. 'Jest a mile or so. I have to think of you, you know. I should feel more easy. If we was locked up, you know—not that I should mind on my own account.'

They rode with a streaky, gray sea coming and going on their left hand. Every mile they put between themselves and Chichester Mr. Hoopdriver felt a little less conscience-striken, and a little more of the gallant desperado. Here he was riding on a splendid machine with a Slap-up girl beside him. What would they think of it in the Emporium if any of them were to see him? He imagined in detail the astonishment of Miss Isaacs and of Miss Howe. 'Why! It's Mr. Hoopdriver,' Miss Isaacs would say. '*Never!*' emphatically from Miss Howe. Then he played with Briggs, and then tried the 'G.V.' in a shay. 'Fancy introjuicing 'em to her—my sister *pro tem.*' He was her brother Chris—Chris what? Confound it!—Harringon, Hartington—something like that. Have to keep off that topic until he could remember. Wish he'd told her the truth now—almost. He glanced at her. She was riding with her eyes straight ahead of her. Thinking. A little perplexed she seemed. He noticed how well she rode, and that she rode with her lips closed—a thing he could never manage.

Mr. Hoopdriver's mind came round to the future. What was she going to do? What were they both going to do? His thoughts took a graver color. He had rescued her. This was fine, manly rescue work he was engaged upon. She ought to go home, in spite of that stepmother. He must insist gravely but firmly upon that. She was the spirited sort, of course, but still—wonder if she had any money? Wonder what the second-class fare from Havant to London is? Of course he would have to pay that—it was the regular thing, he being a gentleman. Then should he take her home? He began to rough in a moving sketch of the return. The stepmother, repentant of her indescribable cruelties, would be present—even these rich people have their troubles—probably an uncle or two. The footman would announce, Mr.—bother that name!—and Miss Milton. Then two women weeping together, and a knightly figure in the background dressed in a handsome Norfolk jacket, still conspicuously new. He would conceal his feeling until the very end. Then, leaving, he would pause in the doorway in such an attitude as Mr. George Alexander might assume, and say, slowly and dwindlingly: 'Be to kind to her—*be* kind to her,' and so depart, heartbroken to the meanest intelligence. But that was a matter for the future. He would have to begin discussing the return soon. There was no traffic along the road, and he came up beside her (he had fallen behind in his musing). She began to talk. 'Mr. Denison,' she began, and then, doubtfully, 'that *is* your name? I'm very stupid—'

'It is,' said Mr. Hoopdriver. (Denison was it? Denison, Denison, Denison. What was she saying?)

'I wonder how far you are willing to help me?'

Confoundedly hard to answer a question like that on the spur of the moment, without steering wildly. 'You may rely,' said Mr. Hoopdriver, recovering from a violent wabble. 'I can assure you—I want to help you very much. Don't consider me at all. Leastways, consider me entirely at your service.' (Nuisance not to be able to say this kind of thing right.)

'You see, I am so awkwardly situated.'

'If I can only help you—you will make me very happy—' There was a pause. Round a bend in the road they came upon a grassy space between hedge and road, set with yarrow and meadowsweet, where a felled tree lay among the green. There she dismounted, and propping her machine against a stone sat down. 'Here we can talk,' she said.

'Yes,' said Mr. Hoopdriver, expectant.

She answered after a little while, sitting, elbow on knee, with her chin in her hand, and looking straight in front of her. 'I don't know—I am resolved to Live my Own Life.'

'Of course,' said Mr. Hoopdriver. 'Naturally.'

'I want to Live, and I want to see what life means. I want to learn. Every one is hurrying me; everything is hurrying me; I want time to think.'

Mr. Hoopdriver was puzzled, but admiring. It was wonderful how clear and ready her words were. But then one might well speak well with a throat and lips like that. He knew he was inadequate, but he tried to meet the occasion. 'If you let them rush you into anything you might repent of, of course you'd be very silly,' he said.

'Don't *you* want to learn?' she asked.

'I was wondering only this morning,' he began, and stopped.

She was too intent upon her own thoughts to notice this insufficiency. 'I find myself in life, and it terrifies me. I seem to be like a little speck whirling on a wheel, suddenly caught up. "What am I here for?" I ask. Simply to be here a time—I asked it a week ago, I asked it yesterday, and I ask it to-day. And mother takes me shopping, people come to tea, there is a new play to pass the time, or a concert, or a novel. The wheels of the world go on turning, turning. It is horrible. I want to do a miracle like Joshua and stop the whirl until I have thought it out. At home—it's impossible.'

Mr. Hoopdriver stroked his moustache. 'It *is* so,' he said, in a meditative tone. 'Things *will* go on.' The faint breath of summer stirred the trees, and a bunch of dandelion puff lifted among the meadowsweet and struck and broke into a dozen separate threads against his knee. They flew on apart, and sank, as the breeze fell, among the grass: some to germinate, some to perish. His eye followed them until they had vanished.

'I can't go back to Surbiton,' said the Young Lady in Gray.

'*Eigh?*' said Mr. Hoopdriver, catching at his moustache. This was an unexpected development.

'I want to write, you see,' said the Young Lady in Gray, 'to write Books and alter things. To do Good. I want to lead a Free Life and Own myself. I can't go back. I want to obtain a position as a Journalist. I have been told—but I know no one to help me at once. No one that I could go to. There is one person—she was a mistress at my school. If I could write to her—but then, how could I get her answer?'

'H'mp,' said Mr. Hoopdriver, very grave.

'I can't trouble you much more. You have come—you have risked things—'

'That don't count,' said Mr. Hoopdriver. 'It's double pay to let me do it, so to speak.'

'It is good of you to say that. Surbiton is so Conventional. I am resolved to be Unconventional—at any cost. But we are so hampered. If I could only burgeon out of all that hinders me! I want to struggle, to take my place in the world. I want to be my own mistress, to shape my own career. But my step-mother objects so. She does as she likes herself, and is strict with me to ease her conscience. And if I go back now, go back owning myself beaten—' She left the rest to his imagination.

'I see that,' agreed Mr. Hoopdriver. He *must* help her. Within his skull he was doing some intricate arithmetic with five pounds six and twopence. In some vague way he inferred from all this that Jessie was trying to escape from an undesirable marriage, but was saying these things out of modesty. His circle of ideas was so limited.

'You know, Mr.— I've forgotten your name again.'

Mr. Hoopdriver seemed lost in abstraction. 'You can't go back, of course, quite like that,' he said thoughtfully. His ears were suddenly red and his cheeks flushed.

'But what *is* your name?'

'Name!' said Mr. Hoopdriver. 'Why!—Benson, of course.'

'Mr. Benson—yes—it's really very stupid of me. But I can never remember names. I must make a note on my cuff.' She clicked a little silver pencil and wrote the name down. 'If I could write to my friend, I believe she would be able to help me to an independent life. I could write to her—or telegraph. Write, I think. I could scarcely explain in a telegram. I know she would help me.'

Clearly there was only one course open to a gentleman under the circumstances. 'In that case,' said Mr. Hoopdriver, 'if you don't mind trusting yourself to a stranger, we might continue as we are perhaps—for a day or so; until you heard' (Suppose thirty shillings a day, that gives four days, say four thirties is hun' and twenty, six quid—well, three days, say; four ten.)

'You are very good to me.'

His expression was eloquent.

'Very well, then, and thank you. It's wonderful—it's more than I deserve that you—' She dropped the theme abruptly. 'What was our bill at Chichester?'

'*Eigh?*' said Mr. Hoopdriver, feigning a certain stupidity. There was a brief discussion. Secretly he was delighted at her insistence in paying. She carried her point. Their

31

talk came round to their immediate plans for the day. They decided to ride easily, through Havant, and stop, perhaps, at Fareham or Southampton; for the previous day had tried them both. Holding the map extended on his knee, Mr. Hoopdriver's eye fell by chance on the bicycle at his feet. 'That bicycle,' he remarked, quite irrelevantly, 'wouldn't look the same machine if I got a big double Elarum instead of that little bell.'

'Why?'

'Jest a thought.' A pause.

'Very well, then—Havant and lunch,' said Jessie, rising.

'I wish, somehow, we could have managed it without stealing that machine,' said Hoopdriver. 'Because it *is* stealing it, you know, come to think of it.'

'Nonsense. If Mr. Bechamel troubles you—I will tell the world—if need be.'

'I believe you would,' said Mr. Hoopdriver, admiring her. 'You're plucky enough—goodness knows.'

Discovering suddenly that she was standing, he, too, rose, and picked up her machine. She took it and wheeled it into the road. Then he took his own. He paused, regarding it. 'I say!' said he. 'How'd this bike look, now, if it was enameled gray?'

She looked over her shoulder at his grave face. 'Why try and hide it in that way?'

'It was jest a passing thought,' said Mr. Hoopdriver airily.

As they were riding on to Havant it occurred to Mr. Hoopdriver in a transitory manner that the interview had been quite other than his expectation. But that was the way with everything in Mr. Hoopdriver's experience. And though his Wisdom looked grave within him, and Caution was chinking coins, and an ancient prejudice in favor of Property shook her head, something else was there too, shouting in his mind to drown all these saner consideration, the intoxicating thought of riding beside Her all to-day, all to-morrow, perhaps for other days after that. Of talking to her familiarly, being brother of all her slender strength and freshness, of having a golden, real, and wonderful time beyond all his imaginings. His old familiar fancyings gave place to anticipations as impalpable and fluctuating and beautiful as the sunset of a summer day.

At Havant he took an opportunity to purchase, at a small hairdresser's in the main street, a tooth-brush, a pair of nail scissors, and a little bottle of stuff to darken the moustache, an article the shop man introduced to his attention, recommended highly, and sold in the excitement of the occasion.

## CHAPTER XXIX
### THE UNEXPECTED ANECDOTE OF THE LION

They rode on to Cosham, and lunched lightly but expensively there. Jessie went out and posted her letter to her schoolmistress. Then the green height of Portsdown Hill tempted them, and leaving their machines in the village, they clambered up the slope to the silent red-brick fort that crowned it. Thence they had a view of Portsmouth and its cluster of sister towns, the crowded narrows of the harbor, the Solent, and the Isle of Wight like a blue cloud through the hot haze. Jessie by some miracle had become a skirted woman in the Cosham inn. Mr. Hoopdriver lounged gracefully on the turf, smoked a Red Herring cigarette, and lazily regarded the fortified town that spread like a map away there, the inner line of defense like toy fortifications, a mile off perhaps; and beyond that a few little fields and then the beginnings of Landport suburb and the smoky cluster of the multitudinous houses. To the right, at the head of the harbor shallows, the town of Porchester rose among the trees. Mr. Hoopdriver's anxiety receded to some remote corner of his brain and that florid, half-voluntary imagination of his shared the stage with the image of Jessie. He began to speculate on the impression he was creating. He took stock of his suit optimistically again, and reviewed, with some complacency, his actions for the last four-and-twenty hours. Then he was dashed at the thought of her infinite perfections.

She had been observing him quietly, rather more closely during the last hour or so. She did not look at him directly, because he seemed always looking at her. Her own troubles had quieted down a little, and her curiosity about the chivalrous, worshipping, but singular gentleman in brown, was awakening. She had recalled, too, the curious incident of their first encounter. She found him hard to explain to herself. You must understand that her knowledge of the world was rather less than nothing, having been obtained entirely from books. You must not take a certain ignorance for foolishness.

She had begun with a few experiments. He did not know French except '*sivver-play*,' a phrase he seemed to regard as a very good light table joke in itself. His English was uncertain, but not such as books informed her distinguished the lower classes. His manners seemed to her good on the whole, but a trifle over-respectful and out of fashion. He called her 'Madam' once. He seemed a person of means and leisure, but he knew nothing of recent concerts, theatres, or books. How did he spend his time? He was certainly chivalrous, and a trifle simple-minded. She fancied (so much is there in a change of costume) that she had never met with such a man before. What *could* he be?

'Mr. Benson,' she said, breaking a silence devoted to landscape.

He rolled over and regarded her, chin on knuckles, 'At your service.'

'Do you paint? Are you an artist?'

'Well,' Judicious pause. 'I should hardly call myself a Nartist, you know. I *do* paint a little. And sketch, you know—skitty kind of things.'

He plucked and began to nibble a blade of grass. It was really not so much lying as his quick imagination that prompted him to add: 'In Papers, you know, and all that.'

'I see,' said Jessie, looking at him thoughtfully. Artists were a very heterogeneous class certainly, and geniuses had a trick of being a little odd. He avoided her eye and bit his grass. 'I don't do *much*, you know.'

'It's not your profession?'

'Oh no,' said Hoopdriver, anxious now to hedge. 'I don't make a regular thing of it, you know. Jest now and then something comes into my head and down it goes. No—I'm not a *regular* artist.'

'Then you don't practice any regular profession?'

Mr. Hoopdriver looked into her eyes and saw their quiet unsuspicious regard. He had vague ideas of resuming the detective role. 'It's like this,' he said, to gain time. 'I have a sort of profession. Only there's a kind of reason—nothing much, you know—'

'I beg your pardon for cross-examining you.'

'No trouble,' said Mr. Hoopdriver. 'Only I can't very well—I leave it to you, you know. I don't want to make any mystery of it, so far as that goes.' Should he plunge boldly and be a barrister? That anyhow was something pretty good. But she might know about barristry.

'I think I could guess what you are.'

'Well—guess,' said Mr. Hoopdriver.

"You come from one of the colonies?'

'Dear me!' said Mr. Hoopdriver, veering round to the new wind. 'How did you find out *that*? (The man was born in a London suburb, dear Reader.)

'I guessed,' she said.

He lifted his eyebrows as one astonished, and clutched a new piece of grass.

'You were educated up country.'

'Good again,' said Hoopdriver, rolling over again upon his elbow. 'You're a *clairvoy* ant.' He bit at the grass, smiling. 'Which colony was it?'

'That I don't know.'

'You must guess,' said Hoopdriver.

'South Africa,' she said 'I strongly incline to South Africa.'

'South Africa's quite a large place,' he said.

'But South Africa is right?'

'You're warm,' said Hoopdriver, 'anyhow'; and the while his imagination was eagerly exploring this new province.

'South Africa *is* right?' she insisted.

He turned over again and nodded, smiling reassuringly into her eyes.

'What made me think of South Africa was that novel of Olive Schreiner's, you know—*The Story of an African Farm*. Gregory Rose is so like you.'

'I never read *The Story of an African Farm*,' said Hoopdriver. 'I must. What's he like?'

'You must read the book. But it's a wonderful place, with its mixture of races, and its brand-new civilization jostling the old savagery. Were you near Khama?'

'He was a long way off from our place,' said Mr. Hoopdriver. 'We had a little ostrich farm, you know—just a few hundred of 'em, out Johannesburg way.'

'On the Karroo—was it called?'

'That's the term. Some of it was freehold though. Luckily. We got along very well in the old days. But there's no ostriches on that farm now.' He had a diamond mine in his head, just at the moment, but he stopped and left a little to the girl's imagination. Besides which it occurred to him with a kind of shock that he was lying.

'What became of the ostriches?'

'We sold 'em off, when we parted with the farm. Do you mind if I have another cigarette? That was when I was quite a little chap, you know, that we had this ostrich farm.'

'Did you have blacks and Boers about you?'

'Lots,' said Mr. Hoopdriver, striking a match on his instep, and beginning to feel hot at the new responsibility he had brought upon himself.

'How interesting! Do you know, I've never been out of England except to Paris and Mentone and Switzerland.'

'One gets tired of traveling (*puff*) after a bit, of course.'

'You must tell me about your farm in South Africa. It always stimulates my imagination to think of these places. I can fancy all the tall ostriches being driven out by a black herd to—graze, I suppose. How do ostriches feed?'

'Well,' said Hoopdriver. 'That's rather various. They have their fancies, you know. There's fruit, of course, and that kind of thing; and chicken food, and so forth. You have to use judgment.'

'Did you ever see a lion?'

'They weren't very common in our district,' said Hoopdriver, quite modestly. 'But I've seen them of course. Once or twice.'

'Fancy seeing a lion! Weren't you frightened?'

Mr. Hoopdriver was now thoroughly sorry he had accepted that offer of South Africa. He puffed his cigarette and regarded the Solent languidly as he settled the fate of that lion in his mind. 'I scarcely had time,' he said. 'It all happened in a minute.'

'Go on,' she said.

'I was going across the inner paddock where the fatted ostriches were.'

'Did you *eat* ostriches, then? I did not know—'

'Eat them! — often. Very nice they *are* too, properly stuffed. Well, we—I, rather—was going across this paddock, and I saw something standing up in the moonlight and looking at me.' Mr. Hoopdriver was in a hot perspiration now. His invention seemed to have gone limp. 'Luckily I had my father's gun with me. I *was* scared, though, I can tell you. (*Puff.*) I just aimed at the end that I thought was the head. And let fly. (*Puff.*) And over it went, you know.'

'Dead?'

'*As* dead. It was one of the luckiest shots I ever fired. And I wasn't much over nine at the time neither.'

'*I* should have screamed and run away.'

'There's some things you can't run away from,' said Mr. Hoopdriver. 'To run would have been Death.'

'I don't think I ever met a lion-killer before,' she remarked, evidently with a heightened opinion of him.

There was pause. She seemed meditating further questions. Mr. Hoopdriver drew his watch hastily. 'I say,' said Mr. Hoopdriver, showing it to her, 'don't you think we ought to be getting on?'

35

His face was flushed, his ears bright red. She ascribed his confusion to modesty. He rose with a lion added to the burthens of his conscience, and held out his hand to assist her. They walked down into Cosham again, resumed their machines, and went on at a leisurely pace along the northern shore of the big harbor. But Mr. Hoopdriver was no longer happy. This horrible, this fulsome lie, stuck in his memory. Why *had* he done it! She did not ask for any more South African stories, happily—at least until Porchester was reached—but talked instead of Living One's Own Life, and how custom hung on people like chains. She talked wonderfully, and set Hoopdriver's mind fermenting. By the Castle, Mr. Hoopdriver caught several crabs in little shore pools. At Fareham they stopped for a second tea, and left the place towards the hour of sunset, under such invigorating circumstances as you shall in due course hear.

# from *The Island of Doctor Moreau* (1896)

*For some stretches* The Island of Doctor Moreau *is sheer horror story. It is also a meditation on evolution and on the nature of the human animal. By calling it a "theological grotesque," and thereby drawing attention to how much Moreau takes on the creative possibilities of a god, Wells himself pointed to important thematic issues at play. Beyond the issues of Moreau's science there lurk profound questions about Prendick's, the narrator's, own responsibility in this bizarre situation: how much has he compromised his own moral standing by going along with Moreau? The novel is told through the eyes of Prendick, a man who has been saved from shipwreck and then stranded on Moreau's island by the vindictive captain. Prendick has slowly become aware that most of the "men" on the island are strange. At first he thinks they are humans whom Moreau has changed into beasts. The two brief selections come from the middle of the novel, as Prendick comes to a clearer understanding of the actual state of affairs on the island. The novel raises its thematic issues in an artful fashion. Humans may claim to speak for "the law," but they are no more responsible or moral than the beast men with their recitations of "the law," the obedience to which supposedly makes them human.*

from CHAPTERS XII and XVI
THE SAYERS OF THE LAW

Then something cold touched my hand. I started violently, and saw close to me a dim pinkish thing, looking more like a flayed child than anything else in the world. The creature had exactly the mild but repulsive features of a sloth, the same low forehead and slow gestures. As the first shock of the change of light passed, I saw about me more distinctly. The little sloth-like creature was standing and staring at me. My conductor had vanished.

The place was a narrow passage between high walls of lava, a crack in its knotted flow and on either side interwoven heaps of sea-mat, palm fans and reeds leaning against the rock, formed rough and impenetrably dark dens. The winding way up the ravine between these was scarcely three yards wide, and was disfigured by lumps of decaying fruit pulp and other refuse which accounted for the disagreeable stench of the place.

The little pink sloth creature was still blinking at me when my Ape Man reappeared at the aperture of the nearest of these dens, and beckoned me in. As he did so a slouching monster wriggled out of one of the places further up this strange street, and stood up in featureless silhouette against the bright green beyond, staring at me. I hesitated—had half a mind to bolt the way I had come—and then, determined to go through with the adventure, gripped my nailed stick about the middle, and crawled into the little evil-smelling lean-to after my conductor.

It was a semicircular space, shaped like the half of a bee-hive, and against the rocky wall that formed the inner side of it was a pile of variegated fruits, cocoa-nuts and others. Some rough vessels of lava and wood stood about the floor, and one on a rough stool. There was no fire. In the darkest corner of the hut sat a shapeless mass of darkness that grunted "Hey!" as I came in, and my Ape Man stood in the dim light of the doorway and held out a spilt cocoa-nut to me as I crawled into the other corner and squatted down. I took it and began gnawing it, as serenely as possible in spite of my tense trepidation and the nearly intolerable closeness of the den. The little pink sloth creature stood in the aperture of the hut, and something else with a drab face and bright eyes came staring over its shoulder.

"Hey," came out of the lump of mystery opposite. "It is a man! It is a man!" gabbled my conductor—"a man, a man, a live man, like me."

"Shut up!' said the voice from the dark, and grunted. I gnawed my cocoa-nut amid an impressive silence. I peered hard into the blackness, but could distinguish nothing. "It is a man," the voice repeated. "He comes to live with us?" It was a thick voice with something in it, a kind of whistling overtone, that struck me as peculiar, but the English accent was strangely good.

The Ape Man looked at me as though he expected something. I perceived the pause was interrogative.

"He comes to live with you," I said.

"It is a man. He must learn the Law."

I began to distinguish now a deeper blackness in the black, a vague outline of a hunched-up figure. Then I noticed the opening of the place was darkened by two more heads. My hand tightened on my stick. The thing in the dark repeated in a louder tone, "Say the words." I had missed its last remark. "Not to go on all-Fours; that is the Law"—it repeated in a kind of sing-song.

I was puzzled. "Say the words," said the Ape Man, repeating, and the figures in the doorway echoed this with a threat in the tone of their voices. I realized I had to repeat this idiotic formula. And then began the insanest ceremony. The voice in the dark began intoning a mad litany, line by line, and I and the rest to repeat it. As they did so, they swayed from side to side, and beat their hands upon their knees, and I followed their example. I could have imagined I was already dead and in another world. The dark hut, these grotesque dim figures, just flecked here and there by a glimmer of light, and all of them swaying in unison and chanting:

"Not to go on all-Fours; *that* is the Law. Are we not Men?"

"Not to suck up Drink; *that* is the Law. Are we not Men?"

"Not to eat Flesh or Fish; *that* is the Law. Are we not Men?"

"Not to claw Bark of Trees; *that* is the Law. Are we not Men?"

"Not to chase other Men; *that* is the Law. Are we not Men?"

And so from the prohibition of these acts of folly, on to the prohibition of what I thought then were the maddest, most impossible and most indecent things one could well imagine. A kind of rhythmic fervor fell on all of us; we gabbled and swayed faster and faster, repeating this amazing law. Superficially the contagion of these brute men was upon me, but deep down within me laughter and disgust struggled together. We ran through a long list of prohibitions, and then the chant swung round to a new formula:

"*His* is the House of Pain.

"*His* is the Hand that makes.

"*His* is the Hand that wounds.

"*His* is the Hand that heals.

And so on for another long series, mostly quite incomprehensible gibberish to me, about *Him*, whoever he might be. I could have fancied it was a dream, but never before have I heard chanting in a dream.

"*His* is the lightning-flash," we sang. "*His* is the deep salt sea."

A horrible fancy came into my head that Moreau, after animalizing these men, had infected their dwarfed brains with a kind of deification of himself. However, I was too keenly aware of white teeth and strong claws about me to stop my chanting on the account. "*His* are the stars in the sky."

At last that song ended. I saw the Ape Man's face shining with perspiration, and my eyes being now accustomed to the darkness, I saw more distinctly the figure in the corner from which the voice came. It was the size of a man, but it seemed covered with a dull gray hair almost like a Skye terrier. What was it? What were they all? Imagine yourself surrounded by all the most horrible cripples and maniacs it is possible to conceive, and you may understand a little of my feelings with these grotesque caricatures of humanity about me.

"He is a five-man, a five-man, a five-man . . . like me," said the Ape Man.

I held out my hands. The gray creature in the corner leant forward. "Not to run on all-Fours; that is the Law. Are we not Men?" he said. He put out a strangely distorted talon, and gripped my fingers. The thing was almost like the hoof of a deer produced into claws. I could have yelled with surprise and pain. His face came forward and peered at my nails, came forward into the light of the opening of the hut, and I saw with a quivering disgust that it was like the face of neither man nor beast, but a mere shock of gray hair, with three shadowy overarchings to mark the eyes and mouth.

"He has little nails," said the grisly creature in his hairy beard. "It is well. Many are troubled with big nails."

He threw my hand down, and instinctively I gripped my stick.

"Eat roots and herbs—it is His will," said the Ape Man.

"I am the Sayer of the Law," said the gray figure. "Here come all that be new, to learn the Law. I sit in the darkness and say the Law."

"It is even so," said one of the beasts in the doorway.

"Evil are the punishments of those who break the Law. None escape."

"None escape," said the Beast folk, glancing furtively at each other.

"None, none," said the Ape Man. "None escape. See! I did a little thing, a wrong thing once. I jabbered, jabbered, stopped talking. None could understand. I am burnt, branded in the hand. He is great, he is good!"

"None escape," said the great creature in the corner.

"None escape," said the Beast People, looking askance at one another.

"For every one the want that is bad," said the gray Sayer of the Law. "What you will want, we do not know. We shall know. Some want to follow things that move, to watch and slink and wait and spring, to kill and bite, bite deep and rich, sucking the blood . . . It is bad. 'Not to chase other Men; that is the Law. *Are we not Men?* Not to eat Flesh nor Fish: that is the Law. *Are we not Men?'*"

"None escape," said a dappled brute standing in the doorway.

"For every one the want that is bad," said the gray Sayer of the Law. "Some want to go tearing with teeth and hands into the roots of things, snuffing into the earth . . . It is bad."

"None escape," said the men in the door.

"Some go clawing trees, some go scratching at the graves of the dead; some go fighting with foreheads or feet or claws; some bite suddenly, none giving occasion; some love uncleanness."

"None escape," said the Ape Man, scratching his calf.

"None escape," said the little pink sloth creature.

"Punishment is sharp and sure. Therefore learn the Law. Say the words," and incontinently he began again the strange litany of the Law, and again I and all these creatures began singing and swaying. My head reeled with this jabbering and the close stench of the place, but I kept on, trusting to find presently some chance of a new development. "Not to go on all-Fours; that is the Law. *Are We Not Men?*"

We were making such a noise that I noticed nothing of a tumult outside, until someone, who, I think was one of the two Swine Men I had seen, thrust his head over the little pink sloth creature and shouted something excitedly, something that I did not catch. Incontinently those at the opening of the hut vanished, my Ape man rushed out, the thing that had sat in the dark followed him—I only observed it was big and clumsy, and covered with silvery hair, and I was left alone.

Then before I reached the aperture I heard the yelp of a staghound.

In another moment I was standing outside the hovel, my chair-rail in my hand, every muscle of me quivering. Before me were the clumsy backs of perhaps a score of these Beast People, their misshapen heads half-hidden by their shoulder-blades. They were gesticulating excitedly. Other half-animal faces glared interrogation out of the hovels. Looking in the direction in which they faced I saw coming through the haze under the trees beyond the end of the passage of dens the dark figure and aw-

ful white face of Moreau. He was holding the leaping staghound back, and close behind him came Montgomery, revolver in hand.

For a moment I stood horror-struck.

\* \* \* \* \*

First to arrive was the Satyr, strangely unreal for all that he cast a shadow, and tossed
the dust with his hoofs; after him from the brake came a monstrous lout, a thing of
horse and rhinoceros, chewing a straw as it came; and then appeared the Swine
Woman and two Wolf Women; then the Fox-Bear Witch with her red eyes in her
peaked red face, and then others—all hurrying eagerly. As they came forward they
began to cringe towards Moreau and chant, quite regardless of one another, fragments of the latter half of the litany of the Law: "*His* is the Hand that wounds, *His* is
the Hand that heals," and so forth.

As soon as they had approached within a distance of perhaps thirty yards they
halted, and bowing on knees and elbows, began flinging the white dust upon their
heads. Imagine the scene if you can. We three blue-clad men, with our misshapen black-
faced attendant, standing in a wide expanse of sunlit yellow dust under the blazing blue
sky, and surrounded by this circle of crouching and gesticulating monstrosities, some almost human save in their subtle expression and gestures, some like cripples, some so
strangely distorted as to resemble nothing but the denizens of our wildest dreams. And
beyond, the reedy lines of a cane brake in one direction and a dense tangle of palm-trees
on the other, separating us from the ravine with the huts, and to the north the hazy horizon of the Pacific Ocean.

"Sixty-two, sixty-three," counted Moreau. "There are four more."

"I do not see the Leopard Man," said I.

Presently Moreau sounded the great horn again, and at the sound of it all the
Beast People writhed and groveled in the dust. Then, slinking out of the cane brake,
stooping near the ground, and trying to join the dust-throwing circle behind
Moreau's back, came the Leopard man. And I saw that his forehead was bruised. The
last of the Beast People to arrive was the little Ape Man. The earlier animals, hot and
weary with their groveling, shot vicious glances at him.

"Cease," said Moreau, in his firm loud voice, and the Beast People sat back upon
their hams and rested from their worshipping.

"Where is the Sayer of the Law?" said Moreau, and the hairy gray monster
bowed his face in the dust.

"Say the words," said Moreau, and forthwith all in the kneeling assembly,
swaying from side to side and dashing up the sulphur with their hands, first the
right hand and a puff of dust, and then the left, began once more to chant their
strange litany.

When they reached "Not to eat Flesh or Fish; that is the Law," Moreau held up
his lank white hand. "*Stop!*" he cried, and there fell absolute silence upon them all.

41

I think they all knew and dreaded what was coming. I looked round at their strange faces. When I saw their wincing attitudes and the furtive dread in their bright eyes, I wondered that I had ever believed them to be men.

"That Law has been broken," said Moreau.

"None escape," from the faceless creature with the Silvery Hair. "None escape," repeated the kneeling circle of Beast People.

"Who is he?" cried Moreau, and looked round at their faces, cracking his whip. I fancied the Hyaena-Swine looked dejected, so too did the Leopard Man. Moreau stopped, facing this creature, who cringed towards him with the memory and dread of infinite torment. "Who is he?' repeated Moreau, in a voice of thunder.

"Evil is he who breaks the Law," chanted the Sayer of the Law.

Moreau looked into the eyes of the Leopard Man, and seemed to be dragging the very soul out of the creature.

"Who breaks the Law—" said Moreau, taking his eyes off his victim and turning towards us. It seemed to me there was a touch of exultation in his voice.

"—goes back to the House of Pain," they all clamored; "goes back to the House of Pain, O Master!"

"Back to the House of Pain—back to the House of Pain," gabbled the Ape Man, as though the idea was sweet to him.

"Do you hear?" said Moreau, turning back to the criminal, "my friend . . . Hullo!"

For the Leopard man, released from Moreau's eye, had risen straight from his knees, and now, with eyes aflame and his huge feline tusks flashing out from under his curling lips, leapt towards his tormentor. I am convinced that only the madness of unendurable fear could have prompted this attack. The whole circle of three-score monsters seemed to rise about us. I drew my revolver. The two figures collided. I saw Moreau reeling back from the Leopard Man's blow. There was a furious yelling and howling all about us. Everyone was moving rapidly. For a moment I thought it was a general revolt.

The furious face of the Leopard Man flashed by mine, with M'ling close in pursuit. I saw the yellow eyes of the Hyaena-Swine blazing with excitement, his attitude as if he were half-resolved to attack me. The Satyr, too, glared at me over the Hyaena-Swine's hunched shoulders. I heard the crack of Moreau's pistol, and saw the pink flash dart across the tumult. The whole crowd seemed to swing round in the direction of the glint of fire, and I, too, was swung round by the magnetism of the movement. In another second I was running, one of the tumultuous shouting crowd, in pursuit of the escaping Leopard Man.

That is all I can tell definitely. I saw the Leopard man strike Moreau, and then everything spun about me, until I was running headlong.

M'ling was ahead, close in pursuit of the fugitive. Behind, their tongues already lolling out, ran the Wolf-Women in great leaping strides. The Swine-Folk followed, squealing with excitement, and the two Bull Men in their swathings of white. Then came Moreau in a cluster of the Beast People, his wide-brimmed straw hat blown off, his revolver in hand, and his lank white hair streaming out. The Hyaena-Swine ran beside me, keeping pace with me, and glancing furtively at me out of his feline eyes, and the others came pattering and shouting behind us.

The Leopard Man went bursting his way through the long canes, which sprang back as he passed and rattled in M'ling's face. We others in the rear found a trampled path for us when we reached the brake. The chase lay through the brake for perhaps a quarter of a mile, and then plunged into a dense thicket that retarded our movements exceedingly, though we went through it in a crowd together—fronds flicking into our faces, ropy creepers catching us under the chin, or gripping our ankles, thorny plants hooking into the tearing cloth and flesh together.

"He has gone on all-fours though this," panted Moreau, now just ahead of me.

"None escape," said the Wolf-Bear, laughing into my face with the exultation of hunting.

We burst out again among rocks, and saw the quarry ahead, running lightly on all-fours, and snarling at us over his shoulder. At that the Wolf-Folk howled with delight. The thing was still clothed, and, at a distance, its face still seemed human, but the carriage of its four limbs was feline, and the furtive droop of its shoulder was distinctly that of a hunted animal. It leapt over some thorny yellow flowering bushes and was hidden. M'ling was half-way across the space.

Most of us now had lost the first speed of the chase, and had fallen into a longer and steadier stride. I saw, as we traversed the open, that the pursuit was now spreading from a column into a line. The Hyaena-Swine still ran close to me, watching me as it ran, every now and then puckering its muzzle with a snarling laugh.

At the edge of the rocks the Leopard Man, realizing he was making for the projecting cape upon which he had stalked me on the night of my arrival, had doubled in the undergrowth. But Montgomery had seen the maneuver, and turned him again.

So, panting, tumbling against rocks, torn by brambles, impeded by ferns and reeds, I helped to pursue the Leopard Man who had broken the Law, and the Hyaena-Swine ran, laughing savagely, by my side. I staggered on, my head reeling, and my heart beating against my ribs, tired almost to death, and yet not daring to lose sight of the chase, lest I should be left alone with this horrible companion. I staggered on in spite of infinite fatigue and the dense heat of the tropical afternoon.

And at last the fury of the hunt slackened. We had pinned the wretched brute into a corner of the island. Moreau, whip in hand, marshaled us all into an irregular line, and we advanced now slowly, shouting to one another as we advanced, and tightening the cordon about our victim. He lurked, noiseless and invisible, in the bushes through which I had run from him during the midnight pursuit.

"Steady!" cried Moreau; "steady!" as the ends of the line crept round the tangle of undergrowth, and hemmed the brute in.

"'Ware a rush!" came the voice of Montgomery from beyond the thicket.

I was on the slope above the bushes. Montgomery and Moreau beat along the beach beneath. Slowly we pushed in among the fretted network of branches and leaves. The quarry was silent.

43

"Back to the House of Pain, the House of Pain, the House of Pain!" yelped the voice of the Ape Man, some twenty yards to the right.

When I heard that I forgave the poor wretch all the fear he had inspired in me.

I heard the twigs snap and the boughs swish aside before the heavy tread of the Horse-rhinoceros upon my right. Then suddenly, through a polygon of green, in the half-darkness under the luxuriant growth, I saw the creature we were hunting. I halted. He was crouched together into the smallest possible compass, his luminous green eyes turned over his shoulder regarding me.

It may seem a strange contradiction in me—I cannot explain the fact—but now, see-ing the creature there in a perfectly animal attitude, with the light gleaming in its eyes, and its imperfectly human face distorted with terror, I realized again the fact of its hu-manity. In another moment other of its pursuers would see it, and it would be over-powered and captured, to experience once more the horrible tortures of the enclosure. Abruptly I slipped out my revolver, aimed between his terror-struck eyes and fired.

As I did so the Hyaena-Swine saw the thing, and flung itself upon it with an ea-ger cry, thrusting thirsty teeth into its neck. All about me the green masses of the thicket were swaying and cracking as the Beast People came rushing together. One face and then another appeared.

"Don't kill it, Prendick!" cried Moreau. "Don't kill it!" and I saw him stooping as he pushed through the under fronds of the big ferns.

In another moment he had beaten off the Hyaena-Swine with the handle of his whip, and he and Montgomery were keeping away the excited carnivorous Beast People, and particularly M'ling from the still quivering body. The Hairy Gray Thing came sniffing at the corpse under my arm. The other animals, in their animal ardor, jostled me to get a nearer view.

"Confound you, Prendick!" said Moreau. "I wanted him."

"I'm sorry," said I, though I was not. "It was the impulse of the moment." I felt sick with exertion and excitement. Turning, I pushed my way out of the crowding Beast People and went on alone up the slope towards the higher part of the headland. Under the shouted instructions of Moreau, I heard the three white-swathed Bull Men begin dragging the victim down towards the water.

It was easy now for me to be alone. The Beast People manifested a quite human curiosity about the dead body, and followed it in a thick knot, sniffing and growling at it, as the Bull Men dragged it down the beach. I went to the headland, and watched the Bull Men, black against the evening sky, as they carried the weighted dead body out to sea, and, like a wave across my mind, came the realization of the unspeakable aimlessness of things upon the island.

\* \* \* \* \*

44

# from *The Invisible Man* (1897)

*Griffen, the protagonist of* The Invisible Man, *is the least admirable of Wells's scientific heroes, and he appears in a novel with the most comic ordinary people. Griffen may have our sympathy during the early chapters when we slowly become aware of who he is and what his plight is—he has to cover himself so as not to be invisible, and he needs to find an antidote to invisibility. As the story proceeds, however, he is revealed as having been self-serving from the beginning (he risked burning down the apartment house for his experiments), and a homicidal figure out of nightmare at the end. The comedy is of the sort that Wells has mastered before, but in this context it lends a surreal tonality to the story. Conrad admired this novel very much, and one can see why. The idea of invisibility is made plausible, and its implications are thought through in remarkable detail. The selection comes from the middle of the novel, as the townspeople begin to suspect what they have to deal with.*

## Chapter 5
### The Burglary at the Vicarage

The facts of the burglary at the vicarage came to us chiefly through the medium of the vicar and his wife. It occurred in the small hours of Whit-Monday—the day devoted in Iping to the Club festivities. Mrs. Bunting, it seems, woke up suddenly in the stillness that comes before the dawn, with the strong impression that the door of their bedroom had opened and closed. She did not arouse her husband at first, but sat up in bed listening. She then distinctly heard the pad, pad, pad of bare feet coming out of the adjoining dressing-room and walking along the passage towards the staircase. As soon as she felt assured of this, she aroused the Rev. Mr. Bunting as quietly as possible. He did not strike a light, but putting on his spectacles, her dressing-gown, and his bath slippers, he went out on the landing to listen. He heard quite distinctly a fumbling going on at his study desk downstairs, and then a violent sneeze.

At that he returned to his bedroom, armed himself with the most obvious weapon, the poker, and descended the staircase as noiselessly as possible. Mrs. Bunting came out on the landing.

The hour was about four, and the ultimate darkness of night was past. There was a faint shimmer of light in the hall, but the study doorway yawned impenetrably black. Everything was still except the faint creaking of the stairs under Mr. Bunting's tread, and the slight movements in the study. Then something snapped, the drawer was opened, and there was a rustle of papers. Then came an imprecation, and a match was struck and the study was flooded with yellow light. Mr. Bunting was now in the hall, and through the crack of the door he could see the desk and the open drawer and a candle burning on the desk. But the robber he could not see. He stood there in the hall undecided what to do, and Mrs. Bunting, her face white and intent, crept slowly downstairs after him. One thing kept up Mr. Bunting's courage: the persuasion that this burglar was a resident in the village.

They heard the chink of money, and realized that the robber had found the housekeeping reserve of gold—two pounds ten in half-sovereigns altogether. At that sound Mr. Bunting was nerved to abrupt action. Gripping the poker firmly, he rushed into the room, closely followed by Mrs. Bunting, fiercely, and then stopped amazed. Apparently the room was perfectly empty.

Yet their conviction that they had, that very moment, heard somebody moving in the room had amounted to a certainty. For half a minute, perhaps, they stood gaping, then Mrs. Bunting went across the room and looked behind the screen, while Mr. Bunting, by a kindred impulse, peered under the desk. Then Mrs. Bunting turned back the window-curtains, and Mr. Bunting looked up the chimney and probed it with the poker. Then Mrs. Bunting scrutinized the waste-paper basket and Mr. Bunting opened the lid of the coal-scuttle. Then they came to a stop and stood with eyes interrogating each other.

"I could have sworn—" said Mr. Bunting.

"The candle!" said Mrs. Bunting. "Who lit the candle?"

"The drawer!" said Mrs. Bunting "And the money's gone!"

She went hastily to the doorway.

"Of all the extraordinary occurrences—"

There was a violent sneeze in the passage. They rushed out, and as they did so the kitchen door slammed. "Bring the candle," said Mr. Bunting, and led the way. They both heard a sound of bolts being hastily shot back.

As he opened the kitchen door he saw through the scullery that the back door was just opening, and the faint light of early dawn displayed the dark masses of the garden beyond. He was certain that nothing went out of the door. It opened, stood open for a moment, and then closed with a slam. As it did so, the candle Mrs. Bunting was carrying from the study flickered and flared. It was a minute or more before they entered the kitchen.

The place was empty. They refastened the back door, examined the kitchen, pantry, and scullery thoroughly, and at last went down into the cellar. There was not a soul to be found in the house, search as they would.

Daylight found the vicar and his wife, a quaintly-costumed little couple, still marveling about on their own ground floor by the unnecessary light of a guttering candle.

## CHAPTER 6
### THE FURNITURE THAT WENT MAD

Now it happened that in the early hours of Whit-Monday, before Millie was hunted out for the day, Mr. Hall and Mrs. Hall both rose and went noiselessly down into the cellar.

46

Their business there was of a private nature, and had something to do with the specific gravity of their beer. They had hardly entered the cellar when Mrs. Hall found she had forgotten to bring down a bottle of sarsaparilla from their joint-room. As she was the expert and principal operator in this affair, Hall very properly went upstairs for it.

On the landing he was surprised to see that the stranger's door was ajar. He went on into his own room and found the bottle as he had been directed.

But returning with the bottle, he noticed that the bolts of the front door had been shot back, that the door was in fact simply on the latch. And with a flash of inspiration he connected this with the stranger's room upstairs and suggestions of Mr. Teddy Henfrey. He distinctly remembered holding the candle while Mrs. Hall shot those bolts overnight. At the sight he stopped, gaping, then with the bottle still in his hand went upstairs again. He rapped at the stranger's door. There was no answer. He rapped again; then pushed the door wide open and entered.

It was as he expected. The bed, the room also, was empty. And what was stranger, even to his heavy intelligence, on the bedroom chair and along the rail of the bed were scattered the garments, the only garments so far as he knew, and the bandages of their guest. His big slouch hat even was cocked jauntily over the bedpost.

As Hall stood there he heard his wife's voice coming out of the depth of the cellar, with that rapid telescoping of the syllables and interrogative cocking up of the final words to a high note, by which the West Sussex villager is wont to indicate a brisk impatience.

"Gearge! You gart what a wand?"

At that he turned and hurried down to her. "Janny," he said over the rail of the cellar steps, " 'tas the truth what Henfrey sez. 'E's not in uz room, 'e ent. And the front door's unbolted."

At first Mrs. Hall did not understand, and as soon as she did she resolved to see the empty room for herself. Hall, still holding the bottle, went first. "If 'e ent there," he said, "his close are. And what's 'e doing' without his close, then? 'Tas a most curious basness."

As they came up the cellar steps, they both, it was afterwards ascertained, fancied they heard the front door open and shut, but seeing it closed and nothing there, neither said a word to the other about it at the time. Mrs. Hall passed her husband in the passage and ran on first upstairs. Some one sneezed on the staircase. Hall, following six steps behind, thought that he heard her sneeze. She, going on first, was under the impression that Hall was sneezing. She flung open the door and stood regarding the room. "Of all the curious!" she said.

She heard a sniff close behind her head as it seemed, and, turning, was surprised to see Hall a dozen feet off on the top-most stair. But in another moment he was beside her. She bent forward and put her hand on the pillow and then under the clothes.

"Cold," she said. "He's been up this hour or more."

As she did so, a most extraordinary thing happened—the bed-clothes gathered themselves together, leapt up suddenly into a sort of peak, and then jumped headlong over the bottom rail. It was exactly as if a hand had clutched them in the center and flung them aside. Immediately after, the stranger's hat hopped off the bed-post, described a whirling flight in the air through the better part of a circle, and then dashed straight at Mrs. Hall's face. Then as swiftly came the sponge from the washstand; and then the chair, flinging the stranger's coat and trousers carelessly aside, and laughing dryly in a voice singularly like the stranger's, turned itself up with is four legs at Mrs. Hall, seemed to take aim at her for a moment, and charged at her. She screamed and turned, and then the chair legs came gently but firmly against her back and impelled her and Hall out of the room. The door slammed violently and was locked. The chair and bed seemed to be executing a dance of triumph for a moment, and then abruptly everything was still.

Mrs. Hall was left almost in a fainting condition in Mr. Hall's arms on the landing. It was with the greatest difficulty that Mr. Hall and Millie, who had been roused by her scream of alarm, succeeded in getting her downstairs, and applying the restoratives customary in these cases.

" 'Tas sperrits," said Mrs. Hall. "I know 'tas sperrits. I've read in papers of en. Tables and chairs leaping and dancing—!"

"Take a drop more, Janny," said Hall. " 'Twill stedy ye."

"Lock him out," said Mrs. Hall. "Don't let him come in again. I half guessed—I might ha' known. With them goggling eyes and bandaged head, and never going to church of a Sunday. And all they bottles—more'n it's right for any one to have. He's put the sperrits into the furniture. My good old furniture! 'Twas in that very chair my poor dear mother used to sit when I was little girl. To think it should rise up against me now!"

"Just a drop more, Janny," said Hall. "Your nerves is all upset."

They sent Millie across the street through the golden five o'clock sunshine to rouse up Mr. Sandy Wadgers, the blacksmith. Mr. Hall's compliments and the furniture upstairs was behaving most extraordinary. Would Mr. Wadgers come round? He was a knowing man, was Mr. Wadgers, and very resourceful. He took quite a grave view of the case. "Arm darmed ef thet ent witchcraft," was the view of Mr. Sandy Wadgers. "You warnt horseshoes for such gentry as he."

He came round greatly concerned. They wanted him to lead the way upstairs to the room, but he didn't' seem to be in any hurry. He preferred to talk in the passage. Over the way Huxter's apprentice came out and began taking down the shutters of the tobacco window. He was called over to join the discussion. Mr. Huxter naturally followed in the course of a few minutes. The Anglo-Saxon genius for parliamentary government asserted itself; there was a great deal of talk and no decisive action. "Let's have the facts first," insisted Mr. Sandy Wadgers. "Let's be sure we'd be acting perfectly right in bustin' that there door open. A door onbust is always open to bustin', but ye can't onbust a door once you've busted en."

And suddenly and most wonderfully the door of the room upstairs opened of its own accord, and as they looked up in amazement, they saw descending the stairs the muffled figure of the stranger staring more blackly and blankly than ever with those unreasonably large blue glass eyes of his. He came down stiffly and slowly, staring all the time; he walked across the passage staring, then stopped.

"Look there!" he said, and their eyes followed the direction of his gloved finger and saw a bottle of sarsaparilla hard by the cellar door. Then he entered the parlor, and suddenly, swiftly, viciously slammed the door in their faces.

Not a word was spoken until the last echoes of the slam had died away. They stared at one another. "Well, if that don't lick everything!" said Mr. Wadgers, and left the alternative unsaid.

"I'd go in and ask'n 'bout it," said Wadgers, to Mr. Hall. "I'd d'mand an explanation."

It took some time to bring the landlady's husband up to that pitch. At last he rapped, opened the door, and got as far as, "Excuse me—"

"Go to the devil!" said the stranger in a tremendous voice, and "Shut the door after you." So that brief interview terminated.

## CHAPTER 7
### THE UNVEILING OF THE STRANGER

The stranger went into the little parlor of the Coach and Horses about half-past five in the morning, and there he remained until near midday, the blinds down, the door shut, and none, after Hall's repulse, venturing near him.

All that time he must have fasted. Thrice he rang his bell, the third time furiously and continuously, but no one answered him. "Him and his 'go to the devil' indeed!" said Mrs. Hall. Presently came an imperfect rumor of the burglary at the vicarage, and two and two were put together. Hall, assisted by Wadgers, went off to find Mr. Shuckleforth, the magistrate, and take his advice. No one ventured upstairs. How the stranger occupied himself is unknown. Now and then he would stride violently up and down, and twice came an outburst of curses, a tearing of paper, and a violent smashing of bottles.

The little group of scared but curious people increased. Mrs. Huxter came over; some gay young fellows resplendent in black ready-made jackets and *pique* paper ties, for it was Whit-Monday, joined the group with confused interrogations. Young Archie Harker distinguished himself by going up the yard and trying to peep under the window-blinds. He could see nothing, but gave reason for supposing that he did, and others of the Iping youth presently joined him.

It was the finest of all possible Whit-Mondays, and down the village street stood a row of nearly a dozen booths and a shooting gallery, and on the grass by the forge were three yellow and chocolate wagons and some picturesque strangers of both sexes putting up a cocoanut shy. The gentlemen wore blue jerseys, the ladies white aprons and quite fashionable hats with heavy plumes. Wodger of the Purple Fawn and Mr. Jaggers the cobbler, who also sold second-hand ordinary bicycles, were stretching a string of union-jacks and royal ensigns (which had originally celebrated the Jubilee) across the road . . .

And inside, in the artificial darkness of the parlor, into which only one thin jet of sunlight penetrated, the stranger, hungry we must suppose, and fearful, hidden in his uncomfortable hot wrappings, pored through his dark glasses upon his paper and chinked his dirty little bottles, and occasionally swore savagely at the boys, audible if invisible, outside the windows. In the corner by the fireplace lay the fragments of half a dozen smashed bottles, and a pungent tang of chlorine tainted the air. So much we know from what was heard at the time and from what was subsequently seen in the room.

About noon he suddenly opened his parlor door and stood glaring fixedly at the three or four people in the bar. "Mrs. Hall," he said. Somebody went sheepishly and called for Mrs. Hall.

Mrs. Hall appeared after an interval, a little short of breath, but all the fiercer for that. Hall was still out. She had deliberated over the scene, and she came holding a little tray with an unsettled bill upon it. "Is it your bill you're wanting, sir?" she said.

"Why wasn't my breakfast laid? Why haven't you prepared my meals and answered my bell? Do you think I live without eating?"

"Why isn't my bill paid?" said Mrs. Hall. "That's what I want to know."

"I told you three days ago I was awaiting a remittance—"

"I told you two days ago I wasn't going to await no remittances. You can't grumble if your breakfast waits a bit, if my bill's been waiting these five days, can you?"

The stranger swore briefly but vividly.

"Nar, nar!" from the bar.

"And I'd thank you kindly, sir, if you'd keep your swearing to yourself, sir," said Mrs. Hall.

The stranger stood looking more like an angry diving-helmet than ever. It was universally felt in the bar that Mrs. Hall had the better of him. His next words showed as much.

"Look here, my good woman—" he began.

"Don't good woman *me*," said Mrs. Hall.

"I've told you my remittance hasn't come—"

"Remittance indeed!" said Mrs. Hall.

"Still I daresay in my pocket—"

"You told me two days ago that you hadn't anything but a sovereign's worth of silver upon you—"

"Well, I've found some more—"

" 'Ul-*lo!*" from the bar.

"I wonder where you found it!" said Mrs. Hall.

That seemed to annoy the stranger very much. He stamped his foot. "What do you mean?" he said.

"That I wonder where you found it," said Mrs. Hall. "And before I take any bills or get any breakfasts, or do any such things whatsoever, you got to tell me one or two

50

things I don't understand, and what nobody don't understand and what everybody is very anxious to understand. I want to know what you been doing t' my chair upstairs, and I want know how 'tis your room was empty, and how you got in again. Them as stops in this house comes in by the doors—that's the rule of the house, and that you *didn't* do, and what I want know is how you *did* come in. And I want to know—"

Suddenly the stranger raised his gloved hands clenched, stamped his foot, and said, "Stop!" with such extraordinary violence that he silenced her instantly.

"You don't understand," he said, "who I am or what I am. I'll show you. By Heaven! I'll show you." Then he put his open palm over his face and withdrew it. The center of his face became a black cavity. "Here," he said. He stepped forward and handed Mrs. Hall something which she, staring at his metamorphosed faced, accepted automatically. Then, when she saw what it was, she screamed loudly, dropped it, and staggered back. The nose—it was the stranger's nose! pink and shining—rolled on the floor.

Then he removed his spectacles, and every one in the bar gasped. He took off his hat, and with a violent gesture tore at his whiskers and bandages. For a moment they resisted him. A flash of horrible anticipation passed through the bar. "Oh, my Gard!" said some one. Then off they came.

It was worse than anything. Mrs. Hall standing open-mouthed and horror-struck, shrieked at what she saw, and made for the door of the house. Everyone began to move. They were prepared for scars, disfigurements, tangible horrors, but *nothing!* The bandages and false hair flew across the passage into the bar, making a hobbledehoy jump to avoid them. Every one tumbled on every one else down the steps. For the man who stood there shouting some incoherent explanation, was a solid gesticulating figure up to the coat-collar of him, and then—nothingness, no visible thing at all!

People down the village heard shouts and shrieks, and looking up the street saw the Coach and Horses violently firing out its humanity. They saw Mrs. Hall fall down and Mr. Teddy Henfrey jump to avoid tumbling over her, and then they heard the frightful screams of Millie, who, emerging suddenly from the kitchen at the noise of the tumult, had come upon the headless stranger from behind.

Forthwith every one all down the street, the sweet-stuff seller, cocoanut shy proprietor and his assistant, the swing man, little boys and girls, rustic dandies, smart wenches, smocked elders and aproned gypsies, began running towards the inn; and in a miraculously short space of time a crowd of perhaps forty people, and rapidly increasing, swayed and hooted and inquired and exclaimed and suggested, in front of Mrs. Hall's establishment. Everyone seemed eager to talk at once, and the result was babel. A small group supported Mrs. Hall, who was picked up in a state of collapse. There was a conference, and the incredible evidence of a vociferous eye-witness. "O'Bogey!" "What's he been doin', then?" "Ain't hurt the girl, 'as 'e?" "Run at en with a knife, I believe." "No 'ed, I tell ye. I don't mean no manner of speaking, I mean *marn 'ithout ' ed!*" "Narnsense! 'tas some conjuring trick." "Fetched off 'is wrappin's, 'e did—"

In its struggles to see in through the open door, the crowd formed itself into a straggling wedge, with the more adventurous apex nearest the inn. "He stood for a moment, I heerd the gal scream, and he turned. I saw her skirts whisk, and he went after her. Didn't take ten seconds. Back he comes with a knife in uz hand and a loaf; stood just as if he was staring. Not a moment ago. Went in that there door. I tell 'e, 'e ain't gart no 'ed 't all. You just missed en—"

There was a disturbance behind, and the speaker stopped to step aside for a little procession that was marching very resolutely towards the house—first Mr. Hall, very red and determined, then Mr. Bobby Jaffers, the village constable, and then the wary Mr. Wadgers. They had come now armed with a warrant.

People shouted conflicting information of the recent circumstances. " 'Ed or no 'ed," said Jaffers, "I got to 'rest en, and 'rest en I *will*."

Mr. Hall marched up the steps, marched straight to the door of the parlor and flung it open. "Constable," he said, "do your duty."

Jaffers marched in, Hall next, Wadgers last. They saw in the dim light the headless figure facing them, with a gnawed crust of bread in one gloved hand and a chunk of cheese in the other.

"That's him!" said Hall.

"What the devil's this?" came in a tone of angry expostulation from above the collar of the figure.

"You're a damned rum customer, mister," said Mr. Jaffers. "But 'ed or no 'ed, the warrant says 'body,' and duty's duty—"

"Keep off!" said the figure, starting back.

Abruptly he whipped down the bread and cheese, and Mr. Hall just grasped the knife on the table in time to save it. Off came the stranger's left glove and was slapped in Jaffers' face. In another moment Jaffers, cutting short some statement concerning a warrant, had gripped him by the handless wrist and caught his invisible throat. He got a sounding kick on the shin that made him shout, but he kept his grip. Hall sent the knife sliding along the table to Wadgers, who acted as goal-keeper for the offensive, so to speak, and then stepped forward as Jaffers and the stranger swayed and staggered towards him, clutching and hitting in. A chair stood in the way, and went aside with a crash as they came down together.

"Get the feet," said Jaffers between his teeth.

Mr. Hall, endeavoring to act on instructions, receiving a sounding kick in the ribs that disposed of him for a moment, and Mr. Wadgers, seeing the decapitated stranger had rolled over and got the upper side of Jaffers, retreated towards the door, knife in hand, and so collided with Mr. Huxter and the Siddermorton carter coming to the rescue of law and order. At the same moment down came three or four bottles from the chiffonier and shot a web of pungency into the air of the room.

"I'll surrender," cried the stranger, though he had Jaffers down, and in another moment he stood up panting, a strange figure, headless and handless—for he had pulled off his right glove now a well as his left. "It's no good," he said, as if sobbing for breath.

It was the strangest thing in the world to hear that voice coming as if out of empty space, but Sussex peasants are perhaps the most matter-of-fact people under the sun. Jaffers got up also and produced a pair of handcuffs. Then he started.

"I say!" said Jaffers, brought up short by a dim realization of incongruity of the whole business. "Darm it! Can't use 'em as I can see."

The stranger ran his arm down his waistcoat, and as if by a miracle the buttons to which his empty sleeve pointed became undone. Then he said something about his shin, and stooped down. He seemed to be fumbling with his shoes and socks.

"Why!" said Huxter, suddenly, "that's not a man at all. It's just empty clothes. Look! You can see down his collar and the linings of his clothes. I could put my arm—"

He extended his hand; it seemed to meet something in mid-air, and he drew it back with a sharp exclamation. "I wish you'd keep your fingers out of my eye," said the aerial voice, in a tone of savage expostulation. "The fact is, I'm all here: head, hands, legs, and all the rest of it, but it happens I'm invisible. It's a confounded nuisance, but I am. That's no reason why I should be poked to pieces by every stupid bumpkin in Iping, is it?"

The suit of clothes, now all unbuttoned and hanging loosely upon its unseen supports, stood up, arms akimbo.

Several other of the men folks had now entered the room, so that it was closely crowded. "Invisible, eigh?" said Huxter, ignoring the stranger's abuse. "Who ever heard the likes of that?"

"It's strange, perhaps, but it's not a crime. Why am I assaulted by a policeman in this fashion?"

"Ah! that's a different matter," said Jaffers. "No doubt you are a bit difficult to see in this light, but I got a warrant, and it's all correct. What I'm after ain't no invisibility—it's burglary. There's a house been broken into and money took."

"Well?"

"And circumstances certainly point—"

"Stuff and nonsense!" said the Invisible Man.

"I hope so, sir: but I've got my instructions."

"Well," said the stranger, "I'll come. I'll *come*. But no handcuffs."

"It's the regular thing," said Jaffers.

"No handcuffs," stipulated the stranger.

"Pardon me," said Jaffers.

Abruptly the figure sat down, and before any one could realize what was being done, the slippers, socks, and trousers had been kicked off under the table. Then he sprang up again and flung off his coat.

"Here, stop that," said Jaffers, suddenly realizing what was happening. He gripped the waistcoat; it struggled, and the shirt slipped out of it and left it limp and empty in his hand. "Hold him!" said Jaffers loudly. "Once he gets they things off—!"

"Hold him!" cried every one, and there was a rush at the fluttering white shirt which was now all that was visible of the stranger.

The shirt-sleeve planted a shrewd blow in Hall's face that stopped his open-armed advance, and sent him backward into old Toothsome the sexton, and in another moment the garment was lifted up and became convulsed and vacantly flapping about the arms, even as a shirt that is being thrust over a man's head. Jaffers clutched at it, and only helped to pull it off; he was struck in the mouth out of the air, and incontinently drew his truncheon and smote Teddy Henfrey savagely upon the crown of his head.

"Look out!" said everybody, fencing at random and hitting at nothing. "Hold him! Shut the door! Don't let him loose! I got something! Here he is!" A perfect bable of noises they made. Everybody, it seemed, was being hit all at once, and Sandy Wadgers, knowing as ever and his wits sharpened by a frightful blow in the nose, re-opened the door and led the rout. The others, following incontinently, were jammed for a moment in the corner by the doorway. The hitting continued. Phipps, the Unitarian, had a front tooth broke, and Henfrey was injured in the cartilage of his ear. Jaffers was struck under the jaw, and, turning, caught at something that intervened between him and Huxter in the melee, and prevented their coming together. He felt a muscular chest, and in another moment the whole mass of struggling excited men shot out in the crowded hall.

"I got him!" shouted Jaffers, choking and reeling through them all, and wrestling with purple face and swelling veins against his unseen enemy.

Men staggered right and left as the extraordinary conflict swayed swiftly towards the house door, and went spinning down the half-dozen steps of the inn. Jaffers cried in a strangled voice—holding tight, nevertheless, and making play with his knee—spun round, and fell heavily undermost with his head on the gravel. Only then did his fingers relax.

There were excited cries of "Hold him!" "Invisible!" and so forth, and a young fellow, a stranger in the place whose name did not come to light, rushed in at once, caught something, missed his hold, and fell over the constable's prostrate body. Halfway across the road, a woman screamed as something pushed by her; a dog, kicked apparently, yelped and ran howling into Huxter's yard, and with that the transit of the Invisible Man was accomplished. For a space people stood amazed and gesticulating, and then came Panic, and scattered them abroad through the village as a gust scatters dead leaves.

But Jaffers lay quite still, face upward and knees bent.

# from *The War of the Worlds* (1898)

*From its opening lines, with their sober and chilling meditation on cosmic vulnerability,* The War of the Worlds *challenges the self-satisfaction of turn-of-the-century Britain. Wells adapts the popular invasion story, and depicts in detail the process by which a smug and proud society is humbled and made aware of its common lot with all the other animals in the Darwinian struggle for survival. Book I, entitled "The Coming of the Martians" depicts with wonderfully even pacing the movement from complacency, to fear, to terror, to despair. The selections from various parts of the novel depict the arrival of the first Martian capsule, the coming awareness of what the invasion means, and the narrator's meeting with the curate. Book I ends with one of Wells's greatest descriptive passages, the pyrrhic victory of the Thunderchild. The selection from the second book depicts the defeat of the Martians. It is typical of Wells's complex sense of what is involved in such situations that he can depict this moment of human triumph also as a tragedy.*

BOOK I

THE COMING OF THE MARTIANS

CHAPTER THE FIRST

THE EVE OF THE WAR

No one would have believed in the last years of the nineteenth century that this world was being watched keenly and closely by intelligences greater than man's and yet as mortal as his own; that as men busied themselves about their various concerns they were scrutinized and studied, perhaps almost as narrowly as a man with a microscope might scrutinize the transient creatures that swarm and multiply in a drop of water. With infinite complacency men went to and fro over this globe about their little affairs, serene in their assurance of their empire over matter. It is possible that the infusoria under the microscope do the same. No one gave a thought to the older worlds of space as sources of human danger, or thought of them only to dismiss the idea of life upon them as impossible or improbable. It is curious to recall some of the mental habits of those departed days. At most, terrestrial men fancied there might be other men upon Mars, perhaps inferior to themselves and ready to welcome a missionary enterprise. Yet across the gulf of space, minds that are to our minds as ours are to those of the beasts that perish, intellects vast and cool and unsympathetic, regarded this earth with envious eyes, and slowly and surely drew their plans against us. And early in the twentieth century came the great disillusionment.

The planet Mars, I scarcely need remind the reader, revolves about the sun at a mean distance of 140,000,000 miles, and the light and heat it receives from the sun is barely half of that received by this world. It must be, if the nebular hypothesis has any truth, older than our world; and long before this earth ceased to be molten, life upon its surface must have begun its course. The fact that it is scarcely one-seventh of the volume of the earth must have accelerated its cooling to the temperature at which life could begin. It has air and water and all that is necessary for the support of animated existence.

Yet so vain is man and so blinded by his vanity, that no writer, up to the very end of the nineteenth century, expressed any idea that intelligent life might have developed there far, or indeed at all, beyond its earthly level. Nor was it generally understood that since Mars is older than our earth, with scarcely a quarter of the superficial area and remoter from the sun, it necessarily follows that it is not only more distant from life's beginning but nearer its end.

The secular cooling that must some day overtake our planet had already gone far indeed with our neighbor. Its physical condition is still largely a mystery, but we know now that even in its equatorial region that mid-day temperature barely approaches that of our coldest winter. Its air is much more attenuated than ours, its oceans have shrunk until they cover but a third of its surface, and as its slow seasons change huge snow-caps gather and melt about either pole and periodically inundate its temperate zones. That last stage of exhaustion, which to us is still incredibly remote, has become a present-day problem for the inhabitants of Mars. The immediate pressure of necessity has brightened their intellects, enlarged their powers, and hardened their hearts. And looking across space with instruments, and intelligences such as we have scarcely dreamed of, they see, at its nearest distance only 135,00,000 of miles sunward of them, a morning star of hope, our own warmer planet, green with vegetation and gray with water, with a cloudy atmosphere eloquent of fertility, with glimpses through its drifting cloud-wisps of broad stretches of populous country and narrow, navy-crowded seas.

And we men, the creatures who inhabit this earth, must be to them at least as alien and lowly as are the monkeys and lemurs to us. The intellectual side of man already admits that life is an incessant struggle for existence, and it would seem that this too is the belief of the minds upon Mars. Their world is far gone in its cooling and this world is still crowded with life, but crowded only with what they regard as inferior animals. To carry warfare sunward is, indeed, their only escape from the destruction that generation after generation creeps upon them.

And before we judge of them too harshly we must remember what ruthless and utter destruction our own species has wrought, not only upon animals, such as the vanished bison and the dodo, but upon its own inferior races. The Tasmanians, in spite of their human likeness, were entirely swept out of existence in a war of extermination waged by European immigrants, in the space of fifty years. Are we such apostles of mercy as to complain if the Martian warred in the same spirit?

The Martians seem to have calculated their descent with amazing subtlety—their mathematical learning is evidently far in excess of ours—and to have carried out their preparations with a well-nigh perfect unanimity. Had our instruments permitted it, we might have seen the gathering trouble far back in the nineteenth century. Men like Schiaparelli watched the red planet—it is odd, by-the-bye, that for countless centuries Mars has been the star of war—but failed to interpret the fluctuating appearances of the marking they mapped so well. All that time the Martians must have been getting ready.

During the opposition of 1894 a great light was seen on the illuminated part of the disk, first at the Lick Observatory, then by Perrotin of Nice, and then by other observers. English readers heard of it first in the issue of *Nature* dated August 2nd. I am inclined to think that this blaze may have been the casting of the huge gun, in the vast pit sunk into their planet, from which their shots were fired at us. Peculiar markings, as yet unexplained, were seen near the site of that outbreak during the next two oppositions.

The storm burst upon us six years ago now. As Mars approached opposition, Lavelle of Java set the wires of the astronomical exchange palpitating with the amazing intelligence of a huge outbreak of incandescent gas upon the planet. It had occurred towards midnight of the 12th; and the spectroscope, to which he had at once resorted, indicated a mass of flaming gas, chiefly hydrogen, moving with an enormous velocity towards this earth. This jet of fire had become invisible about a quarter past twelve. He compared it to a colossal puff of flame suddenly and violently squirted out of the planet, "as flaming gases rushed out of a gun."

A singularly appropriate phrase it proved. Yet the next day there was nothing of this in the papers except a little note in the *Daily Telegraph*, and the world went in ignorance of some of the gravest dangers that ever threatened the human race. I might not have heard of the eruption at all had I not met Ogilvy, the well-known astronomer, at Ottershaw. He was immensely excited at the news, and in the excess of his feelings invited me up to take a turn with him that night in a scrutiny of the red planet.

In spite of all that has happened since, I still remember that vigil very distinctly: the black and silent observatory, the shadowed lantern throwing a feeble glow upon the floor in the corner, the steady ticking of the clockwork of the telescope, the little slit in the roof—an oblong profundity with the star-dust streaked across it. Ogilvy moved about, invisible but audible. Looking through the telescope, one saw a circle of deep blue and the little round planet swimming in the field. It seemed such a little thing, so bright and small and still, faintly marked with transverse stripes, and slightly flattened from the perfect round. But so little it was, so silvery warm—a pin's-head of light! It was as if it quivered, but really this was the telescope vibrating with the activity of the clockwork that kept the planet in view.

As I watched, the planet seemed to grow larger and smaller and to advance and recede, but that was simply that my eye was tired. Forty millions of miles it was from us—more than forty millions of miles of void. Few people realize the immensity of vacancy in which the dust of the material universe swims.

Near it in the field, I remember, were three faint points of light, three telescopic stars infinitely remote, and all around it was the unfathomable darkness of empty space. You know how that blackness looks on a frosty starlight night. In a telescope it seems far profounder. And invisible to me because it was so remote and small, flying swiftly and steadily towards me across that incredible distance, drawing nearer every minute by so many thousands of miles, came the Thing they were sending us, the Thing that was to bring so much struggle and calamity and death to the earth. I never dreamed of it then as I watched; no one on earth dreamed of that unerring missile.

That night, too, there was another jetting out of gas from the distant planet. I saw it. A reddish flash at the edge, the slightest projection of the outline just as the chronometer struck midnight; and at that I told Ogilvy and he took my place. The night was warm and I was thirsty, and I went, stretching my legs clumsily and feeling my way in the darkness, to the little table where the siphon stood, while Ogilvy exclaimed at the streamer of gas that came out towards us.

That night another invisible missile started on its way to the earth from Mars, just a second or so under twenty-four hours after the first one. I remember how I sat on the table there in the blackness, with patches of green and crimson swimming before my eyes. I wished I had a light to smoke by, little suspecting the meaning of the minute gleam I had seen and all that it would presently bring me. Ogilvy watched till one, and then gave it up; and we lit the lantern and walked over to his house. Down below in the darkness were Ottershaw and Chertsey and all their hundred of people, sleeping in peace.

He was full of speculation that night about the condition of Mars, and scoffed at the vulgar idea of its having inhabitants who were signaling us. His idea was that meteorites might be falling in a heavy shower upon the planet, or that a huge volcanic explosion was in progress. He pointed out to me how unlikely it was that organic evolution had taken the same direction in the two adjacent planets.

"The chances against anything man-like on Mars are a million to one," he said.

Hundreds of observers saw the flame that night and the night after about midnight, and again the night after; and so for ten nights, a flame each night. Why the shots ceased after the tenth no one on earth has attempted to explain. It may be the gases of the firing caused the Martians inconvenience. Dense clouds of smoke or dust, visible through a powerful telescope on earth as little gray, fluctuating patches, spread through the clearness of the planet's atmosphere and obscured its more familiar features.

Even the daily papers woke up to the disturbances at last, and popular notes appeared here, there, and everywhere concerning the volcanoes upon Mars. The serio-comic periodical *Punch*, I remember, made a happy use of it in the political cartoon. And, all unsuspected, those missiles the Martians had fired at us drew earthward, rushing now at a pace of many miles a second through the empty gulf of space, hour by hour and day by day, nearer and nearer. It seems to me now almost incredibly wonderful that, with that swift fate hanging over us, men could go about their petty concerns as they did. I remember how jubilant Markham was at securing a new photograph of the planet for the illustrated paper he edited in those days. People in these latter times scarcely realize the abundance and enterprise of our nineteenth-century papers. For my own part, I was much occupied in learning to ride the bicycle, and busy upon a series of papers discussing the probable developments of moral ideas as civilization progressed.

One night (the first missile then could scarcely have been 10,000,000 miles away) I went for a walk with my wife. It was starlight, and I explained the Signs of the Zodiac to her, and pointed out Mars, a bright dot of light creeping zenithward, towards which so many telescopes were pointed. It was a warm night. Coming home, a party of excursionists from Chertsey or Isleworth passed us singing and playing music. There were lights in the upper windows of the houses as the people went to bed. From the railway station in the distance came the sound of shunting trains, ringing and rumbling, softened almost into melody by the distance. My wife pointed out to me the brightness of the red, green, and yellow signal lights hanging in a framework against the sky. It seemed so safe and tranquil.

CHAPTER THE SECOND<br>THE FALLING-STAR

Then came the night of the first falling-star. It was seen early in the morning rushing over Winchester eastward, a line of flame high in the atmosphere. Hundreds must have seen it, and taken it for an ordinary falling-star. Albin described it as leaving a greenish streak behind it that glowed for some seconds. Denning, our greatest authority on meteorites, stated that the height of its first appearance was about ninety or one hundred miles. It seemed to him that it fell to earth about one hundred miles east of him.

I was at home at that hour and writing in my study; and although my French windows face towards Ottershaw and the blind was up (for I loved in those days to look up at the night sky), I saw nothing of it. Yet this strangest of all things that ever came to earth from outer space must have fallen while I was sitting there, visible to me had I only looked up as it passed. Some of those who saw its flight say it traveled with a hissing sound. I myself heard nothing of that. Many people in Berkshire, Surrey, and Middlesex must have seen the fall of it, and, at most, have thought that another meteorite had descended. No one seems to have troubled to look for the fallen mass that night.

But very early in the morning poor Ogilvy, who had seen the shooting-star and who was persuaded that a meteorite lay somewhere on the common between Horsell, Ottershaw, and Woking, rose early with the idea of finding it. Find it he did, soon after dawn, and not far from the sand-pits. An enormous hole had been made

59

by the impact of the projectile, and the sand and gravel had been flung violently in every direction over the heath, forming heaps visible a mile and a half away. The heather was on fire eastward, and a thin blue smoke rose against the dawn.

The Thing itself lay almost entirely buried in sand, amidst the scattered splinters of a fir-tree it had shivered to fragments in its descent. The uncovered part had the appearance of a huge cylinder, caked over and its outline softened by a thick scaly dun-colored incrustation. It had a diameter of about thirty yards. He approached the mass, surprised at the size and more so at the shape, since most meteorites are rounded more or less completely. It was, however, still so hot from its flight through the air as to forbid his near approach. A stirring noise within its cylinder he ascribed to the unequal cooling of its surface; for at that time it had not occurred to him that it might be hollow.

He remained standing at the edge of the pit that the Thing had made for itself, staring at its strange appearance, astonished chiefly at its unusual shape and color, and dimly perceiving even then some evidence of design in its arrival. The early morning was wonderfully still, and the sun, just clearing the pine-trees towards Weybridge, was already warm. He did not remember hearing any birds that morning, there was certainly no breeze stirring, and the only sounds were the faint movements from within the cindery cylinder. He was all alone on the common.

Then suddenly he noticed with a start that some of the gray clinker, the ashy incrustation that covered the meteorite, was falling off the circular edge of the end. It was dropping off in flakes and raining down upon the sand. A large piece suddenly came off and fell with a sharp noise that brought his heart into his mouth.

For a minute he scarcely realized what this meant, and, although the heat was excessive, he clambered down into the pit close to the bulk to see the Thing more clearly. He fancied even then that the cooling of the body might account for this, but what disturbed that idea was the fact that the ash was falling only from the end of the cylinder.

And then he perceived that, very slowly, the circular top of the cylinder was rotating on its body. It was such a gradual movement that he discovered it only through noticing that a black mark that had been near him five minutes ago was now at the other side of the circumference. Even then he scarcely understood what this indicated, until he heard a muffled grating sound and saw the black mark jerk forward an inch or so. Then the thing came upon him in a flash. The cylinder was artificial—hollow—with an end that screwed out! Something within the cylinder was unscrewing the top!

"Good heavens!" said Ogilvy. "There's a man in it—men in it! Half roasted to death! Trying to escape!"

At once, with a quick mental leap, he linked the Thing with the flash upon Mars.

\* \* \* \* \*

FROM THE WAR OF THE WORLDS

## CHAPTER THE FIFTH
## THE HEAT-RAY

After the glimpse I had had of the Martians emerging from the cylinder in which they had come to the earth from their planet, a kind of fascination paralyzed my actions. I remained standing knee-deep in the heather, staring at the mound that hid them. I was a battle-ground of fear and curiosity.

I did not dare to go back towards the pit, but I felt a passionate longing to peer into it. I began walking, therefore, in a big curve, seeking some point of vantage and continually looking at the sand-heaps that hid these new-comers to our earth. Once a leash of thin black whips, like the arms of an octopus, flashed across the sunset and was immediately withdrawn, and afterwards a thin rod rose up, joint by joint, bearing at its apex a circular disk that spun with a wobbling motion. What could be going on there?

Most of the spectators had gathered in one or two groups—one a little crowd toward Woking, the other a knot of people in the direction of Chobham. Evidently they shared my mental conflict. There were few near me. One man I approached—he was, I perceived, a neighbor of mine, though I did not know his name—and accosted. But it was scarcely a time for articulate conversation.

"What ugly *brutes!*" he said. "Good God! What ugly brutes!" He repeated this over and over again.

"Did you see a man in the pit?" I said; but he made no answer to that. We became silent, and stood watching for a time side by side, deriving, I fancy, a certain comfort in one another's company. Then I shifted my position to a little knoll that gave me the advantage of a yard or more of elevation, and when I looked for him presently he was walking towards Woking.

The sunset faded to twilight before anything further happened. The crowd far away on the left, towards Woking, seemed to grow and I heard now a faint murmur from it. The little knot of people towards Chobham dispersed. There was scarcely an intimation of movement from the pit.

It was this, as much as anything, that gave people courage, and I suppose the new arrivals from Woking also helped to restore confidence. At any rate, as the dusk came on a slow, intermittent movement upon the sand-pits began, a movement that seemed to gather force as the stillness of the evening about the cylinder remained unbroken. Vertical black figures in twos and threes would advance, stop, watch and advance again, spreading out as they did so in a thin irregular crescent that promised to enclose the pit in its attenuated horns. I, too, on my side began to move towards the pit.

Then I saw some cabmen and others had walked boldly into the sand-pits, and heard the clatter of hoofs and the grind of wheels. I saw a lad trundling off the barrow of apples. And then, within thirty yards of the pit, advancing from the direction of Horsell, I noted a little black knot of men, the foremost of whom was waving a white flag.

This was the Deputation. There had been a hasty consultation, and since the Martians were evidently, in spite of their repulsive forms, intelligent creatures, it had been resolved to show them, by approaching them with signals, that we too were intelligent.

Flutter, flutter, went the flag, first to the right, then to the left. It was too far for me to recognize any one there, but afterwards I learned that Ogilvy, Stent, and Henderson were with others in this attempt at communication. This little group had in its advance dragged inwards, so to speak, the circumference of the now almost complete circle of people, and a number of dim black figures followed it at discreet distances.

Suddenly there was a flash of light, and a quantity of luminous greenish smoke came out of the pit in three distinct puffs, which drove up, one after the other, straight into the still air.

This smoke (or flame, perhaps, would be the better word for it) was so bright that the deep blue sky overhead and the hazy stretches of brown common towards Chertsey, set with black pine-trees, seemed to darken abruptly as these puffs arose, and to remain the darker after their dispersal. At the same time a faint hissing sound became audible.

Beyond the pit stood the little wedge of people with the white flag at its apex, arrested by these phenomena, a little knot of small vertical black shapes upon the black ground. As the green smoke arose, their faces flashed out pallid green, and faded again as it vanished. Then slowly the hissing passed into a humming into a long, loud, droning noise. Slowly a humped shape rose out of the pit, and the ghost of a beam of light seemed to flicker out from it.

Forthwith flashes of actual flame, a bright glare leaping from one to another, sprang from the scattered group of men. It was as if some invisible jet impinged upon them and flashed into white flame. It was as if each man were suddenly and momentarily turned to fire.

Then, by the light of their own destruction, I saw them staggering and falling, and their supporters turning to run.

I stood staring, not as yet realizing that this was death leaping from man to man in that little distant crowd. All I felt was that it was something very strange. An almost noiseless and blinding flash of light, and a man fell headlong and lay still; and as the unseen shaft of heat passed over them, pine-trees burst into fire and every dry furze-bush became with one dull thud a mass of flames. And far away towards Knaphill I saw the flashes of trees and hedges and wooden building suddenly set alight.

It was sweeping round swiftly and steadily, this flaming death, this invisible, inevitable sword of heat. I perceived it coming towards me by the flashing bushes it touched, and was too astounded and stupefied to stir. I heard the crackle of fire in the sand-pits and the sudden squeal of a horse that was as suddenly stilled. Then it was as if an invisible yet intensely heated finger were drawn through the heather between me and the Martians, and all along a curving line beyond the sand-pits the dark ground smoked and crackled. Something fell with a crash far away to the left where the road from Woking station opens out on the common. Forthwith the hissing and humming ceased, and the black, dome-like object sank slowly out of sight into the pit.

All this had happened with such swiftness that I had stood motionless, dumbfounded and dazzled by the flashes of light. Had that death swept through a full circle, it must inevitably have slain me in my surprise. But it passed and spared me, and left the night about me suddenly dark and unfamiliar.

The undulating common seemed now dark almost to blackness, except where its roadways lay gray and pale under the deep-blue sky of the early night. It was dark, and suddenly void of men. Overhead the stars were mustering, and in the west the sky was still a pale, bright, almost greenish blue. The tops of the pine-trees and the roofs of Horsell came out sharp and black against the western afterglow. The Martians and their appliances were altogether invisible, save for that thin mast upon which their restless mirror wobbled. Patches of brush and isolated trees here and there smoked and glowed still, and the houses towards Woking station were sending up spires of flame into the stillness of the evening air.

Nothing was changed save for that and a terrible astonishment. The little group of black specks with the flag of white had been swept out of existence, and the stillness of the evening, so it seemed to me, had scarcely been broken.

It came to me that I was upon this dark common, helpless, unprotected, and alone. Suddenly, like a thing falling upon me from without, came—fear.

With an effort I turned and began a stumbling run through the heather.

The fear I felt was no rational fear, but a panic terror not only of the Martians, but of the dusk and stillness all about me. Such an extraordinary effect in unmanning me it had that I ran weeping silently as a child might do. Once I had turned, I did not dare to look back.

I remember I felt an extraordinary persuasion I was being played with, that presently, when I was upon the very verge of safety, this mysterious death—as swift as the passage of light—would leap after me from the pit about the cylinder and strike me down.

\* \* \* \* \*

### Chapter the Thirteenth
### How I Fell in with the Curate

\* \* \* \* \*

For a long time I drifted, so painful and weary was I after the violence I had been through, and so intense the heat upon the water. Then my fears got the better of me again, and I resumed my paddling. The sun scorched my bare back. At last, as the bridge at Walton was coming into sight round the bend, my fever and faintness overcame my fears, and I landed on the Middlesex bank and lay down, deadly sick, amid the long grass. I suppose the time was then about four or five o'clock. I got up presently, walked perhaps half a mile without meeting a soul, and then lay down again in the shadow of a hedge. I seem to remember talking, wonderingly, to myself during that last spurt. I was also very thirsty, and bitterly regretful I had drunk no more water. It is a curious thing that I felt angry with my wife; I cannot account for it, but my impotent desire to reach Leatherhead worried me excessively.

I do not clearly remember the arrival of the curate, so that probably I dozed. I became aware of him as a seated figure in soot-smudged shirt-sleeves, and with his up-turned, clean-shaven face staring at a faint flickering that danced over the sky. The sky was what is called a mackerel sky—rows of faint down-plumes of cloud, just tinted with the midsummer sunset.

I sat up, and at the rustle of my motion he looked at me quickly.

"Have you any water?" I asked abruptly.

He shook his head.

"You have been asking for water for the last hour," he said.

For a moment we were silent, taking stock of each other. I dare say he found me a strange enough figure, naked, save for my water-soaked trousers and socks, scalded and my face and shoulders blackened by the smoke. His face was a fair weakness, his chin retreated, and his hair lay in crisp, almost flaxen curls on this low forehead; his eyes were rather large, pale-blue, and blankly staring. He spoke abruptly, looking vacantly away from me.

"What does it mean?" he said. "What do these things mean?"

I stared at him and made no answer.

He extended a thin white hand and spoke in almost a complaining tone.

"Why are these things permitted? What sins have we done? The morning service was over, I was walking through the roads to clear my brain for the afternoon, and then—fire, earthquake, death! As if it were Sodom and Gomorrah! All our work undone, all the work—What are these Martians?"

"What are we?" I answered, clearing my throat.

He gripped his knees and turned to look at me again. For half a minute, perhaps, he stared silently.

"I was walking through the roads to clear my brain," he said. "And suddenly— fire, earthquake, death!"

He relapsed into silence, with his chin now sunken almost to his knees.

Presently he began waving his hand.

"All the work—all the Sunday-schools—What have we done—what has Weybridge done? Everything gone—everything destroyed. The church! We rebuilt it only three years ago. Gone!—swept out of existence! Why?"

Another pause, and he broke out again like one demented.

"The smoke of her burning goeth up for ever and ever!" he shouted.

His eyes flamed, and he pointed a lean finger in the direction of Weybridge.

By this time I was beginning to take his measure. The tremendous tragedy in which he had been involved—it was evident he was a fugitive from Weybridge—had driven him to the very verge of his reason.

"Are we far from Sunbury?" I said, in a matter-of-fact tone.

"What are we to do?" he asked. "Are these creatures everywhere? Has the earth been given over to them?"

"Are we far from Sunbury?"

"Only this morning I officiated at early celebration—"

"Things have changed," I said, quietly. "You must keep your head. There is still hope."

"Hope!"

"Yes. Plentiful hope—for all this destruction!"

I began to explain my view of our position. He listened at first, but as I went on the interest dawning in this eyes gave place to their former stare, and his regard wandered from me.

"This must be the beginning of the end," he said, interrupting me. "The end! The great and terrible day of the Lord! When men shall call upon the mountains and the rocks to fall upon them and hide them—hide them from the face of Him that sitteth upon the throne!"

I began to understand the position. I ceased my labored reasoning, struggled to my feet, and, standing over him, laid my hand on his shoulder.

"Be a man!" said I. "You are scared out of your wits! What good is religion if it collapses under calamity? Think of what earthquakes and floods, wars and volcanoes, have done before to men! Did you think God had exempted Weybridge? He is not an insurance agent."

For a time he sat in blank silence.

"But how can we escape?" he asked, suddenly. "They are invulnerable, they are pitiless."

"Neither the one nor, perhaps, the other," I answered. "And the mightier they are the more sane and wary should we be. One of them was killed yonder not three hours ago."

"Killed!" he said, staring about him. "How can God's ministers be killed?"

"I saw it happen." I proceeded to tell him. "We have chanced to come in for the thick of it," said I, "and that is all."

"What is that flicker in the sky?" he asked abruptly.

I told him it was the heliograph signaling—that it was the sign of human help and effort in the sky.

"We are in the midst of it," I said, "quiet as it is. That flicker in the sky tells of the gathering storm. Yonder, I take it, are the Martians, and Londonward, where those hills rise about Richmond and Kingston and the trees give cover, earthworks are being thrown up and guns are being placed. Presently the Martians will be coming this way again."

65

And even as I spoke he sprang to his feet and stopped me by a gesture. "Listen!" he said.

From beyond the low hills across the water came the dull resonance of distant guns and a remote weird crying. Then everything was still. A cockchafer came droning over the hedge and past us. High in the west the crescent moon hung faint and pale above the smoke of Weybridge and Shepperton and the hot, still splendor of the sunset.

"We had better follow this path," I said, "northward."

\* \* \* \* \*

### CHAPTER THE SEVENTEENTH
### THE "THUNDER CHILD"

Had the Martians aimed only at destruction, they might on Monday have annihilated the entire population of London, as it spread itself slowly through the home countries. Not only along the road through Barnet, but also through Edgware and Waltham Abbey, and along the roads eastward to Southend and Shoeburyness, and south of the Thames to Deal and Broadstairs, poured the same frantic rout. If one could have hung that June morning in a balloon in the blazing blue above London every northward and eastward road running out of the tangled maze of streets would have seemed stippled black with the streaming fugitives, each dot a human agony of terror and physical distress. I have set forth at length in the last chapter my brother's account of the road through Chipping Barnet, in order that my readers may realize how that swarming of black dots appeared to one of those concerned. Never before in the history of the world had such a mass of human beings moved and suffered together. The legendary hosts of Goths and Huns, the hugest armies Asia has ever seen, would have been but a drop in that current. And this was no disciplined march; it was a stampede—a stampede gigantic and terrible—without order and without a goal, six million people, unarmed and unprovisioned, driving headlong. It was the beginning of the rout of civilization, of the massacre of mankind.

Directly below him the balloonist would have seen the network of streets far and wide, houses, churches, squares, crescents, gardens—already derelict—spread out like a huge map, and in the southward *blotted.* Over Ealing, Richmond, Wimbledon, it would have seemed as if some monstrous pen had flung ink upon the chart. Steadily, incessantly, each black splash grew and spread, shooting out ramifications this way and that, now banking itself against rising ground, now pouring swiftly over a crest into a newfound valley, exactly as a gout of ink would spread itself upon blotting-paper.

And beyond, over the blue hills that rise southward of the river, the glittering Martians went to and fro, calmly and methodically spreading their poison-cloud over

66

this patch of country and then over that, laying it again with their stream jets when it had served its purpose, and taking possession of the conquered country. They do not seem to have aimed at extermination so much as at complete demoralization and the destruction of any opposition. They exploded any stores of powder they came upon, cut every telegraph, and wrecked the railways here and there. They were hamstringing mankind. They seemed in no hurry to extend the field of their operations, and did not come beyond the central part of London all that day. It is possible that a very considerable number of people in London stuck to their houses through Monday morning. Certain it is that many died at home suffocated by the Black Smoke.

Until about mid-day the Pool of London was an astonishing scene. Steamboats and shipping of all sorts lay there, tempted by the enormous sums of money offered by fugitives, and it is said that many who swam out to these vessels were thrust off with boathooks and drowned. About one o'clock in the afternoon the thinning remnant of a cloud of the black vapor appeared between the arches of Blackfriars Bridge. At that the Pool became a scene of mad confusion, fighting, and collision, and for some time a multitude of boats and barges jammed in the northern arch of the Tower Bridge, and the sailors and lightermen had to fight savagely against the people who swarmed upon them from the river front. People were actually clambering down the piers of the bridge from above.

When, an hour later, a Martian appeared beyond the Clock Tower and waded down the river, nothing but wreckage floated above Limehouse.

Of the falling of the fifth cylinder I have presently to tell. The sixth star fell at Wimbledon. My brother, keeping watch beside the women in the chaise in a meadow, saw the green flash of it far beyond the hills. On Tuesday the little party, still set upon getting across the sea, made its way through the swarming country towards Colchester. The news that the Martians were now in possession of the whole of London was confirmed. They had been seen at Highgate, and even, it was said, at Neasden. But they did not come into my brother's view until the morrow.

That day the scattered multitudes began to realize the urgent need of provisions. As they grew hungry the rights of property ceased to be regarded. Farmers were out to defend their cattle-sheds, granaries, and ripening root crops with arms in their hands. A number of people now, like my brother, had their faces eastward, and there were some desperate souls even going back towards London to get food. These were chiefly people from the northern suburbs, whose knowledge of the Black Smoke came by hearsay. He heard that about half the members of the government had gathered at Birmingham, and that enormous quantities of high explosives were being prepared to be used in automatic mines across the Midland counties.

He was also told that the Midland Railway Company had replaced the desertions of the first day's panic, had resumed traffic, and was running northward trains from St. Albans to relieve the congestion of the home counties. There was also a placard in Chipping Ongar announcing that large stores of flour were available in the northern towns and that within twenty-four hours bread would be distributed among the starving people in the neighborhood. But this intelligence did not deter him from the plan of escape he had formed, and the three pressed eastward all day, and heard no more of the bread distribution than this promise. Nor, as a matter of fact, did anyone else hear more of it. That night fell the seventh star, falling upon Primrose Hill. It fell while Miss Elphinstone was watching, for she took that duty alternately with my brother. She saw it.

On Wednesday the three fugitives—they had passed the night in a field of unripe wheat—reached Chelmsford, and there a body of the inhabitants, calling itself the Committee of Public Supply seized the pony as provisions, and would give nothing in exchange for it but the promise of a share in it the next day. Here there were rumors of Martians at Epping, and news of the destruction of Waltham Abbey Powder Mills in a vain attempt to blow up one of the invaders.

People were watching for Martians here from the church towers. My brother, very luckily for him as it chanced, preferred to push on at once to the coast rather than wait for food, although all three of them were very hungry. By mid-day they passed through Tillingham, which, strangely enough, seemed to be quite silent and deserted, save for a few furtive plunderers hunting for food. Near Tillingham they suddenly came in sight of the sea, and the most amazing crowd of shipping of all sorts that it is possible to imagine.

For after the sailors could no longer come up the Thames, they came on to the Essex coast, to Harwich and Walton and Clacton, and afterwards to Foulness and Shoebury, to bring off the people. They lay in a huge sickle-shaped curve that vanished into mist at last towards the Naze. Close inshore was a multitude of fishing-smacks—English, Scotch, French, Dutch, and Swedish; steam-launches from the Thames, yachts, electric boats; and beyond were ships of large burden, a multitude of filthy colliers, trim merchantmen, cattle-ships, passenger-boats, petroleum-tanks, ocean tramps, an old white transport even, neat white and gray liners from Southampton and Hamburg; and along the blue coast across the Blackwater my brother could make out dimly a dense swarm of boats chaffering with the people on the beach, a swarm which also extended up the Blackwater almost to Maldon.

About a couple of miles out lay an ironclad, very low in the water, almost, to my brother's perception, like a water-logged ship. This was the ram *Thunder Child*. It was the only war-ship in sight, but far away to the right over the smooth surface of the sea—for that day there was a dead calm—lay a serpent of black smoke to mark the next ironclads of the Channel Fleet, which hovered in an extended line, steam up and ready for action, across the Thames estuary during the course of the Martian conquest, vigilant and yet powerless to prevent it.

At the sight of the sea, Mrs. Elphinstone, in spite of the assurances of her sister-in-law, gave way to panic. She had never been out of England before, she would rather die than trust herself in a foreign country, and so forth. She seemed, poor woman, to imagine that the French and the Martians might prove very similar. She

68

had been growing increasingly hysterical, fearful, and depressed during the two days' journeyings. Her great idea was to return to Stanmore. Things had been always well and safe at Stanmore. They would find George at Stanmore.

It was with the greatest difficulty they could get her down to the beach, where presently my brother succeeded in attracting the attention of some men on a paddle steamer from the Thames. They sent a boat and drove a bargain for thirty-six pounds for the three. The steamer was going, these men said, to Ostend.

It was about two o'clock when my brother, having paid their fares at the gangway, found himself safely aboard the steamboat with his charges. There was food aboard, albeit at exorbitant prices, and the three of them contrived to eat a meal on one of the seats forward.

There were already a couple of score of passengers aboard, some of whom had expended their last money in securing a passage, but the captain lay off the Blackwater until five in the afternoon, picking up passengers until the seated decks were even dangerously crowded. He would probably have remained longer had it not been for the sound of guns that began about that hour in the south. As if in answer, the ironclad seaward fired a small gun and hoisted a string of flags. A jet of smoke sprang out of her funnels.

Some of the passengers were of opinion that this firing came from Shoeburyness until it was noticed that it was growing louder. At the same time, far away in the south-east the masts and upper-works of three ironclads rose one after the other out of the sea, beneath clouds of black smoke. But my brother's attention speedily reverted to the distant firing in the south. He fancied he saw a column of smoke rising out of the distant gray haze.

The little steamer was already flapping her way eastward of the big crescent of shipping, and the low Essex coast was growing blue and hazy, when a Martian appeared, small and faint in the remote distance, advancing along the muddy coast from the direction of Foulness. At that the captain on the bridge swore at the top of his voice with fear and anger at his own delay, and the paddles seemed infected with his terror. Every soul aboard stood at the bulwarks or on the seats of the steamer and stared at the distant shape, higher than the trees or church towers inland, and advancing with a leisurely parody of a human stride.

It was the first Martian my brother had seen, and he stood, more amazed then terrified, watching this Titan advancing deliberately towards the shipping, wading farther and farther into the water as the coast fell away. Then, far away beyond the Crouch, came another, striding over some stunted trees, and then yet another, still farther off, wading deeply through a shiny mudflat that seemed to hang half-way between sea and sky. They were all stalking seaward, as if to intercept the escape of the multitudinous vessels that were crowded between Foulness and the Naze. In spite of the throbbing exertions of the engines of the little paddle-boat, and the pouring foam that her wheels flung behind her, she receded with terrifying slowness from this ominous advance.

69

Glancing, north-westward, my brother saw the large crescent of shipping already writhing with the approaching terror; one ship passing behind another, another coming round from broadside to end on, steamships whistling and giving off volumes of steam, sails being let out, launches rushing hither and thither. He was so fascinated by this and by the creeping danger away to the left that he had no eyes for anything seaward. And then a swift movement of the steamboat (she had suddenly come round to avoid being run down) flung him headlong from the seat upon which he was standing. There was a shouting all about him, a trampling of feet, and a cheer that seemed to be answered faintly. The steamboat lurched and rolled him over upon his hands.

He sprang to his feet and saw to starboard and not a hundred yards from their heeling, pitching boat, a vast iron bulk like the blade of a plough tearing through the water, tossing it on either side in huge waves of foam that leaped towards the steamer, flinging her paddles helplessly in the air, and then sucking her deck down almost to the water-line.

A douche of spray blinded my brother for a moment. When his eyes were clear again he saw the monster had passed and was rushing landward. Big iron upper-works rose out of this headlong structure, and from that twin funnels projected and spat a smoking blast shot with fire. It was the torpedo-ram, *Thunder Child*, steaming headlong, coming to the rescue of the threatened shipping.

Keeping his footing on the heaving deck by clutching the bulwarks, my brother looked past this charging leviathan at the Martians again, and he saw the three of them now close together, and standing so far out to sea that their tripod supports were almost entirely submerged. Thus sunken, and seen in remote perspective, they appeared far less formidable than the huge iron bulk in whose wake the steamer was pitching so helplessly. It would seem they were regarding this new antagonist with astonishment. To their intelligence, it may be, the giant was even such another as themselves. The *Thunder Child* fired no gun, but simply drove full speed towards them. It was probably her not firing that enabled her to get so near the enemy as she did. They did not know what to make of her. One shell, and they would have sent her to the bottom forthwith with the Heat-Ray.

She was steaming at such as pace that in a minute she seemed half-way between the steamboat and the Martians—a diminishing black bulk against the receding horizontal expanse of the Essex coast.

Suddenly the foremost Martian lowered his tube and discharged a canister of the black gas at the ironclad. It hit her larboard side and glanced off in an inky jet that rolled away to seaward, an unfolding torrent of Black Smoke, from which the ironclad drove clear. To the watchers from the steamer, low in the water and with the sun in their eyes, it seemed as though she were already among the Martians.

They saw the gaunt figures separating and rising out of the water as they retreated shoreward, and one of them raised the camera-like generator of the Heat-Ray. He held it pointing obliquely downward, and a bank of steam sprang from the water at its touch. It must have driven through the iron of the ship's side like a white-hot iron rod through paper.

A flicker of flame went up through the rising steam, and then the Martian reeled and staggered. In another moment he was cut down, and a great body of water and steam shot high in the air. The guns of the *Thunder Child* sounded through the reek, going off one after the other, and one shot splashed the water high close by the steamer, ricocheted towards the other flying ships to the north, and smashed a smack to match-wood.

But no one heeded that very much. At the sight of the Martian's collapse the captain on the bridge yelled inarticulately, and all the crowding passengers on the steamer's stern shouted together. And then they yelled again. For, surging out beyond the white tumult drove something long and black, the flames streaming from its middle parts, its ventilators and funnels spouting fire.

She was alive still; the steering-gear, it seems, was intact and her engines working. She headed straight for a second Martian, and was within a hundred yards of him when the Heat-Ray came to bear. Then with a violent thud, a blinding flash, her decks, her funnels, leaped upward. The Martian staggered with the violence of her explosion, and in another moment the flaming wreckage, still driving forward with the impetus of its pace, had struck him and crumpled him up like a thing of card-board. My brother shouted involuntarily. A boiling tumult of steam hid everything again.

"Two!" yelled the captain.

Every one was shouting. The whole steamer from end to end rang with frantic cheering that was taken up first by one and then by all in the crowding multitude of ships and boats that was driving out to sea.

The steam hung upon the water for many minutes, hiding the third Martian and the coast altogether. And all this time the boat was paddling steadily out to sea and away from the fight; and when at last the confusion cleared, the drifting bank of black vapor intervened, and nothing of the *Thunder Child* could be made out, nor could the third Martian be seen. But the ironclads to seaward were now quite close and standing in towards shore past the steamboat.

The little vessel continued to beat its way seaward, and the ironclads receded slowly towards the coast, which was hidden still by a marbled bank of vapor, part steam, part black gas, eddying and combining in the strangest way. The fleet of refugees was scattering to the north-east; several smacks were sailing between the ironclads and the steamboat. After a time, and before they reached the sinking cloud-bank, the warships turned northward, and then abruptly went about and passed into the thickening haze of evening southward. The coast grew faint, and at last indistinguishable amid the low banks of clouds that were gathering about the sinking sun.

Then suddenly out of the golden haze of the sunset came the vibration of guns, and a form of black shadows moving. Every one struggled to the rail of the steamer and peered into the blinding furnace of the west, but nothing was to be distinguished clearly. A mass of smoke rose slanting and barred the face of the sun. The steamboat throbbed on its way through an interminable suspense.

The sun sank into grey clouds, the sky flushed and darkened, the evening star trembled into sight. It was deep twilight when the captain cried out and pointed. My brother strained his eyes. Something rushed up into the sky out of the grayness— rushed slantingly upward and very swiftly into the luminous clearness about the clouds in the western sky; something flat and broad and very large, that swept round in a vast curve, grew smaller, sank slowly, and vanished again into the grey mystery of the night. And as it flew it rained darkness upon the land.

BOOK II

THE EARTH UNDER THE MARTIANS

* * * * *

CHAPTER THE EIGHTH
DEAD LONDON

After I had parted from the artilleryman, I went down the hill, and by the High Street across the bridge to Fulham. The red weed was tumultuous at that time, and nearly choked the bridge roadway; but its fronds were already whitened in patches by the spreading disease that presently removed it so swiftly.

At the corner of the lane that runs to Putney Bridge station I found a man lying. He was as black as a sweep with the black dust, alive, but helplessly and speechlessly drunk. I could get nothing from him but curses and furious lunges at my head. I think I should have stayed by him but for the brutal expression of his face.

There was black dust along the roadway from the bridge onwards, and it grew thicker in Fulham. The streets were horribly quiet. I got food—sour, hard, and moldy, but quite eatable—in a baker's shop here. Some way towards Walham Green the streets became clear of powder, and I passed a white terrace of houses on fire; the noise of the burning was an absolute relief. Going on towards Brompton, the streets were quiet again.

Here I came once more upon the black powder in the streets and upon dead bodies. I saw altogether about a dozen in the length of the Fulham Road. They had been dead many days, so that I hurried quickly past them. The black powder covered them over, and softened their outlines. One or two had been disturbed by dogs.

Where there was no black powder, it was curiously like a Sunday in the City, with the closed shops, the houses locked up and the blinds drawn, the desertion, and the stillness. In some places plunderers had been at work, but rarely at other than the provision and wine shops. A jeweler's window had been broken open in one place, but apparently the thief had been disturbed, and a number of gold chains and a watch lay scattered on the pavement. I did not trouble to touch them. Farther on was a tattered woman in a heap on a doorstep; the hand that hung over her knee was gashed and bled down her rusty brown dress, and a smashed magnum of champagne formed a pool across the pavement. She seemed asleep, but she was dead.

The farther I penetrated into London, the profounder grew the stillness. But it was not so much the stillness of death—it was the stillness of suspense, of expectation. At any time the destruction that had already singed the north-western borders of the metropolis, and had annihilated Ealing and Kilburn, might strike among these houses and leave them smoking ruins. It was a city condemned and derelict. . . .

In South Kensington the streets were clear of dead and of black powder. It was near South Kensington that I first head the howling. It crept almost imperceptibly upon my senses. It was a sobbing alternation of two notes, "Ulla, ulla, ulla, ulla," keeping on perpetually. When I passed streets that ran northward it grew in volume, and houses and buildings seemed to deaden and cut it off again. It came in a full tide down Exhibition Road. I stopped, staring towards Kensington Gardens, wondering at this strange, remote wailing. It was as if that mighty desert of houses had found a voice for its fear and solitude.

"Ulla, ulla, ulla, ulla," wailed that superhuman note—great waves of sound sweeping down the broad, sunlit roadway, between the tall building on each side. I turned northwards, marveling, towards the iron gates of Hyde Park. I had half a mind to break into the Natural History Museum and find my way up to the summits of the towers, in order to see across the park. But I decided to keep to the ground, where quick hiding was possible, and so went on up the Exhibition Road. All the large mansions on each side of the road were empty and still, and my footsteps echoed against the sides of the houses. At the top, near the park gate, I came upon a strange sight—a bus overturned, and the skeleton of a horse picked clean. I puzzled over this for a time, and then went on to the bridge over the Serpentine. The voice grew stronger and stronger, though I could see nothing above the house-tops on the north side of the park, save a haze of smoke to the north-west.

"Ulla, ulla, ulla, ulla," cried the voice, coming, as it seemed to me, from the district about Regent's Park. The desolating cry worked upon my mind. The mood that had sustained me passed. The wailing took possession of me. I found I was intensely weary, footsore, and now again hungry and thirsty.

It was already past noon. Why was I wandering alone in this city of the dead? Why was I alone when all London was lying in state, and in its black shroud? I felt intolerably lonely. My mind ran on old friends that I had forgotten for years. I thought of the poisons in the chemists' shops, of the liquors the wine-merchants stored; I recalled the two sodden creatures of despair, who so far as I knew, shared the city with myself. . . .

I came into Oxford Street by the Marble Arch, and here again were black powder and several bodies, and an evil, ominous smell from the gratings of the cellars of some of the houses. I grew very thirsty after the heat of my long walk. With infinite trouble I managed to break into a public-house and get food and drink. I was weary after eating, and went into the parlor behind the bar, and slept on a black horsehair sofa I found there.

I awoke to find that dismal howling still in my ears, "Ulla, ulla, ulla, ulla." It was now dusk, and after I had routed out some biscuits and a cheese in the bar—there was a meat-safe, but it contained nothing but maggots—I wandered on through the silent residential squares to Baker Street—Portman Square is the only one I can name—and so came out at last upon Regent's Park. And as I emerged from the top of Baker Street, I saw far away over the trees in the clearness of the sunset the hood of the Martian giant from which this howling proceeded. I was not terrified. I came upon him as if it were a matter of course. I watched him for some time, but he did not move. He appeared to be standing and yelling, for no reason that I could discover.

I tried to formulate a plan of action. That perpetual sound of "Ulla, ulla, ulla, ulla," confused my mind. Perhaps I was too tired to be very fearful. Certainly I was more curious to know the reason of this monotonous crying than afraid. I turned back away from the park and struck into Park Road, intending to skirt the park, went along under the shelter of the terraces, and got a view of this stationary, howling Martian from the direction of St. John's Wood. A couple of hundred yards out of Baker Street I heard a yelping chorus, and saw, first a dog with a piece of putrescent red meat in his jaws coming headlong towards me, and then a pack of starving mongrels in pursuit of him. He made a wide curve to avoid me, as though he feared I might prove a fresh competitor. As the yelping died away down the silent road, the wailing sounds of "Ulla, ulla, ulla, ulla," reasserted itself.

I came upon the wrecked handling-machine halfway to St. John's Wood station. At first I thought a house had fallen across the road. It was only as I clambered among the ruins that I saw, with a start, this mechanical Samson lying, with its tentacles bent and smashed and twisted, among the ruins it had made. The forepart was shattered. It seemed as if it had driven blindly straight at the house, and had been overwhelmed in its overthrow. It seemed to me then that this might have happened by a handling-machine escaping from the guidance of its Martian. I could not clamber among the ruins to see it, and the twilight was now so far advanced that the blood with which its seat was smeared, and the gnawed gristle of the Martian that the dogs had left, were invisible to me.

Wondering still more at all that I had seen, I pushed on towards Primrose Hill. Far away, through a gap in the trees, I saw a second Martian, as motionless as the first, standing in the park towards the Zoological Gardens, and silent. A little beyond the ruins about the smashed handling-machine I came upon the red weed again, and found the Regent's Canal, a spongy mass of dark-red vegetation.

As I crossed the bridge, the sound of "Ulla, ulla, ulla, ulla," ceased. It was, as it were, cut off. The silence came like a thunderclap.

The dusky houses about me stood faint and tall and dim; the trees towards the park were growing black. All about me the red weed clambered among the ruins, writhing to get above me in the dimness. Night, the mother of fear and mystery, was coming upon me. But while that voice sounded the solitude, the desolation, had been endurable; by virtue of it London had still seemed alive, and the sense of life about me had upheld me. Then suddenly a change, the passing of something— I knew not what—and then a stillness that could be felt. Nothing but this gaunt quiet.

London about me gazed at me spectrally. The windows in the white houses were like the eye-sockets of skulls. About me my imagination found a thousand noiseless enemies moving. Terror seized me, a horror of my temerity. In front of me the road became pitchy black as though it was tarred, and I saw a contorted shape lying across the pathway. I could not bring myself to go on. I turned down St. John's Wood Road, and ran headlong from this unendurable stillness towards Kilburn. I hid from the night and the silence, until long after midnight, in a cabmen's shelter in Harrow Road. But before the dawn my courage returned, and while the stars were still in the sky I turned once more towards Regent's Park. I missed my way among the streets, and presently saw down a long avenue, in the half-light of the early dawn, the curve of Primrose Hill. On the summit, towering up to the fading stars, was a third Martian, erect and motionless like the others.

An insane resolve possessed me. I could die and end it. And I would save myself even the trouble of killing myself. I marched on recklessly towards this Titan, and then, as I drew nearer and the light grew, I saw that a multitude of black birds was circling and clustering about the hood. At that my heart gave a bound, and I began running along the road.

I hurried through the red weed that choked St. Edmund's Terrace (I waded breast-high across a torrent of water that was rushing down from the waterworks towards the Albert Road), and emerged upon the grass before the rising of the sun. Great mounds had been heaped about the crest of the hill, making a huge redoubt of it—it was the final and largest place the Martians had made—and from behind these heaps there rose a thin smoke against the sky. Against the sky-line an eager dog ran and disappeared. The thought that had flashed into my mind grew real, grew credible. I felt not fear, only a wild, trembling exultation, as I ran up the hill towards the motionless monster. Out of the hood hung lank shreds of brown, at which the hungry birds pecked and tore.

In another moment I had scrambled up the earthen rampart and stood upon its crest, and the interior of the redoubt was below me. A mighty space it was, with gigantic machines here and there within it, huge mounds of material and strange shelter-places. And scattered about it, some in their overturned war-machines, some in the now rigid handling-machines, and a dozen of them stark and silent and laid in a row, were the Martians—*dead!*—slain by the putrefactive and disease bacteria against which their systems were unprepared; slain as the red weed was being slain; slain, after all man's devices had failed, by the humblest things that God, in his wisdom, has put upon this earth.

75

For so it had come about, as indeed I and many men might have foreseen had not terror and disaster blinded our minds. These germs of disease have taken toll of humanity since the beginning of things—taken toll of our prehuman ancestors since life began here. But by virtue of this natural selection of our kind we have developed resisting power; to no germs do we succumb without a struggle, and to many—those that cause putrefaction in dead matter, for instance—our living frames are altogether immune. But there are no bacteria in Mars, and directly these invaders arrived, directly they drank and fed, our microscopic allies began to work their overthrow. Already when I watched them they were irrevocably doomed, dying and rotting even as they went to and fro. It was inevitable. By the toll of a billion deaths man has bought his birthright of the earth, and it is his against all comers; it would still be his were the Martians ten times as mighty as they are. For neither do men live nor die in vain.

\* \* \* \* \*

# from *The First Men in the Moon* (1901)

*Bedford, a bankrupt playwright and a con-man, tells the story of the invention of Cavorite, of the trip to the Moon, of the descent to the interior and finding the strange race of Selenites, and of his heroic return to Earth. His own narrative asks to be criticized. From the start, Bedford has seen in Cavor—the eccentric, obsessed, and unworldly scientist—a possibility for profit. On the Moon, drunk with lunar mushrooms, Bedford lets loose a rant about racial and imperial conquest. At the end Cavor, in messages that he sends back to Earth by radio, suggests that Bedford had needlessly provoked the crisis that caused the two humans to flee and finally to become separated. Cavor goes silent, but his last communications are entirely enigmatic, and the final terrifying scene of his being menaced by the Selenites has no basis in fact; it is only Bedford's "vivid dream." This revision casts the whole adventure narrative into a new mode, not one simply of dangerous escapes, but one of utopian and dystopian possibilities of the sort discussed in the introduction. The selection reprints all of the novel except the comic beginning scenes in which Bedford meets Cavor, makes sure he will profit from Cavorite, and with some reluctance accompanies the intrepid Cavor on a trip to the moon. We pick up just as the spacecraft (a sphere that can selectively negate gravity) carrying Bedford and Cavor comes to rest on the Moon.*

\* \* \* \* \*

### CHAPTER THE SIXTH
### THE LANDING ON THE MOON

Came a thud, and I was half buried under the bale of our possessions, and for a space everything was still. Then I could hear Cavor puffing and grunting and the snapping of a shutter in its sash. I made an effort, thrust back our blanket-wrapped luggage, and emerged from beneath it. Our open windows were just visible as a deeper black set with stars.

We were still alive, and we were lying in the darkness of the shadow of the wall of the great crater into which we had fallen.

We sat getting our breath again and feeling the bruises on our limbs. I think neither of us had had a very clear expectation of such rough handling as we had received. I struggled painfully to my feet. "And now," said I, "to look at the landscape of the moon! But!—It's tremendously dark, Cavor!"

The glass was dewy, and as I spoke I wiped at it with my blanket. "We're half an hour or so beyond the day," he said. "We must wait."

77

It was impossible to distinguish anything. We might have been in a sphere of steel for all that we could see. My rubbing with the blanket simply smeared the glass, and as fast as I wiped it, it became opaque again with freshly-condensed moisture, mixed with an increasing quantity of blanket hairs. Of course I ought not to have used the blanket. In my efforts to clear the glass I slipped upon the damp surface and hurt my skin against one of the oxygen cylinders that protruded from our bale.

The thing was exasperating—it was absurd. Here we were just arrived upon the moon, amidst we knew not what wonders, and all we could see was the gray and streaming wall of the bubble in which we had come.

"Confound it," I said, "but at this rate we might have stopped at home!" and I squatted on the bale and shivered and drew my blanket closer about me.

Abruptly the moisture turned to spangles and fronds of frost. "Can you reach the electric heater?" said Cavor. "Yes—that black knob. Or we shall freeze."

I did not wait to be told twice. "And now," said I, "what are we to do?"

"Wait," he said.

"Wait?"

"Of course. We shall have to wait until our air gets warm again, and then this glass will clear. We can't do anything till then. It's night here yet—we must wait for the day to overtake us. Meanwhile, don't you feel hungry?"

For a space I did not answer him, but sat fretting. I turned reluctantly from the crater wall. These hummocks looked like snow. At the time I thought they were snow. But they were not—they were mounds and masses of frozen air!

So it was at first; and then, sudden, swift, and amazing, came the lunar day.

The sunlight had crept down the cliff, it touched the drifted masses at its base, and incontinently came striding with seven-leagued boots towards us. The distant cliff seemed to shift and quiver, and at the touch of the sun a reek of gray vapor poured upwards from the crater floor, whirls and puffs and drifting wraiths of gray, thicker and broader and denser, until at last the whole westward plain was steaming like a wet handkerchief held before the fire, and the westward cliffs were no more than a refracted glare beyond.

"It is air," said Cavor, "It must be air—or it would not rise like this—at this mere touch of a sunbeam. And at this pace . . ."

He peered upwards. "Look!" he said.

"What?" I asked.

"In the sky. Already. On the blackness—a little touch of blue. See! The stars seem larger; the little ones and all those dim nebulosities we saw in empty space—they are hidden!"

Swiftly, steadily the day approached us. Gray summit after gray summit was overtaken by the blaze, and turned to a smoking white intensity. At last there was nothing to the west of us but a bank of surging fog, the tumultuous advance and ascent of cloudy haze. The distant cliff had receded farther and farther, had loomed and changed through the whirl, had foundered and vanished at last in its confusion.

78

Nearer came that steaming advance, nearer and nearer, coming as fast as the shadow of a cloud before the south-west wind. About us rose a thin, anticipatory haze.

Cavor gripped my arms. "What?" I said.

"Look! The sunrise! The sun!"

He turned me about and pointed to the brow of the eastward cliff, looming above the haze about us, scarcely lighter than the darkness of the sky. But now its line was marked by strange reddish shapes—tongues of vermilion flame that writhed and danced. I fancied it must be spirals of vapor that had caught the light and made this crest of fiery tongues against the sky, but indeed it was the solar prominences I saw, a crown of fire about the sun that is forever hidden from earthly eyes by our atmospheric veil.

And then—the sun!

Steadily, inevitably, came a brilliant line—came a thin edge of intolerable effulgence that took a circular shape, became a bow, became a blazing scepter, and hurled a shaft of heat at us as though it were a spear.

It seemed verily to stab my eyes! I cried aloud and turned about blinded, groping for my blanket beneath the bale.

And with the incandescence came a sound, the first sound that had reached us from without since we left the earth, a hissing and rustling, the stormy trailing of the aerial garment of the advancing day. And with the coming of the sound and the light the sphere lurched, and, blinded and dazzled, we staggered helplessly against each other. It lurched again, and the hissing grew louder. I had shut my eyes perforce; I was making clumsy efforts to cover my head with my blanket, and this second lurch sent me helplessly off my feet. I fell against the bale, and, opening my eyes, had a momentary glimpse of the air just outside our glass. It was running—it was boiling—like snow into which a white-hot rod is thrust. What had been solid air had suddenly, at the touch of the sun, become a paste, a mud, a slushy liquefaction that hissed and bubbled into gas.

There came a still more violent whirl of the sphere, and we had clutched each other. In another moment we were spun about again. Round we went and over, and then I was on all fours. The lunar dawn had hold of us. It meant to show us little men what the moon could do with us.

I caught a second glimpse of things without, puffs of vapor, half-liquid slush, excavated, sliding, falling, sliding. We dropped into darkness. I went down with Cavor's knees in my chest. Then he seemed to fly away from me, and for a moment I lay, with all the breath out of my body, staring upwards. A huge landslip, as it were, of melting stuff had splashed from us. I saw the bubbles dancing on the glass above. I heard Cavor exclaiming feebly.

Then some huge landslip in the thawing air had caught us and, spluttering expostulation, we began to roll down a slope, rolling faster and faster, leaping crevasses and rebounding from banks, faster and faster, westward into the white-hot boiling tumult of the lunar day.

Clutching at each other we spun about, pitched this way and that, our bale of packages leaping at us, pounding at us. We collided, we gripped, we were torn asunder—our heads met, and the whole universe burst into fiery darts and stars! On the earth we should have smashed each other a dozen times, but on the moon luckily for us our weight was only one-sixth of what it is terrestrially, and we fell very mercifully. I recall a sensation of utter sickness, a feeling as if my brain were upside down within my skill, and then—

Something was at work upon my face; some thin feelers worried my ears. Then I discovered the brilliance of the landscape around was mitigated by blue spectacles. Cavor bent over me, and I saw his face upside down, his eyes also protected by tinted goggles. His breath came regularly, and his lip was bleeding from a bruise. "Better?" he said, wiping the blood with the back of his hand.

Everything seemed swaying for a space, but that was simply my giddiness. I perceived that he had closed some of the shutters in the outer sphere to save me from the direct blaze of the sun. I was aware that everything about us was very brilliant.

"Lord!" I gasped. "But this—"

I craned my neck to see. I perceived the blinding glare outside, an utter change from the gloomy darkness of our first impressions. "Have I been insensible long?" I asked.

"I don't know—the chronometer is broke. Some little time. . . . My dear chap! I have been afraid . . . "

I lay for a space taking this in. I saw his face still bore evidences of emotion. For a while I said nothing. I passed an inquisitive hand over my contusions, and surveyed his face for similar damages. The back of my right hand had suffered most, and was skinless and raw. My forehead was bruised and had bled. He handed me a measure with some of the restorative—I forgot the name of it—he had brought with us. After a time I felt a little better. I began to stretch my limbs carefully. Soon I could talk.

"It wouldn't have done," I said, as though there had been no interval.

"No it *wouldn't!*"

He thought, his hands hanging over his knees. He peered through the glass and then stared at me. "Good Lord!" he said. "No!"

"What has happened?" I asked after a pause; "have we jumped to the tropics?"

"It was as I expected. This air has evaporated. If it is air. At any rate it has evaporated, and the surface of the moon is showing. We are lying on a bank of earthy rock. Here and there bare soil is exposed; a queer sort of soil."

It occurred to him that it was unnecessary to explain. He assisted me into a sitting position, and I could see with my own eyes.

CHAPTER THE SEVENTH
A LUNAR MORNING

The harsh emphasis, the pitiless black and white of the scenery had altogether disappeared. The glare of the sun had taken upon itself a faint tinge of amber; the shadows upon the cliff on the crater wall were deeply purple. To the eastward a dark bank of fog still crouched and sheltered from the sunrise, but to the westward the sky was blue and clear. I began to realize the length of my insensibility.

We were no longer in a void. An atmosphere had risen about us. The outline of things had gained in character, had grown acute and varied; save for a shadowed space of white substance here and there, white substance that was no longer air but snow, the Arctic appearance had gone altogether. Everywhere broad, rusty-brown spaces of bare and tumbled earth spread to the blaze transient little pools and eddies of water, the only things stirring in that expanse of barrenness. The sunlight inundated the upper two-thirds of our sphere and turned our climate to high summer, but our feet were still in shadow and the sphere was lying upon a drift of snow.

And scattered here and there upon the slope, and emphasized by little white threads of unthawed snow upon their shady sides, were shapes like sticks—dry, twisted sticks of the same rusty hue as the rock upon which they lay. That caught one's thoughts sharply. Sticks! On a lifeless world? Then as my eye grew more accustomed to the texture of their substance I perceived that almost all this surface had a fibrous texture, like the carpet of brown needles one finds beneath the shade of pine trees.

"Cavor!" I said.

"Yes?"

"It may be a dead world now—but once—"

Something arrested my attention. I had discovered among these needles a number of little round objects. It seemed to me that one of these had moved.

"Cavor," I whispered.

"What?"

But I did not answer at once. I stared incredulous. For an instant I could not believe my eyes. I gave an inarticulate cry. I gripped his arm. I pointed. "Look!" I cried, finding my tongue. "There! Yes! And there!"

His eyes followed my pointing finger. "Eh?" he said.

How can I describe the thing I saw? It is so petty a thing to state, and yet it seemed so wonderful, so pregnant with emotion. I have said that amidst the stick-like litter were these round bodies, these little oval bodies that might have passed as very small pebbles. And now first one and then another had stirred, had rolled over and cracked, and down the crack of each of them showed a minute line of yellowish green, thrusting outward to meet the hot encouragement of the newly risen sun. For a moment that was all, and then there stirred and burst a third!

"It is a seed," said Cavor. And then I herd him whisper, very softly: "*Life!*"

"Life!" and immediately it poured upon us that our vast journey had not been made in vain, that we had come to no arid waste of minerals, but to a world that lived and moved! We watched intensely. I remember I kept rubbing the glass before me with my sleeve, jealous of the faintest suspicion of mist.

81

The picture was clear and vivid only in the middle of the field. All about that center the dead fibers and seeds were magnified and distorted by the curvature of the glass. But we could see enough! One after another all down the sunlit slope these miraculous little brown bodies burst and gaped apart, like seed-pods, like the husks of fruits; opened mouths that drank in the heat and light pouring in a cascade from the newly risen sun.

Every moment more of these seed-coats ruptured, and even as they did so the swelling pioneers overflowed their rent-distended seed-cases and passed into the second stage of growth. With a steady assurance, a swift deliberation, these amazing seeds thrust a rootlet downward to the earth and a queer bundle-like bud into the air. In a little while the whole slope was dotted with minute plantlets standing at attention in the blaze of the sun.

They did not stand for long. The bundle-like buds swelled and strained and opened with a jerk, thrusting out a coronet of red sharp tips, spreading a whorl of tiny, spiky, brownish leaves, that lengthened rapidly, lengthened visibly even as we watched. The movement was slower than any animal's, swifter than any plant's I have ever seen before. How can I suggest it to you—the way that growth went on? The leaf tips grew so that they moved onward even while we looked at them. The brown seed-case shriveled and was absorbed with an equal rapidity. Have you ever on a cold day taken a thermometer into your warm hand and watched the little thread of mercury creep up the tube? These moon-plants grew like that.

In a few minutes, as it seemed, the buds of the more forward of these plants had lengthened into a stem, and were even putting forth a second whorl of leaves, and all the slope that had seemed so recently a lifeless stretch of litter was now dark with the stunted, olive-green herbage of bristling spikes that swayed with the vigor of their growing.

I turned about, and behold! Along the upper edge of a rock to the eastward a similar fringe, in a scarcely less forward condition, swayed and bent, dark against the blinding glare of the sun. And beyond this fringe was the silhouette of a plant mass, branching clumsily like a cactus and swelling visibly, swelling like a bladder that fills with air.

Then to the westwards also I discovered another such distended form was rising over the scrub. But here the light fell upon its sleek sides, and I could see that its color was a vivid orange. It rose as one watched it; if one looked away from it for a minute and then back, its outline had changed: it thrust out blunt, congested branches, until in a little time it rose a coralline shape of many feet in height. Compared with such a growth the terrestrial puff-ball which will sometimes swell a foot in diameter in a single night, would be a hopeless laggard. But then the puff-ball grows against a gravitational pull of six times that of the moon. Beyond, out of gullies and flats that had been hidden from us but not from the quickening sun, over reefs and banks of shining rock, a bristling beard of spiky fleshy vegetation was straining into view, hurrying tumultuously to take advantage of the brief day in which it must flower and fruit and seed again and die. It was like a miracle, that growth. So, one must imagine, the trees and plants arose at the Creation, and covered the desolation of the new-made earth.

Imagine it! imagine that dawn! The resurrection of the frozen air, the stirring and quickening of the soil, and then this silent uprising of vegetation, this unearthly ascent of fleshliness and spikes. Conceive it all lit by a blaze that would make the intensest sunlight of earth seem watery and weak. And still amidst this stirring jungle wherever there was shadow lingered banks of bluish snow. And to have the picture of our impression complete you must bear in mind that we saw it all through a thick bent glass, distorting it as things are distorted by a lens, acute only in the center of the picture and very bright there, and towards the edges magnified and unreal.

CHAPTER THE EIGHTH
PROSPECTING BEGINS

We ceased to gaze. We turned to each other, the same thought, the same question in our eyes. For these plants to grow there must be some air, however attenuated—air that we also should be able to breathe.

"The manhole?" I said.

"Yes," said Cavor; "if it is air we see!"

"In a little while," I said, "These plants will be as high as we are. Suppose—suppose, after all—Is it certain? How do you know that stuff *is* air? It may be nitrogen; it may be carbonic acid even!"

"That is easy," he said, and set about proving it. He produced a big piece of crumpled paper from the bale, lit it, and thrust it hastily through the manhole valve. I bent forward and peered down through the thick glass for its appearance outside, that little flame on whose evidence depended so much!

I saw the paper drop out and lie lightly upon the snow. The pink flame of its burning vanished. For an instant it seemed to be extinguished. . . . And then I saw a little blue tongue upon the edge of it that trembled and crept and spread!

Quietly that whole sheet, save where it lay in immediate contact with the snow, charred and shriveled and sent up a quivering thread of smoke. There was no doubt left to me: the atmosphere of the moon was either pure oxygen or air, and capable therefore unless its tenuity were excessive, of supporting our alien life. We might emerge—and live!

I sat down with my legs on either side of the manhole and prepared to unscrew it, but Cavor stopped me. "There is first a little precaution," he said. He pointed out that, although it was certainly an oxygenated atmosphere outside, it might still be so rarefied as to cause us grave injury. He reminded me of mountain sickness and of the bleeding that often afflicts aeronauts who have ascended too swiftly, and he spent some time in the preparation of a sickly tasting drink which he insisted on my sharing. It made me feel a little numb, but otherwise had no effect on me. Then he permitted me to begin unscrewing.

Presently the glass stopper of the manhole was so far undone that the denser air within our sphere began to escape along the thread of the screw, singing as a kettle signs before it boils. There-upon he made me desist. It speedily became evident that the pressure outside was very much less than it was within. How much less it was we had no means of telling.

I sat grasping the stopper with both hands ready to close it again if, in spite of our intense hope, the lunar atmosphere should after all prove too rarefied for us, and Cavor sat with a cylinder of compressed oxygen at hand to restore our pressure. We looked at each other in silence, and then at the fantastic vegetation that swayed and grew visibly and noiselessly without. And ever that shrill piping continued.

The blood-vessels began to throb in my ears, and the sound of Cavor's movements diminished. I noted how still everything had become because of the thinning of the air.

As our air sizzled out from the screw the moisture of it condensed in little puffs.

Presently I experienced a peculiar shortness of breath—that lasted, indeed, during the whole of the time of our exposure to the moon's exterior atmosphere, and a rather unpleasant sensation about the ears and fingernails and the back of the throat grew on my attention, and presently passed off again.

But then came vertigo and nausea that abruptly changed the quality of my courage. I gave the lid of the manhole half a turn and made a hasty explanation to Cavor, but now he was the more sanguine. He answered me in a voice that seemed extraordinarily small and remote because of the thinness of the air that carried the sound. He recommended a nip of brandy, and set me the example, and presently I felt better. I turned the manhole stopper back again. The throbbing in my ears grew louder, and then I remarked that the piping note of the outrush had ceased. For a time I could not be sure that it had ceased.

"Well?" said Cavor, in the ghost of a voice.

"Well?" said I.

"Shall we go on?"

I thought. "Is this all?"

"If you can stand it."

By way of answer I went on unscrewing. I lifted the circular operculum from its place and laid it carefully on the bale. A flake or so of snow whirled and vanished as that thin and unfamiliar air took possession of our sphere. I knelt and then seated myself at the edge of the manhole, peering over it. Beneath, within a yard of my face, lay the untrodden snow of the moon.

There came a little pause. Our eyes met.

"It doesn't distress your lungs too much?" said Cavor.

"No," I said. "I can stand this."

He stretched out his hand for his blanket, thrust his head through its central hole, and wrapped it about him. He sat down on the edge of the manhole; he let his feet drop until they were within six inches of the lunar snow. He hesitated for a moment, then thrust himself forwards, dropped these intervening inches, and stood upon the untrodden soil of the moon.

As he stepped forwards he was refracted grotesquely by the edge of the glass. He stood for a moment looking this way and that. Then he drew himself together and leaped.

The glass distorted everything, but it seemed to me even then to be an extremely big leap. He had at one bound become remote. He seemed twenty or thirty feet off. He was standing high upon a rocky mass and gesticulating back to me. Perhaps he was shouting—but the sound did not reach me. But how the deuce had he done this? I felt like a man who has just seen a new conjuring trick.

Still in a puzzled state of mind, I too dropped though the manhole. I stood up. Just in front of me the snow-drift had fallen away and made a sort of ditch. I made a step and jumped.

I found myself flying through the air, saw the rock on which he stood coming to meet me, clutched it, and clung in a state of infinite amazement. I gasped a painful laugh. I was tremendously confused. Cavor bent down and shouted in piping tones for me to be careful. I had forgotten that on the moon, with only an eighth part of the earth's mass and a quarter of its diameter, my weight was barely a sixth what it was on earth. But now that fact insisted on being remembered.

"We are out of Mother Earth's leading-strings now," he said.

With a guarded effort I raised myself to the top and, moving as cautiously as a rheumatic patient, stood up beside him under the blaze of sun. The sphere lay behind us on its dwindling snow-drift thirty feet away.

As far as the eyes could see over the enormous disorder of rocks that formed the crater floor the same bristling scrub that surrounded us was starting into life, diversified here and there by bulging masses of a cactus form, and scarlet and purple lichens that grew so fast they seemed to crawl over the rocks. The whole area of the crater seemed to me then to be one similar wilderness up to the very foot of the surrounding cliff.

This cliff was apparently bare of vegetation save at its base, and with buttresses and terraces and platforms that did not very greatly attract our attention at the time. It was many miles away from us in every direction; we seemed to be almost at the center of the crater, and we saw it through a certain haziness that drove before the wind. For there was even a wind now in the thin air—a swift yet weak wind that chilled exceedingly, but exerted little pressure. It was blowing round the crater, as it seemed, to the hot, illuminated side from the foggy darkness under the sunward wall. It was difficult to look into this eastward fog; we had to peer with half-closed eyes beneath the shade of our hands because of the fierce intensity of the motionless sun.

"It seems to be deserted," said Cavor, "absolutely desolate."

I looked about me again. I retained even then a clinging hope of some quasi-human evidence, some pinnacle of building, some house or engine; but everywhere spread the tumbled rocks in peaks and crests, and the darting scrub and those bulging cacti that swelled and swelled, a flat negation as it seemed of all such hope.

"It looks as though these plants had it to themselves," I said. "I see no trace of any other creature."

"No insects—no birds—no! Not a trace, not a scrap or particle of animal life. If there was—what would they do in the night? . . . No; there's just these plants alone."

I shaded my eyes with my hand. "It's like a landscape of a dream. These things are less like earth land plants than the things one imagines among the rocks at the bottom of the sea. Look at that, yonder! One might imagine it a lizard changed into a plant. And that glare!"

"This is only the fresh morning," said Cavor.

He sighed and looked about him. "This is no world for men," he said. "And yet in a way . . . it appeals."

He became silent for a time, then commenced his meditative humming. I started at a gentle touch, and found a thin sheet of livid lichen lapping over my shoe. I kicked at it; it fell to powder, and each speck began to grow. I heard Cavor exclaim sharply, perceived that one of the fixed bayonets of the scrub had pricked him.

He hesitated, his eyes sought among the rocks about us. A sudden blaze of pink had crept up a ragged pillar of crag. It was a most extraordinary pink, a livid magenta.

"Look!" said I, turning, and behold Cavor had vanished.

For an instant I stood transfixed. Then I made a hasty step to look over the verge of the rock. But, in my surprise at his disappearance, I forgot once more that we were on the moon. The thrust of my foot that I made in striding would have carried me six—a good five yards over the edge. For the moment the thing had something of the effect of one of those nightmares when one falls and falls. For while one falls sixteen feet in the first second of a fall on earth, on the moon one falls two, and with only a sixth of one's weight. I fell, or rather I jumped down, about ten yards I supposed. It seemed to take a long time—five or six seconds, I should think. I floated through the air and fell like a feather, knee-deep in a snow-drift in the bottom of a gully of blue-gray, white-veined rock.

I looked about me. "Cavor!" I cried, but no Cavor was visible.

"Cavor!" I cried louder, and the rocks echoed me.

I turned fiercely to the rocks and clambered to the summit of them. "Cavor," I cried. My voice sounded like the voice of a lost lamb.

The sphere too was not in sight, and for a moment a horrible feeling of desolation pinched my heart.

Then I saw him. He was laughing and gesticulating to attract my attention. He was on a bare patch of rock twenty or thirty yards away. I could not hear his voice, but "Jump!" said his gestures. I hesitated, the distance seemed enormous. Yet I reflected that surely I must be able to clear a greater distance than Cavor.

I made a step back, gathered myself together, and leaped with all my might. I seemed to shoot up in the air as if I should never come down.

It was horrible and delightful, and as wild as a nightmare to go flying off in this fashion. I realized my leap had been altogether too violent. I flew clean over Cavor's head, and beheld a spiky confusion in a gully spreading to meet my fall. I gave a yelp of alarm. I put out my hands and straightened my legs.

I hit a huge fungoid bulk that burst all about me, scattering a mass of orange spores in every direction, and covering me with orange powder. I rolled over spluttering, and came to rest convulsed with breathless laughter.

I became aware of Cavor's little round face peering over a bristling hedge. He shouted some faded inquiry. "Eh?" I tried to shout, but could not do so for want of breath. He made his way towards me, coming gingerly among the bushes. "We've got to be careful!" he said. "This moon has no discipline. She'll let us smash ourselves."

He helped me to my feet. "You exerted yourself too much," he said, dabbing at the yellow stuff with his hand to remove it from my garments.

I stood passive and panting, allowing him to beat off the jelly from my knees and elbows and lecture me upon my misfortunes. "We don't quite allow for the gravitation. Our muscles are scarcely educated yet. We must practice a little. When you have got your breath."

I pulled two or three little thorns out of my hand, and sat for a time on a boulder of rock. My muscles were quivering, and I had that feeling of personal disillusionment that comes to the learner of cycling on earth at his first fall.

It suddenly occurred to Cavor that the cold air in the gully after the brightness of the sun might give me a fever. So we clambered back into the sunlight. We found that beyond a few abrasions I had received no serious injuries from my tumble, and at Cavor's suggestion we were presently looking round for some safe and easy landing-place for my next leap. We chose a rocky slab some ten yards off, separated from us by a little thicket of olive-green spikes.

"Imagine it there!" said Cavor, who was assuming airs of a trainer, and he pointed to a spot about four feet from my toes. This leap I managed without difficulty, and I must confess I found a certain satisfaction in Cavor's falling short by a foot or so and tasting the spikes of the scrub. "One has to be careful, you see," he said, pulling out his thorns, and with that he ceased to be my mentor and became my fellow-learner in the art of lunar locomotion.

We chose a still easier jump and did it without difficulty, and then leaped back again and to and fro several times, accustoming our muscles to the new standard. I could never have believed, had I not experienced it, how rapid that adaptation would be. In a very little time indeed, certainly after fewer than thirty leaps, we could judge the effort necessary for a distance with almost terrestrial assurance.

And all this time the lunar plants were growing around us, higher and denser and more entangled, every moment thicker and taller spiked plants, green cactus masses, fungi, fleshy and lichenous things, strange radiate and sinuous shapes. But we were so intent upon our leaping that for a time we gave no head to their unfaltering expansion.

An extraordinary elation had taken possession of us. Partly I think it was our sense of release from the confinement of the sphere. Mainly, however, the thin sweetness of the air, which I am certain contained a much larger proportion of oxygen than our terrestrial atmosphere. In spite of the strange quality of all about us, I felt as adventurous and experimental as a Cockney placed for the first time among mountains; and I do not think it occurred to either of us, face to face though we were with the Unknown, to be very greatly afraid.

We were bitten by a spirit of enterprise. We selected a lichenous kopje, perhaps fifteen yards away, and landed neatly on its summit one after the other. "Good!" we cried to each other, "good"; and Cavor made three steps and went off to a tempting slope of snow a good twenty yards and more beyond. I stood for a moment struck by the grotesque effect of his soaring figure, his dirty cricket cap and spiky hair, his little round body, his arms and his knickerbockered legs tucked up tightly against the weird spaciousness of the lunar scene. A gust of laughter seized me, and then I stepped off to follow. Plump! I dropped beside him.

We made a few Gargantuan strides, leaped three or four times more, and sat down at last in a lichenous hollow. Our lungs were painful. We sat holding our sides and recovering our breath, looking appreciation at each other. Cavor panted something about "amazing sensations." And then came a thought into my head. For the moment it did not seem a particularly appalling thought, simply a natural question arising out of the situation.

"By the way," I said, "Where exactly is the sphere?"

Cavor looked at me. "Eh?"

The full meaning of what we were saying struck me sharply.

"Cavor!" I cried, laying a hand on his arm. "Where is the sphere?"

## CHAPTER THE NINTH
### LOST MEN IN THE MOON

His face caught something of my dismay. He stood up and stared about him at the scrub that fenced us in and rose about us, straining upwards in a passion of growth. He put a dubious hand to his lips. He spoke with a sudden lack of assurance. "I think," he said slowly, "we left it . . . somewhere . . . about *there*."

He pointed a hesitating finger that wavered in an arc.

"I'm not sure." His look of consternation deepened. "Anyhow," he said with his eyes on me, "it can't be far."

We had both stood up. We made unmeaning ejaculations.

All about us on the sunlit slopes frothed and swayed the darting shrubs, the swelling cactus, the creeping lichens, and wherever the shade remained the snow-drifts lingered. North, south, east and west spread an identical monotony of unfamiliar forms. And somewhere, buried already among this tangled confusion, was our sphere, our home, our only provision, our only hope of escape from this fantastic wilderness of ephemeral growths into which we had come.

"I think after all," he said, pointing suddenly, "it might be over there."

"No," I said. "We have turned in a curve. See! Here is the mark of my heels. It's clear the thing must be more to the eastward, much more. No! the sphere must be over there."

"I *think*," said Cavor, "I kept the sun upon my right all the time."

"Every leap, it seems to me," I said, "my shadow flew before me."

We stared into each other's eyes. The area of the crater had become enormously vast to our imaginations, the growing thickets already impenetrably dense.

"Good heavens! What fools we have been!"

"It's evident that we must find it again," said Cavor, "and that soon. The sun grows stronger. We should be fainting with the heat already if it wasn't so dry. And . . . I'm hungry."

I stared at him. I had not suspected this aspect of the matter before. But it came to me at once—a positive craving. "Yes," I said with emphasis, "I am hungry, too."

He stood up with a look of active resolution. "Certainly we must find the sphere."

As calmly as possible we surveyed the interminable reefs and thickets that formed the floor of the crater, each of us weighing in silence the chances of our finding the sphere before we were overtaken by heat and hunger.

"It can't be fifty yards from here," said Cavor, with indecisive gestures. "The only thing is to beat round about until we come upon it."

"That is all we can do," I said, without any alacrity to begin our hunt. "I wish this confounded spike bush did not grow so fast!"

"That's just it," said Cavor. "But it was lying on a bank of snow."

I stared about me in the vain hope of recognizing some knoll or shrub that had been near the sphere. But everywhere was a confusing sameness, everywhere the aspiring bushes, the distending fungi, the dwindling snow-banks, steadily and inevitably changed. The sun scorched and stung; the faintness of an unaccountable hunger mingled with our infinite perplexity. And even as we stood there, confused and lost amidst unprecedented things, we became aware for the first time of a sound upon the moon other than the stir of the growing plants, the faint sighing of the wind, or those that we ourselves had made.

Boom . . . Boom . . . Boom . . .

It came from beneath our feet, a sound in the ground. We seemed to hear it with our feet as much as with our ears. Its dull resonance was muffled by distance, thick with the quality of intervening substance. No sound that I can imagine could have astonished us more, nor have changed more completely the quality of things about us. For this sound, rich, slow, and deliberate, seemed to us like the striking of some gigantic buried clock.

Boom . . . Boom . . . Boom . . .

We questioned each other in faint and faded voices. "A clock?"

"Like a clock!"

"What is it?"

"What can it be?"

"Count," was Cavor's belated suggestion, and at that word the striking ceased.

The silence, the rhythmic disappointment of the silence, came as a fresh shock. For a moment one could doubt whether one had ever hear a sound. Or whether it might not still be going on! Had I indeed heard a sound?

I felt the pressure of Cavor's hand upon my arm. He spoke in an undertone, as if he feared to wake some sleeping thing. "Let us keep together," he whispered, "and look for the sphere. We must get back to the sphere. This is beyond our understanding."

"Which way shall we go?"

He hesitated. An intense persuasion of presences, of unseen things about us and near us, dominated our minds. What could they be? Where could they be? Was this arid desolation, alternately frozen and scorched, only the outer rind and mask of some subterranean world? And if so, what sort of world? What sort of inhabitants might it not presently disgorge upon us?

And then stabbing the aching stillness, as vivid and sudden as an unexpected thunder-clap came a clang and rattle as though great gates of metal had suddenly been flung apart.

It arrested our steps. We stood gaping helplessly. Then Cavor stole towards me.

"I do not understand!" he whispered, close to my face. He waved his hand vaguely skywards, the vague suggestions of still vaguer thoughts.

"A hiding-place! If anything came—"

I looked about us. I nodded my head in assent to him.

We started off, moving stealthily, with the most exaggerated precautions against noise. We went towards a thicket of scrub. A clangor as of hammers flung about a boiler hastened our steps. "We must crawl," whispered Cavor.

The lower leaves of the bayonet plants, already overshadowed by the newer ones above, were beginning to wilt and shrivel so that we could thrust our way among the thickening stems without any serious injury. A stab in the face or arm we did not heed. At the heart of the thicket I stopped and stared panting into Cavor's face.

"Subterranean," he whispered. "Below."

"They may come out."

"We must find the sphere!"

"Yes," I said, "but how?"

"Crawl till we come to it."

"But if we don't?"

"Keep hidden. See what they are like."

"We will keep together," said I.

He thought. "Which way shall we go?"

"We must take our chance."

We peered this way and that. Then very circumspectly we began to crawl though the lower jungle, making so far as we could judge a circuit, halting now at every waving fungus, at every sound, intent only on the sphere from which we had so foolishly emerged. Ever and again from out of the ground beneath us came concussions, beatings, strange inexplicable, mechanical sounds, and once and then again we thought we heard something, a faint rattle and tumult, borne to us through the air. But fearful as we were we dared attempt no vantage-point to survey the crater. For long we saw nothing of the beings whose sounds were so abundant and insistent. But for the faintness of our hunger and the drying of our throats that crawling would have had the quality of a very vivid dream. It was so absolutely unreal. The only element with any touch of reality was these sounds.

Picture it to yourself. About us the dreamlike jungle, with the silent bayonet leaves darting overhead, and the silent, vivid sun-splashed lichens under our hands and knees, waving with the vigor of their growth as a carpet waves when the wind gets beneath it. Ever and again one of the bladder fungi, building and distending under the sun, loomed upon us. Ever and again in vivid color some novel shape obtruded. The very cells that built up these plants were as large as my thumb, like beads of colored glass. And all these things were saturated in the unmitigated glare of the sun were seen against a sky that was bluish-black and spangled still, in spite of the sunlight, with a few surviving stars. Strange! The very forms and texture of the stones were strange. It was all strange: the feeling of one's body was unprecedented, every other movement ended in a surprise. The breath sucked thin in one's throat, the blood flowed through one's ears in a throbbing tide, thud, thud, thud, thud . . .

And ever and again came gusts of turmoil, hammering, the clanging and throb of machinery, and presently—the bellowing of great beasts!

### CHAPTER THE TENTH
### THE MOONCALF PASTURES

So we two poor terrestrial castaways, lost in that wild-growing moon jungle, crawled in terror before the sounds that had come upon us. We crawled as it seemed a long time before we saw either Selenite or mooncalf, though we heard the bellowing and gruntulous noises of these latter continually drawing nearer to us. We crawled through stony ravines, over snow slopes, amidst fungi that ripped like thin bladders at our thrust, emitting a watery humor over a perfect pavement of things like puffballs and beneath interminable thickets of scrub. And ever more hopelessly our eyes sought for our abandoned sphere. The noise of the moon-calves would at times be a vast, flat, calf-like sound, at times it rose to an amazed and wrathy bellowing, and again it would become a clogged, bestial sound as though these unseen creatures had sought to eat and bellow at the same time.

Our first view was but an inadequate, transitory glimpse, yet none the less disturbing because it was incomplete. Cavor was crawling in front at the time, and he first was aware of their proximity. He stopped, arresting me with a single gesture.

91

A crackling and smashing of the scrub appeared to be advancing directly upon us, and then, as we squatted close and endeavored to judge of the nearness and direction of this noise, there came a terrific bellow behind us, so close and vehement that the tops of the bayonet scrub bent before it, and one felt the breath of it hot and moist. Turning about we saw indistinctly through a crowd of swaying stems the mooncalf's shining sides and the long line of its back looming against the sky.

Of course it is hard for me now to say how much I saw at that time, because my impressions were corrected by subsequent observation. First of all was its enormous size: the girth of its body was some fourscore feet, its length perhaps two hundred. Its sides rose and fell with its labored breathing. I perceived that its gigantic flabby body lay along the ground and that its skin was of corrugated white, dappling into blackness along the backbone. But of its feet we saw nothing. I think also that we saw then the profile at least of the almost brainless head, with its fat-encumbered neck, it's slobbering, omnivorous mouth, its little nostrils, and tight shut eyes. (For the mooncalf invariably shuts its eyes in the presence of the sun.) We had a glimpse of a vast red pit as it opened its mouth to bleat and bellow again, we had a breath from the pit, and then the monster heeled over like ship, dragged forward along the ground, creasing all his leathery skin, rolled again, and so wallowed past us, smashing a path amidst the scrub, and was speedily hidden from our eyes by the dense interlacing beyond. Another appeared more distantly, and then another, and then, as though he was driving these animated lumps of provender to their pasture, a Selenite came momentarily into view. My grip upon Cavor's foot became convulsive at the sight of him, and we remained motionless and peering long after he had passed out of our range.

By contrast with the mooncalves he seemed a trivial being, a mere ant, scarcely five feet high. He was wearing garments of some leathery substance so that no portion of his actual body appeared—but of this of course we were entirely ignorant. He presented himself, therefore, as a compact bristling creature, having much of the quality of a complicated insect, with whip-like tentacles, and a clanging arm projecting from his shining cylindrical body-case. The form of his head was hidden by his enormous, many-spiked helmet—we discovered afterwards that he used the spikes for prodding refractory mooncalves—and a pair of goggles of darkened glass set very much at the side gave a bud-like quality to the metallic apparatus that covered his face. His arms did not project beyond his body-case, and he carried himself upon short legs that wrapped though they were in warm coverings, seemed to our terrestrial eyes inordinately flimsy. They had very short thighs, very long shanks, and little feet.

In spite of his heavy-looking clothing he was progressing with what would be from the terrestrial point of view very considerable strides, and his clanging arm was busy. The quality of his motion during the instant of his passing suggested haste and a certain anger, and soon after we had lost sight of him we heard the bellow of a mooncalf change abruptly into a short, sharp squeal, followed by the scuffle of its acceleration. And gradually that bellowing receded, and then came to an end, as if the pastures sought had been reached.

We listened. For a space the moon world was still. But it was some time before we resumed our crawling search for the vanished sphere.

When next we saw mooncalves they were some little distance away from us, in a place of tumbled rocks. The sloping surfaces of the rocks were thick with a speckled green plant, growing in dense, mossy clumps, upon which these creatures were browsing. At the sight of them we stopped on the margin of the reeds amidst which we were crawling, peering through at them and looking round for a second glimpse of a Selenite. They lay against their food like stupendous slugs, huge, greasy hulls, eating greedily and noisily, with a sort of sobbing avidity. They seemed monsters of mere fatness, clumsy and overwhelmed to a degree that would make a Smithfield ox seem a model of agility. Their busy, writhing, chewing mouths, their closed eyes, together with the appetizing sound of their munching, made up an effect of animal enjoyment that was singularly stimulating to our empty frames.

"Hogs!" said Cavor, with unusual passion. "Disgusting hogs!" and after one glare of angry envy crawled off through the bushes to our right. I stayed long enough to see that the speckled plant was quite hopeless for human nourishment, then crawled after him, nibbling a quill of it between my teeth.

Presently we were arrested again by the proximity of a Selenite, and this time we were able to observe him more exactly. Now we could see that the Selenite covering was indeed clothing, and not a sort of crustacean integument. He was similar in costume to the former one we had glimpsed, except that ends of something like wadding were protruding from his neck, and he stood on a promontory of rock and moved his head this way and that as though he was surveying the crater. We lay quite still, fearing to attract his attention if we moved, and after a time he turned about and disappeared.

We came upon another drove of mooncalves bellowing up a ravine, and then we passed over a place of sounds, sounds of beating machinery, as if some huge hall of industry came near the surface there. And while these sounds were still about us we came to the edge of a great open space, perhaps two hundred yards in diameter, and perfectly level. Save for a few lichens that advanced from its margin, this space was bare, and presented a powdery surface of dusty yellow color. We were afraid to strike out across this space, but as it presented less obstruction to our crawling than the scrub, we went down upon it and began very circumspectly to skirt its edge.

For a little while the noises below ceased, and everything, save for the faint stir of the growing vegetation, was very still. Then abruptly there began an uproar, louder, more vehement, and nearer than any we had so far heard. Of a certainty it came from below. Instinctively we crouched as flat as we could, ready for a prompt plunge into the thicket beside us. Each knock and throb seemed to vibrate through our bodies. Louder grew this throbbing and beating, and that irregular vibration increased until the whole moon world seemed to be jerking and pulsing.

"Cover," whispered Cavor, and I turned towards the bushes.

At that instant came a thud like the thud of a gun, and then a thing happened—it still haunts me in my dreams. I had turned my head to look at Cavor's face, and thrust out my hand in front of me as I did so. My hand met nothing! I plunged suddenly into a bottomless hole!

My chest hit something hard, and I found myself with my chin on the edge of an unfathomable abyss that had suddenly opened beneath me, my hand extended stiffly into the void. The whole of that flat circular area was no more than a gigantic lid, that was now sliding sideways from off the pit it had covered into a slot prepared for it.

Had it not been for Cavor I think I should have remained rigid, hanging over this margin and staring into the enormous gulf below until at last the edges of the slot scraped me off and hurled me into its depths. But Cavor had not received the shock that had paralyzed me. He had been a little distance from the edge when the lid had first opened, and, perceiving the peril that held me helpless, gripped my legs and pulled me backward. I came into a sitting position, crawled away from the edge for a space on all fours, then staggered up and ran after him across the thundering, quivering sheet of metal. It seemed to be swinging open with a steadily-accelerated velocity, and the bushes in front of me shifted sideways as I ran.

I was none too soon. Cavor's back vanished amidst the bristling thicket, and as I scrambled up after him the monstrous valve came into its position with a clang. For a long time we lay panting, not daring to approach the pit.

But at last, very cautiously, and bit by bit, we crept into a position from which we could peer down. The bushes about us creaked and waved with the force of a breeze that was blowing down the shaft. We could see nothing at first except smooth, vertical walls descending at last into an impenetrable black. And then gradually we became aware of a number of faint and little lights going to and fro.

For a time that stupendous gulf of mystery held us so that we forgot even our sphere. In time as we grew more accustomed to the darkness we could make out very small dim illusive shapes moving about among those needle-point illuminations. We peered, amazed and incredulous, understanding so little that we could find no words to speak. We could distinguish nothing that would give us a clue to the meaning of the faint shapes we saw.

"What can it be?" I asked; "what can it be?"

"The engineering! . . . They must live in these caverns during the night and come out during the day."

"Cavor!" I said. "Can they be—*that*—it was something like—men?"

*That* was not a man."

"No."

"We dare risk nothing!"

"We dare do nothing until we find the sphere," he assented with a groan, and stirred himself to move. He stared about him for a space, sighed, and indicated a direction. We struck out through the jungle. For a time we crawled resolutely, then with diminishing vigor. Presently among great shapes of flabby purple there came a noise of trampling and of cries about us. We lay close, and for a long time the sounds went to and fro and very near. But this time we saw nothing. I tried to whisper to Cavor that I could hardly go without food much longer, but my mouth had become too dry for whispering.

"Cavor," I said, "I must have food."

He turned a face full of dismay towards me. "It's a case for holding out," he said.

"But I *must*," I said; "and look at my lips!"

"I've been thirsty some time."

"If only some of the snow had remained!"

"It's clean gone! We're driving from Arctic to tropical at the rate of a degree a minute. . . ."

I gnawed my hand.

"The sphere!" he said. "There is nothing for it but the sphere." We roused ourselves to another spurt of crawling. My mind ran entirely on edible things, on the hissing profundity of summer drinks; more particularly I craved for beer. I was haunted by the memory of the eighteen-gallon cask that had swaggered in my Lympne cellar. I thought of the adjacent larder, and especially of steak and kidney pie—tender steak and plenty of kidney, and rich, thick gravy between. Ever and again I was seized with fits of hungry yawning. We came to flat places overgrown with fleshy red things, monstrous coralline growths; as we pushed against them they snapped and broke. I noted the quality of the broken surfaces. The confounded stuff certainly looked of a bitable texture.

I picked up a fragment and sniffed at it.

"Cavor," I said, in a hoarse undertone.

He glanced at me with his face screwed up. "Don't," he said. I put down the fragment, and we crawled on through this tempting fleshiness for a space.

"Cavor," I asked, "why not?"

"Poison," I heard him say, but he did not look round.

We crawled some way before I decided.

"I'll chance it," said I.

He made a belated gesture to prevent me. I stuffed my mouth full. He crouched, watching my face, his own twisted into the oddest expression. "It's good," I said.

"Oh, Lord!" he cried.

He watched me munch, his face wrinkled between desire and disapproval, then suddenly succumbed to appetite, and began to tear off huge mouthfuls. For a time we did nothing but eat.

The stuff was not unlike a terrestrial mushroom, only it was much laxer in texture, and as one swallowed it, it warmed the throat. At first we experienced a mere mechanical satisfaction in eating. Then our blood began to run warmer, and we tingled at the lips and fingers, and then new and slightly irrelevant ideas came bubbling up in our minds.

"It's good," said I. "Infernally good! What a home for our surplus population! Our poor surplus population," and I broke off another large portion.

It filled me with a curiously benevolent satisfaction that there was such good food on the moon. The depression of my hunger gave way to an irrational exhilaration. The dread and discomfort in which I had been living vanished entirely. I perceived the moon no longer as a planet from which I must earnestly desire the means of escape, but as a possible refuge for human destitution. I think I forgot the Selenites, the mooncalves, the lid, and the noises completely as soon as I had eaten that fungus.

Cavor replied to my third repetition of my "surplus population" remark with similar words of approval. I felt that my head swam, but I put this down to the stimulating effect of food after a long fast. "Ess'lent discov'ry, yours, Cavor," said I. "S'end on'y to the 'tato?"

"Whajer mean?" asked Cavor. "'Scovery of the moon—se'nd on'y to the 'tato?"

I looked at him, shocked at his suddenly hoarse voice and by the badness of his articulation. It occurred to me in a flash that he was intoxicated, possibly by the fungus. It also occurred to me that he erred in imagining that he had discovered the moon—he had not discovered it, he had only reached it. I tried to lay my hand on his arm and explain this to him, but the issue was too subtle for his brain. It was also unexpectedly difficult to express. After a momentary attempt to understand me—I remember wondering if the fungus had made my eyes as fishy as his—he set off upon some observations on his own account.

"We are," he announced, with a solemn hiccup, "the creashurs o' what we eat and drink."

He repeated this, and as I was now in one of my subtle moods I determined to dispute it. Possibly I wandered a little from the point. But Cavor certainly did not attend at all properly. He stood up as well as he could, putting a hand on my head to steady himself, which was disrespectful, and stood staring about him, quite devoid now of any fear of the moon beings.

I tried to point out that this was dangerous, for some reason that was not perfectly clear to me; but the word "dangerous" had somehow got mixed with "indiscreet," and come out rather more like "injuries" than either, and after an attempt to disentangle them I resumed my argument, addressing myself principally to the unfamiliar but attentive coralline growths on either side. I felt that it was necessary to clear up this confusion between the moon and a potato at once—I wandered into a long parenthesis on the importance of precision of definition in argument. I did my best to ignore the fact that my bodily sensations were no longer agreeable.

In some way that I have now forgotten my mind was led back to projects of colonization. "We must annex this moon," I said. "There must be no shilly-shally. This is part of the White Man's Burden. Cavor—we are—*hic*—Satap—mean Satraps! N'mpire Caesar never dreamt. B'in all the newspapers. Cavorecia. Bedfordecia. Bedfordecia. Hic—Limited. Mean—unlimited! Practically."

Certainly I was intoxicated. I embarked upon an argument to show the infinite benefits our arrival would confer upon the moon. I involved myself in a rather difficult proof that the arrival of Columbus was, after all, beneficial to America. I found I had forgotten the line of argument I had intended to pursue, and continued to repeat "sim'lar to C'lumbus" to fill up time.

From that point my memory of the action of that abominable fungus becomes confused. I remember vaguely that we declared our intention of standing no nonsense from any confounded insects, that we decided it ill became men to hide shamefully upon a mere satellite, that we equipped ourselves with huge armfuls of the fungi—whether for missile purposes or not I do not know—and, heedless of the stabs of the bayonet shrub, we started forth into the sunshine.

Almost immediately we must have come upon the Selenites. There were six of them, and they were marching in single file over a rocky place, making the most remarkable piping and whining sounds. They all seemed to become aware of us at once, all instantly became silent and motionless like animals, with their faces turned towards us.

For a moment I was sobered.

"Insects," murmured Cavor, "insects!—and they think I'm going to crawl about on my stomach—on my vertebrated stomach!"

"Stomach," he repeated, slowly, as though he chewed the indignity.

Then suddenly, with a sort of fury, he made three vast strides and leaped towards them. He leaped badly; he made a series of somersaults in the air, whirled right over them, and vanished with an enormous splash amidst the cactus bladders. What the Selenites made of this amazing, and to my mind undignified, irruption from another planet, I have no means of guessing. I seem to remember the sight of their backs as they ran in all directions—but I am not sure. All these last incidents before oblivion came are vague and faint in my mind. I know I made a step to follow Cavor, and tripped and feel headlong among the rocks. I was, I am certain, suddenly and vehemently ill. I seem to remember a violent struggle, and being gripped by metallic clasps. . . .

My next clear recollection is that we were prisoners at we knew not what depth beneath the moon's surface; we were in darkness and amidst strange, distracting noises; our bodies covered with scratches and bruises, and our heads racked with pain.

### Chapter the Eleventh
### The Selenite's Face

I found myself sitting crouched together in a tumultuous darkness. For a long time I could not understand where I was nor how I had come to this perplexity. I thought of the cupboard into which I had been thrust at times when I was a child, and then of a very dark and noisy bedroom in which I had slept during an illness. But these sounds about me were not noises I had known and there was a thin flavor in the air like the wind of a stable. Then I supposed we must still be at work on the sphere, and that somehow I had got into the cellar of Cavor's house. I remembered we had finished the sphere, and fancied I must still be in it and traveling through space.

"Cavor," I said "cannot we have some light?"

There came no answer.

"Cavor!" I insisted.

I was answered by a groan. "My head!" I heard him say, "my head!"

I attempted to press my hands to my brow, which ached, and discovered they were tied together. This startled me very much. I brought them up to my mouth and felt the cold smoothness of metal. They were chained together. I tried to separate my legs and made out they were similarly fastened, and also I was fastened to the ground by a much thicker chain about the middle of my body.

I was more frightened than I had yet been by anything in all our strange experiences. For a time I tugged silently at my bonds.

"Cavor!" I cried out, sharply, "why am I tied? Why have you tied my hand and foot?"

"I haven't tied you," he answered. "It's the Selenites."

The Selenites! My mind hung on that for a space. Then my memories came back to me; the snowy desolation, the thawing of the air, the growth of the plants, our strange hopping and crawling among the rocks and vegetation of the crater. All the distress of our frantic search for the sphere returned to me. . . . Finally the opening of the great lid that covered the pit!

Then as I strained to trace our later movements down to our present plight the pain in my head became intolerable. I came to an insurmountable barrier, an obstinate blank.

"Cavor!"

"Yes."

"Where are we?"

"How should I know?"

"Are we dead?"

"What nonsense!"

"They've got us, then!"

He made no answer but a grunt. The lingering traces of the poison seemed to make him oddly irritable.

"What do you mean to do?"

"How should I know what to do?"

"Oh, very well," said I, and became silent. Presently, I was roused from a stupor, "Oh, Lord!" I cried, "I wish you'd stop that buzzing."

We lapsed into silence again, listening to the dull confusion of noises, like the muffled sounds of a street or factory, that filled our ears. I could make nothing of it; my mind pursued first one rhythm and then another, and questioned it in vain. But after a long time I became aware of a new and sharper element, not mingling with the rest, but standing out, as it were, against that cloudy background of sound. It was a series of little definite sounds, tappings and rubbings like a loose spray of ivy against a window or a bird moving about upon a box. We listened and peered about us, but the darkness was a velvet pall. There followed a noise like a subtle movement of the wards of a well-oiled lock. And then there appeared before me, hanging as it seemed in an immensity of black, a thin bright line.

"Look!" whispered Cavor, very softly.

"What is it?"

"I don't know."

We stared.

The thin bright line became a band, broader and paler. It took upon itself the quality of a bluish light falling upon a whitewashed wall. It ceased to be parallel sided; it developed a deep indentation on one side. I turned to remark this to Cavor, and was amazed to see his ear in a brilliant illumination—all the rest of him in shadow. I twisted my head round as well as my bonds would permit. "Cavor!" I said, "it's behind!"

His ear vanished—gave place to an eye.

Suddenly the crack that has been admitting the light broadened out and revealed itself as the space of an opening door. Beyond was a sapphire vista, and in the doorway stood a grotesque outline silhouetted against the glare.

We both made convulsive efforts to turn, and, failing, sat staring over our shoulder at this. My first impression was of some clumsy quadruped with lowered head. Then I perceived it was the slender, pinched body and short and extremely attenuated bandy legs of a Selenite, with his head depressed between his shoulders. He was without the helmet and body-covering they wear upon the exterior.

He was a blank figure to us, but instinctively our imagination supplied features to his very human outline. I at least took it instantly that he was somewhat hunchbacked, with a high forehead and long features.

He came forward three steps and paused for a time. His movements seemed absolutely noiseless. Then he came forward again. He walked like a bird—his feet fell one in front of the other. He stepped out of the ray of light that came through the doorway and it seemed that he vanished altogether in the shadow.

For a moment my eyes sought him in the wrong place, and then I perceived him standing facing us both in the full light. Only the human features I had attributed to him were not there at all!

Of course I ought to have expected that, only I did not. It came to me as an absolute, for a moment an overwhelming, shock. It seemed as though it wasn't a face; as though it must needs be a mask, a horror, a deformity that would presently be disavowed or explained. There was no nose, and the thing had bulging eyes at the side—in the silhouette I had supposed they were ears . . . I have tried to draw one of these heads, but I cannot.

There was a mouth, downwardly curved, like a human mouth in a face that stared ferociously.

The neck on which the head was poised was jointed in three places, almost like the short joints in the leg of a crab. The joints of the limbs I could not see because of the puttee-like straps in which they were swathed, and which formed the only clothing this being wore.

At the time my mind was taken up by the mad impossibility of the creature. I suppose he also was amazed—and with more reason, perhaps, for amazement than we. Only, confound him, he did not show it. We did at least know what had brought about this meeting of incompatible creatures. But conceive how it would seem to decent Londoners, for example, to come upon a couple of living things, as big as men and absolutely unlike any other earthly animals, careering about among the sheep in Hyde Park!

It must have taken him like that.

Imagine us! We were bound hand and foot, fagged and filthy, our beards two inches long, our faces scratched and bloody. Cavor you must imagine in his knickerbockers (torn in several places by the bayonet scrub), his Jaeger shirt and old cricket cap, his wiry hair wildly disordered, a tail to every quarter of the heavens. In that blue light his face did not look red, but very dark; his lips and the drying blood upon his hands seemed black. If possible I was in a worse plight than he, on account of the yellow fungus into which I had jumped. Our jackets were unbuttoned, and our shoes had been taken off and lay at our feet. We were sitting with our backs to the queer, bluish light peering at such a monster as Dürer might have invented.

Cavor broke the silence, started to speak, went hoarse, and cleared his throat. Outside began a terrific bellowing, as of mooncalf in trouble. It ended in a shriek, and everything was still again.

Presently the Selenite turned about, flickered into a shadow, stood for a moment retrospective at the door, and then closed it on us, and once more we were in the murmurous mystery of darkness into which we had awakened.

### CHAPTER THE TWELFTH
### MR. CAVOR MAKES SOME SUGGESTIONS

For a time neither of us spoke. To focus all the things we had brought upon ourselves seemed beyond my mental powers.

"They've got us," I said at last.

"It was that fungus."

"Well, if I hadn't taken it we should have fainted and starved."

"We might have found the sphere."

I lost my temper at his persistence and swore to myself. For a time we hated each other in silence. I drummed with my finger on the floor between my knees and ground the links of my fetters together. Presently I was forced to talk again.

"What do you make of it, anyhow?" I asked humbly.

"They are reasonable creatures—they can make things and do things. Those lights we saw . . . "

He stopped. It was clear he could make nothing of it.

When he spoke again it was to confess. "After all, they are more human than we had a right to expect. I suppose—"

He stopped irritatingly.

"Yes?"

"I suppose anyhow—on any planet, where there is an intelligent animal, it will carry its brain case upward, and have hands and walk erect . . . "

Presently he broke away in another direction.

"We are some way in," he said. "I mean—perhaps a couple of thousand feet or more."

"Why?"

"It's cooler. And our voices are so much louder. That faded quality—it has altogether gone. And the feeling in one's ears and throat."

I had not noted that, but I did now.

"The air is denser. We must be some depth—a mile even we may be—inside the moon."

"We never thought of a world inside the moon."

"No."

"How could we?"

"We might have done. Only—one gets into habits of mind."

He thought for a time.

"Now," he said "it seems such an obvious thing. Of course! The moon must be enormously cavernous with an atmosphere within, and at the center of its caverns a sea. One knew that the moon had a lower specific gravity than the earth; one knew that it had little air or water outside; one knew, too, that it was sister planet to the earth and that it was unaccountable that it should be different in composition. The inference that it was hollowed out was as clear as day. And yet one never saw it as a fact. Kepler, of course—" His voice had the interest now of a man who has discovered a pretty sequence of reasoning.

"Yes," he said, "Kepler, with his *subvolvani*, was right after all."

"I wish you had taken the trouble to find that out before we came," I said.

He answered nothing, buzzing to himself softly as he pursued his thoughts. My temper was going. "What do you think has become of the sphere, anyhow?" I asked.

"Lost," he said, like a man who answers an uninteresting question.

"Among those plants?"

"Unless they find it."

"And then?"

"How can I tell?"

"Cavor," I said, with a sort of hysterical bitterness, "things look bright for my Company."

He made no answer.

"Good Lord!" I exclaimed. "Just think of all the trouble we took to get into this pickle! What did we come for? What are we after? What was the moon to us, or we

101

to the moon? We wanted too much, we tried too much. We ought to have started the little things first. It was you proposed the moon! Those Cavorite spring blinds! I am certain we could have worked them for terrestrial purposes. Certain! Did you really understand what I proposed? A steel cylinder—"

"Rubbish!" said Cavor.

We ceased to converse.

For a time Cavor kept up a broken monologue without much help to me.

"If they find it," he began; "if they find it . . . what will they do with it? Well, that's the question! It may be that's *the* question. They won't understand it, anyhow. If they understood that sort of thing they would have come long since to the earth. Would they? Why shouldn't they? But they would have sent something—They couldn't keep their hands off such a possibility. No! But they will examine it. Clearly they are intelligent and inquisitive. They will examine it—get inside it—trifle with the studs. Off! . . .That would mean the moon for us for all the rest of our lives. Strange creatures, strange knowledge. . . . "

"As for strange knowledge—!" said I, and language failed me.

"Look here, Bedford," said Cavor. "You came on this expedition of your own free will."

"You said to me—'call it prospecting.'"

"There are always risks in prospecting."

"Especially when you do it unarmed and without thinking out every possibility."

"I was so taken up with the sphere. The thing rushed on us and carried us away."

"Rushed on *me*, you mean."

"Rushed on me just as much. How was I to know when I set to work on molecular physics that the business would bring me here—of all places?"

"It's this accursed Science," I cried. "It's the very Devil. The medieval priests and persecutors were right, and the moderns are all wrong. You tamper with it and it offers you gifts. And directly you take them it knocks you to pieces in some unexpected way. Old passions and new weapons—now it upsets your religion, now it upsets your social ideas, now it whirls you off to desolation and misery!"

"Anyhow, it's no use you quarrelling with me now. These creatures—the Selenites—or whatever we choose to all them, have got us tied hand and foot. Whatever temper you choose to go through with it in, you will have to go through with it...We have experiences before us that will need all our coolness."

He paused as if he required my assent. But I sat sulking. "Confound your science!" he said.

"The problem is communication. Gestures, I fear, will be different. Pointing, for example. No creatures but men and monkeys point."

That was too obviously wrong for me. "Pretty nearly every animal," I cried, "points with its eyes or nose."

Cavor meditated over that. "Yes," he said at last, "and we don't. There are such differences! Such differences!"

"One might . . . But how can I tell? There is speech. The sounds they make, a sort of fluting and piping. I don't see how we are to imitate that. Is it their speech, that sort of thing? They may have different senses, different means of communication. Of course they are minds and we are minds—there must be something in common. Who knows how far we may not get to an understanding?"

"The things are outside us," I said. "They're more different from us than the strangest animals on earth. They are a different clay. What is the good of talking like this?"

Cavor thought. "I don't see that. Where there are minds, they will have something similar—even though they have been evolved on different planets. Of course, if it was a question of instinct—if we or they were no more than animals—"

"Well, are they? They're much more like ants on their hind legs than human beings, and who ever got to any sort of understanding with ants?"

"But these machines and clothing! No, I don't hold with you, Bedford. The difference is wide—"

"It's insurmountable."

"The resemblance must bridge it. I remember reading once a paper by the late Professor Galton on the possibility of communication between the planets. Unhappily at that time it did not seem probable that it would be of any material benefit to me, and I fear I did not give it the attention I should have done, in view of this state of affairs. Yet . . . Now, let, me see!

"His idea was to begin with those broad truths that must underlie all conceivable mental existences and establish a basis on those. The great principles of geometry, to begin with. He proposed to take some leading proposition of Euclid's, and show by construction that its truth was known to us; to demonstrate, for example, that the angles at the base of an isosceles triangle are equal, and that if the equal sides be produced the angles on the other side of the base are equal also; or that the square of the hypotenuse of a right-triangle is equal to the sum of the squares of the two other sides. By demonstrating our knowledge of these things we should demonstrate our possession of a reasonable intelligence . . . Now, suppose I . . . I might draw the geometrical figure with a wet finger or ever trace it in the air . . . "

He fell silent. I sat meditating his words. For a time his wild hope of communication, of interpretation with these weird beings, held me. Then that angry despair that was a part of my exhaustion and physical misery resumed its sway. I perceived with a sudden novel vividness the extraordinary folly of everything I had ever done. "Ass!" I said, "oh, ass, unutterable ass . . . I seem to exist only to go about doing preposterous things . . . Why did we ever leave the sphere? . . . Hopping about looking for patents and concessions in the craters of the moon! . . . If only we had had the sense to fasten a handkerchief to a stick to show where we had left the sphere!"

I subsided fuming.

"It is clear," meditated Cavor, "they are intelligent. One can hypothecate certain things. As they have not killed us at once they must have ideas of mercy.

Mercy! At any rate of restraint. Possibly of intercourse. They may meet us. And this apartment and the glimpses we had of its guardian! These fetters! A high degree of intelligence . . . "

"I wish to Heaven," cried I, "I'd thought even twice. Plunge after plunge. First one fluky start and then another. It was my confidence in you. Why didn't I stick to my play? That was what I was equal to. That was my world and the life I was made for. I could have finished that play. I'm certain . . . it was a good play. I had the scenario as good as done. Then . . . Conceive it! leaping to the moon! Practically—I've thrown my life away! That old woman in the inn near Canterbury had better sense."

I looked up, and stopped in mid-sentence. The darkness had given place to that bluish light again. The door was opening, and several noiseless Selenites were coming into the chamber. I became quite still staring at their grotesque faces.

Then suddenly my sense of disagreeable strangeness changed to interest. I perceived that the foremost and second carried bowls. One elemental need at least our minds could understand in common. They were bowls of some metal that, like our fetters, looked dark in that bluish light; and each contained a number of whitish fragments. All the cloudy pain and misery that oppressed me rushed together and took the shape of hunger. I eyed these bowls wolfishly. It seemed that at the end of the arms that lowered one towards me were not hands, but a sort of flap and thumb, like the end of an elephant's truck.

The stuff in the bowl was loose in texture and whitish-brown in color—rather like lumps of some cold soufflé, and it smelt faintly like mushrooms. From a partly-divided carcass of a mooncalf that we presently saw I am inclined to believe it must have been mooncalf flesh.

My hands were so tightly chained that I could barely contrive to reach the bowl, but when they saw the effort I made two of them dexterously released one of the turns about my wrist. Their tentacle hands were soft and cold to my skin. I immediately seized a mouthful of the food. It had the same laxness in texture that all organic structures seem to have upon the moon; it tasted rather like a *gauffre*, or a damp meringue, but in no way was it disagreeable. I took two other mouthfuls. "I wanted—food!" said I, tearing off a still larger piece . . .

For a time we ate with an utter absence of self-consciousness. We ate and presently drank like tramps in a soup kitchen. Never before, nor since, have I been hungry to the ravenous pitch, and save that I have had this very experience I could never have believed that a quarter of a million of miles out of our proper world, in utter perplexity of soul, surrounded, watched, touched by beings more grotesque and inhuman than the worst creatures of a nightmare, it would be possible for me to eat in utter forgetfulness of all these things. They stood about us, watching us, and ever and again making a slight elusive twittering that stood them, I suppose, in the stead of speech. I did not even shiver at their touch. And when the first zeal of my feeding was over I could note that Cavor too had been eating with the same shameless abandon.

104

## Chapter the Thirteenth
### Experiments in Intercourse

When at last we had made an end of eating, the Selenites linked our hands closely together again, and then untwisted the chains about our feet and rebound them, so as to give us a limited freedom of movement. Then they unfastened the chains about our waists. To do all this they had to handle us freely, and ever and again one of their queer heads came down close to my face, or a soft tentacle-hand touched my head or neck. I do not remember that I was afraid then or repelled by their proximity. I think that our incurable anthropomorphism made us imagine there were human heads inside their masks. The skin, like everything else, looked bluish, but that was on account of the light, and it was hard and shiny quite in the beetle-wing fashion, not soft or moist or hairy as a vertebrated animal's would be. Along the crest of the head was a low ridge of whitish spines running from back to front, and a much larger ridge curved on each side over the eyes. The Selenite who untied me used his mouth to help his hands.

"They seem to be releasing us," said Cavor. "Remember, we are on the moon! Make no sudden movements!"

"Are you going to try that geometry?"

"If I get a chance. But, of course, they may make an advance first."

We remained passive, and the Selenites, having finished their arrangements stood back from us, and seemed to be looking at us. I say seemed to be because as their eyes were at the sides and not in front one had the same difficulty in determining the direction in which they were looking as one has in the case of a hen or a fish. They conversed with one another in their reedy tones, that seemed to me impossible to imitate or define. The door behind us opened wider, and glancing over my shoulder I saw a vague large space beyond in which a little crowd of Selenites were standing. They seemed a curiously miscellaneous rabble.

"Do they want us to imitate those sounds?" I asked Cavor.

"I don't think so," he said.

"It seems to me that they are trying to make us understand something."

"I can't make anything of their gestures. Do you notice this one, who is worrying with his head like a man with an uncomfortable collar?"

"Let us shake our heads at him."

We did that, and finding it ineffectual, attempted an imitation of the Selenite's movements. That seemed to interest them. At any rate, they all set up the same movement. But as that seemed to lead to nothing we desisted at last, and so did they, and fell into a piping argument among themselves. Then one of them, shorter and very much thicker than the other, and with a particularly wide mouth, squatted down suddenly beside Cavor, and put his hands and feet in the same posture as Cavor's were bound, and then by a dexterous movement stood up.

"Cavor," I shouted, "they want us to get up!"

He stared open-mouthed. "That's it!' he said.

And with much heaving and grunting, because our hands were tied together, we contrived to struggle to our feet. The Selenites made way for our elephantine heavings, and seemed to twitter more volubly. As soon as we were on our feet the thick-set Selenites came and patted each of our faces with his tentacles, and walked towards the open doorway. That also was plain enough and we followed him. We saw that four of the Selenies standing in the doorway were much taller than the others, and clothed in the same manner as those we had seen in the crater, namely, with spiked, round helmets and cylindrical body-cases, and that each of the four carried a goad, with spike and guard made of that same dull-looking metal as the bowls. These four closed about us one on either side of each of us, as we emerged from our chamber into the cavern from which the light had come.

We did not get our impression of that cavern all at once. Our attention was taken up by the movements and attitudes of the Selenites immediately about us, and by the necessity of controlling our motion, lest we should startle and alarm them and ourselves by some excessive stride. In front of us was the short, thick-set being who had solved the problem of asking us to get up, moving with gestures that seemed, almost all of them, intelligible to us, inviting us to follow him. His spout-like face turned from one of us to the other with a quickness that was clearly interrogative. For a time, I say, we were taken up with these things.

But at last the great place that formed a background to our movements asserted itself. It became apparent that the source of much at least of the tumult of sounds which had filled our ears ever since we had recovered from the stupefaction of the fungus was a vast mass of machinery in active movement, whose flying and whirling parts were visible indistinctly over the heads and between the bodies of the Selenites who walked about us. And not only did the web of sounds that filled the air proceed from this mechanism, but also the peculiar blue light that irradiated the whole place. We had taken it as a natural thing that a subterranean cavern should be artificially lit, and even now, though the fact was patent to my eyes, I did not really grasp its import until presently the darkness came. The meaning and structure of this huge apparatus I cannot explain, because we neither of us learnt what it was for or how it worked. One after another, big shafts of metal flung out and up from its center, their head traveling in what seemed to me to be a parabolic path; each dropped a sort of dangling arm as it rose towards the apex of its flight and plunged down into a vertical cylinder, forcing this down before it. About it moved the shapes of tenders, little figures that seemed vaguely different from the beings about us. As each of the three dangling arms of the machine plunged down, there was a clank and then a roaring, and out of the top of the vertical cylinder came pouring this incandescent substance, that lit the place and ran over as milk runs over a boiling pot and dripped luminously into a tank of light below. It was a cold blue light, a sort of phosphorescent glow, but infinitely brighter, and from the tanks into which it fell it ran in conduits athwart the cavern.

Thud, thud, thud, thud, came the sweeping arms of this unintelligible apparatus, and the light substance hissed and poured. At first the thing seemed only reasonably large and near to us; and then I saw how exceedingly little the Selenites upon it seemed, and I realized the full immensity of cavern and machine. I looked from this tremendous affair to the faces of the Selenites with a new respect. I stopped, and stared at this thunderous engine.

"But this is stupendous!" I said. "What can it be for?"

Cavor's blue-lit face was full of an intelligent respect. "I can't dream! Surely these beings—Men could not make a thing like that! Look at those arms: are they on connecting rods?"

The thick-set Selenite had gone some paces unheeded. He came back and stood between us and the great machine. I avoided seeing him, because I guessed somehow that his idea was to beckon us onward. He walked away in the direction he wished us to go, and turned and came back, and flicked our faces to attract our attention.

Cavor and I looked at each other.

"Cannot we show him we are interested in the machine?" I said.

"Yes," said Cavor. "We'll try that." He turned to our guide, and smiled, and pointed to the machine, and pointed again, and then to his head, and then to the machine. By some defect of reasoning he seemed to imagine that broken English might help these gestures. "Me look'im" he said; "Me think'im very much. Yes."

His behavior seemed to check the Selenites in their desire for our progress for a moment. They faced one another, their queer heads moved, the twittering voices came quick and liquid. Then one of them, a lean, tall creature, with a sort of mantle added to the puttee in which the others were dressed, twisted his elephant trunk of a hand about Cavor's waist, and pulled him gently to follow our guide, who again went on ahead.

Cavor resisted. "We may just as well begin explaining ourselves now! They may think we are new animals, a new sort of mooncalf, perhaps! It is most important that we should show an intelligent interest from the outset."

He began to shake his head violently. "No, no," he said; "me not come on one minute. Me look at 'im."

"Isn't there some geometrical point you might bring in apropos of that affair?" I suggested, as the Selenites conferred again.

"Possibly a parabolic—" he began.

He yelled loudly and leaped six feet or more!

One of the four armed moon-men had pricked him with a goad!

I turned on the goad-bearer behind me with a swift, threatening gesture and he started back. This and Cavor's sudden shout and leap clearly astonished all the Selenites. They receded hastily, facing us. For one of those moments that seem to last for ever we stood in angry protest, with a scattered semicircle of these inhuman beings about us.

"He pricked me!" said Cavor, with a catching of the voice.

"I saw him," I answered.

"Confound it!" I said to the Selenties; "we're not going to stand that! What on earth do you take us for?"

I glanced quickly right and left. Far away across the blue wilderness of cavern I saw a number of other Selenites running towards us; broad and slender they were and one with a larger head than the others. The cavern spread wide and low, and receded in every direction into darkness. Its roof, I remember, seemed to bulge down as if with the weight of the vast thickness of rocks that prisoned us. There was no way out of it—no way out of it. Above, below, in every direction, was the unknown, and these inhuman creatures with goads and gestures confronting us, and we two unsupported men!

CHAPTER THE FOURTEENTH
THE GIDDY BRIDGE

Just for a moment that hostile pause endured. I suppose that both we and the Selenites did some very rapid thinking. My clearest impression was that there was nothing to put my back against and that we were bound to be surrounded and killed. The overwhelming folly of our presence there loomed over me in black, enormous reproach. Why had I ever launched myself on this mad, inhuman expedition?

Cavor came to my side and laid his hand on my arm. His pale and terrified face was ghastly in the blue light.

"We can't do anything," he said. "It's a mistake. They don't understand. We must go—as they want us to go."

I looked down at him, and then at the fresh Selenites who were coming to help their fellows. "If I had my hands free—"

"It's no use," he panted.

"No."

"We'll go."

And he turned about and led the way in the direction that had been indicated for us.

I followed, trying to look as subdued as possible, and feeling at the chains about my wrists. My blood was boiling. I noted nothing more of the cavern, though it seemed to take a long time before we had marched across it, or if I noted anything I forgot it as I saw it. My thoughts were concentrated, I think, upon my chains and the Selenites, and particularly upon the helmeted ones with the goads. At first they marched parallel with us, and at a respectful distance, but presently they were overtaken by three others, and then they drew nearer until they were within arms' length again. I winced like a spurred horse as they came near to us. The shorter, thicker Selenite marched at first on our right flank, but presently came in front of us again.

How well the picture of that grouping has bitten into my brain: the back of Cavor's downcast head just in front of me, and the dejected droop of his shoulders, and our guide's gaping visage, perpetually jerking about him, and the goad-bearers on each side, watchful yet open-mouthed—a blue monochrome. And after all, I do re-

108

member one other thing besides the purely personal affair, which is that a sort of gutter came presently across the floor of the cavern and then ran along by the side of the path of rock we followed. It was full of the same bright blue luminous stuff that flowed out of the great machine. I walked close beside it, and I can testify it radiated not a particle of heat. It was brightly shining, and yet it was neither warmer nor colder than anything else in the cavern.

Clang, clang, clang, we passed under the thumping levers of another vast machine, and so came at last to a wide tunnel, in which we could even hear the pad, pad of our shoeless feet, and which, save for the trickling thread of blue to the right of us, was quite unlit. The shadows made gigantic travesties of our shapes and those of the Selenites on the irregular wall and roof of the tunnel. Ever and again crystals in the walls scintillated like gems, ever and again the passage expanded into a stalactitic cavern, or gave off branches that vanished into darkness.

We seemed to be marching down that tunnel for a long time. "Trickle, trickle," went the flowing light very softly, and our footfalls, and their echoes made an irregular paddle, paddle. My mind settled down to the question of my chains. If I were to slip off one turn, *so*, and then to twist it *so* . . .

If I tried to do it very gradually, would they see I was slipping my wrist out of the looser turn? If they did, what would they do?

"Bedford," said Cavor, "it goes down. It keeps on going down."

His remark roused me from my sullen preoccupation. "If they wanted to kill us," he said, dropping back to come level with me, "There is no reason why they should not have done it."

"No," I admitted; "that's true."

"They don't understand us," he said; "they think we are merely strange animals, some wild sort of mooncalf birth, perhaps. It will be only when they observe us better that they will begin to think we have minds—"

"When you trace those geometrical problems?" said I.

"It may be that."

We tramped on for a space.

"You see," said Cavor, "these may be Selenites of a lower class."

"The infernal fools," said I, viciously, glancing at their exasperating faces.

"If we endure what they do to us—"

"We've got to endure it," said I.

"There may be others less stupid. This is the mere outer fringe of their world. It must go down and down, cavern, passage, tunnel, down at last to the sea, hundreds of miles below."

His words made me think of the mile or so of rock and tunnel that might be over our heads already. It was like a weight dropping on my shoulders. "Away from the sun and air," I said. "Even a mine half a mile deep is stuffy."

"This is not—anyhow. It's probable—Ventilation! The air would blow from the dark side of the moon to the sunlit, and all the carbonic acid would well out there and feed those plants. Up this tunnel, for example—there is quite a breeze. And what a world it must be! The earnest we have in that shaft, and those machines—"

"And the goad," I said. "Don't forget the goad!"

He walked a little in front me for a time.

"Even that goad—" he said.

"Well?"

"I was angry at the time. But—it was perhaps necessary we should get on. They have different skins and probably different nerves. They may not understand our objection—just as a being from Mars might not like our earthly habit of nudging."

"They'd better be careful how they nudge me."

"And about that geometry. After all, their way is a way of understanding too. They begin with the elements of life and not of thought. Food. Compulsion. Pain. They strike at fundamentals."

"There's no doubt about that," I said.

He went on to talk of the enormous and wonderful world into which we were being taken. I realized slowly from his tone that even now he was not absolutely in despair at the prospect of going ever deeper into this inhuman planet burrow. His mind ran on machines and invention to the exclusion of a thousand dark things that beset me. It wasn't that he intended to make any use of these things: he simply wanted to know them.

"After all," he said, "this is a tremendous occasion. It is the meeting of two worlds. What are we going to see? Think of what is below us here."

"We shan't see much if the light isn't better," I remarked.

"This is only the outer crust. Down below—On this scale—There will be everything. Do you notice how different they seem one from another? The story we shall take back!"

"Some rare sort of animal," I said, "might comfort himself in that way while they were bringing him to the Zoo . . . it doesn't follow that we are going to be shown all these things."

"When they find we have reasonable minds," said Cavor, "they will want to learn about the earth. Even if they have no generous emotions they will teach in order to learn . . . And the things they must know! The unanticipated things!"

He went on to speculate on the possibility of their knowing things he had never hoped to learn on earth, speculating in that way, with a raw wound from that goad already in his skin! Much that he said I forgot, for my attention was drawn to the fact that the tunnel along which we had been marching was opening out wider and wider. We seemed from the feeling of the air to be going out into a huge space. But how big the space might really be we could not tell, because it was unlit. Our little stream of light ran in a dwindling thread and vanished far ahead. Presently the rocky walls had disappeared altogether on either hand. There was nothing to be seen but the path in front of us and the trickling, hurrying rivulet of blue phosphorescence. The figures of Cavor and guiding Selenite marched before me; the sides of their legs and heads that were towards the rivulet were clear and bright blue; their darkened sides, now that the reflection of the tunnel wall no longer lit them, merged indistinguishably in the darkness beyond.

And soon I perceived that we were approaching a declivity of some sort, because the little blue stream dipped suddenly out of sight.

I another moment, as it seemed, we had reached the edge. The shining stream gave one meander of hesitation and then rushed over. It fell to a depth at which the sound of its descent was absolutely lost to us. Far below was a bluish glow, a sort of blue mist. And the darkness the stream dropped out of became utterly void and black, save that a thing like a plank projected from the edge of the cliff and stretched out and faded and vanished altogether. There was a warm air blowing up out of the gulf.

For a moment Cavor and I stood as near the edge as we dared peering into a blue tinged profundity. And then our guide was pulling at my arm.

He left me and walked to the end of that plank and stepped upon it, looking back. When he perceived we watched him, he turned about and went on over it, walking as surely as though he was on firm earth. For a moment his form was distinct, then he became a blue blur, and vanished into the obscurity. I was aware of some vague shape looming darkly out of the black.

There was a pause. "Surely—!" said Cavor.

One of the other Selenites walked a few paces out upon the plank and turned and looked back at us unconcernedly. The others stood ready to follow us. Our guide's expectant figure reappeared. He was returning to see why we had not advanced.

"What is that beyond there?" I asked.

"I can't see."

"We can't cross this at my price," said I.

"I could not go three steps on it," said Cavor, "even with my hands free."

We looked at each other's drawn faces in blank consternation.

"They can't know what it is to be giddy." Said Cavor.

"It's quite impossible for us to walk that plank."

"I don't believe they see as we do. I've been watching them. I wonder if they know this is simply blackness for us. How can we make them understand?"

"Anyhow, we must make them understand."

I think we said these things with a vague half hope the Selenites might somehow understand. I knew quite clearly that all that was needed was an explanation. Then, as I saw their faces, I realized that an explanation was impossible. Just here it was that our resemblances were not going to bridge our differences. Well, I wasn't going to walk the plank anyhow. I slipped one wrist very quickly out of the coil of chain that was loose, and then began to twist both in opposite directions. I was standing nearest to the bridge, and as I did this two of the Selenites laid hold of me and pulled me gently towards it.

I shook my head violently. "No go," I said, "no use. You don't understand."

Another Selenite added his compulsion. I was forced to step forward.

"I've got an idea," said Cavor, but I knew his ideas.

111

"Look here!" I exclaimed to the Selenites. "Steady on! It's all very well for you—"

I swung round upon my heel; I burst out into curses. For one of the armed Selenites had stabbed my behind with his goad.

I wrenched my wrist free from the little tentacles that held them. I turned on the goad-bearer. "Confound you!" I cried. "I've warned you of that. What on earth do you think I'm made of, to stick that into me? If you touch me again—!"

By way of answer he pricked me forthwith.

I heard Cavor's voice in alarm and entreaty. Even then I think he wanted to compromise with these creatures. "I say, Bedford," he cried, "I know a way!" but the sting of that second stab seemed to set free some pent-up reserve of energy in my being. Instantly a link of the wrist-chain snapped, and with it snapped all considerations that had held us unresisting in the hands of these moon-creatures. For that second, at least, I was mad with fear and anger. I took no thought of consequences. I hit straight out at the face of the thing with the goad. The chain was twisted round my fist . . .

Then came another of those beastly surprises of which the moon world is full.

My mailed hand seemed to go clean through him. He smashed like some sort of sweetmeat with liquid in it. He broke right in. He squelched and splashed. It was like hitting a damp toadstool. The flimsy body went spinning a dozen yards and fell with a flabby impact. I was astonished. I was incredulous that any living thing could be so flimsy. For an instant I could have believed the whole thing a dream.

Then it had become real and imminent again. Neither Cavor nor the other Selenites seemed to have done anything from the time when I had turned about to the time when the dead Selenite hit the ground. Everyone stood back from us two, everyone alert. That arrest seemed to last at least a second after the Selenite was down. Everyone must have been taking the thing in. I seem to remember myself standing with my arm half retracted, trying also to take it in. "What next?" clamored my brain; "what next?" Then in a moment everyone was moving!

I perceived we must get our chains loose, and that before we could do this these Selenites had to be beaten off. I faced towards the group of the three goad-bearers. Instantly one threw his goad at me. It swished over my head, and I suppose went flying into the abyss behind.

I leaped right at him with all my might as the goad flew over me. He turned to run as I jumped, and I bore him to the ground, came down right upon him, and slipped upon his smashed body and fell. He seemed to wriggle under my feet.

I came into a sitting position, and on every hand the blue backs of the Selenites were receding into the darkness. I bent a link by main force and untwisted the chain that had hampered me about the ankles, and sprang to my feet, with the chain in my hand. Another goad, flung javelin-wise, whistled by me, and I made a rush towards the darkness out of which it had come. Then I turned back towards Cavor, who was still standing in the light of the rivulet near the gulf, convulsively busy with his wrists, and at the same time jabbering nonsense about his idea.

"Come on!" I cried.

"My hands!" he answered.

Then, realizing that I dared not run back to him because my ill-calculated steps might carry me over the edge, he came shuffling towards me, with his hands held out before him.

I gripped his chains at once to unfasten them.

"Where are they?" he panted.

"Run away. They'll come back. They're throwing things! Which way shall we go?"

"By the light. To that tunnel. Eh?"

"Yes," said I, and his hands were free.

I dropped on my knees and fell to work on his ankle bonds. Whack came something—I know not what—and splashed the livid streamlet into drops about us. Far away on our right a piping and whistling began.

I whipped the chain off his feet, and put it in his hand. "Hit with that!" I said, and without waiting for an answer set off in big bounds along the path by which we had come. I had a nasty feeling that these things could jump out of the darkness on to my back. I heard the impact of Cavor's leaps come following after me.

We ran in vast strides. But that running, you must understand, was an altogether different thing from any running on earth. On earth one leaps and almost instantly hits the ground again; but on the moon, because of its weaker pull, one shot through the air for several seconds before one came to earth. In spite of our violent hurry this gave an effect of long pauses, pauses in which one might have counted seven or eight. Step, and one soared off. All sorts of questions ran through my mind: "Where are the Selenites? What will they do? Shall we ever get to that tunnel? Is Cavor far behind? Are they likely to cut him off?" Then, whack, stride, and off again for another step.

I saw a Selenite running in front of me, his legs going exactly as a man's would go on earth, saw him glance over his shoulder, and heard him shriek as he ran aside out of my way into the darkness. He was, I think, our guide, but I am not sure. Then in another vast stride the walls of rock had come into view on either hand, and in two more strides I was in the tunnel, and tempering my pace to its low roof. I went on to a bend, then stopped and turned back, and plug, plug, plug, Cavor came into view, splashing into the stream of blue light at every stride, and grew larger and blundered into me. We stood clutching each other. For a moment, at least, we had shaken off our captors and were alone.

We were both very much out of breath. We spoke in panting, broken sentences.

"You spoiled it all!" panted Cavor.

"Nonsense," I cried. "It was that or death."

"What are we to do?"

"Hide."

"How can we?"

"It's dark enough."

"But where?"

"Up one of these side caverns."

"And then?"

"Think."

"Right—come on."

We strode on, and presently came to a radiating, dark cavern. Cavor was in front. He hesitated, and chose a black mouth that seemed to promise good hiding. He went towards it and turned.

"It's dark," he said.

"Your legs and feet will light us. You're wet with luminous stuff."

"But—"

A tumult of sounds, and in particular a sound like a clanging gong became audible advancing up the main tunnel. It was horribly suggestive of a tumultuous pursuit. We made a bolt for the unlit cavern forthwith. As we ran our way was lit by the irradiation of Cavor's legs. "It's lucky," I panted, "they took off our boots, or we should fill this place with clatter." On we rushed, taking the smallest steps we could to avoid striking the roof of the cavern. After a time we seemed to be gaining on the uproar. It became muffled, it dwindled, it died away.

I stopped and looked back and I heard the pad, pad of Cavor's feet receding. Then he stopped also. "Bedford," he whispered, "there's a sort of light in front of us."

I looked, and at first could see nothing. Then I perceived his head and shoulders dimly outline against a fainter darkness. I saw also that this mitigation of the darkness was not blue as all the other light within the moon had been, but a pallid gray, a very vague faint white, the daylight color. Cavor noted this difference as soon or sooner than I did, and I think, too, that it filled him with much the same wild hope.

"Bedford," he whispered, and his voice trembled, "that light—it is possible—"

He did not dare to say the thing he hoped. There came a pause. Suddenly I knew by the sound of his feet that he was striding towards that pallor. I followed him with a beating heart.

### CHAPTER THE FIFTEENTH
### POINTS OF VIEW

The light grew stronger as we advanced. In a little time it was nearly as strong as the phosphorescence on Cavor's legs. Our tunnel was expanding into a cavern and this new light was at the farther end of it. I perceived something that set my hopes leaping and bounding.

"Cavor," I said, "it comes from above! I am certain it comes from above!"

He made no answer, but hurried on.

Indisputably it was a grey light, a silvery light.

114

In another moment we were beneath it. It filtered down through a chink in the walls of the cavern, and as I stared up, drip, came a huge drop of water upon my face. I started, and stood aside; drip, fell another drop quite audibly on the rocky floor.

"Cavor," I said, "if one of us lifts the other, he can reach that crack!"

"I'll lift you," he said, and incontinently hoisted me as though I were a baby.

I thrust an arm into the crack, and just at my finger-tips found a little ledge by which I could hold. The white light was very much brighter now. I pulled myself up by two fingers with scarcely an effort, though on earth I weigh twelve stone, reached to a still higher corner of rock, and so got my feet on the narrow ledge. I stood up and searched up the rocks with my fingers; the cleft broadened out upwardly. "It's climbable," I said to Cavor. "Can you jump up to my hand if I hold it down to you?"

I wedged myself between the sides of the cleft, rested knee and foot on the ledge, and extended a hand. I could not see Cavor, but I could hear the rustle of his movements as he crouched to spring. Then whack, and he was hanging to my arm—and no heavier than a kitten! I lugged him up until he had a hand on my ledge and could release me.

"Confound it!" I said, "anyone could be a mountaineer on the moon," and so set myself in earnest to climbing. For a few minutes I clambered steadily, and then I looked up again. The cleft opened out gradually, and the light was bright. Only—

It was not daylight after all!

In another moment I could see what it was, and at the sight I could have beaten my head against the rocks with disappointment. For I beheld simply an irregularly sloping open space, and all over its slanting floor stood a forest of little club-shaped fungi, each shining gloriously with that pinkish, silver light. For a moment I stared at their soft radiance, then sprang forward and upward among them. I plucked up half a dozen and flung them against the rocks, and then sat down, laughing bitterly, as Cavor's ruddy face came into view.

"It's phosphorescence again," I said. "No need to hurry. Sit down and make yourself at home." And as he spluttered over our disappointment I began to fling more of these growths into the cleft.

"I thought it was daylight," he said.

"Daylight!" cried I. "Daybreak, sunset, clouds, and windy skies! Shall we ever see such things again?"

As I spoke a little picture of our world seemed to rise before me, bright and dainty and clear, like the background of some old Italian picture. "The sky that changes, and the sea that changes, and the hills and the green trees, and the towns and cities shining in the sun. Think of a wet roof at sunset, Cavor! Think of the windows of a westward house!"

He made no answer.

"Here we are burrowing in this beastly world that isn't a world, with its inky ocean hidden in some abominable blackness below, and outside that torrid day and that death stillness of night. And all those things that are chasing us now, beastly men

115

of leather—insect men, that come out of a nightmare! After all, they're right! What business have we here, smashing them and disturbing their world? For all we know the whole planet is up and after us already. In a minute we may hear them whimpering and their gongs going. What are we to do? Where are we to go? Here we are as comfortable as snakes from Jamrach's loose in a Surbiton villa!"

"It was your fault," said Cavor.

"My fault!" I shouted. "Good Lord!"

"I had an idea."

"Curse your ideas!"

"If we had refused to budge—"

"Under those goads?"

"Yes. They would have carried us."

"Over that bridge?"

"Yes. They must have carried us from outside."

"I'd rather be carried by a fly across a ceiling. Good Heavens!"

I resumed my destruction of the fungi. Then suddenly I saw something that struck me even then.

"Cavor," I said, "these chains are of gold!"

He was thinking intently, with his hands gripping his cheeks. He turned his head slowly and stared at me and, when I had repeated my words, at the twisted chain about his right hand. "So they are," he said, "so they are." His face lost its transitory interest even as he looked. He hesitated for a moment, then went on with his interrupted meditation. I sat for a space puzzling over the fact that I had only just observed this, until I considered the blue light in which we had been and which had taken all the color out of the metal. And from that discovery I started upon a train of thought that carried me wide and far. I forgot that I had just been asking what business we had in the moon. Gold . . . .

It was Cavor who spoke first. "It seems to me that there are two courses open to us."

"Well?"

"Either we can attempt to make our way—fight our way if necessary—out to the exterior and then hunt for our sphere until either we find it or the cold of the night comes to kill us, or else—"

He paused. "Yes," I said, though I knew what was coming.

"We might attempt once more to establish some sort of understanding with the minds of the people in the moon."

"So far as I'm concerned—it's first."

"I doubt."

"I don't."

"You see," said Cavor, "I do not think we can judge the Selenites by what we have seen of them. Their central world, their civilized world, will be far below in the profounder caverns about their sea. This region of the crust in which we are is an outly-

116

ing district, a pastoral region. At least, that is my interpretation. These Selenites we have seen may be only the equivalent of cowboys and engine-tenders. Their use of goads—in all probability mooncalf goads—the lack of imagination they show in expecting us to be able to do just what they can do, their indisputable brutality, all seem to point to something of that sort. But if we endured—"

"Neither of us could endure a six-inch plank across the bottomless pit for very long."

"No," said Cavor, "but then—"

"I *won't*," I said.

He discovered a new line of possibilities. "Well," suppose we got ourselves into some corner, where we could defend ourselves against these hinds and laborers. If, for example, we could hold out for a week or so, it is probable that the news of our appearance would filter down to the more intelligent and populous parts—"

"If they exist."

"They must exist, or whence come those tremendous machines?"

"That's possible, but it's the worst of the two chances."

"We might write up inscriptions on walls—"

"How do we know their eyes could see the marks we made?"

"If we cut them—"

"That's possible of course."

I took up a new thread of thought. "After all," I said, "I suppose you don't think these Selenites so infinitely wiser than men?"

"They must know a lot more—or at least a lot of different things."

"Yes, but—" I hesitated. "I think you'll admit, Cavor, that you're rather an exceptional man."

"How?"

"Well, you—you're a rather lonely man; have been, that is. You haven't married."

"Never wanted to. But why?"

"And you never grew richer than you happened to be?"

"Never wanted that either."

"You've just rooted after knowledge."

"Well, a certain curiosity is nartural—"

"You think so. That's just it. You think every other mind wants to know. I remember once, when I asked you why you conducted all these researches, you said you wanted yours F.R.S., and to have the stuff called Cavorite, and things like that. You know perfectly well you didn't do it for that; but at the time my question took you by surprise, and you felt you ought to have something to look like a motive. Really, you conducted researches because you had to. It's your twist."

"Perhaps it is—"

"It isn't one man in a million has that twist. Most men want—well, various things, but very few want knowledge for its own sake. I don't. I know perfectly well. Now these Selenites seem to be a driving, busy sort of people, but how do you know that even the most intelligent will take an interest in us or our world? I don't believe they'll even know we have a world. They never come out at night—they'd freeze if they did. They've probably never seen any heavenly body at all except blazing sun. How are they to know there is another world? What does it matter to them if they do? Well, even if they have had a glimpse of a few stars or even of the earth crescent, what of that? Why should people living inside a planet trouble to observe that sort of thing? Men wouldn't have done it except for the seasons and sailing; why should the moon people? . . .

"Well, suppose there a few philosophers like yourself. They are just the very Selenites who'll never hear of our existence. Suppose a Selenite had dropped on the earth when you were at Lympne; you'd have been the last man in the world to hear he had come. You never read a newspaper. You see the chances against you. Well, it's for these chances we're sitting here doing nothing while precious time is flying. I tell you we've got into a fix. We've come unarmed, we've lost our sphere, we've got no food, we've shown ourselves to the Selenites and made them think we're strange, strong, dangerous animals, and unless these Selenites are perfect fools they'll take us if they can and kill us if they can't, and that's the end of the matter. After they take us they'll probably kill us through some misunderstanding. After we're done for they may discuss us, perhaps, but we shan't get much fun out of that."

"Go on."

"On the other hand, here's gold knocking about like cast-iron at home. If only we can get some of it back, if only we can find our sphere again before they do and get back, then—"

"Yes?"

"We might put the thing on a sounder footing. Come back in a bigger sphere with us."

"Good Lord!" cried Cavor, as though the idea was horrible.

I shied another luminous fungus down the cleft.

"Look here, Cavor," I said, "I've half the voting power anyhow in this affair, and this is a case for a practical man. I'm a practical man, and you are not. I'm not going to trust to Selenites and geometrical diagrams again if I can help it. . . . That's all. Get back. Drop all this secrecy—or most of it. And come again."

He reflected. "When I came to the moon," he said, "I ought to have come alone."

"The question before the meeting," I said, "is how to get back to the sphere."

For a time we nursed our knees in silence. Then he seemed to decide to accept my reasons.

"I think," he said, "one can get data. It is clear that, while the sun is on this side of the moon, the air will be blowing through this planet sponge from the dark side hither. On this side, at any rate, the air will be expanding and flowing out of the moon caverns into the crater. . . .Very well, there's a draught here."

"So there is."

"And that means that this is not a dead end, somewhere behind us this cleft goes on and up. The draught is blowing up, and that is the way we have to go. If we try to get up any sort of chimney or gully there is, we shall not only get out of these passages where they are hunting for us—"

"But suppose the gully is too narrow."

"We'll come down again."

"Ssh!" I said, suddenly; "what's that?"

We listened. At first it was an indistinct murmur, and then one picked out the clang of a gong. "They must think we are mooncalves," said I, "to be frightened at that."

"They're coming along that passage," said Cavor. "They must be."

"They'll not think of the cleft. They'll go past."

I listened again for a space. "This time," I whispered, "they're likely to have some sort of weapon."

Then suddenly I sprang to my feet. "Good heavens, Cavor!" I cried. "But they *will*. They'll see the fungi I have been pitching down. They'll—"

I didn't finish my sentence. I turned about and made a leap over the fungus-tops towards the upper end of the cavity. I saw that the space turned upwards and became a draughty cleft again, ascending to impenetrable darkness. I was about to clamber up into this, and then with a happy inspiration turned back.

"What are you doing?" asked Cavor.

"Go on!" said I, and went back and got two of the shining fungi, and putting one into the breast pocket of my flannel jacket so that is stuck out to light our climbing, went back with the other for Cavor. The noise of the Selenites was now so loud that it seemed they must be already beneath the cleft. But it might be they would have difficulty in clambering into it, or might hesitate to ascend it against our possible resistance. At any rate we had now the comforting knowledge of the enormous muscular superiority that was the gift of our birth on another planet. The next moment I was clambering with gigantic vigor after Cavor's blue-lit heels.

### CHAPTER THE SIXTEENTH
### THE FIGHT IN THE CAVE OF THE MOON BUTCHERS

I do not know how far we clambered before we came to the grating. It may be we ascended only a few hundred feet, but at the time it seemed to me we might have hauled and jammed and hopped and wedged ourselves through a mile or more of vertical ascent. Whenever I recall that time there comes into my head the heavy clank of our golden chains that followed every movement. Very soon my knuckles and knees were raw, and I had a bruise on one cheek. After a time the first violence of our efforts diminished, and our movements became more deliberate and less painful.

The noise of the pursuing Selenites had died away altogether. It seemed almost as if they had not traced us up the crack after all, in spite of the tell-tale heap of broken fungi that must have lain beneath it. At times the cleft narrowed so much that we could scarce squeeze into it, at others it expanded into great drusy cavities studded with prickly crystals, or thickly beset with dull, shining fungoid pimples. Sometimes it twisted spirally and at other times slanted down nearly to the horizontal direction. Ever and again there was the intermittent drip and trickle of water by us. Once or twice it seemed to us that small living things had rustled out of our reach, but what they were we never saw. They may have been venomous beasts for all I know, but they did us no harm, and we were now tuned to a pitch when a weird creeping thing more or less mattered little. And at last, far above came the familiar bluish light again, and then we saw that it filtered through a grating that barred our way.

We whispered as we pointed this out to each other and became more and more cautious in our ascent. Presently we were close under the grating, and by pressing my face against its bars I could see a limited portion of the cavern beyond. It was clearly a large space, and lit no doubt by some rivulet of the same blue light that we had seen flow from the beating machinery. An intermittent trickle of water dropped ever and again between the bars near my face.

My first endeavor was naturally to see what might be upon the floor of the cavern, but our grating lay in a depression whose rim hid all this from our eyes. Our foiled attention then fell back upon the suggestion of the various sounds we heard, and presently my eye caught a number of faint shadows that played across the dim, roof, far overhead.

Indisputably there were several Selenites, perhaps a considerable number in this space, for we could hear the noises of their intercourse and faint sounds that I identified as their footfalls. There was also a succession of regularly repeated sounds, chid, chid, chid, which began and ceased, suggestive of a knife or spade hacking at some soft substance. Then came a clank as of chains, a whistle and a rumble as of a truck running over a hollowed place, and then again that chid, chid, chid, resumed. The shadows told of shapes that moved quickly and rhythmically in agreement with that regular sound, and rested when it ceased.

We put our heads close together and began to discuss these things in noiseless whispers.

"They're occupied," I said; "they are occupied in some way."

"Yes."

"They're not seeking us or thinking of us."

"Perhaps they have not heard us."

"Those others are hunting about below. If suddenly we appeared here—"

We looked at each other.

"There might be a chance to parley," said Cavor.

"No," I said, "not as we are."

For a space we remained, each occupied with his own thoughts.

Chid, chid, chid went the chipping and the shadows moved to and fro.

I looked at the grating. "It's flimsy," I said. "We might bend two of the bars and crawl through."

We wasted a little time in vague discussion. Then I took one of the bars in both hands, and got my feet up against the rock until they were almost on a level with my head, and so thrust against the bar. It bent so suddenly that I almost slipped. I clambered about and bent the adjacent bar in the opposite direction, and then took the luminous fungus from my pocket and dropped it down the fissure.

"Don't do anything hastily," whispered Cavor, as I twisted myself up through the opening I had enlarged. I had a glimpse of busy figures as I came through the grating, and immediately bent down, so that the rim of the depression in which the grating lay hid me from their eyes, and so lay flat, signaling advice to Cavor as he also prepared to come through. Presently we were side by side in the depression, peering over the edge at the cavern and its occupants.

It was a much larger cavern than we had supposed from our first glimpse of it, and we looked up from the lowest portion of its sloping floor. It widened out as it receded from us, and its roof came down and hid the remoter portion altogether. Lying in a line along its length, vanishing at last far away in that tremendous perspective, were a number of huge shapes, huge pallid hulls, upon which the Selenites were busy. At first they seemed big white cylinders of vague import. Then I noted the heads upon them lying towards us, eyeless and skinless like the heads of sheep at a butcher's, and perceived they were the carcasses of mooncalves being cut up, much as the crew of a whaler might cut up a moored whale. They were cutting off the flesh in strips, and on some of the farther trunks the white ribs were showing. It was the sound of their hatchets that made that chid, chid, chid. Some distance away a thing like a trolley, cable-drawn and loaded with chunks of lax meat, was running up the slope of the cavern floor. That enormous busy avenue of hulls that were destined to be food gave us a sense of the vast populousness of the moon world second only to the effect of our first glimpse down the shaft.

It seemed to me at first that the Selenites must be standing on trestle-supported planks,* and then I saw that the planks and supports and the hatchets were really of the same leaden hue as my fetters had seemed before white light came to bear on them. A number of very thick-looking crowbars lay about the floor and had apparently assisted to turn the dead mooncalf over on its side. They were perhaps six feet long, with shaped handles; very tempting looking weapons. The whole place was lit by three transverse streams of the blue fluid.

We lay for a long time noting all these things in silence. "Well?" said Cavor at last.

I crouched lower and turned to him. I had come upon a brilliant idea. "Unless they lowered those bodies by a crane," I said "we must be nearer the surface than I thought."

"Why?"

---

* I do not remember seeing any wooden things on the moon; doors, tables, everything corresponding to our terrestrial journey was made of metal, and I believe for the most part of gold, which as a metal would, of course, naturally recommend itself—other things being equal—on account of the ease in working it and its toughness and durability.

"The mooncalf doesn't hop and it hasn't got wings."

He peered over the edge of the hollow again. "I wonder now—" he began. "After all we have never gone far from the surface."

I stopped him by a grip on his arm. I had heard a noise from the cleft below us!

We twisted ourselves about and lay as still as death, with every sense alert. In a little while I did not doubt that something was quietly ascending the cleft. Very slowly and quite noiselessly I assured myself of a good grip on my chain, and waited for that something to appear.

"Just look at those chaps with the hatchets again," I said

"They're all right," said Cavor.

I took a quick provisional aim at the gap in the grating. I could hear now quite distinctly the soft twittering of the ascending Selenites, the dab of their hands against the rock, and the falling of dust from their grips as they clambered.

Then I could see that there was something moving dimly in the blackness below the grating, but what it might be I could not distinguish. The whole thing seemed to hang fire just for a moment; then, smash! I had sprung to my feet, struck savagely at something that had flashed out at me. It was the keen point of a spear. I have thought since that its length in the narrowness of the cleft must have prevented its being sloped to reach me. Anyhow, it shot out from the grating like the tongue of a snake and missed, and flew back and flashed again. But the second time I snatched and caught it, and wrenched it away, but not before another had darted ineffectually at me.

I shouted with triumph as I felt the hold of the Selenite resist my pull for a moment and give, and then I was jabbing down through the bars, amidst squeals from the darkness, and Cavor had snapped off the other spear, and was leaping and flourishing through the grating, and then an axe hurtled through the air and whacked against the rocks beyond to remind me of the fleshers at the carcasses up the cavern.

I turned, and they were all coming towards us in open order, waving their axes. They were short thick little beggars with long arms, strikingly different from the ones we had seen before. If they had not heard of us before they must have realized the situation with incredible swiftness. I stared at them for a moment, spear in hand. "Guard the grating Cavor," I cried, and howling to intimidate them, I rushed to meet them. Two of them missed with their hatchets, and the rest fled incontinently. Then the two also were sprinting away up the cavern, with hands clenched and heads down. I never saw men run like them.

I knew the spear I had was useless for me. It was thin and flimsy, only effectual for a thrust, and too long for a quick recovery. So I only chased the Selenites as far as the first carcass, and stopped there and picked up one of the crowbars that were lying about. It felt comfortably heavy and equal to smashing any number of Selenites. I threw away my spear, and picked up a second crowbar for the other hand. I felt five times better than I had with the spear. I shook the two threateningly at the Selenites, who had come to a halt in a little crowd far away up the cavern, and then turned about to look at Cavor.

He was leaping from side to side of the grating making threatening jabs with his broken spear. That was all right. It would keep the Selenites down—for a time at least. I looked up the cavern again. What on earth were we going to do now?

We were cornered already. But these butchers up the cavern had been surprised; they were probably scared, and they had no special weapons, only those little hatchets of theirs. And that way lay escape. Their sturdy little forms—ever so much shorter and thicker than the mooncalf herders—were scattered up the slope in a way that was eloquent of indecision. I had the moral advantage of a mad bull in a street. But for all that there seemed a tremendous crowd of them. Very probably there was. Those Selenites down the cleft had certainly some infernally long spears. It might be they had other surprises for us. . . . But, confound it! if we charged up the cave we should let them up behind us; and if we didn't, those little brutes up the cave would probably be reinforced. Heaven alone knew what tremendous engines of warfare—guns, bombs, terrestrial torpedoes—this unknown world below our feet, this vaster world of which we had only picked the outer cuticle, might not presently send up to our destruction. It became clear the only thing to do was to charge! It became clearer as the legs of a number of fresh Selenites appeared running down the cavern towards us.

"Bedford!" cried Cavor, and behold! He was halfway between me and the grating.

"Go back!" I cried. "What are you doing—"

"They've got—it's like a gun!"

And struggling in the grating between those defensive spears appeared the head and shoulders of a singularly lean and angular Selenite bearing some complicated apparatus.

I realized Cavor's utter incapacity for the fight we had in hand. For a moment I hesitated. Then I rushed past him whirling my crowbars, and shouting to confound the aim of the Selenite. He was aiming in the queerest way with the thing against his stomach.

"*Chuzz!*" The thing wasn't a gun; it went off more like a crossbow, and dropped me in the middle of a leap.

I didn't fall down—I simply came down a little shorter than should have done if I hadn't been hit, and from the feel of my shoulder the thing might have tapped me and glanced off. Then my left hand hit against the shaft, and I perceived there was a sort of spear sticking half through my shoulder. The moment after, I got home with the crowbar in my right hand, and hit the Selenite fair and square. He collapsed—crushed and crumpled—his head smashed like an egg.

I dropped a crowbar, pulled the spear out of my shoulder, and began to jab it down the grating into the darkness. At each jab came a shriek and twitter. Finally I hurled the spear down upon them with all my strength, leaped up, picked up the crowbar again, and started for the multitude up the cavern.

"Bedford!" cried Cavor, "Bedford!" as I flew past him.

I seem to remember his footsteps coming on behind me.

Step, leap . . . whack, step, leap. . . . Each leap to last ages. With each, the cave opened out and the number of visible Selenites increased. At first they seemed all

123

running about like ants in a disturbed ant-hill one or two waving hatchets and coming to meet me, more running away, some bolting sidewise into the avenue of carcasses; then presently others came in sight carrying spears, and then others. I saw a most extraordinary thing, all hands and feet, bolting for cover. The cavern grew darker farther up. Flick! Something flew over my head. Flick! As I soared in mid-stride I saw a spear hit and quiver in one of the carcasses to my left. Then as I came down one hit the ground before me and I heard the remote chuzz! with which their things were fired. Flick! Flick! For a moment it was a shower. They were volleying!

I stopped dead.

I don't think I thought clearly then. I seem to remember a stereotyped phrase running through my mind: "Zone of fire, seek cover!" I know I made a dash for the space between two of the carcasses, and stood there, panting and feeling very wicked.

I looked round for Cavor, and for a moment it seemed as if he had vanished from the world. Then he came out of the darkness between the row of the carcasses and the rocky wall of the cavern. I saw his little face, dark and blue, and shining with perspiration and emotion.

He was saying something, but what it was I did not heed. I had realized that we might work from mooncalf to mooncalf up the cave until we were near enough to charge home. It was charge or nothing. "Come on!" I said, and led the way.

"Bedford!" he cried, unavailingly.

My mind was busy as we went up that narrow alley between the dead bodies and the wall of the cavern. The rocks curved about—they could not enfilade us. Though in that narrow space we could not leap yet with our earth-born strength we were still able to go very much faster than the Selenites. I reckoned we should presently come among them. Once we were on them they would be hardly as formidable as black beetles. Only there would first of all be a volley. I thought of a stratagem. I whipped off my flannel jacket as I ran.

"Bedford!" panted Cavor, behind me.

I glanced back. "What?" said I.

He was pointing upward over the carcasses. "White light" he said. "White light again!"

I looked, and it was even so; a faint white ghost of twilight in the remoter cavern roof. That seemed to give me double strength.

"Keep close," I said. A flat long Selenite dashed out of the darkness and squealed and fled. I halted and stopped Cavor with my hand. I hung my jacket over my crowbar, ducked round the next carcass, dropped jacket and crowbar, showed myself, and darted back.

"Chuzz—flick," just one arrow came. We were close on the Selenites, and they were standing in a crowd, broad, short and tall together, with a little battery of their shooting implements pointing down the cave. Three of four other arrows followed the first, and then their fire ceased.

124

I stuck out my head, and escaped by a hair's breadth. This time I drew a dozen shots or more, and heard the Selenites shouting and twittering as if with excitement as they shot. I picked up jacket and crowbar again.

"Now!" said I, and thrust out the jacket.

"Chuzz-zz-zz-zz! Chuzz!" In an instant my jacket had grown a thick beard of arrows, and they were quivering all over the carcass behind us. Instantly I slipped the crowbar out of the jacket, dropped the jacket—for all I know to the contrary it is lying up there in the moon now—and rushed out upon them.

For a minute perhaps it was massacre. I was too fierce to discriminate, and the Selenites were probably too scared to fight. At any rate they made no sort of fight against me. I saw scarlet, as the saying is. I remember I seemed to be wading among these leathery things as a man wades through tall grass mowing and hitting, first right then left—smash, smash! Little drops of moisture flew about. I trod on things that crushed and piped and went slippery. The crowd seemed to open and close and flow like water. They seemed to have no combined plan whatever. There were spears flying about me; I was grazed over the ear by one. I was stabbed once in the arm and once in the cheek, but I only found that out afterwards when the blood had had time to run and cool and feel wet.

What Cavor did I do not know. For a space it seemed that this fighting had lasted for an age and must needs go on forever. Then suddenly it was all over, and there was nothing to be seen but the backs of heads bobbing up and down as their owners ran in all directions . . . I seemed altogether unhurt. I ran forward some paces, shouting, then turned about. I was amazed.

I had come through them in vast flying strides. They were all behind me, and running hither and thither to hide.

I felt an enormous astonishment at the evaporation of the great fight into which I had hurled myself, and not a little exultation. It did not seem to me that the Selenites were unexpectedly flimsy, but that I was unexpectedly strong. I laughed stupidly. This fantastic moon!

I glanced for a moment at the smashed and writhing bodies that were scattered over the cavern floor with a vague idea of further violence, then hurried on after Cavor.

## CHAPTER THE SEVENTEENTH
### IN THE SUNLIGHT

Presently we saw that the cavern before us opened on a hazy void. In another moment we had emerged upon a slanting gallery that projected into a vast circular space, a huge cylindrical pit running vertically up and down. Round this pit the slanting gallery ran without any parapet or protection for a turn and a half, and then plunged high above into the rock again. Somehow it reminded me then of one of those spiral turns of the railway through the Saint Gothard. It was all tremendously huge. I can scarcely hope to convey to you the titanic proportion of all that place—the titanic effect of it. Our eyes followed up the vast declivity of the pit wall, and overhead and far above we beheld a round opening set with faint stars, and half of the lip above it well-nigh blinding with the white light of the sun. At that we cried aloud simultaneously.

"Come on!" I said, leading the way.

"But there?" said Cavor, and very carefully stepped nearer the edge of the gallery. I followed his example, craned forward and looked down, but I was dazzled by that gleam of light above, and I could see only a bottomless darkness with spectral patches of crimson and purple floating therein. Yet if I could not see I could hear. Out of this darkness came a sound—a sound out of that enormous hollow, it may be, for miles beneath our feet . . .

For a moment I listened, then tightened my grip on my crowbar and led the way up the gallery.

"This must be the shaft we looked down upon," said Cavor. "Under that lid."

"And below there is where we saw the lights."

"The lights!" said he. "Yes—the lights of the world that now we shall never see."

"We'll come back," I said, for now we had escaped so much I was rashly sanguine that we should recover the sphere.

His answer I did not catch.

"Eh?" I asked.

"It doesn't matter," he answered, and we hurried on in silence.

I suppose that slanting lateral way was four or five miles long, allowing for its curvature, and it ascended at a slope that would have made it almost impossibly steep on earth, but which we strode up easily. We saw only two Selenites during all that portion of our flight, and as soon as they became aware of us they ran headlong. It was clear that the knowledge of our strength and violence had reached them. Our way to the exterior was unexpectedly plain. The spiral gallery straightened into a steeply ascendant tunnel, its floor bearing abundant traces of the mooncalves, and so straight and short in proportion to its vast arch that no part of it was absolutely dark. Almost immediately in began to lighten, and then far off and high up and quite blindingly brilliant appeared its opening on the exterior, a slope of Alpine steepness surmounted by a crest of bayonet shrub, tall but broken down now and dry and dead, in spiky silhouette against the sun.

And it is strange that we men, to whom this very vegetation had seemed so weird and horrible a little time ago, should now behold it with the emotion a home-coming exile might feel at sight of his native land. We welcomed even the rareness of the air that made us pant as we ran and which rendered speaking no longer the easy thing it had been. Larger grew the sunlit circle above us and larger, and all the nearer tunnel sank into a rim of indistinguishable black. We saw the dead bayonet shrub no longer with any touch of green in it, but brown and dry and thick, and the shadow of its upper branches high out of sight made a densely interlaced pattern upon the tumbled rocks. And at the immediate mouth of the tunnel was a wide trampled space where the mooncalves had come and gone.

We came out upon this space at last into a light and heat that hit and pressed upon us. We traversed the exposed area painfully, and clambered up a slope among the scrub-stems, and sat down at last panting in a high place beneath the shadow of a mass of twisted lava. Even in the shade the rock felt hot.

The air was intensely hot, and we were in great physical discomfort, but for all that we were no longer in a nightmare. We seemed to have come to our own province again, beneath the stars. All the fear and stress of our flight through the dim passages and fissures below had fallen from us. That last fight had filled us with an enormous confidence in ourselves so far as the Selenites were concerned. We looked back almost incredulously at the black opening from which we had just emerged. Down there, in a blue glow that now in our memories seemed the next thing to absolute darkness, we had met with things like mad mockeries of men, helmet-headed creatures, and had walked in fear before them, and had submitted to them until we could submit no longer. And behold, they had smashed like wax and scattered like chaff, and fled and vanished like the creatures of a dream!

I rubbed my eyes, doubting whether we had not slept and dreamt these things by reason of the fungus we had eaten, and suddenly discovered the blood upon my face, and then that my shirt was sticking painfully to my shoulder and arm.

"Confound it!" I said, gauging my injuries with an investigatory hand; suddenly that distant tunnel-mouth became, as it were, a watching eye.

"Cavor!" I said, "what are they going to do now? And what are we going to do?"

He shook his head, with his eyes fixed upon the tunnel. "How can one tell what they will do?"

"It depends on what they think of us, and I don't see how we can begin to guess that. And it depends upon what they have in reserve. It's as you say, Cavor: we have touched the merest outside of this world. They may have all sorts of things inside here. Even with those shooting things they might make it bad for us . . .

"Yet, after all," I said, "even if we don't find the sphere at once, there is a chance for us. We might hold out. Even through the night. We might go down there again and make a fight for it."

I stared about me with speculative eyes. The character of the scenery had altered altogether by reason of the enormous growth and subsequent drying of the scrub. The crest on which we sat was high and commanded a wide prospect of the crater and landscape and we saw it now all sere and dry in the late autumn slopes and fields of trampled brown where the mooncalves had pastured, and far away in the full blaze of the sun a drove of them basked slumberously, scattered shapes, each with a blot of shadow against it like sheep on the side of a down. But not a sign of Selenite was to be seen. Whether they had fled on our emergence from the interior passages or whether they were accustomed to retire after driving out the mooncalves I cannot guess. At the time I believed the former was the case.

"If we were to set fire to all this stuff," I said, "we might find the sphere among the ashes."

Cavor did not seem to hear me. He was peering under his hand at the stars, that still, in spite of the intense sunlight, were abundantly visible in the sky. "How long do you think we have been here?" he asked at last.

"Been where?"

"On the moon."

'Two earthly days, perhaps."

"More nearly ten. Do you know, the sun is past its zenith, and sinking in the west? In four days' time or less it will be night."

"But—we've only eaten once!"

"I know that. And—but there are the stars!"

"But why should time seem different because we are on a smaller planet?"

"I don't know. There it is!"

"How does one tell time?"

"Hunger—fatigue—all those things are different. Everything is different. Everything. To me it seems that since first we came out of the sphere it has been only a question of hours—long hours. At most."

"Ten days," I said; "that leaves—" I looked up at the sun for a moment and then saw that it was halfway from the zenith to the western edge. "Four days! . . . Cavor, we mustn't sit here and dream. How do you think we can begin?"

I stood up. "We must get a fixed point which we can recognize. We might hoist a flag, or a handkerchief or something—and quarter the ground and work round that."

He stood up beside me.

"Yes," he said, "there is nothing for it but to hunt for the sphere. Nothing. We may find it—certainly we may find it. And if not—"

"We must keep on looking."

He looked this way and that, glanced up at the sky and down at the tunnel and astonished me by a sudden gesture of impatience. "Oh! But we have done foolishly! To have come to his pass! Think how it might have been and the things we might have done!"

"We may do something yet."

"Never the thing we might have done. Here below our feet is a world. Think of what that world must be! Think of that machine we saw and the lid and the shaft! They were just remote outlying suggestions, and those creatures we have seen and fought with, no more than ignorant peasants, dwellers in the outskirts, yokels and laborers half akin to brutes. Down below! Caverns beneath caverns, tunnels, structures, ways…It must open out and be greater and wider and more populous as one descends. Assuredly. Right down at last to the central sea that washes round the core of the moon. Think of its inky waters under the spare lights! If indeed their eyes need lights. Think of the cascading tributaries pouring down their channels to feed it. Think of the tides upon its surface and the rush and swirl of its ebb and flow. Perhaps they have ships that go upon it, perhaps down there are mighty cities and swarming ways and wisdom and order passing the wit of man. And we may die here upon it

128

and never see the masters who must be—ruling over these things! We may freeze and die here and the air will freeze and thaw upon us, and then—! They will come upon us, come on our stiff and silent bodies and find the sphere we cannot find and they will understand at last, too late, all the thought and effort that ended here in vain!" His voice through all that speech sounded like the voice of someone heard in a telephone weak and far away.

"But the darkness," I said.

"One might get over that."

"How?"

"I don't know. How am I to know? One might carry a torch, one might have a lamp—The others—might understand."

He stood for a moment with his hands held down and a rueful face, staring out over the waste that defied him. Then with a gesture of renunciation he turned towards me with proposals for the systematic hunting of the sphere.

"We can return," I said.

He looked about him. "First of all we shall have to get to earth."

"We could bring back lamps to carry and climbing irons and a hundred necessary things."

"Yes," he said.

"We can take back an earnest of success in this gold."

He looked at my golden crowbars and said nothing for a space. He stood with his hands clasped behind his back staring across the crater. At last he sighed and spoke. "It was I found the way here, but to find a way isn't always to be master of a way. If I take my secret back to earth what will happen? I do not see how I can keep my secret for a year, for even a part of a year. Sooner or later it must come out, even if other men rediscover it. And then . . . Governments and powers will struggle to get hither, they will fight against one another and against these moon people. It will only spread warfare and multiply the occasions of war. In a little while, in a very little while if I tell my secret, this planet to its deepest galleries will be strewn with human dead. Other things are doubtful, but that is certain . . . It is not as though man had any use for the moon. What good would the moon be to men? Even of their own planet what have they made but a battle ground and theatre of infinite folly? Small as his world is, and short as his time, he has still in his little life down there far more than he can do. No! Science has toiled too long forging weapons for fools to use. It is time she held her hand. Let him find it out for himself again—in a thousand years' time."

"There are methods of secrecy," I said.

He looked up at me and smiled. "After all," he said, "why should one worry? There is little chance of our finding the sphere and down below trouble is brewing for us. It's simply the human habit of hoping till we die, that makes us think of return. Our troubles are only beginning. We have shown these moonfolk violence, we have given them a taste of our quality and our chances are about as good as a tiger's that has got loose and killed a man in Hyde Park. The news of us must be running down from gallery to gallery, down towards the central parts . . . No sane beings will ever let us take that sphere back to earth, after so much as they have seen of us."

"We aren't improving our chances" said I, "by sitting here." We stood up side by side.

"After all," he said, "we must separate. We must fasten up a handkerchief on these tall spikes here and stick it firmly and from this as a center we must work over the crater. You must go westward, moving out in semicircles to and from the setting sun. You must move first with your shadow on your right until it is at right angles with the direction of your handkerchief and then with your shadow on your left. And I will do the same to the east. We will look into every gully, examine ever skerry of rocks, we will do all we can to find my sphere. If we see Selenites we will hide from them as well as we can. For drink we must take snow, and if we feel the need of food we must kill a mooncalf, if we can, and eat such flesh as it has—raw, and so each will go his own way."

"And if one of us comes upon the sphere?"

"He must come back to the white handkerchief and stand by it and signal to the other."

"And if neither—"

Cavor glanced up at the sun. "We go on seeking until the night and cold overtake us."

"Suppose the Selenites have found the sphere and hidden it?"

He shrugged his shoulders.

"Or if presently they come hunting us?"

He made no answer.

"You had better take a club," I said.

He shook his head and stared away from me across the waste.

But for a moment he did not start. He looked round at me shyly, hesitated. "*Au revoir*," he said.

I felt an odd stab of emotion. A sense of how we had galled each other and particularly how I must have galled him came to me. "Confound it!" thought I, "We might have done better!" I was on the point of asking him to shake hands—for that was how I felt just then—when he put his feet together and leaped away from me towards the north. He drifted through the air as a dead leaf would do, fell lightly and leaped again. I stood for a moment watching him, then faced westward reluctantly, pulled myself together, and, with something of the feeling of a man who leaps into icy water, selected a point and plunged forward to explore my solitary half of the moon world. I dropped rather clumsily among rocks, stood up and looked about me, clambered to a rocky slab and leaped again. . . . When presently I looked for Cavor he was hidden from my eyes, but the handkerchief showed out bravely on its headland, white in the blaze of the sun.

I determined not to lose sight of that handkerchief whatever might betide.

FROM *The First Men in the Moon*

## Chapter the Eighteenth
## Mr. Bedford Alone

In a little while it seemed to me as if I had always been alone on the moon. I hunted for a time with a certain intentness, but the heat was still very great and the thinness of the air felt like a hoop about one's chest. I came presently into a hollow basin bristling with tall brown dry fronds about its edge and I sat down under these to rest and cool. I intended to stay for only a little while. I put down my club beside me and sat resting my chin on my hands. I saw with a colorless interest that the rocks of the basin, where here and there the crackling dry lichens had shrunk away to show them, were all veined and splattered with gold, that here and there bosses of rounded and wrinkled gold projected from among the litter. What did that matter now? A sort of languor had possession of my limbs and mind, I did not believe for a moment that we should ever find the sphere in the vast desiccated wilderness. I seemed to lack a motive for effort until the Selenites should come. Then I supposed I should exert myself, obeying that unreasonable imperative that urges a man before all things to preserve and defend this life, albeit he may preserve it only to die more painfully in a little while.

Why had we come to the moon?

The thing presented itself to me as a perplexing problem. What is this spirit in man that urges him forever to depart from happiness and security, to toil, to place himself I danger, even to risk a reasonable certainty of death? It dawned upon me up there in the moon as a thing I ought always to have known, that man is not made simply to go about being safe and comfortable and well fed and amused. Against his interest, against his happiness he is constantly being driven to do unreasonable things. Some force not himself impels him and go he must. But why? Why? Sitting there in the midst of that useless moon gold, amidst the things of another world, I took count of all my life. Assuming I was to die a castaway upon the moon, I failed altogether to see what purpose I had served; I got no light on that point, but it was clearer to me than it had ever been in my life before that I was not serving my own purpose; that all my life I had in truth never served the purposes of my private life. Whose purpose was I serving? . . . I ceased to speculate on why we had come to the moon and took a wider sweep. Why had I come to the earth? Why had I a private life at all? . . . I lost myself at last in bottomless speculation.

My thoughts became vague and cloudy, no longer leading in definite directions. I had not felt heavy or weary—I cannot imagine one doing so upon the moon—but I suppose I was greatly fatigued. At any rate I slept.

Slumbering there rested me greatly, and the sun was setting and the violence of the heat abating through all the time I slumbered. When at last I was roused from my slumbers by a remote clamor, I felt active and capable again. I rubbed my eyes and stretched my arms. I rose to my feet—I was a little stiff—and at once prepared to resume my search. I shouldered my golden clubs one on each shoulder and went on out of the ravine of the gold-veined rocks.

The sun was certainly lower, much lower than it had been, the air was very much cooler. I perceived I must have slept some time. It seemed to me that a faint touch of misty blueness hung about the western cliff. I leaped to a little boss of rock, and surveyed the crater. I could see no signs of mooncalves or Selenites, nor could I see Cavor, but I could see my handkerchief afar off spread out on its thicket of thorns. I looked about me, and then sprang forward to the next convenient viewpoint.

I beat my way round in a semicircle and back again in a still remoter crescent. It was very fatiguing and hopeless. The air was really very much cooler and it seemed to me that the shadow under the westward cliff was growing broad. Ever and again I stopped and reconnoitered, but there was no sign of Cavor, no sign of Selenites, and it seemed to me the mooncalves must have been driven in to the interior again—I could see none of them. I became more and more desirous of seeing Cavor. The winged outline of the sun had sunk now until it was scarcely the distance of its diameter from the rim of the sky. I was oppressed by the idea that the Selenites would presently close their lids and valves and shut us out under the inexorable onrush of the lunar night. It seemed to me high time that he abandoned his search and that we took counsel together. I felt how urgent it was that we should decide soon as to our course. We had failed to find the sphere, we no longer had time to seek it. once these valves were closed, with us outside, we were lost men. The great night of space would descend upon us, that blackness of the void which is the only absolute death. All my being shrank from that approach. We must get into the moon again, though we were slain in doing it. I was haunted by a vision of our freezing to death, of our hammering with our last strength on the valve of the great pit.

I took no thought any more of the sphere. I thought only of finding Cavor again. I was half inclined to go back into the moon without him rather than seek him until it was too late. I was already halfway back towards our handkerchief, when suddenly—

I saw the sphere!

I did not find it so much as it found me. It was lying much farther to the westward than I had gone and the sloping rays of the sinking sun reflected from its glass had suddenly proclaimed its presence in a dazzling beam. For an instant I though this was some new device of the Selenites against us, and then I understood.

I threw up my arms, shouted a ghostly shout and set off in vast leaps towards it. I missed one of my leaps and dropped into a deep ravine and twisted my ankle and after that I stumbled at almost every leap. I was in a state of hysterical agitation, trembling violently and quite breathless long before I got to it. Three times at least I had to stop with my hands resting on my sides, and in spite of the thin dryness of the air the perspiration was wet upon my face.

I thought of nothing but the sphere until I reached it, I forgot even my trouble of Cavor's whereabouts. My last leap flung me with my hands hard against its glass; then lay against it panting and trying vainly to shout, "Cavor! Here is the sphere!" When I had recovered a little I peered through the thick glass and the things inside seemed tumbled. I stooped to peer closer. Then I attempted to get in. I had to hoist it over a little to get my head through the manhole. The screw stopper was inside and I could see now that nothing had been touched, nothing had suffered. It lay there as we had left it when we had dropped out amidst the snow. For a time I was wholly occupied in making and remaking this inventory. I found I was trembling violently. It was good to see that familiar dark interior again! I cannot tell you how good. Presently I crept inside and sat down among the things. I looked through the glass at the moon world and shivered. I placed my gold clubs upon the bale and sought out and took a little food, not so much because I wanted it but because it was there. Then it occurred to me that it was time to go out and signal for Cavor. But I did not go out and signal for Cavor forthwith. Something held me to the sphere.

After all, everything was coming right. There would still be time for us to get more of the magic stone that gives one mastery over men. There was gold for the picking up, and the sphere would travel as well half full of gold as though it were empty. We could go back now masters of ourselves and our world, and then—

I roused myself at last and with an effort got myself out of the sphere. I shivered as I emerged, for the evening air was growing very cold. I stood in the hollow, staring about me. I scrutinized the bushes round me very carefully before I leaped to the rocky shelf hard by and took once more what had been my first leap in the moon. But this time I made it with no effort whatever.

The growth and decay of the vegetation had gone on apace and the whole aspect of the rocks had changed, but still it was possible to make out the slope on which the seeds had germinated and the rocky mass from which we had taken our first view of the crater. But the spiky shrub on the slope stood brown and sere now and thirty feet high, and cast long shadows that stretched out of sight; and the little seeds that clustered in its upper branches were brown and ripe. Its work was done, it was brittle and ready to fall and crumple under the freezing air, so soon as the nightfall came. And the huge cacti that had swollen as we watched them had long since burst and scattered their spores to the four quarters of the moon. Amazing little corner of the universe—the landing place of men!

Some day, thought I, I will have an inscription standing there right in the midst of the hollow. It came to me if only this teeming world within could know of the full import of that moment how curious its tumult would become!

But as yet it could scarcely be dreaming of the significance of our coming. For if it did the crater would surely be an uproar of pursuit. I looked about for some place from which I might signal to Cavor, and saw that same patch of rock to which he had leaped from my present standpoint still bare and barren in the sun. For a moment I hesitated at going so far from the sphere. Then with a pang of shame at that hesitation I leaped . . .

From this vantage point I surveyed the crater again. Far away at the top of the enormous shadow I cast was the little white handkerchief fluttering on the bushes. It was very little and very far. Cavor was not in sight. It seemed to me that by this time he ought to be looking for me. That was the agreement. But he was nowhere to be seen.

I stood waiting and watching, hands shading my eyes, expecting every moment to distinguish him. Very probably I stood there for a long time. I tried to shout and was reminded of the thinness of the air. I made an undecided step back towards the sphere. But a lurking dread of the Selenites made me hesitate to signal my where-abouts by hoisting one of our sleeping blankets on to the adjacent scrub. My eyes searched the crater again.

It had an effect of emptiness that chilled me. All sounds of the Selenites in the world beneath had died away. It was as still as death. Save for the faint stir of the shrub about me in the little breeze that was rising, there was no sounds, no shadow of a sound. And the breeze blew chill.

Confound Cavor!

I took a deep breath. I put my hands to the sides of my mouth. "Cavor!" I bawled and the sound was like some mannikin shouting far away.

I looked at the handkerchief, I looked behind me at the broadening shadow of the westward cliff, I looked under my hand at the sun. It seemed to me that almost visi-bly it was creeping down the sky.

I felt I must act instantly if I was to save Cavor. I whipped off my vest and hung it as a mark on sere bayonets of the shrubs behind me, and then set off in a straight line towards the handkerchief. Perhaps it was a couple of miles away—a matter of a few hundred leaps and strides. I have already told how one seemed to hang through those lunar leaps. In each suspense I sought Cavor and marveled why he should be hidden. In each leap I could feel the sun setting behind me. Each time I touched the ground I was tempted to go back.

A last leap and I was in the depression below our handkerchief, a stride and I stood on our former vantage point within arm's reach of it. I stood straight and scanned the world about me, between its lengthening bars of shadow. Far away, down a long declivity, was the opening of the tunnel up which we had fled, and my shadow reached towards it, reached towards it and touched it like a finger of the night.

Not a sign of Cavor, not a sound in all the stillness, only that the stir and waving of the scrub and of the shadows increased. And suddenly and violently I shivered. "Cav'—" I began and realized once more the uselessness of human voice in that thin air.

Silence. The silence of death.

Then it was my eye caught something—a little thing, lying perhaps fifty yards away down the slope, amidst a litter of bent and broken branches. What was it? I knew, and yet for some reason I would not know.

I went nearer to it. It was the little cricket cap Cavor had worn. I did not touch it. I stood looking at it.

I saw then that the scattered branches about it had been forcibly smashed and trampled. I hesitated, stepped forward and picked it up.

I stood with Cavor's cap in my hand, staring at the trampled reeds and thorns about me. On some of them were little smears of something dark, something I dared not touch. A dozen yards away, perhaps, the rising breeze dragged something into view, something small and vividly white.

It was a little piece of paper crumpled as though it had been clutched tightly. I picked it up, and on it were smears of red. My eye caught faint pencil marks. I smoothed it out and saw uneven broken writing ending at last in a crooked streak upon the paper.

I set myself to decipher this.

"I have been inured about the knee, I think my kneecap is hurt, and I cannot run or crawl," it began—pretty distinctly written.

Then less legibly: "They have been chasing me for some time and it is only a question of"—the word "time" seemed to have been written here and erased in favor of something illegible—"before they get me. They are beating all about me."

Then the writing became convulsive. "I can hear them," I guessed the tracing meant; and then it was quite unreadable for a space. Then came a little string of words that were quite distinct, "a different sort of Selenite altogether, who appear to be directing the—" The writing became a mere hasty confusion again.

"They have larger brain cases—much larger, and slender bodies and very short legs. They make gentle noises and move with organized deliberation . . .

"And though I am wounded and helpless here, their appearance still gives me hope." That was like Cavor. "They have not shot at me or attempted—injury. I intend—"

Then came the sudden streak of the pencil across the paper, and on the back and edges—blood!

And as I stood there, stupid and perplexed, with this dumbfounding relic in my hand, something very, very soft and light and chill touched my hand for a moment and ceased to be, and then a thing, a little white speck drifted athwart a shadow. It was a tiny snowflake, the first snowflake, the herald of the night.

I looked up with a start and the sky had darkened now almost to blackness and was thick with a gathering multitude of coldly watchful stars. I looked eastward, and the light of that shriveled world was touched with a somber bronze, westward, and the sun—robbed now by a thickening white mist of half its heat and splendor—was touching the crater rim, was sinking out of sight and all the shrubs and jagged and tumbled rocks stood out against it in a bristling disorder of black shapes. Into the great lake of darkness westward, a vast wreath of mist was sinking. A cold wind set all the crater shivering. Suddenly for a moment I was in a puff of falling snow and all the world about me gray and dim.

And then it was I heard, not loud and penetrating as at first, but faint and dim like a dying voice, that tolling, that same tolling that had welcomed the coming of the day: Boom . . . Boom . . . Boom . . .

135

It went about the crater; it seemed to throb with the throbbing of the greater stars: the blood-red crescent of the sun's disc sank as it tolled out: Boom . . . Boom . . . Boom . . .

What had happened to Cavor? All through the tolling I stood there stupidly, and at last the tolling ceased. And suddenly the open mouth of the tunnel down below there shut like an eye and vanished out of sight.

Then indeed was I alone.

Over me, about me, closing in on me, embracing me ever nearer was the Eternal, that which was before the beginning and that which triumphs over the end; that enormous void in which all light and life and being is but the thin and vanishing splendor of a falling star, the cold, the stillness, the silence—the infinite and final Night of space.

The sense of solitude and desolation became the sense of an overwhelming Presence, that stooped towards me, that almost touched me.

"No," I cried, "no! Not yet! Not yet! Wait. Wait! Oh wait!" My voice went up to a faint shriek. I flung the crumpled paper from me, scrambled back to the crest to take my bearings, and then, with all the will that was in me, leaped out towards the mark I had left, dim and distant now in the very margin of the shadow.

Leap, leap, leap, and each leap was seven ages.

Before me the pale serpent-girdled sector of the sun sank and sank and the advancing shadow swept to seize the sphere before I could reach it. I was two miles away—a hundred leaps of more—and the air about was thinning out as it thins under an air pump, and the cold was gripping at my joints. But had I died, I should have died leaping. Once, and then again my foot slipped on the gathering snow and shortened my leap; once I fell short into bushes that crashed and smashed into dusty chips and nothingness, and once I stumbled as I dropped and rolled head over heels into a gully and rose bruised and bleeding and confused as to my direction.

But such incidents were as nothing to the intervals, those awful pauses when one drifted through the air towards that pouring tide of night. My breathing made a piping noise, and it was as though knives were whirling in my lungs. My heart seemed to beat against the top of my brain. "Shall I reach it? Oh Heaven! Shall I reach it?"

My whole being became anguish.

"Lie down," screamed my pain and despair, "Lie down."

The nearer I struggled, the more impossibly remote it seemed. I was numb, I stumbled, I bruised and cut myself and did not bleed.

It was in sight.

I fell on all fours and my lungs whooped.

I crawled. The frost gathered on my lips, icicles hung from my moustache and beard, I was white with the freezing atmosphere.

I was a dozen yards from it. My eyes had become dim. "Lie down," screamed despair, "lie down!"

I fought stiffly with it. I was on the manhole lip, a stupefied half dead being. The snow was all about me. I pulled myself in. There lurked within a little warmer air. The snowflakes—the airflakes—danced in about me, as I tried with chilling hands to thrust the valve in and spin it tight and hard. I sobbed, "I *will*." I chattered on my teeth. And then with fingers that quivered and felt brittle I turned to the shutter studs.

As I fumbled with the switches—for I had never controlled them before—I could see dimly through the steaming glass, the blazing red streamers of the sinking sun, dancing and flickering through the snowstorm and the black forms of the scrub thickening and bending and breaking beneath the accumulating snow. Thicker whirled the snow and thicker, black against the light. What if even now the switches overcame me?

Then something clicked under my hands and in an instant that last vision of the moon world was hidden from my eyes. I was in the silence and darkness of the interplanetary sphere.

## CHAPTER THE NINETEENTH
### MR. BEDFORD IN INFINITE SPACE

It was almost as though I had been killed. Indeed I could imagine a man suddenly and violently killed would feel very much as I did. One moment, a passion of agonizing existence and fear; the next, darkness and stillness, neither light nor life nor sun, moon nor stars, the black Infinite. Although the thing was done by my own act, although I had already tasted this very effect in Cavor's company, I felt astonished, dumbfounded and overwhelmed. I seemed to be born upwards into an enormous darkness. My fingers floated off the studs, I hung as if I were annihilated, and at last very softly and gently I came against the bale and the golden chain and the crowbars that had drifted to the middle of the sphere.

I do not know how long that drifting took. In the sphere, of course, even more than on the moon one's earthly time-sense was ineffectual. At the touch of the bale it was as if I had awakened from a dreamless sleep. I immediately perceived that if I wanted to keep awake and alive I must get a light or open a window so to get a grip of something with my eyes. And besides I was cold. I kicked off from the bale therefore, clawed on to the thin cords within the glass, crawled along until I got to the manhole rim, and so got my bearings for the light and blind studs, took a shove off, and flying once round the bale and getting a scare from something big and flimsy that was drifting loose, I got my hand on the cord quite close to the studs and reached them. I lit the little lamp first of all to see what it was I had collided with, and discovered that old copy of *Lloyd's News* had slipped its moorings, and was adrift in the void. That brought me out of the Infinite to my own proper dimensions again. It made me laugh and pant for a time and suggested the idea of a little oxygen from one of the cylinders. After that I lit the heater until I felt warm and then I took food. Finally I set to work in a very gingerly fashion on the Cavorite blinds to see if I could guess by any means how the sphere was traveling.

The first blind I opened I shut at once, and hung for a time flattened and blinded by the sunlight that had hit me. After thinking a little I started upon the widows at right angles to this one, and got the huge crescent moon and the second time the little crescent earth behind it. I was amazed to find how far I was from the moon. I had reckoned that not only should I have little or none of the "kick-off" that the earth's atmosphere had given us at our start, but that the tangential "fly-off" of the moon's spin would be at least twenty-eight times less than the earth's. I had expected to discover myself hanging over our crater and on to the edge of the night, but all that was now only a part of the outline of the white crescent that filled the sky. And Cavor—?

He was already infinitesimal.

I tried to imagine what could have happened to him. But at that time I could think of nothing but death. I seemed to see him bent and smashed at the foot of some interminably high cascade of blue. And all about him the stupid insects stared . . .

Under the inspiring touch of the drifting newspaper I became very practical again for a while. It was quite clear to me that what I had to do was to get back to earth, but as far as I could see I was drifting away from it. Whatever had happened to Cavor, even if he was still alive, which seemed to me incredible after that bloodstained scrap, I was powerless to help him. There he was, living or dead behind the mantle of that rayless night, and there he must remain at least until I could summon our fellow-men to his assistance. Should I do that ? Something of the sort I had in my mind; to come back to earth, if it were possible, and then as maturer consideration might determine, either to show and explain the sphere to a few discreet persons and act with them, or else to keep my secret, sell my gold, obtain weapons, provisions and an assistant, and return with these advantages to deal on equal terms with the flimsy people of the moon ; to rescue Cavor if that were still possible, and at any rate to procure a sufficient supply of gold to place my subsequent proceedings on a firmer basis.

But that was hoping far; I had first to get back. I set myself to decide just exactly how the return to earth could be contrived. As I struggled with that problem I ceased to worry about what I should do when I got there. My only care was to get back.

I puzzled out at last that my best chance would be to drop back towards the moon as near as I dared in order to gather velocity, then to shut my windows and fly behind it, and when I was past to open my earthward windows and so get off at a good pace homeward. But whether I should ever reach the earth by that device or whether I might simply find myself spinning about it in some hyperbolic or parabolic curve or other, I could not tell. Later I had a happy inspiration, and by opening certain windows to the moon, which had appeared in the sky in front of the earth, I turned my course aside so as to head off the earth, behind which without some such expedient it had become evident to me I must pass. I did a very great deal of complicated thinking over these problems—for I am no mathematician—and in the end I am certain it was much more my good luck than my reasoning that enabled me to hit the earth. Had I known then, as I know now, the mathematical chances that were against me, I doubt if I should have troubled even to touch the studs to make any attempt. And having puzzled out what I considered the thing to do, I opened all my moonward windows, and squatted down—the effort lifted me for a time some foot or so into the air and I hung there in the oddest way—and waited for the crescent to get bigger and bigger until I felt I was near enough for safety. Then I would shut the windows, fly past the moon with the velocity I had got from it—if I did not smash upon it—and so go on towards the earth.

And that is what I did.

At last I felt my moonward start was sufficient. I shut out the sight of the moon from my eyes, and in a state of mind that was, I now recall, incredibly free from anxiety or any distressful quality, I sat down to begin a vigil in that little speck of matter in infinite space that would last until I should strike the earth. The heater had made the sphere tolerably warm, the air had been refreshed by the oxygen, and except for that faint congestion of the head that was always with me while I was away from earth, I felt entire physical comfort. I had extinguished the light again lest it should fail me in the end; I was in darkness save for the earthshine and the glitter of the stars below me. Everything was so absolutely silent and still that I might indeed have been the only being in the universe, and yet, strangely enough, I had no more feeling of loneliness or fear than if I had been lying in bed on earth. Now this seems all the stranger to me since during my last hours in the crater of the moon the sense of my utter loneliness had been an agony . . .

Incredible as it will seem, this interval of time that I spent in space has no sort of proportion to any other interval of time in my life. Sometimes it seemed as though I sat through immeasurable eternities like some god upon a lotus leaf, and again as though there was a momentary pause as I journeyed from moon to earth. In truth, it was altogether some weeks of earthly time. But I had done with care and anxiety, hunger or fear, for that space. I floated, thinking with a strange breadth and freedom of all that we had undergone and of all my life and motives and the secret issues of my being. I seemed to myself to have grown greater and greater, to have lost all sense of movement, to be floating amidst the stars; and always the sense of earth's littleness and the infinite littleness of my life upon it, was in my thoughts.

I can't profess to explain what happened in my mind. No doubt it could all be traced directly or indirectly to the curious physical conditions under which I was living. I set it down here just for what it is worth and without any comment. The most prominent quality of it was a pervading doubt of my own identity. I became, if I may so express it, dissociate from Bedford, I looked down on Bedford as a trivial incidental thing with which I chanced to be connected, I saw Bedford in many relations—as an ass or as a poor beast where I had hitherto been inclined to regard him with a quiet pride as a very spirited and rather forcible person. I saw him not only as an ass, but as the son of many generations of asses. I reviewed his schooldays and his early manhood and his first encounter with love very much as one might review the proceedings of ant in the sand . . . I regret that something of that period of lucidity still hangs about me, and I doubt if I shall ever recover the full-blooded self-satisfaction of my early days. But at the time, the thing was not in the least painful, because I had that extraordinary persuasion that as a matter of fact I was no more Bedford than I was anyone else, but only a mind floating in the still serenity of space. Why should I be disturbed about this Bedford's shortcomings? I was not responsible for him or them.

For a time I struggled against this really very grotesque delusion. I tried to summon the memory of vivid moments, of tender or intense emotions to my assistance; I felt that if I could recall one genuine twinge of feeling the growing rupture would be stopped. But I could not do it. I saw Bedford rushing down Chancery Lane, hat on the back of his head, coat tails flying out, *en route* for his public examination. I saw him dodging and bumping against and even saluting other similar little creatures in that swarming gutter of people. Me? I saw Bedford that same evening in the sitting-room of a certain lady, and his hat was on the table beside him and it badly wanted brushing and he was in tears. Me? I saw him with the lady in various attitudes and emotions—I never felt so detached before . . . I saw him hurrying off to Lympne to write a play, and accosting Cavor, and in his shirt sleeves working at the sphere, and walking out to Canterbury because he was afraid to come. Me? I did not believe it.

I still reasoned that all this was hallucination due to my solitude and the fact that I had lost all weight and sense of resistance. I had endeavored to recover that sense by hanging myself about the sphere, by pinching my hands and clasping them together. Among other things I lit the light, captured that torn copy of *Lloyd's* and read those convincingly realistic advertisements again, about the Cutaway bicycle, and the gentleman of private means and the lady in distress who was selling those "forks and spoons." There was no doubt *they* existed surely enough, and, said I: "This is your world, and you are Bedford and you are going back to live among things like that for all the rest of you life." But the doubts within me could still argue: "It is not you that is reading, it is Bedford—but *you are not Bedford*, you know. That's just where the mistake comes in."

"Confound it!" I cried, "and if I am not Bedford, what *am* I?"

But in that direction no light was forthcoming, though the strangest fancies came drifting into my brain, queer remote suspicions like shadows seen from far away. . . . Do you know I had an idea that really I was something quite outside not only the world, but all worlds, and out of space and time, and that this poor Bedford was just a peephole through which I looked at life . . .

Bedford! However I disavowed him, there I was most certainly bound up with him, and I knew that wherever and whatever I might be I must needs feel the stress of his desires and sympathize with all his joys and sorrows until his life should end. And with the dying of Bedford—what then? . . .

140

Enough of this remarkable phase of my experiences. I tell it there simply to show how one's isolation and departure from this planet touched not only the functions and feeling of every organ of the body but indeed also the very fabric of the mind with strange and unanticipated disturbances. All through the major portion of the vast space-journey I hung thinking of such immaterial things, hung dissociated and apathetic, a cloudy megalomaniac as it were amidst the stars and planets in the void of space, and not only the world to which I was returning, but the blue-lit caverns of the Selenites, their helmet faces, their gigantic and wonderful machines, and the fate of Cavor, dragged helpless into that world, were facts infinitely minute and altogether trivial.

Until at last I began to feel the pull of the earth upon my being, drawing me back again to the life that is real for men. And then indeed it grew clearer and clearer to me that I was quite certainly Bedford after all, and returning after amazing adventures to this world of ours, and with a life that I was very likely to lose in this return. I set myself to puzzle out the conditions under which I must fall to earth.

## CHAPTER THE TWENTIETH
### MR. BEDFORD AT LITTLESTONE

My line of flight was about parallel with the surface as I came into the upper air. The temperature of the sphere began to rise forthwith. I knew it behoved me to drop at once. Far below me in a darkling twilight stretched a great expanse of sea. I opened every window I could and fell—out of sunshine into evening and out of evening into night. Vaster grew the earth and vaster, swallowing up the stars, and the silvery translucent starlit veil of cloud it wore spread out to catch me. At last the world seemed no longer a sphere, but flat, and then concave. It was no longer a planet in the sky, but the world of Man. I shot all but an inch or so of earthward window and dropped with a slackening velocity. The broadening water, now so near that I could see the dark glitter of the waves, rushed up to meet me. I snapped the last strip of window and sat scowling and biting my knuckles waiting for the impact . . .

The sphere hit the water with a huge splash: it must have sent it fathoms high. At the splash I flung the Cavorite shutters open. Down I went, but slower and slower, and then I felt the sphere pressing against my feet and so drove up again as a bubble drives. And at the last I was floating and rocking upon the surface of the sea and my journey in space was at an end.

The night was dark and overcast. Two yellow pin-points far away showed the passing of a ship, and nearer was a red glare that came and went. Had not the electricity of my glow lamp exhausted itself, I could have got picked up that night. In spite of the inordinate fatigue I was beginning to feel, I was excited now and for a time hopeful in a feverish, impatient way that so my traveling might end.

But at last I ceased to move about, and sat, wrists on knees staring at a distant red light. I swayed up and down, rocking, rocking. My excitement passed. I realized I had yet to spend at least another night in the sphere. I perceived myself infinitely heavy and fatigued. And so I fell asleep.

A change in the rhythmic motion awakened me. I peered though the refracting glass and saw that I had come aground upon a huge shallow of sand. Far away I saw houses and trees, and seaward a curved vague distortion of a ship hung between sea and sky.

I stood up and staggered. My one desire was to emerge. The manhole was upward and I wrestled with the screw. Slowly I opened the manhole. At last the air was singing in again as once it had sung out. But this time I did not wait until the pressure was adjusted. In another moment I had the weight of the window on my hands and it was open, to the old familiar sky of earth.

The air hit me on the chest so that I gasped. I dropped the glass screw. I cried out, put my hands to my chest and sat down. For a time I was in pain. Then I took deep breaths. At last I could rise and move about again.

I tried to thrust my head through the manhole, and the sphere rolled over. It was as though something had lugged my head down as it emerged. I ducked back sharply or I should have been pinned face under water. After some wriggling and shoving I managed to crawl out upon sand, over which the retreating waves still came and went.

I did not attempt to stand up. It seemed to me that my body must be suddenly changed to lead. Mother Earth had her grip on me now—no Cavorite intervening. I sat down heedless of the water that came over my feet.

It was dawn, a gray dawn, rather overcast but showing here and there a long patch of greenish gray. Some way out a ship was lying at anchor, a pale silhouette of a ship with one yellow light. The water came rippling in in long shallow waves. Away to the right curved the land, a shingle bank with little hovels, and at last a lighthouse, a sailing mark and a point. Inland stretched a space of level sand, broken here and there by pools of water and ending a mile away perhaps in a low shore of scrub. To the north-east some isolated watering-place was visible; a row of gaunt lodging houses, the tallest objects that I could see on earth, dull dabs against the brightening sky. What strange men can have reared these vertical piles in such an amplitude of space I do not know. There they are like pieces of Brighton lost in the waste.

For a long time I sat there, yawning and rubbing my face. At last I struggled to rise. It made me feel that I was lifting a weight. I stood up.

I stared at the distant houses. For the first time since our starvation in the crater I thought of earthly food. "Bacon," I whispered, "eggs. Good toast and good coffee…And how the devil am I going to get all this stuff to Lympe?" I wondered where I was. It was an east shore, anyhow, and I had seen Europe before I dropped.

I heard footsteps crunching in the sand and a little round-faced friendly looking man in flannels, with a bathing towel wrapped about his shoulders and his bathing dress over his arm, appeared up the beach. I knew instantly that I must be in England. He was staring most intently at the sphere and me. He advanced, staring. I dare say I looked a ferocious savage enough—dirty, unkempt to an indescribable degree, but it did not occur to me at the time. He stopped at a distance of twenty yards. "Hul-lo, my man!" he said doubtfully.

"Hullo yourself!" said I.

He advanced reassured by that. "What on earth is that thing?" he asked.

"Can you tell me where I am?" I asked.

"That's Littlestone," he said, pointing to the houses; "and that's Dungeness! Have you just landed? What's that thing you've got? Some sort of machine?"

"Yes."

"Have you floated ashore? Have you been wrecked or something? What is it?"

I meditated swiftly. I made an estimate of the little man's appearance as he drew nearer. "By Jove!" he said, "You've had a time of it! I thought you—Well—Where were you cast away? Is that a sort of floating thing for saving life?"

I decided to take that line for the present. I made a few vague affirmatives. "I want help" I said hoarsely. "I want to get some stuff up the beach—stuff I can't very well leave about." I became aware of three other pleasant looking young men with towels and blazers and straw hats coming down the sand towards me. Evidently the early bathing section of this Littlestone.

"Help!" said the young man; "rather!" He became vaguely active. "What particularly do you want done?" He turned round and gesticulated. The three young men accelerated their pace. In a minute they were about me plying me with questions I was disinclined to answer. "I'll tell all that later," I said. "I'm dead beat. I'm a rag."

"Come up to the hotel," said the foremost little man. "We'll look after that thing there."

I hesitated. "I can't," I said. "In that sphere there's two big bars of gold."

They looked incredulously at one another, then at me with a new inquiry. I went to the sphere, stooped, crept in and presently they had the Selenites' crowbars and the broken chain before them. If I had not been so horribly fagged I could have laughed at them. It was like kittens round a beetle. They didn't know what to do with the stuff. The fat little man stooped and lifted the end of one of the bars and then dropped it with a grunt. Then they all did.

"It's lead or gold!' said one.

"Oh, it's gold!" said another.

"Gold right enough," said the third.

Then they all stared at me and then they all stared at the ship lying at anchor.

"I say!" cried the little man. "But where did you get that?"

I was too tired to keep up a lie. "I got it in the moon."

I saw them stare at one another.

"Look here!" said I, "I'm not going to argue now. Help me carry these lumps of gold up to the hotel—I guess with rests two of you can manage one and I'll trail this chain thing—and I'll tell you more when I've had some food."

"And how about that thing?'

"It won't hurt there," I said. "Anyhow—confound it!—it must stop there now. If the tide comes up, it will float all right."

And in a state of enormous wonderment these young men most obediently hoisted my treasures on their shoulders, and with limbs that felt like lead I headed a procession towards that distant fragment of "sea-front." Halfway there we were reinforced by two awe-stricken little girls with spades, and later appeared a lean little boy with a penetrating sniff. He was, I remember, wheeling a bicycle and he accompanies us at a distance of about a hundred yards on our right flank and then I suppose gave us up as uninteresting, mounted his bicycle and rode off over the level sands in the direction of the sphere.

I glanced back after him.

"He won't touch it," said the stout young man reassuringly, and I was only too willing to be reassured.

At first something of the gray of the morning was in my mind, but presently the sun disengage itself from the level clouds of the horizon and lit the world and turned the leaden sea to glittering waters. My spirits rose. A sense of the vast importance of the things I had done and had yet to do came with the sunlight into my mind. I laughed aloud as the foremost man staggered under my gold. When indeed I took my place in the world, how amazed the world would be!

If it had not been for my inordinate fatigue the landlord of the Littlestone hotel would have been amusing as he hesitated between my gold and my respectable company on one hand and my filthy appearance on the other. But at last I found myself in a terrestrial bathroom once more; had warm water to wash myself with and a change of raiment, preposterously small indeed, but clean, that the genial little man had lent me. He lent me a razor, too, but I could not screw up my resolution to attack even the outposts of the bristling beard that covered my face.

I sat down to an English breakfast and ate with a sort of languid appetite, an appetite many weeks old and very decrepit and stirred myself to answer the questions of the four young men. And I told them the truth.

"Well," said I, "as you press me—I got it in the moon."

"The moon?"

"Yes, the moon in the sky."

"But how do you mean?"

"What I say, confound it!"

"That you have just come from the moon?"

"Exactly! Through space—in that ball." And I took a delicious mouthful of egg. I made a private note that when I went back to the moon I would take a box of eggs.

I could see clearly that they did not believe one word of what I told them, but evidently they considered me the most respectable liar they had ever met. They glanced at one another and then concentrated the fire of their eyes on me. I fancy they expected a clue to me in the way I helped myself to salt. They seemed to find something significant in my peppering my egg. Those strangely shaped masses of gold they had staggered under held their minds. There the lumps lay in front of me, each worth thousand of pounds and as impossible for anyone to steal as a house or a piece of land. As I looked at their curious faces over my coffee cup I realized something of the enormous wilderness of explanations into which I should have to wander to render myself comprehensible again.

"You don't really mean," began the youngest young man in the tone of one who speaks to an obstinate child.

"Just pass me the toast rack," I said, and shut him up completely.

"But look here, I say," began one of the others. "We're not going to believe that, you know."

"Ah, well," said I, and shrugged my shoulders.

"He doesn't want to tell us," said the youngest young man in a stage voice aside, and then with an appearance of great *sang-friod:* "You don't mind if I have a cigarette?"

I waved him a cordial assent, and proceeded with my breakfast. Two of the others went and looked out of the farther window and talked inaudibly. I was struck by a thought. "The tide," I said, "is running out?"

There was a pause as to who should answer me. "It's near the ebb," said the little fat man.

"Well, anyhow," I said, "it won't float far."

I decapitated my third egg and began a little speech. "Look here," I said. "Please don't imagine I'm surly or telling you uncivil lies or anything of that sort. I'm forced almost to be a little short and mysterious. I can quite understand this is as queer as it can be and that your imaginations must be going it. I can assure you, you're in at a memorable time. But I can't make it clear to you now—it's impossible. I give you my word of honor I've come from the moon, and that's all I can tell you. . . . All the same I'm tremendously obliged to you, you know, tremendously. I hope that my manner hasn't in any way given you offence."

"Oh no, not in the least!" said the youngest young man affably. "We can quite understand," and staring hard at me all the time he heeled his chair back until it very nearly upset, and recovered with some exertion. "Not a bit of it," said the fat young man. "Don't you imagine that!" and they all got up and dispersed and walked about and lit cigarettes and generally tried to show they were perfectly amiable and disengaged and entirely free from the slightest curiosity about me and the sphere. "I'm going to keep an eye on that ship out there all the same," I heard on of them remarking in an undertone. If only they could have forced themselves to it they would, I believe, even have gone out and left me. I went on with my third egg.

"The weather," the fat little man remarked presently, "has been immense, has it not? I don't know when we have had such a summer . . . "

Phoo-whizz! Like a tremendous rocket!

And somewhere a window was broken.

"What's that?" said I.

"It isn't—?" cried the little man and rushed to the corner window.

All the others rushed to the window likewise. I sat staring at them.

Suddenly I leaped up, knocked over my third egg, and rushed for the window also. I had just thought of something. "Nothing to be seen there," cried the little man rushing for the door.

"It's that boy!" I cried, bawling in hoarse fury; "it's that accursed boy!" and turning about I pushed the waiter aside—he was just bringing me some more toast—and rushed violently out of the room and down and out upon the queer little esplanade in front of the hotel.

The sea, which had been smooth, was rough now with hurrying cat's-paws, and all about where the sphere had been was tumbled water like the wake of a ship. Above, a little puff of cloud whirled like dispersing smoke, and the three or four people on the beach were staring up with interrogative faces towards the point of that unexpected report. And that was all! Boots and waiter and the four young men in blazers came rushing out behind me. Shouts came from windows and doors and all sorts of worrying people came into sight—agape.

For a time I stood there too overwhelmed by this new development to think of the people. At first I was too stunned to see the thing as any definite disaster—I was just stunned as a man is by some accidental violent blow. It is only afterwards he begins to appreciate his specific injury.

"Good Lord!"

I felt as though somebody was pouring funk out of a can down the back of my neck. My legs became feeble. I had got the first intimation of what the disaster meant for me. There was that confounded boy—sky high! I was utterly "left." There was the gold in the coffee room, my only possession on earth. How would it all work out? The general effect was of a gigantic unmanageable confusion.

"I say," said the voice of the little man behind, "I say, you know."

I wheeled about and there were twenty or thirty people all bombarding me with dumb interrogation, with infinite doubt and suspicion. I felt that compulsion of their eyes intolerably. I groaned aloud.

"I can't," I shouted. "I tell you, I can't! I'm not equal to it! You must puzzle and—and be damned to you!"

I gesticulated convulsively. He receded a step as though I had threatened him. I made a bolt through them into the hotel. I charged back into the coffee-room, rang the bell furiously. I gripped the waiter as he entered. "D'y hear?" I shouted. "Get help and carry these bars up to my room right away."

He failed to understand me and I shouted and raved at him. A scared looking little old man in a green apron appeared and two of the young men in flannels. I made a dash at them and commandeered their services. As soon as the gold was in my room I felt free to quarrel. "Now get out," I shouted; "all o' you get out if you don't want to see man go mad before your eyes!" And I helped the waiter by the

146

shoulder as he hesitated in the doorway. And then as soon as I had the door locked on them all I tore off the little man's clothes again, shied them right and left and got into bed forthwith. And there I lay swearing and panting and cooling for a long time.

At last I was calm enough to get out of bed and ring up the round-eyed waiter for a flannel nightshirt, a soda and whisky and some good cigars. And these things being procured after an exasperating delay that drove me several times to the bell, I locked the door again and proceeded very deliberately to look the entire situation in the face.

The net result of the great experiment presented itself as an absolute failure. It was a rout and I was the sole survivor. It was an absolute collapse and this was the final disaster. There was nothing for it but to save myself, and as much as I could in the way of prospects from our *débacle*. At one fatal crowning blow all my vague resolutions of return and recovery had vanished. My intention of going back to the moon, of getting a sphereful of gold and afterwards of having a fragment of Cavorite analyzed and so recovering the great secret, perhaps finally even of recovering Cavor's body, all these ideas vanished altogether.

I was the sole survivor, and that was all.

I think that going to bed was one of the luckiest ideas I have ever had in an emergency. I really believe I should either have got looseheaded or done some fatal, indiscreet thing. But there, locked in and secure from all interruption I could think out the position in all its bearings and make my arrangements at leisure.

Of course what had happened to the boy was quite clear to me. He had crawled into the sphere, meddled with the studs, shut the Cavorite windows and gone up. It was highly improbable he had screwed in the manhole stopper, and even if he had the chances were a thousand to one against his getting back. It was fairly evident that he would gravitate with my bales to somewhere near the middle of the sphere and remain there and so cease to be a legitimate terrestrial interest however remarkable he might seem to the inhabitants of some remote quarter of space. I very speedily convinced myself on that point. And as for any responsibility I might have in the matter, the more I reflected the clearer it became that if only I kept quiet, I need not trouble myself about that. If I was faced by sorrowing parents demanding their lost boy, I had merely to demand my lost sphere—or ask them what they meant. At first I had had a vision of weeping parents and guardians and all sorts of complications, but now I saw that I simply had to keep my mouth shut and nothing in that way could arise. And indeed the more I lay and smoked and thought the more evident became the wisdom of impenetrability.

It is within the right to every British citizen, provided he does not commit damage nor indecorum, to appear suddenly wherever he please and as ragged and filthy as he please, and with whatever amount of virgin gold he sees fit to encumber himself, and no one has any right at all to hinder and retain him in this procedure. I formulated that at last to myself and repeated it over as a sort of private Magna Charta of my liberty.

Once I had put that issue on one side I could take up and consider in an equable manner certain considerations I had scarcely dared think of before, namely, those arising out of the circumstances of my bankruptcy. But now looking at this matter calmly and at leisure, I could see that if only I suppressed my identity by a temporary assumption of some less well-known name, and retained my two months' beard, the risks of any annoyance from the spiteful creditors to whom I have already alluded became very small indeed. From that to a definite course of rational wordly action was plain sailing. It was all amazingly petty, no doubt, but what was there remaining for me to do? Whatever I did I was resolved that I would keep myself level and right side up.

I ordered up writing materials and addressed a letter to the new Romney bank—the nearest, the waiter informed me—telling the manager I wished to open an account with him and requesting him to send two trustworthy persons properly authenticated in a cab with a good horse to fetch some hundredweight of gold with which I happened to be encumbered. I signed the letter "Wells," which seemed to me to be a thoroughly respectable sort of name. This done, I got a Folkestone blue book, chose an outfitter, and asked him to send a cutter to measure me for a drab tweed suit, ordering at the same time a valise, dressing bag, brown boots, shirts, hat (to fit), and so forth, and from a watchmaker I also ordered a watch. And these letters being dispatched, I had up as good a lunch as the hotel could give, and then lay smoking a cigar, as calm as possible until in accordance with my instructions two duly authenticated clerks came from the bank and weighed and took away my gold. After that I pulled the clothes over my ears in order to drown any knocking and went very comfortably to sleep.

I went to sleep. No doubt it was a prosaic thing for the first man back from the moon to do, and I can imagine that the young and imaginative reader will find my behavior disappointing. But I was horribly fatigued and bothered, and, confound it! what else was there to do? There certainly was not the remotest chance of my being believed, if I had told my story then, and it would certainly have subjected me to intolerable annoyances. I went to sleep. When at last I awoke I was ready to face the world, as I have always been accustomed to face it since I came to years of discretion. And so I got away to Italy and there it is I am writing this story. If the world will not have it as a fact, then the world may take it as fiction. It is no concern of mine.

And now that the account is finished, I am amazed to think how completely this adventure is gone and done with. Everybody believes that Cavor was a not very brilliant scientific experimenter who blew up his house and himself at Lympne, and they explain the bang that followed my arrival at Littlestone by a reference to the experiments with explosives that are going on continually at the government establishment of Lydd, two miles away. I must confess that hitherto I have not acknowledged my share in the disappearance of Master Tommy Simmons, which was that little boy's name. That perhaps may prove a difficult bit of corroboration to explain away. They account for my appearance in rags with two bars of indisputable gold upon the Littlestone beach in various ingenious ways—it doesn't worry me what they think of me. They say I have strung all these things together to avoid being questioned too closely as to the source of my wealth. I would like to see the man who could invent a story that would hold together like this one. Well, they must take it as fiction—there it is.

I have told my story—and now I suppose I have to take up the worries of this terrestrial life again. Even if one has been to the moon, one has still to earn a living. So I am working here at Amalfi on the scenario of that play I sketched before Cavor came walking into my world, and I am trying to piece my life together as it was before ever I saw him. I must confess that I find it hard to keep my mind on the play when the moonshine comes into my room. It is full moon here, and the last night I was out on the pergola for hours staring away at the shining blankness that hides so much. Imagine it! Tables and chairs and trestles and bars of gold! Confound it!—if only one could hit on that Cavorite again! But such a thing as that doesn't come twice in a life. Here I am, a little better off than I was in Lympne, and that is all. And Cavor has sought death in a more elaborate way than any human being ever did before. So the story closes as finally and completely as a dream. It fits in so little with all the other things of life, so much of it is so utterly remote from all human experience, the leaping, the queer eating, the hard breathing of those weightless times, that indeed there are moments when, in spite of my moon gold, I do more than half believe myself that the whole thing was a dream.

## CHAPTER THE TWENTY-FIRST
### THE ASTONISHING COMMUNICATION OF MR. JULIUS WENDIGEE

When I had finished the account of my return to the earth at Littlestone I wrote "The End," made a flourish and threw my pen aside, fully believing that the whole story of the First Men in the Moon was told. Not only had I done this, but I had placed my manuscript in the hands of a literary agent, had permitted it to be sold, had seen the greater portion of it appear in *The Strand Magazine,* and was setting to work again upon the scenario of the play I had commenced at Lympne before I realized that the end was not yet. Following me from Amalfi to Algiers, there reached me (it is now about six weeks ago) one of the most astounding communications I have even been fated to receive. Briefly, it informed me that Mr. Julius Wendigee, a Dutch electrician, who has been experimenting with certain apparatus akin to the apparatus used by Mr. Tesla in America, in the hope of discovering some method of communication with Mars, was receiving day by day a curiously fragmentary message in English which was indisputably emanating from Mr. Cavor in the moon.

At first I thought the thing was an elaborate practical joke by someone who had seen the manuscripts of my narrative. I answered Mr. Wendigee jestingly, but he replied in a manner that put such suspicion altogether aside, and in a state of inconceivable excitement I hurried from Algiers to the little observatory upon the Monte Rosa in which he was working. In the presence of his record and his appliances—and above all of the messages from Mr. Cavor that were coming to hand—my lingering doubts vanished. I decided at once to accept his proposal to remain with him, assisting him to take down the record from day to day, and endeavoring with him to send a message back to the moon. Cavor, we learnt, was not only alive but free in the midst of an almost inconceivable community of these ant-like beings, these ant-men, in the blue darkness of the lunar caves. He was lamed, it seemed, but otherwise in quite good health—in better health, he distinctly said, than he usually enjoyed on earth. He had had a fever, but it had left no bad effects. And naturally enough he seemed to be laboring under a conviction that I was either dead in the moon crater or lost in the deep of space.

Mr. Wendigee was engaged in quite a different investigation when he received the first message from the moon. The reader will no doubt recall the little excitement that began the century, arising about of an announcement by Mr. Nikola Tesla, the American electrical celebrity, that he had received a message from Mars. His announcement recalled attention to a fact that had long been familiar to scientific people, namely: that from some unknown source in space, waves of electro-magnetic disturbance, entirely similar to those used by Signor Marconi for his wireless telegraphy, are constantly reaching the earth. Besides Mr. Tesla several other observers have been engaged in perfecting apparatus for receiving and recording these vibrations, though few would go so far as to consider them actual messages from some extra-terrestrial sender. Among those few however we must certainly count Mr. Wendigee. Ever since 1898 he had devote himself almost entirely to this subject, and being a man of ample means he had erected an observatory on the flanks of Monte Rosa, in a position adapted in every way for such observations.

My scientific attainments, I must admit, are not great, but so far as they enable me to judge, Mr. Wendigee's contrivances for detecting and recording any disturbances in the electro-magnetic conditions of space are eminently original and ingenious. And by a happy combination of circumstances, they were set up and in operation about two months before Cavor made his first attempt to call up the earth. Consequently we have fragments of his communications even from the beginning. Unhappily, they are only fragments, and the most momentous of all the things that he had to tell humanity, the instructions, that is, for the making of Cavorite, if indeed he ever transmitted them, have throbbed themselves away, unrecorded in space. We never succeeded in getting a response back to Cavor. He did not know therefore what we had received or what we had missed; nor indeed did he certainly know that anyone on earth was really aware of his efforts to reach us. And the persistence he displayed in sending eighteen long descriptions of lunar affairs—as they would be if we had them complete—shows how much his mind must have turned back towards his native planet since he left it two years ago.

150

You can imagine how amazed Mr. Wendigee must have been when he discovered his record of electro-magnetic disturbances interlaced by Cavor's straight-forward English. Mr. Wendigee knew nothing of our wild journey moonward, and suddenly—this English out of the void!

It is well the reader should understand the conditions under which these messages were sent. Somewhere within the moon Cavor certainly had access for a time to a considerable amount of electrical apparatus, and it would seem he rigged up—perhaps furtively—a transmitting arrangement of the Marconi type. This he was able to operate at irregular intervals: sometimes for only half an hour or so, sometimes for three or four hours at a stretch. At these times he transmitted his earthward message, regardless of the fact that the relative position of the moon and points upon the earth's surface is constantly altering. As a consequence of this and of the necessary imperfections of our recording instruments his communication comes and goes in our records in an extremely fitful manner; it becomes blurred; it "fades out" in a mysterious and altogether exasperating way. And added to this is the fact that he was not an expert operator; he had partly forgotten, or never completely mastered, the code in general use, and as he became fatigued he dropped words and misspelt in a curious manner.

Altogether we have probably missed quite half of the communications he made, and much we have is damaged, broken, and partly effaced. In the abstract that follows the reader must be prepared therefore for a considerable amount of break, hiatus, and change of topic. Mr. Wendigee and I are collaborating in a complete and annotated edition of the Cavor record, which we hope to publish together with a detailed account of the instruments employed, beginning with the first volume in January next. That will be the full and scientific report, of which this is only the popular first transcript. But here we give at least sufficient to complete the story I have told, and to give the broad outlines of the state of the kindred world so near, and yet so dissimilar to our own.

### CHAPTER THE TWENTY-SECOND
### AN ABSTRACT OF THE SIX MESSAGES FIRST RECEIVED FROM MR. CAVOR

The two earlier messages of Mr. Cavor may very well be reserved for that larger volume. They simply tell with greater brevity and with a difference in several details that is interesting, but not of any vital importance, the bare facts of the making of the sphere and our departure from the world. Throughout, Cavor speaks of me as a man who is dead, but with a curious change of temper as he approaches our landing on the moon. "Poor Bedford," he says of me, and "this poor young man," and he blames himself for inducing a young man, "by no means well equipped for such adventures," to leave a planet "on which he was indisputably fitted to succeed" on so precarious a mission. I think he underrates the part my energy and practical capacity played in bringing about the realization of his theoretical sphere. "We arrived," he says, with no more account of our passage through space than if we made a journey in a railway train.

And then he becomes increasingly unfair to me. Unfair, indeed, to an extent I should not have expected in a man trained in the search for truth. Looking back over my previously written account of these things I must insist that I have been altogether juster to Cavor than he has been to me. I have extenuated little and suppressed nothing. But his account is:

"It speedily became apparent that the entire strangeness of our circumstances and surroundings—great loss of weight, attenuated but highly oxygenated air, consequent exaggeration of the results of muscular effort, rapid development of weird plants from obscure spores, lurid sky—was exciting my companion unduly. On the moon his character seemed to deteriorate. He became impulsive, rash, and quarrelsome. In a little while his folly in devouring some gigantic vesicles and his consequent intoxication led to our capture by the Selenites—before we had had the slightest opportunity of properly observing their ways . . . "

(He says, you observe, nothing of his own concession to those same "vesicles.")

And he goes on from that point to say: "We came to a difficult passage with them, and Bedford, mistaking certain gestures of theirs"—pretty gestures they were!—"gave way to a panic violence. He ran amuck, killed three, and perforce I had to flee with him after the outrage. Subsequently we fought with a number who endeavored to bar our way, and slew seven or eight more. It says much for tolerance of these beings that on my recapture I was not instantly slain. We made our ways to the exterior and to increase our chances of recovering our sphere separated in the crater of our arrival. But presently I came upon a body of Selenites led by two who were curiously different, even in form, from any of those we had seen hitherto, with larger heads and smaller bodies and much more elaborately wrapped about. After evading them for some time I fell into a crevasse, cut my head rather badly and displaced my patella, and, finding crawling very painful, decided to surrender—if they would still permit me to do so. This they did, and perceiving my helpless condition carried me with them again into the moon. And of Bedford I have heard or seen nothing more nor, so far as I can gather, has any Selenite. Either the night overtook him in the crater, or else, which is more probable, he found the sphere, and desiring to steal a march upon me made off with it—only, I fear, to find it uncontrollable, and to a more lingering fate in outer space."

And with that Cavor dismisses me and goes on to more interesting topics. I dislike the idea of seeming to use my position as his editor to deflect his story in my own interest, but I am obliged to protest here against the turn he gives these occurrences. He says nothing about that gasping message on the blood-stained paper in which he told, or attempted tell, a very different story. The dignified self-surrender is an altogether new view of the affair that has come to him, I must insist, since he began to feel secure among the lunar people; and as for the "stealing a march" conception, I am quite willing to let the reader decide between us on what he has before him. I know I am not a model man—I have made no pretence to be. But am I *that?*

However, that is the sum of wrongs. From this point I can edit Cavor with an untroubled mind, for he mentions me no more.

It would seem that the Selenites who came upon him carried him to some point in the interior down "a great shaft" by means of what he describes as "a sort of balloon." We gather from the rather confused passage in which he describes this, and from a number of chance allusions and hints in other and subsequent messages, that this "great shaft" is one of an enormous system of artificial shafts that run, each from what is called a lunar "crater" downwards for very nearly a hundred miles towards the central portion of our satellite. These shafts communicate by transverse tunnels, they throw out abysmal caverns and expand into great globular places; the whole of the moon's substance for a hundred miles inwards, indeed, is a mere sponge of rock. "Partly," says Cavor, "this sponginess is natural, but very largely it is due to the enormous industry of the Selenites in the past. The great circular mounds of the excavated rock and earth that from these great circles about the tunnels are known to earthly astronomers (misled by a false analogy) as volcanoes."

It was down this shaft they took him, in this "sort of balloon" he speaks of, at first into an inky blackness and then into a region of continually increasing phosphorescence. Cavor's dispatches show him to be, for a scientific man, curiously regardless of detail, but we gather that this light was due to the streams and cascades of water— "no doubt containing some phosphorescent organism"—that flowed ever more abundantly downward towards the Central Sea. And as he descended, he says: "The Selenites also became luminous." And at last far below him he saw as it were a lake of heatless fire, the waters of the Central Sea, glowing and eddying in strange perturbation "like luminous blue milk that is about to boil."

"This Lunar Sea," says Cavor, in a later passage, "is not a stagnant ocean; a solar tide sends it in a perpetual flow around the lunar axis and strange storms and boilings and rushings of its waters occur, and at times cold winds and thunderings that ascend out of it into the busy ways of the great ant-hill above. It is only when the water is in motion that it gives out light; in its rare seasons of calm it is black. Commonly, when one sees it, its waters rise and fall in an oily swell, and flakes and big rafts of shining, bubbly foam drift with the sluggish, faintly-glowing current. The Selenites navigate its cavernous straits and lagoons in little shallow boats of a canoe-like shape: and even before my journey to the galleries about the Grand Lunar, who is Master of the Moon, I was permitted to make a brief excursion on its waters.

"The caverns and passages are naturally very tortuous. A large proportion of these ways are known only to expert pilots among the fisherman, and not infrequently Selenites are lost for ever in their labyrinths. In their remoter recesses, I am told, strange creatures lurk, some of them so terrible and dangerous that all the science of the moon has been unable to exterminate them. There is particularly the

Rapha, an inextricable mass of clutching tentacles that one hacks to pieces only to multiply; and the Tzee, a darting creature that is never seen, so subtly and suddenly does it slay . . . "

He gives us a gleam of description.

"I was reminded on this excursion of what I have read of the Mammoth Caves; if only I had a yellow flambeau instead of pervading blue light, and a solid-looking boatman with an oar instead of a scuttle-faced Selenite working an engine at the back of a canoe, I could have imagined I had suddenly got back to earth. The rocks about us varied, sometimes black, sometimes pale blue and veined, and once they flashed and glittered as though we had come into a mine of sapphires. And below one saw the ghostly phosphorescent fishes flash and vanish in the hardly less phosphorescent deep. Then presently a long ultramarine vista down the turgid stream of one of the channels of traffic, and a landing-stage, and then perhaps a glimpse up the enormous crowded shaft of one of the vertical ways.

"In one great place heavy with glistening stalactites a number of boats was anchored. We went alongside one of these and watched the long-armed fishing Selenites winding in a net. They were little, hunch-backed insects with very strong arms, shorts, bandy legs, and crinkled face-masks. As they pulled, the net seemed the heaviest thing I had come upon in the moon; it was loaded with weights—no doubt of gold—and it took a long time to draw, for in those waters the larger and more edible fish lurk deep. The fish in the net came up like a blue moonrise—a blaze of darting tossing blue.

"Among their catch was a many-tentaculate evil-eyed black thing, ferociously active, whose appearance they greeted with shrieks and twitters, and which they hacked to pieces with quick nervous movements. All its disserved limbs continues to lash and writhe in a vicious manner. Afterwards when fever had hold of me I dreamt again and again of that bitter, furious creature rising so vigorous and active out of the unknown sea. It was the most active and malignant thing of all the living creatures I have yet seen in this world inside the moon. . . .

"The surface of this sea must be very nearly two hundred miles (if not more) below the level of the moon's exterior; all the cities of the moon lie, I learned, immediately above this Central Sea, in such cavernous spaces and artificial galleries as I have described, and they communicate with the exterior by enormous vertical shafts which open invariably in what are called by earthly astronomers the 'craters' of the moon. The lid covering one such aperture I had already seen during the wanderings that had preceded my capture.

"Upon the condition of the less central portion of the moon I have not yet arrived at very precise knowledge. There is an enormous system of caverns in which the mooncalves shelter during the night; and there are abattoirs and the like—in one of these it was that Bedford and I fought with the Selenite butchers—and I have seen since balloons laden with meat descending out of the upper dark. I have as yet scarcely learnt as much of these things as a Zulu in London will learn about the

British corn supplies in the same time. It is clear, however, that these vertical shafts and the vegetation of the surface must play an essential *role* in ventilating and keeping fresh the atmosphere of the moon. At one time, and particularly on my first emergence from my prison, there was certainly a cold wind blowing *down* the shaft, and later there was a kind of sirocco upwards that corresponded with my fever. For at the end of about three weeks I fell ill of an indefinable fever, and in spite of sleep and the quinine tabloids that very fortunately I had brought in my pocket, I remained ill and fretting miserably, almost to the time when I was taken into the palace of the Grand Lunar, who is Master of the Moon.

"I will not dilate on the wretchedness of my condition," he remarks, "during those days of ill-health." Nevertheless he goes on with great amplitude with details I omit here. "My temperature," he concludes, "kept abnormally high for a long time, and I lost all desire for food. I had stagnant waking intervals and sleep tormented by dreams, and at one phase I was, I remember, so weak as to be earth-sick and almost hysterical. I longed almost intolerably for color to break the everlasting blue . . . "

He reverts again presently to the topic of this sponge-caught lunar atmosphere. I am told by astronomers and physicists that all he tells is in absolute accordance with what was already known of the moon's condition. Had earthly astronomers had the courage and imagination to push home a bold induction, says Mr. Wendigee, they might have foretold almost everything that Cavor has to say of the general structure of the moon. They know now pretty certainly that moon and earth are not so much satellite and primary as smaller and greater sisters, made out of one mass, and consequently made of the same material. And since the density of the moon is only three-fifths that of the earth, there can be nothing for it but that she is hollowed out by a great system of caverns. There was no necessity, said Sir Jabez Flap, F.R.S., that most entertaining exponent of the facetious side of the stars, that we should ever have gone to the moon to find out such easy inferences, and points the pun with an allusion to Gruyere; but he certainly might have announced his knowledge of the hollowness of the moon before. And if the moon is hollow, then the apparent absence of air and water is, of course, quite easily explained. The sea lies within at the bottom of the caverns, and the air travels through the great sponge of galleries, in accordance with simple physical laws. The caverns of the moon, on the whole, are very windy places. As the sunlight comes round the moon, the air in the outer galleries on that side is heated, its pressure increases, some flows out on the exterior and mingles with the evaporating air of the craters (where the plants remove its carbonic acid), while the greater portion flows round through the galleries to replace the shrinking air of the cooling side that the sunlight had left. There is, therefore, a constant eastward breeze in the air of the outer galleries, and an up-flow during the lunar days up the shafts, complicated, of course very greatly by the varying shape of the galleries and the ingenious contrivances of the Selenite mind . . .

### CHAPTER THE TWENTY-THIRD
### THE NATURAL HISTORY OF THE SELENITES

The messages of Cavor from the sixth up to the sixteenth are for the most part so much broken, and so abounding in repetitions, that they scarcely form a consecutive narrative. They will be given in full, of course, in the scientific report, but here it will be far more convenient to continue simply to abstract and quote as in the former chapter. We have subjected every word to a keen critical scrutiny, and my own brief memories and impressions of lunar things have been of inestimable help in interpreting what would otherwise have been impenetrably dark. And, naturally, as living beings, our interest centers far more upon the strange community of lunar insects in which he is living, it would seem as an honored guest, than upon the mere physical condition of their world.

I have already made it clear, I think, that the Selenites I saw resembled man in maintaining the erect attitude and in having four limbs, and I have compared the general appearance of their heads and the jointing of their limbs to that of insects. I have mentioned too the peculiar consequence of the smaller gravitation of the moon on their fragile slightness. Cavor confirms me upon all these points. He calls them "animals," though of course they fall under no division of the classification of earthly creatures, and he points out "the insect type of anatomy had, fortunately for men, never exceeded a relatively very small size on earth." The largest terrestrial insects, living or extinct, do not as a matter of fact measure six inches in length; "but here, against the lesser gravitation of the moon, a creature certainly as much insect as vertebrate seems to have been able to attain to human and ultra-human dimensions."

He does not mention the ant, but throughout his allusions the ant is continually brought before my mind, in its sleepless activity, its intelligence, its social organization, and, more particularly, the fact that it displays, in addition to the two forms, the male and the sexless creatures, workers, soldiers and the like, differing from one another in structure, character, power and use and yet all members of the same species. And these Selenites are of course, if only by reason of this widely extended adaptation, incomparably greater than ants. And in place of the existing four or five different forms of ant there are almost innumerably different forms of Selenites. I have endeavored to indicate the very considerable difference observable in such Selenites of the outer crust as I happened to encounter; the differences in size, hue, and shape were certainly as wide as the difference between the most widely separated races of men. But such differences as I saw fade absolutely to nothing in comparison with the huge distinctions of which Cavor tells. It would seem the exterior Selenites I saw were, indeed, mostly of one color and occupation—mooncalf hinds, butchers, fleshers, and the like. But within the moon practically unsuspected by me, there are, it seems, a host of variations. The moon is indeed a kind of super-anthill. But in place of the five distinctive types, the worker, soldier, winged male, queen and slave of the ant-world, there are amongst the moon-folk not only hundreds of differentiations, but, within each, and linking one to the other, a whole series of fine gradations. And these Selenites are not merely colossally superior to ants, but, according to Cavor, colossally, in intelligence, morality, and social wisdom, higher than man.

It would seem the discovery came upon Cavor very speedily. I infer rather than learn from his narrative that he was captured by the mooncalf hinds under the direction of those other Selenites who "have larger brain-cases (heads?) and very much shorter legs." Finding he would not walk even under the goad, they carried him into darkness, crossed a narrow, plank-like bridge that may have been the very bridge I had refused, and put him down in something that must have seemed at first to be some sort of lift. This was the balloon—it had certainly been absolutely invisible to us in the darkness—and what had seemed to me a mere plank-walking into the void was really, no doubt, the passage of the gangway. In this he descended towards constantly more luminous strata of the moon. At first they descended in silence—save for the twitterings of the Selenites—and then into a stir of windy movement. In a little while the profound blackness had made his eyes so sensitive that he began to see more and more of the things about him, and at last the vague took shape.

"Conceive an enormous cylindrical space," says Cavor in his seventh message, "a quarter of a mile across, perhaps; very dimly lit at first and then bright, with big platforms twisting down its sides in a spiral that vanishes at last below in a blue profundity; and lit ever more brightly—one could not tell how or why. Think of the well of the very largest spiral staircase or lift-shaft that you have ever looked down, and magnify that by a hundred. Imagine it at twilight seen through blue glass. Imagine yourself looking down that; only imagine also that you feel extraordinarily light and have got rid of any giddy feeling you might have on earth, and you will have the first conditions of my impression. Round this enormous shaft imagine a broad gallery running in a much steeper spiral than would be credible on earth, and forming a steep road protected from the gulf only by a little parapet that vanishes at last in perspective a couple of miles below.

"Looking up I saw the very fellow of the downward vision; it had of course the effect of looking into a very steep cone. A wind was blowing down the shaft, and far above I fancied I heard, growing fainter and fainter, the bellowing of the mooncalves that were being driven down again from their evening pasturage on the exterior. And up and down the spiral galleries were scattered numerous moon people, pallid, faintly self-luminous insects, regarding our appearance or busied on unknown errands.

"Either I fancied it or a flake of snow, came drifting swiftly down on the icy breeze. And then, falling like a snowflake, a little figure, a little man-insect clinging to a parachute, drove down very swiftly towards the central places of the moon.

"The big-headed Selenite sitting beside me, seeing me move my head with the gesture of one who saw, pointed with his trunklike 'hand' and indicated a sort of jetty coming into sight very far below: a little landing-stage, as it were, hanging into the void. As it swept up towards us our pace diminished very rapidly, and in a few moments as it seemed we were abreast of it and at rest. A mooring-place was flung and grasped, and I found myself pulled down to a level with a great crowd of Selenites, who jostled to see me.

"It was an incredible crowd. Suddenly and violently there was forced upon my attention the vast amount of difference there is amongst these beings of the moon.

"Indeed, there seemed no two alike in all that jostling multitude. They differed in shape, they differed in size! Some bulged and overhung, some ran about among the feet of their fellows, some twined and interlaced like snakes. All of them had the grotesque and disquieting suggestion of an insect that has somehow contrived to burlesque humanity; all seemed to present an incredible exaggeration of some particular feature; one had a vast right forelimb, an enormous antennal arm, as it were; one seemed all leg, poised, as it were, on stilts; another protruded an enormous nose-like organ beside a sharply speculative eye that made him startlingly human until one saw his expressionless mouth. One has seen punchinellos made of lobster claws—he was like that. The strange and (except for the want of mandibles and palps) most insectlike head of the mooncalf-minders underwent astounding transformations; here it was broad and low, here high and narrow, here its vacuous brow was drawn out into horns and strange features, here it was whiskered and divided, and there with a grotesquely human profile. There were several brain-cases distended like bladders to a huge size. The eyes, too, were strangely varied, some quite elephantine in their small alertness, some huge pits of darkness. There were amazing forms with heads reduced to microscopic proportions and blobby bodies; and fantastic, flimsy things that existed it would seem only as a basis of vast, white-rimmed, glaring eyes. And oddest of all, two or three of these weird inhabitants of a subterranean world, a world sheltered by innumerable miles of rock from sun or rain, *carried umbrellas* in their tentaculate hands!—real terrestrial-looking umbrellas! And then I thought of the parachutist.

"These moon people behaved exactly as a human-crowd might have done in similar circumstances: they jostled and thrust one another, they shoved one another aside, they even clambered upon one another to get a glimpse of me. Every moment they increased in numbers, and pressed more urgently upon the discs of my ushers"—Cavor does not explain what he means by this—"every moment fresh shapes forced themselves upon my astounded attention. And presently I was signed and helped into a sort of litter, and lifted up on the shoulders of strong-armed bearers and so borne over this seething nightmare towards the apartments that were provided for me in the moon. All about me were eyes, faces, masks, tentacle, a leathery noise like the rustling of beetle wings, and a great bleating and twittering of Selenite voices."

We gather he was taken to a "hexagonal apartment," and there for a space he was confined. Afterwards he was given a much more considerable liberty; indeed, almost as much freedom as one has in a civilized town on earth. And it would appear that the mysterious being who is the ruler and master of the moon appointed two Selenites "with large heads" to guard and study him, and to establish whatever mental communications were possible with him. Amazing and incredible as it may seem, these two creatures, these fantastic men-insects, these beings of another world, were presently communicating with Cavor by means of terrestrial speech.

Cavor speaks of them as Phi-oo and Tsi-puff. Phi-oo, he says, was about five feet high; he had small, slender legs about eighteen inches long, and slight feet of the common lunar pattern. On these balanced a little body, throbbing with the pulsations of his heart. He had long, soft, many-jointed arms ending in a tentacled grip, and his neck was many-jointed in the usual way, but exceptionally short and thick. "His head," says Cavor—apparently alluding to some previous description that has gone astray in space—"is of the common lunar type, but strangely modified. The mouth has the usual expressionless gape, but it is unusually small and pointing downwards, and the mask is reduced to the size of a large flat nose-flap. On either side are the little hen-like eyes. The rest of the head is distended into a huge globe, and the chitinous leathery cuticle of the mooncalf hinds thins out to a mere membrane, through which the pulsating brain movements are distinctly visible. He is a creature, indeed, with a tremendously hypertrophied brain, and with the rest of his organism both relatively and absolutely dwarfed." In another passage Cavor compares the back view of him to Atlas supporting the world. Tsi-puff, it seems, was a similar insect, but his "face" was drawn out to a considerable length, and the brain hypertrophy being in different regions, his head was not round but pear-shaped, with the stalk downward. There were also in Cavor's retinue litter-carriers, lop-sided beings with enormous shoulders, very spidery ushers, and a squat foot-attendant.

The manner in which Phi-oo and Tsi-puff attacked the problem of speech was fairly obvious. They came into this "hexagonal cell" in which Cavor was confined, and began imitating every sound he made, beginning with a cough. He seems to have grasped their intention with great quickness, and to have begun repeating words to them and pointing to indicate the application. The procedure was probably always the same. Phi-oo would attend to Cavor for a space, then point also and say the word he had heard. The first word he mastered was "man," and the second "mooney"—which Cavor on the spur of the moment seems to have used instead of "Selenite" for the moon race. As soon as Phi-oo was assured of the meaning of a word he repeated it to Tsi-puff, who remembered it infallibly. They mastered over one hundred English nouns at their first session.

Subsequently it seems they brought an artist with them to assist the work of explanation with sketches and diagrams—Cavor's drawings being rather crude. "He was," says Cavor, "a being with an active arm and an arresting eye," and he seemed to draw with incredible swiftness.

The eleventh message is undoubtedly only a fragment of a longer communication. After some broken sentences, the record of which is unintelligible, it goes on:

"But it will interest only linguists, and delay me too long, to give the details of the series of intent parleys of which these were the beginning, and, indeed, I very much doubt if I could give in anything like the proper order all the twistings and

159

turnings that we made in our pursuit of mutual comprehension. Verbs were soon plain sailing—at least, such active verbs as I could express by drawings; some adjectives were easy, but when it came to abstract nouns, to prepositions, and the sort of hackneyed figures of speech by means of which so much is expressed on earth, it was like diving in cork jackets. Indeed, these difficulties were insurmountable until to the sixth lesson came a fourth assistant, a being with a huge football-shaped head, whose *forte* was clearly the pursuit of intricate analogy. He entered in a preoccupied manner, stumbling against a stool, and the difficulties that arose had to be presented to him with a certain amount of clamor and hitting and pricking before they reached his apprehension. But once he was involved his penetration was amazing. Whenever there came a need of thinking beyond Phi-oo's by no means limited scope, this prolate-headed person was in request, but he invariably told the conclusion to Tsi-puff, in order that it might be remembered; Tsi-puff was ever the arsenal for the facts. And so we advanced again.

"It seemed long and yet brief—a matter of days before I was positively talking with these insects of the moon. Of course, at first it was an intercourse infinitely tedious and exasperating, but imperceptibly it has grown to comprehension. And my patience has grown to meet its limitations. Phi-oo it is who does all the talking. He does it with a vast amount of meditative provisional 'M'm—M'm,' and he has caught up one or two phrases. 'If I may say,' 'If you understand,' and adorns all his speech with them.

"Thus he would discourse. Imagine him explaining his artist.

"'M'm—M'm—he—if I may say—draw. Eat little—drink little—draw. Love draw. No other thing. Hate all who not draw like him. Angry. Hate all who draw like him better. Hate most people. Hate all who not think all world for to draw. Angry. M'm. All things mean nothing to him—only draw. He likes you . . . if you understand . . . New things to draw. Ugly—striking. Eh?"

"'He'—turning to Tsi-puff—'love remember words. Remember wonderful more than any. Think no, draw no—remember. Say'—here he referred to his gifted assistant for a word—'histories—all things. He hear once—say ever.'

"It is more wonderful to me than the most wonderful dream to hear these extraordinary creatures—for even familiarity fails to weaken the inhuman effect of their appearance—continually piping a nearer approach to coherent earthly speech asking question, giving answers. I feel that I am casting back to the fable-hearing period of childhood again when the ant and the grasshopper talked together and the bee judged between them . . . "

And while these linguistic exercises were going on Cavor seems to have experienced a considerable relaxation of his confinement. The first dread and distrust our unfortunate conflict aroused was being, he says, "continually effaced by the deliberate rationality of all I do . . . I am now able to come and go as I please, or I am restricted only for my own good. So it is I have been able to get at this apparatus, and, assisted by a happy find among the material that is littered in this enormous store-cave, I have contrived to dispatch these messages. So far not the slightest attempt has been made to interfere with me in this, though I have made it quite clear to Phi-oo that I am signaling to the earth.

"'You talk to other?' he asked, watching me.

"'Others,' said I.

"'Others,' he said, 'Oh, yes. Men?'

"'And I went on transmitting."

Cavor was continually making corrections in his previous accounts of the Selenites, as fresh facts flowed in upon him to modify his conclusions, and accordingly one gives the quotations that follow with a certain amount of reservation. They are quoted from the ninth, thirteenth, and sixteenth messages, and, altogether vague and fragmentary as they are, they probably give us as complete a picture of the social life of this strange community as mankind can now hope to have for some generations.

"In the moon," says Cavor, "every citizen knows this place. He is born to that place, and the elaborate discipline of training and education and surgery he undergoes fits him at last so completely to it that he has neither ideas nor organs for any purpose beyond it. 'Why should he?' Phi-oo would ask. If, for example, a Selenite is destined to be a mathematician, his teachers and trainers set out at once to that end. They check any incipient disposition to other pursuits, they encourage his mathematical bias with a perfect psychological skill. His brain grows, or at least the mathematical faculties of his brain grow, and the rest of him only so much as is necessary to sustain this essential part of him. At last, save for rest and food, his one delight lies in the exercise and display of his faculty, his one interest in its application, his sole society the other specialists in his own line. His brain grows continually larger, at least so far as the portions engaging in mathematics are concerned; they bulge ever larger and seem to suck all life and vigor from the rest of his frame. His limbs shrivel, his heart and digestive organs diminish, his insect face is hidden under its bulging contours. His voice becomes a mere squeak for the stating of formulae; he seems deaf to all but properly enunciated problems. The faculty of laughter, save for the sudden discovery of some paradox, is lost to him; his deepest emotion is the evolution of a novel computation. And so he attains his end.

"Or again, a Selenite appointed to be minder of mooncalves is from his earliest years induced to think and live mooncalf, to find his pleasure in mooncalf lore, his exercise in their ending and pursuit. He is trained to become wiry and active, his eyes are indurated to the tight wrappings, the angular contours that constitute a 'smart mooncalfishness.' He takes at last no interest in the deeper part of the moon; he regards all Selenites not equally versed in mooncalves with indifference, derision, or hostility. His thoughts are of mooncalf pastures, and his dialect an accomplished mooncalf technique. So also he loves his work, and discharges in perfect happiness the duty that justifies his being. And so it is with all sorts and conditions of Selenites—each is a perfect unit in a world machine . . .

"These beings with big heads to whom the intellectual labors fall, form a sort of aristocracy in this strange society, and at the head of them, quintessential of the moon, is that marvelous gigantic ganglion the Grand Lunar, into whose presence I am finally to come. The unlimited development of the minds of the intellectual class is rendered possible by the absence in the lunar anatomy of bony skull, that strange box of bone that clamps about the developing brain of man, imperiously insisting 'thus far and no farther' to all his possibilities. They fall into three main classes differing greatly in influence and respect. These are the administrators, of whom Phi-oo was one, Selenites of considerable initiative and versatility, responsible each for a certain cubic content of the moon's bulk; the experts, like the football-headed thinkers who are trained to perform certain special operations; and the erudite, who are repositories of all knowledge. To this latter class belongs, Tsi-puff, the first lunar professor of terrestrial languages. With regard to these latter it is a curious little thing to note that the unlimited growth of the lunar brain has rendered unnecessary the invention of all those mechanical aids to brain work which have distinguished the career of man. There are no books, no records of any sort, no libraries, nor inscriptions. All knowledge is stored in distended brains much as the honey-ants of Texas store honey in their distended abdomens. The lunar Somerset House and the lunar British Museum Library are collections of living brains . . .

"The less specialized administrators, I note, do for the most part take a very lively interest in me whenever they encounter me. They will come out of their way and stare at me and ask questions to which Phi-oo will reply. I see them going hither and thither with a retinue of bearers, attendants, shouters, parachute-carriers, and so forth—queer groups to see. The experts for the most part ignore me completely, even as they ignore each other, or notice me only to begin a clamorous exhibition of their distinctive skill. The erudite with very few exceptions are rapt in impervious and apoplectic complacence from which only a denial of their erudition can rouse them. Usually they are led about by little watchers and attendants, and often there are small and active-looking creatures, small females usually, that I am inclined to think are a sort of wife to them; but some of the profounder scholars are altogether too great for locomotion, and are carried from place to place in a kind of sedan tub, wabbling jellies of knowledge that enlist my respectful astonishment. I have just passed one in coming to this place where I am permitted to amuse myself with these electrical toys, a vast, shaven, shaky head, bald and thin-skinned, carried on his grotesque stretcher. In front and behind came his bearers, and curious almost trumpet-faced, news disseminators shrieked his fame.

"I have already mentioned the retinues that accompanied most of the intellectuals: ushers, bearers, valets, extraneous tentacles and muscles as it were, to replace the abortive physical powers of these hypertrophied minds. Porters almost invariably accompany them. There are also extremely swift messengers with spider-like legs, and 'hands' for grasping parachutes, and attendants with vocal organs that could well-nigh wake the dead. Apart from their controlling intelligence, these subordinates are as inert and helpless as umbrellas in a stand. They exist only in relation to the orders they have to obey, the duties they have to perform.

"The bulk of these insects, however, who go to and fro upon the spiral ways, who fill the ascending balloons and drop past me clinging to flimsy parachutes, are, I gather, of the operative class. "Machine hands," indeed some of these are in actual fact—it is no figure of speech; the single tentacle of the mooncalf hind is replaced by huge single or paired bunches of three, or five, or seven digits for clawing, lifting, guiding, the rest of them no more than subordinate appendages to these important parts. Some, who I suppose deal with a bell-striking mechanism, have enormous rabbit-like ears just behind the eyes; some whose work lies in delicate chemical operations project a vast olfactory organ; others again have fat feet for treadles with anchylosed joints; and others—who I have been told are glass-blowers—seem mere lung-bellows. But every one of these common Selenites is exquisitely adapted to the social need it meets. Fine work is done by fined-down workers amazingly dwarfed and neat. Some I could hold on the palm of my hand. There is even a sort of turn-spit Selenite, very common, whose duty and only delight it is to supply the motive power for various small appliances. And to rule over these things and order any erring tendency there might be in some aberrant natures are the finest muscular beings I have seen in the moon, a sort of lunar police, who must have been trained from their earliest years to give a perfect respect and obedience to the swollen heads.

"The making of these various sorts of operative must be a very curious and interesting process. I am still much in the dark about it, but quite recently I came upon a number of young Selenites, confined in jars from which only the fore limbs protruded, who were being compressed to become machine-minders of a special sort. The extended 'hand' in this highly developed system of technical education is stimulated by irritants and nourished by injection while the rest of the body is starved. Phi-oo, unless I misunderstood him, explained that in the earlier stages these queer little creatures are apt to display signs of suffering in their various cramped situations, but they easily become indurated to their lot; and he took me on to where a number of flexible-limbed messengers were being drawn out and broken in. It is quite unreasonable, I know, but these glimpses of the educational methods of these beings have affected me disagreeably. I hope, however, that may pass off and I may be able to see more of this aspect of this wonderful social order. That wretched-looking hand sticking out of its jar seemed to appeal for lost possibilities; it haunts me still, although, of course, it is really in the end a far more humane proceeding than our earthly method of leaving children to grow into human beings, and then making machines of them.

"Quite recently, too—I think it was on the eleventh or twelfth visit I made to this apparatus—I had a curious light upon the lives of these operatives. I was being guided through a short cut hither instead of going down the spiral and by the quays

163

of the Central Sea. From the devious windings of a long, dark gallery we emerged into a vast, low cavern, pervaded by an earthy smell and rather brightly lit. The light came from a tumultuous growth of livid fungoid shapes—some indeed singularly like our terrestrial mushrooms, but standing as high or higher than a man.

"'Mooneys eat these' said I to Phi-oo.

"'Yes, food.'

"'Goodness me!' I cried, 'what's that?'

"My eye had just caught the figure of an exceptionally big and ungainly Selenite lying motionless among the stems, face downwards. We stopped.

"'Dead?' I asked. For as yet I have seen no dead in the moon, and I have grown curious.

"'*No!*' exclaimed Phi-oo. 'Him—worker—no work to do. Get little drink then—make sleep—till we him want. What good him wake, eh? No want him walking about.'

"'There's another!' cried I.

"And indeed all that huge extent of mushroom ground was, I found, peppered wit these prostrate figures sleeping under an opiate until the moon had need of them. There were scores of them of all sorts, and we were able to turn some of them over and examine them more precisely than I had been able to do previously. When disturbed they breathed noisily, but did not wake. One I remember very distinctly; he left a strong impression, I think, because some trick of the light and of his attitude was strongly suggestive of a drawn-up human figure. His fore-limbs were long, delicate tentacles—he was some kind of refined manipulator—and the pose of his slumber suggested a submissive suffering. No doubt it was quite a mistake for me to interpret his expression in that way, but I did. And as Phi-oo rolled him over into the darkness among the livid fleshiness again, I felt a distinctly unpleasant sensation, although as he rolled the insect in him was confessed.

"It simply illustrates the unthinking way in which one acquires habits of thought and feeling. To drug the worker one does not want and toss him aside is surely far better than to expel him from his factory to wander starving in the streets. In every complicated social community there is necessarily a certain intermittency in the occupation of all specialized labor, and in this way the trouble of an unemployed problem is altogether anticipated. And yet, so unreasonable are even scientifically trained minds, I still do not like the memory of those prostrate forms amidst those quiet, luminous arcades of fleshy growth, and I avoid that short cut in spite of the inconveniences of its longer, more noisy, and more crowded alternative.

"My alternative route takes me round by a huge, shadowy cavern, very crowded and clamorous, and here it is seen peering out of the hexagonal opening of a sort of honeycomb wall, or parading a large open space behind, or selecting the toys and amulets made to please them by the acephalic dainty-fingered jewelers who work in kennels below, the mothers of the moon-world—the queen bees, as it were, of the hive. They are noble-looking beings, fantastically and sometimes quite beautifully adorned, with a proud carriage and, save for their mouths, almost microscopic heads . . .

"Of the condition of the moon sexes, marrying and giving in marriage, and of birth and so forth among the Selenites, I have as yet been able to learn very little. With the steady progress of Phi-oo in English, however, my ignorance will no doubt as steadily disappear. I am of opinion that, as with the ants and bees, there is in this community a large majority of the members of the neuter sex. Of course on earth in our cities there are now many who never live that life of parentage which is the natural life of man. Here as with the ants, this thing has become a normal condition of the race; and the whole of such replacement as is necessary falls upon this special and by no means numerous class of matrons, the mothers of the moon-world, large and stately beings beautifully fitted to bear the larval Selenite. Unless I misunderstand an explanation of Phi-oo's, they are absolutely incapable of cherishing the young they bring into the moon; periods of foolish indulgence alternate with moods of aggressive violence; and as soon as possible the little creatures, who are quite soft and flabby and pale colored, are transferred to the charge of a variety of celibate females, women 'workers,' as it were, who in some cases possess brains of almost masculine dimensions."

Just at this point, unhappily, this message broke off. Fragmentary and tantalizing as the matter constituting this chapter is, it does nevertheless give a vague, broad impression of an altogether strange and wonderful world—a world with which our own must now prepare to reckon sooner or later. This intermittent trickle of messages, this whispering of a record needle in the darkness of the mountain slopes, is the first warning of such a change in human conditions as mankind has scarcely imagined heretofore. In that planet there are new elements, new appliances, new traditions, an overwhelming avalanche of new ideas, a strange race with whom we must inevitably struggle for mastery—gold as common as iron or wood . . .

## CHAPTER THE TWENTY-FOURTH
## THE GRAND LUNAR

The penultimate message describes, occasionally even with elaborate detail, the encounter between Cavor and the Grand Lunar, who is the ruler or Master of the Moon. Cavor seems to have sent most of it without interference, but to have been interrupted in the concluding portion. The second came after an interval of a week.

The first message begins: "At last I am able to resume this—"; it then becomes illegible for a space, and after a time resumes in mid-sentence.

The missing words of the following sentence are probably "The crowd." There follows quite clearly: "grew even denser as we drew near the palace of the Grand Lunar—if I may call a series of excavations a palace. Everywhere faces stared at me—blank, chitinous gapes and masks, big eyes peering over tremendous forehead plates; below, an undergrowth of smaller creatures dodged and yelped; and grotesque heads poised on sinuous, swanlike, long-jointed necks appeared craning over shoulders and beneath arm-pits. Keeping a welcome space about me marched a cordon of stolid, scuttle-headed guards who had joined us on our leaving the boat in which we had come along the channels of the Central Sea. The flea-like artist with the little brain joined us also, and a thick bunch of lean porter-ants swayed and struggled under the multitude of conveniences that were considered essential to my state. I was carried in a litter during the final stage of our journey. It was made of some very ductile metal that looked dark to me, meshed and woven and with bars of paler metal, and about me as I advanced there grouped itself a long and complicated procession.

"In front, after the manner of heralds, marched four trumpet-faced creatures making a devastating bray; and then came squat, almost beetle-like ushers before and behind, and on either hand a galaxy of learned heads, a sort of animated encyclopedia, who were, Phi-oo explained, to stand about the Grand Lunar for purposes of reference. Not a thing in lunar science, not a point of view or method of thinking, that these wonderful beings did not carry in their heads. Followed guards and porters, and then Phi-oo's shivering brain borne also on a litter. Then came Tsi-puff in a lightly less important litter; then myself on a littler of greater elegance than any other and surrounded by my food and drink attendants. More trumpeters came next, splitting the ear with vehement outcries, and then several big brains, special correspondents one might well call them or historiographers, charged with the task of observing and remembering every detail of this epoch-making interview. A company of attendants, bearing and dragging banners and masses of scented fungi and curious symbols, completed the procession. The way was lined by ushers and officers in caparisons that gleamed like steel, and beyond their line the heads and tentacles of that enormous crowd surged on either hand.

"I will own that I am still by no means induriated to the peculiar effect of the Selenite appearance, and to find myself as it were adrift on this broad sea of excited entomology was by no means agreeable. Just for a space I had something like the 'horrors.' It had come to me before in these lunar caverns, when on occasion I have found myself weaponless and with an undefended back amidst a crowd of these Selenites, but never quite so vividly. It is, of course, as absolutely irrational a feeling as one could well have, and I hope gradually to subdue it. But just for a moment, as I swept forward into the welter of the vast crowd, it was only by gripping my litter tightly and summoning all my will-power that I succeeded in stifling an outcry or some such manifestation. It lasted perhaps three minutes; then I had myself in hand again.

"We ascended the spiral of a vertical way for some time and then passed through a series of huge halls, dome-roofed, and gloriously decorated. The approach to the Grand Lunar was certainly contrived to give one a vivid impression of his greatness. The halls—all happily sufficiently luminous for my terrestrial eye—were a cunning and elaborate crescendo of space and decoration. The effect of their progressive size was enhanced by the steady diminution in the lighting, and by a thin haze of incense that thickened as one advanced. In the earlier ones the vivid, clear light made everything finite and concrete to me. I seemed to advance continually to something larger, dimmer, and less material.

"I must confess that all this splendor made me feel extremely shabby and unworthy. I was unshaven and unkempt; I had brought no razor; I had a coarse beard over my mouth. On earth I have always been inclined to despise any attention to my person beyond a proper care for cleanliness; but under the exceptional circumstances in which I found myself, representing, as I did, my planet and my kind, and depending very largely upon the attractiveness of my appearance for a proper reception, I would have given much for something a little more artistic and dignified than the husks I wore. I had been so serene in the belief that the moon was uninhabited as to overlook such precautions altogether. As it was I was dressed in a flannel jacket, knickerbockers, and golfing stockings, stained with every sort of dirt the moon offered; slippers (of which the left heel was wanting), and a blanket, through a hole in which I thrust my head. (These clothes, indeed, I still wear.) Sharp bristles are anything but an improvement to my cast of features, and there was an unmended tear at the knee of my knickerbockers that showed conspicuously as I squatted in my litter; my right stocking, too, persisted in getting about my ankle. I am fully alive to the injustice my appearance did humanity, and if by any expedient I could have improvised something a little out of the way and imposing I would have done so. But I could hit upon nothing. I did what I could with my blanket—folding it somewhat after the fashion of a toga, and for the rest I sat as upright as the swaying of my litter permitted.

"Imagine the largest hall you have ever been in, elaborately decorated with blue and whitish-blue majolica, lit by blue light, you know not how, and surging with metallic or livid-white creatures of such a mad diversity as I have hinted. Imagine this hall to end in an open archway beyond which is a still larger hall, and beyond this yet another and still larger one, and so on. At the end of the vista a flight of steps, like the steps of Ara Coeli at Rome, ascends out of sight. Higher and higher these steps appear to go as one draws nearer their base. But at last I came under a huge archway and beheld the summit of these steps, and upon it the Grand Lunar exalted on his throne.

"He was seated in a blaze of incandescent blue. A hazy atmosphere filled the place so that its walls seemed invisibly remote. This gave him an effect of floating in a blue-black void. He seemed at first a small, self-luminous cloud, brooding on his glaucous throne; his brain-case must have measured many yards in diameter. For some reason that I cannot fathom a number of blue search-lights coming from behind the throne gave a star-like radiance to the halo immediately surrounding him. About him, and little and indistinct in this glow, a number of body-servants sustained and supported him, and overshadowed and standing in a huge semicircle beneath him were his intellectual subordinates, his remembrancers and computators and searchers, his flatterers and servants, and all the distinguished insects of the court of the moon. Still lower stood ushers and messengers, and then all down the countless steps of the throne were guards, and at the base, enormous, various, indistinct, a vast swaying multitude of the minor dignitaries of the moon. Their feet made a perpetual scraping whisper on the rocky floor, their limbs moved with a rustling murmur.

"As I entered the penultimate hall the music rose and expanded into an imperial magnificence of sound, and the shrieks of the news-bearers died away . . .

"My procession opened out like a fan. My ushers and guards went right and left, and the three litters bearing myself and Phi-oo and Tsi-puff marched across a shiny waste of floor to the foot of the giant stairs. Then began a vast throbbing hum that mingled with the music. The two Selenites dismounted, but I was bidden to remain seated—I imagine as a special honor. The music ceased, but not that humming, and by a simultaneous movement of ten thousand respectful eyes, my attention was directed to the enhaloed supreme intelligence that hovered about us.

"At first as I peered into the radiating blaze, this quintessential brain looked very much like a thin, featureless bladder with dim, undulating ghosts of convolutions writhing visibly within. Then beneath its enormity and just above the edge of the throne one saw with a start minute elfin eyes peering out of the blaze. No face, but eyes, as if they peered through holes. At first I could see no more than these two staring little eyes, and then below I distinguished the little dwarfed body and its insect-jointed limbs, shriveled and white. The eyes stared down at me with a strange intensity, and the lower part of the swollen globe was wrinkled. Ineffectual-looking little hand-tentacles steadied this shape on the throne . . .

"It was great. It was pitiful. One forgot the hall and the crowd.

"I ascended the staircase by jerks. It seemed to me that the purple glowing brain-case above us spread over me, and took more and more of the whole effect into itself as I drew nearer. The tiers of attendants and helpers grouped about their master seemed to dwindle and fade into the glare. I saw that the shadowy attendants were busy spraying that great brain with a cooling spray, and patting and sustaining it. For my own part I sat gripping my swaying litter and staring at the Grand Lunar, unable to turn my gaze aside. And at last, as I reached a little landing that was separated only by ten steps or so from the supreme seat, the woven splendor of the music reached a climax and ceased, and I was left naked, as it were, in the vastness, beneath the still scrutiny of the Grand Lunar's eyes.

"He was scrutinizing the first man he had ever seen . . .

"My eyes dropped at last from his greatness to the faint figures in the blue mist about him, and then down the steps to the massed Selenites, still and expectant in their thousands, packed on the floor below. Once again an unreasonable horror reached out towards me . . . and passed.

"After the pause came the salutation. I was assisted from my litter, and stood awkwardly while a number of curious and no doubt deeply symbolical gestures were vicariously performed for me by two slender officials. The encyclopedic galaxy of the learned that had accompanied me to the entrance of the last hall appeared two steps above me and left and right of me, in readiness for the Grand Lunar's need, and Phi-oo's white brain placed itself about halfway up to the throne in such a position as to communicate easily between us without turning his back on either the Grand Lunar or myself. Tsi-puff took up a position behind him. Dexterous ushers sidled sidewise towards me, keeping a full face to the Presence. I seated myself Turkish fashion, and Phi-oo and Tsi-puff also knelt down above me. There came a pause. The eyes of the nearer court went from me to the Grand Lunar and came back to me, and a hissing and piping of expectation passed across the hidden multitudes below and ceased.

"That humming ceased.

"For the first and last time in my experience the moon was silent.

"I became aware of a faint wheezy noise. The Grand Lunar was addressing me. It was like the rubbing of a finger upon a pane of glass.

"I watched him attentively for a time and then glanced at the alert Phi-oo. I felt amidst those filmy beings ridiculously thick and fleshy and solid, my head all jaw and black hair. My eyes went back to the Grand Lunar. He had ceased; his attendants were busy, and his shining superficies was glistening and running with cooling spray.

"Phi-oo meditated through an interval. He consulted Tsi-puff. Then he began piping his recognizable English—at first a little nervously, so that he was not very clear.

"'M'm—the Grand Lunar—wished to say—wishes to say—he gathers you are—m'm—men—that you are a man from the planet earth. He wishes to say that he welcomes you—and wished to learn—learn, if I may use the word—the state of your world, and the reasons why you came to this.'

"He paused. I was about to reply when he resumed. He proceeded to remarks of which the drift was not very clear, though I am inclined to think they were intended to be complimentary. He told me that the earth was to the moon what the sun is to the earth, and that the Selenites desired very directly to learn about the earth and men. He then told me, no doubt in compliment also, the relative magnitude and diameter of earth and moon, and the perpetual wonder and speculation with which the Selenites had regarded our planet. I meditated with downcast eyes and decided to reply that men too had wondered what might lie in the moon, and had judged it dead, little recking on such magnificence as I had seen that day. The Grand Lunar, in token of recognition, caused his blue search-light to rotate in a very confusing manner, and all about the great hall ran the pipings and whispering and rustlings of the report of what I had said. He then proceeded to put to Phi-oo a number of inquiries which were easier to answer.

"He understood, he explained, that we lived on the surface of the earth, that our air and sea were outside the globe; the latter part, indeed, he already knew from his astronomical specialists. He was very anxious to have more detailed information of what he called this extraordinary state of affairs, for from the solidity of the earth there had always been a disposition to regard it as uninhabitable. He endeavored first to ascertain the extremes of temperature to which we earth beings were exposed, and he was deeply interested by my descriptive treatment of clouds and rain. His imagination was assisted by the fact that the lunar atmosphere in the outer galleries of the night side is not infrequently very foggy. He seemed inclined to marvel that we did

169

not find the sunlight too intense for our eyes, and was interested in my attempt to explain that the sky was tempered to a bluish color through the refraction of the air, though I doubt if he clearly understood that. I explained how the iris of the human eyes can contract the pupil and save the delicate internal structure from the excess of sunlight, and was allowed to approach within a few feet of the Presence in order that this structure might be seen. This led to a comparison of the lunar and terrestrial eyes. The former is not only excessively sensitive to such light as men can see, but it can also *see* heat, and every difference in temperature within the moon renders objects visible to it.

"The iris was quite a new organ to the Grand Lunar. For a time he amused himself by flashing his rays into my face and watching my pupils contract. As a consequence, I was dazzled and blinded for some little time. . . .

"But in spite of that discomfort, I found something reassuring by insensible degrees in the rationality of this business of question and answer. I could shut my eyes, think of my answer, and almost forget that the Grand Lunar has no face. . . .

"When I had descended again to my proper place the Grand Lunar asked how we sheltered ourselves from heat and storms, and I expounded to him the arts of building and furnishing. Here we wandered into misunderstandings and cross-purposes, due largely, I must admit, to the looseness of my expressions. For a long time I had great difficulty in making him understand the nature of a house. To him and his attendant Selenites it seemed no doubt the most whimsical thing in the world that men should build houses when they might descend into excavations, and an additional complication was introduced by the attempt I made to explain that men had originally begun their homes in caves, and that they were now taking their railways and many establishments beneath the surface. Here I think a desire for intellectual completeness betrayed me. There was also a considerable tangle due to an equally unwise attempt on my part to explain about mines. Dismissing this topic at last in an incomplete state, the Grand Lunar inquired what we did with the interior of our globe.

"A tide of twittering and piping swept into the remotest corners of that great assembly when it was at last made clear that we men know absolutely nothing of the contents of the world upon which the immemorial generations of our ancestors have been evolved. Three time had I to repeat that of all the 4,000 miles of substance between the earth and its centre men knew only to the depth of a mile, and that very vaguely. I understood the Grand Lunar to ask why I had come to the moon seeing we had scarcely touched our own planet yet, but he did not trouble me at that time to proceed to an explanation, being too anxious to pursue the details of this mad inversion of all his ideas.

"He reverted to the question of weather, and I tried to describe the perpetually changing sky, and snow, and frost and hurricanes. 'But when the night comes,' he asked, 'is it not cold?'

"I told him it was colder than by day.

"'And does not your atmosphere freeze?'

"I told him no; that it was never cold enough for that, because our nights were so short.

"Not even liquefy?'

"I was about to say 'No,' but then it occurred to me that one part at least of our atmosphere, the water vapor of it, does sometimes liquefy and form dew and sometimes freeze and form frost—a process perfectly analogous to the freezing of all the external atmosphere of the moon during its longer night. I made myself clear on this point, and from there Grand Lunar went on to speak with me of sleep. For the need of sleep that comes so regularly every twenty-four hours to all things is part also of our earthly inheritance. On the moon they rest only at rare intervals and after exceptional exertions. Then I tried to describe to him the soft splendors of a summer night, and from that I passed to a description of those animals that prowl by night and sleep by day. I told him of lions and tigers, and here it seemed that we had come to a deadlock. For, save in their waters, there are no creatures in the moon not absolutely domestic and subject to his will, and so it has been for immemorial years. They have monstrous water creatures, but no evil beasts, and the idea of anything strong and large existing 'outside' in the night is very difficult for them."

*[The record is here too broken to transcribe for the space of perhaps twenty words or more.]*

"He talked with his attendants, as I suppose, upon the strange superficiality and unreasonableness of (man), who lives on the mere surface of a world, a creature of waves and winds and all the chances of space, who cannot even unite to overcome the beasts that prey upon his kind, and yet who dares to invade another planet. During this aside I sat thinking, and then at his desire I told him of the different sorts of men. He searched me with questions. 'And for all sorts of work you have the same sort of men. But who thinks? Who governs?'

"I gave him an outline of the democratic method.

"When I had done he ordered cooling sprays upon his brow and then requested me to repeat my explanation, conceiving something had miscarried.

"Do they not do different things then?' said Phi-oo.

"Some I admitted were thinkers and some officials; some hunted, some were mechanics, some artists, some toilers. 'But *all* rule,' I said.

"'And have they not different shapes to fit them to their different duties?'

"'None that you can see,' I said, 'except perhaps their clothes. Their minds perhaps differ a little,' I reflected.

"'Their minds must differ a great deal,' said the Grand Lunar, 'or they would all want to do the same things.'

"In order to bring myself into a closer harmony with his preconceptions, I said that his surmise was right. 'It was all hidden in the brain,' I said; 'but the difference was there. Perhaps if one could see the minds and souls of men they would be as varied and unequal as the Selenites. There were great men and small men, men who could reach out far and wide, and men who could go swiftly; noisy, trumpet-minded men, and men who could remember without thinking. . . . '"

*[The record is indistinct for three words.]*

"He interrupted me to recall me to my previous statement. 'But you said all men rule?' he pressed.

"He reached out to a salient fact. 'Do you mean,' he asked, 'that there is no Grand Earthly?'

"I thought of several people, but assured him finally there was none. I explained that such autocrats and emperors as we had tried upon earth had usually ended in drink, or vice, or violence, and that the large and influential section of the people of the earth to which I belonged, the Anglo-Saxons, did not mean to try that sort of thing again. At which the Grand Lunar was even more amazed.

"'But how do you keep even such wisdom as you have?' he asked; and I explained to him the way we helped our limited . . ."

*[A word omitted here, probably "brains."]*

"with libraries of books. I explained to him how our science was growing by the united labours of innumerable little men, and on that he made no comment save that it was evident we had mastered much in spite of our social savagery, or we could not have come to the moon. Yet the contrast was very marked. With knowledge the Selemites grew and changed; mankind stored their knowledge about them and remained brutes—equipped. He said this . . . "

*[Here there is a short piece of the record indistinct.]*

"He then caused me to describe how we went about this earth of ours, and I described to him our railways and ships. For a time he could not understand that we had the use of steam only one hundred years, but when he did he was clearly amazed. I may mention as a singular thing that the Selenites use years to count by, just as we do on earth, though I can make nothing of their numeral system. That, however, does not matter, because Phi-oo understands ours. From that I went on to tell him that mankind had dwelt in cities only for nine or ten thousand years, and that we were still not united in one brotherhood, but under many different forms of government. This astonished the Grand Lunar very much, when it was made clear to him. At first he thought we referred merely to administrative areas.

"Our States and Empires are still the rawest sketches of what order will some day be,' I said, and so I came to tell him . . . "

*[At this point a length of record that probably represents thirty or forty words is totally illegible.]*

"The Grand Lunar was greatly impressed by the folly of men in clinging to the inconvenience of diverse tongues. 'They want to communicate and yet not to communicate,' he said , and then for a long time he questioned me closely concerning war.

"He was at first perplexed and incredulous. 'You mean to say,' he asked, seeking confirmation, 'that you run above over the surface of your world—this world, whose riches you have scarcely begun to scrape—killing one another for beasts to eat?'

"I told him that was perfectly correct.

"He asked for particulars to assist his imagination. 'But do not your ships and your poor little cities get injured?' he asked and I found the waste of property and conveniences seemed to impress upon him almost as much as the killing. 'Tell me more,' said the Grand Lunar; 'make me see pictures. I cannot conceive these things.'

"And so, for a space, though something loth, I told him the story of earthly War.

"I told him of the first orders and ceremonies of war, of warnings and ultimatums, and the marshalling and marching of troops. I gave him an idea of maneuvers and positions and battle joined. It told him of sieges and assaults, of starvation and hardship in trenches, and of sentinels freezing in the snow. I told him of routs and surprises, and desperate last stands and faint hopes, and the pitiless pursuit of fugitives and the dead upon the field. I told, too, of the past, of invasions and massacres, of the Huns and Tartars, and the wars of Mahomet and the Caliphs and of the Crusades. And as I went on, and Phi-oo translated, the Selenites cooed and murmured in a steadily intensified emotion.

"I told them an ironclad could fire a shot of a ton twelve miles, and go through twenty feet of iron—and how we could steer torpedoes under water. I went on to describe a Maxim gun in action and what I could imagine of the Battle of Colenso. The Grand Lunar was so incredulous that he interrupted the translation of what I had said in order to have my verification of my account. They particularly doubted my description of the men cheering and rejoicing as they went into battle.

"'But surely they do not like it!' translated Phi-oo.

"I assured them men of my race considered battle the most glorious experience of life, at which the whole assembly was stricken with amazement.

"'But what good is this war?' asked the Grand Lunar, sticking to his theme.

"'Oh! as for *good*!' said I, 'it thins the population!'

"'But why should there be a need—?'

"There came a pause, the cooling sprays impinged upon his brow, and then he spoke again."

*At this point there suddenly becomes predominant in the record a series of undulations that have been apparent as a perplexing complication as far back as Cavor's description of the silence that fell before the first speaking of the Grand Lunar. These undulations are evidently the result of radiations proceeding from the lunar source, and their persistent approximation to the alternating signals of Cavor is curiously suggestive of some operator deliberately seeking to mix them in with his message and render it illegible. At first they are small and regular, so that with a little care and the loss of very few words we have been able to disentangle Cavor's message; then they become broad and larger, then suddenly they are irregular, with an irregularity that gives the effect at last of someone scribbling through a line of writing. For a long time nothing can be made of this madly zigzagging trace; then quite abruptly the interruption ceases, leaves a few words clear, and then resumes and continues for all the rest of the message, completely obliterating whatever Cavor was attempting to transmit. Why, if this is indeed a deliberate intervention, the Selenites should have preferred to let Cavor go on transmitting his message in happy ignorance of their obliteration of its record, when it was clearly quite in their power and much more easy and convenient for them to stop his proceedings at any time, is a problem to which I can contribute nothing. The thing seems to have happened so, and that is all I can say. This last rag of his description of the Grand Lunar begins in mid-sentence:*

"Interrogated me very closely upon my secret. I was able in a little while to get to an understanding with them, and at last to elucidate what has been a puzzle to me ever since I realized the vastness of their science, namely, how it is they themselves have never discovered 'Cavorite.' I find they know of it as a theoretical substance, but they have always regarded it as a practical impossibility, because for some reason there is no helium in the moon, and helium—"

*[Across the last letters of helium slashes the resumption of that obliterating trace. Note the word "secret," for on that, and that alone, I base my interpretation of the last message, as both Mr. Wendigee and myself now believe it to be, that he is ever likely to send us.]*

CHAPTER THE TWENTY-FIFTH<br>THE LAST MESSAGE CAVOR SENT TO THE EARTH

In this unsatisfactory manner the penultimate message of Cavor dies out. One seems to see him there amidst his blue-lit apparatus intently signaling us to the last, all unaware of the curtain of confusion that drops between us; all unaware, too, of the final dangers that even then must have been creeping upon him. His disastrous want of vulgar common sense had utterly betrayed him. He had talked of war, he had talked of all the strength and irrational violence of men, of their insatiable aggressions, their tireless futility of conflict. He had filled the whole moon-world with this impression of our race, and then I think it plain he admitted that upon himself alone hung the possibility—at least for a long time—of any other men reaching the moon. The line the cold, inhuman reason of the moon would take seems plain enough to me, and a suspicion of it, and then perhaps some sudden sharp realization of it, must have come to him. One imagines him going about the moon with the remorse of this fatal indiscretion growing in his mind. During a certain time most assuredly the Grand Lunar was deliberating the new situation, and for all that time Cavor went as free as ever he had gone. We imagine that obstacles of some sort prevented his getting to his electro-magnetic apparatus again after that last message I have given. For some days we received nothing. Perhaps he was having fresh audiences, and trying to evade his previous admissions. Who can hope to guess?

And then suddenly, like a cry in the night, like a cry that is followed by a stillness, came the last message. It is the briefest fragment, the broken beginnings of two sentences.

The first was:

"I was mad to let the Grand Lunar know—"

There was an interval of perhaps a minute. One imagines some interruption from without. A departure from the instrument—a dreadful hesitation among the looming masses of apparatus in that dim, blue-lit cavern—a sudden rush back to it, full of resolve that came too late. Then, as if it were hastily transmitted came:

"Cavorite made as follows: take—"

There followed one word, a quite unmeaning word as it stands—

"uless."

And that is all.

It may be he made a hasty attempt to spell "useless" when his fate was close upon him. Whatever it was that was happening about that apparatus, we cannot tell. Whatever it was we shall never, I know, receive another message from the moon. For my own part a vivid dream has come to my help, and I see, almost as plainly as though I had seen it in actual fact, a blue-lit disheveled Cavor struggling in the grip of a great multitude of those insect Selenites, struggling ever more desperately and hopelessly as they swarm upon him, shouting, expostulating, perhaps even at last fighting, and being forced backward step by step out of all speech or sign of his fellows, for evermore into the Unknown—into the dark, into that silence that has no end.

# from *The Food of the Gods* (1904)

*The Food of the Gods appears a few years after the half-decade that produced the great scientific romances, but it begins with a situation that comes straight out of that tradition: the invention of "Boomfood," or what its inventors name "Herakleophorbia," a chemical that causes continuous and extraordinary growth. At first Boomfood causes disaster. Unlike the usual scientific romance, however, before it is half through* The Food of the Gods *has begun to realize a second possibility for such stupendous growth, and it takes increasingly seriously the mental and moral enlargement that takes place in the few children fed Boomfood. In the last section, when some sixty humans have achieved an adult height of about forty feet and strife is beginning between the two "species" of humans, the novel ends abruptly with the utopian possibilities the giants represent alive and full of potential. The comedy of the beginning becomes not just a satire on scientific overreaching but a rendering of the very limitations that the Giants will supposedly overcome. The selection describes those early horrific events. The inventors of Boomfood, Mr. Bensington and Professor Redwood, establish an "Experimental Farm" run by two incompetents, Mr. and Mrs. Skinner. Mr. Skinner speaks with a severe lisp. The scenes show Wells at his comic peak.*

\* \* \* \* \*

### from Chapter the Second
### The Experimental Farm
#### 1

Mr. Bensington proposed originally to try this stuff, so soon as he was really able to prepare it, upon tadpoles. One always does try this sort of thing upon tadpoles to begin with; that being what tadpoles are for. And it was agreed that he should conduct the experiments and not Redwood, because Redwood's laboratory was occupied with the ballistic apparatus and animals necessary for an investigation into the Diurnal Variation in the Butting Frequency of the Young Bull Calf, an investigation that was yielding curves of an abnormal and very perplexing sort, and the presence of glass globes of tadpoles was extremely undesirable while this particular research was in progress.

But when Mr. Bensington conveyed to his cousin Jane something of what he had in mind, she put a prompt veto upon the importation of any considerable number of tadpoles, or any such experimental creatures, into their flat. She had no objection whatever to his use of one of the rooms of the flat for the purposes of a non-explosive

176

chemistry that so far as she was concerned came to nothing; and she let him have a gas furnace and a sink and a dust-tight cupboard of refuge from the weekly storm of cleaning she would not forgo. And having known people addicted to drink, she regarded his solicitude for distinction in learned societies as an excellent substitute for the coarser form of depravity. But any sort of living things in quantity, "wriggly" as they were bound to be alive, and "smelly" dead, she could not and would not abide. She said these things were certain to be unhealthy, and Bensington was notoriously a delicate man—it was nonsense to say he wasn't. And when Bensington tried to make the enormous importance of this possible discovery clear, she said that it was all very well, but if she consented to his making everything nasty and unwholesome in the place (and that was what it all came to) then she was certain he would be the first to complain.

And Mr. Bensington went up and down the room, regardless of his corns, and spoke to her quite firmly and angrily without the slightest effect. He said that nothing ought to stand in the way of the Advancement of Science, and she said that the Advancement of Science was one thing and having a lot of tadpoles in a flat was another; he said that in Germany it was an ascertained fact that a man with an idea like his would at once have twenty thousand properly-fitted cubic feet of laboratory placed at his disposal, and she said she was glad and always had been glad that she was not a German; he said that it would make him famous for ever, and she said it was much more likely to make him ill to have a lot of tadpoles in a flat like theirs; he said he was master in his own house, and she said that rather than wait on a lot of tadpoles she'd go as matron to a school; and then he asked her to be reasonable, and she asked *him* to be reasonable then and give up all this about tadpoles; and he said she might respect his ideas, and she said not if they were smelly she wouldn't; and then he gave way completely and said—in spite of the classical remarks of Huxley upon the subject—a bad word. Not a very bad word it was, but bad enough.

And after that she was greatly offended and had to be apologized to, and the prospect of ever trying the Food of the Gods upon tadpoles in their flat at any rate vanished completely in the apology.

So Bensington had to consider some other way of carrying out these experiments in feeding that would be necessary to demonstrate his discovery, so soon as he had his substance isolated and prepared. For some days he meditated upon the possibility of boarding out his tadpoles with some trustworthy person, and then the chance sight of the phrase in a newspaper turned his thoughts to an Experimental Farm.

And chicks. Directly he thought of it, he thought of it as a poultry farm. He was suddenly taken with a vision of wildly growing chicks. He conceived a picture of coops and runs, outsize and still more outsize coops, and runs progressively larger. Chicks are so accessible, so easily fed and observed, so much drier to handle and measure, that for his purpose tadpoles seemed to him now, in comparison with them, quite wild and uncontrollable beasts. He was quite puzzled to understand why he had not thought of chicks instead of tadpoles from the beginning. Among other

177

things it would have saved all this trouble with his cousin Jane. And when he suggested this to Redwood, Redwood quite agreed with him.

Redwood said he was convinced that in working so much upon needlessly small animals experimental physiologists made a great mistake. It is exactly like making experiments in chemistry with an insufficient quantity of material; errors of observation and manipulation become disproportionately large. It was of extreme importance just at present that scientific men should assert their right to have their material *big*. That was why he was doing his present series of experiments at the Bond Street College upon Bull Calves, in spite of a certain amount of inconvenience to the students and professors of other subjects caused by their incidental levity in the corridors. But the curves he was getting were quite exceptionally interesting, and would, when published, amply justify his choice. For his own part, were it not for the inadequate endowment of science in this country, he would never, if he could avoid it, work on anything smaller than a whale. But a Public Vivarium on a scale sufficient to render this possible was, he feared, at present, in this country at any rate, a Utopian demand. In Germany—Etc.

As Redwood's bull calves needed his daily attention, the selection and equipment of the Experimental Farm fell largely on Bensington. The entire cost also, it was understood, was to be defrayed by Bensington, at least until a grant could be obtained. Accordingly he alternated his work in the laboratory of his flat with farm-hunting up and down the lines that run southward out of London, and his peering spectacles, his simple baldness, and his lacerated cloth shoes filled the owners of numerous undesirable properties with vain hopes. And he advertised in several daily papers, and *Nature* for a responsible couple (married), punctual, active, and used to poultry, to take entire charge of an Experimental Farm of three acres.

He found the place he seemed in need of at Hickleybrow, near Urshot in Kent. It was a queer little isolated place, in a dell surrounded by old pine woods that were black and forbidding at night. A humped shoulder of down cut it off from the sunset, and a gaunt well with a shattered penthouse dwarfed the dwelling. The little house was creeperless, several windows were broken, and the cart shed had a black shadow at midday. It was a mile and a half from the end house of the village, and its loneliness was very doubtfully relieved by an ambiguous family of echoes.

The place impressed Bensington as being eminently adapted to the requirements of scientific research. He walked over the premises sketching out coops and runs with a sweeping arm, and he found the kitchen capable of accommodating a series of incubators and foster mothers with the very minimum of alternation. He took the place then and there; on his way back to London he stopped at Dunton Green and closed with an eligible couple that had answered his advertisements, and that same evening he succeeded in isolating a sufficient quantity of Herakleophorbia II to more than justify these engagements.

The eligible couple who were destined under Mr. Bensington to be the first almoners on earth of the Food of the Gods, were not only very perceptibly aged, but

178

also extremely dirty. This latter point Mr. Bensington did not observe, because nothing destroys the powers of general observation quite so much as a life of experimental science. They were named Skinner, Mr. and Mrs. Skinner, and Mr. Bensington interviewed them in a small room with hermetically sealed windows, a spotted overmantel looking-glass, and some ailing calceolarias.

Mrs. Skinner was a very little old woman, capless, with dirty white hair drawn back very, very tightly from a face that had begun by being chiefly, and was now through the loss of teeth and chin and the wrinkling up of everything else, ending by being almost exclusively—nose. She was dressed in slate color (so far as her dress had any color) slashed in one place with red flannel. She let him in and talked to him guardedly and peered at him round and over her nose, while Mr. Skinner she alleged made some alteration in his toilette. She had one tooth that got into her articulation, and she held her two long wrinkled hands nervously together. She told Mr. Bensington that she had managed fowls for years, and knew all about incubators; in fact, they themselves had run a Poultry Farm at one time, and it had only failed at last through the want of pupils. "It's the pupils as pay," said Mrs. Skinner.

Mr. Skinner, when he appeared, was a large-faced man with a lisp, and a squint that made him look over the top of your head, slashed slippers that appealed to Mr. Bensington's sympathies, and a manifest shortness of buttons. He held his coat and shirt together with one hand and traced patterns on the black and gold tablecloth with the index finger of the other, while his disengaged eye watched Mr. Bensington's sword of Damocles, so to speak, with an expression of sad detachment. "You don't want to run thith Farm for profit. No, Thir. Ith all the thame, Thir. Ekthperimenth! Prethithely."

He said they could go to the farm at once. He was doing nothing at Dunton Green except a little tailoring. "It ithn't the thmart pathe I thought it wath, and what I get ithent thkarthley worth having," he said, "tho that if it ith any convenienth to you for uth to come . . ."

And in a week Mr. and Mrs. Skinner were installed in the farm, and the jobbing carpenter from Hickleybrow was diversifying the task of erecting runs and hen-houses with a systematic discussion of Mr. Bensington.

"I haven't theen much of 'im yet," said Mr. Skinner. "But ath far ath I can make 'im out 'e theemth to be a thtewpid o' fool."

"*I* thought 'e seemed a bit dotty," said the carpenter form Hickleybrow.

"'E fanthieth 'imthelf about poultry," said Mr. Skinner. "O my goodneth! You'd think nobody knew nothin' about poultry thept 'im"

"'E *looks* like a 'en," said the carpenter from Hickleybrow; "what with them spectacles of 'is.'"

Mr. Skinner came closer to the carpenter from Hickleybrow and spoke in a confidential manner, and one sad eye regarded the distant village and one was bright and wicked. "Got to be meathured every blethed day—every blethed 'en, 'e thayth. Tho ath to thee they grow properly. What oh . . . eh? Every blethed 'en—every blethed day."

And Mr. Skinner put up his hand to laugh behind it in a refined and contagious manner, and humped his shoulders very much—and only the other eye of him failed to participate in his laughter. Then doubting if the carpenter had quite got the point of it, he repeated in a penetrating whisper: "*Meathured!*"

"'E's worse than our old guvnor; I'm dratted if 'e ain't," said the carpenter from Hickleybrow.

## 2

Experimental work is the most tedious thing in the world (unless it be the reports of it in the *Philosophical Transactions*), and it seemed a long time to Mr. Bensington before his first dream of enormous possibilities was replaced by a crumb of realization. He had taken the Experimental Farm in October, and it was May before the first inklings of success began. Herakleophorbia I. and II. and III. had to be tried, and failed; there was trouble with the rats of the Experimental Farm, and there was trouble with the Skinners. The only way to get Skinner to do anything he was told to do was to dismiss him. Then he would rub his unshaven chin—he was always unshaven most miraculously and yet never bearded—with a flattened hand, and look at Mr. Bensington with one eye, and over him with the other, and say, "Oo, of courthe, Thir—if you're *theriouth* . . . !"

But at last success dawned. And its herald was a letter in the long slender handwriting of Mr. Skinner.

"The new Brood are out," wrote Mr. Skinner, "and don't quite like the look of them. Growing very rank—quite unlike what the similar lot was before your last directions was given. The last before the cat got them was a very nice stocky chick, but these are Growing like thistles. I never saw. They peck so hard, striking above boot top, that am unable to give exact Measures as requested. They are regular Giants and eating as such. We shall want more corn very soon, for you never saw such chicks to eat. Bigger than Bantams. Going on at this rate they ought to be a bird for show, rank as they are. Plymouth Rocks won't be in it. Had a scare last night thinking that cat was at them, and when I looked out at the window could have sworn I see her getting in under the wire. The chicks was all awake and pecking about hungry when I went out, but could not see anything of the cat. So gave them a peck of corn, and fastened up safe. Shall be glad to know if the Feeding to be continued as directed. Food you mixed is pretty near all gone, and do not like to mix any more myself on account of the accident with the pudding. With best wishes from us both, and soliciting continuance of esteemed favors,

"Respectfully yours,
"ALFRED NEWTON SKINNER."

The allusion towards the end referred to a milk pudding with which some Herakleophorbia II. had got itself mixed, with painful and very nearly fatal results to the Skinners.

But Mr. Bensington, reading between the lines, saw in this rankness of growth the attainment of his long-sought goal. The next morning he alighted at Urshot station, and in the bag in his hand he carried, sealed in three tins, a supply of the Food of the Gods sufficient for all the chicks in Kent.

It was a bright and beautiful morning late in May, and his corns were so much better that he resolved to walk through Hickleybrow to his farm. It was three miles and a half altogether, through the park and village and then along the green glades of the Hickleybrow preserves. The trees were all dusted with the green spangles of high spring, the hedges were full of stitchwort and campion and the woods of blue hyacinths and purple orchids, and everywhere there was a great noise of birds, thrushes, blackbirds, robins, finches, and many more; and in one warm corner of the park some bracken was unrolling, and there was a leaping and rushing of fallow deer.

These things brought back to Mr. Bensington his early and forgotten delight in life; before him the promise of his discovery grew bright and joyful, and it seemed to him that indeed he must have come upon the happiest day in his life. And when in the sunlit run by the sandy bank under the shadow of the pine trees he saw the chicks that had eaten the food he had mixed for them, gigantic and gawky, bigger already than many a hen that is married and settled; and still growing, still in their first soft yellow plumage (just faintly marked with brown along the back), he knew indeed that his happiest day had come.

At Mr. Skinner's urgency he went into the run; but after he had been pecked through the cracks in his shoes once or twice he got out again, and watched these monsters through the wire netting. He peered close to the netting, and followed their movements as though he had never seen a chick before in his life.

"What they'll be when they're gown up ith impothible to think," said Mr. Skinner.

"Big as a horse," said Mr. Bensington.

"Pretty near," said Mr. Skinner.

"Several people could dine off a wing!" said Mr. Bensington. "They'd cut up into joints like butcher's meat."

"They won't go on growing at thith pathe though," said Mr. Skinner.

"No?" said Mr. Bensington.

"No," said Mr. Skinner. "I know thith thort. They begin rank, but they don't go on, bleth you! No."

There was a pause.

"It'th management," said Mr. Skinner modestly.

Mr. Bensington turned his glasses on him suddenly.

"We got 'em almoth ath big at the other plathe," said Mr. Skinner, with his better eye piously uplifted and letting himself go a little; "me and the mithith."

Mr. Bensington made his usual general inspection of the premises, but he speedily returned to the new run. It was, you know, in truth ever so much more than he had dared to expect. The course of science is so tortuous and so slow; after the clear promises and before the practical realization arrives there comes almost always year after year of intricate contrivance, and here—here was the Food of the Gods arriving after less than a year of testing! It seemed too good—too good. That Hope Deferred which is the daily food of the scientific imagination was to be his no more! So at least it seemed to him then. He came back and stared at these stupendous chicks of his time after time.

"Let me see," he said. "They're ten days old. And by the side of an ordinary chick I should fancy—about six or seven times as big. . . ."

"It'th about time we artht for a rithe in thkrew," said Mr. Skinner to his wife. "He'th ath pleathed ath Punth about the way we got thoth chickth on in the further run—pleathed ath Punth he ith."

He bent confidentially towards her. "Thinkth it'th that old food of hith," he said behind his hand, and made a noise of suppressed laughter in his pharyngeal cavity. . . .

Mr. Bensington was indeed a happy man that day. He was in no mood to find fault with details of management. The sunshine certainly brought out the accumulating slovenliness of the Skinner couple more vividly than he had ever seen it before. But his comments were of the gentlest. The fencing of many of the runs was out of order, but he seemed to consider it quite satisfactory when Mr. Skinner explained that it was a "fokth or a dog or thomething" did it. He pointed out that the incubator had not been cleaned.

"That it *asn't*, Sir," said Mrs. Skinner with her arms folded, smiling coyly behind her nose. "We don't seem to have had time to clean it not since we been 'ere. . . ."

He went upstairs to see some ratholes that Skinner said would justify a trap—they certainly were enormous—and discovered that the room in which the Food of the Gods was mixed with meal and bran was in a quite disgraceful disorder. The Skinners were the sort of people who find a use for cracked saucers and old cans and pickle jars and mustard boxes, and the place was littered with these. In one corner a great pile of apples that Skinner had saved was decaying and from a nail in the sloping part of the ceiling hung several rabbit skins upon which he proposed to test his gift as a furrier. ("There ithn't mutth about furth and thingth that *I* don't know," said Skinner.)

Mr. Bensington certainly sniffed critically at this disorder, but he made no unnecessary fuss, and even when he found a wasp regaling itself in a gallipot half full of Herakleophorbia IV., he simply remarked mildly that his substance was better sealed from the damp than exposed to the air in that manner.

And he turned from these things at once to remark—what had been for some time in his mind—"I *think*, you know, Skinner—I shall kill one of these chicks—as a specimen. I think we will kill it this afternoon, and I will take it back with me to London."

He pretended to peer into another gallipot and then took off his spectacles to wipe them.

"I should like," he said, "I should like very much to have some relic—some memento—of this particular brood at this particular day.

"By-the-by," he said, "you don't give those little chicks meat?"

"Oh! *no*, Thir," said Skinner, "I can athure you, Thir, we know far too much about the management of fowlth of all detheriptionth to do anything of that thort."

"Quite sure you don't throw your dinner refuse—I thought I noticed the bones of a rabbit scattered about the far corner of the run—"

But when they came to look at them they found they were the larger bones of a cat picked very clean and dry.

* * * * *

from CHAPTER THE THIRD<br>THE GIANT RATS<br>1

It was two nights after the disappearance of Mr. Skinner that the Podbourne doctor was out late near Hankey, driving in his buggy. He had been up all night assisting another undistinguished citizen into this curious world of ours; and his task accomplished, he was driving homeward in a drowsy mood enough. It was about two o'clock in the morning, and the waning moon was rising. The summer night had gone cold, and there was a low-lying whitish mist that made things indistinct. He was quite alone—for his coachman was ill in bed—and there was nothing to be seen on either hand but a drifting mystery of hedge running athwart the yellow glare of his lamps, and nothing to hear but the clitter clatter of his horse and the gride and hedge echo of his wheels. His horse was as trustworthy as himself, and one does not wonder that he dozed. . . .

You know that intermittent drowsing as one sits, the drooping of the head, the nodding to the rhythm of the wheels, then chin upon breast, and at once the sudden start up again.

*Pitter, litter, patter.*

"What was that?"

It seemed to the doctor he had heard a thin shrill squeal close at hand. For a moment he was quite awake. He said a word or two of underserved rebuke to his horse, and looked about him. He tried to persuade himself that he had heard a distant squeal of a fox—or perhaps a young rabbit gripped by a ferret.

*Swish, swish, swish, pitter, patter, swish—* . . .

"What was that?"

He felt he was getting fanciful. He shook his shoulders and told his horse to get on. He listened and heard nothing.

Or was it nothing?

He had the queerest impression that something had just peeped over the hedge at him, a queer big head. With round ears! He peered hard, but he could see nothing.

"Nonsense," said he.

He sat up with an idea that he had dropped into a nightmare, gave his horse the slightest touch of the whip, spoke to it and peered again over the hedge. The glare of his lamp, however, together with the mist, rendered things indistinct, and he could distinguish nothing. It came into his head, he says, that there could be nothing there, because if there was his horse would have shied at it. Yet for all that his senses remained nervously awake.

Then he heard quite distinctly a soft pattering of feet in pursuit along the road.

He would not believe his ears about that. He could not look round, for the road just there had a sinuous curve. He whipped up his horse and glanced sideways again. And then he saw quite distinctly where a ray from his lamp leapt a low stretch of hedge, the curved back of—some big animal, he couldn't tell what, going along in quick convulsive leaps.

He says he thought of the old tales of witchcraft—the thing was so utterly unlike any animal he knew, and he tightened his hold on the reins for fear of the fear of his horse. Educated man as he was, he admits he asked himself if this could be something that his horse could not see.

Ahead, and drawing near in silhouette against the rising moon, was the outline of the little hamlet of Hankey, comforting, though it showed never a light, and he cracked his whip and spoke again and then in a flash the rats were at him!

He had passed a gate, and as he did so, the foremost rat came leaping over into the road. The thing sprang upon him out of vagueness into the utmost clearness, the sharp, eager, round-eared face, the long body exaggerated by its movement; and what particularly struck him, the pink webbed forefeet of the beast. What must have made it more horrible to him at the time, was that he had no idea the thing was any created beast he knew. He did not recognize it as a rat, because of its size. His horse gave a bound as the thing dropped into the road beside it. The little lane woke into tumult at the report of the whip and the doctor's shout. The whole thing suddenly went fast.

*Rattle-clatter, clash, clatter.*

The doctor, one gathers, stood up, shouted to his horse, and slashed with all his strength. The rat winced and swerved most reassuringly at his blow—in the glare of his lamp he could see the fur furrow under the lash—and he slashed again and again, heedless and unaware of the second pursuer that gained upon his offside.

He let the reins go, and glanced back to discover the third rat in pursuit behind. . . .

His horse bounded forward. The buggy leapt high at a rut. For a frantic minute perhaps everything seemed to be going in leaps and bounds. . . .

It was sheer good luck the horse came down in Hankey and not either before or after the houses had been passed.

No one knows how the horse came down, whether it stumbled or whether the rat on the offside really got home with one of those slashing down strokes of the incisors (given with the full weight of the body); and the doctor never discovered that he himself was bitten until he was inside the brickmaker's house, much less did he discover when the bite occurred, though bitten he was and badly—a long slash like the slash of a double tomahawk that had cut two parallel ribbons of flesh from his left shoulder.

He was standing up in his buggy at one moment, and in the next he had leapt to the ground, and with his ankle, though he did no know it, badly sprained, he was cutting furiously at a third rat that was flying directly at him. He scarcely remembers the leap he must have made over the top of the wheel as the buggy came over, so obliteratingly hot and swift did his impressions rush upon him. I think myself the horse reared up with the rat biting again at his throat, and fell sideways, and carried the whole affair over; and that the doctor sprang, as it were, instinctively. As the buggy came down, the receiver of the lamp smashed, and suddenly poured a flare of blazing oil, a thud of white flame into the struggle.

That was the first thing the brickmaker saw.

He had heard the clatter of the doctor's approach and—though the doctor's memory has nothing of this—wild shouting. He had got out of bed hastily, and as he did so came the terrific smash, and up shot the glare outside the rising blind. "It was brighter than day," he says. He stood, blind cord in hand, and stared out of the window at a nightmare transformation of the familiar road before him. The black figure of the doctor with its whirling whip danced out against the flame. The horse kicked indistinctly, half hidden by the blaze, with a rat at its throat. In the obscurity against the churchyard wall, the eyes of a second monster shone wickedly. Another—a mere dreadful blackness with red-lit eyes and flesh-colored hands—clutched unsteadily on the wall coping to which it had leapt at the flash of the exploding lamp.

You know the keen face of a rat, those two sharp teeth, those pitiless eyes. Seen magnified to near six times its linear dimensions, and still more magnified by darkness and amazement and the leaping fancies of a fitful blaze, it must have been an ill sight for the brickmaker—still more than half asleep.

Then the doctor had grasped the opportunity, that momentary respite the flare afforded, and was out of the brickmaker's sight below battering the door with the butt of his whip.

The brickmaker would not let him in until he had got a light.

There are those who have blamed the man for that, but until I know my own courage better, I hesitate to join their number.

The doctor yelled and hammered. . . .

The brickmaker says he was weeping with terror when at last the door was opened.

"Bolt," gasped the doctor, "bolt," and could say no more. He tried to move to the door to help and sank down on the chair beside the clock while the brickmaker fastened the door.

"I don't know what they *are*!" he repeated several times. "I don't know what they *are*"—with a high note on the "are."

185

The brickmaker would have got him whisky, but the doctor would not be left alone with nothing but a flickering light just then.

It was long before the brickmaker could get him to go upstairs . . .

And when the fire was out the giant rats came back, took the dead horse, dragged it across the churchyard into the brickfield and ate it until it was dawn, none even then daring to disturb them. . . .

* * * * *

# "The Country of the Blind"
# (1904)

*"The Country of the Blind" is a kind a parable and, like many parables, its meaning is enigmatic. It has been common for critics to see it simply as an allegory of the oppression of the gifted genius (Nunez, who can see) by the mass of common people (the society of The Blind). Certainly, this is a start, but Wells has complicated the allegory, first by making it clear that Nunez does not have the blind people's happiness in mind at all when he sets out to become their King; second by showing with great ingenuity how well-adapted the blind are to their environment. It is not at all clear that Nunez has anything to contribute to their society or their lives. In the late 1930s Wells rewrote the end of the story: despite warnings from Nunez, who can see an earthquake high in the mountains, the blind stay in their valley and are destroyed. The change diminishes some of the ambiguity. At the end of the revised version, however, when Medina-saroté declines the possibility of sight, we may still wonder whether she is wise or simply cowardly. The original version of the story, printed here, renders Nunez's escape deeply and irresolvably ambiguous: he revels in sight, but it may well be his dying moment. Is Nunez a visionary like the philosopher who escapes Plato's cave? Or is he an egomaniac, like Griffen? Or is he simply an incompetent, like the scientists in* The Food of the Gods?

Three hundred miles and more from Chimborazo, one hundred from the snows of Cotopaxi, in the wildest wastes of Ecuador's Andes, there lies that mysterious mountain valley, cut off from the world of men, the Country of the Blind. Long years ago that valley lay so far open to the world that men might come at last through frightful gorges and over an icy pass into its equable meadows; and thither indeed men came, a family or so of Peruvian half-breeds fleeing from the lust and tyranny of an evil Spanish ruler. Then came the stupendous outbreak of Mindobamba, when it was night in Quito for seventeen days, and the water was boiling at Yaguachi and all the fish floating dying even as far as Guayaquil; everywhere along the Pacific slopes there were landslips and swift thawings and sudden floods, and one whole side of the old Arauca crest slipped and came down in thunder, and cut off the Country of the Blind forever from the exploring feet of men. But one of these early settlers had chanced to be on the hither side of the gorges when the world had so terribly shaken itself, and he perforce had to forget his wife and his child and all the friends and possessions he had left up there, and start life over again in the lower world. He started it again but ill, blindness overtook him, and he died of punishment in the mines; but the story he told begot a legend that lingers along the length of the Cordilleras of the Andes to this day.

He told of his reason for venturing back from that fastness, into which he had first been carried lashed to a llama, beside a vast bale of gear, when he was a child. The valley he said, had in it all that the heart of man could desire—sweet water, pasture, an even climate, slopes of rich brown soil with tangles of a shrub that bore an excellent fruit, and on one side great hanging forests of pine that held the avalanches high. Far overhead, on three sides, vast cliffs of gray-green rock were capped by cliffs of ice; but the glacier stream came not to them but flowed away by the farther slopes, and only now and then huge ice masses fell on the valley side. In this valley it neither rained nor snowed, but the abundant springs gave a rich green pasture, that irrigation would spread over all the valley space. The settlers did well indeed there. Their beasts did well and multiplied and but one thing marred their happiness. Yet it was enough to mar it greatly. A strange disease had come upon them, and had made all the children born to them there—and, indeed, several older children also—blind. It was to seek some charm or antidote against this plague of blindness that he had with fatigue and danger and difficulty returned down the gorge. In those days, in such cases, men did not think of germs and infections but of sins; and it seemed to him that the reason of this affliction must lie in the negligence of these priestless immigrants to set up a shrine so soon as they entered the valley. He wanted a shrine—a handsome, cheap, effectual shrine—to be erected in the valley; he wanted relics and such-like potent things of faith, blessed objects and mysterious medals and prayers. In his wallet he had a bar of native silver for which he would not account; he insisted there was none in the valley with something of the insistence of an inexpert liar. They had all clubbed their money and ornaments together, having little need for such treasure up there, he said, to buy them holy help against their ill. I figure this dim-eyed young mountaineer, sunburnt, gaunt, and anxious, hat-brim clutched feverishly, a man all unused to the ways of the lower world, telling this story to some keen-eyed, attentive priest before the great convulsion; I can picture him presently seeking to return with pious and infallible remedies against that trouble, and the infinite dismay with which he must have faced the tumbled vastness where the gorge had once come out. But the rest of his story of mischances is lost to me, save that I know of his evil death after several years. Poor stray from that remoteness! The stream that had once made the gorge now bursts from the mouth of a rocky cave, and the legend his poor, ill-told story set going developed into the legend of a race of blind men somewhere "over there" one may still hear to-day.

And amidst the little population of that now isolated and forgotten valley the disease ran its course. The old became groping and purblind, the young saw but dimly, and the children that were born to them saw never at all. But life was very easy in that snow-rimmed basin, lost to all the world, with neither thorns nor briars, with no evil insects nor any beasts save the gentle breed of llamas they had lugged and thrust and followed up the beds of the shrunken rivers in the gorges up which they had come. The seeing had become purblind so gradually that they scarcely noted their loss. They guided the sightless youngsters hither and thither until they knew the whole valley marvelously, and when at last sight died out among them the race lived on. They had even time to adapt themselves to the blind control of fire, which they made carefully in stoves of stone. They were a simple strain of people at the first, unlettered, only slightly touched with the Spanish civilization, but with something of a tradition of the arts of old Peru and of its lost philosophy. Generation followed generation. They forgot many things; they devised many things. Their tradition of the greater world they came from became mythical in color and uncertain. In all things save sight they were strong and able; and presently the chance of birth and heredity sent one who had an original mind and who could talk and persuade among them, and then afterwards another. These two passed, leaving their effects, and the little community grew in numbers and in understanding, and met and settled social and economic problems that arose. Generation followed generation. There came a time when a child was born who was fifteen generations from that ancestor who went out of the valley with a bar of silver to seek God's aid, and who never returned. Thereabouts it chanced that a man came into this community from the outer world. And this is a story of that man.

He was a mountaineer from the country near Quito, a man who had been down to the sea and had seen the world, a reader of books in an original way, an acute and enterprising man, and he was taken on by a party of Englishmen who had come out to Ecuador to climb mountains, to replace one of their three Swiss guides who had fallen ill. He climbed here and he climbed there, and then came the attempt on Parascotopetl, the Matterhorn of the Andes, in which he was lost to the outer world. The story of the accident has been written a dozen times. Pointer's narrative is the best. He tells how the party worked their difficult and almost vertical way up to the very foot of the last and greatest precipice, and how they built a night shelter amidst the snow up on a little shelf of rock, and, with a touch of real dramatic power, how presently they found Nunez had gone from them. They shouted, and there was no reply; shouted and whistled, and for the rest of that night they slept no more.

As the morning broke they saw the traces of his fall. It seems impossible he could have uttered a sound. He had slipped eastward towards the unknown side of the mountain; far below he had struck a steep slope of snow, and ploughed his way down it in the midst of a snow avalanche. His track went straight to the edge of a frightful precipice, and beyond that everything was hidden. Far, far below, and hazy with distance, they could see trees rising out of a narrow, shut-in valley—the lost Country of the Blind. But they did not know it was the lost Country of the Blind, nor distinguish it in any way from any other narrow streak of upland valley. Unnerved by the disaster, they abandoned their attempt in the afternoon,

189

and Pointer was called away to the war before he could make another attack. To this day Parascotopetl lifts an unconquered crest, and Pointer's shelter crumbles unvisited amidst the snows.

And the man who fell survived.

At the end of the slope he fell a thousand feet, and came down in the midst of a cloud of snow upon a snow slope even steeper than the one above. Down this he was whirled, stunned and insensible, but without a bone broken in his body; and then at last came to gentler slopes, and at last rolled out and lay still, buried amidst a softening heap of the white masses that had accompanied and saved him. He came to himself with a dim fancy that he was ill in bed; then realized his position with a mountaineer's intelligence, and worked himself loose and, after a rest or so, out until he saw the stars. He rested flat upon his chest for a space, wondering where he was and what had happened to him. He explored his limbs, and discovered that several of his buttons were gone and his coat turned over his head. His knife had gone from his pocket, and his hat was lost, though he had tied it under his chin. He recalled that he had been looking for loose stones to raise his piece of the shelter wall. His ice-axe had disappeared.

He decided he must have fallen, and looked up to see, exaggerated by the ghastly light of the rising moon, the tremendous flight he had taken. For a while he lay, gazing blankly at that vast pale cliff towering above, rising moment by moment out of a subsiding tide of darkness. Its phantasmal, mysterious beauty held him for a space, and then he was seized with a paroxysm of sobbing laughter. . . .

After a great interval of time he became aware that he was near the lower edge of the snow. Below, down what was now a moonlit and practicable slope, he saw the dark and broken appearance of rock-strewn turf. He struggled to his feet, aching in every joint and limb, got down painfully from the heaped loose snow about him, went downward until he was on the turf, and there dropped rather than lay beside a boulder, drank deep from the flask in his inner pocket, and instantly fell asleep. . . .

He was awakened by the singing of birds in the trees far below.

He sat up and perceived he was on a little alp at the foot of a vast precipice, that was grooved by the gully down which he and his snow had come. Over against him another wall of rock reared itself against the sky. The gorge between these precipices ran east and west and was full of the morning sunlight, which lit to the westward the mass of fallen mountain that closed the descending gorge. Below him it seemed there was a precipice equally steep, but behind the snow in the gully he found a sort of chimney-cleft dripping with snow-water down which a desperate man might venture. He found it easier than it seemed, and came at last to another desolate alp, and then after a rock climb of no particular difficulty to a steep slope of trees. He took his bearings and turned his face up the gorge, for he saw it opened out above upon green meadows, among which he now glimpsed quite distinctly a cluster of stone huts of unfamiliar fashion. At times his progress was like clambering along the face of a wall, and after a time the rising sun ceased to strike along the gorge, the voices of the

190

singing birds died away, and the air grew cold and dark about him. But the distant valley with its houses was all the brighter for that. He came presently to talus, and among the rocks he noted—for he was an observant man—an unfamiliar fern that seemed to clutch out of the crevices with intense green hands. He picked a frond or so and gnawed its stalk and found it helpful.

About midday he came at last out of the throat of the gorge into the plain and the sunlight. He was stiff and weary; he sat down in the shadow of a rock, filled up his flask with water from a spring and drank it down, and remained for a time resting before he went on to the houses.

They were very strange to his eyes, and indeed the whole aspect of that valley became, as he regarded it, queerer and more unfamiliar. The greater part of its surface was lush green meadow, starred with many beautiful flowers, irrigated with extraordinary care, and bearing evidence of systematic cropping piece by piece. High up and ringing the valley about was a wall, and what appeared to be a circumferential water-channel, from which the little trickles of water that fed the meadow plants came, and on the higher slopes above this flocks of llamas cropped the scanty herbage. Sheds, apparently shelters or feeding-places for the llamas, stood against the boundary wall here and there. The irrigation streams ran together into a main channel down the center of the valley, and this was enclosed on either side by a wall breast high. This gave a singularly urban quality to this secluded place, a quality that was greatly enhanced by the fact that a number of paths paved with black and white stones, and each with a curious little curb at the side, ran hither and thither in an orderly manner. The houses of the central village were quite unlike the casual and higgledly-piggledy agglomeration of the mountain villages he knew; they stood in a continuous row on either side of a central street of astonishing cleanness; here and there their parti-colored façade was pierced by a door, and not a solitary window broke their even frontage. They were parti-colored with extraordinary irregularity; smeared with a sort of plaster that was sometimes gray, sometimes drab, sometimes slate-colored or dark brown; and it was the sight of this wild plastering first brought the word "blind" into the thoughts of the explorer. "The good man who did that," he thought, "must have been as blind as a bat."

He descended a steep place, and so came to the wall and channel that ran about the valley, near where the latter spouted out its surplus contents into the deeps of the gorge in a thin and wavering thread of cascade. He could now see a number of men and women resting on piled heaps of grass, as if taking a siesta, in the remote part of the meadow, and nearer the village a number of recumbent children, and then nearer at hand three men carrying pails on yokes along a little path that ran from the encircling wall towards the houses. These latter were clad in garments of llama cloth and boots and belts of leather, and they wore caps of cloth with back and ear flaps. They followed one another in single file, walking slowly and yawning as they walked, like men who have been up all night. There was something so reassuringly prosperous and respectable in their bearing that after a moment's hesitation Nunez stood forward as conspicuously as possible upon his rock, and gave vent to a mighty shout that echoes round the valley.

The three men stopped, and moved their heads as though they were looking about them. They turned their faces this way and that, and Nunez gesticulated with freedom. But they did not appear to see him for all his gestures, and after a time, directing themselves towards the mountains far away to the right, they shouted as if in answer. Nunez bawled again, and then once more, and as he gestured ineffectually the word "blind" came up to the top of his thoughts. "The fools must be blind," he said.

When at last, after much shouting and wrath, Nunez crossed the stream by a little bridge, came through a gate in the wall, and approached them, he was sure that they were blind. He was sure that this was the Country of the Blind of which the legends told. Conviction had sprung upon him, and a sense of great and rather enviable adventure. The three stood side by side, not looking at him, but with their ears directed towards him, judging him by his unfamiliar steps. They stood close together like men a little afraid, and he could see their eyelids closed and sunken, as though the very balls beneath had shrunk away. There was an expression near awe on their faces.

"A man," one said, in hardly recognizable Spanish—"a man it is—a man or a spirit—coming down from the rocks."

But Nunez advanced with the confident steps of a youth who enters upon life. All the old stories of the lost valley and the Country of the Blind had come back to his mind, and through his thoughts ran this old proverb, as if it were a refrain—

"In the Country of the Blind the One-eyed Man is King."

"In the Country of the Blind the One-eyed Man is King."

And very civilly he gave them greeting. He talked to them and used his eyes.

"Where does he come from, brother Pedro?" asked one.

"Down out of the rocks."

"Over the mountains I come," said Nunez, "out of the country beyond there—where men can see. From near Bogota, where there are a hundred thousands of people, and where the city passes out of sight."

"Sight?" muttered Pedro. "Sight?"

"He comes," said the second blind man, "out of the rocks."

The cloth of their coats Nunez saw was curiously fashioned, each with a different sort of stitching.

They startled him by a simultaneous movement towards him, each with a hand outstretched. He stepped back from the advance of these spread fingers.

"Come hither," said the third blind man, following his motion and clutching him neatly.

And they held Nunez and felt him over, saying no word further until they had done so.

192

"Carefully," he cried, with a finger in his eye, and found they thought that organ, with its fluttering lids, a queer thing in him. They went over it again.

"A strange creature, Correa," said the one called Pedro. "Feel the coarseness of his hair. Like a llama's hair."

"Rough he is as the rocks that begot him," said Correa, investigating Nunez's unshaven chin with a soft and slightly moist hand. "Perhaps he will grow finer." Nunez struggled a little under their examination because they gripped him firm.

"Carefully," he said again.

"He speaks," said the third man. "Certainly he is a man."

"Ugh!" said Pedro, at the roughness of his coat.

"And you have come into the world?" asked Pedro.

"*Out* of the world. Over mountain and glaciers; right over above there, half-way to the sun. Out of the great big world that goes down, twelve days' journey to the sea."

They scarcely seemed to heed him. "Our fathers have told us men may be made by the forces of Nature," said Correa. "It is the warmth of things and moisture, and rottenness—rottenness."

"Let us lead him to the elders," said Pedro.

"Shout first," said Correa, "lest the children be afraid. This is a marvelous occasion."

So they shouted, and Pedro went first and took Nunez by the hand to lead him to the houses.

He drew his hand away. "I can see," he said.

"See?" said Correa.

"Yes, see," said Nunez, turning towards him, and stumbled against Pedro's pail.

"His senses are still imperfect," said the third blind man. "He stumbles, and talks unmeaning words. Lead him by the hand."

"As you will," said Nunez, and was led along, laughing.

It seemed they knew nothing of sight.

Well, all in good time he would teach them.

He heard people shouting, and saw a number of figures gathering together in the middle roadway of the village.

He found it taxed his nerve and patience more than he had anticipated, that first encounter with the population of the Country of the Blind. The place seemed larger as he drew near to it, and the smeared plasterings queerer, and a crowd of children and men and women (the women and girls, he was pleased to note, had some of them quite sweet faces, for all that their eyes were shut and sunken) came about him, holding on to him, touching him with soft, sensitive hands, smelling at him, and listening at every word he spoke. Some of the maidens and children, however, kept aloof as if afraid, and indeed his voice seemed coarse and rude beside their softer notes. They mobbed him. His three guides kept close to him with an effect of proprietorship, and said again and again, "A wild man out of the rocks."

"Bogota," he said. "Bogota. Over the mountain crests."

"A wild man, using wild words," said Pedro. "Did you hear that—*Bogota*? His mind is hardly formed yet. He has only the beginnings of speech."

A little boy nipped his hand. "Bogota! he said mockingly.

"Ay! A city to your village. I come from the great world—where men have eyes and see."

"His name's Bogota," they said.

"He stumbled," said Correa; "stumbled twice as we came hither."

"Bring him to the elders."

And they thrust him suddenly through a doorway into a room as black as pitch, save at the end there faintly glowed a fire. The crowd closed in behind him and shut out all but the faintest glimmer of day, and before he could arrest himself he had fallen headlong over the feet of a seated man. His arm, outflung, struck the face of someone else as he went down; he felt the soft impact of features and heard a cry of anger, and for a moment he struggled against a number of hands that clutched him. It was a one-sided fight. An inkling of the situation came to him, and he lay quiet.

"I fell down," he said; "I couldn't see in this pitchy darkness."

There was a pause as if the unseen persons about him tried to understand his words. Then the voice of Correa said: "He is but newly formed. He stumbles as he walks and mingles words that mean nothing with his speech."

Others also said things about him that he heard or understood imperfectly.

"May I sit up?" he asked, in a pause. "I will not struggle against you again."

They consulted and let him rise.

The voice of an older man began to question him, and Nunez found himself trying to explain the great world out of which he had fallen, and the sky and mountain and sight and such-like marvels, to these elders who sat in darkness in the Country of the Blind. And they would believe and understand nothing whatever he told them, a thing quite outside his expectation. They would not even understand many of his words. For fourteen generations these people had been blind and cut off from all the seeing world; the names for all the things of sight had faded and changed; the story of the outer world was faded and changed to a child's story; and they had ceased to concern themselves with anything beyond the rocky slopes above their circling wall. Blind men of genius had arisen among them and questioned the shreds of belief and tradition they had brought with them from their seeing days, and had dismissed all these things as idle fancies, and replaced them with new and saner explanations. Much of their imagination had shriveled with their eyes, and they had made for themselves new imaginations with their ever more sensitive ears and finger-tips. Slowly Nunez realized this; that his expectation of wonder and reverence at his origin and his gifts was not to be borne out; and after his poor attempt to explain sight to them had been set aside as the confused version of a new-made being describing the marvels of his incoherent sensations, he subsided, a little dashed, into listening to their instruction. And the eldest of the blind men explained to him life and philosophy and religion, how that the world (meaning their valley) had been first an empty hollow in the rocks, and then had come, first inanimate things without the gift of touch, and llamas and a few other creatures that had little sense, and then men, and at last angels, whom one could hear singing and making fluttering sounds, but whom no one could touch at all, which puzzled Nunez greatly until he thought of the birds.

He went on to tell Nunez how this time had been divided into the warm and the cold, which are the blind equivalents of day and night, and how it was good to sleep in the warm and work during the cold, so that now, but for his advent, the whole town of the blind would have been asleep. He said Nunez must have been specially created to learn and serve the wisdom they had acquired, and for that all his mental incoherency and stumbling behavior he must have courage, and do his best to learn, and at that all the people in the doorway murmured encouragingly. He said the night—for the blind call their day night—was now far gone, and it behooved every one to go back to sleep. He asked Nunez if he knew how to sleep, and Nunez said he did, but that before sleep he wanted food.

They brought him food—llama's milk in a bowl, and rough salted bread—and led him into a lonely place to eat out of their hearing, and afterwards to slumber until the chill of the mountain evening roused them to begin their day again. But Nunez slumbered not at all.

Instead, he sat up in the place where they had left him, resting his limbs and turning the unanticipated circumstances of his arrival over and over in his mind.

Every now and then he laughed, sometimes with amusement, and sometimes with indignation.

"Unformed mind!" he said. "Got no senses yet! They little know they've been insulting their heaven-sent king and master. I see I must bring them to reason. Let me think—let me think."

He was still thinking when the sun set.

Nunez had an eye for all beautiful things, and it seemed to him that the glow upon the snowfields and glaciers that rose about the valley on every side was the most beautiful thing he had ever seen. His eyes went from that inaccessible glory to the village and irrigated fields, fast sinking into the twilight, and suddenly a wave of emotion took him, and he thanked God from the bottom of his heart that the power of sight had been given him.

He heard a voice calling to him from out of the village.

"Ya ho there, Bogota! Come hither!"

At that he stood up smiling. He would show these people once and for all what sight would do for a man. They would seek him, but not find him.

"You move not, Bogota," said the voice.

He laughed noiselessly, and made two stealthy steps aside from the path.

"Trample not on the grass, Bogota; that is not allowed."

195

Nunez had scarcely heard the sound he made himself. He stopped amazed.

The owner of the voice came running up the piebald path towards him.

He stepped back into the pathway. "Here I am," he said.

"Why did you not come when I called you?" said the blind man. "Must you be led like a child? Cannot you hear the path as you walk?"

Nunez laughed. "I can see it," he said.

"There is no such word as *see*," said the blind man, after a pause. "Cease this folly, and follow the sound of my feet."

Nunez followed a little annoyed.

"My time will come," he said.

"You'll learn," the blind man answered. "There is much to learn in the world."

"Has no one told you, 'In the Country of the Blind the One-eyed Man is King'?"

"What is blind?" asked the blind man carelessly over his shoulder.

Four days passed, and the fifth found the King of the Blind still incognito, as a clumsy and useless stranger among his subjects.

It was, he found, much more difficult to proclaim himself than he had supposed, and in the meantime, while he meditated his *coup d'etat*, he did what he was told and learned the manners and customs of the Country of the Blind. He found working and going about at night a particularly irksome thing, and he decided that that should be the first thing he would change.

They led a simple, and laborious life, these people with all the elements of virtue and happiness, as these things can be understood by men. They toiled, but not oppressively; they had food and clothing sufficient for their needs; they had days and seasons of rest; they made much of music and singing, and there was love among them, and little children.

It was marvelous with what confidence and precision they went about their ordered world. Everything, you see, had been made to fit their needs; each of the radiating paths of the valley area had a constant angle to the others, and was distinguished by a special notch upon its kerbing; all obstacles and irregularities of path or meadow had long since been cleared away; all their methods and procedure arose naturally from their special needs. Their senses had become marvelously acute; they could hear and judge the slightest gesture of a man a dozen paces away—could hear the very beating of his heart. Intonation had long replaced expression with them, and touches gesture, and their work with hoe and spade and fork was as free and confident as garden work can be. Their sense of smell was extraordinarily fine; they could distinguish individual differences as readily as a dog can, and they went about the tending of the llamas, who lived among the rocks above and came to the wall for food and shelter, with ease and confidence. It was only when at last Nunez sought to assert himself that he found how easy and confident their movements could be.

He rebelled only after he had tried persuasion.

He tried at first on several occasions to tell them of sight. "Look you here, you people," he said. "There are things you do not understand in me."

Once or twice one or two of them attended to him; they sat with faces downcast and ears turned intelligently towards him, and he did his best to tell them what it was to see. Among his hearers was a girl, with eyelids less red and sunken than the others, so that one could almost fancy she was hiding eyes, whom especially he hoped to persuade. He spoke of the beauties of sight, of watching the mountains, of the sky and the sunrise, and they heard him with amused incredulity that presently became condemnatory. They told him there were indeed no mountains at all, but that the end of the world; thence sprang a cavernous roof of the universe, from which the dew and the avalanches fell; and when he maintained stoutly the world had neither end nor roof such as they supposed, they said his thoughts were wicked. So far as he could describe sky and clouds and stars to them it seemed to them a hideous void, a terrible blankness in the place of the smooth roof to things in which they believed—it was an article of faith with them that the cavern roof was exquisitely smooth to the touch. He saw that in some manner he shocked them, and gave up that aspect of the matter altogether, and tried to show them the practical value of sight. One morning he saw Pedro in the path called Seventeen and coming towards the central houses, but still too far off for hearing or scent, and he told them as much. "In a little while," he prophesied, "Pedro will be here." An old man remarked that Pedro had no business on path Seventeen, and then as if in confirmation, that individual as he drew near turned and went transversely into path Ten and so back with nimble paces towards the outer wall. They mocked Nunez when Pedro did not arrive, and afterwards, when he asked Pedro questions to clear his character, Pedro denied and outfaced him, and was afterwards hostile to him.

Then he induced them to let him go a long way up the sloping meadows towards the wall with one complacent individual, and to him he promised to describe all that happened among the houses. He noted certain goings and comings, but the things that really seemed to signify to these people happened inside of or behind the windowless houses—the only things they took note of to test him by—and of these he could see or tell nothing; and it was after the failure of this attempt, and the ridicule they could not repress, that he resorted to force. He thought of seizing a spade and suddenly smiting one or two of them to earth and so in fair combat showing the advantage of eyes. He went so far with that resolution as to seize his spade, and then he discovered a new thing about himself, and that was that it was impossible for him to hit a blind man in cold blood.

He hesitated, and found them all aware that he snatched up the spade. They stood alert, with their heads on one side, and bent ears towards him for what he could do next.

"Put that spade down," said one, and he felt a sort of helpless horror. He came near obedience.

Then he thrust one backwards against a house wall, and fled past him and out of the village.

He went athwart one of their meadows, leaving a track of trampled grass behind his feet, and presently sat down by the side of one of their ways. He felt something of the buoyancy that comes to all men in the beginning of a fight, but more perplexity. He began to realize that you cannot even fight happily with creatures who stand upon a different mental basis to yourself. Far away he saw a number of men carrying spades and sticks come out of the street of houses, and advance in a spreading line along the several paths towards him. They advanced slowly, speaking frequently to one another, and ever and again the whole cordon would halt and sniff the air and listen.

The first time they did this Nunez laughed. But afterwards he did not laugh.

One struck his trail in the meadow grass, and came stooping and feeling his way along it.

For five minutes he watched the slow extension of the cordon, and then his vague disposition to do something forthwith became frantic. He stood up, went a pace or so towards the circumferential wall, turned, and went back a little way. There they all stood in a crescent, still and listening.

He also stood still, gripping his spade very tightly in both hands. Should he charge them?

The pulse in his ears ran into the rhythm of "In the Country of the Blind the One-eyed Man is King!"

Should he charge them?

He looked back at the high and unclimbable wall behind—unclimbable because of its smooth plastering, but withal pierced with many little doors, and at the approaching line of seekers. Behind these, others were now coming out of the street of houses.

Should he charge them?

"Bogota!" called one. "Bogota! where are you?"

He gripped his spade still tighter, and advanced down the meadows towards the place of habitations, and directly he moved they converged near him. "I'll hit them if they touch me," he swore; "by Heaven, I will. I'll hit." He called aloud. "Look here, I'm going to do what I like in this valley. Do you hear? I'm going to do what I like and go where I like!"

They were moving in upon him quickly, groping, yet moving rapidly. It was like playing blind man's buff, with everyone blindfolded except one. "Get hold of him!" cried one. He found himself in the arc of a loose curve of pursuers. He felt suddenly he must be active and resolute.

"You don't understand," he cried in a voice that was meant to be great and resolute, and which broke. "You are blind, and I can see. Leave me alone!"

"Bogota! Put down that spade, and come off the grass!"

The last order, grotesque in its urban familiarity, produced a gust of anger.

"I'll hurt you," he said, sobbing with emotion. "By Heaven, I'll hurt you. Leave me alone!"

He began to run, not knowing clearly where to run. He ran from the nearest blind man, because it was a horror to hit him. He stopped, and then made a dash to escape from their closing ranks. He made for where a gap was wide, and the men on either side, with a quick perception of the approach of his paces, rushed in on one another. He sprang forward, and then saw he must be caught, and *swish!* The spade and struck. He felt the soft thud of hand and arm, and the man was down with a yell of pain, and he was through.

Through! And then he was close to the street of houses again, and blind men, whirling spades and stakes, were running with a sort of reasoned swiftness hither and thither.

He heard steps behind him just in time, and found a tall man rushing forward and swiping at the sound of him. He lost his nerve, hurled his spade a yard wide at his antagonist and whirled about and fled, fairly yelling as he dodged another.

He was panic-stricken. He ran furiously to and fro, dodging when there was no need to dodge, and in his anxiety to see on every side of him at once, stumbling. For a moment, he was down and they heard his fall. Far away in the circumferential wall a little doorway looked like heaven, and he set off in a wild rush for it. He did not even look round at his pursuers until it was gained, and he had stumbled across the bridge, clambered a little way among the rocks, to the surprise and dismay of a young llama, who went leaping out of sight, and lay down sobbing for breath.

And so his *coup d'etat* came to an end.

He stayed outside the wall of the Valley of the Blind for two nights and days without food or shelter, and meditated upon the unexpected. During these mediations he repeated very frequently and always with a profounder note of derision the exploded proverb: "In the Country of the Blind the One-eyed Man is King." He thought chiefly of ways of fighting and conquering these people, and it grew clear that for him no practicable way was possible. He had no weapons, and now it would be hard to get one.

The canker of civilization had got to him even in Bogota, and he could not find it in himself to go down and assassinate a blind man. Of course, if he did that, he might then dictate terms on the threat of assassinating them all. But—sooner or later he must sleep!...

He tried also to find food among the pine trees, to be comfortable under pine boughs while the frost fell at night, and—with less confidence—to catch a llama by artifice in order to try to kill it—perhaps by hammering it with a stone—and so finally, perhaps, to eat some of it. But the llamas had a doubt of him and regarded him with distrustful brown eyes, and spat when he drew near. Fear came on him the second day and fits of shivering. Finally he crawled down to the wall of the Country of the Blind and tried to make terms. He crawled along by the stream, shouting, until two blind men came out to the gate and talked to him.

"I was mad," he said. "But I was only newly made."

They said that was better.

He told them he was wiser now, and repented of all he had done.

Then he wept without intention, for he was very weak and ill now, and they took that as a favorable sign.

They asked him if he still thought he could "*see.*"

"No," he said. "That was folly. The word means nothing—less than nothing!"

They asked him what was overhead.

"About ten times ten the height of a man there is a roof above the world—of rock—and very, very smooth." . . . He burst again into hysterical tears. "Before you ask me any more, give me some food or I shall die."

He expected dire punishments, but these blind people were capable of toleration. They regarded his rebellion as but one more proof of his general idiocy and inferiority; and after they had whipped him they appointed him to do the simplest and heaviest work they had for anyone to do, and he, seeing no other way of living, did submissively what he was told.

He was ill for some days, and they nursed him kindly. That refined his submission. But they insisted on his lying in the dark, and that was a great misery. And blind philosophers came and talked to him of the wicked levity of his mind, and reproved him so impressively for his doubts about the lid of rock that covered their cosmic casserole that he almost doubted whether indeed he was not the victim of hallucination in not seeing it overhead.

So Nunez became a citizen of the Country of the Blind, and these people ceased to be a generalized people and became individualities and familiar to him, while the world beyond the mountains became more and more remote and unreal. There was Yacob, his master, a kindly man when not annoyed; there was Pedro, Yacob's nephew; and there was Medina-saroté, who was the youngest daughter of Yacob. She was little esteemed in the world of the blind, because she had a clear-cut face, and lacked that satisfying, glossy smoothness that is the blind man's ideal of feminine beauty; but Nunez thought her beautiful at first, and presently the most beautiful thing in the whole creation. Her closed eyelids were not sunken and red after the common way of the valley, but lay as though they might open again at any moment; and she had long eyelashes, which were considered a grave disfigurement. And her voice was strong, and did not satisfy the acute hearing of the valley swains. So that she had no lover.

There came a time when Nunez thought that, could he win her, he would be resigned to live in the valley for all the rest of his days.

He watched her; he sought opportunities of doing her little services, and presently he found that she observed him. Once at a rest-day gathering they sat side by side in the dim starlight, and the music was sweet. His hand came upon hers and he dared to clasp it. Then very tenderly she returned his pressure. And one day, as they were at their meal in the darkness, he felt her hand very softly seeking him, and as it chanced the fire leaped, then he saw the tenderness of her face.

He sought to speak to her.

He went to her one day when she was sitting in the summer moonlight spinning. The light made her a thing of silver and mystery. He sat down at her feet and told her he loved her, and told her how beautiful she seemed to him. He had a lover's voice, he spoke with a tender reverence that came near to awe, and she had never before been touched by adoration. She made him no definite answer, but it was clear his words pleased her.

After that he talked to her whenever he could take an opportunity. The valley became the world for him, and the world beyond the mountains where men lived in sunlight seemed no more than a fairy tale he would some day pour into her ears. Very tentatively and timidly he spoke to her of sight.

Sight seemed to her the most poetical of fancies, and she listened to his description of the stars and the mountains and her own sweet white-lit beauty as though it was a guilty indulgence. She did not believe, she could only half understand, but she was mysteriously delighted, and it seemed to him that she completely understood.

His love lost its awe and took courage. Presently he was for demanding her of Yacob and the elders in marriage, but she became fearful and delayed. And it was one of her elder sisters who first told Yacod that Medina-saroté and Nunez were in love.

There was from the first very great opposition to the marriage of Nunez and Medina-saroté; not so much because they valued her as because they held him as a being apart, an idiot, incompetent thing below the permissible level of a man. Her sisters opposed it bitterly as bringing discredit on them all; and old Yacob, though he had formed a sort of liking for his clumsy, obedient serf, shook his head and said the thing could not be. The young men were all angry at the idea of corrupting the race, and one went so far as to revile and strike Nunez. He struck back. Then for the first time he found an advantage in seeing, even by twilight, and after that fight was over no one was disposed to raise a hand against him. But they still found his marriage impossible.

Old Yacob had a tenderness for his last little daughter, and was grieved to have her weep upon his shoulder.

"You see, my dear, he's an idiot. He has delusions; he can't do anything right."

"I know," wept Medina-saroté. "But he's better than he was. He's getting better. And he's strong, dear father, and kind—stronger and kinder than any other man in the world. And he loves me—and, father, I love him."

Old Yacob was greatly distressed to find her inconsolable, and besides—what made it more distressing—he liked Nunez for many things. So he went and sat in the windowless council-chamber with the other elders and watched the trend of the talk, and said, at the proper time, "He's better than he was. Very likely, some day, we shall find him as sane as ourselves."

Then afterwards one of the elders, who thought deeply, had an idea. He was the great doctor among these people, their medicine-man, and he had a very philosophical and inventive mind, and the idea of curing Nunez of his peculiarities appealed to him. One day when Yacob was present he returned to the topic of Nunez.

201

"I have examined Bogota," he said, "and the case is clearer to me. I think very probably he might be cured."

"That is what I have always hoped," said old Yacob.

"His brain is affected," said the blind doctor.

The elders murmured assent.

"Now, *what* affects it?"

"Ah!" said old Yacob.

"*This*," said the doctor, answering his own question. "Those queer things that are called the eyes, and which exist to make an agreeable soft depression in the face, are diseased, in the case of Bogota, in such a way as to affect his brain. They are greatly distended, he has eyelashes, and his eyelids move, and consequently his brain is in a state of constant irritation and destruction."

"Yes?" said old Yacob. "Yes?"

"And I think I may say with reasonable certainty that, in order to cure him completely, all that we need do is a simple and easy surgical operation—namely, to remove these irritant bodies."

"And then he will be sane?"

"Then he will be perfectly sane, and a quite admirable citizen."

"Thank Heaven for science!" said old Yacob, and went forth at once to tell Nunez of his happy hopes.

But Nunez's manner of receiving the good news struck him as being cold and disappointing.

"One might think," he said, "from the tone you take, that you did not care for my daughter."

It was Medina-saroté who persuaded Nunez to face the blind surgeons.

"*You* do not want me," he said, "to lose my gift of sight?"

She shook her head.

"My world is sight."

Her head drooped lower.

"There are the beautiful things, the beautiful little things—the flowers, the lichens among the rocks, the lightness and softness on a piece of fur, the far sky with its drifting down of clouds, the sunsets and the stars. And there is *you*. For you alone it is good to have sight, to see your sweet, serene face, your kindly lips, your dear, beautiful hands folded together. . . . It is these eyes of mine you won, these eyes that hold me to you, that these idiots seek. Instead, I must touch you, hear you, and never see you again. I must come under that roof of rock and stone and darkness, that horrible roof under which your imagination stoops. . . . No; you would not have me do that?"

A disagreeable doubt had arisen in him. He stopped, and left the thing a question.

"I wish," she said, "sometimes—" She paused.

"Yes?" said he, a little apprehensively.

"I wish sometimes—you would not talk like that."

202

"Like what?"

"I know it's pretty—it's your imagination. I love it, but *now*—"

He felt cold. "*Now*?" he said faintly.

She sat quite still.

"You mean—you think—I should be better, better perhaps—"

He was realizing things very swiftly. He felt anger, indeed, anger at the dull course of fate, but also sympathy for her lack of understanding—a sympathy near akin to pity.

"*Dear*," he said, and he could see by her whiteness how intensely her spirit pressed against the things she could not say. He put his arms about her, he kissed her ear, and they sat for a time in silence.

"If I were to consent to this?" he said at last, in a voice that was very gentle.

She flung her arms about him, weeping wildly. "Oh, if you would," she sobbed, "if only you would!"

For a week before the operation that was to raise him from his servitude and inferiority to the level of a blind citizen, Nunez knew nothing of sleep, and all through the warm sunlit hours, while the others slumbered happily, he sat brooding or wandered aimlessly, trying to bring his mind to bear on his dilemma. He had given his answer, he had given his consent, and still he was not sure. And at last work-time was over, the sun rose in splendor over the golden crests, and his last day of vision began for him. He had a few minutes with Medina-saroté before she went apart to sleep.

"To-morrow," he said, "I shall see no more."

"Dear heart!" she answered, and pressed his hands with all her strength.

"They will hurt you but little," she said; "and you are going through this pain—you are going through it, dear lover, for *me*. . . . Dear, if a woman's heart and life can do it, I will repay you. My dearest one, my dearest with the tender voice, I will repay."

He was drenched in pity for himself and her.

He held her in his arms, and pressed his lips to hers, and looked on her sweet face for the last time. "Good-bye!" he whispered at that dear sight, "good-bye!"

And then in silence he turned away from her.

She could hear his slow retreating footsteps, and something in the rhythm of them threw her into a passion of weeping.

He had fully meant to go to a lonely place where the meadows were beautiful with white narcissus, and there remain until the hour of his sacrifice should come, but as he went he lifted up his eyes and saw the morning, the morning like an angel in golden armor, marching down the steeps. . . .

It seemed to him that before this splendor he, and this blind world in the valley, and his love, and all, were no more than a pit of sin.

He did not turn aside as he had meant to do, but went on, and passed through the wall of the circumference and out upon the rock, and his eyes were always upon the sunlit ice and snow.

He saw their infinite beauty, and his imagination soared over them to the things beyond he was now resign for ever.

He thought of that great free world he was parted from, the world that was his own, and he had a vision of those further slopes, distance beyond distance, with Bogota, a place of multitudinous stirring beauty, a glory by day, a luminous mystery by night. A place of palaces and fountains and statues and white houses, lying beautifully in the middle distance. He thought how for a day or so one might come down through the passes, drawing nearer and nearer to its busy streets and ways. He thought of the river journey, day by day, from great Bogota to the still vast world beyond, through towns and villages, forest and desert places, the rushing river day by day, until its banks receded and the big steamers came splashing by, and one had reached the sea—the limitless sea, with its thousands of islands, and its ships seen dimly far away in their incessant journeyings round and about that greater world. And then, unpent by mountains, one saw the sky—the sky, not such a disc as one saw it here, but an arch of immeasurable blue, a deep of deeps in which the circling stars were floating. . . .

His eyes scrutinized the great curtain of the mountains with a keener inquiry.

For example, if one went so, up that gully and to that chimney there, then one might come out high among those stunted pines that ran round in a sort of shelf and rose still higher and higher as it passed above the gorge. And then? That talus might be managed. Thence perhaps a climb might be found to take him up to the precipice that came below the snow; and if that chimney failed, then another farther to the east might serve his purpose better. And then? Then one would be out upon the amber-lit snow there, and half-way up to the crest of those beautiful desolations.

He glanced back at the village, then turned right round and regarded it steadfastly.

He thought of Medina-saroté, and she had become small and remote.

He turned again towards the mountain wall, down which the day had come to him.

Then very circumspectly he began to climb.

When sunset came he was no longer climbing, but he was far and high. He had been higher, but he was still very high. His clothes were torn, his limbs were bloodstained, he was bruised in many places, but he lay as if he were at his ease, and there was a smile on his face.

From where he rested the valley seemed as if it were in a pit and nearly a mile below. Already it was dim with haze and shadow, though the mountain summits around him were things of light and fire. The mountain summits around him were things of light and fire, and the little details of the rocks near at hand were drenched with subtle beauty—a vein of green mineral piercing the grey, the flash of crystal faces here and there, a minute, minutely beautiful orange lichen close beside his face. There were deep mysterious shadows in the gorge, blue deepening into purple, and purple into a luminous darkness, and overhead was the illimitable vastness of the sky. But he heeded these things no longer, but lay quite inactive there, smiling as if he were satisfied merely to have escaped from the valley of the Blind in which he had thought to be King.

The glow of the sunset passed, and the night came, and still he lay peacefully contented under the cold stars.

# from *In the Days of The Comet*
# (1906)

In the Days of the Comet, *notorious in its own time for the suggestions of radical sexual possibilities, is a breakthrough novel. For almost a decade Wells had been drawing versions of the world his own adolescence prepared him for—a stunting, tiresome, ignorant, and outrageously unjust society that offered no escape for its victims. This new novel brazenly combines the genre of social realism with that of the scientific romance. In a finely paced exercise in cross-cutting, Wells brings to simultaneous crisis the love plot, the industrial strike, the international war, and the collision of Earth with the comet. The crowded, melodramatic stage is then suddenly and quietly suspended, and in its place appears a new dawn, sane, without rage, one in which all participants easily and generously confess their previous selfishness and immediately set about putting matters straight. Only in the slow working out of the love dilemma does Wells remind us (off in a corner, so to speak) that he knows that old behaviors do not simply evaporate. In the epilogue a man from our own time, a reader like ourselves, speaks of the skepticism to which the bright, monotone utopian optimism blinds us. The selection contains all of the first section of the novel, a bit of the second describing the awakening after the comet, and the chapters on love from the third. Sections recounting Leadford's work with the Prime Minister after the change and the death of Leadford's mother have be omitted. As the last chapter begins, Leadford has renounced Nettie and is ready to marry Anna, who has accompanied him through the death of his mother*

## PROLOGUE
### THE MAN WHO WROTE IN THE TOWER

I saw a grey-haired man, a figure of hale age, sitting at a desk and writing.

He seemed to be in a room in a tower, very high, so that through the tall window on his left one perceived only distances, a remote horizon of sea, a headland, and that vague haze and glitter in the sunset that many miles away marks a city. All the appointments of this room were orderly and beautiful, and in some subtle quality, in this small difference and that, new to me and strange. They were in no fashion I could name, and the simple costume the man wore suggested neither period nor country. It might, I thought, be the Happy Future, or Utopia; an errant mote of memory, Henry James's phrase and story of "The Great Good Place," twinkled across my mind, and passed and left no light.

The man I saw wrote with a thing like a fountain pen, a modern touch that prohibited any historical reference, and as he finished each sheet, writing in an easy flowing hand, he added it to a growing pile upon a graceful little table under the window. His last done sheets lay loose, partly covering others that were clipped together into fascicles.

*Clearly he was unaware of my presence, and I stood waiting until his pen should come to a pause. Old as he certainly was he wrote with a steady hand. . . .*

*I discovered that a concave speculum hung slantingly high over his head; a movement in this caught my attention sharply, and I looked up to see, distorted and made fantastic but bright and beautifully coloured, the magnified, reflected, evasive rendering of a palace, of a terrace, of the vista of a great roadway with many people, people exaggerated, impossible-looking because of the curvature of the mirror, going to and fro. I turned my head quickly that I might see more clearly through the window behind me, but it was too high for me to survey this nearer scene directly, and after a momentary pause I came back to that distort-ing mirror again.*

*But now the writer was leaning back in his chair. He put down his pen and sighed the half resentful sigh—"ah! you work, you! how you gratify and tire me!"—of a man who has been writing to his satisfaction.*

*"What is this place," I asked, "and who are you?"*

*He looked around with the quick movement of surprise.*

*"What is this place?" I repeated, "and where am I?"*

*He regarded me steadfastly for a moment under his wrinkled brows, and then his expres-sion softened to a smile. He pointed to a chair beside the table. "I am writing," he said.*

*"About this?"*

*"About the Change."*

*I sat down. It was a very comfortable chair, and well placed under the light.*

*"If you would like to read—" he said.*

*I indicated the manuscript. "This explains?" I asked.*

*"That explains," he answered.*

*He drew a fresh sheet of paper towards him as he looked at me.*

*I glanced from him about his apartment and back to the little table. A fascicle marked very distinctly "I" caught my attention, and I took it up. I smiled in his friendly eyes. "Very well," said I, suddenly at my ease, and he nodded and went on writing. And in a mood between con-fidence and curiosity, I began to read.*

*This is the story that happy, active-looking old man in that pleasant place had written.*

### BOOK I
### THE COMET
### CHAPTER THE FIRST
### DUST IN THE SHADOWS
### 1

I have set myself to write the story of the Great Change, so far as it has affected my own life and the lives of one or two people closely connected with me, primarily to please myself.

Long ago, in my crude unhappy youth I conceived a desire to write a book. To scribble secretly and dream of authorship was one of my chief alleviations, and I read with a sympathetic envy every scrap I could get about the world of literature and the lives of literary people. It is something even amidst this present happiness, to find leisure and opportunity to take up and partially realise these old and hopeless dreams. But that alone, in a world where so much of vivid and increasing interest presents itself to be done, even by an old man, would not, I think, suffice to set me at this desk. I find some such recapitulation of my past as this will involve, is becoming necessary to my own secure mental continuity. The passage of years brings a man at last to retrospection; at seventy-two one's youth is far more important than it was at forty. And I am out of touch with my youth. The old life seems so cut off from the new, so alien and so unreasonable, that at times I find it bordering upon the incredible. The data have gone, the buildings and places. I stopped dead the other afternoon in my walk across the moor, where once the dismal outskirts of Swathinglea straggled towards Leet, and asked, "Was it here indeed that I crouched among the weeds and refuse and broken crockery and loaded my revolver ready for murder? Did ever such a thing happen in my life? Was such a mood and thought and intention ever possible to me? Rather, has not some queer nightmare spirit out of dreamland slipped a pseudo-memory into the records of my vanished life?" There must be many alive still who have the same perplexities. And I think too that those who are now growing up to take our places in the great enterprise of mankind, will need many such narratives as mine for even the most partial conception of the old world of shadows that came before our day. It chances too that my case is fairly typical of the Change; I was caught midway in a gust of passion; and a curious accident put me for a time in the very nucleus of the new order. . . .

My memory takes me back across the interval of fifty years to a little ill-lit room with a sash window open to a starry sky, and instantly there returns to me the characteristic smell of that room the penetrating odour of an ill-trimmed lamp, burning cheap paraffin. Lighting by electricity had then been perfected for fifteen years, but still the larger portion of the world used these lamps. All this first scene will go, in my mind at least, to that olfactory accompaniment. That was the evening smell of the room. By day it had a more subtle aroma, a closeness, a peculiar sort of faint pungency that I associate—I know not why—with dust.

Let me describe this room to you in detail. It was perhaps eight feet by seven in area and rather higher than either of these dimensions; the ceiling was of plaster, cracked and bulging in places, grey with the soot of the lamp, and in one place discoloured by a system of yellow and olive-green stains caused by the percolation of damp from above. The walls were covered with dun-coloured paper, upon which had been printed in oblique reiteration a crimson shape, something of the nature of a curly ostrich feather, or an acanthus flower, that had in its less faded moments a sort of dingy gaiety. There were several big plaster-rimmed wounds in this, caused by Parload's ineffectual attempts to get nails into the wall, whereby there might hang pictures. One nail had hit between two bricks and got home, and from this depended, sustained a little insecurely by frayed and knotted blind-cord, Parload's hanging bookshelves, planks painted over with a treacly blue enamel and further decorated by a fringe of pinked American cloth insecurely fixed by tacks. Below this was a little table that behaved with a mulish vindic-tiveness to any knee that was thrust beneath it suddenly; it was covered with a cloth whose pattern of red and black had been rendered less monotonous by the accidents of Parload's versatile ink bottle, and on it, *leit motif* of the whole, stood and stank the lamp. This lamp, you must understand, was of some whitish translucent substance that was neither china nor glass, it had a shade of the same substance, a shade that did not protect the eyes of a reader in any measure, and it seemed admirably adapted to bring into pitiless prominence the fact that, after the lamp's trimming, dust and paraffin had been smeared over its exterior with a reckless generosity.

The uneven floor boards of this apartment were covered with scratched enamel of chocolate hue, on which a small island of frayed carpet dimly blossomed in the dust and shadows.

There was a very small grate, made of cast-iron in one piece and painted buff, and a still smaller misfit of a cast-iron fender that confessed the grey stone of the hearth. No fire was laid, only a few scraps of torn paper and the bowl of a broken corn-cob pipe were visible behind the bars, and in the corner and rather thrust away was an angular japanned coal-box with a damaged hinge. It was the custom in those days to warm every room separately from a separate fireplace, more prolific of dirt than heat, and the rickety sash window, the small chimney, and the loose-fitting door were ex-pected to organise the ventilation of the room among themselves without any further direction.

Parload's truckle bed hid its grey sheets beneath an old patchwork counterpane on one side of the room, and veiled his boxes and such-like oddments, and invading the two corners of the window were an old whatnot and the washhandstand, on which were distributed the simple appliances of his toilet.

This washhandstand had been made of deal by someone with an excess of turn-ery appliances in a hurry, who had tried to distract attention from the rough eco-nomics of his workmanship by an arresting ornamentation of blobs and bulbs upon the joints and legs. Apparently the piece had then been placed in the hands of some person of infinite leisure equipped with a pot of ochreous paint, varnish, and a set of flexible combs. This person had first painted the article, then, I fancy, smeared it with varnish, and then sat down to work with the combs to streak and comb the varnish into a weird imitation of the grain of some nightmare timber. The washhandstand so made had evidently had a prolonged career of violent use, had been chipped, kicked, splintered, punched, stained, scorched, hammered, desiccated, damped, and defiled, had met indeed with almost every possible adventure except conflagration or a scrubbing, until at last it had come to this high refuge of Parload's attic to sustain the simple requirements of Parload's personal cleanliness. There were, in chief, a basin and a jug of water and slop-pail of tin, and, further, a piece of yellow soap in a tray, a tooth-brush, a rat-tailed shaving brush, one huckaback towel, and one or two other minor articles. In those days only very prosperous people had more than such an equipage, and it is to be remarked that every drop of water Parload used had to be carried by an unfortunate servant girl—the "slavey," Parload called her—up from the basement to the top of the house and subsequently down again. Already we begin to forget how modern an invention is personal cleanliness. It is a fact that Parload had never stripped for a swim in his life; never had a simultaneous bath all over his body since his childhood. Not one in fifty of us did in the days of which I am telling you.

A chest, also singularly grained and streaked, of two large and two small drawers, held Parload's reserve of garments, and pegs on the door carried his two hats and completed this inventory of a "bed-sitting-room" as I knew it before the Change. But I had forgotten—there was also a chair with a "squab" that apologised inadequately for the defects of its cane seat. I forgot that for the moment because I was sitting on the chair on the occasion that best begins this story.

I have described Parload's room with such particularity because it will help you to understand the key in which my earlier chapters are written, but you must not imagine that this singular equipment or the smell of the lamp engaged my attention at that time to the slightest degree. I took all this grimy unpleasantness as if it were the most natural and proper setting for existence imaginable. It was the world as I knew it. My mind was entirely occupied then by graver and intenser matters, and it is only now in the distant retrospect that I see those details of environment as being remarkable, as significant, as indeed obviously the outward visible manifestations of the old world disorder in our hearts.

## 2

Parload stood at the open window, opera-glass in hand, and sought and found and was uncertain about and lost again, the new comet.

I thought the comet no more than a nuisance then because I wanted to talk of other matters. But Parload was full of it. My head was hot, I was feverish with interlacing annoyances and bitterness, I wanted to open my heart to him—at least I wanted to relieve my heart by some romantic rendering of my troubles—and I gave but little heed to the things he told me. It was the first time I had heard of this new speck among the countless specks of heaven, and I did not care if I never head of the thing again.

We were two youths much of an age together; Parload was two and twenty, and eight months older than I. He was—I think his proper definition was "engrossing clerk" to a little solicitor in Overcastle, while I was third in the office staff of Rawdon's pot-bank in Clayton. We had met first in the "Parliament" of the Young Men's Christian Association of Swathinglea; we had found we attended simultaneous classes in Overcastle, he in science and I in shorthand, and had started a practice of walking home together, and so our friendship came into being. (Swathinglea, Clayton, and Overcastle were contiguous towns, I should mention, in the great industrial area of the Midlands.) We had shared each other's secret of religious doubt, we had confided to one another a common interest in Socialism, he had come twice to supper at my mother's on a Sunday night, and I was free of his apartment. He was then a tall, flaxen-haired, gawky youth, with a disproportionate development of neck and wrist, and capable of vast enthusiasm; he gave two evenings a week to the evening classes of the organised science school in Overcastle, physiography was his favourite "subject," and through this insidious opening of his mind the wonder of outer space had come to take possession of his soul. He had commandeered an old opera-glass from his uncle who farmed at Leet over the moors, he had bought a cheap paper planisphere and *Whitaker's Almanack*, and for a time day and moonlight were mere blank interruptions to the one satisfactory reality in his life—star-gazing. It was the deeps that had seized him, the immensities, and the mysterious possibilities that might float unlit in that unplumbed abyss. With infinite labour and the help of a very precise article in *The Heavens*, a little monthly magazine that catered for those who were under this obsession, he had at last got his opera-glass upon the new visitor to our system from outer space. He gazed in a sort of rapture upon that quivering little smudge of light among the shining pin-points—and gazed. My troubles had to wait for him.

"Wonderful," he sighed, and then as though his first emphasis did not satisfy him, "wonderful!"

He turned to me. "Wouldn't you like to see?"

I had to look, and then I had to listen, how that this scarce-visible intruder was to be, was presently to be, one of the largest comets this world has ever seen, how that its course must bring it within at most—so many score of millions of miles from the earth, a mere step, Parload seemed to think that; how that the spectroscope was already sounding its chemical secrets, perplexed by the unprecedented band in the green, how it was even now being photographed in the very act of unwinding—in an unusual direction—a sunward tail (which presently it wound up again), and all the while in a sort of undertow I was thinking first of Nettie Stuart and the letter she had just written me, and then of old Rawdon's detestable face as I had seen it that afternoon. Now I planned answers to Nettie and now belated repartees to my employer, and then again "Nettie" was blazing all across the background of my thoughts. . . .

Nettie Stuart was daughter of the head gardener of the rich Mr. Verrall's widow, and she and I had kissed and become sweethearts before we were eighteen years old. My mother and hers were second cousins and old schoolfellows, and though my mother had been widowed untimely by a train accident, and had been reduced to letting lodgings (she was the Clayton curate's landlady), a position esteemed much lower than that of Mrs. Stuart, a kindly custom of occasional visits to the gardener's cottage at Checkshill Towers still kept the friends in touch. Commonly I went with her. And I remember it was in the dusk of one bright evening in July, one of those long golden evenings that do not so much give way to night as admit at last, upon courtesy, the moon and a choice retinue of stars, that Nettie and I, at the pond of goldfish where the yew-bordered walks converged, made our shy beginners' vow. I remember still—something will always stir in me at that memory—the tremulous emotion of that adventure. Nettie was dressed in white, her hair went off in waves of soft darkness from above her dark shining eyes; there was a little necklace of pearls about her sweetly modelled neck, and a little coin of gold that nestled in her throat, I kissed her half-reluctant lips, and for three yeas of my life thereafter—nay! I almost think for all the rest of her life and mine—I could have died for her sake.

You must understand—and every year it becomes increasingly difficult to understand—how entirely different the world was then from what it is now. It was a dark world; it was full of preventable disorder, preventable diseases, and preventable pain, of harshness and stupid unpremeditated cruelties; but yet, it may be even by virtue of the general darkness, there were moments of a rare and evanescent beauty that seem no longer possible in my experience. The great Change has come for ever more, happiness and a beauty are our atmosphere, there is peace on earth and good will to all men. None would dare to dream of returning to the sorrows of the former time, and yet that misery was pierced, ever and again its grey curtain was stabbed through and through by joys of an intensity, by perceptions of a keenness that it seems to me are now altogether gone out of life. Is it the Change, I wonder, that has robbed life of its extremes, or is it perhaps only this, that youth has left me—even the strength of middle years leaves me now—and taken its despairs and raptures, leaving me judgment perhaps, sympathy, memories?

I cannot tell. One would need to be young now and to have been young then as well, to decide that impossible problem.

Perhaps a cool observer even in the old days would have found little beauty in our grouping. I have our two photographs at hand in this bureau as I write, and they show me a gawky youth in ill-fitting ready-made clothing, and Nettie—indeed Nettie is badly dressed, and her attitude is more than a little stiff; but I can see her through the picture, and her living brightness and something of that mystery of charm she had for me, comes back again to my mind. Her face had triumphed over the photographer—or I would long ago have cast this picture away.

The reality of beauty yields itself to no words. I wish that I had the sister art and could draw in my margin something that escapes description. There was a sort of gravity in her eyes. There was something, a matter of the minutest difference, about her upper lip so that her mouth closed sweetly and broke very sweetly to a smile. That grave, sweet smile!

After we had kissed and decided not to tell our parents for a while of the irrevocable choice we had made the time came for us to part, shyly and before others, and I and my mother went off back across the moonlit park—the bracken thickets rustling with startled deer—to the railway station at Checkshill and so to our dingy basement in Clayton, and I saw no more of Nettie—except that I saw her in my thoughts—for nearly a year. But at our next meeting it was decided that we must correspond, and this we did with much elaboration of secrecy, for Nettie would have no one at home, not even her only sister, know of her attachment. So I had to send my precious documents sealed and under cover by way of a confidential schoolfellow of hers who lived near London. . . . I could write that address down now, though house and street and suburb have gone beyond any man's tracing.

Our correspondence began our estrangement, because for the first time we came into more than sensuous contact and our minds sought expression.

Now you must understand that the world of thought in those days was in the strangest condition, it was choked with obsolete inadequate formulae, it was tortuous to a maze-like degree with secondary contrivance and adaptations, suppressions, conventions, and subterfuges. Base immediacies fouled the truth on every man's lips. I was brought up by my mother in a quaint old-fashioned narrow faith in certain religious formulae, certain rules of conduct, certain conceptions of social and political order, that had no more relevance to the realities and needs of everyday contemporary life than if they were clean linen that had been put away with lavender in a drawer. Indeed, her religion did actually smell of lavender; on Sundays she put away all the things of reality, the garments and even the furnishings of everyday, hid her hands, that were gnarled and sometimes chapped with scrubbing, in black, carefully mended gloves, assumed her old black silk dress and bonnet and took me, unnaturally clean and sweet also, to church. There we sang and bowed and heard sonorous prayers and joined in sonorous responses, and rose with a congregational sigh refreshed and relieved when the doxology, with its opening "Now to God the Father, God the Son," bowed out the tame, brief sermon. There was a hell in that religion of my mother's, a red-haired hell of curly flames that had once been very terrible; there was a devil who was also *ex officio* the British King's enemy, and much denunciation of the wicked lusts of the flesh; we were expected to believe that most of our poor unhappy world was to atone for its muddle and trouble here by suffering exquisite torments for ever after, world without end, Amen. But indeed those curly flames looked rather jolly. The whole thing had been mellowed and faded into a gentle unreality long before my time; if it had much terror even in my childhood I have forgotten it, it was not so terrible as the giant who was killed by the Beanstalk, and I see it all now as a setting for my poor old mother's worn and grimy face, and almost lovingly as a part of her. And Mr. Gabbitas, our plump little lodger, strangely transformed in his vestments and lifting his voice manfully to the quality of those Elizabethan prayers, seemed, I think, to give her a special and peculiar interest with God. She radiated her own tremulous gentleness upon Him, and redeemed Him from all the implications of vindictive theologians; she was in truth, had I but perceived it, the effectual answer to all she would have taught me.

So I see it now, but there is something harsh in the earnest intensity of youth; and having at first taken all these things quite seriously, the fiery hell and God's vindictiveness at any neglect, as though they were as much a matter of fact as Bladden's ironworks and Rawdon's pot-bank, I presently with an equal seriousness flung them out of my mind again.

Mr. Gabbitas, you see, did sometimes, as the phrase went, "take notice" of me, he had induced me to go on reading after I left school, and with the best intentions in the world and to anticipate the poison of the times he had lent me Burble's "Scepticism Answered," and drawn my attention to the library of the Institute in Clayton.

The excellent Burble was a great shock to me. It seemed clear from his answer to the sceptic that the case for doctrinal orthodoxy and all that faded and by no means awful hereafter, which I had hitherto accepted as I accepted the sun, was an extremely poor one, and to hammer home that idea the first book I got from the Institute happened to be an American edition of the collected works of Shelley, his gassy prose as well as his atmospheric verse. I was soon ripe for blatant unbelief. And at the Young Men's Christian Association I presently made the acquaintance of Parload, who told me, under promises of the most sinister secrecy, that he was "a Socialist out and out." He lent me several copies of a periodical with the clamant title of *The Clarion*, which was just taking up a crusade against the accepted religion. The adolescent years of any fairly intelligent youth lie open, and will always lie healthily open, to the contagion of philosophical doubts, of scorns and new ideas, and I will confess I had the fever of that phase badly. Doubt, I say, but it was not so much doubt—which is a complex thing—as startled emphatic denial. "Have I believed *this!*" And I was also, you must remember, just beginning love-letters to Nettie.

We live now in these days, when the Great Change has been in most things accomplished, in a time when everyone is being educated to a sort of intellectual gentleness, a gentleness that abates nothing from our vigour, and it is hard to understand the stifled and struggling manner in which my generation of common young men did its thinking. To think at all about certain questions was an act of rebellion that set one oscillating between the furtive and the defiant. People begin to find Shelley—for all his melody—noisy and ill-conditioned now because his Anarchs have vanished, yet there was a time when novel thought *had* to go to that tune of breaking glass. It becomes a little difficult to imagine the yeasty state of mind, the disposition to shout and say, "Yah!" at constituted authority, to sustain a persistent note of provocation such as we raw youngsters displayed. I began to read with avidity such writing as Carlyle, Browning, and Heine have left for the perplexity of posterity, and not only to read and admire but to imitate. My letters to Nettie, after one or two genuinely intended displays of perfervid tenderness, broke out towards theology, sociology, and the cosmos in turgid and startling expressions. No doubt they puzzled her extremely.

I retain the keenest sympathy and something inexplicably near to envy for my own departed youth, but I should find it difficult to maintain my case against anyone who would condemn them altogether as having been a very silly, posturing, emotional hobbledehoy indeed and quite like my faded photograph. And when I try to recall what exactly must have been the quality and tenor of my more sustained efforts to write memorably to my sweetheart, I confess I shiver. . . . Yet I wish they were not all destroyed.

Her letters to me were simple enough, written in a roundish, unformed hand and badly phrased. Her first two or three showed a shy pleasure in the use of the word "dear," and I remember being first puzzled and then, when I understood, delighted, because she had written "Willie *asthore*" under my name. "Asthore," I gathered, meant "darling." But when the evidences of my fermentation began, her answers were less happy.

I will not weary you with the story of how we quarrelled in our silly youthful way, and how I went the next Sunday, all uninvited, to Checkshill, and made it worse, and how afterwards I wrote a letter that she thought was "lovely," and mended the matter. Nor will I tell of all our subsequent fluctuations of misunderstanding. Always I was the offender and the final penitent until this last trouble that was now beginning; and in between we had some tender near moments, and I loved her very greatly. There was this misfortune in the business, that in the darkness, and alone, I thought with great intensity of her, of her eyes, of her touch, of her sweet and delightful presence, but when I sat down to write I thought of Shelley and Burns and myself, and other such irrelevant matters. When one is in love in this fermenting way, it is harder to make love than it is when one does not love at all. And as for Nettie, she loved, I know, not me but those gentle mysteries. It was not my voice should rouse her dreams to passion. . . . So our letters continued to jar. Then suddenly she wrote me one doubting whether she could ever care for anyone who was a Socialist and did not believe in Church, and then hard upon it came another note with unexpected novelties of phrasing. She thought we were not suited to each other, we differed so in tastes and ideas, she had long thought of releasing me from our engagement. In fact, though I really did not apprehend it fully at the first shock, I was dismissed. Her letter had reached me when I came home after old Rawdon's none too civil refusal to raise my wages. On this particular evening of which I write, therefore, I was in a state of feverish adjustment to two new and amazing, two nearly overwhelming facts, that I was neither indispensable to Nettie nor at Rawdon's. And to talk of comets!

Where did I stand!

I had grown so accustomed to think of Nettie as inseparably mine—the whole tradition of "true love" pointed me to that—that for her to face about with these precise small phrases towards abandonment, after we had kissed and whispered and come so close in the little adventurous familiarities of the young, shocked me profoundly. I! I! And Rawdon didn't find me indispensable either. I felt I was suddenly repudiated by the universe and threatened with effacement, that in some positive and emphatic way I must at once assert myself. There was no balm of the religion I had learned, or in the irreligion I had adopted, for wounded self-love.

Should I fling up Rawdon's place at once and then in some extraordinary, swift manner make the fortune of Frobisher's adjacent and closely competitive pot-bank?

215

The first part of that programme at any rate would be easy of accomplishment, to go to Rawdon and say, "You will hear from me again," but for the rest, Frobisher might fail me. That, however, was a secondary issue. The predominant affair was with Nettie. I found my mind thick-shot with flying fragments of rhetoric that might be of service in the letter I would write her. Scorn, irony, tenderness—what was it to be? . . .

"Bother!" said Parload suddenly.

"What?" said I.

"They're firing up at Bladden's iron-works, and the smoke comes right across my bit of sky."

The interruption came just as I was ripe to discharge my thoughts upon him.

"Parload," said I, "very likely I shall have to leave all this. Old Rawdon won't give me a rise in my wages, and after having asked I don't think I can stand going on upon the old terms any more. See? So I may have to clear out of Clayton for good and all."

### 3

That made Parload put down the opera-glass and look at me.

"It's a bad time to change just now," he said after a little pause.

Rawdon had said as much, in a less agreeable tone.

But with Parload I felt always a disposition to the heroic note. "I'm tired," I said, "of humdrum drudgery for other men. One may as well starve one's body out of a place as starve one's soul in one."

"I don't know about that altogether," began Parload, slowly. . . .

And with that we began one of our interminable conversations, one of those long, wandering, intensely generalising, diffusely personal talks that will be dear to the hearts of intelligent youths until the world comes to an end. The Change has not abolished that, anyhow.

It would be an incredible feat of memory for me now to recall all that meandering haze of words, indeed I recall scarcely any of it, though its circumstances and atmosphere stand out, a sharp, clear picture in my mind. I posed after my manner and behaved very foolishly no doubt, a wounded, smarting egotist, and Parload played his part of the philosopher preoccupied with the deeps.

We were presently abroad, walking through the warm summer's night and talking all the more freely for that. But one thing that I said I can remember. "I wish at times," said I, with a gesture at the heavens "that comet of yours or some such thing would indeed strike this world—and wipe us all away, strikes, wars, tumults, loves, jealousies, and all the wretchedness of life!"

"Ah!" said Parload, and the thought seemed to hang about him.

"It could only add to the miseries of life," he said irrelevantly when presently I was discoursing of other things.

"What would?"

"Collision with a comet. It would only throw things back. It would only make what was left of life more savage than it is at present."

"But why should anything be left of life?" said I. . . .

That was our style, you know, and meanwhile we walked together up the narrow street outside his lodging, up the stepway and the lanes towards Clayton Crest and the high road.

But my memories carry me back so effectually to those days before the Change that I forget that now all these places have been altered beyond recognition, that the narrow street and the stepway and the view from Clayton Crest, and indeed all the world in which I was born and bred and made, has vanished clean away, out of space and out of time, and well-nigh out of the imagination of all those who are younger by a generation than I. You cannot see, as I can see, the dark empty way between the mean houses, the dark empty way lit by a bleary gas-lamp at the corner, you cannot feel the hard checkered pavement under your boots, you cannot mark the dimly lit windows here and there, and the shadows upon the ugly and often patched and crooked blinds of the people cooped within. Nor can you presently pass the beer-house with its brighter gas and its queer, screening windows, nor get a whiff of foul air and foul language from its door, nor see the crumpled furtive figure—some rascal child—that slinks past us down the steps.

We crossed the longer street, up which a clumsy steam tram, vomiting smoke and sparks, made its clangorous way, and adown which one saw the greasy brilliance of shop fronts and the naphtha flares of hawkers' barrows dripping fire into the night. A hazy movement of people swayed along that road, and we heard the voice of an itinerant preacher from a waste place between the houses. You cannot see these things as I can see them, nor can you figure—unless you know the pictures that great artist Hyde has left the world—the effect of the hoarding by which we passed, lit below by a gas-lamp and towering up to a sudden sharp black edge against the pallid sky.

Those hoardings! They were the brightest coloured things in all that vanished world. Upon them, in successive layers of paste and paper, all the rough enterprises of that time joined in chromatic discord; pill vendors and preachers, theatres and charities, marvelous soaps and astonishing pickles, typewriting machines and sewing machines, mingled in a sort of visualised clamour. And passing that there was a muddy lane of cinders, a lane without a light, that used its many puddles to borrow a star or so from the sky. We splashed along unheeding as we talked.

Then across the allotments, a wilderness of cabbages and evil-looking sheds, past a gaunt abandoned factory, and so to the highroad. The high road ascended in a curve past a few houses and a beerhouse or so, and round until all the valley in which four industrial towns lay crowded and confluent was overlooked.

I will admit that with the twilight there came a spell of weird magnificence over all that land and brooded on it until dawn. The horrible meanness of its details was veiled, the hutches that were homes, the bristling multitudes of chimneys, the ugly patches of unwilling vegetation amidst the makeshift fences of barrelstave and wire. The rusty scars that framed the opposite ridges where the iron ore was taken and the barren mountains of slag from the blast furnaces were veiled; the reek and boiling smoke and dust from foundry, pot-bank, and furnace, transfigured and assimilated by the night. The dust-laden atmosphere that was grey oppression through the day became at sundown a mystery of deep translucent colours of blues and purples, of sombre and vivid reds, of strange bright clearnesses of green and yellow athwart the darkling sky. Each upstart furnace, when its monarch sun had gone, crowned itself with flames, the dark cinder heaps began to glow with quivering fires, and each pot-bank squatted rebellious in a volcanic coronet of light. The empire of the day broke into a thousand feudal baronies of burning coal. The minor streets across the valley picked themselves out with gas-lamps of faint yellow, that brightened and mingled at all the principal squares and crossings with the greenish pallor of incandescent mantles and the high cold glare of the electric arc. The interlacing railways lifted bright signal-boxes over their intersections, and signal stars of red and green in rectangular constellations. The trains became articulated black serpents breathing fire. . . .

Moreover, high overhead, like a thing put out of reach and near forgotten, Parload had rediscovered a realm that was ruled by neither sun nor furnace, the universe of stars.

This was the scene of many a talk we two had held together. And if in the daytime we went right over the crest and looked westward there was farmland, there were parks and great mansions, the spire of a distant cathedral, and sometimes when the weather was near raining, the crests of remote mountains hung clearly in the sky. Beyond the range of sight indeed, out beyond, there was Checkshill; I felt it there always, and in the darkness more than I did by day. Checkshill, and Nettie!

And to us two youngsters, as we walked along the cinder path beside the rutted road and argued out our perplexities, it seemed that this ridge gave us compendiously a view of our whole world.

There on the one hand in a crowded darkness, about the ugly factories and work-places, the workers herded together, ill clothed, ill nourished, ill taught, badly and expressively served at every occasion in life, uncertain even of their insufficient livelihood from day to day, the chapels and churches and public-hoses swelling up amidst their wretched homes like saprophytes amidst a general corruption, and on the other, in space, freedom, and dignity, scarce heeding the few cottages, as overcrowded as they were picturesque, in which the labourers festered, lived the landlords and masters who owned pot-banks and forge and farm and mine. Far away, distant, beautiful, irrelevant, from out of a little cluster of a second-hand bookshops, ecclesiastical residences, and the inns and incidentals of a decaying market town, the cathedral of Lowchester pointed a beautiful, unemphatic spire to vague incredible skies. So it seemed to us that the whole world was planned in those youthful first impressions.

218

We saw everything simple, as young men will. We had our angry, confident solutions, and whosoever would criticise them was a friend of the robbers. It was a clear case of robbery, we held, visibly so; there in those great houses lurked the Landlord and the Capitalist, with his scoundrel the Lawyer, with his cheat the Priest, and we others were all victims of their deliberate villainies. No doubt they winked and chuckled over their rare wines, amidst their dazzling, wickedly dressed women, and plotted further grinding for the faces of the poor. And amidst all the squalor on the other hand, amidst brutalities, ignorance, and drunkenness, suffered multitudinously their blameless victim, the Working Man. And we, almost at the first glance, had found all this out, it had merely to be asserted now with sufficient rhetoric and vehemence to change the face of the whole world. The Working Man would arise—in the form of a Labour Party, and with young men like Parload and myself to represent him—and come to his own, and then—?

Then the robbers would get it hot, and everything would be extremely satisfactory.

Unless my memory plays me strange tricks, that does no injustice to the creed of thought and action that Parload and I held as the final result of human wisdom. We believed it with heat, and rejected with heat the most obvious qualification of its harshness. At times in our great talks we were full of heady hopes for the near triumph of our doctrine, more often our mood was hot resentment at the wickedness and stupidity that delayed so plain and simple a reconstruction of the order of the word. Then we grew malignant, and thought of barricades and significant violence. I was very bitter, I know, upon this night of which I am now particularly telling; and the only face upon the hydra of Capitalism and Monopoly that I could see at all clearly, smiled exactly as old Rawdon had smiled when he refused to give me more than a paltry twenty shillings a week.

I wanted intensely to salve my self-respect by some revenge upon him, and I felt that if that could be done by slaying the hydra, I might drag its carcass to the feet of Nettie, and settle my other trouble as well. "What do you think of me now, Nettie?"

That at any rate comes near enough to the quality of my thinking then, for you to imagine how I gesticulated and spouted to Parload that night. You see us as little black figures, unprepossessing in outline, set in the midst of that desolating night of flaming industrialism, and my little voice with a rhetorical twang protesting, denouncing. . . .

You will consider those notions of my youth poor silly violent stuff; particularly if you are of the younger generation born since the Change you will be of that opinion. Nowadays the whole world thinks clearly, thinks with deliberation, pellucid certainties; you find it impossible to imagine how any other thinking could have been possible. Let me tell you then how you can bring yourself to something like the condition of our former state. In the first place you must get yourself out of health by unwise drinking and eating, and out of condition by neglecting your exercise; then you must contrive to be worried very much and made very anxious and uncomfortable, and then you must work very hard for four or five days and for long hours every day at something too petty to be interesting, too complex to be mechanical, and without any personal significance to you whatever. This done, get straightway into a room that is not ventilated at all, and that is already full of foul air, and there set yourself to think out some very complicated problem. In a little while you will find yourself in a state of intellectual muddle, annoyed, impatient, snatching at the obvious, presently choosing and rejecting conclusions haphazard. Try to play chess under such conditions and you will play stupidly and lose your temper. Try to do anything that taxes the brain or temper and you will fail.

Now the whole world before the Change was as sick and feverish as that; it was worried and overworked and perplexed by problems that would not get stated simply, that changed and evaded solution, it was in an atmosphere that had corrupted and thickened past breathing; there was no thorough cool thinking in the world at all. There was nothing in the mind of the world anywhere but half-truths, hasty assumptions, hallucinations, and emotions. Nothing. . . .

I know it seems incredible, that already some of the younger men are beginning to doubt the greatness of the Change our world has undergone, but read—read the newspapers of that time. Every age becomes mitigated and a little ennobled in our minds as it recedes into the past. It is the past of those who like myself have stories of that time to tell, to supply, by a scrupulous spiritual realism, some antidote to that glamour.

4

Always with Parload I was chief talker.

I can look back upon myself with, I believe, an almost perfect detachment. Things have so changed that indeed now I am another being, with scarce anything in common with that boastful foolish youngster whose troubles I recall. I see him vulgarly theatrical, egotistical, insincere; indeed I do not like him save with that instinctive material sympathy that is the fruit of incessant intimacy. Because he was myself I may be able to feel and write understandingly about motives that will put him out of sympathy with nearly every reader, but why should I palliate or defend his quality?

Always, I say, I did the talking, and it would have amazed me beyond measure if anyone had told me that mine was not the greater intelligence in these wordy encounters. Parload was a quiet youth, and stiff and restrained in all things, while I had that supreme gift of young men and democracies, the gift of copious expression. Parload I diagnosed in my secret heart as a trifle dull; he posed as pregnant quiet, I thought, and was obsessed by the congenial notion of "scientific caution." I did not remark that while my hands were chiefly useful for gesticulation or holding a pen, Parload's hands could do all sorts of things; and I did not think therefore that fibres must run from those fingers to something in his brain. Nor, though I bragged perpetually of my shorthand, of my literature, of my indispensable share in Rawdon's business, did Parload lay stress on the conics and calculus he "mugged" in the organised science school. Parload is a famous man now, a great figure in a great time, his work upon intersection radiations had broadened the intellectual horizon of mankind for ever; and I, who am at best a hewer of intellectual wood, a drawer of living water, can smile, and he can smile, to think how I patronised and posed and jabbered over him in the darkness of those early days.

That night I was shrill and eloquent beyond measure. Rawdon was, of course, the hub upon which I went round—Rawdon and the Rawdonesque employer and the injustice of "wages slavery" and all the immediate conditions of that industrial blind alley up which it seemed our lives were thrust. But ever and again I glanced at other things. Nettie was always there in the background of my mind, regarding me enigmatically. It was part of my pose to Parload that I had a romantic love-affair somewhere way beyond the sphere of our intercourse, and that note gave a Byronic resonance to many of the nonsensical things I produced for his astonishment.

I will not weary you with too detailed an account of the talk of a foolish youth who was also distressed and unhappy, and whose voice was balm for the humiliations that smarted in his eyes. Indeed now in many particulars I cannot disentangle this harangue of which I tell from many of the things I may have said in other talks to Parload. For example I forget if it was then or before or afterwards that, as it were by accident, I let out what might be taken as an admission that I was addicted to drugs.

"You shouldn't do that," said Parload, suddenly. "It won't do to poison your brains with that."

My brains, my eloquence, were to be very important assets to our party in the coming revolution. . . .

But one thing does clearly belong to this particular conversation I am recalling. When I started out it was quite settled in the back of my mind that I must not leave Rawdon's. I simply wanted to abuse my employer to Parload. But I talked myself quite out of touch with all the cogent reasons there were for sticking to my place, and I got home that night irrevocably committed to a spirited—not to say a defiant—policy with my employer.

"I can't stand Rawdon's much longer," I said to Parload by way of a flourish.

"There's hard times coming," said Parload.

"Next winter."

"Sooner. The Americans have been overproducing, and they mean to dump. The iron trade is going to have convulsions."

"I don't care. Pot-banks are steady."

"With a corner in borax? No. I've heard—"

"What have you heard?"

"Office secrets. But it's no secret there's trouble coming to potters. There's been borrowing and speculation. The masters don't stick to one business as they used to do. I can tell that much. Half the valley may be 'playing' before two months are out."

221

Parload delivered himself of this unusually long speech in his most pithy and weighty manner.

"Playing" was our local euphemism for a time when there was no work and no money for a man, a time of stagnation and dreary hungry loafing day after day. Such interludes seemed in those days a necessary consequence of industrial organisation.

"You'd better stick to Rawdon's," said Parload.

"Ugh," said I, affecting a noble disgust.

"There'll be trouble" said Parload.

"Who cares?" said I. "Let there be trouble—the more the better. This system has got to end, sooner or later. These capitalists with their speculation and corners and trusts make things go from bad to worse. Why should I cower in Rawdon's office, like a frightened dog, while hunger walks the streets? Hunger is the master revolutionary. When he comes we ought to turn out and salute him. Anyway, I'm going to do so now."

"That's all very well," began Parload.

"I'm tired of it," I said. "I want to come to grips with all these Rawdons. I think perhaps if I was hungry and savage I could talk to hungry men—"

"There's your mother," said Parload, in his slow judicial way.

That was a difficulty.

I got over it by a rhetorical turn. "Why should one sacrifice the future of the world—why should one even sacrifice one's own future—because one's mother is totally destitute of imagination?"

## 5

It was late when I parted from Parload and came back to my own home.

Our house stood in a highly respectable little square near the Clayton parish church. Mr. Gabbitas, the curate of all work, lodged on our ground floor, and upstairs there was an old lady, Miss Holroyd, who painted flowers on china and maintained her blind sister in an adjacent room; my mother and I lived in the basement and slept in the attics. The front of the house was veiled by a Virginian creeper that defined the Clayton air and clustered in untidy dependent masses over the wooden porch.

As I came up the steps I had a glimpse of Mr. Gabbitas printing photographs by candle light in his room. It was the chief delight of his little life to spend his holiday abroad in the company of a queer little snapshot camera, and to return with a great multitude of foggy and sinister negatives that he had made in beautiful and interesting places. These the camera company would develop for him on advantageous terms, and he would spend his evenings the year through in printing from them in order to inflict copies upon his undeserving friends. There was a long frameful of his work in the Clayton National School, for example, inscribed in old English lettering, "Italian Travel Pictures, by the Rev. E. B. Gabbitas." For this it seemed he lived and travelled and had his being. It was his only real joy. By his shaded light I could see his sharp little nose, his little pale eyes behind his glasses, his mouth pursed up with the endeavor of his employment. . . .

"Hireling Liar," I muttered, for was not he also part of the system, part of the scheme of robbery that made wages serfs of Parload and me?—though his share in the proceedings was certainly small.

"Hireling Liar," said I, standing in the darkness, outside even his faint glow of travelled culture. . . .

My mother let me in.

She looked at me, mutely, because she knew there was something wrong and that it was no use for her to ask what.

"Good night, mumm," said I, and kissed her a little roughly, and lit and took my candle and went off at once up the staircase to bed, not looking at her.

"I've kept some supper for you, dear."

"Don't want any supper."

"But, dearie—"

"Good night, mother," and I went up and slammed my door upon her, blew out my candle, and lay down at once upon my bed, lay there a long time before I got up to undress.

There were times when that dumb beseeching of my mother's face irritated me unspeakably. It did so that night. I felt I had to struggle against it, that I could not exist if I gave way to its pleadings, and it hurt me and divided me to resist it, almost beyond endurance. It was clear to me that I had to think out for myself religious problems, social problems, questions of conduct, questions of expediency, that her poor dear simple beliefs could not help me at all—and she did not understand! Hers was the accepted religion, her only social ideas were blind submissions to the accepted order—to laws, to doctors, to clergymen, lawyers, masters, and all respectable persons in authority over us, and with her to believe was to fear. She knew from a thousand little signs—though still at times I went to church with her—that I was passing out of touch of all these things that ruled her life, into some terrible unknown. From things I said she could infer such clumsy concealments as I made. She felt my socialism, felt my spirit in revolt against the accepted order, felt the impotent resentments that filled me with bitterness against all she held sacred. Yet, you know, it was not her dear gods she sought to defend so much as me! She seemed always to be wanting to say to me, "Dear, I know it's hard—but revolt is harder. Don't make war on it, dear—don't! Don't do anything to offend it. I'm sure it will hurt you if you do—it will hurt you if you do."

She had been cowed into submission, as so many women of that time had been, by the sheer brutality of the accepted thing. The existing order dominated her into a worship of abject observances. It had bent her, aged her, robbed her of eyesight so that at fifty-five she peered through cheap spectacles at my face and saw it only dimly, filled herewith a habit of anxiety, made her hands—Her poor dear hands! Not in the whole world now could you find a woman with hands so grimy, so needle-worn, so misshapen by toil, so chapped and coarsened, so evilly entreated. . . . At any rate, there is this I can say for myself, that my bitterness against the world and fortune was for her sake as well as for my own.

Yet that night I pushed by her harshly. I answered her curtly, left her concerned and perplexed in the passage, and slammed my door upon her.

And for a long time I lay raging at the hardship and evil of life, at the contempt of Rawdon and the loveless coolness of Nettie's letter, at my weakness and insignificance, at the things I found intolerable, and the things I could not mend. Over and over went my poor little brain, tired out and unable to stop on my treadmill of troubles. Nettie. Rawdon. My mother. Gabbitas. Nettie. . . .

Suddenly I came upon emotional exhaustion. Some clock was striking midnight. After all, I was young; I had these quick transitions. I remember quite distinctly, I stood up abruptly, undressed very quickly in the dark, and had hardly touched my pillow again before I was asleep.

But how my mother slept that night I do not know.

Oddly enough, I do not blame myself for behaving like this to my mother, though my conscience blames me acutely for my arrogance to Parload. I regret my behaviour to my mother before the days of the Change, it is a scar among my memories that will always be a little painful to the end of my days, but I do not see how something of the sort was to be escaped under those former conditions. In that time of the muddle and obscurity people were overtaken by needs and toil and hot passions before they had the chance of even a year or so of clear thinking; they settled down to an intense and strenuous application to some partial but immediate duty, and the growth of thought ceased in them. They set and hardened into narrow ways. Few women remained capable of a new idea after five and twenty, few men after thirty-one or two. Discontent with the thing that existed was regarded as immoral, it was certainly an annoyance, and the only protest against it, the only effort against that universal tendency in all human institutions to thicken and clog, to work loosely and badly, to rust and weaken towards catastrophes, came from the young—the crude unmerciful young. It seemed in those days to thoughtful men the harsh law of being—that either we must submit to our elders and be stifled, or disregard them, disobey them, thrust them aside, and make our little step of progress before we too ossified and became obstructive in our turn.

My pushing past my mother, my irresponsive, departure to my own silent meditations, was, I now perceive, a figure of the whole hard relationship between parents and son in those days. There appeared no other way; that perpetually recurring tragedy was, it seemed, part of the very nature of the progress of the word. We did not think, then that minds might grow ripe without growing rigid, or children honour their parents and still think for themselves. We were angry and hasty because we stifled in the darkness, in a poisoned and vitiated air. That deliberate animation of the intelligence which is now the universal quality, that vigour with consideration, that judgment with confident enterprise which shine through all our world, were things disintegrated and unknown in the corrupting atmosphere of our former state.

*(So the first fascicle ended. I put it aside and looked for the second.*

*"Well?" said the man who wrote.*

*"This is fiction?"*

*"It's my story."*

*"But you—Amidst this beauty—You are not this ill-conditioned, squalidly bred lad of whom I have been reading?"*

*He smiled. "There intervenes a certain Change," he said. "Have I not hinted at that?"*

*I hesitated upon a question, then saw the second fascicle at hand, and picked it up.)*

CHAPTER THE SECOND

NETTIE

1

I cannot now remember (the story resumed) what interval separated that evening on which Parload first showed me the comet—I think I only pretended to see it then— and the Sunday afternoon I spent at Checkshill.

Between the two there was time enough for me to give notice and leave Rawdon's, to seek for some other situation very strenuously in vain, to think and say many hard and violent things to my mother and to Parload, and to pass through some phases of very profound wretchedness. There must have been a passionate correspondence with Nettie, but all the froth and fury of that has faded now out of my memory. All I have clear now is that I wrote one magnificent farewell to her, casting her off for ever, and that I got in reply a prim little note to say that even if there was to be an end to everything, that was no excuse for writing such things as I had done, and then I think I wrote again in a vein I considered satirical. To that she did not reply. That interval was at least three weeks, and probably four, because the comet which had been on the first occasion only a dubious speck in the sky, certainly visible only when it was magnified, was now a great white presence, brighter than Jupiter, and casting a shadow on its own account. It was now actively present in the world of human thought, everyone was talking about it, everyone was looking for its waxing splendour as the sun went down—the papers, the music-halls, the hoardings, echoed it.

Yes, the comet was already dominant before I went over to make everything clear to Nettie. And Parload had spent two hoarded pounds in buying himself a spectroscope, so that he could see for himself, night after night, that mysterious, that stimulating line—the unknown line in the green. How many times I wonder did I look at the smudgy, quivering symbol of the unknown things that were rushing upon us out of the inhuman void before I rebelled? But at last I could stand it no longer, and I reproached Parload very bitterly for wasting his time in "astronomical dilettantism."

"Here," said I, "we're on the verge of the biggest lockout in the history of this countryside; here's distress and hunger coming, here's all the capitalistic competitive system like a wound inflamed, and you spend you time gaping at that damned silly streak of nothing in the sky!"

Parload stared at me. "Yes, I do," he said slowly, as though it was a new idea. "Don't I? . . . I wonder why."

"*I* want to start meetings of an evening on Howden's Waste."

"You think they'd listen?"

"They'd listen fast enough now."

"They didn't before," said Parload, looking at his pet instrument.

"There was a demonstration of unemployed at Swathinglea on Sunday. They got to stone throwing."

Parload said nothing for a little while and I said several things. He seemed to be considering something.

"But, after all," he said at last, with an awkward movement towards his spectroscope, "that does signify something."

"The comet?"

"Yes."

"What can it signify? You don't want me to believe in astrology. What does it matter what flames in the heavens—when men are starving on earth?"

"It's—it's science."

"Science! What we want now is socialism—not science."

He still seemed reluctant to give up his comet.

"Socialism's all right," he said, "but if that thing up there was to hit the earth it might matter."

"Nothing matters but human beings."

"Suppose it killed them all."

"Oh," said I, "that's Rot."

"I wonder," said Parload, dreadfully divided in his allegiance.

He looked at the comet. He seemed on the verge of repeating his growing information about the nearness of the paths of the earth and comet, and all that might ensue from that. So I cut in with something I had got out of a now forgotten writer called Ruskin, a volcano of beautiful language and nonsensical suggestions, who prevailed very greatly with eloquent excitable young men in those days. Something it was about the insignificance of science and the supreme importance of Life. Parload stood listening, half turned towards the sky with the tips of his fingers on his spectroscope. He seemed to come to a sudden decision.

"No. I don't agree with you, Leadford," he said. "You don't understand about science."

Parload rarely argued with that bluntness of opposition. I was so used to entire possession of our talk that his brief contradiction struck me like a blow. "Don't agree with me!" I repeated.

"No," said Parload.

"But how?"

"I believe science is of more importance than socialism," he said. "Socialism's a theory. Science—science is something more."

And that was really all he seemed to be able to say.

We embarked upon one of those queer arguments illiterate young men used always to find so heating. Science or Socialism? It was, of course, like arguing which is right, left-handedness or a taste for onions; it was altogether impossible opposition. But the range of my rhetoric enabled me at last to exasperate Parload, and his mere repudiation of my conclusions sufficed to exasperate me, and we ended in the key of a positive quarrel. "Oh, very well!" said I. "So long as I know where we are!"

I slammed his door as though I dynamited his house, and went raging down the street but I felt that he was already back at the window worshipping his blessed line in the green, before I got round the corner.

I had to walk for an hour or so, before I was cool enough to go home.

And it was Parload who had first introduced me to Socialism!

Recreant!

The most extraordinary things used to run through my head in those days. I will confess that my mind ran persistently that evening upon revolutions after the best French pattern, and I sat on a Committee of Safety and tried backsliders. Parload was there, among the prisoners, backsliderissimus, aware too late of the error of his ways. His hands were tied behind his back ready for the shambles; through the open door one heard the voice of justice, the rude justice of the people. I was sorry, but I had to do my duty.

"If we punish those who would betray us to Kings," said I, with a sorrowful deliberation, "how much the more must we punish those who would give over the State to the pursuit of useless knowledge"; and so with a gloomy satisfaction sent him off to the guillotine.

"Ah, Parload! Parload! If only you'd listened to me earlier, Parload! . . ."

None the less that quarrel made me extremely unhappy. Parload was my only gossip, and it cost me much to keep away from him and think evil of him with no one to listen to me, evening after evening.

That was a very miserable time for me, even before my last visit to Checkshill. My long unemployed hours hung heavily on my hands. I kept away from home all day, partly to support a fiction that I was sedulously seeking another situation, and partly to escape the persistent question in my mother's eyes. "Why did you quarrel with Mr. Rawdon? Why did you? Why do you keep on going about with a sullen face and risk offending *it* more?" I spent most of the morning in the newspaper-room of the public library, writing impossible applications for impossible posts—I remember that among other things of the sort I offered my services to a firm of private detectives, a sinister breed of traders upon base jealousies now happily vanished from the world, and wrote apropos of an advertisement for "stevedores" that I did not know what the duties of a stevedore might be, but that I was apt and willing to learn—and in the afternoons and evenings I wandered through the strange lights and shadows of my native valley and hated all created things. Until my wanderings were checked by the discovery that I was wearing out my boots.

The stagnant inconclusive malaria of that time!

I perceive that I was an evil-tempered, ill-disposed youth with a great capacity for hatred, but—

There was an excuse for hate.

It was wrong of me to hate individuals, to be rude, harsh, and vindictive to this person or that, but indeed it would have been equally wrong to have taken the manifest offer life made me, without resentment. I see now clearly and calmly what I then felt obscurely and with an unbalanced intensity, that my conditions were intolerable. My work was tedious and laborious and it took up an unreasonable proportion of my time; I was ill clothed, ill fed, ill housed, ill educated and ill trained; my will was suppressed and cramped to the pitch of torture: I had no reasonable pride in myself and no reasonable chance of putting anything right. It was a life hardly worth living. That a large proportion of the people about me had no better a lot, that many had a worse, does not affect these facts. It was a life in which contentment would have been disgraceful. If some of them were contented or resigned, so much the worse for everyone. No doubt it was hasty and foolish of me to throw up my situation, but everything was so obviously aimless and foolish in our social organisation that I do not feel disposed to blame myself even for that, except in so far as it pained my mother and caused her anxiety.

Think of the one comprehensive fact of the lock-out!

That year was a bad year, a year of world-wide economic disorganisation. Through their want of intelligent direction the great "Trust" of American ironmasters, a gang of energetic, narrow-minded furnace owners, had smelted far more iron than the whole world had any demand for. (In those days there existed no means of estimating any need of that sort beforehand.) They had done this without even consulting the ironmasters of any other country. During their period of activity they had drawn into their employment a great number of workers, and had erected a huge productive plant. It is manifestly just that people who do headlong stupid things of this sort should suffer, but in the old days it was quite possible, it was customary, for the real blundereers in such disasters to shift nearly all the consequences of their incapacity. No one thought it wrong for a light-witted "captain of industry" who had led his work-people into overproduction, into the disproportionate manufacture, that is to say, of some particular article, to abandon and dismiss them, nor was there anything to prevent the sudden frantic underselling of some trade rival in order to surprise and destroy his trade, secure his customers for one's own destined needs, and shift a portion of one's punishment upon him. This operation of spasmodic underselling was known as "dumping." The American ironmasters were now dumping on the British market. The British employers were, of course, taking their loss out of their work-people as much as possible, but in addition they were agitating for some legislation that would prevent—not stupid relative excess in production, but "dumping"—not the disease, but the consequences of the disease. The necessary knowledge to prevent either dumping or its cause, the uncorrelated production of commodities, did not exist, but this hardly weighed with them at all; and in answer to their demands there had arisen a curious party of retaliatory-protectionists who combined vague proposals for spasmodic responses to these convulsive attacks from foreign manufacturers, with the very evident intention of achieving financial adventures. The dishonest and reckless elements were indeed so evident in this movement as to add very greatly to the general atmosphere of distrust and insecurity, and in the recoil from the prospect of fiscal power in the hands of the class of men known as the "New Financiers," one heard frightened old-fashioned statesmen assuming with passion that "dumping" didn't occur, or that it was a very charming sort of thing to happen. Nobody would face and handle the rather intricate truth of the business. The whole effect upon the mind of a cool observer was of a covey of unsubstantial jabbering minds drifting over a series of irrational economic cataclysms, prices and employment tumbled about like towers in an earthquake, and amidst the shifting masses were the common work-people going on with their lives as well as they could, suffering, perplexed, unorganised, and for anything but violent, fruitless protests, impotent. You cannot hope now to understand the infinite want of adjustment in the old order of things. At one time there were people dying of actual starvation in India, while men were burning unsaleable wheat in America. It sounds like the account of a particularly mad dream, does it not? It was a dream, a dream from which no one on earth expected an awakening.

To us youngsters with the positiveness, the rationalism of youth, it seemed that the strikes and lockouts, the overproduction and misery could not possibly result simply from ignorance and want of thought and feeling. We needed more dramatic factors than these mental fogs, these mere atmospheric devils. We fled therefore to that common refuge of the unhappy ignorant, a belief in callous insensate plots—we called them "plots"—against the poor.

You can still see how we figured it in any museum by looking up the caricatures of capital and labour that adorned the German and American socialistic papers of the old time.

## 2

I had cast Nettie off in an eloquent epistle, had really imagined the affair was over for ever—"I've done with women," I said to Parload—and then there was silence for more than a week.

Before that week was over I was wondering with a growing emotion what next would happen between us.

I found myself thinking constantly of Nettie, picturing her—sometimes with stern satisfaction, sometimes with sympathetic remorse—mourning, regretting, realising the absolute end that had come between us. At the bottom of my heart I no more believed that there was an end between us, than that an end would come to the world. Had we not kissed one another, had we not achieved an atmosphere of whispering nearness, breached our virgin shyness with one another? Of course she was mine, of course I was hers, and separations and final quarrels and harshness and distance were no more than flourishes upon that eternal fact. So at least I felt the thing, however I shaped my thoughts.

Whenever my imaginations got to work as that week drew to its close, she came in as a matter of course. I thought of her recurrently all day and dreamt of her at night. On Saturday night I dreamt of her very vividly. Her face was flushed and wet with tears her hair a little disordered, and when I spoke to her she turned away. In some manner this dream left in my mind a feeling of distress and anxiety. In the morning I had a raging thirst to see her.

That Sunday my mother wanted me to go to church very particularly. She had a double reason for that; she thought that it would certainly exercise a favourable influence upon my search for a situation throughout the next week, and in addition Mr. Gabbitas, with certain mystery behind his glasses, had promised to see what he could do for me, and she wanted to keep him up to that promise. I half consented, and then my desire for Nettie took hold of me. I told my mother I wasn't going to church, and set off about eleven to walk the seventeen miles to Checkshll.

It greatly intensified the fatigue of that long tramp that the sole of my boot presently split at the toe, and after I had put the flapping portion off, a nail worked through and began to torment me. However, the boot looked all right after that operation and gave no audible hint of my discomfort. I got some bread and cheese at a little inn on the way, and was in Checkshill park about four. I did not go by the road past the house and so round to the gardens, but cut over the crest beyond the second keeper's cottage, along a path Nettie used to call her own. It was a mere deer track. It led up a miniature valley and through a pretty dell in which we had been accustomed to meet, and so through the hollies and along a narrow path close by the wall of the shrubbery to the gardens.

In my memory that walk through the park before I came upon Nettie stands out very vividly. The long tramp before it is fore-shortened to a mere effect of dusty road and painful boot, but the bracken valley and sudden tumult of doubts and unwonted expectations that came to me, stands out now as something significant, as something unforgettable, something essential to the meaning of all that followed. Where should I meet her? What would she say? I had asked these questions before and found an answer. Now they came again with a trail of fresh implications and I had no answer for them at all. As I approached Nettie she ceased to be the mere butt of my egotistical self-projection, the custodian of my sexual pride, and drew together and became over

230

and above this a personality of her own, a personality and a mystery, a sphinx I had evaded only to meet again.

I find a little difficulty in describing the quality of the old-world love-making so that it may be understandable now.

We young people had practically no preparation at all for the stir and emotions of adolescence. Toward the young the world maintained a conspiracy of stimulating silences. There came no initiation. There were books, stories of a curiously conventional kind that insisted on certain qualities in every love-affair and greatly intensified one's natural desire for them, perfect trust, perfect loyalty, lifelong devotion. Much of the complex essentials of love were altogether hidden. One read these things, got accidental glimpses of this and that, wondered and forgot, and so one grew. Then strange emotions, novel alarming desires, dreams strangely charged with feeling; an inexplicable impulse of self-abandonment began to trickle queerly amongst the familiar purely egotistical and materialist things of boyhood and girlhood. We were like misguided travellers who had camped in the dry bed of a tropical river. Presently we were knee keep and neck deep in the flood. Our beings were suddenly going out from ourselves seeking other beings we knew not why. This novel craving for abandonment to some one of the other sex, bore us away. We were ashamed and full of desire. We kept the thing a guilty secret, and were resolved to satisfy it against all the world. In this state it was we drifted in the most accidental way against some other blindly seeking creature, and linked like nascent atoms.

We were obsessed by the books we read, by all the talk about us that once we had linked ourselves we were linked for life. Then afterwards we discovered that other was also an egotism, a thing of ideas and impulses, that failed to correspond with ours.

So it was, I say, with the young of my class and most of the young people in our world. So it came about that I sought Nettie on the Sunday afternoon and suddenly came upon her, light bodied, slenderly feminine, hazel eyed, with her soft sweet young face under the shady brim of her hat of straw, the pretty Venus I had resolved should be wholly and exclusively mine.

There, all unaware of me still, she stood, my essential feminine, the embodiment of the inner thing in life for me—and moreover an unknown other, a person like myself.

She held a little book in her hand, open as if she were walking along and reading it. That chanced to be her pose, but indeed she was standing quite still, looking away towards the grey and lichenous shrubbery wall and, as I think now, listening. Her lips were a little apart, curved to that faint sweet shadow of a smile.

### 3

I recall with a vivid precision her queer start when she heard the rustle of my approaching feet, her surprise, her eyes almost of dismay for me. I could recollect, I believe, every significant word she spoke during our meeting, and most of what I said to her. At least, it seems I could, though indeed I may deceive myself. But I will not make the attempt. We were both too ill-educated to speak our full meanings, we stamped out our feelings with clumsy stereotyped phrases; you who are better taught would fail to catch our intention. The effect would be inanity. But our first words I may give you, because though they conveyed nothing to me at the time, afterwards they meant much.

"You, Willie!" she said.

"I have come," I said—forgetting in the instant all the elaborate things I had intended to say. "I thought I would surprise you—"

"Surprise me?"

"Yes."

She stared at me for a moment. I can see her pretty face now as it looked at me—her impenetrable dear face. She laughed a queer little laugh and her colour went for a moment, and then so soon as she had spoken, came back again.

"Surprise me at what?" she said with a rising note.

I was too intent to explain myself to think of what might lie in that.

"I wanted to tell you," I said, "that I didn't mean quite . . . the things I put in my letter."

4

When I and Nettie had been sixteen we had been just of an age and contemporaries altogether. Now we were a year and three-quarters older, and she—her metamorphosis was almost complete, and I was still only at the beginning of a man's long adolescence.

In an instant she grasped the situation. The hidden motives of her quick-ripened little mind flashed out their intuitive scheme of action. She treated me with that neat perfection of understanding a young woman has for a boy.

"But how did you come?" she asked.

I told her I had walked.

"Walked!" In an instant she was leading me towards the gardens. I must be tired. I must come home with her at once and sit down. Indeed it was near tea-time (the Stuarts had tea at the old-fashioned hour of five). Everyone would be so surprised to see me. Fancy walking! Fancy! But she supposed a man thought nothing of seventeen miles. When could I have started!

All the while, keeping me at a distance, without even the touch of her hand.

"But, Nettie! I came over to talk to you!"

"My dear boy! Tea first, if you please! And besides—aren't we talking?"

The "dear boy" was a new note, that sounded oddly to me.

She quickened her pace a little.

"I wanted to explain—" I began.

Whatever I wanted to explain I had no chance to do so. I said a few discrepant things that she answered rather by her intonation than her words.

When we were well past the shrubbery, she slackened a little in her urgency, and so we came along the slope under the beeches to the garden. She kept her bright, straightforward-looking girlish eyes on me as we went; it seemed she did so all the time, but now I know, better than I did then, that every now and then she glanced over me and behind me towards the shrubbery. And all the while, behind her quick breathless, inconsecutive talk, she was thinking.

Her dress marked the end of her transition.

Can I recall it?

Not, I am afraid, in the terms a woman would use. But her bright brown hair, which had once flowed down her back in a jolly pig-tail tied with a bit of scarlet ribbon, was now caught up into an intricacy of pretty curves above her little ear and cheek, and the soft long lines of her neck; her white dress had descended to her feet; her slender waist, which had once been a mere geographical expression, an imaginary line like the equator, was now a thing of flexible beauty. A year ago she had been a pretty girl's face sticking out from a little unimportant frock that was carried upon an extremely active and efficient pair of brown-stockinged legs. Now there was coming a strange new body that flowed beneath her clothes with a sinuous insistence. Every movement, and particularly the novel droop of her hand and arm to the unaccustomed skirts she gathered about her, and a graceful forward inclination that had come to her, called softly to my eyes. A very fine scarf—I suppose you would call it a scarf—of green gossamer, that some new-wakened instinct had told her to fling about her shoulders, clung now closely to the young undulations of her body, and now streamed fluttering out for a moment in a breath of wind, and like some shy independent tentacle with a secret to impart, came into momentary contact with my arm.

She caught it back and reproved it.

We went through the green gate in the high garden wall. I held it open for her to pass through, for this was one of my restricted stock of stiff politenesses, and then for a second she was near touching me. Se we came to the trim array of flower-beds near the head gardener's cottage and the vistas of "glass" on our left. We walked between the box edgings and beds of begonias, and into the shadow of a yew hedge within twenty yards of that very pond with the gold-fish at whose brim we had plighted our vows, and so we came to the wistaria-smothered porch.

The door was wide open, and she walked in before me. "Guess who has come to see us!" she cried.

Her father answered indistinctly from the parlour, and a chair creaked. I judged he was disturbed in his nap.

"Mother!" she called in her clear young voice. "Puss!"

Puss was her sister.

She told them in a marvelling key that I had walked all the way from Clayton, and they gathered about me and echoed her notes of surprise.

233

"You'd better sit down, Willie," said her father; "now you have got here. How's your mother?"

He looked at me curiously as he spoke.

He was dressed in his Sunday clothes, a sort of brownish tweeds, but the waistcoat was unbuttoned for greater comfort in his slumbers. He was a brown-eyed ruddy man, and I still have now in my mind the bright effect of the red-golden hairs that started out from his cheek to flow down into his beard. He was short but strongly built, and his beard and moustache were the biggest things about him. She had taken all the possibility of beauty he possessed, his clear skin, his bright hazel-brown eyes, and wedded them to a certain quickness she got from her mother. Her mother I remember as a sharp-eyed woman of great activity; she seems to me now to have been perpetually bringing in or taking out meals or doing some such service, and to me—for my mother's sake and my own—she was always welcoming and kind. Puss was a youngster of fourteen perhaps of whom a hard bright stare, and a pale skin like her mother's, are the chief traces on my memory. All these people were very kind to me, and among them there was a common recognition, sometimes very agreeably finding expression, that I was—"clever." They all stood about me as if they were a little at a loss.

"Sit down!" said her father. "Give him a chair, Puss."

We talked a little stiffly—they were evidently surprised by my sudden apparition, dusty, fatigued, and white-faced; but Nettie did not remain to keep the conversation going.

"There!" she cried suddenly, as if she were vexed. "I declare!" and she darted out of the room.

"Lord! What a girl it is!" said Mrs. Stuart. "I don't know what's come to her."

It was half an hour before Nettie came back. It seemed a long time to me, and yet she had been running, for when she came in again she was out of breath. In the meantime, I had thrown out casually that I had given up my place at Rawdon's. "I can do better than that," I said.

"I left my book in the dell," she said, panting. "Is tea ready?" and that was her apology. . . .

We didn't shake down into comfort even with the coming of the tea-things. Tea at the gardener's cottage was a serious meal, with a big cake and little cakes, and preserves and fruit, a fine spread upon a table. You must imagine me, sullen, awkward, and preoccupied, perplexed by the something that was inexplicably unexpected in Nettie, saying little, and glowering across the cake at her, and all the eloquence I had been concentrating for the previous twenty-four hours, miserably lost somewhere in the back of my mind. Nettie's father tried to set me talking; he had a liking for my gift of ready speech, for his own ideas came with difficulty, and it pleased and astonished him to hear me pouring out my views. Indeed, over there I was, I think, even more talkative than with Parload, though to the world at large I was a shy young lout. "You ought to write it out for the newspapers," he used to say. "That's what you ought to do. I never heard such nonsense."

234

Or, "You've got the gift of the gab, young man. We ought to ha' made a lawyer of you."

But that afternoon, even in his eyes, I didn't shine. Failing any other stimulus, he reverted to my search for a situation, but even that did not engage me.

## 5

For a long time I feared I should have to go back to Clayton without another word to Nettie, she seemed insensible to the need I felt for a talk with her, and I was thinking even of a sudden demand for that before them all. It was a transparent maneuver of her mother's, who had been watching my face, that sent us out at last together to do something—I forget now what—in one of the greenhouses. Whatever that little mission may have been it was the merest, most barefaced excuse, a door to shut, or a window to close, and I don't think it got done.

Nettie hesitated and obeyed. She led the way through one of the hot-houses. It was a low, steamy, brick-floored alley between staging that bore a close crowd of pots and ferns, and behind big branching plants that were spread and nailed overhead so as to make an impervious cover of leaves, and in that close green privacy she stopped and turned on me suddenly like a creature at bay.

"Isn't the maidenhair fern lovely?" she said, and looked at me with eyes that said, "Now."

"Nettie," I began, "I was a fool to write to you as I did."

She startled me by the assent that flashed out upon her face. But she said nothing, and stood waiting.

"Nettie," I plunged, "I can't do without you. I—I love you."

"If you loved me," she said trimly, watching the white fingers she plunged among the green branches of a selaginella, "could you write the things you do to me?"

"I don't mean them," I said. "At least not always."

I thought really they were very good letters, and that Nettie was stupid to think otherwise, but I was for the moment clearly aware of the impossibility of conveying that to her.

"You wrote them."

"But then I tramp seventeen miles to say I don't mean them."

"Yes. But perhaps you do."

I think I was at a loss; then I said, not very clearly, "I don't."

"You think you—you love me, Willie. But you don't."

"I do. Nettie! You know I do."

For answer she shook her head.

I made what I thought was a most heroic plunge. "Nettie," I said, "I'd rather have you than—than my own opinions."

The selaginella still engaged her. "You think so now," she said.

I broke out into protestations.

"No," she said shortly. "It's different now."

"But why should two letters make so much difference?" I said.

"It isn't only the letters. But it is different. It's different for good."

She halted a little with that sentence, seeking expression. She looked up abruptly into my eyes and moved, indeed slightly, but with the intimation that she thought our talk might end.

But I did not mean it to end like that.

"For good?" said I. "No! . . . Nettie! Nettie! You don't mean that!"

"I do," she said deliberately, still looking at me, and with all her pose conveying her finality. She seemed to brace herself for the outbreak that must follow.

Of course I became wordy. But I did not submerge her. She stood intrenched, firing her contradictions like guns into my scattered discursive attack. I remember that our talk took the absurd form of disputing whether I could be in love with her or not. And there was I, present in evidence, in a deepening and widening distress of soul because she could stand there, defensive, brighter and prettier than ever, and in some inexplicable way cut off from me and inaccessible.

You know, we had never been together before without little enterprises of endearment, without a faintly guilty, quite delightful excitement.

I pleaded, I argued. I tried to show that even my harsh and difficult letters came from my desire to come wholly into contact with her. I made exaggerated fine statements of the longing I felt for her when I was away, of the shock and misery of finding her estranged and cool. She looked at me, feeling the emotion of my speech and impervious to its ideas. I had no doubt—whatever poverty in my words, coolly written down now, might convey—that I was eloquent then. I meant most intensely what I said, indeed I was wholly concentrated upon it. I was set upon conveying to her with absolute sincerity my sense of distance, and the greatness of my desire. I toiled towards her painfully and obstinately through a jungle of words.

Her face changed very slowly—by such imperceptible degrees as when at dawn light comes into a clear sky. I could feel that I touched her, that her hardness was in some manner melting, her determination softening towards hesitations. The habit of an old familiarity lurked somewhere within her. But she would not let me reach her.

"No," she cried abruptly, starting into motion.

She laid a hand on my arm. A wonderful new friendliness came into her voice. "It's impossible, Willie. Everything is different now—everything. We made a mistake. We two young sillies made a mistake and everything is different for ever. Yes, yes."

She turned about.

"Nettie!" cried I, and, still protesting, pursued her along the narrow alley between the staging toward the hot-house door. I pursued her like an accusation, and she went before me like one who is guilty and ashamed. So I recall it now.

She would not let me talk to her again.

Yet I could see that my talk to her had altogether abolished the clear-cut distance of our meeting in the park. Ever and again I found her hazel eyes upon me. They expressed something novel—a surprise, as though she realised an unwonted relationship, and a sympathetic pity. And still—something defensive.

When we got back to the cottage, I fell talking rather more freely with her father about the nationalisation of railways, and my spirits and temper had so far mended at the realisation that I could still produce an effect upon Nettie, that I was even playful with Puss. Mrs. Stuart judged from that that things were better with me than they were, and began to beam mightily.

But Nettie remained thoughtful and said very little. She was lost in perplexities I could not fathom, and presently she slipped away from us and went upstairs.

<h1 style="text-align:center">6</h1>

I was, of course, too footsore to walk back to Clayton, but I had a shilling and a penny in my pocket for the train between Checkshill and Two-Mile Stone, and that much of the distance I proposed to do in the train. And when I got ready to go, Nettie amazed me by waking up to the most remarkable solicitude for me. I must, she said, go by the road. It was altogether too dark for the short way to the lodge gates.

I pointed out that it was moonlight. "With the comet thrown in," said old Stuart.

"No," she insisted, "you must go by the road."

I still disputed.

She was standing near me. "To please me," she urged, in a quick undertone, and with a persuasive look that puzzled me. Even in the moment I asked myself why should this please her.

I might have agreed had she not followed that up with, "The hollies by the shrubbery are as dark as pitch. And there's the deer-hounds."

"I'm not afraid of the dark," said I. "Nor of the deer-hounds, either."

"But those dogs! Supposing one was loose!"

That was a girl's argument, a girl who still had to understand that fear is an overt argument only for her own sex. I thought too of those grisly lank brutes straining at their chains and the chorus they could make of a night when they heard belated footsteps along the edge of the Killing Wood, and the thought banished my wish to please her. Like most imaginative natures I was acutely capable of dreads and retreats, and constantly occupied with their suppression and concealment, and to refuse the short cut when it might appear that I did it on account of half a dozen almost certainly chained dogs was impossible.

So I set off in spite of her, feeling valiant and glad to be so easily brave, but a little sorry that she should think herself crossed by me.

A thin cloud veiled the moon, and the way under the beeches was dark and indistinct. I was not so preoccupied with my love-affairs as to neglect what I will confess was always my custom at night across that wild and lovely park. I made myself a club by fastening a big flint to one end of my twisted handkerchief and tying the other about my wrist, and with this in my pocket, went on comforted.

And it chanced that as I emerged from the hollies by the corner of the shrubbery I was startled to come unexpectedly upon a young man in evening dress smoking a cigar.

I was walking on turf, so that the sound I made was slight. He stood clear in the moonlight, his cigar glowed like a blood-red star, and it did not occur to me at the time that I advanced towards him almost invisibly in an impenetrable shadow.

"Hullo," he cried, with a sort of amiable challenge. "I'm here first!"

I came out into the light. "Who cares if you are?" said I.

I had jumped at once to an interpretation of his words. I knew that there was an intermittent dispute between the House people and the villager public about the use of this track, and it is needless to say where my sympathies fell in that dispute.

"Eh!" he cried in surprise.

"Thought I would run away, I suppose," said I, and came close up to him.

All my enormous hatred of his class had flared up at the sight of his costume, at the fancied challenge of his words. I knew him. He was Edward Verrall, son of the man who owned not only this great estate but more than half of Rawdon's pot-bank, and who had interests and possessions, collieries and rents, all over the district of the Four Towns. He was a gallant youngster, people said, and very clever. Young as he was there was talk of parliament for him; he had been a great success at the university, and he was being sedulously popularised among us. He took with a light confidence, as a matter of course, advantages that I would have faced the rack to get, and I firmly believed myself a better man than he. He was, as he stood there, a concentrated figure of all that filled me with bitterness. One day he had stopped in a motor outside our house, and I remember the thrill of rage with which I had noted the dutiful admiration in my mother's eyes as she peered through her blind at him. "That's young Mr. Verrall," she said, "They say he's very clever."

"They would," I answered. "Damn them and him!"

But that is by the way.

He was clearly astonished to find himself face to face with a man. His note changed.

"Who the devil are you!" he asked.

My retort was the cheap expedient of re-echoing, "Who the devil are you?"

"Well," he said.

"I'm coming along this path if I like," I said. "See! It's a public path—just as this used to be public land. You've stolen the land—you and yours, and now you want to steal the right of way. You'll ask us to get off the face of the earth next. I shan't oblige. See?"

I was shorter and I suppose a couple of years younger than he, but I had the improvised club in my pocket gripped ready, and I would have fought with him very cheerfully. But he fell a step backward as I came towards him.

"Socialist, I presume?" he said, alert and quiet and with the faintest note of bad-inage.

"One of many."

"We're all socialists nowadays,' he remarked philosophically, "and I haven't the faintest intention of disputing your right of way."

"You'd better not," I said.

"No!"

"No."

He replaced his cigar, and there was a brief pause. "Catching a train?" he threw out.

It seemed absurd not to answer. "Yes," I said shortly.

He said it was a pleasant evening for a walk.

I hovered for a moment and there was my path before me, and he stood aside. There seemed nothing to do but go on. "Good night," said he, as that intention took effect.

I growled a surly good night.

I felt like a bombshell of swearing that must presently burst with some violence as I went on my silent way. He had so completely got the best in our encounter.


7

There comes a memory, an odd intermixture of two entirely divergent things, that stands out with the intensest vividness.

As I went across the last open meadow, following the short cut to Checkshill station, I perceived I had two shadows.

The thing jumped into my mind and stopped its tumid flow for a moment. I remember the intelligent detachment of my sudden interest. I turned sharply, and stood looking at the moon and the great white comet, that the drift of the clouds had now rather suddenly unveiled.

The comet was perhaps twenty degrees from the moon. What a wonderful thing it looked floating there, a greenish-white apparition in the dark blue deeps! It looked brighter than the moon because it was smaller, but the shadow it cast, though clearer cut, was much fainter than the moon's shadow. . . . I went on noting these facts, watching my two shadows precede me.

I am totally unable to account for the sequence of my thoughts on this occasion. But suddenly, as if I had come on this new fact round a corner, the comet was out of my mind again, and I was face to face with an absolutely new idea. I wonder sometimes if the two shadows I cast, one with a sort of feminine faintness with regard to the other and not quite so tall, may not have suggested the word or the thought of an assignation to my mind. All that I have clear is that with the certitude of intuition I knew what it was that had brought the youth in evening dress outside the shrubbery. Of course! He had come to meet Nettie!

239

Once the mental process was started it took no time at all. The day which had been full of perplexities for me, the mysterious invisible thing that had held Nettie and myself apart, the unaccountable strange something in her manner, was revealed and explained.

I knew now why she had looked guilty at my appearance, what had brought her out that afternoon why she had hurried me in, the nature of the "book" she had run back to fetch, the reason why she had wanted me to go back by the high-road, and why she had pitied me. It was all in the instant clear to me.

You must imagine me a black little creature, suddenly stricken still—for a moment standing rigid—and then again suddenly becoming active with an impotent gesture, becoming audible with an inarticulate cry, with two little shadows mocking my dismay, and about this figure you must conceive a great wide space of moonlit grass, rimmed by the looming suggestion of distant trees—trees very low and faint and dim, and over it all the domed serenity of that wonderful luminous night.

For a little while this realisation stunned my mind. My thoughts came to a pause, staring at my discovery. Meanwhile my feet and my previous direction carried me through the warm darkness to Checkshill station with its little lights, to the ticket-office window, and so to the train.

I remember myself as it were waking up to the thing—I was alone in one of the dingy "third-class" compartments of that time—and the sudden nearly frantic insurgence of my rage. I stood up with the cry of an angry animal, and smote my fist with all my strength against the panel of wood before me. . . .

Curiously enough I have completely forgotten my mood after that for a little while, but I know that later, for a minute perhaps, I hung for a time out of the carriage with the door open, contemplating a leap from the train. It was to be a dramatic leap, and then I would go storming back to her, denounce her, overwhelm her; and I hung, urging myself to do it. I don't remember how it was I decided not to do this, at last, but in the end I didn't.

When the train stopped at the next station I had given up all thoughts of going back. I was sitting in the corner of the carriage with my bruised and wounded hand pressed under my arm, and still insensible to its pain, trying to think out clearly a scheme of action—action that should express the monstrous indignation that possessed me.

## CHAPTER THE THIRD
## THE REVOLVER
### 1

"That comet is going to hit the earth!"

So said one of the two men who got into the train and settled down.

"Ah!" said the other man.

"They do say that it is made of gas, that comet. We shan't blow up, shall us! . . ."

What did it matter to me?

I was thinking of revenge—revenge against the primary conditions of my being. I was thinking of Nettie and her lover. I was firmly resolved he should not have her— though I had to kill them both to prevent it. I did not care what else might happen, if only that end was insured. All my thwarted passions had turned to rage. I would have accepted eternal torment that night without a second thought, to be certain of revenge. A hundred possibilities of action, a hundred stormy situations, a whirl of violent schemes, chased one another through my shamed, exasperated mind. The sole prospect I could endure was of some gigantic, inexorably cruel vindication of my humiliated self.

And Nettie? I loved Nettie still, but now with the intensest jealousy, with the keen, unmeasuring hatred of wounded pride, and baffled, passionate desire.

## 2

As I came down the hill from Clayton Crest—for my shilling and a penny only permitted my travelling by train as far as Two-Mile Stone, and thence I had to walk over the hill—I remember very vividly a little man with a shrill voice who was preaching under a gas-lamp against a hoarding to a thin crowd of Sunday evening loafers. He was a short man, bald, with a little fair curly beard and hair, and watery blue eyes, and he was preaching that the end of the world drew near.

I think that is the first time I heard anyone link the comet with the end of the world. He had got that jumbled up with international politics and prophecies from the Book of Daniel.

I stopped to hear him only for a moment or so. I do not think I should have halted at all but his crowd blocked my path, and the sight of his queer wild expression, the gesture of his upward-pointing finger, held me.

"There is the end of all your Sins and Follies," he bawled. "There! There is the Star of Judgments, the Judgments of the most High God! It is appointed unto all men to die—unto all men to die"—his voice changed to a curious flat chant—"and after death, the Judgment! The Judgment!"

I pushed and threaded my way through the bystanders and went on, and his curious harsh flat voice pursued me. I went on with the thoughts that had occupied me before—where I could buy a revolver, and how I might master its use—and probably I should have forgotten all about him had he not taken a part in the hideous dream that ended the little sleep I had that night. For the most part I lay awake thinking of Nettie and her lover.

Then came three strange days—three days that seem now to have been wholly concentrated upon one business.

This dominant business was the purchase of my revolver. I held myself resolutely to the idea that I must either restore myself by some extraordinary act of vigour and violence in Nettie's eyes or I must kill her. I would not let myself fall away from that.

I felt that if I let this matter pass, my last shred of pride and honour would pass with it, that for the rest of my life I should never deserve the slightest respect or any woman's love. Pride kept me to my purpose between my guests of passion.

Yet it was not easy to buy that revolver.

I had a kind of shyness of the moment when I should have to face the shopman, and I was particularly anxious to have a story ready if he should see fit to ask questions why I bought such a thing. I determined to say I was going to Texas, and I thought it might prove useful there. Texas in those days had the reputation of a wild lawless land. As I knew nothing of caliber or impact, I wanted also to be able to ask with a steady face at what distance a man or woman could be killed by the weapon that might be offered me. I was pretty cool-headed in relation to such practical aspects of my affair. I had some little difficulty in finding a gunsmith. In Clayton there were some rook-rifles and so forth in a cycle shop, but the only revolvers these people had impressed me as being too small and toylike for my purpose. It was in a pawnshop window in the narrow High Street of Swathinglea that I found my choice, a reasonably clumsy and serious-looking implement ticketed "As used in the American army."

I had drawn out my balance from the savings bank, a matter of two pounds and more, to make this purchase, and I found it at last a very easy transaction. The pawnbroker told me where I could get ammunition, and I went home that night with bulging pockets, an armed man.

The purchase of my revolver was, I say, the chief business of those days, but you must not think I was so intent upon it as to be insensible to the stirring things that were happening in the streets through which I went seeking the means to effect my purpose. They were full of murmurings: the whole region of the Four Towns scowled lowering from its narrow doors. The ordinary healthy flow of people going to work, people going about their business, was chilled and checked. Numbers of men stood about the streets in knots and groves as corpuscles gather and catch in the blood-vessels in the opening stages of inflammation. The women looked haggard and worried. The iron-workers had refused the proposed reduction of their wages, and the lockout had begun. They were already at "play." The Conciliation Board was doing its best to keep the coal-miners and masters from a breach, but young Lord Redcar, the greatest of our coal-owners and landlord of all Swathinglea and half Clayton, was taking a fine upstanding attitude that made the breach inevitable. He was a handsome young man, a gallant young man; his pride revolted at the idea of being dictated to by a "lot of bally miners," and he meant, he said, to make a fight for it. The world had treated him sumptuously from his earliest years; the shares in the common stock of five thousand people had gone to pay for his handsome upbringing, and large, romantic, expensive ambitions filled his generously nurtured mind. He had early distinguished himself at Oxford by his scornful attitude towards democracy. There was something that appealed to the imagination in his fine antagonism to the crowd—on the one hand, was the brilliant young nobleman, picturesquely alone; on the other, the ugly, inexpressive multitude, dressed inelegantly in shop-clothes, under-educated, under-fed, envious, base, and with a wicked disinclination for work and a wicked appetite for the good things it could so rarely get. For common imaginative purposes one left out the policeman from the design, the stalwart policeman protecting his lordship, and ignored the fact that while Lord Redcar had his hands immediately and legally on the workman's shelter and bread, they could touch him to the skin only by some violent breach of the law.

He lived at Lowchester House, five miles or so beyond Checkshill; but partly to show how little he cared for his antagonists, and partly no doubt to keep himself in touch with the negotiations that were still going on, he was visible almost every day in and about the Four Towns, driving that big motor-car of his that could take him sixty miles an hour. The English passion for fair play one might have thought sufficient to rob this bold procedure of any dangerous possibilities, but he did not go altogether free from insult, and on one occasion at least an intoxicated Irish woman shook her first at him. . . .

A dark, quiet crowd, that was greater each day, a crowd more than half women, brooded as a cloud will sometimes brood permanently upon a mountain crest, in the market-place outside the Clayton Town Hall, where the conference was held. . . .

I considered myself justified in regarding Lord Redcar's passing automobile with a special animosity because of the leaks in our roof.

We held our little house on lease; the owner was a mean, saving old man named Pettigrew, who lived in a villa adorned with plaster images of dogs and goats, at Overcastle, and in spite of our specific agreement, he would do no repairs for us at all. He rested secure in my mother's timidity. Once, long ago, she had been behind-hand with her rent, with half of her quarter's rent, and he had extended the days of grace a month; her sense that some day she might need the same mercy again made her his abject slave. She was afraid even to ask that he should cause the roof to be mended for fear he might take offence. But one night the rain poured in on her bed and gave her a cold, and stained and soaked her poor old patchwork counterpane. Then she got me to compose an excessively polite letter to old Pettigrew, begging him as a favour to perform his legal obligations. It is part of the general imbecility of those days that such one-sided law as existed was a profound mystery to the common people, its provisions impossible to ascertain, its machinery impossible to set in motion. Instead of the clearly written code, the lucid statements of rules and principles that are now at the service of everyone, the law was the muddled secret of the legal profession. Poor people, overworked people, had constantly to submit to petty wrongs because of the intolerable uncertainty not only of law but of cost, and of the demands upon time and energy proceedings might make. There was indeed no justice for anyone too poor to command a good solicitor's deference and loyalty; there was nothing but rough police protection and the magistrate's grudging or eccentric advice for the mass of the population. The civil law, in particular, was a mysterious upper-class weapon, and I can imagine no injustice that would have been sufficient to induce my poor old mother to appeal to it.

All this begins to sound incredible. I can only assure you that it was so.

But I, when I learned that old Pettigrew had been down to tell my mother all about his rheumatism, to inspect the roof, and to allege that nothing was needed, gave way to my most frequent emotion in those days, a burning indignation, and took the matter into my own hands. I wrote and asked him, with a withering air of technicality, to have the roof repaired "as per agreement," and added, "if not done in one week from now we shall be obliged to take proceedings." I had not mentioned this high line of conduct to my mother at first, and so when old Pettigrew came down in a state of great agitation with my letter in his hand, she was almost equally agitated.

"How could you write to old Mr. Pettigrew like that?" she asked me.

I said that old Pettigrew was a shameful old rascal, or words to that effect, and I am afraid I behaved in a very undutiful way to her when she said that she had settled everything with him—she wouldn't say how, but I could guess well enough—and that I was to promise her, promise her faithfully, to do nothing more in the matter. I wouldn't promise her.

And—having nothing better to employ me then—I presently went raging to old Pettigrew in order to put the whole thing before him in what I considered the proper light. Old Pettigrew evaded my illumination; he saw me coming up his front steps—I can still see his queer old nose and the crinkled brow over his eye and the little wisp of grey hair that showed over the corner of his window blind—and he instructed his servant to put up the chain when she answered the door, and to tell me that he would not see me. So I had to fall back upon my pen.

Then it was, as I had no idea what were the proper "proceedings" to take, the brilliant idea occurred to me of appealing to Lord Redcar as the ground landlord, and, as it were, our feudal chief, and pointing out to him that his security for his rent was depreciating in old Pettigrew's hands. I added some general observations on lease holds, the taxation of ground rents, and the private ownership of the soil. And Lord Redcar, whose spirit revolted at democracy and who cultivated a pert humiliating manner with his inferiors to show as much, earned my distinguished hatred for ever by causing his secretary to present his compliments to me, and his request that I would mind my own business and leave him to manage his. At which I was so greatly enraged that I first tore this note into minute innumerable pieces, and then dashed it dramatically all over the floor of my room—from which, to keep my mother from the job, I afterwards had to pick it up laboriously on all-fours.

I was still meditating a tremendous retort, an indictment of all Lord Redcar's class, their manners, morals, economic and political crimes, when my trouble with Nettie arose to slump all minor troubles. Yet not so completely but that I snarled aloud when his lordship's motor-car whizzed by me, as I went about upon my long meandering quest for a weapon. And I discovered after a time that my mother had

244

bruised her knee and was lame. Fearing to irritate me by bringing the thing before me again, she had set herself to move her bed out of the way of the drip without my help, and she had knocked her knee. All her poor furnishings, I discovered, were cowering now close to the peeling bedroom walls; there had come a vast discoloration of the ceiling, and a washing-tub was in occupation of the middle of her chamber. . . .

It is necessary that I should set these things before you, should give the key of inconvenience and uneasiness in which all things were arranged, should suggest the breath of trouble that stirred along the hot summer streets, the anxiety about the strike, the rumours and indignations, the gatherings and meetings, the increasing gravity of the policemen's faces, the combative headlines of the local papers, the knots of picketers who scrutinised anyone who passed near the silent, smokeless forges, but in my mind, you must understand, such impressions came and went irregularly; they made a moving background, changing undertones, to my pre-occupation by that darkly shaping purpose to which a revolver was so imperative an essential.

Along the darkling streets, amidst the sullen crowds, the thought of Nettie, my Nettie, and her gentleman lover made ever a vivid inflammatory spot of purpose in my brain.

### 3

It was three days after this—on Wednesday, that is to say—that the first of those sinister outbreaks occurred that ended in the bloody affair of Peacock Grove and the flooding out of the entire line of the Swathinglea collieries. It was the only one of these disturbances I was destined to see, and at most a mere trivial preliminary of that struggle.

The accounts that have been written of this affair vary very widely. To read them is to realise the extraordinary carelessness of the truth that dishonoured the press of those latter days. In my bureau I have several files of the daily papers of the old time—I collected them, as a matter of fact—and three or four of about that date I have just this moment taken out and looked through to refresh my impression of what I saw. They lie before me—queer, shrivelled, incredible things; the cheap paper has already become brittle and brown and split along the creases, the ink faded or smeared, and I have to handle them with the utmost care when I glance among their raging headlines. As I sit here in this serene place, their quality throughout, their arrangement, their tone, their arguments and exhortations, read as though they came from drugged and drunken men. They give one the effect of faded bawling, of screams and shouts heard faintly in a little gramophone. . . . It is only on Monday I find, and buried deep below the war news, that these publications contain any intimation that unusual happenings were forward in Clayton and Swathinglea.

What I saw was towards evening. I had been learning to shoot with my new possession. I had walked out with it four or five miles across a patch of moorland and

245

down to a secluded little coppice full of blue-bells, half-way along the high-road between Leet and Stafford. Here I had spent the afternoon, experimenting and practising with careful deliberation and grim persistence. I had brought an old kite-frame of cane with me, that folded and unfolded, and each shot-hole I made I marked and numbered to compare with my other endeavours. At last I was satisfied that I could hit a playing-card at thirty paces nine times out of ten; the light was getting too bad for me to see my pencilled bull's-eye, and in that state of quiet moodiness that sometimes comes with hunger to passionate men, I returned by the way of Swathinglea towards my home.

The road I followed came down between banks of wretched-looking workingmen's houses, in close-packed rows on either side, and took upon itself the role of Swathinglea High Street, where, at a lamp and a pillar-box, the steam-trams began. So far that dirty hot way had been unusually quiet and empty, but beyond the corner, where the first group of beershops clustered, it became populous. It was very quiet still, even the children were a little inactive, but there were a lot of people standing dispersedly in little groups, and with a general direction towards the gates of the Bantock Burden coal-pit.

The place was being picketed, although at that time the miners were still nominally at work and the conferences between masters and men still in session at Clayton Town Hall. But one of the men employed at the Bantock Burden pit, Jack Briscoe, was a Socialist, and he had distinguished himself by a violent letter upon the crisis to the leading socialistic paper in England, *The Clarion*, in which he had adventured among the motives of Lord Redcar. The publication of this had been followed by instant dismissal. As Lord Redcar wrote a day or so later to *The Times*—I have that *Times*, I have all the London papers of the last month before the Change—

"The man was paid off and kicked out. Any self-respecting employer would do the same." The thing had happened overnight, and the men did not at once take a clear line upon what was, after all a very intricate and debatable occasion. But they came out in a sort of semi-official strike from all Lord Redcar's collieries beyond the canal that besets Swathinglea. They did so without formal notice, committing a breach of contract by this sudden cessation. But in the long labour struggles of the old days the workers were constantly putting themselves in the wrong and committing illegalities through that overpowering craving for dramatic promptness natural to uneducated minds.

All the men had not come out of the Bantock Burden pit. Something was wrong there, an indecision if nothing else; the mine was still working, and there was a rumour that men from Durham had been held in readiness by Lord Redcar, and were already in the mine. Now it is absolutely impossible to ascertain certainly how things stood at that time. The newspapers say this and that, but nothing trustworthy remains.

I believe I should have gone striding athwart the dark stage of that stagnant industrial drama without asking a question, if Lord Redcar had not chanced to come upon the scene about the same time as myself and incontinently end its stagnation.

He had promised that if the men wanted a struggle he would put up the best fight they had ever had, and he had been active all the afternoon in meeting the quarrel half-way, and preparing as conspicuously as possible for the scratch force of "blacklegs"—as we called them—who were he said and we believed, to replace the strikers in his pits.

I was an eye-witness of the whole of the affair outside the Bantock Burden pit, and—I do not know what happened.

Picture to yourself how the thing came to me.

I was descending a steep, cobbled, excavated road between banked-up footways, perhaps six feet high, upon which, in a monotonous series, opened the living-room doors of rows of dark, low cottages. The perspective of squat blue slate roofs and clustering chimneys drifted downward towards the irregular open space before the colliery—a space covered with coal, wheel-scarred mud, with a patch of weedy dump to the left and the colliery gates to the right. Beyond, the High Street with shops resumed again in good earnest and went on, and the lines of the steam-tramway that started out from before my feet, and were here shining and acutely visible with reflected skylight and here lost in a shadow, took up for one acute moment the greasy yellow irradation of a newly lit gas-lamp as they vanished round the bend. To the left spread a darkling marsh of homes, an infinitude of little smoking hovels, meagre churches, public-houses, Board schools, and other buildings out of which the prevailing chimneys of Swathinglea rose detachedly. To the right, very clear and relatively high, the Bantock Burden pit-mouth was marked by a gaunt lattice bearing a great black wheel, sharp and distinct in the twilight, and beyond, in an irregular perspective, were others following the lie of the seams. The general effect, as one came down the hill, was of a dark compressed life beneath a very high and wide and luminous evening sky, against which these pit-wheels rose. And ruling the calm spaciousness of that heaven was the great comet, now green-white, and wonderful for all who had eyes to see.

The fading afterglow of the sunset threw up all the contours and skyline to the west, and the comet rose eastward out of the pouring tumult of smoke from Bladden's forges. The moon had still to rise.

By this time the comet had begun to assume the cloudlike form still familiar through the medium of a thousand photographs and sketches. At first it had been an almost telescopic speck; it had brightened to the dimensions of the greatest star in the heavens: it had still grown, hour by hour, in its incredibly swift, noiseless and inevitable rush upon our earth, until it had equalled and surpassed the moon. Now it was the most splendid thing this sky of earth has ever held. I have never seen a photograph that gave a proper idea of it. Never at any time did it assume the conventional tailed outline comets are supposed to have. Astronomers talked of its double tail, one preceding it and one trailing behind it, but these were foreshortened to

247

nothing, so that it had rather the form of a bellying puff of luminous smoke with an intenser, brighter heart. It rose a hot yellow colour, and only began to show its distinctive greenness when it was clear of the mists of the evening.

It compelled attention for a space. For all my earthly concentration of mind, I could but stare at it for a moment with a vague anticipation that, after all, in some way so strange and glorious an object must have significance, could not possibly be a matter of absolute indifference to the scheme and values of my life.

But how?

I thought of Parload. I thought of the panic and uneasiness that was spreading in this very matter, and the assurances of scientific men that the thing weighed so little—at the utmost a few hundred tons of thinly diffused gas and dust—that even were it to smite this earth fully, nothing could possibly ensue. And after all, said I, what earthly significance has anyone found in the stars?

Then, as one still descended, the houses and buildings rose up, the presence of those watching groups of people, the tension of the situation; and one forgot the sky.

Preoccupied with myself and with my dark dream about Nettie and my honour, I threaded my course through the stagnating threat of this gathering, and was caught unawares when suddenly the whole scene flashed into drama. . . .

The attention of everyone swung round with an irresistible magnetism towards the High Street, and caught me as a rush of waters might catch a wisp of hay. Abruptly the whole crowd was sounding one note. It was not a word, it was a sound that mingled threat and protest, something between a prolonged "Ah!" and "Ugh!" Then with a hoarse intensity of anger came a low heavy booing, "Boo! boo—oo!" a note stupidly expressive of animal savagery. "Toot, too!" said Lord Redcar's automobile in ridiculous repartee. "Toot, too!" One heard it whizzing and throbbing as the crowd obliged it to slow down.

Everybody seemed in motion towards the colliery gates; I, too, with the others.

I heard a shout. Through the dark figures about me I saw the motor-car stop and move forward again, and had a glimpse of something writhing on the ground. . . .

It was alleged afterwards that Lord Redcar was driving, and that he quite deliberately knocked down a little boy who would not get out of his way. It is asserted with equal confidence that the boy was a man who tried to pass across the front of the motor-car as it came slowly through the crowd, who escaped by a hair's breath, and then slipped on the tram-rail and fell down. I have both accounts set forth, under screaming headlines, in two of these sere newspapers upon my desk. No one could ever ascertain the truth. Indeed, in such a blind tumult of passion, could there be any truth?

There was a rush forward, the horn of the car sounded, everything swayed violently to the right for perhaps ten yards or so, and there was a report like a pistol-shot.

For a moment everyone seemed running away. A woman, carrying a shawl-wrapped child, blundered into me, and sent me reeling back. Everyone thought of firearms, but as a matter of fact something had gone wrong with the motor, what in those old-fashioned contrivances was called a backfire. A thin puff of bluish smoke hung in the air behind the thing. The majority of the people scattered back in a disorderly fashion and left a clear space about the struggle that centered upon the motor-car.

The man or boy who had fallen was lying on the ground with no one near him, a black lump, an extended arm and two sprawling feet. The motor-car had stopped, and its three occupants were standing up. Six or seven black figures surrounded the car, and appeared to be holding on to it as if to prevent it from starting again; one—it was Mitchell a well-known labour leader—argued in fierce low tones with Lord Redcar. I could not hear anything they said, I was not near enough. Behind me the colliery gates were open, and there was a sense of help coming to the motor-car from that direction. There was an unoccupied muddy space for fifty yards, perhaps, between car and gate, and then the wheels and head of the pit rose black against the sky. I was one of a rude semicircle of people that hung as yet indeterminate in action about this dispute.

It was natural, I suppose, that my fingers should close upon the revolver in my pocket.

I advanced with the vaguest intentions in the world, and not so quickly but that several men hurried past me to join the little knot holding up the car.

Lord Redcar, in his big furry overcoat, towered up over the group about him; his gestures were free and threatening, and his voice loud. He made a fine figure there, I must admit; he was a big, fair, handsome young man with a fine tenor voice and an instinct for gallant effect. My eyes were drawn to him at first wholly. He seemed a symbol, a triumphant symbol, of all that the theory of aristocracy claims, of all that filled my soul with resentment. His chauffeur sat crouched together, peering at the crowd under his lordship's arm. But Mitchell showed as a sturdy figure also, and his voice was firm and loud.

"You've hurt that lad," said Mitchell, over and over again. "You'll wait here till you see if he's hurt."

"I'll wait here or not as I please," said Redcar; and to the chauffeur, "Here! Get down and look at it!"

"You'd better not get down," said Mitchell; and the chauffeur stood bent and hesitating on the step.

The man on the back seat stood up, leant forward, and spoke to Lord Redcar, and for the first time my attention was drawn to him. It was young Verrall! His handsome face shone clear and fine in the green pallor of the comet.

I ceased to hear the quarrel that was raising the voice of Mitchell and Lord Redcar. This new fact sent them spinning into the background. Young Verrall!

It was my own purpose coming to meet me half-way.

There was to be a fight here, it seemed certain to come to a scuffle, and here we were—

What was I to do? I thought very swiftly. Unless my memory cheats me, I acted with prompt decision. My hand tightened on my revolver, and then I remembered it was unloaded. I had thought my course out in an instant. I turned round and pushed my way out of the angry crowd that was now surging back towards the motor-car.

It would be quiet and out of sight, I thought, among the dump heaps across the road, and there I might load unobserved. . . .

A big young man striding forward with his fists clenched, halted for one second at the sight of me.

"What!" said he. "Ain't afraid of them, are you?"

I glanced over my shoulder and back at him, was near showing him my pistol, and the expression changed in his eyes. He hung perplexed at me. Then with a grunt he went on.

I heard the voices growing loud and sharp behind me.

I hesitated, half turned towards the dispute, then set off running towards the heaps. Some instinct told me not to be detected loading. I was cool enough therefore to think of the aftermath of the thing I meant to do.

I looked back once again towards the swaying discussion—or was it a fight now? And then I dropped into the hollow, knelt among the weeds, and loaded with eager trembling fingers. I loaded one chamber, got up and went back a dozen paces, thought of possibilities, vacillated, returned and loaded all the others. I did it slowly because I felt a little clumsy, and at the end came a moment of introspection—had I forgotten anything? And then for a few seconds I crouched before I rose, resisting the first gust of reaction against my impulse. I took thought, and for a moment that great green-white meteor overhead swam back into my conscious mind. For the first time then I linked it clearly with all the fierce violence that had crept into human life. I joined up that with what I meant to do. I was going to shoot young Verrall under the benediction of that green glare.

But about Nettie?

I found it impossible to think out that obvious complication.

I came up over the heap again, and walked slowly back towards the wrangle.

Of course I had to kill him. . . .

Now I would have you believe I did not want to murder young Verrall at all at that particular time. I had not pictured such circumstances as these, I had never thought of him in connection with Lord Redcar and our black industrial world. He was in that distant other world of Checkshill, the world of parks and gardens, the world of sunlit emotions and Nettie. His appearance here was disconcerting. I was taken by surprise. I was too tired and hungry to think clearly, and the hard implication of our antagonism prevailed with me. In the tumult of my past emotions I had thought constantly of conflicts, confrontations, deeds of violence; and now the memory of these things took possession of me as though they were irrevocable resolutions.

There was a sharp exclamation, the shriek of a woman, and the crowd came surging back. The fight had begun.

Lord Redcar, I believe, had jumped down from his car and felled Mitchell, and men were already running out to his assistance from the colliery gates.

I had some difficulty in shoving through the crowd; I can still remember very vividly being jammed at one time between two big men so that my arms were pinned to my sides, but all the other details are gone out of my mind until I found myself almost violently projected forward into the "scrap."

I blundered against the corner of the motor-car, and came round it face to face with young Verrall, who was descending from the back compartment. His face was touched with orange from the automobile's big lamps, which conflicted with the shadows of the comet light, and distorted him oddly. That effect lasted but an instant, but it put me out. Then he came a step forward, and the ruddy lights and queerness vanished.

I don't think he recognised me, but he perceived immediately I meant attacking. He struck out at once at me a haphazard blow, and touched me on the cheek.

Instinctively I let go of the pistol, snatched my right hand out of my pocket and brought it up in a belated parry, and then let out with my left full in his chest.

It sent him staggering, and as he went back I saw recognition mingle with astonishment in his face.

"You know me, you swine," I cried and hit again.

Then I was spinning sideways, half-stunned, with a huge lump of a fist under my jaw. I had an impression of Lord Redcar as a great furry bulk, towering like some Homeric hero above the fray. I went down before him—it made him seem to rush up—and he ignored me further. His big flat voice counselled young Verrall:

"Cut, Teddy! It won't do. The picketa's got i'on bahs. . . ."

Feet swayed about me, and some hobnailed miner kicked my ankle and went stumbling. There were shouts and curses, and then everything had swept past me. I rolled over on my face and beheld the chauffeur, young Verrall, and Lord Redcar—the latter holding up his long skirts of fur, and making a grotesque figure—one behind the other, in full bolt across a coldly comet-lit interval, towards the open gates of the colliery.

I raised myself up on my hands.

Young Verrall!

I had not even drawn my revolver—I had forgotten it. I was covered with coaly mud—knees, elbows, shoulders, back. I had not even drawn my revolver! . . .

A feeling of ridiculous impotence overwhelmed me. I struggled painfully to my feet.

I hesitated for a moment towards the gates of the colliery, and then went limping homeward, thwarted, painful, confused and ashamed. I had not the heart nor desire to help in the wrecking and burning of Lord Redcar's motor.

### 4

In the night, fever, pain, fatigue—it may be the indigestion of my supper of bread and cheese—roused me at last out of a hag-rid sleep to face despair. I was a soul lost amidst desolations and shame, dishonoured, evilly treated, hopeless. I raged against the God I denied, and cursed him as I lay.

And it was in the nature of my fever which was indeed only half fatigue and illness, and the rest the disorder of passionate youth, that Nettie, a strangely distorted Nettie, should come through the brief dreams that marked the exhaustions of that vigil, to dominate my misery. I was sensible, with an exaggerated distinctness, of the intensity of her physical charm for me, of her every grace and beauty; she took to herself the whole gamut of desire in me and the whole gamut of pride. She, bodily, was my lost honour. It was not only loss but disgrace to lose her. She stood for life and all that was denied; she mocked me as a creature of failure and defeat. My spirit raised itself towards her, and then the bruise upon my jaw glowed with a dull heat, and I rolled in the mud again before my rivals.

There were times when something near madness took me, and I gnashed my teeth and dug my nails into my hands and ceased to curse and cry out only by reason of the insufficiency of words. And once towards dawn I got out of bed, and sat by my looking-glass with my revolver loaded in my hand. I stood up at last and put it carefully in my drawer and locked it—out of reach of any hasty impulse. After that I slept for a little while.

Such nights were nothing rare and strange in that old order of the world. Never a city, never a night the whole year round, but amidst those who slept were those who waked, plumbing the deeps of wrath and misery. Countless thousands there were so ill, so troubled, they agonised near to the very border-line of madness, each one the centre of a universe darkened and lost. . . .

The next day I spent in gloomy lethargy.

I had intended to go to Checkshill that day, but my bruised ankle was too swollen for that to be possible. I sat indoors in the ill-lit downstairs kitchen, with my foot bandaged, and mused darkly and read. My dear old mother waited on me, and her brown eyes watched me and wondered at my black silences, my frowning preoccupations. I had not told her how it was my ankle came to be bruised and my clothes muddy. She had brushed my clothes in the morning before I got up.

Ah well! Mothers are not treated in that way now. That I suppose must console me. I wonder how far you will be able to picture that dark, grimy, untidy room, with its bare deal table, its tattered wall-paper, the saucepans and kettle on the narrow, cheap, but by no means economical range, the ashes under the fireplace, the rust-spotted steel fender on which my bandaged foot rested; I wonder how near you can come to seeing the scowling pale-faced hobbledehoy I was, unshaven and collarless, in the Windsor chair, and the little timid, dirty, devoted old woman who hovered about me with love peering out from her puckered eyelids. . . .

When she went to buy some vegetables in the middle of the morning she got me a half-penny journal. It was just such a one as these upon my desk, only that the copy I read was damp from the press, and these are so dry and brittle they crack if I touch them. I have a copy of the actual issue I read that morning; it was a paper called emphatically the *New Paper*, but everybody bought it and everybody called it the "yell." It was full that morning of stupendous news and still more stupendous headlines, so stupendous that for a little while I was roused from my egotistical broodings to wider interests. For it seemed that Germany and England were on the brink of war.

Of all the monstrous irrational phenomena of the former time, war was certainly the most strikingly insane. In reality it was probably far less mischievous than such quieter evils as, for example the general acquiescence in the private ownership of land, but its evil consequences showed so plainly that even in those days of stifling confusion one marvelled at it. On no conceivable grounds was there any sense in modern war. Save for the slaughter and mangling of a multitude of people, the destruction of vast quantities of material, and the waste of innumerable units of energy, it effected nothing. The old war of savage and barbaric nations did at least change humanity, you assumed yourselves to be a superior tribe in physique and discipline, you demonstrated this upon your neighbours, and if successful you took their land and their women and perpetuated and enlarged your superiority. The new war changed nothing but the colour of maps, the design of postage stamps, and the relationship of a few accidentally conspicuous individuals. In one of the last of these international epileptic fits, for example the English, with much dysentery and bad poetry and a few hundred deaths in battle, conquered the South African Boers at a gross cost of about three thousand pounds per head—they could have bought the whole of the preposterous imitation of a nation for a tenth of that sum—and except for a few substitutions of personalities, this group of partially corrupt officials in the place of that, and so forth, the permanent change was altogether insignificant. (But an excitable young man in Austria committed suicide when at length the Transvaal ceased to be a "nation.") Men went through the seat of that war after it was all over, and found humanity unchanged except for a general impoverishment and the convenience of an unlimited supply of empty ration tins and barbed wire and cartridge cases—unchanged and resuming with a slight perplexity all its old habits and misunderstandings, the nigger still in his slum-like kraal, the white in his ugly ill-managed shanty. . . .

But we in England saw all these things, or did not see them, through the mirage of the *New Paper*, in a light of mania. All my adolescence from fourteen to seventeen went to the music of that monstrous resonating futility, the cheering, the anxieties, the songs and the waving of flags, the wrongs of generous Buller and the glorious heroism of De Wet—who *always* got away; that was the great point about the heroic De Wet—and it never occurred to us that the total population we fought against was less than half the number of those who lived cramped ignoble lives within the compass of the Four Towns.

But before and after that stupid conflict of stupidities, a greater antagonism was coming into being, was slowly and quietly defining itself as a thing inevitable, sinking now a little out of attention only to resume more emphatically, now flashing into

253

some acute definitive expression and now percolating and pervading some new region of thought, and that was the antagonism of Germany and Great Britain.

When I think of that growing proportion of readers who belong entirely to the new order, who are growing up with only the vaguest early memories of the old world, I find the greatest difficulty in writing down the unintelligible confusions that were matter of fact to their fathers.

Here were we British, forty-one millions of people, in a state of almost indescribably aimless economic and moral muddle that we had neither the courage, the energy, nor the intelligence to improve, that most of us had hardly the courage to think about, and with our affairs hopelessly entangled with the entirely different confusions of three hundred and fifty million other persons scattered about the globe, and here were the Germans over against us, fifty-six millions, in a state of confusion no whit better that our own; and the noisy little creatures who directed papers and wrote books and gave lectures, and generally in that time of world-dementia pretended to be the national mind, were busy in both countries, with a sort of infernal unanimity, exhorting—and not only exhorting but successfully persuading—the two peoples to divert such small common store of material, normal and intellectual energy as either possessed, into the purely destructive and wasteful business of war. And—I have to tell you these things even if you do not believe them, because they are vital to my story—there was not a man alive who could have told you of any real permanent benefit, of anything whatever to counter-balance the obvious waste and evil, that would result from a war between England and Germany, whether England shattered Germany or was smashed and overwhelmed, or whatever the end might be.

The thing was, in fact, an enormous irrational obsession; it was, in the microcosm of our nation, curiously parallel to the egotistical wrath and jealousy that swayed my individual microcosm. It measured the excess of common emotion over the common intelligence, the legacy of inordinate passion we have received from the brute from which we came. Just as I had become the slave of my own surprise and anger and went hither and thither with a loaded revolver, seeking and intending vague fluctuating crimes, so these two nations went about the earth, hot eared and muddle headed, with loaded navies and armies terribly ready at hand. Only there was not even a Nettie to justify their stupidity. There was nothing but quiet imaginary thwarting on either side.

And the press was the chief instrument that kept these two huge multitudes of people directed against one another.

The press—those newspapers that are now so strange to us—like the "Empires," the "Nations," the "Trusts," and all the other great monstrous shapes of that extraordinary time—was in the nature of an unanticipated accident. It had happened, as weeds happen in abandoned gardens, just as all our world has happened—because there was no clear Will in the world to bring about anything better. Towards the end this "press" was almost entirely under the direction of youngish men of that eager, rather unintelligent type that is never able to detect itself aimless, that pursues nothing with incredible pride and zeal; and if you would really understand this mad era the comet brought to an end, you must keep in mind that every phase in the production of these queer old things was pervaded by a strong aimless energy and happened in a concentrated rush.

Let me describe to you, very briefly, a newspaper day.

Figure first, then, a hastily erected and still more hastily designed building in a dirty, paper-littered back street of old London, and a number of shabbily dressed men coming and going in this with projectile swiftness, and within this factory companies of printers, tensely active with nimble fingers—they were always speeding up the printers—ply their type-setting machines, and cast and arrange masses of metal in a sort of kitchen inferno, above which, in a beehive of little brightly lit rooms, dishevelled men sit and scribble. There is a throbbing of telephones and a clicking of telegraph needles, a rushing of messengers, a running to and from of heated men, clutching proofs and copy. Then begins a clatter roar of machinery catching the infection, going faster and faster, and whizzing and banging—engineers, who have never had time to wash since their birth, flying about with oil-cans, while paper runs off its rolls with a shudder of haste. The proprietor you must suppose arriving explosively on a swift motor-car, leaping out before the thing is at a standstill, with letters and documents clutched in his hand, rushing in, resolute to "hustle," getting wonderfully in everybody's way. At the sight of him even the messenger boys who are waiting, get up and scamper to and fro. Sprinkle your vision with collisions, curses, incoherencies. You imagine all the parts of this complex lunatic machine working hysterically towards a crescendo of haste and excitement as the night wears on. At last the only things that seem to travel deliberately in all those tearing vibrating premises are the hands of the clock.

Slowly things draw on towards publication, the consummation of all those stresses. Then in the small hours, into the now dark and deserted streets comes a wild whirl of carts and men, the place spurts papers at every door, bales, heaps, torrents of papers, that are snatched and flung about in what looks like a free fight, and off with a rush and clatter east, west, north, and south. The interest passes outwardly; the men from the little rooms are going homeward, the printers disperse yawning, the roaring presses slackened. The paper exists. Distribution follows manufacture, and we follow the bundles.

Our vision becomes a vision of dispersal. You see those bundles hurling into stations, catching trains by a hair's breadth, speeding on their way, breaking up, smaller bundles of them hurled with a fierce accuracy out upon the platforms that rush by, and then everywhere a division of these smaller bundles into still smaller bundles, into dispersing parcels, into separate papers, and the dawn happens unnoticed amidst a great running and shouting of boys, a shoving through letter slots, openings of windows, spreading out upon book-stalls. For the space of a few hours you must figure the whole country dotted white with rustling papers—placards everywhere vociferating the hurried lie for the day; men and women in trains, men and women eating and reading, men by study-fenders, people sitting up in bed, mothers and sons and daughters waiting for father to finish—a million scattered people reading—reading headlong—or feverishly ready to read. It is just as if some vehement jet had sprayed that white foam of papers over the surface of the land. . . .

And then you know, wonderfully gone—gone utterly, vanished as foam might vanish upon the sand.

Nonsense! The whole affair a noisy paroxysm of nonsense, unreasonable excitement, witless mischief and waste of strength—signifying nothing. . . .

And one of those white particles was the paper I held in my hands as I sat with a bandaged foot on the steel fender in that dark underground kitchen of my mother's, clean roused from my personal troubles by the yelp of the headlines. She sat, sleeves tucked up from her ropy arms, peeling potatoes as I read.

It was like one of a flood of disease germs that have invaded a body, that paper. There I was, one corpuscle in the big amorphous body of the English community, one of forty-one million such corpuscles; and, for all my preoccupations, these potent headlines, this paper ferment, caught me and swung me about. And all over the country that day, millions read as I read, and came round into line with me, under the same magnetic spell, came round—how did we say it!—Ah!—"to face the foe."

The comet had been driven into obscurity overnight. The column headed "Distinguished Scientist says Comet will Strike our Earth. Does it Matter?" went unread. "Germany"—I usually figured this mythical malignant creature as a corseted stiff-moustached Emperor enhanced by heraldic black wings and a large sword—had insulted our flag. That was the message of the *New Paper*, and the monster towered over me, threatening fresh outrages, visibly spitting upon my faultless country's colours. Somebody had hoisted a British flag on the right bank of some tropical river I had never heard of before, and a drunken German officer under ambiguous instructions had torn it down. Then one of the convenient abundant natives of the country, a British subject indisputably, had been shot in the leg. But the facts were by no means clear. Nothing was clear except that we were not going to stand any nonsense from Germany. Whatever had or had not happened we meant to have an apology for, and apparently they did not mean apologising.

### "Has War Come at Last?"

That was the headline. One's heart leaped to assent. . . .

There were hours that day when I clean forgot Nettie, in dreaming of battles and victories by land and sea, of shell fire, and entrenchments, and the heaped slaughter of many thousands of men.

But the next morning I started for Checkshill, started, I remember, in a curiously hopeful state of mind, oblivious of comets, strikes, and wars.

5

You must understand that I had no set plan of murder when I walked over to Check-shill. I had no set plan of any sort. There was a great confusion of dramatically conceived intentions in my head, scenes of threatening and denunciation and terror, but I did not mean to kill. The revolver was to turn upon my rival my disadvantage in age and physique. . . . But that was not it really! The revolver!—I took the revolver because I had the revolver and was a foolish young lout. It was a dramatic sort of thing to take. I had, I say, no plan at all.

Ever and again during that second trudge to Checkshill I was irradiated with a novel unreasonable hope. I had awakened in the morning with the hope, it may have been the last unfaded train of some obliterated dream, that after all Nettie might relent towards me, that her heart was kind towards me in spite of all that I imagined had happened. I even thought it possible that I might have misinterpreted what I had seen. Perhaps she would explain everything. My revolver was in my pocket for all that.

I limped at the outset, but after the second mile my ankle warmed to forgetfulness, and rest of the way I walked well. Suppose, after all, I was wrong?

I was still debating that, as I came through the park. By the corner of the paddock near the keeper's cottage, I was reminded by some belated blue hyacinths of a time when I and Nettie had gathered them together. It seemed impossible that we could really have parted for good and all. A wave of tenderness flowed over me, and still flooded me as I came through the little dell and drew towards the hollies. But there the sweet Nettie of my boy's love faded, and I thought of the new Nettie of desire and the man I had come upon in the moonlight, I thought of the narrow, hot purpose that had grown so strongly out of my springtime's freshness and my mood darkened to night.

I crossed the beech wood and came towards the gardens with a resolute and sorrowful heart. When I reached the green door in the garden wall I was seized for a space with so violent a trembling that I could not grip the latch to lift it, for I no longer had any doubt how this would end. That trembling was succeeded by a feeling of cold and whiteness and self-pity. I was astonished to find myself grimacing, to feel my cheeks wet, and thereupon I gave way completely to a wild passion of weeping. I must take just a little time before the thing was done. . . . I turned away from the door and stumbled for a short distance sobbing loudly, and lay down out of sight among the bracken, and so presently became calm again. I lay there some time. I had half a mind to desist, and then my emotion passed like the shadow of a cloud, and I walked very coolly into the gardens.

Through the open door of one of the glasshouses I saw old Stuart. He was leaning against the staging, his hands in his pockets, and so deep in thought he gave no heed to me. . . .

I hesitated and went on towards the cottage, slowly.

257

Something struck me as unusual about the place, but I could not tell at first what it was. One of the bedroom windows was open, and the customary short blind, with its brass upper rail partly unfastened, drooped obliquely across the vacant space. It looked negligent and odd, for usually everything about the cottage was conspicuously trim.

The door was standing wide open, and everything was still. But giving that usually orderly hall an odd look—it was about half-past two in the afternoon—was a pile of three dirty plates, with used knives and forks upon them, on one of the hall chairs.

I went into the hall, looked into either room and hesitated.

Then I fell to upon the door-knocker and gave a loud rat-tat-too, and followed this up with an amiable "Hel-lo!"

For a time no one answered me, and I stood listening and expectant, with my fingers about my weapon. Someone moved about upstairs presently, and was still again. The tension of waiting seemed to brace my nerves.

I had my hand on the knocker for the second time, when Puss appeared in the doorway.

For a moment we remained staring at one another without speaking. Her hair was dishevelled, her face dirty, tear-stained, and irregularly red. Her expression at the sight of me was pure astonishment. I thought she was about to say something, and then she had darted away out of the house again.

"I say, Puss!" I said. "Puss!"

I followed her out of the door. "Puss! What's the matter? Where's Nettie?"

She vanished round the corner of the house.

I hesitated, perplexed whether I should pursue her. What did it all mean? Then I heard someone upstairs.

"Willie!" cried the voice of Mrs. Stuart. "Is that you?"

"Yes," I answered. "Where's everyone? Where's Nettie? I want to have a talk with her."

She did not answer, but I heard her dress rustle as she moved. I judged she was upon the landing overhead.

I paused at the foot of the stairs, expecting her to appear and come down.

Suddenly came a strange sound, a rush of sounds, words jumbled and hurrying, confused and shapeless, borne along upon a note of throaty distress that at last submerged the words altogether and ended in a wail. Except that it came from a woman's throat it was exactly the babbling sound of a weeping child with a grievance. "I can't," she said, "I can't," and that was all I could distinguish. It was to my young ears the strangest sound conceivable from a kindly motherly little woman whom I had always thought of chiefly as an unparalleled maker of cakes. It frightened me. I went upstairs at once in a state of infinite alarm, and there she was upon the landing, leaning forward over the top of the chest of drawers beside her open bedroom door, and weeping. I never saw such weeping. One thick strand of black hair had escaped, and hung with a spiral twist down her back; never before had I noticed that she had grey hairs.

As I came upon the landing her voice rose again "Oh that I should have to tell you, Willie! Oh that I should have to tell you!" She dropped her head again, and a fresh gust of tears swept all further words away.

I said nothing, I was too astonished; but I drew nearer to her, and waited. . . .

I never saw such weeping; the extraordinary wetness of her dripping handkerchief abides with me to this day.

"That I should have lived to see this day!" she wailed. "I had rather a thousand times she was struck dead at my feet."

I began to understand.

"Mrs. Stuart," I said, clearing my throat; "what has become of Nettie?"

"That I should have lived to see this day!" she said by way of reply.

I waited till her passion abated.

There came a lull. I forgot the weapon in my pocket. I said nothing, and suddenly she stood erect before me, wiping her swollen eyes. "Willie," she gulped, "she's gone!"

"Nettie?"

"Gone! . . . Run away. . . . Run away from her home. Oh, Willie, Willie! The shame of it! The sin and shame of it!"

She flung herself upon my shoulder, and clung to me, and began again to wish her daughter lying dead at our feet.

"There, there," said I, and all my being was a-tremble. "Where has she gone?" I said as softly as I could.

But for the time she was preoccupied with her own sorrow, and I had to hold her there and comfort her with the blackness of finality spreading over my soul.

"Where has she gone?" I asked for the fourth time.

"I don't know—we don't know. And oh, Willie, she went out yesterday morning! I said to her, 'Nettie,' I said to her, 'you're mighty fine for a morning call.' 'Fine clo's for a fine day,' she said, and that was her last words to me!—Willie!—the child I suckled at my breast!"

"Yes, yes. But where has she gone?" I said.

She went on with sobs, and now telling her story with a sort of fragmentary hurry: "She went out bright and shining, out of this house for ever. She was smiling, Willie—as if she was glad to be going. ('Glad to be going.' I echoed with soundless lips.) 'You're mighty fine for the morning,' I says: 'mighty fine.' 'Let the girl be pretty,' says her father, 'while she's young!' And somewhere she'd got a parcel of her things hidden to pick up, and she was going off—out of this house for ever!"

She became quiet.

"Let the girl be pretty," she repeated; 'let the girl be pretty while she's young'. . . . Oh! how can he go on *living*, Willie? . . . He doesn't show it, but he is like a stricken beast. He's wounded to the heart. She was always his favourite. He never seemed to care for Puss like he did for her. And she's wounded him—"

"Where has she gone?" I reverted at last to that.

259

"We don't know. She leaves her own blood, she trusts herself—Oh, Willie, it'll kill me! I wish she and me together were lying in our graves."

"But"—I moistened my lips and spoke slowly—"she may have gone to marry."

"If that was so! I've prayed to God it might be so, Willie. I've prayed that he'd take pity on her—him, I mean, she's with."

I jerked out: "Who's that?"

"In her letter, she said he was a gentleman. She did say he was a gentleman."

"In her letter. Has she written? Can I see her letter?"

"Her father took it."

"But if she writes—When did she write?"

"It came this morning."

"But where did it come from? You can tell—"

"She didn't say. She said she was happy. She said love took one like a storm—"

"Curse that! Where is her letter? Let me see it. And as for this gentleman—"

She stared at me.

"You know who it is."

"Willie!" she protested.

"You know who it is, whether she said or not?" Her eyes made a mute unconfident denial.

"Young Verrall?"

She made no answer. "All I could do for you, Willie," she began presently.

"Was it young Verrall?" I insisted.

For a second, perhaps, we faced one another in stark understandings. . . . Then she plumped back to the chest of drawers, and her wet pocket-handkerchief, and I knew she sought refuge from my relentless eyes.

My pity for her vanished. She knew it was her mistress's son as well as I! And for some time she had known, she had felt.

I hovered over her for a moment, sick with amazed disgust. I suddenly bethought me of old Stuart, out in the greenhouse, and turned and went downstairs. As I did so I looked up to see Mrs. Stuart moving droopingly and lamely back into her own room.


## 6

Old Stuart was pitiful.

I found him still inert in the greenhouse where I had first seen him. He did not move as I drew near him; he glanced at me, and then stared hard again at the flowerpots before him.

"Eh Willie," he said, "this is a black day for all of us."

"What are you going to do?" I asked.

"The missus takes on so," he said. "I came out here."

"What do you mean to do?"

"What is a man to do in such a case?"

"Do!" I cried, "why—Do!"

"He ought to marry her," he said.

"By god, yes!" I cried. "He must do that anyhow."

"He ought to. It's—it's cruel. But what am I to do? Suppose he won't? Likely he won't. What then?"

He drooped with an intensified despair.

"Here's this cottage," he said, pursuing some contracted argument. "We've lived here all our lives, you might say. . . .Clear out. At my age. . . . One can't die in a slum."

I stood before him for a space, speculating what thoughts might fill the gaps between these broken words. I found his lethargy, and the dimly shaped mental attitudes his words indicated, abominable. I said abruptly, "You have her letter?"

He dived into his breast-pocket, became motionless for ten seconds, then woke up again and produced her letter. He drew it clumsily from its envelope, and handed it to me silently.

"Why!" he cried, looking at me for the first time, "What's come to your chin, Willie?"

"It's nothing," I said. "It's a bruise;" and I opened the letter.

It was written on greenish tinted fancy note-paper, and with all and more than Nettie's usual triteness and inadequacy of expression. Her handwriting bore no traces of emotion; it was round and upright and clear as though it had been done in a writing lesson. Always her letters were like masks upon her image; they fell like curtains before the changing charm of her face; one altogether forgot the sound of her light clear voice, confronted by a perplexing stereotyped thing that had mysteriously got a hold upon one's heart and pride. How did that letter run?—

"MY DEAR MOTHER,

"Do not be distressed at my going away. I have gone somewhere safe, and with someone who cares for me very much. I am sorry for your sakes, but it seems that it had to be. Love is a very difficult thing, and takes hold of one in ways one does not expect. Do not think I am ashamed about this, I glory in my love, and you must not trouble too much about me. I am very, very happy (deeply underlined).

"Fondest love to Father and Puss.

"Your loving

"NETTIE."

That queer little document! I can see it now for the childish simple thing it was, but at the time I read it in a suppressed anguish of rage. It plunged me into a pit of hopeless shame; there seemed to remain no pride for me in life until I had revenge. I stood staring at those rounded upstanding letters, not trusting myself to speak or move. At last I stole a glance at Stuart.

He held the envelop in his hand, and stared down at the postmark between his horny thumbnails.

"You can't even tell where she is," he said, turning the thing round in a hopeless manner, and then desisting. "It's hard on us, Willie. Here she is; she hadn't anything to complain of; a sort of pet for all of us. Not even made to do her share of the housework. And she goes off and leaves us like a bird that's learnt to fly. Can't trust us, that's what takes me. Puts 'erself—But there! What's to happen to him?"

He shook his head to show that problem was beyond him.

"You'll go after her," I said in an even voice; "you'll make him marry her?"

"Where am I to go?" he asked helplessly, and held out the envelope with a gesture; "and what could I do? Even if I knew—How could I leave the gardens?"

"Great God!" I cried, "not leave these gardens! It's your Honour, man! If she was my daughter—if she was my daughter—I'd tear the world to pieces! . . ." I choked. "You mean to stand it?"

"What can I do?"

"Make him marry her! Horsewhip him! Horsewhip him, I say!—I'd strangle him!"

He scratched slowly at his hairy check, opened his mouth, and shook his head. Then, with an intolerable note of sluggish gentle wisdom, he said, "People of our sort, Willie, can't do things like that."

I came near to raving. I had a wild impulse to strike him in the face. Once in my boyhood I happened upon a bird terribly mangled by some cat, and killed it in a frenzy of horror and pity. I had a gust of that same emotion now, as this shameful mutilated soul fluttered in the dust before me. Then, you know, I dismissed him from the case.

"May I look?" I asked.

He held out the envelope reluctantly.

"There it is," he said, and pointing with his garden-rough forefinger. "I.A.P.A.M.P. What can you make of that?"

I took the thing in my hands. The adhesive stamp customary in those days was defaced by a circular postmark, which bore the name of the office of departure and the date. The impact in this particular case had been light or made without sufficient ink, and half the letters of the name had left no impression. I could distinguish—

I A P A M P

and very faintly below D.S.O.

I guessed the name in an instant flash of intuition. It was Shaphambury. The very gaps shaped that to mind. Perhaps in a sort of semi-visibility other letters were there, at least hinting themselves. It was a place somewhere on the east coast, I knew, either in Norfolk or Suffolk.

"Why!" cried I—and stopped.

What was the good of telling him?

Old Stuart had glanced up sharply, I am inclined to think almost fearfully, into my face. "You—you haven't got it?" he said.

Shaphambury—I should remember that.

"You don't think you got it?" he said.

I handed the envelope back to him.

"For a moment I thought it might be Hampton," I said.

"Hampton," he repeated. "Hampton. How could you make Hampton?" He turned the envelope about. "H.A.M.—why, Willie, you're a worse hand at the job than me!"

He replaced the letter in the envelope and stood erect to put it back in his breast pocket.

I did not mean to take any risks in this affair. I drew a stump of pencil from my waistcoat pocket, turned a little away from him and wrote "Shaphambury" very quickly on the frayed and rather grimy shirt cuff.

"Well," said I, with an air of having done nothing remarkable.

I turned to him with some unimportant observation—I have forgotten what.

I never finished whatever vague remark I commenced.

I looked up to see a third person waiting at the greenhouse door.

### 7

It was old Mrs. Verrall.

I wonder if I can convey the effect of her to you. She was a little old lady with extraordinary flaxed hair, her weak aquiline features were pursed up into an assumption of dignity, and she was richly dressed. I would like to underline that "richly dressed," or have the words printed in florid old English or Gothic lettering. No one on earth is now quite so richly dressed as she was, no one old or young indulges in so quiet and yet so profound a sumptuosity. But you must not imagine any extravagance of outline or any beauty or richness of colour. The predominant colours were black and fur browns, and the effect of richness was due entirely to the extreme costliness of the materials employed. She affected silk brocades with rich and elaborate patterns, priceless black lace over creamy or purple satin, intricate trimmings through which threads and bands of velvet wriggled, and in the winter rare furs. Her gloves fitted exquisitely, and ostentatiously simple chains of fine gold and pearls and a great number of bracelets laced about her little person. One was forced to feel that the slightest article she wore cost more than all the wardrobe of a dozen girls like Nettie; her bonnet affect the simplicity that is beyond rubies. Richness, that is the first quality about this old lady that I would like to convey to you, and the second was cleanliness. You felt that old Mrs. Verrall was exquisitely clean. If you had boiled my poor dear old mother in soda for a month you couldn't have got her so clean as Mrs. Verrall constantly and manifestly was. And pervading all her presence shone her third great quality, her manifest confidence in the respectful subordination of the world.

She was pale and a little out of breath that day, but without any loss of her ultimate confidence; and it was clear to me that she had come to interview Stuart upon the outbreak of passion that had bridged the gulf between their families.

263

And here again I find myself writing in an unknown language, so far as my younger readers are concerned. You who know only the world that followed the Great Change will find much that I am telling inconceivable. Upon these points I cannot appeal, as I have appealed for other confirmations, to the old newspapers; these were the things that no one wrote about because everyone understood and everyone had taken up an attitude. There were in England and America, and indeed throughout the world, two great informal divisions of human beings—the Secure and the Insecure. There was not and never had been in either country a nobility—it was and remains a common error that the British peers were noble—neither in law nor custom were there noble families, and we altogether lacked the edification one found in Russia, for example, of a poor nobility. A peerage was an hereditary possession that, like the family land, concerned only the eldest sons of the house; it radiated no lustre of noblesse oblige. The rest of the world was in law and practice common—and all America was common. But through the private ownership of land that had resulted from the neglect of feudal obligations in Britain and the utter want of political foresight in the Americas, large masses of property had become artificially stable in the hands of a small minority, to whom it was necessary to mortgage all new public and private enterprises, and who were held together not by any tradition of service and nobility but by the natural sympathy of common interests and a common large scale of living. It was a class without any very definite boundaries; vigorous individualities, by methods for the most part violent and questionable, were constantly thrusting themselves from insecurity to security, and the sons and daughters of secure people, by marrying insecurity or by wild extravagance or flagrant vice, would sink into the life of anxiety and insufficiency which was the ordinary life of man. The rest of the population was landless and, except by working directly or indirectly for the Secure, had no legal right to exist. And such was the shallowness and insufficiency of our thought, such the stifled egotism of all our feelings before the Last Days, that very few indeed of the Secure could be found to doubt that this was the natural and only conceivable order of the world.

It is the life of the Insecure under the old order that I am displaying, and I hope that I am conveying something of its hopeless bitterness to you; but you must not imagine that the Secure lived lives of paradisiacal happiness. The pit of insecurity below them made itself felt, even though it was not comprehended. Life about them was ugly; the sight of ugly and mean houses, of ill-dressed people, the vulgar appeals of the dealers in popular commodities, were not to be escaped. There was below the threshold of their minds an uneasiness; they not only did not think clearly about social economy but they displayed an instinctive disinclination to think. Their security was not so perfect that they had not a dread of falling towards the pit, they were always lashing themselves by new ropes, their cultivation of "connections," of interests, their desire to confirm and improve their positions, was a constant ignoble preoccupation. You must read Thackeray to get the full flavour of their lives. Then the bacterium was apt to disregard class distinctions, and they were never really happy

264

in their servants. Read their surviving books. Each generation bewails the decay of that "fidelity" of servants no generation ever saw. A world that is squalid in one corner is squalid altogether, but that they never understood. They believed there was not enough of anything to go round, they believed that this was the intention of God and an incurable condition of life, and they held passionately and with a sense of right to their disproportionate share. They maintained a common intercourse as "Society" of all who were practically secure, and their choice of that word is exhaustively eloquent of the quality of their philosophy. But, if you can master these alien ideas upon which the old system rested, just in the same measure will you understand the horror these people had for marriages with the Insecure. In the case of their girls and women it was extraordinarily rare, and in the case of either sex it was regarded as a disastrous social crime. Anything was better than that.

You are probably aware of the hideous fate that was only too probably the lot, during those last dark days, of every girl of the insecure classes who loved and gave way to the impulse of self-abandonment without marriage, and so you will understand the peculiar situation of Nettie with young Verrall. One or other had to suffer. And as they were both in a state of great emotional exaltation and capable of strange generosities towards each other, it was an open question and naturally a source of great anxiety to a mother in Mrs. Verrall's position, whether the sufferer might not be her son—whether, as the outcome of that glowing irresponsible commerce, Nettie might not return prospective mistress of Checkshill Towers. The chances were greatly against that conclusion, but such things did occur.

These laws and customs sound, I know, like a record of some nasty-minded lunatic's inventions. They were invincible facts in that vanished world into which, by some accident, I had been born, and it was the dream of any better state of things that was scouted as lunacy. Just think of it! This girl I loved with all my soul, for whom I was ready to sacrifice my life, was not good enough to marry young Verrall. And I had only to look at his even, handsome, characterless face to perceive a creature weaker and no better than myself. She was to be his pleasure until he chose to cast her aside, and the poison of our social system had so saturated her nature—his evening dress, his freedom and his money had seemed so fine to her and I so clothed in squalor—that to this prospect she had consented. And to resent the social conventions that created their situation, was called "class envy," and gently born preachers reproached us for the mildest resentment against an injustice no living man would now either endure or consent to profit by.

What was the sense of saying "peace" when there was no peace? If there was one hope in the disorders of that old world it lay in revolt and conflict to the death.

But if you can really grasp the shameful grotesqueness of the old life, you will begin to appreciate the interpretation of old Mrs. Verrall's appearance that leaped up at once in my mind.

She had come to compromise the disaster!

And the Stuarts *would* compromise! I saw that only too well.

265

An enormous disgust at the prospect of the imminent encounter between Stuart and his mistress made me behave in a violent and irrational way. I wanted to escape seeing that, seeing even Stuart's first gesture in that, at any cost.

"I'm off," said I, and turned my back on him without any further farewell.

My line of retreat lay by the old lady, and so I advanced towards her.

I saw her expression change, her mouth fell a little way open, her forehead wrinkled, and her eyes grew round. She found me a queer customer even at the first sight, and there was something in the manner of my advance that took away her breath.

She stood at the top of the three or four steps that descended to the level of the hothouse floor. She receded a pace or two, with a certain offended dignity at the determination of my rush.

I gave her no sort of salutation.

Well, as a matter of fact, I did give her a sort of salutation. There is no occasion for me to begin apologising now for the thing I said to her—I strip these things before you—if only I can get them stark enough you will understand and forgive. I was filled with a brutal and overpowering desire to insult her.

And so I addressed this poor little expensive old woman in the following terms, converting her by a violent metonymy into a comprehensive plural. "You infernal land thieves!" I said point-blank into her face. "*Have you come to offer them money?*"

And without waiting to test her powers of repartee, passed rudely beyond her and vanished, striding, with my fists clenched, out of her world again. . . .

I have tried since to imagine how the thing must have looked to her. So far as her particular universe went I had not existed at all, or I had existed only as a dim black thing, an insignificant speck, far away across her park in irrelevant, unimportant transit, until this moment when she came, sedately troubled, into her own secure gardens and sought for Stuart among the greenhouses. Then abruptly I flashed into being down that green-walled, brick-floored vista as a black-advised, ill-clad young man, who first stared and then advanced scowling towards her. Once in existence I developed rapidly. I grew larger in perspective and became more and more important and sinister every moment. I came up the steps with inconceivable hostility and disrespect in my bearing, towered over her, becoming for an instant at least a sort of second French Revolution, and delivered myself with the intensest concentration of those wicked and incomprehensible words. Just for a second I threatened annihilation. Happily that was my climax.

And then I had gone by, and the Universe was very much as it had always been except for the wild swirl in it, and the faint sense of insecurity my episode left in its wake.

The thing that never entered my head in those days was that a large proportion of the rich were rich in absolute good faith. I thought they saw things exactly as I saw them, and wickedly denied. But indeed old Mrs. Verrall was no more capable of doubting the perfection of her family's right to dominate a wide countryside, than she was of examining the Thirty-nine Articles or dealing with any other of the adamantine pillars upon which her universe rested in security.

No doubt I startled and frightened her tremendously. But she could not understand.

None of her sort of people ever did seem to understand such livid flashes of hate, as ever and again lit the crowded darkness below their feet. The thing leaped out of the black for a moment and vanished, like a threatening figure by a desolate roadside lit for a moment by one's belated carriage-lamp and then swallowed up by the night. They counted it with nightmares, and did their best to forget what was evidently as insignificant as it was disturbing.

CHAPTER THE FOURTH

WAR

1

From that Moment when I insulted old Mrs. Verrall I became representative, I was a man who stood for all the disinherited of the world. I had no hope of pride or pleasure left in me, I was raging rebellion against God and mankind. There were no more vague intentions swaying me this way and that; I was perfectly clear now upon what I meant to do. I would make my protest and die.

I would make my protest and die. I was going to kill Nettie—Nettie, who had smiled and promised and given herself to another, and who stood now for all the conceivable delightfulnesses, the lost imaginations of the youthful heart, the unattainable joys in life; and Verrall, who stood for all who profited by the incurable injustice of our social order. I would kill them both. And that being done I would blow my brains out and see what vengeance followed my blank refusal to live.

So indeed I was resolved. I raged monstrously. And above me, abolishing the stars, triumphant over the yellow waning moon that followed it below, the giant meteor towered up towards the zenith!

"Let me only kill!" I cried. "Let me only kill!"

So I shouted in my frenzy. I was in a fever that defied hunger and fatigue; for a long time I had prowled over the heath towards Lowchester talking to myself, and now that night had fully come I was tramping homeward, walking the long seventeen miles without a thought of rest. And I had eaten nothing since the morning.

I suppose I must count myself mad, but I can recall my ravings.

There were times when I walked weeping through that brightness that was neither night nor day. There were times when I reasoned in a topsy-turvy fashion with what I called the Spirit of All Things. But always I spoke to that white glory in the sky.

"Why am I here only to suffer ignominies?" I asked. "Why have you made me with pride that cannot be satisfied, with desires that turn and rend me? Is it a jest, this world—a joke you play on your guests? I—even I—have a better humour than that!

267

"Why not learn from me a certain decency of mercy? Why not undo? Have I ever tormented—day by day, some wretched worm—making filth for it to trail through, filth that disgusts it, starving it, bruising it, mocking it? Why should you? Your jokes are clumsy. Try—try some milder fun up there; do you hear? Something that doesn't hurt so infernally.

"You say this is your purpose—your purpose with me. You are making something with me—birth pangs of a soul. Ah! How can I believe you? You forget I have eyes for other things. Let my own case go, but what of that frog beneath the cartwheel, God?—and the bird the cat had torn?"

And after such blasphemies I would fling out a ridiculous little debating society hand. "Answer me that!"

A week ago it had been moonlight, white and black and hard across the spaces of the park, but now the light was livid and full of the quality of haze. An extraordinary low white mist, not three feet above the ground, drifted broodingly across the grass, and the trees rose ghostly out of that phantom sea. Great and shadowy and strange was the world that night, no one seemed abroad; I and my little cracked voice drifted solitary through the silent mysteries. Sometimes I argued as I have told, sometimes I stumbled along in moody vacuity, sometimes my torment was vivid and acute.

Abruptly out of apathy would come a boiling paroxysm of fury, when I thought of Nettie mocking me and laughing, and of her and Verrall clasped in one another's arms.

"I will not have it so!" I screamed. "I will not have it so!"

And in one of these raving fits I drew my revolver from my pocket and fired into the quiet night. Three times I fired it.

The bullets tore through the air, the startled trees told one another in diminishing echoes the thing I had done, and then, with a slow finality, the vast and patient night healed again to calm. My shots, my curses and blasphemies, my prayers—for anon I prayed—that Silence took them all.

It was—how can I express it?—a stifled outcry tranquillised, lost, amid the serene assumptions, the overwhelming empire of that brightness. The noise of my shots, the impact upon things, had for the instant been enormous; then it had passed away. I found myself standing with the revolver held up, astonished, my emotions penetrated by something I could not understand. Then I looked up over my shoulder at the great star, and remained staring at it.

"Who are you?" I said at last.

I was like a man in a solitary desert who has suddenly heard a voice. . . .

That, too, passed.

As I came over Clayton Crest I recalled that I missed the multitude that now night after night walked out to stare at the comet; and the little preacher in the waste beyond the hoardings, who warned sinners to repent before the Judgment was not in his usual place.

It was long past midnight, and everyone had gone home. But I did not think of this at first, and the solitude perplexed me and left a memory behind. The gas-lamps were all extinguished because of the brightness of the comet, and that too was unfamiliar. The little news-agent in the still High Street had shut up and gone to bed, but one belated board had been put out late and forgotten, and it still bore its placard.

The word upon it—there was but one word upon it in staring letters—was: "WAR."

You figure that empty mean street, emptily echoing to my footsteps—no soul awake and audible but me. Then my halt at the placard. And amidst that sleeping stillness, smeared hastily upon the board, a little askew and crumpled but quite distinct beneath that cool meteoric glare, preposterous and appalling, the measureless evil of that word—

"WAR!"

## 2

I awoke in that state of equanimity that so often follows an emotional drenching.

It was late, and my mother was beside my bed. She had some breakfast for me on a battered tray.

"Don't get up yet, dear," she said. "You've been sleeping. It was three o'clock when you got home last night. You must have been tired out."

"Your poor face," she went on, "was as white as a sheet and your eyes shining. . . It frightened me to let you in. And you stumbled on the stairs."

My eyes went quietly to my coat pocket, where something still bulged. She probably had not noticed. "I went to Checkshill," I said. "You know—perhaps—?"

"I got a letter last evening, dear," and as she bent near me to put the tray upon my knees, she kissed my hair softly. For a moment we both remained still, resting on that, her cheek just touching my head.

I took the tray from her to end the pause.

"Don't touch my clothes, mummy," I said sharply, as she moved towards them. "I'm still equal to a clothes-brush."

And then, as she turned away, I astonished her by saying, "You dear mother, you! A little—I understand. Only now—dear mother, oh! Let me be! Let me be!"

And with the docility of a good servant, she went from me. Dear heart of submission that the world and I had used so ill!

It seemed to me that morning that I could never give way to a gust of passion again. A sorrowful firmness of the mind possessed me. My purpose seemed now as inflexible as iron; there was neither love nor hate nor fear left in me—only I pitied my mother greatly for all that was still to come. I ate my breakfast slowly, and thought where I could find out about Shaphambury, and how I might hope to get there. I had not five shillings in the world.

I dressed methodically, choosing the least frayed of my collars, and shaving much more carefully that was my wont; then I went down to the Public Library to consult a map.

Shaphambury was on the coast of Essex, a long and complicated journey from Clayton. I went to the railway-station and made some memoranda from the time-tables. The porters I asked were not very clear about Shaphambury, but the booking-office clerk was helpful, and we puzzled out all I wanted to now. Then I came out into the coaly street again. At the least I ought to have two pounds.

I went back to the Public Library and into the newspaper room to think over this problem.

A fact intruded itself upon me. People seemed in an altogether exceptional stir about the morning journals, there was something unusual in the air of the room, more people and more talking than usual, and for a moment I was puzzled. Then I bethought me: "This war with Germany, of course!" A naval battle was supposed to be in progress in the North Sea. Let them! I returned to the consideration of my own affairs.

Parload?

Could I go and make it up with him, and then borrow? I weighed the chances of that. Then I thought of selling or pawning something, but that seemed difficult. My winter overcoat had not cost a pound when it was new, my watch was not likely to fetch many shillings. Still, both these things might be factors. I thought with a certain repugnance of the little store my mother was probably making for the rent. She was very secretive about that, and it was locked in an old tea-caddy in her bedroom. I knew it would be almost impossible to get any of that money from her willingly, and though I told myself that in this issue of passion and death no detail mattered, I could not get rid of tormenting scruples whenever I thought of that tea-caddy. Was there no other course? Perhaps after every other source had been tapped I might supplement with a few shillings frankly begged from her. "These others," I said to myself, thinking without passion for once of the sons of the Secure, "would find it difficult to run their romances on a pawnshop basis. However, we must manage it."

I felt the day was passing on, but I did not get excited about that. "Slow is swiftest," Parload used to say, and I meant to get everything thought out completely, to take a long aim and then to act as a bullet flies.

I hesitated at a pawnshop on my way home to my midday meal, but I determined not to pledge my watch until I could bring my overcoat also.

I ate silently, revolving plans.

### 3

After our midday dinner—it was a potato-pie, mostly potato with some scraps of cabbage and bacon—I put on my overcoat and got it out of the house while my mother was in the scullery at the back.

A scullery in the old world was, in the case of such houses as ours, a damp, unsavoury, mainly subterranean region behind the dark living-room kitchen, that was rendered more than typically dirty in our case by the fact that into it the coal-cellar, a yawning pit of black uncleanness, opened, and diffused small crunchable particles about the uneven brick floor. It was the region of "washing-up," that greasy, damp function that followed every meal; its atmosphere had ever a cooling steaminess and the memory of boiled cabbage, and the sooty black stains where saucepan or kettle had been put down for a minute, scraps of potato-peel caught by the strainer of the escape-pipe, and rags of a quite indescribable horribleness of acquisition, called "dish-clouts," rise in my memory at the name. The altar of this place was the "sink," a tank of stone, revolting to a refined touch, grease-filmed and unpleasant to see, and above this was a tap for cold water, so arranged that when the water descended it splashed and wetted whoever had turned it on. This tap was our water supply. And in such a place you must fancy a little old woman, rather incompetent and very gentle, a soul of unselfishness and sacrifice, in dirty clothes, all come from their original colours to a common dusty dark grey, in worn, ill-fitting boots, with hands distorted by ill use, and untidy greying hair—my mother. In the winter her hands would be "chapped," and she would have a cough. And while she washes up I go out, to sell my overcoat and watch in order that I may desert her.

I gave way to queer hesitations in pawning my two negotiable articles. A weak indisposition to pawn in Clayton, where the pawnbroker knew me, carried me to the door of the place in Lynch Street, Swathinglea, where I had bought my revolver. Then came an idea that I was giving too many facts about myself to one man, and I came back to Clayton after all. I forget how much money I got, but I remember that it was rather less than the sum I had made out to be the single fare to Shaphambury. Still deliberate, I went back to the Public Library to find out whether it was possible, by walking for ten or twelve miles anywhere, to shorten the journey. My boots were in a dreadful state, the sole of the left one also was now peeling off, and I could not help perceiving that all my plans might be wrecked if at this crisis I went on shoe leather in which I could only shuffle. So long as I went softly they would serve, but not for hard walking. I went to the shoemaker in Hacker Street, but he would not promise any repairs for me under forty-eight hours.

I got back home about five minutes to three, resolved to start by the five train for Birmingham in any case, but still dissatisfied about my money. I thought of pawning a book or something of that sort, but I could think of nothing of obvious value in the house. My mother's silver—two gravy-spoons and a salt-cellar—had been pawned for some weeks, since, in fact, the June quarterday. But my mind was full of hypothetical opportunities.

As I came up the steps to our door, I remarked that Mr. Gabbitas looked at me suddenly round his dull red curtains with a sort of alarmed resolution in his eye and vanished, and as I walked along the passage he opened his door upon me and intercepted me.

You are figuring me, I hope, as a dark and sullen lout in shabby, cheap, old-world clothes that are shiny at all the wearing surfaces, and with a discoloured red tie and frayed linen. My left hand keeps in my pocket as though there is something it prefers to keep a grip upon there. Mr. Gabbitas was shorter than I, and the first note he struck in the impression he made upon anyone was of something bright and birdlike. I think he wanted to be birdlike, he possessed the possibility of an avian charm but, as a matter of fact, there was nothing of the glowing vitality of the bird in his being. And a bird is never out of breath and with an open mouth. He was in the clerical dress of that time, that costume that seems now almost the strangest of all our old-world clothing, and he presented it in its cheapest form—black of a poor texture, ill-fitting, strangely cut. Its long skirts accentuated the tubbiness of his body, the shortness of his legs. The white tie below his all-round collar, beneath his innocent large-spectacled face, was a little grubby, and between his not very clean teeth he held a briar pipe. His complexion was whitish, and although he was only thirty-three or four perhaps, his sandy hair was already thinning from the top of his head.

To your eye, now, he would seem the strangest figure, in the utter disregard of all physical beauty or dignity about him. You would find him extraordinarily odd, but in the old days he met not only with acceptance but respect. He was alive until within a year or so ago, but his later appearance changed. As I saw him that afternoon he was a very slovenly, ungainly little human being indeed; not only was his clothing altogether ugly and queer, but had you stripped the man stark, you would certainly have seen in the bulging paunch that comes from flabby muscles and flabbily controlled appetites, and in the rounded shoulders and flawed and yellowish skin, the same failure of any effort towards clean beauty. You had an instinctive sense that so he had been from the beginning. You felt he was not only drifting through life, eating what came in his way, believing what came in his way, doing without any vigour what came in his way, but that into life also he had drifted. You could not believe him the child of pride and high resolve, or of any splendid passion of love. He had just happened. . . . But we all happened then. Why am I taking this tone over this poor little curate in particular?

"Hello!" he said, with an assumption of a friendly ease. "Haven't seen you for weeks! Come in and have a gossip."

An invitation from the drawing-room lodger was in the nature of a command. I would have liked very greatly to have refused it, never was invitation more inopportune, but I had not the wit to think of an excuse. "All right," I said awkwardly, and he held the door open for me.

"I'd be very glad if you would," he amplified. "One doesn't get much opportunity of intelligent talk in this parish."

What the devil was he up to, was my secret preoccupation. He fussed about me with a nervous hospitality, talking in jumpy fragments, rubbing his hands together, and taking peeps at me over and round his glasses. As I sat down in his leather-covered armchair, I had an odd memory of the one in the Clayton's dentists' operating room—I know not why.

"They're going to give us trouble in the North Sea, it seems," he remarked with a sort of innocent zest. "I'm glad they mean fighting."

There was an air of culture about his room that always cowed me, and that made me constrained even on this occasion. The table under the window was littered with photographic material and the later albums of his continental souvenirs, and on the American cloth trimmed shelves that filled the recesses on either side of the fireplace were what I used to think in those days a quite incredible number of books—perhaps eight hundred altogether, including the reverend gentleman's photograph albums and college and school text-books. This suggestion of learning was enforced by the little wooden shield bearing a college coat-of-arms that hung over the looking-glass, and by a photograph of Mr. Gabbitas in cap and gown in an Oxford frame that adorned the opposite wall. And in the middle of that wall stood his writing-desk, which I knew to have pigeon-holes when it was open and which made him seem not merely cultured but literary. At that he wrote sermons, composing them himself!

"Yes," he said, taking possession of the hearthrug, "the war had to come sooner or later. If we smash their fleet for them now—well, there's an end to the matter!"

He stood on his toes and then bumped down on his heels, and looked blandly through his spectacles at a water-colour by his sister—the subject was a bunch of violets—above the sideboard which was his pantry and tea-chest and cellar. "Yes," he said as he did so.

I coughed, and wondered how I might presently get away.

He invited me to smoke—that queer old practice!—and then when I declined, began talking in a confidential tone of this "dreadful business" of the strikes. "The war won't improve that outlook," he said, and was very grave for a moment.

He spoke of the want of thought for their wives and children shown by the colliers in striking merely for the sake of the union, and this stirred me to controversy, and distracted me a little from my resolution to escape.

"I don't quite agree with that," I said, clearing my throat. "If the men didn't strike for the union now, if they let that be broken up, where would they be when the pinch of reductions did come?"

To which he replied that they couldn't expect to get top-price wages when the masters were selling bottom-price coal. I replied, "That isn't it. The masters don't treat them fairly. They have to protect themselves."

To which Mr. Gabbitas answered, "Well, I don't know. I've been in the Four Towns some time, and I must say I don't think the balance of injustice falls on the masters' side."

"It falls on the men," I agreed, willfully misunderstanding him.

And so we worked our way towards an argument. "Confound this argument!" I thought; but I had no skill in self-extraction, and my irritation crept into my voice. Three little spots of colour came into the cheeks and nose of Mr. Gabbitas, but his voice showed nothing of his ruffled temper.

"You see," I said, "I'm a Socialist. I don't think this world was made for a small minority to dance on the faces of everyone else."

273

"My dear fellow," said the Rev. Gabbitas, "I'm a Socialist too. Who isn't? But that doesn't lead me to class hatred."

"You haven't felt the heel of this confounded system. I have."

"Ah!" said he; and catching him on that note came a rap at the front door, and, as he hung suspended, the sound of my mother letting someone in and a timid rap.

"Now," thought I, and stood up resolutely, but he would not let me. "No, no, no!" said he. "It's only for the Dorcas money."

He put his hand against my chest with an effect of physical compulsion, and cried, "Come in!"

"Our talk's just getting interesting," he protested; and there entered Miss Ramell, an elderly little young lady who was mighty in Church help in Clayton.

He greeted her—she took no notice of me—and went to his bureau, and I remained standing by my chair but unable to get out of the room. "I'm not interrupting?" asked Miss Ramell.

"Not in the least," he said; drew out the carriers and opened his desk. I could not help seeing what he did.

I was so fretted by my impotence to leave him that at the moment it did not connect at all with the research of the morning that he was taking out money. I listened sullenly to his talk with Miss Ramell, and saw only, as they say in Wales, with the front of my eyes, the small flat drawer that had, it seemed, quite a number of sovereigns scattered over its floor. "They're so unreasonable," complained Miss Ramell. Who could be otherwise in a social organisation that bordered on insanity?

I turned away from them, put my foot on the fender, stuck my elbow on the plush-fringed mantel-board, and studied the photographs, pipes, and ashtrays that adorned it. What was it I had to think out before I went to the station.

Of course! My mind made a queer little reluctant leap—it felt like being forced to leap over a bottomless chasm—and alighted upon the sovereigns that were just disappearing again as Mr. Gabbitas shut his drawer.

"I won't interrupt your talk further," sad Miss Ramell, receding doorward.

Mr. Gabbitas played round her politely, and opened the door for her and conducted her into the passage, and for a moment or so I had the fullest sense of proximity to those—it seemed to me there must be ten or twelve—sovereigns. . . .

The front door closed and he returned. My chance of escape had gone.

### 4

"I must be going," I said, with a curiously reinforced desire to get away out of that room.

"My dear chap!" he insisted, "I can't think of it. Surely—there's nothing to call you away." Then with an evident desire to shift the venue of our talk, he asked, "You never told me what you thought of Burble's little book."

I was now, beneath my dull display of submission, furiously angry with him. It occurred to me to ask myself why I should defer and qualify my opinions to him.

Why should I pretend a feeling of intellectual and social inferiority towards him. He asked what I thought of Burble. I resolved to tell him—if necessary with arrogance. Then perhaps he would release me. I did not sit down again, but stood by the corner of the fireplace.

"That was the little book you lent me last summer?" I said.

"He reasons closely, eh?" he said, and indicated the armchair with a flat hand, and beamed persuasively.

I remained standing. "I didn't think much of his reasoning powers," I said.

"He was one of the cleverest bishops London ever had."

"That may be. But he was dodging about in a jolly feeble case," said I.

"You mean?"

"That he's wrong. I don't think he proves his case. I don't think Christianity is true. He knows himself for the pretender he is. His reasoning's—Rot."

Mr. Gabbitas went, I think, a shade paler than his wont, and propitiation vanished from his manner. His eyes and mouth were round, his face seemed to get round, his eyebrows curved at my remarks.

"I'm sorry you think that," he said at last, with a catch in his breath.

He did not repeat his suggestion that I should sit. He made a step or two towards the window and turned. "I suppose you will admit—" he began, with a faintly irritating note of intellectual condescension. . . .

I will not tell you of his arguments or mine. You will find if you care to look for them, in out-of-the-way corners of our book museums, the shrivelled cheap publications—the publications of the Rationalist Press Association, for example—on which my arguments were based. Lying in that curious limbo with them, mixed up with them and indistinguishable, are the endless "Replies" of orthodoxy, like the mixed dead in some hard-fought trench. All those disputes of our fathers, and they were sometimes furious disputes, have gone now beyond the range of comprehension. You younger people, I know, read them with impatient perplexity. You cannot understand how sane creatures could imagine they had joined issue at all in most of these controversies. All the old methods of systematic thinking, the queer absurdities of the Aristotelian logic, have followed magic numbers and mystical numbers, and the Rumpelstiltskin magic names now into the blackness of the unthinkable. You can no more understand our theological passions than you can understand the fancies that made all ancient peoples speak of their gods only by circumlocutions, that made savages pine away and die because they had been photographed, or an Elizabethan farmer turn back from a day's expedition because he had met three crows. Even I, who have been through it all, recall our controversies now with something near incredulity.

Faith we can understand to-day, all men live by faith; but in the old time everyone confused quite hopelessly Faith and a forced, incredible Belief in certain pseudo-concrete statements. I am inclined to say that neither believers nor unbelievers had faith as we understand it—they had insufficient intellectual power. They could not trust unless they had something to see and touch and say, like their barbarous ancestors who could not make a bargain without exchange of tokens. If they no longer worshipped sticks and stones, or eked out their needs with pilgrimages and images, they still held fiercely to audible images, to printed words and formulae.

But why revive the echoes of the ancient logomachies?

Suffice it that we lost our tempers very readily in pursuit of God and Truth, and said exquisitely foolish things on either side. And on the whole—from the impartial perspective of my three and seventy years—I adjudicate that if my dialectic was bad, that of the Rev. Gabbitas was altogether worse.

Little pink spots came into his cheeks, a squealing note into his voice. We interrupted each other more and more rudely. We invented faces and appealed to authorities whose names I mispronounced; and, finding Gabbitas shy of the higher criticism and the Germans, I used the names of Karl Marx and Engels as Bible exegetes with no little effect. A silly wrangle! A preposterous wrangle!—you must imagine our talk becoming louder, with a developing quarrelsome note—my mother no doubt hovering on the staircase and listening in alarm as who should say, "My dear, don't offend it! Oh, don't offend it! Mr. Gabbitas enjoys its friendship. Try to think whatever Mr. Gabbias says"—though we still kept in touch with a pretence of mutual deference. The ethical superiority of Christianity to all other religions came to the fore—I know not how. We dealt with the matter in bold, imaginative generalisations, because of the insufficiency of our historical knowledge. I was moved to denounce Christianity as the ethic of slaves, and declare myself a disciple of a German writer of no little vogue in those days, named Nietzsche.

For a disciple I must confess I was particularly ill acquainted with the works of the master. Indeed, all I knew of him had come to me through a two-column article in *The Clarion* for the previous week. . . . But the Rev. Gabbitas did not read *The Clarion*.

I am, I know, putting a strain upon your credulity when I tell you that I now have little doubt that the Rev. Gabbias was absolutely ignorant even of the name of Nietzsche, although that writer presented a separate and distinct attitude of attack upon the faith that was in the reverend gentleman's keeping.

"I'm a disciple of Nietzsche," said I, with an air of extensive explanation.

He shied away so awkwardly at the name that I repeated it at once.

"But do you know what Nietzsche says?" I pressed him viciously.

"He has certainly been adequately answered," said he, still trying to carry it off.

"Who by?" I rapped out hotly. "Tell me that!" and became mercilessly expectant.

### 5

A happy accident relieved Mr. Gabbitas from the embarrassment of that challenge, and carried me another step along my course of personal disaster.

It came on the heels of my question in the form of a clatter of horses without, and the grind and cessation of wheels. I glimpsed a straw-hatted coachman and a pair of greys. It seemed an incredibly magnificent carriage for Clayton.

"Eh!" said the Rev. Gabbitas, going to the window. "Why, it's old Mrs. Verrall! It's old Mrs. Verrall. Really! What can she want with me?"

He turned to me, and the flush of controversy had passed and his face shone like the sun. It was not every day, I perceived, that Mrs. Verrall came to see him.

"I get so many interruptions," he said, almost grinning. "You must excuse me a minute! Then—then I'll tell you about that fellow. But don't go. I pray you don't go. I can assure you . . . most interesting."

He went out of the room waving vague prohibitory gestures.

"I must go," I cried after him.

"No, no, no!" in the passage. "I've got your answer," I think it was he added, and "quite mistaken"; and I saw him running down the steps to talk to the old lady.

I swore. I made three steps to the window, and this brought me within a yard of that accursed drawer.

I glanced at it, and then at that old woman who was so absolutely powerful, and instantly her son and Nettie's face were flaming in my brain. The Stuarts had, no doubt, already accepted accomplished facts. And I too—

What was I doing here?

What was I doing here while judgment escaped me?

I woke up. I was injected with energy. I took one reassuring look at the curate's obsequious back, at the old lady's projected nose and quivering hand, and then with swift, clean movements I had the little drawer open, four sovereigns in my pocket, and the drawer shut again. Then again at the window—they were still talking.

That was all right. He might not look in that drawer for hours. I glanced at his clock. Twenty minutes still before the Birmingham train. Time to buy a pair of boots and get away. But how was I to get to the station?

I went out boldly into the passage, and took my hat and stick. . . . Walk past him?

Yes. That was all right! He could not argue with me while so important a person engaged him. . . . I came boldly down the steps.

"I want a list made, Mr. Gabbitas, of all the really deserving cases," old Mrs. Verrall was saying.

It is curious, but it did not occur to me that here was a mother whose son I was going to kill. I did not see her in that aspect at all. Instead, I was possessed by a realisation of the blazing imbecility of a social system that gave this palsied old woman the power to give or withhold the urgent necessities of life from hundreds of her fellow-creatures just according to her poor, foolish old fancies of desert.

"We could make a provisional list of that sort," he was saying, and glanced round with a preoccupied expression at me.

"I must go," I said at his flash of inquiry, and added, "I'll be back in twenty minutes," and went on my way. He turned again to his patroness as though he forgot me on the instant. Perhaps after all he was not sorry.

I felt extraordinarily cool and capable, exhilarated, if anything, by this prompt, effectual theft. After all, my great determination would achieve itself. I was no longer oppressed by a sense of obstacles. I felt I could grasp accidents and turn them to my advantage. I would go now down Hacker Street to the little shoemaker's—get a sound, good pair of boots—ten minutes—and then to the railway-station—five minutes more—and off! I felt as efficient and non-moral as if I was Nietzsche's Over-man already come. It did not occur to me that the curate's clock might have a considerable margin of error.

6

I missed the train.

Partly that was because the curate's clock was slow, and partly it was due to the commercial obstinacy of the shoemaker, who would try on another pair after I had declared my time was up. I bought the final pair however, gave him a wrong address for the return of the old ones, and only ceased to feel like the Nietzchean Over-man when I saw the train running out of the station.

Even then I did not lose my head. It occurred to me almost at once that in the event of a prompt pursuit there would be a great advantage in not taking a train from Clayton; that, indeed, to have done so would have been an error from which only luck had saved me. As it was, I had already been very indiscreet in my inquiries about Shaphambury, for once on the scent the clerk could not fail to remember me. Now the chances were against his coming into the case. I did not go into the station therefore at all, I made no demonstration of having missed the train, but walked quietly past, down the road, crossed the iron footbridge, and took the way back circuitously by White's brickfields and the allotments to the way over Clayton Crest to Two-Mile Stone, where I calculated I should have an ample margin for the 6.13 train.

I was not very greatly excited or alarmed then. Suppose, I reasoned, that by some accident the curate goes to that drawer at once; will he be certain to miss four out of ten or eleven sovereigns? If he does, will he at once think I have taken them? If he does, will he act at once or wait for my return? If he acts at once, will he talk to my mother or call in the police? Then there are a dozen roads and even railways out of the Clayton region; how is he to know which I have taken? Suppose he goes straight at once to the right station, they will not remember my departure for the simple reason that I didn't depart. But they may remember about Shaphambury? It was unlikely.

I resolved not to go directly to Shaphambury from Birmingham, but to go thence to Monkshampton, thence to Wyvern, and then come down on Shaphambury from the north. That might involve a night at some intermediate stopping-place, but it would effectually conceal me from any but the most persistent pursuit. And this was not a case of murder yet, but only the theft of four sovereigns.

I had argued away all anxiety before I reached Clayton Crest.

At the Crest I looked back. What a world it was! And suddenly it came to me that I was looking at it for the last time. If I overtook the fugitives and succeeded, I should die with them—or hang. I stopped and looked back more attentively at that wide ugly valley.

It was my native valley, and I was going out of it, I thought, never to return; and yet in that last prospect the group of towns that had borne me and dwarfed and crippled and made me, seemed in some indefinable manner strange. I was, perhaps, more used to seeing it from this comprehensive viewpoint when it was veiled and softened by night; now it came out in all its week-day reek, under a clear afternoon sun. That may account a little for its unfamiliarity. And perhaps, too, there was something in the emotions through which I had been passing for a week and more, to intensify my insight, to enable me to pierce the unusual, to question the accepted. But it came to me then, I am sure, for the first time how promiscuous, how higgledy-piggledy was the whole of that jumble of mines and homes, collieries and pot-banks, railway yards, canals, schools, forges and blast furnaces, churches, chapels, allotment hovels, a vast irregular agglomeration of ugly smoking accidents in which men lived as happy as frogs in a dustbin. Each thing jostled and damaged the other things about it, each thing ignored the other things about it; the smoke of the furnace defiled the pot-bank clay, the clatter of the railway deafened the worshippers in church, the public-house thrust corruption at the school doors, the dismal homes squeezed miserably amidst the monstrosities of industrialism, with an effect of groping imbecility. Humanity choked amidst its products, and all its energy went in increasing its disorder, like a blind stricken thing that struggles and sinks in a morass.

I did not think these things clearly that afternoon. Much less did I ask how I, with my murderous purpose, stood to them all. I write down that realisation of disorder and suffocation here and now as though I had thought it, but indeed then I only felt it, felt it transitorily as I looked back, and then stood with the thing escaping from my mind.

I should never see that countryside again.

I came back to that. At any rate I wasn't sorry. The chances were I should die in sweet air, under a clean sky.

From distant Swathinglea came a little sound, the minute ululation of a remote crowd, and then rapidly three shots.

That held me perplexed for a space. . . . Well, anyhow I was leaving it all! Thank God I was leaving it all! Then, as I turned to go on, I thought of my mother.

It seemed an evil world in which to leave one's mother. My thoughts focused upon her very vividly for a moment. Down there, under that afternoon light, she was going to and from unaware as yet that she had lost me, bent and poking about in the darkling underground kitchen, perhaps carrying a lamp into the scullery to trim, or sitting patiently, staring into the fire, waiting tea for me. A great pity for her, a great remorse at the blacker troubles that lowered over her innocent head, came to me. Why, after all, was I doing this thing?

Why?

279

I stopped again dead, with the hill crest rising between me and home. I had more than half a mind to return to her.

Then I thought of the curate's sovereigns. If he had missed them already, what should I return to? And even if I returned, how could I put them back?

And what of the night after I renounced my revenge? What of the time when young Verrall came back? And Nettie?

No! The thing had to be done.

But at least I might have kissed my mother before I came away, left her some message, reassured her at least for a little while. All night she would listen and wait for me. . . .

Should I send her a telegram from Two-Mile Stone?

It was no good now; too late, too late. To do that would be to tell the course I had taken, to bring pursuit upon me swift and sure, if pursuit there was to be. No. My mother must suffer!

I went on grimly towards Two-Mile Stone, but now as if some greater will than mine directed my footsteps thither.

I reached Birmingham before darkness came, and just caught the last train for Monkshampton, where I had planned to pass the night.

CHAPTER THE FIFTH
THE PURSUIT OF THE TWO LOVERS
1

As the train carried me on from Birmingham to Monkshampton, it carried me not only into a country where I had never been before, but out of the commonplace daylight and the touch and quality of ordinary things, into the strange unprecedented night that was ruled by the giant meteor of the last days.

There was at that time a curious accentuation of the common alternation of night and day. They became separated with a widening difference of value in regard to all mundane affairs. During the day the comet was an item in the newspapers, it was jostled by a thousand more living interests, it was as nothing in the skirts of the war storm that was now upon us. It was an astronomical phenomenon somewhere away over China, millions of miles away in the deeps. We forgot it. But directly the sun sank one turned ever and again towards the east, and the meteor resumed its sway over us.

One waited for its rising, and yet each night it came as a surprise. Always it rose brighter than one had dared to think, always larger and with some wonderful change in its outline, and now with a strange, less luminous, greener disc upon it that grew with its growth, the umbra of the earth. It shone also with its own light, so that this shadow was not hard or black but it shone phosphorescently and with a diminishing intensity where the stimulus of the sun's rays was withdrawn. As it ascended towards the zenith, as the last trailing daylight went after the abdicating sun, its greenish white illumination banished the realities of day, diffused a bright ghostliness over

280

all things. It changed the starless sky about it to an extraordinary deep blue, the profoundest colour in the world, such as I have never seen before or since. I remember, too, that as I peered from the train that was rattling me along to Monkshampton, I perceived and was puzzled by a coppery red light that mingled with all the shadows that were cast by it.

It turned our ugly English industrial towns to phantom cities. Everywhere the local authorities discontinued street lighting—one could read small print in the glare— and so at Monkshamptom I went about through pale, white, unfamiliar streets, whose electric globes had shadows on the path. In windows here and there burnt ruddy orange, like holes cut in some dream curtain that hung before a furnace. A policeman with noiseless feet showed me an inn woven of moonshine, a green-faced man opened to us, and there I abode the night. And the next morning it opened with a mighty clatter, and was a dirty little beerhouse that stank of beer, and there was a fat and grimy landlord with red spots upon his neck, and much noisy traffic going by on the cobbles outside.

I came out, after I had paid my bill, into a street that echoed to the bawlings of two news-vendors and to the noisy yappings of a dog they had raised to emulation. They were shouting: "Great British disaster in the North Sea. A battleship lost with all hands!"

I bought a paper, went on to the railway station reading such details as were given of this triumph of the old civilisation, of the blowing up of this great iron ship, full of guns and explosives and the most costly and beautiful machinery of which that time was capable, together with nine hundred able-bodied men, all of them above the average, by a contact mine towed by a German submarine. I read myself into a fever of warlike emotion. Not only did I forget the meteor, but for a time I forgot even the purpose that took me on to the railway station, bought my ticket, and was now carrying me onward to Shaphambury.

So the hot day came to its own again, and people forgot the night.

Each night there shone upon us more and more insistently, beauty, wonder, the promise of the deeps; and we were hushed, and marvelled for a space. And at the first grey sounds of dawn again, at the shooting of bolts and the noise of milk-carts, we forgot, and the dusty habitual day came yawning and stretching back again. The stains of coal smoke crept across the heavens, and we rose to the soiled disorderly routine of life.

"Thus life has always been," we said; "thus it will always be."

The glory of those nights was almost universally regarded as spectacular merely. It signified nothing to us. So far as western Europe went, it was only a small and ignorant section of the lower classes who regarded the comet as a portent of the end of the world. Abroad, where there were peasantries, it was different, but in England the peasantry had already disappeared. Everyone read. The newspaper, in the quiet days before our swift quarrel with Germany rushed to its climax, had absolutely dispelled all possibilities of a panic in this matter. The very tramps upon the high-roads, the

281

children in the nursery, had learned that at the utmost the whole of that shining cloud could weigh but a few score tons. This fact had been shown quite conclusively by the enormous deflections that had at last swung it round squarely at our world. It had passed near three of the smallest asteroids without producing the minutest perceptible deflection in their course; while, on its own part, it had described a course though nearly three degrees. When it struck our earth there was to be a magnificent spectacle, no doubt, for those who were on the right side of our planet to see; but beyond that nothing. It was doubtful whether we were on the right side. The meteor would loom larger and larger in the sky, but with the umbra of our earth eating its heart of brightness out, and at last it would be the whole sky, a sky of luminous green clouds, with a white brightness about the horizon west and east. Then a pause—a pause of not very exactly definite duration—and then, no doubt, a great blaze of shooting stars. They might be of some unwonted colour because of the unknown element that line in the green revealed. For a little while the zenith would spout shooting stars. Some, it was hoped, would reach the earth and be available for analysis.

That, science said, would be all. The green clouds would whirl and vanish, and there might be thunderstorms. But through the attenuated wisps of comet shine, the old sky, the old stars, would reappear, and all would be as it had been before. And since this was to happen between one and eleven in the morning of the approaching Tuesday—I slept at Monkshampton on Saturday night—it would be only partially visible, if visible at all, on our side of the earth. Perhaps, if it came late, one would see no more than a shooting star low down in the sky. All this we had with the utmost assurances of science. Still it did not prevent the last nights being the most beautiful and memorable of human experiences.

The nights had become very warm, and when next day I had ranged Shaphambury in vain, I was greatly tormented, as that unparalleled glory of the night returned, to think that under its splendid benediction young Verrall and Nettie made love to one another.

I walked backward and forward, backward and forward, along the seafront, peering into the faces of the young couples who promenaded, with my hand in my pocket ready and a curious ache in my heart that had no kindred with rage. Until at last all the promenaders had gone home to bed, and I was alone with the star.

My train from Wyvern to Shaphambury that morning was a whole hour late; they said it was on account of the movement of troops to meet a possible raid from the Elbe.


## 2

Shaphambury seemed an odd place to me even then. But something was quickening in me at that time to feel the oddness of many accepted things. Now in the retrospect I see it as intensely queer. The whole place was strange to my untravelled eyes; the sea even was strange. Only twice in my life had I been at the seaside before, and then I had gone by excursion to places on the Welsh coast whose great cliffs of rock and mountain backgrounds made the effect of the horizon very different from what it is upon the East Anglia seaboard. Here what they call a cliff was a crumbling bank of whitey-brown earth not fifty feet high.

So soon as I arrived I made a systematic exploration of Shaphambury. To this day I retain the clearest memories of the plan I shaped out then, and how my inquiries were incommoded by the overpowering desire of everyone to talk of the chances of a German raid, before the Channel Fleet got round to us. I slept at a small public-house in a Shaphambury back street on Sunday night. I did not get on to Shapham-bury from Wyvern until two in the afternoon, because of the infrequency of Sunday trains, and I got no clue whatever until late in the afternoon of Monday. As the little local train bumped into sight of the place round the curve of a swelling hill, one saw a series of undulating grassy spaces, amidst which a number of conspicuous notice-boards appealed to the eye and cut up the distant sea horizon. Most of these referred to comestibles or to remedies to follow the comestibles; and they were coloured with a view to be memorable rather than beautiful, to "stand out" amidst the gentle grey-ish tones of the east-coast scenery. The greater number, I may remark, of the adver-tisements that were so conspicuous a factor in the life of those days, and which ren-dered our vast tree-pulp newspapers possible, referred to foods, drinks, tobacco, and the drugs that promised a restoration of the equanimity these other articles had de-stroyed. Wherever one went one was reminded in glaring letters that, after all, man was little better than a worm, that eyeless, earless thing that burrows and lives un-complainingly amidst nutritious dirt, "an alimentary canal with the subservient ap-pendages thereto." But in addition to such boards there were also the big black-and-white boards of various grandiloquently named "estates." The individualistic enterprise of that time had led to the plotting out of nearly all the country round and seaside towns into roads and building-plots—all but a small portion of the south and east coast was in this condition, and had the promises of those schemes been realised the entire population of the island might have been accommodated upon the sea frontiers. Nothing of the sort happened, of course; the whole of this uglification of the coast-line was done to stimulate a little foolish gambling in plots, and one saw every-where agents' boards in every state of freshness and decay, ill-made exploitation, roads overgrown with grass, and here and there at a corner, a label, "Trafalgar Av-enue," or "Sea View Road." Here and there, too, some small investor, some shopman with "savings," had delivered his soul to the local builders and built himself a house; and there it stood, ill-designed, mean-looking, isolated, ill-placed on a cheaply fenced plot, athwart which his domestic washing fluttered in the breeze amidst a bleak des-olation of enterprise. Then presently our railway crossed a high road, and a row of mean yellow-brick houses—workmen's cottages, and the filthy black sheds that made the "allotments" of that time a universal eyesore, marked our approach to the more central areas of—I quote the local guidebook—"one of the most delightful resorts in the East Anglian poppy land." Then more mean houses, the gaunt ungainliness of the electric force station—it had a huge chimney, because no one understood how to make combustion of coal complete—and then we were in the railway station, and barely three-quarters of a mile from the centre of this haunt of health and pleasure.

I inspected the town thoroughly before I made my inquiries. The road began badly with a row of cheap, pretentious, insolvent-looking shops, a public-house, and a cab-stand, but, after an interval of little red villas that were partly hidden amidst shrubbery gardens, broke into a confusedly bright but not unpleasing High Street, shuttered that afternoon and sabbatically still. Somewhere in the background a church bell jangled, and children in bright new-looking clothes were going to Sunday-school. Thence through a square of stuccoed lodging houses that seemed a finer and cleaner version of my native square, I came to a garden of asphalt and euonymus—the Sea Front. I sat down on a cast-iron seat, and surveyed first of all the broad stretches of muddy, sandy beach, with its queer wheeled bathing machines painted with the advertisements of somebody's pills, and then at the house fronts that stared out upon these visceral counsels. Boarding-houses, private hotels, and lodging-houses in terraces clustered closely right and left of me, and then came to an end; in one direction scaffolding marked a building enterprise in progress, in the other, after a waste interval, rose a monstrous bulging red shape, a huge hotel, that dwarfed all other things. Northward were low pale cliffs with white denticulations of tents, where the local volunteers, all under arms, lay encamped; and southward, a spreading waste of sandy dunes, with occasional bushes and clumps of stunted pine and an advertisement board or so. A hard blue sky hung over all this prospect, the sunshine cast inky shadows, and eastward was a whitish sea. It was Sunday, and the midday meal still held people indoors. . . .

A queer world! thought I even then—to you now it must seem impossibly queer—and after an interval I forced myself back to my own affair.

How was I to ask? What was I to ask for?

I puzzled for a long time over that—at first I was a little tired and indolent—and then presently I had a flow of ideas.

My solution was fairly ingenious. I invented the following story. I happened to be taking a holiday in Shaphambury, and I was making use of the opportunity to seek the owner of a valuable feather boa, which had been left behind in the hotel of my uncle at Wyvern by a young lady, travelling with a young gentleman—no doubt, a youthful married couple. They had reached Shaphambury somewhen on Thursday. I went over the story many times, and gave my imaginary uncle and his hotel plausible names. At any rate this yarn would serve as a complete justification for all the questions I might wish to ask.

I settled that, but I still sat for a time, wanting the energy to begin. Then I turned towards the big hotel. Its gorgeous magnificence seemed to my inexpert judgment to indicate the very place a rich young man of good family would select.

Huge draught-proof doors were swung round for me by an ironically polite under-porter in a magnificent green uniform, who looked at my clothes as he listened to my question and then with a German accent referred me to a gorgeous head porter, who directed me to a princely young man behind a counter of brass and polish, like a bank—like several banks. This young man, while he answered me, kept his eye on my collar and tie—and I knew that they were abominable.

"I want to find a lady and gentleman who came to Shaphambury on Tuesday," I said.

"Friends of yours?" he asked with a terrible fineness of irony.

I made out at last that here at any rate the young people had not been. They might have lunched there, but they had had no room. But I went out—door opened again for me obsequiously—in a state of social discomfiture, and did not attack any other establishment that afternoon.

My resolution had come to a sort of ebb. More people were promenading, and their Sunday smartness abashed me. I forgot my purpose in an acute sense of myself. I felt that the bulge of my pocket caused by the revolver was conspicuous, and I was ashamed. I went along the sea front away from the town, and presently lay down among pebbles and sea poppies. This mood of reaction prevailed with me all that afternoon. In the evening, about sundown, I went to the station and asked questions of the outporters there. But outporters, I found, were a class of men who remembered luggage rather than people, and I had no sort of idea what luggage young Verrall and Nettie were likely to have with them.

Then I fell into conversation with a salacious wooden-legged old man with a silver ring, who swept the steps that went down to the beach from the parade. He knew much about young couples, but only in general terms, and nothing of the particular young couple I sought. He reminded me in the most disagreeable way of the sensuous aspects of life, and I was not sorry when presently a gunboat appeared in the offing signalling the coastguard and the camp, and cut short his observations upon holidays, beaches, and morals.

I went—and now I was past my ebb—and sat in a seat upon the parade, and watched the brightening of those rising clouds of chilly fire that made the ruddy west seem tame. My midday lassitude was going, my blood was running warmer again. And as the twilight and that filmy brightness replaced the dusty sunlight and robbed this unfamiliar place of all its matter-of-fact queerness, its sense of aimless materialism, romance returned to me, and passion, and my thoughts of honour and revenge. I remember that change of mood as occurring very vividly on this occasion, but I fancy that less distinctly I had felt this before many times. In the old times, night and the starlight had an effect of intimate reality the daytime did not possess. The daytime—as one saw it in towns and populous places—had hold of one, no doubt, but only as an uproar might, it was distracting, conflicting, insistent. Darkness veiled the more salient aspects of those agglomerations of human absurdity, and one could exist—one could imagine.

I had a queer illusion that night, that Nettie and her lover were close at hand, that suddenly I should come on them. I have already told how I went through the dark seeking them in every couple that drew near. And I dropped asleep at last in an unfamiliar bedroom hung with gaudily decorated texts, cursing myself for having wasted a day.


3


I sought them in vain the next morning, but after midday I came in quick succession on a perplexing multitude of clues. After failing to find any young couple that corresponded to young Verrall and Nettie, I presently discovered an unsatisfactory quartet of couples.

Any of these four couples might have been the one I sought; with regard to none of them was there conviction. They had all arrived either on Wednesday or Thursday. Two couples were still in occupation of their rooms, but neither of these were at home. Late in the afternoon I reduced my list by eliminating a young man in drab, with side whiskers and long cuffs, accompanied by a lady of thirty or more, of consciously ladylike type. I was disgusted at the sight of them; the other two young people had gone for a long walk, and though I watched their boarding-house until the fiery cloud shone out above, sharing and mingling in an unusually splendid sunset, I missed them. Then I discovered them dining at a separate table in the bow window, with red-shaded candles between them, peering out ever and again at this splendour that was neither night or day. The girl in her pink evening dress looked very light and pretty to me—pretty enough to enrage me—she had well-shaped arms and white, well-modelled shoulders, and the turn of her cheek and the fair hair about her ears was full of subtle delights; but she was not Nettie, and the happy man with her was that degenerate type our old aristocracy produced with such odd frequency, chinless, large bony nose, small fair head, languid expression, and a neck that had demanded and received a veritable sleeve of collar. I stood outside in the meteor's livid light, hating them and cursing them for having delayed me so long. I stood until it was evident they remarked me, a black shape of envy silhouetted against the glare.

That finished Shaphambury. The question I now had to debate was which of the remaining couples I had to pursue.

I walked back to the parade trying to reason my next step out, and muttering to myself, because there was something in that luminous wonderfulness that touched one's brain and made one feel a little light-headed.

One couple had gone to London; the other had gone to the Bungalow village at Bone Cliff. Where, I wondered, was Bone Cliff?

I came upon my wooden-legged man at the top of his steps.

"Hullo," said I.

He pointed seaward with his pipe, his silver ring shone in the sky light.

"Rum," he said.

"What is?" I asked.

"Searchlights! Smoke! Ships going north! If it wasn't for this blasted Milky Way gone green up there, we might see."

He was too intent to heed my questions for a time. Then he vouchsafed over his shoulder—

"Know Bungalow village?—rather. Artis' and such. Nice goings on! Mixed bathing—something scandalous. Yes."

"But where is it?" I said, suddenly exasperated.

"There!" he said. "What's that flicker? A gunflash—or I'm a lost soul!"

"You'd hear," I said, "long before it was near enough to see a flash."

He didn't answer. Only by making it clear I would distract him until he told me what I wanted to know could I get him to turn from his absorbed contemplation of that phantom dance between the sea rim and the shine. Indeed I gripped his arm and shook him. Then he turned upon me cursing.

"Seven miles," he said, "along this road. And now go to 'ell with yer!"

I answered with some foul insult by way of thanks, and so we parted; and I set off towards the bungalow village.

I found a policeman, standing star-gazing, a little way beyond the end of the parade, and verified the wooden-legged man's directions.

"It's a lonely road, you know," he called after me. . . .

I had an odd intuition that now at last I was on the right track. I left the dark masses of Shaphambury behind me, and pushed out into the dim pallor of that night with the quiet assurance of a traveller who nears his end.

The incidents of that long tramp I do not recall in any orderly succession, the one progressive thing is my memory of a growing fatigue. The sea was for the most part smooth and shining like a mirror, a great expanse of reflecting silver barred by slow broad undulations, but at one time a little breeze breathed like a faint sigh and ruffled their long bodies into faint scaly ripples that never completely died out again. The way was sometimes sandy, thick with silvery colourless sand, and sometimes chalky and lumpy, with lumps that had shining facets; a black scrub was scattered, sometimes in thickets, sometimes in single bunches, among the somnolent hummocks of sand. At one place came grass, and ghostly great sheep looming up among the grey. After a time black pinewoods intervened, and made sustained darknesses along the road, woods that frayed out at the edges to weirdly warped and stunted trees. Then isolated pine witches would appear, and make their rigid gestures at me as I passed. Grotesquely incongruous amidst these forms, I presently came on estate boards, appealing, "Houses can be built to suit purchaser," to the silence, to the shadows, and the glare.

Once I remember the persistent barking of a dog from somewhere inland of me, and several times I took out and examined my revolver very carefully. I must, of course, have been full of my intention when I did that, I must have been thinking of Nettie and revenge, but I cannot now recall these emotions at all. Only I see again very distinctly the greenish gleams that ran over lock and barrel as I turned the weapon in my hand.

Then there was the sky, the wonderful, luminous, starless, moonless sky, and the empty blue deeps of the edge of it, between the meteor and the sea and once—strange phantoms!—I saw far out upon the shine, and very small and distant, three long black warships, without masts, or sails, or smoke, or any lights, dark, deadly, furtive things, travelling very swiftly and keeping an equal distance. And when I looked again they were very small, and then the shine had swallowed them up.

Then once a flash and what I thought was a gun, until I looked up and saw a fading trail of greenish light still hanging in the sky. And after that there was a shiver and whispering in the air, a stronger throbbing in one's arteries, a sense of refreshment, a renewal of purpose. . . .

Somewhere upon my way the road forked, but I do not remember whether that was near Shaphambury or near the end of my walk. The hesitation between two rutted unmade roads alone remains clear in my mind.

At last I grew weary. I came to piled heaps of decaying seaweed and cart tracks running this way and that, and then I had missed the road and was stumbling among sand hummocks quite close to the sea. I came out on the edge of the dimly glittering sandy beach, and something phosporescent drew me to the water's edge. I bent down and peered at the little luminous specks that floated in the ripples.

Presently with a sigh I stood erect, and contemplated the lonely peace of that last wonderful night. The meteor had now trailed its shining nets across the whole space of the sky and was beginning to set; in the east the blue was coming to its own again; the sea was an intense edge of blackness, and now, escaped from that great shine, and faint and still tremulously valiant, one weak elusive star could just be seen, hovering on the verge of the invisible.

How beautiful it was! How still and beautiful! Peace! Peace!—the peace that passeth understanding, robed in light descending! . . .

My heart swelled, and suddenly I was weeping.

There was something new and strange in my blood. It came to me that indeed I did not want to kill.

I did not want to kill. I did not want to be the servant of my passions any more. A great desire had come to me to escape from life, from the daylight which is heat and conflict and desire, into that cool night of eternity—and rest. I had played—I had done.

I stood upon the edge of the great ocean, and I was filled with an inarticulate spirit of prayer, and I desired greatly—peace from myself.

And presently, there in the east, would come again the red discolouring curtain over these mysteries, the finite world again, the grey and growing harsh certainties

288

of dawn. My resolve I knew would take up with me again. This was a rest for me, an interlude; but to-morrow I should be William Leadford once more, ill-nourished, ill-dressed, ill-equipped and clumsy, a thief and shamed, a wound upon the face of life, a source of trouble and sorrow even to the mother I loved; no hope in life left for me now but revenge before my death.

Why this paltry thing, revenge? It entered into my thoughts that I might end the matter now and let these others go.

To wade out into the sea, into this warm lapping that mingled the natures of water and light, to stand there breast-high, to thrust my revolver barrel into my mouth—?

Why not?

I swung about with an effort. I walked slowly up the beach thinking. . . .

I turned and looked back at the sea. No! Something within me said, "No!"

I must think.

It was troublesome to go further because the hummocks and the tangled bushes began. I sat down amidst a black cluster of shrubs, and rested, chin on hand. I drew my revolver from my pocket and looked at it, and held it in my hand. Life? Or Death? . . .

I seemed to be probing the very deeps of being, but indeed imperceptibly I fell asleep, and sat dreaming.

## 4

Two people were bathing in the sea.

I had awakened. It was still that white and wonderful night, and the blue band of clear sky was no wider than before. These people must have come into sight as I fell asleep, and awakened me almost at once. They waded breast-deep in the water, emerging, coming shoreward, a woman, with her hair coiled about her head, and in pursuit of her a man, graceful figures of black and silver with a bright green surge flowing off from them, a pattering of flashing wavelets about them. He smote the water and splashed it towards her, she retaliated, and then they were knee-deep, and then for an instant their feet broke the long silver margin of the sea.

Each wore a tightly fitting bathing dress that hid nothing of the shining, dripping beauty of their youthful forms.

She glanced over her shoulder and found him nearer than she thought, started, gesticulated, gave a little cry that pierced me to the heart, and fled up the beach obliquely towards me, running like the wind, and passed me, vanished amidst the black distorted bushes, and was gone—she and her pursuer, in a moment, over the ridge of sand.

I heard him shout between exhaustion and laughter. . . .

And suddenly I was a thing of bestial fury, standing with hands held up and clenched, rigid in gesture of impotent threatening, against the sky. . . .

For this striving, swift thing of light and beauty was Nettie—and this was the man for whom I have been betrayed!

And, it blazed upon me, I might have died there by the sheer ebbing of my will—unavenged!

In another moment I was running and stumbling, revolver in hand, in quite unsuspected pursuit of them, through the soft and noiseless sand.


## 5

I came up over the little ridge and discovered the bungalow village I had been seeking, nestling in a crescent lap of dunes. A door slammed, and two runners had vanished, and I halted staring.

There was a group of three bungalows nearer to me than the others. Into one of these three they had gone, and I was too late to see which. All had doors and windows carelessly open, and none showed a light.

This place, upon which I had at last happened, was a fruit of the reaction of artistic-minded and carelessly living people against the costly and uncomfortable social stiffness of the more formal seaside resorts of that time. It was, you must understand, the custom of the steam-railway companies to sell their carriages after they had been obsolete for a sufficient length of years, and some genius had hit upon the possibility of turning these into habitable cabins for the summer holiday. The thing had become a fashion with a certain Bohemian-spirited class; they added cabin to cabin, and these little improvised homes, gaily painted and with broad verandahs and supplementary lean-tos added to their accommodation, made the brightest contrast conceivable to the dull rigidities of the decorous resorts. Of course there were many discomforts in such camping that had to be faced cheerfully, and so this broad sandy beach was sacred to high spirits and the young. Art muslin and banjoes, Chinese lanterns and frying, are leading "notes," I find, in the impression of those who once knew such places well. But so far as I was concerned this odd settlement of pleasure-squatters was a mystery as well as a surprise, enhanced rather than mitigated by an imaginative suggestion or so I had received from the wooden-legged man at Shaphambury. I saw the thing as no gathering of light hearts and gay idleness, but grimly—after the manner of poor men poisoned by the suppression of all their cravings after joy. To the poor man, to the grimy workers, beauty and cleanness were absolutely denied; out of a life of greasy dirt, of muddied desires, they watched their happier fellows with a bitter envy and foul, tormenting suspicions. Fancy a world in which the common people held love to be a sort of beastliness, own sister to being drunk! . . .

There was in the old time always something cruel at the bottom of this business of sexual love. At least that is the impression I have brought with me across the gulf of the great Change. To succeed in love seemed such triumph as no other success could give, but to fail was as if one was tainted. . . .

I felt no sense of singularity that this thread of savagery should run through these emotions of mine and become now the whole strand of these emotions. I believed, and I think I was right in believing, that the love of all true lovers was a sort of defiance then, that they closed a system in each other's arms and mocked the world without. You loved against the world, and these two loved *at* me. They had their business with one another, under the threat of a watchful fierceness. A sword, a sharp sword, the keenest edge in life, lay among their roses.

Whatever may be true of this for others, for me and my imagination, at any rate, it was altogether true. I was never for dalliance, I was never a jesting lover. I wanted fiercely; I made love impatiently. Perhaps I had written irrelevant love-letters for that very reason; because with this stark theme I could not play. . . .

The thought of Nettie's shining form, of her shrinking bold abandon to her easy conqueror, gave me now a body of rage that was nearly too strong for my heart and nerves and the tense powers of my merely physical being. I came down among the pale sand heaps slowly towards that queer village of careless sensuality, and now within my puny body I was coldly sharpset for pain and death, a darkly gleaming hate, a sword of evil, drawn.

6

I halted, and stood planning what I had to do.

Should I go to bungalow after bungalow until one of the two I sought answered to my rap? But suppose some servant intervened!

Should I wait where I was—perhaps until morning—watching? And meanwhile—

All the nearer bungalows were very still now. If I walked softly to them, from open windows, from something seen or overheard, I might get a clue to guide me. Should I advance circuitously, creeping upon them, or should I walk straight to the door? It was bright enough for her to recognise me clearly at a distance of many paces.

The difficulty to my mind lay in this, that if I involved other people by questions, I might at last confront my betrayers with these others close about me, ready to snatch my weapon and seize my hands. Besides, what names might they bear here?

"Boom!" the sound crept upon my senses, and then again it came.

I turned impatiently as one turns upon an impertinence, and beheld a great ironclad not four miles out, steaming fast across the dappled silver, and from its funnels sparks, intensely red, poured out into the night. As I turned, came the hot flash of its guns, firing seaward, and answering this, red flashes and a streaming smoke in the line between sea and sky. So I remembered it, and I remember myself

291

staring at it—in a state of stupid arrest. It was an irrelevance. What had these things to do with me?

With a shuddering hiss, a rocket from a headland beyond the village leaped up and burst hot gold against the glare, and the sound of the third and fourth guns reached me.

The windows of the dark bungalows, one after another, leaped out, squares of ruddy brightness that flared and flickered and became steadily bright. Dark heads appeared looking seaward, a door opened, and sent out a brief lane of yellow to mingle and be lost in the comet's brightness. That brought me back to the business in hand.

"Boom! Boom!" and when I looked again at the great ironclad, a little torchlike spurt of flame wavered behind her funnels. I could hear the throb and clangour of her straining engines. . . .

I became aware of the voices of people calling to one another in the village. A white-robed, hooded figure, some man in a bathing wrap, absurdly suggestive of an Arab in his burnous, came out from one of the nearer bungalows, and stood clear and still and shadowless in the glare.

He put his hands to shade his seaward eyes, and shouted to people within.

The people within—my people! My fingers tightened on my revolver. What was this war nonsense to me? I would go round among the hummocks with the idea of approaching the three bungalows inconspicuously from the flank. This fight at sea might serve my purpose—except for that, it had no interest for me at all. Boom! Boom! The huge voluminous concussions rushed past me, beat at my heart and passed. In a moment Nettie would come out to see.

First one and then two other wrapped figures came out of the bungalows to join the first. His arm pointed seaward, and his voice, a full tenor, rose in explanation. I could hear some of the words. "It's a German!" he said. "She's caught."

Someone disputed that, and there followed a little indistinct babble of argument. I went on slowly in the circuit I had marked out, watching these people as I went.

They shouted together with such a common intensity of direction that I halted and looked seaward. I saw the tall fountain flung by a shot that had just missed the great warship. A second rose still nearer us, a third and a fourth, and then a great uprush of dust, a whirling cloud, leaped out of the headland whence the rocket had come, and spread with slow deliberation right and left. Hard on that an enormous crash, and the man with the full voice leaped and cried, "Hit!"

Let me see! Of course, I had to go round beyond the bungalows, and then come up towards the group from behind.

A high-pitched woman's voice called, "Honeymooners! Honeymooners! Come out and see!"

Something gleamed in the shadow of the nearer bungalow, and a man's voice answered from within. What he said I did not catch, but suddenly I heard Nettie calling very distinctly, "We've been bathing."

The man who had first come out shouted, "Don't you hear the guns? They're fighting—not five miles from shore."

"Eh?" answered the bungalow, and a window opened.

"Out there!"

I did not hear the reply, because of the faint rustle of my own movements. Clearly these people were all too much occupied by the battle to look in my direction, and so I walked now straight towards the darkness that held Nettie and the black desire of my heart.

"Look!" cried someone, and pointed skyward.

I glanced up, and behold! The sky was streaked with bright green trails. They radiated from a point halfway between the western horizon and the zenith, and within the shining clouds of the meteor a streaming movement had begun, so that it seemed to be pouring both westwardly and back towards the east, with a crackling sound, as though the whole heaven was stippled over with phantom pistol-shots. It seemed to me then as if the meteor was coming to help me, descending with those thousand pistols like a curtain to fend off this unmeaning foolishness of the sea.

"Boom!" went a gun on the big ironclad, and "boom!" and the guns of the pursuing cruisers flashed in reply.

To glance up at that streaky, stirring light scum of the sky made one's head swim. I stood for a moment dazed, and more than a little giddy. I had a curious instant of purely speculative thought. Suppose, after all, the fanatics were right, and the world was coming to an end! What a score that would be for Parload!

Then it came into my head that all these things were happening to consecrate my revenge! The war below, the heavens above were the thunderous garment of my deed. I heard Nettie's voice cry out not fifty yards away, and my passion surged again. I was to return to her amid these terrors bearing unanticipated death. I was to possess her, with a bullet, amidst thunderings and fear. At the thought I lifted up my voice to a shout that went unheard, and advanced now recklessly, revolver displayed in my hand.

It was fifty yards, forty yards, thirty yards—the little group of people, still heedless of me, was larger and more important now, the green-shot sky and the fighting ships remoter. Someone darted out from the bungalow, with an interrupted question, and stopped, suddenly aware of me. It was Nettie, with some coquettish dark wrap about her, and the green glare shining on her sweet face and white throat. I could see her expression, stricken with dismay and terror at my advance, as though something had seized her by the heart and held her still—a target for my shots.

"Boom!" came the ironclad's gunshot like a command. "Bang!" the bullet leaped from my hand. Do you know, I did not want to shoot her then. Indeed I did not want to shoot her then! Bang! And I had fired again, still striding on, and—each time it seemed I had missed.

She moved a step or so towards me, still staring, and then someone intervened, and near beside her I saw young Verrall.

A heavy stranger, the man in the hooded bathgown, a fat, foreign-looking man, came out of nowhere like a shield before them. He seemed a preposterous interruption. His face was full of astonishment and terror. He rushed across my path with arms extended and open hands, as one might try to stop a runaway horse. He shouted some nonsense. He seemed to want to dissuade me, as though dissuasion had anything to do with it now.

"Not you, you fool!" I said hoarsely. "Not you!" But he hid Nettie nevertheless.

By an enormous effort I resisted a mechanical impulse to shoot through his fat body. Anyhow, I knew I mustn't shoot him. For a moment I was in doubt, then I became very active, turned aside abruptly and dodged his pawing arm to the left, and so found two others irresolutely in my way. I fired a third shot in the air, just over their heads, and ran at them. They hastened left and right; I pulled up and faced about within a yard of a foxy-faced young man coming sideways, who seemed about to grapple me. At my resolute halt he fell back a pace, ducked, and threw up a defensive arm, and then I perceived the course was clear, and ahead of me, young Verrall and Nettie—he was holding her arm to help her—running away. "Of course!" said I.

I fired a fourth ineffectual shot, and then in an access of fury at my misses, started out to run them down and shoot them barrel to backbone. "These people!" I said, dismissing all these interferences. . . . "A yard," I panted, speaking aloud to myself, "a yard! Till then, take care, you mustn't—mustn't shoot again."

Someone pursued me, perhaps several people—I do not know, we left them all behind. . . .

We ran. For a space I was altogether intent upon the swift monotony of flight and pursuit. The sands were changed to a whirl of green moonshine, the air was thunder. A luminous green haze rolled about us. What did such things matter? We ran. Did I gain or lose? That was the question. They ran through a gap in a broken fence that sprang up abruptly out of nothingness, and turned to the right. I noted we were on a road. But this green mist! One seemed to plough through it. They were fading into it, and at that thought I made a spurt that won a dozen feet or more.

She staggered. He gripped her arm, and dragged her forward. They doubled to the left. We were off the road again and on turf. It felt like turf. I tripped and fell at a ditch that was somehow full of smoke, and was up again, but now they were phantoms half gone into the livid swirls about me. . . .

Still I ran.

On, on! I groaned with the violence of my effort. I staggered again and swore. I felt the concussions of great guns tear past me through the murk.

They were gone! Everything was going, but I kept on running. Once more I stumbled. There was something about my feet that impeded me, tall grass or heather, but I could not see what it was, only this smoke that eddied about my knees. There was a noise and spinning in my brain, a vain resistance to a dark green curtain that was falling, falling, falling, fold upon fold. Everything grew darker and darker.

I made one last frantic effort, and raised my revolver, fired my penultimate shot at a venture, and fell headlong to the ground. And behold! The green curtain was a black one, and the earth and I and all things ceased to be.

## BOOK II
### THE GREEN VAPOURS
### FROM CHAPTER THE FIRST
### THE CHANGE
#### 1

I SEEMED to awaken out of a refreshing sleep.

I did not awaken with a start, but opened my eyes, and lay very comfortably looking at a line of extraordinarily scarlet poppies that glowed against a glowing sky. It was the sky of a magnificent sunrise, and an archipelago of gold-beached purple islands floated in a sea of golden green. The poppies too, swan-necked buds, blazing corollas, translucent stout seed-vessels, stoutly upheld, had a luminous quality, seemed wrought only from some more solid kind of light.

I stared unwonderingly at these things for a time, and then there rose upon my consciousness, intermingling with these, the bristling golden green heads of growing barley.

A remote faint question, where I might be, drifted and vanished again in my mind. Everything was very still.

Everything was as still as death.

I felt very light, full of the sense of physical well-being. I perceived I was lying on my side in a little trampled space in a weedy, flowering barley field, that was in some inexplicable way saturated with light and beauty. I sat up, and remained for a long time filled with the delight and charm of the delicate little convolvulus that twined among the barley stems, the pimpernel that laced the ground below.

Then that question returned. What was this place? How had I come to be sleeping here?

I could not remember.

It perplexed me that somehow my body felt strange to me. It was unfamiliar—I could not tell how—and the barley, and the beautiful weeds, and the slowly developing glory of the dawn behind; all those things partook of the same unfamiliarity. I felt as though I was a thing in some very luminous painted window, as though this dawn broke through me. I felt I was part of some exquisite picture painted in light and joy.

A faint breeze bent and rustled the barley-heads and jogged my mind forward.

Who was I? That was a good way of beginning.

I held up my left hand and arm before me, a grubby hand, a frayed cuff; but with a quality of painted unreality, transfigured as a beggar might have been by Botticelli. I looked for a time steadfastly at a beautiful pearl sleeve-link.

I remembered Willie Leadford, who had owned that arm and hand, as though he had been someone else.

Of course! My history—its rough outline rather than the immediate past—began to shape itself in my memory, very small, very bright and inaccessible, like a thing watched through a microscope. Clayton and Swathinglea returned to my mind; the slums and darkness, Düreresque, minute and in their rich dark colours pleasing, and through them I went towards my destiny. I sat hands on knees recalling that queer passionate career that had ended with my futile shot into the growing darkness of the End. The thought of that shot awoke my emotions again.

There was something in it now, something absurd, that made me smile pityingly. Poor little angry, miserable creature! Poor little angry, miserable world!

I sighed for pity, not only pity for myself, but for all the hot hearts, the tormented brains, the straining, striving things of hope and pain, who had found their peace at last beneath the pouring mist and suffocation of the comet. Because certainly that world was over and done. They were all so weak and unhappy, and I was now so strong and so serene. For I felt sure I was dead; no one living could have this perfect assurance of good, this strong and confident peace. I had made an end of the fever called living. I was dead, and it was all right, and these—?

I felt an inconsistency.

These, then, must be the barley fields of God!—the still and silent barley fields of God, full of unfading poppy flowers whose seeds bear peace.

## 2

It was queer to find barley fields in heaven, but no doubt there were many surprises in store for me.

How still everything was! Peace! The peace that passeth understanding. After all it had come to me! But, indeed, everything was very still! No bird sang. Surely I was alone in the world! No birds sang. Yes, and all the distant sounds of life had ceased, the lowing of cattle, the barking of dogs. . . .

Something that was like fear beatified came into my heart. It was all right, I knew; but to be alone! I stood up and met the hot summons of the rising sun, hurrying towards me, as it were, with glad tidings, over the spikes of the barley. . . .

Blinded, I made a step. My foot struck something hard, and I looked down to discover my revolver, a blue-black thing, like a dead snake at my feet.

For a moment that puzzled me.

Then I clean forgot about it. The wonder of the quiet took possession of my soul. Dawn, and no birds singing!

How beautiful was the world! How beautiful, but how still! I walked slowly through the barley towards a line of elder bushes, wayfaring trees and bramble that made the hedge of the field. I noted as I passed along a dead shrew mouse, as it seemed to me, among the halms; then a still toad. I was surprised that this did not leap aside from my foothalls, and I stooped and picked it up. Its body was limp like life, but it made no struggle, the brightness of its eye was veiled, it did not move in my hand.

It seems to me now that I stood holding that lifeless little creature for some time. Then very softly I stooped down and replaced it. I was trembling—trembling with a nameless emotion. I looked with quickened eyes closely among the barley stems, and behold, now everywhere I saw beetles, flies, and little creatures that did not move, lying as they fell when the vapours overcame them; they seemed no more than painted things. Some were novel creatures to me. I was very unfamiliar with natural things. "My God!" I cried; "but is it only I—?"

And then at my next movement something squealed sharply. I turned about, but I could not see it, only I saw a little stir in a rut and heard the diminishing rustle of the unseen creature's flight. And at that I turned to my toad again; and its eye moved and it stirred. And presently, with infirm and hesitating gestures, it stretched its limbs and began to crawl away from me.

But wonder, that gentle sister of fear, had me now. I saw a little way ahead a brown and crimson butterfly perched upon a cornflower. I thought at first it was the breeze that stirred it, and then I saw its wings were quivering. And even as I watched it, it started into life, and spread itself, and fluttered into the air.

I watched it fly, a turn this way, a turn that, until suddenly it seemed to vanish. And now, life was returning to this thing and that on every side of me, with slow stretchings and bendings, with twitterings, with a little start and stir. . . .

I came slowly, stepping very carefully because of these drugged, feebly awakening things, through the barley to the hedge. It was a very glorious hedge, so that it held my eyes. It flowed along and interlaced like splendid music. It was rich with lupin, honeysuckle, campions, and ragged-robin; bed straw, hops, and wild clematis twined and hung among its branches, and all along its ditch border the starry stitchwort lifted its childish faces, and chorused in lines and masses. Never had I seen such a symphony of note-like flowers and tendrils and leaves. And suddenly in its depths, I heard a chirrup and the whir of startled wings.

Nothing was dead, but everything had changed to beauty! And I stood for a time with clean and happy eyes looking at the intricate delicacy before me and marvelling how richly God has made his worlds. . . .

"Tweedle-Tweezle," a lark had shot the stillness with is shining thread of song; one lark, and then presently another, invisibly in the air, making out of that blue quiet a woven cloth of gold. . . .

The earth recreated—only by the reiteration of such phrases may I hope to give the intense freshness of that dawn. For a time I was altogether taken up with the beautiful details of being, as regardless of my old life of jealous passion and impatient sorrow as though I was Adam new made. I could tell you now with infinite particularity of the shut flowers that opened as I looked, of tendrils and grass blades, of a blue-tit I picked up very tenderly—never before had I remarked the great delicacy of feathers—that presently disclosed its bright black eye and judged me, and perched, swaying fearlessly, upon my finger, and spread unhurried wings and flew away, and of a great ebullition of tadpoles in the ditch; like all the things that lived beneath the water they had passed unaltered through the Change. Amid such incidents, I lived those first great moments, losing for a time in the wonder of each little part the mighty wonder of the whole.

A path ran between hedge and barley, and along this, leisurely and content and glad, looking at this beautiful thing and that, moving a step and stopping, then moving on again, I came presently to a stile and deep below it, and overgrown, was a lane.

And on the worn oak of the stile was a round label, and on the label these words, "Swindells' G 90 Pills"

I sat myself astraddle on the stile, not fully grasping all the implications of these words. But they perplexed me even more than the revolver and my dirty cuff.

About me now the birds lifted up their little hearts and sang, ever more birds and more.

I read the label over and over again, and joined it to the fact that I still wore my former clothes, and that my revolver had been lying at my feet. One conclusion stared out at me. This was no new planet, no glorious hereafter such as I had supposed. This beautiful wonderland was the world, the same old world of my rage and death! But at least it was like meeting a familiar house-slut, washed and dignified, dressed in a queen's robes, worshipful and fine. . . .

It might be the old world indeed, but something new lay upon all things, a glowing certitude of health and happiness. It might be the old world, but the dust and fury of the old life was certainly done. At least I had no doubt of that.

I recalled the last phases of my former life, that darkling climax of pursuit and anger and universal darkness and the whirling green vapours of extinction. The comet had struck the earth and made an end to all things; of that too I was assured.

But afterwards? . . .

And now?

The imaginations of my boyhood came back as speculative possibilities. In those days I had believed firmly in the necessary advent of a last day, a great coming out of the sky, trumpetings and fear, the Resurrection, and the Judgment. My roving fancy now suggested to me that this Judgment must have come and passed. That it had passed and in some manner missed me. I was left alone here, in a swept and garnished world (except, of course, for this label of Swindells') to begin again perhaps. . . .

No doubt Swindells had got his deserts.

My mind ran for a time on Swindells, on the imbecile pushfulness of that extinct creature, dealing in rubbish, covering the countryside with lies in order to get—what had he sought?—a silly, ugly, great house, a temper-destroying motor-car, a number of disrespectful, abject servants; thwarted intrigues for a party-fund baronetcy as the crest of his life, perhaps. You cannot imagine the littleness of those former times;

their naïve, queer absurdities! And for the first time in my existence I thought of these things without bitterness. In the former days I had seen wickedness, I had seen tragedy, but now I saw only the extraordinary foolishness of the old life. The ludicrous side of human wealth and importance turned itself upon me, a shining novelty, poured down upon me like the sunrise, and engulfed me in laughter. Swindells! Swindells, damned! My vision of Judgment became a delightful burlesque. I saw the chuckling Angel slayer with his face veiled, and the corporeal presence of Swindells upheld amidst the laughter of the spheres. "Here's a thing, and a very pretty thing, and what's to be done with this very pretty thing?" I saw a soul being drawn from a rotund, substantial-looking body like a whelk from its shell. . . .

I laughed loudly and long. And behold! Even as I laughed the keen point of things accomplished stabbed my mirth, and I was weeping, weeping aloud, convulsed with weeping, and the tears were pouring down my face.

## 3

Everywhere the awakening came with the sunrise. We awakened to the gladness of the morning; we walked dazzled in a light that was joy. Everywhere that was so. It was always morning. It was morning because, until the direct rays of the sun touched it, the changing nitrogen of our atmosphere did not pass into its permanent phase, and the sleepers lay as they had fallen. In its intermediate state the air hung inert, incapable of producing either revival or stupefaction, no longer green, but not yet changed to the gas that now lives in us. . . .

To everyone, I think, came some parallel to the mental states I have already sought to describe—a wonder, an impression of joyful novelty. There was also very commonly a certain confusion of the intelligence, a difficulty in self-recognition. I remember clearly as I sat on my stile that presently I had the clearest doubts of my own identity and fell into the oddest metaphysical questionings. "If this be I," I said, "then how is it I am no longer madly seeking Nettie? Nettie is now the remotest thing—and all my wrongs. Why have I suddenly passed out of all that passion? Why does not the thought of Verrall quicken my pulses? . . ."

I was only one of many millions who that morning had the same doubts. I suppose one knows one's self for one's self when one returns from sleep or insensibility by the familiarity of one's bodily sensations, and that morning all our most intimate bodily sensations were changed. The intimate chemical processes of life were changed, its nervous metaboly. For the fluctuating, uncertain, passion-darkened thought and feeling of the old time came steady, full-bodied, wholesome processes. Touch was different, sight was different, sound and all the senses were subtler; had it not been that our thought was steadier and fuller, I believe great multitudes of men would have gone mad. But, as it was, we understood. The dominant impression I would convey in this account of the Change is one of enormous release, of a vast substantial exaltation. There was an effect, as it were, of light-headedness that was also clear-headedness, and the alteration in one's bodily sensations, instead of producing the mental obfuscation, the loss of identity that was a common mental trouble under former conditions, gave simply a new detachment from the timid passions and entanglements of the personal life.

In this story of my bitter, restricted youth that I have been telling you, I have sought constantly to convey the narrowness, the intensity, the confusion, muddle, and dusty heat of the old world. It was quite clear to me, within an hour of my awakening, that all that was, in some mysterious way, over and done. That, too, was the common experience. Men stood up; they took the new air into their lungs—a deep long breath, and the past fell from them; they could forgive, they could disregard, they could attempt. . . . And it was no new thing, no miracle that sets aside the former order of the world. It was a change in material conditions, a change in the atmosphere, that at one bound had released them. Some of them it had released to death. . . Indeed, man himself had changed not at all. We knew before the Change, the meanest knew, by glowing moments in ourselves and others, by histories and music and beautiful things, by heroic instances and splendid stories, how fine mankind could be, how fine almost any human being could upon occasion be; but the poison in the air, its poverty in all the nobler elements which made such moments rare and remarkable—all that had changed. The air was changed, and the Spirit of Man that had drowsed and slumbered and dreamt dull and evil things, awakened, and stood with wonder-clean eyes, refreshed, looking again on life.

\* \* \* \* \*

**from CHAPTER THE THIRD**
**THE CABINET COUNCIL**
**2**

I remember as one thing that struck me very forcibly at the time, the absence of any discussion, any difference of opinion, about the broad principles of our present state. These men had lived hitherto in a system of conventions and acquired motives, loyalty to a party, loyalty to various secret agreements and understandings, loyalty to the Crown; they had all been capable of the keenest attention to precedence, all capable of the most complete suppression of subversive doubts and inquiries, all had their religious emotions under perfect control. They had seemed protected by invisible but impenetrable barriers from all the heady and destructive speculations, the socialistic, republican, and communistic theories that one may still trace through the literature of the last days of the comet. But now it was as if at the very moment of the awakening those barriers and defences had vanished, as if the green vapours had washed through their minds and dissolved and swept away a hundred once rigid boundaries and obstacles. They had admitted and assimilated at once all that was good in the ill-dressed propagandas that had clamoured so vehemently and vainly at the doors of their minds in the former days. It was exactly like the awakening from an absurd and limiting dream. They had come out together naturally and inevitably upon the broad daylight platform of obvious and reasonable agreement upon which we and all the order of our world now stand.

Let me try to give the chief things that had vanished from their minds. There was, first, the ancient system of "ownership" that made such an extraordinary tangle of our administration of the land upon which we lived. In the old time no one believed in that as either just or ideally convenient, but everyone accepted it. The community which lived upon the land was supposed to have waived its necessary connection with the land, except in certain limited instances of highway and common. All the rest of the land was cut up in the maddest way into patches and oblongs and triangles of various sizes between a hundred square miles and a few acres, and placed under the nearly absolute government of a series of administrators called landowners. They owned the land almost as a man now owns his hat; they bought it and sold it, and cut it up like cheese or ham; they were free to ruin it, or leave it waste, or erect upon it horrible and devastating eyesores. If the community needed a road or a tramway, if it wanted a town or a village in any position, nay, even if it wanted to go to and fro, it had to do so by exorbitant treaties with each of the monarchs whose territory was involved. No man could find foothold on the face of the earth until he had paid toll and homage to one of them. They had practically no relations and no duties to the nominal, municipal, or national Government amidst whose larger areas their own dominions lay. . . . This sounds, I know, like a lunatic's dream, but mankind was that lunatic; and not only in the old countries of Europe and Asia, where this system had arisen out of the delegation of local control to territorial magnates did it obtain, but the "new countries," as we called them then—the United States of America, Cape Colony, Australia, and New Zealand—spent much of the nineteenth century in the frantic giving away of land for ever to any casual person who would take it. Was there coal, was there petroleum or gold, was there rich soil or harbourage, or the site for a fine city, these obsessed and witless Governments cried out for scramblers, and a stream of shabby, tricky, and violent adventurers set out to found a new section of the landed aristocracy of the world. After a brief century of hope and pride, the great republic of the United States of America, the hope as it was deemed of mankind, became for the most part a drifting crowd of landless men; landlords and railway lords, food lords (for the land is food) and mineral lords ruled its life, gave it Universities as one gave coins to a mendicant, and spent its resources upon such vain, tawdry, and foolish luxuries as the world had never seen before. Here was a thing none of these statesmen before the Change would have regarded as anything but the natural order of the world, which not one of them now regarded as anything but the mad and vanished illusion of a period of dementia.

And as it was with the question of the land, so was it also with a hundred other systems and institutions and complicated and disingenuous factors in the life of man. They spoke of trade, and I realised for the first time there could be buying and selling that was no loss to any man; they spoke of industrial organisation, and one saw it under captains who sought no base advantages. The haze of old associations, of personal entanglements and habitual recognitions had been dispelled from every stage and process of the social training of men. Things long hidden appeared discovered with an amazing clearness and nakedness. These men who had awakened, laughed dissolvent laughs, and the old muddle of schools and colleges, books and traditions, the old fumbling, half-figurative, half-formal teaching of the Churches, the complex of weakening and confusing suggestions and hints, amidst which the pride and honour of adolescence doubted and stumbled and fell, became nothing but a curious and pleasantly faded memory. "There must be a common training of the young," said Richover; "a frank initiation. We have not so much educated them as hidden things from them, and set traps. And it might have been so easy—it can all be done so easily."

That hangs in my memory as the refrain of that council, "It can all be done so easily," but when they said it then, it came to my ears with a quality of enormous refreshment and power. It can all be done so easily, given frankness, given courage. Time was when these platitudes had the freshness and wonder of a gospel.

In this enlarged outlook the war with the Germans—that mythical, heroic, armed female, Germany, had vanished from men's imaginations—was a mere exhausted episode. A truce had already been arranged by Melmount, and these ministers, after some marvelling reminiscences, set aside the matter of peace as a mere question of particular arrangements. . . . The whole scheme of the world's government had become fluid and provisional in their minds, in small detail as in great, the unanalysable tangle of wards and vestries, districts and municipalities, counties, states, boards, and nations, the interlacing, overlapping, and conflicting authorities, the felt of little interests and claims, in which an innumerable and insatiable multitude of lawyers, agents, managers, bosses, organisers lived like fleas in a dirty old coat, the web of the conflicts, jealousies, heated patchings up and jobbings apart, of the old order—they flung it all on one side.

"What are the new needs?" said Melmount. "This muddle is too rotten to handle. We're beginning again. Well, let us begin afresh."

3

"Let us begin afresh!" This piece of obvious common sense seemed then to me instinct with courage, the noblest of words. My heart went out to him as he spoke. It was, indeed, that day as vague as it was valiant; we did not at all see the forms of what we were thus beginning. All that we saw was the clear inevitableness that the old order should end. . . .

And then in a little space of time mankind in halting but effectual brotherhood was moving out to make its world anew. Those early years, those first and second decades of the new epoch, were in their daily detail a time of rejoicing toil; one saw chiefly one's own share in that, and little of the whole. It is only now that I look back at it all from these ripe years, from this high tower, that I see the dramatic sequence of its changes, see the cruel old confusions of the ancient time become clarified, simplified, and dissolve and vanish away. Where is that old world now? Where is London, that sombre city of smoke and drifting darkness, full of the deep roar and haunting music of disorder, with its oily, shining, mud-rimmed, barge-crowded river, its black pinnacles and blackened dome, its sad wildernesses of smut-greyed houses it myriads of draggled prostitutes, its millions of hurrying clerks? The very leaves upon its trees were foul with greasy black defilements. Where is lime-white Paris, with its green and disciplined foliage, its hard unflinching tastefulness, its smartly organised viciousness, and the myriads of workers, noisily shod, streaming over the bridges in the grey cold light of dawn? Where is New York, the high city of clangour and infuriated energy, wind swept and competition swept, its huge buildings jostling one another and straining ever upward for a place in the sky, the fallen pitilessly overshadowed? Where are its lurking corners of heavy and costly luxury, the shameful bludgeoning bribing vice of its ill-ruled underways, and all the gaunt extravagant ugliness of its strenuous life? And where now is Philadelphia, with its innumerable small and isolated homes, and Chicago with its interminable bloodstained stockyards, its polyglot underworld of furious discontent?

All these vast cities have given way and gone, even as my native Potteries and the Black Country have gone, and the lives that were caught, crippled, starved, and maimed amidst their labyrinths, their forgotten and neglected maladjustments, and their vast, inhuman, ill-conceived industrial machinery have escaped—to life. Those cities of growth and accident are altogether gone, never a chimney smokes about our world to-day, and the sound of the weeping of children who toiled and hungered, the dull despair of over-burdened women, the noise of brute quarrels in alleys, all shameful pleasures and all the ugly grossness of wealthy pride have gone with them, with the utter change in our lives. As I look back into the past I see a vast exultant dust of house-breaking and removal rise up into the clear air that followed the hour of the green vapours, I live again the Year of Tents, the year of Scaffolding, and like the triumph of a new theme in a piece of music— the great cities of our new days arise. Come Caerlyon and Armedon, the twin cities of lower England, with the winding summer city of the Thames between, and I see the gaunt dirt of old Edinburgh die to rise again white and tall beneath the shadow of her ancient hill; and Dublin too, reshaped, returning enriched, fair, spacious, the city of rich laughter and warm hearts, gleaming gaily in a shaft of sunlight through the soft warm rain. I see the great cities America has planned and made; the Golden City, with ever-ripening fruit along its broad warm ways, and the bell-glad City of a Thousand Spires. I see again as I have seen, the city of theatres and meeting-places, the City of the Sunlight Bright, and the new city that is still called Utah; and dominated by its observatory dome and the plain and dignified lines of the university façade upon the cliff, Martenabar the great white winter city of the upland snows. And the lesser places, too, the

303

townships, the quiet resting-places, villages half forest with a brawl of streams down their streets, villages, laced with avenues of cedar, villages of garden, of roses and wonderful flowers and the perpetual humming of bees. And through all the world go our children, our sons the old world would have made into servile clerks and shopmen, plough drudges and servants; our daughters who were erst anaemic drudges, prostitutes, sluts, anxiety-racked mothers or sere, repining failures; they go about this world glad and brave, learning, living, doing, happy and rejoicing, brave and free. I think of them wandering in the clear quiet of the ruins of Rome, among the tombs of Egypt or the temples of Athens, of their coming to Mainington and its strange happiness, to Orba and the wonder of its white and slender tower. . . . But who can tell of the fullness and pleasure of life, who can number all our new cities in the world?—cities made by the loving hands of men for living men, cities men weep to enter, so fair they are, so gracious and so kind. . . .

Some vision surely of these things must have been vouchsafed me as I sat there behind Melmount's couch, but now my knowledge of accomplished things has mingled with and effaced my expectations. Something indeed I must have foreseen—or else why was my heart so glad?

BOOK III
THE NEW WORLD
from CHAPTER THE FIRST
LOVE AFTER THE CHANGE
1

So far I have said nothing of Nettie. I have departed widely from my individual story. I have tried to give you the effect of the change in relation to the general framework of human life, its effect of swift, magnificent dawn, of an overpowering letting in and inundation of light, and the spirit of living. In my memory all my life before the Change has the quality of a dark passage, with the dimmest side gleams of beauty that come and go. The rest is dull pain and darkness. Then suddenly the walls, the bitter confines, are smitten and vanish, and I walk, blinded, perplexed, and yet rejoicing, in this sweet, beautiful world, in its fair incessant variety, its satisfaction, its opportunities, exultant in this glorious gift of life. Had I the power of music I would make a world-wide motif swell and amplify, gather to itself this theme and that, and rise at last to sheer ecstasy of triumph and rejoicing. It should be all sound, all pride, all the hope of outsetting in the morning brightness, all the glee of unexpected happenings, all the gladness of painful effort suddenly come to its reward; it should be like blossoms new opened and the happy play of children, like tearful, happy mothers holding their first-born, like cities building to the sound of music, and great ships, all hung with flags and wine-bespattered, gliding down through cheering multitudes to their first meeting with the sea. Through it all should march Hope, confident Hope, radiant and invincible, until at last it would be the triumph march of Hope the conqueror, coming with trumpetings and banners through the wide-flung gates of the world.

And then out of that luminous haze of gladness comes Nettie, transfigured.

So she came again to me—amazing, a thing incredibly forgotten.

She comes back, and Verrall is in her company. She comes back into my memories now, just as she came back then, rather quaintly at first—at first not seen very clearly, a little distorted by intervening things, seen with a doubt, as I saw her through the slightly discoloured panes of crinkled glass in the window of the Menton post-office and grocer's shop. It was on the second day after the Change, and I had been sending telegrams for Melmount, who was making arrangements for his departure for Downing Street. I saw the two of them at first as small, flawed figures. The glass made them seem curved, and it enhanced and altered their gestures and paces. I felt it became me to say "Peace" to them, and I went out, to the jangling of the door-bell. At the sight of me they stopped short, and Verrall cried with the note of one who has sought, "Here he is!" and Nettie cried, "Willie!"

I went towards them, and all the perspectives of my reconstructed universe altered as I did so.

I seemed to see these two for the first time; how fine they were, how graceful and human. It was as though I had never really looked at them before, and, indeed, always before I had beheld them through a mist of selfish passion. They had shared the universal darkness and dwarfing of the former time; they shared the universal exaltation of the new. Now suddenly Nettie, and the love of Nettie, a great passion for Nettie, lived again in me. This change which had enlarged men's hearts had made no end to love. Indeed, it had enormously enlarged and glorified love. She stepped into the centre of that dream of world reconstruction that filled my mind and took possession of it all. A little wisp of hair had blown across her cheek, her lips fell apart in that sweet smile of hers; her eyes were full of wonder, of a welcoming scrutiny, of an infinitely courageous friendliness.

I took her outstretched hand, and wonder overwhelmed me. "I wanted to kill you," I said simply, trying to grasp that idea. It seemed now like stabbing the stars, or murdering the sunlight.

"Afterwards we looked for you," said Verrall; "and we could not find you. . . . We heard another shot."

I turned my eyes to him, and Nettie's hand fell from me. It was then I thought of how they had fallen together, and what it must have been to have awakened in that dawn with Nettie by one's side. I had a vision of them as I had glimpsed them last amidst the thickening vapours, close together, hand in hand. The green hawks of the Change spread their darkling wings above their last stumbling paces. So they fell. And awoke—lovers together in a morning of Paradise. Who can tell how bright the sunshine was to them, how fair the flowers, how sweet the singing of the birds? . . .

This was the thought of my heart. But my lips were saying, "When I awoke I threw my pistol away." Sheer blankness kept my thoughts silent for a little while;

I said empty things. "I am very glad I did not kill you—that you are here, so fair and well. . . .

"I am going back to Clayton on the day after to-morrow," I said, breaking away to explanations. "I have been writing shorthand here for Melmount, but that is almost over now. . . ."

Neither of them said a word, and though all facts had suddenly ceased to matter anything, I went on informatively, "he is to be taken to Downing Street, where there is a proper staff, so that there will be no need of me. . . . Of course, you're a little perplexed at my being with Melmount. You see I met him—by accident—directly I recovered. I found him with a broken ankle—in that lane. . . . I am to go now to the Four Towns to help prepare a report. So that I am glad to see you both again"—I found a catch in my voice—"to say good-by to you, and wish you well."

This was after the quality of what had come into my mind when first I saw them through the grocer's window, but it was not what I felt and thought as I said it. I went on saying it because otherwise there would have been a gap. It had come to me that it was going to be hard to part from Nettie. My words sounded with an effect of unreality. I stopped, and we stood for a moment in silence looking at one another.

It was I, I think, who was discovering most. I was realising for the first time how little the Change had altered in my essential nature. I had forgotten this business of love for a time in a world of wonder. That was all. Nothing was lost from my nature, nothing had gone, only the power of thought and restraint had been wonderfully increased, and new interests had been forced upon me. The Green Vapours had passed, our minds were swept and garnished, but we were ourselves still, though living in a new and finer air. My affinities were unchanged; Nettie's personal charm for me was only quickened by the enhancement of my perceptions. In her presence, meeting her eyes, instantly my desire, no longer frantic but sane, was awake again.

It was just like going to Checkshill in the old time, after writing about socialism. . . .

I relinquished her hand. It was absurd to part in these terms.

So we all felt it. We hung awkwardly over our sense of that. It was Verrall, I think, who shaped the thought for me, and said that to-morrow then we must meet and say good-bye, and so turned our encounter into a transitory making of arrangements. We settled we would come to the inn at Menton, all three of us, and take our midday meal together. . . .

Yes, it was clear that was all we had to say . . . now.

We parted a little awkwardly. I went on down the village street, not looking back, surprised at myself, and infinitely perplexed. It was as if I had discovered something overlooked that disarranged all my plans, something entirely disconcerting. For the first time I went back preoccupied and without eagerness to Melmount's work. I wanted to go on thinking about Nettie; my mind had suddenly become voluminously productive concerning her and Verrall.

## 2

The talk we three had together in the dawn of the new time is very strongly impressed upon my memory. There was something fresh and simple about it, something young and flushed and exalted. We took up, we handled with a certain naïve timidity, the most difficult questions the Change had raised for men to answer. I recall we made little of them. All the old scheme of human life had dissolved and passed away, the narrow competitiveness, the greed and base aggression, the jealous aloofness of soul from soul. Where had it left us? That was what we and a thousand million others were discussing. . . .

It chanced that this last meeting with Nettie is inseparably associated—I don't know why—with the landlady of the Menton inn.

The Menton inn was one of the rare pleasant corners of the old order; it was an inn of an unusual prosperity, much frequented by visitors from Shaphambury, and given to the serving of lunches and teas. It had a broad mossy bowling-green, and round about it were creeper-covered arbours amidst beds of snap-dragons, and hollyhock, and blue delphinium, and many such tall familiar summer flowers. These stood out against a background of laurels and holly, and above these again rose the gables of the inn and its signpost—a white-horsed George slaying the dragon—against copper beeches under the sky.

While I waited for Nettie and Verrall in this agreeable trysting-place, I talked to the landlady—a broad-shouldered, smiling, freckled woman—about the morning of the Change. That motherly, abundant, red-haired figure of health was buoyantly sure that everything in the world was now to be changed for the better. That confidence, and something in her voice, made me love her as I talked to her. "Now we're awake," she said, "all sorts of things will be put right that hadn't any sense in them. Why? Oh! I'm sure of it."

Her kind blue eyes met mine in an infinitude of friendliness. Her lips in her pauses shaped in a pretty faint smile.

Old tradition was strong in us; all English inns in those days charged the unexpected, and I asked what our lunch was to cost.

"Pay or not," she said, "and what you like. It's holiday these days. I suppose we'll still have paying and charging, however we manage it, but it won't be the worry it has been—that I feel sure. It's the part I never had no fancy for. Many a time I peeped through the bushes worrying to think what was just and right to me and mine, and what would send 'em away satisfied. It isn't the money I care for. There'll be mighty changes, be sure of that; but here I'll stay, and make people happy—them that go by on the roads. It's a pleasant place here when people are merry; it's only when they're jealous or mean, or tired, or eat up beyond any stomach's digesting, or when they got the drink in 'em that Satan comes into this garden. Many's the happy face I've seen here, and many that come again like friends, but nothing to equal what's going to be, now things are being set right."

She smiled, that bounteous woman, with the joy of life and hope. "You shall have an omelette," she said, "you and your friends; such an omelette—like they'll have 'em in heaven! I feel there's cooking in me these days like I've never cooked before. I'm rejoiced to have it to do. . . ."

It was just then that Nettie and Verrall appeared under a rustic archway of crimson roses that led out from the inn. Nettie wore white and a sun-hat, and Verrall was a figure of grey. "Here are my friends," I said; but for all the magic of the Change, something passed athwart the sunlight in my soul like the passing of the shadow of a cloud. "A pretty couple," said the land lady, as they crossed the velvet green towards us. . . .

They were indeed a pretty couple, but that did not greatly gladden me. No—I winced a little at that.

### 3

This old newspaper, this first reissue of the *New Paper* desiccated last relic of a vanished age, is like the little piece of identification the superstitious of the old days— those queer religionists who brought a certain black-clad Mrs. Piper to the help of Christ—used to put into the hand of a clairvoyant. At the crisp touch of it I look across a gulf of fifty years and see again the three of us sitting about that able in the arbour, and I smell again the smell of the sweet-brier that filled the air about us, and hear in our long pauses the abundant murmuring of bees among the heliotrope of the borders.

It is the dawn of the new time, but we still bear the marks and liveries of the old.

I see myself, a dark, ill-dressed youth, with the bruise Lord Redcar gave me still blue and yellow beneath my jaw; and young Verrall sits cornerwise to me, better grown, better dressed, fair and quiet, two years my senior indeed, but looking no older than I because of his light complexion; and opposite me is Nettie, with dark eyes upon my face, graver and more beautiful than I have ever seen her in the former time. Her dress is still that white one she had worn when I came upon her in the park, and still about her dainty neck she wears her string of pearls and that little coin of gold. She is so much the same, she is so changed; a girl then and now a woman—and all my agony and all the marvel of the Change between! Over the end of the green table about which we sit, a spotless cloth is spread, it bears a pleasant lunch spread out with a simple equipage. Behind me is the liberal sunshine of the green and various garden. I see it all. Again I sit there, eating awkwardly, this paper lies upon the table and Verrall talks of the Change.

"You can't imagine," he says in his sure fine accents, "how much the Change has destroyed of me. I still don't feel awake. Men of my sort are so tremendously *made*; I never suspected it before."

He leans over the table towards me with an evident desire to make himself perfectly understood. "I find myself like some creature that is taken out of its shell—soft and new. I was trained to dress in a certain way, to behave in a certain way, to think in a certain way; I see now it's all wrong and narrow—most of it anyhow—a system of class shibboleths. We were decent to each other in order to be a gang to the rest of the world. Gentlemen indeed! But it's perplexing—"

I can hear his voice saying that now, and see the lift of his eyebrows and his pleasant smile.

He paused. He had wanted to say that, but it was not the thing we had to say.

I leaned forward a little and took hold of my glass very tightly. "You two," I said, "will marry?"

They looked at one another.

Nettie spoke very softly. "I did not mean to marry when I came away," she said.

"I know," I answered. I looked up with a sense of effort and met Verrall's eyes.

He answered me. "I think we two have joined our lives. . . . But the thing that took us was a sort of madness."

I nodded. "All passion," I said, "is madness." Then I fell into a doubting of those words.

"Why did we do these things?" he said, turning to her suddenly.

Her hands were clasped under her chin, her eyes downcast.

"We had to," she said, with her old trick of inadequate expression.

Then she seemed to open out suddenly.

"Willie," she cried with a sudden directness, with her eyes appealing to me, "I didn't mean to treat you badly—indeed I didn't. I kept thinking of you—and of father and mother, all the time. Only it didn't seem to move me. It didn't move me not one bit from the way I had chosen."

"Chosen!" I said.

"Something seemed to have hold of me," she admitted. "It's all so unaccountable. . . ."

She gave a little gesture of despair.

Verrall's fingers played on the cloth for a space. Then he turned his face to me again.

"Something said 'Take her.' Everything. It was a raging desire—for her. I don't know. Everything contributed to that—or counted for nothing. You—"

"Go on," said I.

"When I knew of you—"

I looked at Nettie. "You never told him about me?" I said, feeling, as it were, a sting out of the old time.

Verrall answered for her. "No. But things dropped; I saw you that night, my instincts were all awake. I knew it was you."

"You triumphed over me . . . If I could I would have triumphed over you," I said. "But go on!"

"Everything conspired to make it the finest thing in life. It had an air of generous recklessness. It meant mischief, it might mean failure in that life of politics and affairs for which I was trained, which it was my honour to follow. That made it all the finer. It meant ruin or misery for Nettie. That made it all the finer. No sane or decent man would have approved of what we did. That made it more splendid than ever. I had all the advantages of position and used them basely. That mattered not at all."

Yes," I said; "it is time. And the same dark wave that lifted you, swept me on to follow. With that revolver—and blubbering with hate. And the word to you, Nettie, what was it? 'Give?' Hurl yourself down the steep?"

Nettie's hands fell upon the table. "I can't tell what it was," she said, speaking barehearted straight to me. "Girls aren't trained as men are trained to look into their minds. I can't see it yet. All sorts of mean little motives were there—over and above the 'must.' Mean motives. I kept thinking of his clothes." She smiled—a flash of brightness at Verrall. "I kept thinking of being like a lady and sitting in an hotel—with men like butlers waiting. It's the dreadful truth, Willie. Things as mean as that! Things meaner than that!"

I can see her now pleading with me, speaking with a frankness as bright and amazing as the dawn of the first great morning.

"It wasn't all mean," I said slowly, after a pause.

"No!" They spoke together.

"But a woman chooses more than a man does," Nettie added. "I saw it all in little bright pictures. Do you know—that jacket—there's something—You won't mind my telling you? But you won't now!"

I nodded, "No."

She spoke as if she spoke to my soul, very quietly and very earnestly, seeking to give the truth. "Something cottony in that cloth of yours," she said. "I know there's something horrible in being swung round by things like that, but they did swing me round. In the old time—to have confessed that! And I hated Clayton—and the grime of it. That kitchen! Your mother's dreadful kitchen! And besides, Willie, I was afraid of you. I didn't understand you and I did him. It's different now—but then I knew what he meant. And there was his voice."

"Yes," I said to Verrall, making these discoveries quietly, "yes, Verrall, you have a good voice. Queer I never thought of that before!"

We sat silently for a time before our vivisected passions.

"Gods!" I cried, "and here was our poor little top-hamper of intelligence on all these waves of instinct and wordless desire, these foaming things of touch and sight and feeling, like—like a coop of hens washed overboard and clucking amidst the seas."

Verrall laughed approval of the image I had struck out. "A week ago," he said, trying it further, "we were clinging to our chicken coops and going with the heave and pour. That was true enough a week ago. But to-day—?"

"To-day," I said, "the wind has fallen. The world storm is over. And each chicken coop has changed by a miracle to a vessel that makes head against the sea."

4

"What are we to do?" asked Verrall.

Nettie drew a deep crimson carnation from the bowl before us, and began very neatly and deliberately to turn down the sepals of its calyx and remove, one by one, its petals. I remember that went on through all our talk. She put those ragged crimson shreds in a long row and adjusted them and readjusted them. When at last I was alone with these vestiges the pattern was still incomplete.

"Well," said I, "the matter seems fairly simple. You two"—I swallowed it—"love one another."

I paused. They answered me by silence, by a thoughtful silence.

"You belong to each other. I have thought it over and looked at it from many points of view. I happened to want—impossible things. . . . I behaved badly. I had no right to pursue you." I turned to Verrall. "You hold yourself bound to her?"

He nodded assent.

"No social influence, no fading out of all this generous clearness in the air—for that might happen—will change you back? . . ."

He answered me with honest eyes meeting mine, "No, Leadford, no!"

"I did not know you," I said. "I thought of you as something very different from this."

"I was," he interpolated.

"Now," I said, "it is all changed."

Then I halted—for my thread had slipped away from me.

"As for me," I went on, and glanced at Nettie's downcast face, and then sat forward with my eyes upon the flowers between us, "since I am swayed and shall be swayed by an affection for Nettie, since that affection is rich with the seeds of desire, since to see her yours and wholly yours is not to be endured by me—I must turn about and go from you; you must avoid me and I you. . . . We must divide the world like Jacob and Esau. . . . I must direct myself with all the will I have to other things. After all—this passion is not life! It is perhaps for brutes and savages, but for men— no! We must part and I must forget. What else is there but that?"

I did not look up, I sat very tense with the red petals printing an indelible memory in my brain, but I felt the assent of Verrall's pose. There were some moments of silence. Then Nettie spoke. "But—" she said, and ceased.

I waited for a little while. I sighed and leaned back in my chair. "It is perfectly simple," I smiled, "now that we have cool heads."

"But is it simple?" asked Nettie, and slashed my discourse out of being.

I looked up and found her with her eyes on Verrall. "You see," she said, "I like Willie. It's hard to say what one feels—but I don't want him to go away like that."

"But then," objected Verrall, "how—?"

"No," said Nettie, and swept her half-arranged carnation petals back into a heap of confusion. She began to arrange them very quickly into one long straight line.

"It's so difficult—I've never before in all my life tried to get to the bottom of my mind. For one thing I've not treated Willie properly. He—he counted on me. I know he did. I was his hope. I was a promised delight—something, something to crown life—better than anything he had ever had. And a secret pride. . . . He lived upon me. I knew—when we two began to meet together, you and I—It was a sort of treachery to him—"

"Treachery!" I said. "You were only feeling your way through all these perplexities."

"You thought it treachery."

"I don't know."

"I did. In a sense I think so still. For you had need of me."

I made a slight protest at this doctrine and fell thinking.

"And even when he was trying to kill us," she said to her lover, "I felt for him down in the bottom of my mind. I can understand all the horrible things, the humiliation—the humiliation! He went through."

"Yes," I said, "but I don't see—"

"*I* don't see. I'm only trying to see. But you know, Willie, you are a part of my life. I have known you longer than I have known Edward. I know you better. Indeed I know you with all my heart. You think all your talk was thrown away upon me, that I never understood that side of you, or your ambitions or anything. I did. More than I thought at the time. Now—now it is all clear to me. What I had to understand in you was something deeper than Edward brought me. I have it now. . . . You are a part of my life, and I don't want to cut all that off from me now I have comprehended it, and thrown it away."

"But you love Verrall."

"Love is such a queer thing! . . . Is there one love? I mean, only one love?" She turned to Verrall. "I know I love you. I can speak out about that now. Before this morning I couldn't have done. It's just as though my mind had got out of a scented prison. But what is it, this love for you? It's a mass of fancies—things about you— ways you look, ways you have. It's the senses—and the senses of certain beauties. Flattery too, things you said, hopes and deceptions for myself. And all that had rolled up together and taken to itself the wild heap of those deep emotions that slumbered in my body; it seemed everything. But it wasn't. How can I describe it? It was like having a very bright lamp with a thick shade—everything else in the room was hidden. But you take the shade off and there they are—it is the same light—still there! Only it lights everyone!"

Her voice ceased. For awhile no one spoke, and Nettie, with a quick movement, swept the petals into the shape of a pyramid.

Figures of speech always distract me, and it ran through my mind like some puzzling refrain, "It is still the same light. . . ."

"No woman believes these things," she asserted abruptly.

"What things?"

"No woman ever has believed them."

"You have to choose a man," said Verrall, apprehending her before I did.

"We're brought up to that. We're told—it's in books, in stories, in the way people look, in the way they behave—one day there will come a man. He will be everything, no one else will be anything. Leave everything else; live in him."

"And a man, too, is taught that of some woman," said Verrall.

"Only men don't believe it! They have more obstinate minds. . . . Men have never behaved as though they believed it. One need not be old to know that. By nature they don't believe it. But a woman believes nothing by nature. She goes into a mould hiding her secret thoughts almost from herself."

"She used to," I said.

"You haven't," said Verrall, "anyhow."

"I've come out. It's this comet. And Willie. And because I never really believed in the mould at all—even if I thought I did. It's stupid to send Willie off—shamed, cast out, never to see him again—when I like him as much as I do. It is cruel, it is wicked and ugly, to prance over him as if he was a defeated enemy, and pretend I'm going to be happy just the same. There's no sense in a rule of life that prescribes that. It's selfish. It's brutish. It's like something that has no sense. I—" there was a sob in her voice, "Willie! I *won't*."

I sat lowering, I mused with my eyes upon her quick fingers.

"It is brutish," I said at last, with a careful unemotional deliberation. "Nevertheless—it is in the nature of things. . . . No! . . . You see, after all, we are still half brutes, Nettie. And men, as you say, are more obstinate than women. The comet hasn't altered that; it's only made it clearer. We have come into being through a tumult of blind forces. . . . I come back to what I said just now! We have found our poor reasonable minds, our wills to live well, ourselves, adrift on a wash of instincts, passions, instinctive prejudices, half animal stupidities. . . . Here we are like people clinging to something—like people awakening—upon a raft."

"We come back at last to my question," said Verrall, softly; "what are we to do?"

"Part," I said. "You see, Nettie, these bodies of ours are not the bodies of angels. They are the same bodies—I have read somewhere that in our bodies you can find evidence of the lowliest ancestry; that about our inward ears—I think it is—and about our teeth, there remains still something of the fish, that there are bones that recall little—what is it?—marsupial forbears—and a hundred traces of the ape. Even your beautiful body, Nettie, carries this taint. No! Hear me out." I leaned forward earnestly. "Our emotions, our passions, our desires, the substance of them, like the substance of our bodies, is an animal, a competing thing, as well as a desiring thing. You speak to us now as mind to minds—one can do that when one has had exercise and when one has eaten, when one is not doing anything—but when one turns to live, one turns again to matter."

"Yes," said Nettie, slowly following me, "but you control it."

"Only through a measure of obedience. There is no magic in the business—to conquer matter, we must divide the enemy, and take matter as an ally. Nowadays it is indeed true, by faith a man can remove mountains; he can say to a mountain, Be thou removed and be thou cast into the sea; but he does it because he helps and trusts his brother men, because he has the wit and patience and courage to win over to his side iron, steel, obedience, dynamite, cranes, trucks, the money of other people. . . . To conquer my desire for you, I must not perpetually thwart it by your presence; I must go away so that I may not see you, I must take up other interests, thrust myself into struggles and discussions—"

"And forget?" said Nettie.

"Not forget," I said; "but anyhow—cease to brood upon you."

She hung on that for some moments.

"No," she said, demolished her last pattern and looked up at Verrall as he stirred.

Verrall leaned forward on the table, elbows upon it, and the fingers of his two hands intertwined.

"You know,' he said, "I haven't thought much of these things. At school and the University, one doesn't. . . . It was part of the system to prevent it. They'll alter all that, no doubt. We seem"—he thought—"to be skating about over questions that one came to at last in Greek—with various readings—in Plato, but which it never occurred to any one to translate out of a dead language into living realities. . . ." he halted and answered some unspoken question from his own mind with, "No. I think with Leadford, Nettie, that, as he put it, it is in the nature of things for men to be exclusive; the things that live are the struggle for existence incarnate—and that works out that the men struggle for their mates; for each woman one prevails. The others go away."

"Like animals," said Nettie.

"Yes. . . ."

"There are many things in life," I said, "but that is the rough universal truth."

"But," said Nettie, "you don't struggle. That has been altered because men have minds."

"You choose," I said.

"If I don't choose to choose?"

"You have chosen."

She gave a little impatient "Oh! Why are women always the slaves of sex? Is this great age of Reason and Light that has come to alter nothing of that? And men too! I think it is all—stupid! I do not believe this is the right solution of the thing, or anything but the bad habits of the time that was. . . .Instinct! You don't let your instincts rule you in a lot of other things. Here am I between you. Here is Edward. I—love him because he is gay and pleasant, and because—because I like him! Here is Willie—a part of me—my first secret, my oldest friend! Why must I not have both? Am I not a mind that you must think of me as nothing but a woman? Imagine me always as a thing to struggle for?" She paused; then she made her distressful proposition to me. "Let us three keep together," she said. "Let us not part. To part is lame, Willie. Why should we not anyhow keep friends? Meet and talk?"

"Talk?" I said. "About this sort of thing?"

I looked across at Verrall and met his eyes, and we studied one another. It was the clean, straight scrutiny of honest antagonism. "No," I decided. "Between us, nothing of that sort can be.":

"Ever?" said Nettie.

"Never," I said, convinced.

I made an effort within myself. "We cannot tamper with the law and customs of these things," I said; "these passions are too close to one's essential self. Better surgery than a lingering disease! From Nettie my love—asks all. A man's love is not devotion—it is a demand, a challenge. And besides"—and here I forced my theme—"I have given myself now to a new mistress—and it is I, Nettie, who am unfaithful. Behind you and above you rises the coming City of the World, and I am in the building. Dear heart! You are only happiness—and that—Indeed that calls! If it is only that my life blood shall christen the foundation stones—I could almost hope that should be my part, Nettie—I will join myself in that." I threw all the conviction I could into these words. . . . "No conflict of passion," I added a little lamely, "must distract me."

There was a pause.

"Then we must part," said Nettie, with the eyes of a woman one strikes in the face.

I nodded assent. . . .

There was a little pause, and then I stood up. We stood up, all three. We parted almost sullenly, with no more memorable words, and I was left presently in the arbour alone.

I do not think I watched them go. I only remember myself left there somehow—horribly empty and alone. I sat down again and fell into a deep shapeless musing.

### 5

Suddenly I looked up. Nettie had come back and stood looking down at me.

"Since we talked I have been thinking," she said. "Edward has let me come to you alone. And I feel perhaps I can talk better to you alone."

I said nothing and that embarrassed her.

"I don't think we ought to part," she said.

"No—I don't think we ought to part," she repeated.

"One lives," she said, "in different ways. I wonder if you will understand what I am saying, Willie. It is hard to say what I feel. But I want it said. If we are to part for ever I want it said—very plainly. Always before I have had the woman's instinct and the woman's training which makes one hide. But—Edward is not all of me. Think of what I am saying—Edward is not all of me. . . . I wish I could tell you better how I see it. I am not all of myself. You, at any rate, are a part of me and I cannot bear to leave you. And I cannot see why I should leave you. There is sort of blood link between us, Willie. We grew together. We are in one another's bones. I understand you. Now indeed I understand. In some way I have come to an understanding at a stride. Indeed

315

I understand you and your dream. I want to help you. Edward—Edward has no dreams. . . . It is dreadful to me, Willie, to think we two are to part."

"But we have settled that—part we must."

"But why?"

"I love you."

"Well, and why should I hide it, Willie?—I love you. . . ." Our eyes met. She flushed, she went on resolutely: "You are stupid. The whole thing is stupid. I love you both."

I said, "You do not understand what you say. No!"

"You mean that I must go."

"Yes, yes. Go!"

For a moment we looked at one another, mute, as though deep down in the unfathomable darkness below the surface and present reality of things dumb meanings strove to be. She made to speak and desisted.

"But must I go?" she said at last, with quivering lips, and the tears in her eyes were stars. Then she began, "Willie—"

"Go!" I interrupted her. . . . "Yes."

Then again we were still.

She stood there, a tearful figure of pity, longing for me, pitying me. Something of that wider love that will carry our descendants at last out of all the limits, the hard, clear obligations of our personal life, moved us, like the first breath of a coming wind out of the heaven that stirs and passes away. I had an impulse to take her hand and kiss it, and then a trembling came to me, and I knew that if I touched her, my strength would all pass from me. . . .

And so, standing at a distance one from the other, we parted, and Nettie went, reluctant and looking back, with the man she had chosen, to the lot she had chosen, out of my life—like the sunlight out of my life. . . .

Then, you know, I suppose I folded up this newspaper and put it in my pocket. But my memory of that meeting ends with the face of Nettie turning to go.

\* \* \* \* \*

## from CHAPTER THE THIRD
### BELTANE AND NEW YEAR'S EVE
#### 4

It seems to me as if the intense memory of Nettie vanished utterly out of my mind at the touch of Anna's lips. I loved Anna.

We went to the council of our group—commune it was then called—and she was given me in marriage, and within a year she had borne me a son. We saw much of one another, and talked ourselves very close together. My faithful friend she became and has been always, and for a time we were passionate lovers. Always she has loved me and kept my soul full of tender gratitude and love for her; always when we met our hands and eyes clasped in friendly greeting, all through our lives from that hour we have been each other's secure help and refuge, each other's ungrudging fastness of help and sweetly frank and open speech. . . . And after a little while my love and desire for Nettie returned as though it had never faded away.

No one will have a difficulty now in understanding how that could be, but in the evil days of the world malaria, that would have been held to be the most impossible thing. I should have had to crush that second love out of my thoughts, to have kept it secret from Anna, to have lied about it to all the world. The old-world theory was there was only one love—we who float upon a sea of love find that hard to understand. The whole nature of a man was supposed to go out to the one girl or woman who possessed him, her whole nature to go out to him. Nothing was left over—it was a discreditable thing to have any surplus at all. They formed a secret secluded system of two, two and such children as she bore him. All other women he was held bound to find no beauty in, no sweetness, no interest; and she likewise, in no other man. The old-time men and women went apart in couples, into defensive little houses, like beasts into little pits, and in these "homes" they sat down purposing to love, but really coming very soon to jealous watching of this extravagant mutual proprietorship. All freshness passed very speedily out of their love, out of their conversation, all pride out of their common life. To permit each other freedom was blank dishonour. That I and Anna should love, and after our love-journey together, go about our separate lives and dine at the public tables, until the advent of her motherhood, would have seemed a terrible strain upon our unmitigable loyalty. And that I should have it in me to go on loving Nettie—who loved in different manner both Verrall and me—would have outraged the very quintessence of the old convention.

In the old days love was a cruel proprietary thing. But now Anna could let Nettie live in the world of my mind, as freely as a rose will suffer the presence of white lilies. If I could hear notes that were not in her compass, she was glad, because she loved me, that I should listen to other music than hers. And she, too, could see the beauty of Nettie. Life is so rich and generous now, giving friendship, and a thousand tender interests and helps and comforts, that no one stints another of the full realisation of all possibilities of beauty. For me from the beginning Nettie was the figure of beauty, the shape and colour of the divine principle that lights the world. For everyone there are certain types, certain faces and forms, gestures, voices and intonations that have that inexplicable unanalysable quality. These come through the crowd of kindly friendly fellow-men and women—one's own. These touch one mysteriously, stir deeps that must otherwise slumber, pierce and interpret the world. To refuse this interpretation is to refuse the sun, to darken and deaden all life. . . . I love Nettie, I loved all who were like her, in the measure that they were like her, in voice, or eyes, or form, or smile. And between my wife and me there was no bitterness that the great goddess, the life-giver, Aphrodite, Queen of the Living Seas, came to my

317

imagination so. It qualified our mutual love not at all, since now in our changed world love is unstinted; it is a golden net about our globe that nets all humanity together.

I thought of Nettie much, and always movingly beautiful things restored me to her; all fine music, all pure deep colour, all tender and solemn things. The stars were hers, and the mystery of moonlight; the sun she wore in her hair, powdered finely, beaten into gleams and threads of sunlight in the wisps and strands of her hair. . . . Then suddenly one day a letter came to me from her, in her unaltered clear hand-writing, but in a new language of expression, telling me many things. She had learned of my mother's death, and the thought of me had grown so strong as to pierce the silence I had imposed on her. We wrote to one another—like ordinary friends with a certain restraint between us at first, and with a great longing to see her once more arising in my heart. For a time I left that hunger unexpressed, and then I was moved to tell it to her. And so on New Year's Day in the Year Four, she came to Lowchester and me. How I remember that coming, across the gulf of fifty years! I went out across the park to meet her, so that we might meet alone. The windless morning was clear and cold, the ground new carpeted with snow, and all the trees motionless lace and glitter of frosty crystals. The rising sun had touched the white with spirit of gold, and my heart beat and sang within me. I remember now the snowy shoulder of the down sunlit against the bright blue sky. And presently I saw the woman I loved coming through the white still trees. . . .

I had made a goddess of Nettie, and behold she was a fellow-creature! She came, warm-wrapped and tremulous, to me, with the tender promise of tears in her eyes, with her hands outstretched and that dear smile quivering upon her lips. She stepped out of the dream I had made of her, a thing of needs and regrets and human kindliness. Her hands as I took them were a little cold. The goddess shone through her indeed, glowed in all her body, she was a worshipful temple of love for me—yes. But I could feel, like a thing new discovered, the texture and sinews of her living, her dear personal and mortal hands. . . .

### THE EPILOGUE
### THE WINDOW OF THE TOWER

*This was as much as this pleasant-looking grey-haired man had written. I had been lost in his story throughout the earlier portions of it, forgetful of the writer and his gracious room, and the high tower in which he was sitting. But gradually, as I drew near the end, the sense of strangeness returned to me. It was more and more evident to me that this was a different humanity from any I had know, unreal, having different customs, different beliefs, different interpretations, different emotions. It was no mere change in conditions and institutions the comet had wrought. It had made a change of heart and mind. In a manner it had dehumanised the world, robbed it of its spites, it intense jealousies, its inconsistencies, its humour. At the* end, and particularly after the death of his mother, I felt his story had slipped away from my sympathies altogether. Those Beltane fires had burned something in him that worked living still and unsubdued in me, that rebelled in particular at that return of Nettie. I became inattentive. I no longer felt with him, nor gathered a sense of complete understanding from his phrases. His Lord Eros indeed! He and these transfigured people—they were beautiful and noble people, like the people one sees in great pictures, like the gods of noble sculpture, but they had no nearer fellowship than these to competitive men. As the Change was realised, with every stage of realisation the gulf widened and it was harder to follow his word.

I put down the last fascicle of all, and met his friendly eyes. It was hard to dislike him.

I felt a subtle embarrassment in putting the question that perplexed me. And yet it seemed so material to me I had to put it. "And did you—?" I asked. "Were you—lovers?"

His eyebrows rose. "Of course."

"But your wife—?"

It was manifest he did not understand me.

I hesitated still more. I was perplexed by a conviction of baseness. "But—" I began. "You remained lovers?"

"Yes." I had grave doubts if I understood him. Or he me.

I made a still more courageous attempt. "And had Nettie no other lovers?"

"A beautiful woman like that! I know not how many loved beauty in her, nor what she found in others. But we four from that time were very close, you understand, we were friends, helpers, personal lovers in a world of lovers."

"Four?"

"There was Verrall."

Then suddenly it came to me that the thoughts that stirred in my mind were sinister and base, that the queer suspicions, the coarseness and coarse jealousies of my old world were over and done for these more finely living souls. "You made," I said, trying to be liberal minded, "a home together."

"A home!" He looked at me, and, I know not why, I glanced down at my feet. What a clumsy, ill-made thing a boot is, and how hard and colourless seemed my clothing! How harshly I stood out amidst these perfected things. I had a moment of rebellious detestation. I wanted to get out of all this. After all, it wasn't my style. I wanted intensely to say something that would bring him down a peg, make sure, as it were, of my suspicions by launching an offensive accusation. I looked up and he was standing.

"I forgot," he said. "You are pretending the old world is still going on. A home!"

He put out his hand, and quite noiselessly the great window widened down to us, and the splendid nearer prospect of that dreamland city was before me. There for one clear moment I saw it; its galleries and open spaces, its trees of golden fruit and crystal waters, its music and rejoicing, love and beauty without ceasing flowing through its varied and intricate streets. And the nearer people I saw now directly and plainly, and no longer in the distorted mirror that hung overhead. They really did not justify my suspicions, and yet—! They were such people as one sees on earth—save that they were changed. How can I express that

319

*change. As a woman is changed in the eyes of her lover, as a woman is changed by the love of a lover. They were exalted. . . .*

*I stood up beside him and looked out. I was a little flushed, my ears a little reddened, by the inconvenience of my curiosities, and by my uneasy sense of profound moral differences. He was taller than I. . . .*

*"This is our home" he said smiling, and with thoughtful eyes on me.*

# from *Tono-Bungay*
# (1909)

*As David Lodge argues,* Tono-Bungay *belongs in the tradition of the "State of England" novel, in which character is less important than a rendering of the institutions and procedures that bear responsibility for the way things are. It is a long, sprawling novel that traces George Ponderevo's growth (with many parallels to Wells's own) through different stages and arenas of British life. Few other novels catch the energy of commerce and its fraud so well as* Tono-Bungay. *The title is the name of a quack medicine that George's uncle Teddy Ponderevo concocts and makes a very great fortune selling. George himself, in the following selections, has some qualms about the business. As he overcomes them, we enter an ambiguous world of compromise and excitement. Uncle Teddy is a magnificent comic figure, completely taken by the goal of commercial capitalism, a man who is not a villain but who knows at his heart that he is acting like a scoundrel, full of the "air" of the magnate entrepreneur, able to play the role with bravado and with an eye to the details. Aunt Susan, Teddy's spouse, is one of Wells's most sympathetic women. She manages to nurture Teddy and George in their social adventure without any illusions about the legitimacy of the thing.* Tono-Bungay *ends with economic disaster. After helping his uncle escape his creditors to die with some trace of dignity on the continent, George moves on and becomes a shipbuilder. The final scene, selected here, renders the double quality of dangerous excitement and moral ambiguity that has recurred throughout the novel.*

## BOOK II
### CHAPTER THE SECOND
### THE DAWN COMES, AND MY UNCLE APPEARS IN A NEW SILK HAT
### 1

Throughout my student days I had not seen my uncle. I refrained from going to him in spite of an occasional regret that in this way I estranged myself from my aunt Susan, and I maintained a sulky attitude of mind towards him. And I don't think that once in all that time I gave a thought to that mystic word of his that was to alter all the world for us. Yet I had not altogether forgotten it. It was with a touch of memory, dim transient perplexity if no more—why did this thing seem in some way personal?—that I read a new inscription upon the hoarding:

The Secret of Vigour, Tono-Bungay.

That was all. It was simple and yet in some way arresting. I found myself repeating the word after I had passed, it roused one's attention like the sound of distant guns. "Tono"—what's that? And deep, rich, unhurrying;—"*Bun*-gay!"

Then came my uncle's amazing telegram, his answer to my hostile note, which must have followed him on from place to place; "*Come to me at once you are wanted three hundred a year certain tono-bungay.*"

"By Jove!" I cried, "of course!

"It's something—. A patent-medicine! I wonder what he wants with me?"

In his Napoleonic way my uncle had omitted to give an address. His telegram had been handed in at Farringdon Road, and after complex meditations I replied to Ponderevo, Farringdon Road, trusting to the rarity of our surname to reach him.

"Where are you?" I asked.

His reply came promptly:

"192A, Raggett Street, E.C."

The next day I took an unsanctioned holiday after the morning's lecture. I discovered my uncle in a wonderfully new silk hat—oh, a splendid hat! With a rolling brim that went beyond the common fashion. It was decidedly too big for him—that was its only fault. It was stuck on the back of his head, and he was in a white waistcoat and shirt-sleeves. He welcomed me with a forgetfulness of my bitter satire and my hostile abstinence that was almost divine. His glasses fell off at the sight of me. His round inexpressive eyes shone brightly. He held out his plump short hand.

"Here we are, George! What did I tell you? Needn't whisper it now, my boy. Shout it—*loud*! Spread it about! Tell every one! Tono—TONO—TONO-BUYNGAY!"

Raggett Street, you must understand, was a thoroughfare over which some one had distributed large quantities of cabbage stumps and leaves. It opened out of the upper end of Farringdon Street, and 192A was a shop with the plate-glass front coloured chocolate, on which several of the same bills I had read upon the hoardings had been struck. The floor was covered by street mud that had been brought in on dirty boots, and three energetic young men of the hooligan type, in neck-wraps and caps, were packing wooden cases with papered-up bottles, amidst much straw and confusion. The counter was littered with these same swathed bottles, of a pattern then novel but now amazingly familiar in the world, the blue paper with the coruscating figure of a genial nude giant, and the printed directions of how under practically all circumstances to take Tono-Bungay. Beyond the counter on one side opened a staircase down which I seem to remember a girl descending with a further consignment of bottles, and the rest of the background was a high partition, also chocolate, with "Temporary Laboratory" inscribed upon it in white letters, and over a door that pierced it, "Office." Here I rapped, inaudible amid much hammering, and then entered unanswered to find my uncle, dressed as I have described, one hand gripping a sheaf of letters, and the other scratching his head as he dictated to one of three toiling typewriter girls. Behind him was a further partition and a door inscribed "ABSOLUTELY PRIVATE—NO ADMISSION," thereon. This partition was of wood painted the universal chocolate up to about eight feet from the ground and then of glass. Through the glass I saw dimly a crowded suggestion of crucibles and glass retorts, and—by Jove!—yes!—the dear old Wimblehurst air-pump still! It gave me quite a little thrill—that air-pump! And beside it was the electrical machine—but something—some serious trouble—had happened to that. All these were evidently placed on a shelf just at the level to show.

"Come right into the sanctum," said my uncle, after he had finished something about "esteemed consideration," and whisked me through the door into a room that quite amazingly failed to verify the promise of that apparatus. It was papered with dingy wallpaper that had peeled in places; it contained a fireplace, an easy-chair with a cushion, a table on which stood two or three big bottles, a number of cigar-boxes on the mantel, a whisky Tantalus and a row of soda syphons. He shut the door after me carefully.

"Well, here we are!" he said. "Going strong! Have a whiskey, George? No!—Wise man! Neither will I! You see me at it! At it—hard!"

"Hard at what?"

"Read it," and he thrust into my hand a label—that label that has now become one of the most familiar objects of the chemist's shop, the greenish-blue rather old-fashioned bordering, the legend, the name in good black type, very clear, and the strong man all set about with lightning flashes above the double column of skillful lies in red—the label of Tono-Bungay. "It's afloat," he said, as I stood puzzling at this, "It's afloat. I'm afloat!" And suddenly he burst out singing in that throaty tenor of his—

*"I'm afloat, I'm afloat on the fierce flowing tide,*
*The ocean's my home and my bark is my bride!"*

"Ripping song that is, George. Not so much a bark as a solution, but still—it does! Here we are at it! By-the-bye! Half a mo'! I've thought of a thing." He whisked out, leaving me to examine this nuclear spot at leisure, while his voice became dictatorial without. The den struck me as in its large grey dirty way quite unprecedented and extraordinary. The bottles were all labelled simply A, B, C, and so forth, and that dear old apparatus above, seen from this side, was even more patently "On the shelf" than when it had been used to impress Wimblehurst. I saw nothing for it but to sit down in the chair and await my uncle's explanations. I remarked, a frock-coat with satin lapels behind the door; there was a dignified umbrella in the corner and a clothes-brush and a hat-brush stood on a side-table. My uncle returned in five minutes looking at his watch—a gold watch—"Gettin' lunch-time, George," he said. "You'd better come and have lunch with me!"

"How's Aunt Susan?" I asked.

"Exuberant. Never saw her so larky. This has bucked her up something wonderful—all this."

"All what?"

"Tono-Bungay."

"What is Tono-Bungay?" I asked.

THE H. G. WELLS READER

My uncle hesitated. "Tell you after lunch, George," he said. "Come along!" and having locked up the sanctum after himself, led the way along a narrow dirty pavement, lined with barrows and swept at times by avalanche-like porters bearing burthens to vans, to Farringdon Street. He hailed a passing cab superbly, and the cabman was infinitely respectful. "Schäfers'," he said, and off we went side by side—and with me more and more amazed at all these things—to Schäfers' Hotel, the second of the two big places with huge lace-curtain-covered windows near the corner of Blackfriars Bridge.

I will confess I felt a magic change in our relative proportions as the two colossal, pale-blue-and-red-liveried porters of Schäfers' held open the inner doors for us with a salutation that in some manner they seemed to confine wholly to my uncle. Instead of being about four inches taller, I felt at least the same size as he, and very much slenderer. Still more obsequious waiters relieved him of the new hat and the dignified umbrella, and took his orders for our lunch. He gave them with a fine assurance.

He nodded to several of the waiters.

"They know me, George, already," he said. "Point me out. Lively place! Eye for coming men!"

The detailed business of the lunch engaged our attention for a while, and then I leaned across my plate. "And *now*?" said I.

"It's the secret of vigour. Didn't you read that label?"

"Yes, but—"

"It's selling like hot cakes."

"And what is it?" I pressed.

"Well," said my uncle, and then leaned forward and spoke softly under cover of his hand, "It's nothing more or less than . . . "

(But here an unfortunate scruple intervenes. After all, Tono-bungay is still a marketable commodity and in the hands of purchasers, who bought it from—among other venders—me. No! I am afraid I cannot give it away.)

"You see," said my uncle in a slow confidential whisper, with eyes very wide and a creased forehead, "it's nice because of the" (here he mentioned a flavouring matter and an aromatic spirit), "it's stimulating because of" (here he mentioned two very vivid tonics, one with a marked action on the kidneys). "And the" (here he mentioned two other ingredients) "makes it pretty intoxicating. Cocks their tails. Then there's" (but I touch on the essential secret). "And there you are. I got it out of an old book of recipes—all except the" (here he mentioned the more virulent substance, the one that assails the kidneys), "which is my idea. Modern touch! There you are!"

He reverted to the direction of our lunch.

Presently he was leading the way to the lounge—a sumptuous place in red morocco and yellow glazed crockery, with incredible vistas of settees and sofas and things, and there I found myself grouped with him in two excessively upholstered chairs with an earthenware Moorish table between us bearing coffee and Benedictine, and I was tasting the delights of a tenpenny cigar. My uncle smoked a similar cigar in an habituated manner, and he looked energetic and knowing and luxurious and most unexpectedly a little bounder, round the end of it. It was just a trivial flaw upon our swagger, perhaps, that we both were clear our cigars had to be "mild." He got obliquely across the spaces of his great arm-chair so as to incline confidentially to my ear, he curled up his little legs, and I, in my longer way, adopted a corresponding receptive obliquity. I felt that we should strike an unbiased observer as a couple of very deep and wily and developing and repulsive persons.

"I want to let you into this"—puff—"George," said my uncle round the end of his cigar. "For many reasons."

His voice grew lower and more cunning. He made explanations that to my inexperience did not completely explain. I retain an impression of a long credit and a share with a firm of wholesale chemists, of a credit and a prospective share with some pirate printers, of a third share for a leading magazine and newspaper proprietor.

"I played 'em off one against the other," said my uncle. I took his point in an instant. He had gone to each of them in turn and said the others had come in.

"I put up four hundred pounds," said my uncle, "myself and my all. And you know—"

He assumed a brisk confidence. "I hadn't five hundred pence. At least—"

For a moment he really was just a little embarrassed. "I *did*," he said, "produce capital. You see, there was that trust affair of yours—I ought I suppose—in strict legality—to have put that straight first. Zzzz. . . .

"It was a bold thing to do," said my uncle, shifting the venue from the region of honour to the region of courage. And then with a characteristic outburst of piety, "Thank God it's all come right!

"And now, I suppose, you ask where do *you* come in! Well, fact is I've always believed in you, George. You've got—it's a sort of dismal grit. Bark your shins, rouse you, and you'll go! You'd rush any position you had a mind to rush. I know a bit about character, George—trust me. You've got—" He clenched his hands and thrust them out suddenly, and at the same time said, with explosive violence, "Wooosh! Yes. You have! The way you put away that Latin at Wimblehurst; I've never forgotten it. Wo-oo-oo-osh! Your science and all that! Wo-oo-oo-osh! I know my limitations. There's things I can do, and" (he spoke in a whisper, as though this was the first hint of his life's secret) "there's things I can't. Well, I can create this business, but I can't make it go. I'm too voluminous—I'm a boiler-over, not a simmering stick-at-it. You keep on *hotting up and hotting up*. Papins' digester. That's you, steady and long and piling up,— then, wo-oo-oo-oo-osh. Come in and stiffen these niggers. Teach them that wo-oo-oo-osh. There you are! That's what I'm after. You! Nobody else believes you're more than a body. Come right in with me and be a man. Eh, George? Think of the fun of it—a thing on the go—a Real Live Thing! Wooshing it up! Making it buzz and spin! Whoo-oo-oo."—He made alluring expanding circles in the air with his hand. "Eh?"

His proposal, sinking to confidential undertones again, took more definite shape. I was to give all my time and energy to developing and organising. "You shan't write a single advertisement, or give a single assurance," he declared. "I can do all that."

And the telegram was no flourish; I was to have three hundred a year. Three hundred a year. ("That's nothing," said my uncle, "the thing to freeze on to, when the time comes, is your tenth of the vendor's share.")

Three hundred a year certain, anyhow! It was an enormous income to me. For a moment I was altogether staggered. Could there be that much money in the whole concern? I looked about me at the sumptuous furniture of Schäfers' Hotel. No doubt there were many such incomes.

My head was spinning with unwonted Benedictine and Burgundy.

"Let me go back and look at the game again," I said. "Let me see up-stairs and round about."

I did.

"What do you think of it all?" my uncle asked at last.

"Well, for one thing," I said, "why don't you have those girls working in a decently ventilated room? Apart from any other consideration, they'd work twice as briskly. And they ought to cover the corks before labelling round the bottle—"

"Why?" said my uncle.

"Because—they sometimes make a mucker of the cork job, and then the label's wasted."

"Come and change it, George," said my uncle, with sudden fervour. "Come here and make a machine of it. You can. Make it all slick, and then make it woosh. I know you can. Oh! I know you can."

2

I seem to remember very quick changes of mind after that lunch. The muzzy exaltation of the unaccustomed stimulants gave way very rapidly to a mood of pellucid and impartial clairvoyance which is one of my habitual mental states. It is intermittent; it leaves me for weeks together, I know, but back it comes at last like justice on circuit, and calls up all my impressions, all my illusions, all my willful and passionate proceedings. We came down-stairs again into that inner room which pretended to be a scientific laboratory through its high glass lights, and indeed was a lurking-place. My uncle pressed a cigarette on me, and I took it and stood before the empty fireplace while he propped his umbrella in the corner, deposited the new silk hat that was a little too big for him on the table, blew copiously and produced a second cigar.

It came into my head that he had shrunken very much in size since the Wimble-hurst days, that cannon ball he had swallowed was rather more evident and shameless than it had been, his skin less fresh and the nose between his glasses, which still didn't quite fit, much redder. And just then he seemed much laxer in his muscles and not quite as alertly quick in his movements. But he evidently wasn't aware of the degenerative nature of his changes as he sat there, looking suddenly quite little under my eyes.

"Well, George!" he said, quite happily unconscious of my silent criticism, "what do you think of it all?"

326

"Well," I said; "in the first place—it's a damned swindle!"

"Tut! Tut!" said my uncle. "it's as straight as—It's fair trading!"

"So much the worse for trading," I said.

"It's the sort of thing everybody does. After all, there's no harm in the stuff—and it may do good. It might do a lot of good—giving people confidence, f'rinstance, against an epidemic. See? Why not? I don't see where your swindle comes in."

"H'm," I said. "It's a thing you either see or don't see."

"I'd like to know what sort of trading isn't a swindle in its way. Everybody who does a large advertised trade is selling something common on the strength of saying it's uncommon. Look at Chickson—they made him a baronet. Look at Lord Radmore, who did it on lying about the alkali in soap! Rippin' ads those were of his too!"

"You don't mean to say you think doing this stuff up in bottles and swearing it's the quintessence of strength and making poor devils buy it at that, is straight?"

"Why not, George? How do we know it mayn't be the quintessence to them so far as they're concerned?"

"Oh!" I said, and shrugged my shoulders.

"There's Faith. You put Faith in 'em. . . . I grant our labels are a bit emphatic. Christian Science, really. No good setting people against the medicine. Tell me a solitary trade nowadays that hasn't to be—emphathic. It's the modern way! Everybody understands it—everybody allows for it."

"But the world would be no worse and rather better, if all this stuff of yours was run down a conduit into the Thames."

"Don't see that, George, at all. 'Mong other things, all our people would be out of work. Unemployed! I grant you Tono-Bungay *may* be—not *quite* so good a find for the world as Peruvian bark, but the point is, George—it *makes trade*! And the world lives on trade. Commerce! A romantic exchange of commodities and property. Romance. 'Magination. See? You must look at these things in a broad light. Look at the wood—and forget the trees! And hang it, George! we got to do these things! There's no way unless you do. What do *you* mean to do—anyhow?"

"There's ways of living," I said, "without either fraud or lying."

"You're a bit stiff, George. There's no fraud in this affair, I'll bet my hat! But what do you propose to do? Go as chemist to some one who is running a business, and draw a salary without a share like I offer you. Much sense in that? It comes out of the swindle—as you call it—just the same."

"Some businesses are straight and quiet, anyhow; supply a sound article that is really needed, don't shout advertisements."

"No, George. There you're behind the times. The last of that sort was sold up 'bout five years ago."

"Well, there's scientific research."

"And who pays for that? Who put up that big City and Guilds place at South Kensington? Enterprising business men! They fancy they'll have a bit of science going on, they want a handy Expert ever and again, and there you are! And what do you get for research when you've done it? Just a bare living and no outlook. They just keep you to make discoveries, and if they fancy they'll use 'em they do."

"One can teach."

"How much a year, George? How much a year? I suppose you must respect Carlyle! Well,—you take Carlyle's test—solvency. (Lord! What a book that French Revolution of his is!) See what the world pays teachers and discoverers and what it pays business men! That shows the ones it really wants. There's a justice in these big things, George, over and above the apparent injustice. I tell you it wants trade. It's Trade that makes the world go round! Argosies! Venice! Empire!"

My uncle suddenly rose to his feet.

"You think it over, George. You think it over! And come up on Sunday to the new place—we got rooms in Gower Street now—and see your aunt. She's often asked for you, George—often and often, and thrown it up at me about the bit of property—though I've always said and always will, that twenty-five shillings in the pound is what I'll pay you and interest up to the nail. And think it over. It isn't me I ask you to help. It's yourself. It's your aunt Susan. It's the whole concern. It's the commerce of your country. And we want you badly. I tell you straight, I know my limitations. You could take this place, you could make it go! I can see you at it—looking rather sour. Woosh is the word, George."

And he smiled endearingly.

"I got to dictate a letter," he said, ending the smile and vanished into the outer room.

* * * * *

6

At last I went to the address my uncle had given me in Gower Street, and found my aunt Susan waiting tea for him.

Directly I came into the room I appreciated the change in outlook that the achievement of Tono-Bungay had made almost as vividly as when I saw my uncle's new hat. The furniture of the room struck upon my eye as almost stately. The chairs and sofa were covered with chintz which gave it a dim remote flavour of Bladesover; the mantel, the cornice, the gas pendant were larger and finer than the sort of thing I had grown accustomed to in London. And I was shown in by a real housemaid with real tails to her cap, and great quantities of reddish hair. There was my aunt too, looking bright and pretty, in a blue-patterned tea-wrap with bows that seemed to me the quintessence of fashion. She was sitting in a chair by the open window with quite a pile of yellow-labelled books on the occasional table beside her. Before the large, paper-decorated fireplace stood a three-tiered cake-stand displaying assorted cakes, and a tray with all the tea equipage except the teapot, was on the large central table.

The carpet was thick, and a spice of adventure was given it by a number of dyed sheep-skin mats.

"Hel-*lo!*" said my aunt as I appeared. "It's George!"

"Shall I serve the tea now, Mem?" said the real housemaid, surveying our greetings coldly.

"Not till Mr. Ponderevo comes, Meggie," said my aunt, and grimaced with extraordinary swiftness and virulence as the housemaid turned her back.

"Meggie, she calls herself," said my aunt as the door closed, and left me to infer a certain want of sympathy.

"You're looking very jolly, aunt," said I.

"What do you think of all this old Business he's got?" asked my aunt.

"Seems a promising thing," I said.

"I suppose there is a business somewhere?"

"Haven't you seen it?"

"'Fraid I'd say something *at* it, George, if I did. So he won't let me. It came on quite suddenly. Brooding he was and writing letters and sizzling something awful—like a chestnut going to pop. Then he come home one day saying Tono-Bungay till I thought he was clean off his onion, and singing—what was it?"

"'I'm afloat, I'm afloat,'" I guessed.

"The very thing. You've heard him. And saying our fortunes were made. Took me out to the Ho'born Restaurant, George—dinner, and we had champagne, stuff that blows up the back of your nose and makes you go So, and he said at last he'd got things worthy of me—and we moved here next day. It's a swell house, George. Three pounds a week for the rooms. And he says the Business'll stand it."

She looked at me doubtfully.

"Either do that or smash," I said profoundly.

We discussed the question for a moment mutely with our eyes. My aunt slapped the pile of books from Mudie's.

"I've been having such a Go of reading, George. you never did!"

"What do you think of the business?" I asked.

"Well, they've let him have money," she said, and thought and raised her eyebrows.

"It's been a time," she went on. "The flapping about! Me sitting doing nothing and him on the go like a rocket. He's done wonders. But he wants you, George—he wants you. Sometimes he's full of hope—talks of when we're going to have a carriage and be in society—makes it seem so natural and topsy-turvy, I hardly know whether my old heels aren't up here listening to him, and my old head on the floor. . . . Then he gets depressed. Says he wants restraint. Says he can make a splash but can't keep on. Says if you don't come in everything will smash—But you are coming in?"

She paused and looked at me.

"Well—"

"You don't say you won't come in!"

"But look here, aunt," I said, "do you understand quite? . . . It's a quack medicine. It's trash."

"There's no law against selling quack medicine that I know of," said my aunt. She thought for a minute and became unusually grave. "It's our only chance, George," she said. "If it doesn't go . . ."

There came the slamming of a door, and a loud bellowing from the next apartment through the folding doors. "Here—er Shee *Rulk* lies *Poo* Tom Bo—oling."

"Silly old Concertina! Hark at him, George!" she raised her voice. "Don't sing that, you old Walrus you! Sing 'I'm afloat!'"

One leaf of the folding doors opened and my uncle appeared.

"Hullo, George! Come along at last? Gossome tea-cake, Susan?"

"Thought it over, George?" he said abruptly.

"Yes," said I.

"Coming in?"

I paused for a last moment and nodded yes.

"Ah!" he cried. "Why couldn't you say that a week ago?"

"I've had false ideas about the world," I said. . . . "Oh! They don't matter now! Yes, I'll come, I'll take my chance with you, I won't hesitate again."

And I didn't. I stuck to that resolution for seven long years.

* * * * *

BOOK IV<br>CHAPTER THE THIRD<br>NIGHT AND THE OPEN SEA<br>1

I have tried throughout all this story to tell things as they happened to me. In the beginning—the sheets are still here on the table, grimy and dogs-eared and old-looking—I said I wanted to tell *myself* and the world in which I found myself, and I have done my best. But whether I have succeeded I cannot imagine. All this writing is grey now and dead and trite and unmeaning to me; some of it I know by heart. I am the last person to judge it.

As I turn over the big pile of manuscript before me, certain things become clearer to me, and particularly the immense inconsequence of my experiences. It is, I see now that I have it all before me, a story of activity and urgency and sterility. I have called it *Tono-Bungay*, but I had far better have called it *Waste*. I have told of childless Marion, of my childless aunt, of Beatrice wasted and wasteful and futile. What hope is there for people whose women become fruitless? I think of all the energy I have given to vain things. I think of my industrious scheming with my uncle, of Crest Hill's vast cessation, of his resonant strenuous career. Ten thousand men have envied him and wished to live as he lived. It is all one spectacle of forces running to waste, of people

330

who use and do not replace, the story of a country hectic with a wasting aimless fever of trade and money-making and pleasure-seeking. And now I build destroyers!

Other people may see this country in other terms; this is how I have seen it. In some early chapter in this heap I compared all our present colour and abundance to October foliage before the frosts nip down the leaves. That I still feel was a good image. Perhaps I see wrongly. It may be I see decay all about me because I am, in a sense, decay. To others it may be a scene of achievement and construction radiant with hope. I too have a sort of hope, but it is a remote hope, a hope that finds no promise in this Empire or in any of the great things of our time. How they will look in history I do not know, how time and chance will prove them I cannot guess; that is how they have mirrored themselves on one contemporary mind.

## 2

Concurrently with writing the last chapter of this book I have been much engaged by the affairs of a new destroyer we have completed. It has been an oddly complementary alternation of occupations. Three weeks or so ago this novel had to be put aside in order that I might give all my time day and night to the fitting and finishing of the engines. Last Thursday X2, for so we call her, was done, and I took her down the Thames and went out nearly to Texel for a trial of speed.

It is curious how at times one's impressions will all fuse and run together into a sort of unity and become continuous with things that have hitherto been utterly alien and remote. That rush down the river became mysteriously connected with this book. As I passed down the Thames I seemed in a new and parallel manner to be passing all England in review. I saw it then as I had wanted my readers to see it. The thought came to me slowly as I picked my way through the Pool; it stood out clear as I went dreaming into the night out upon the wide North Sea. . . .

It wasn't so much thinking at the time as a sort of photographic thought that came and grew clear. X2 went ripping through the dirty oily waters as scissors rip through canvas, and the front of my mind was all intent with getting her through under the bridges and in and out among the steamboats and barges and rowing-boats and piers. I lived with my hands and eyes hard ahead. I thought nothing then of any appearances but obstacles, but for all that the back of my mind took the photographic memory of it complete and vivid. . . .

"This," it came to me, "is England. This is what I wanted to give in my book. This!"

We started in the late afternoon. We throbbed out of our yard above Hammersmith Bridge, fussed about for a moment, and headed down-stream. We came at an easy rush down Craven Reach, past Fulham and Hurlingham, past the long stretches of muddy meadow and muddy suburb to Battersea and Chelsea, round the cape of tidy frontage that is Grosvenor Road and under Vauxhall Bridge, and Westminster opened before us. We cleared a string of coal barges, and there on the left in the October sunshine stood the Parliament houses and the flag was flying and Parliament was sitting. . . .

I saw it at the time unseeingly; afterwards it came into my mind as the centre of the whole broad panoramic effect of that afternoon. The stiff square lace of Victorian Gothic with its Dutch clock of a tower came upon me suddenly and stared and whirled past in a slow half pirouette and became still, I know, behind me as if watching me recede. "Aren't you going to respect me, then?" it seemed to say.

Not I! There in that great pile of Victorian architecture the landlords and the lawyers, the bishops, the railway men and the magnates of commerce go to and fro—in their incurable tradition of commercialised Bladesovery, of meretricious gentry and nobility sold for riches. I have been near enough to know. The Irish and the Labour men run about among their feet, making a fuss, effecting little; they've got no better plans that I can see. Respect it indeed! There's a certain paraphernalia of dignity, but whom does it deceive? The King comes down in a gilt coach to open the show and wears long robes and a crown; and there's a display of stout and slender legs in white stockings and stout and broader legs in black stockings and artful old gentlemen in ermine. I was reminded of one congested afternoon I had spent with my aunt amidst a cluster of agitated women's hats in the Royal Gallery of the House of Lords and how I saw the King going to open Parliament, and the Duke of Devonshire looking like a gorgeous pedlar and terribly bored with the cap of maintenance on a tray before him hung by slings from his shoulders. A wonderful spectacle! . . .

It is quaint no doubt, this England—it is even dignified in places—full of mellow associations. That does not alter the quality of the realities these robes conceal. The realities are greedy trade, base profit-seeking, bold advertisement—and kingship and chivalry, in spite of this wearing the treasured robes, are as dead among it all as that crusader my uncle championed against the nettles outside the Duffield church. . . .

I have thought much of that bright afternoon's panorama.

To run down the Thames so is to run one's hand over the pages in the book of England from end to end. One begins in Craven Reach and it is as if one were in the heart of old England. Behind us are Kew and Hamptom Court with their memories of Kings and Cardinals, and one runs at first between Fulham's episcopal garden parties and Hurlingham's playground for the sporting instinct of our race. The whole effect is English. There is space, there are old trees and all the best qualities of the homeland in that upper reach. Putney too, looks Anglican on a dwindling scale. And then for a stretch the newer developments slop over, one misses Bladesover and there come first squalid stretches of mean homes right and left and then the dingy industrialism of the south side, and on the north bank the polite long front of nice houses, artistic, literary, administrative people's residences, that stretches from Cheyne Walk nearly to Westminster and hides a wilderness of slums. What a long slow crescendo that is, mile after mile, with the houses crowding closer, the multiplying succession of church towers, the architectural moments, the successive bridges, until you come out into the second movement of the piece with Lambeth's old palace under your quarter and the houses of Parliament on your bow! Westminster Bridge is ahead of you then and through it you flash, and in a moment the round-faced clock tower cranes up to peer at you again and now Scotland yard squares at you, a fat beef-eater of a policeman disguised miraculously as a Bastille.

For a stretch you have the essential London; you have Charing Cross railway-station, heart of the world, and the Embankment on the north side with its new hotels overshadowing its Georgian and Victorian architecture, and mud and great warehouses and factories, chimneys, shot towers, advertisements on the south. The northward sky-line grows more intricate and pleasing, and more and more does one thank God for Wren. Somerset House is as picturesque as the civil war, one is reminded again of the original England, one feels in the fretted sky the quality of Restoration lace.

And then comes Astor's strong box and the lawyers' Inns . . . .

(I had a passing memory of myself there, how once I had trudged along the Embankment westward, weighing my uncle's offer of three hundred pounds a year. . . .)

Through that central essential London reach I drove, and X2 bored her nose under the foam regardless of it all like a black hound going through reeds—on what trail, even I who made her cannot tell.

And in this reach too, one first meets the sea-gulls and is reminded of the sea. Blackfriars one takes—just under these two bridges and just between them is the finest bridge moment in the world—and behold, soaring up, hanging in the sky over a rude tumult of warehouses, over a jostling competition of traders, irrelevantly beautiful and altogether remote, Saint Paul's! "Of course!" one says, "Saint Paul's!" It is the very figure of whatever fineness the old Anglican culture achieved, detached, a more dignified and chastened Saint Peter's, colder, greyer but still ornate, it has never been overthrown, never disavowed, only the tall warehouses and all the roar of traffic have forgotten it, every one has forgotten it; the steamships, the barges, go heedlessly by regardless of it, intricacies of telephone wires and poles cut blackly into its thin mysteries and presently, when in a moment the traffic permits you and you look round for it, it has dissolved like a cloud into the grey blues of the London sky.

And then the traditional and ostensible England falls from you altogether. The third movement begins, the last great movement in the London symphony, in which the trim scheme of the old order is altogether dwarfed and swallowed up. Comes London Bridge, and the great warehouses tower up about you waving stupendous cranes, the gulls circle and scream in your ears, large ships lie among their lighters, and one is in the port of the world. Again and again in this book I have written of England as a feudal scheme overtaken by fatty degeneration and stupendous accidents of hypertrophy. For the last time I must strike that note as the memory of the dear neat little sunlit ancient Tower of London lying away in a gap among the warehouses comes back to me, that little accumulation of buildings so provincially pleasant and dignified, overshadowed by the vulgarest, most typical exploit of modern England, the sham Gothic casings to the ironwork of the Tower Bridge. That Tower

Bridge is the very balance and confirmation of Westminster's dull pinnacles and tower. That sham Gothic bridge; in the very gates of our mother of change, the Sea!

But after that one is in a world of accident and nature. For the third part of the panorama of London is beyond all law, order, and precedence, it is the seaport and the sea. One goes down the widening reaches through a monstrous variety of shipping, great steamers, great sailing-ships, trailing the flags of all the world, a monstrous confusion of lighters, witches' conferences of brown-sailed barges, wallowing tugs, a tumultuous crowding and jostling of cranes and spars, and wharves and stores, and assertive inscriptions. Huge vistas of dock open right and left of one, and here and there beyond and amidst it all are church towers, little patches of indescribably old-fashioned and worn-out houses, riverside pubs and the like, vestiges of townships that were long since torn to fragments and submerged in these new growths. And amidst it all no plan appears, no intention, no comprehensive desire. That is the very key of it all. Each day one feels that the pressure of commerce and traffic grew, grew insensibly monstrous, and first this man made a wharf and that erected a crane, and then this company set to work and then that, and so they jostled together to make this unassailable enormity of traffic. Through it we dodged and drove, eager for the high seas.

I remember how I laughed aloud at the glimpse of the name of a London Country Council steamboat that ran across me. *Caxton* it was called, and another was *Pepys* and another was *Shakespeare*. They seemed so wildly out of place, splashing about in that confusion. One wanted to take them out and wipe them and put them back in some English gentleman's library. Everything was alive about them, flashing, splashing, and passing, ships moving, tugs panting, hawsers taut, barges going down with men toiling at the sweeps, the water all a-swirl with the wash of shipping scaling into millions of little wavelets, curling and frothing under the whip of the unceasing wind. Past it all we drove. And at Greenwich to the south, you know, there stands a fine stone frontage where all the victories are recorded in a Painted Hall, and beside it is the "Ship" where once upon a time those gentlemen of Westminster used to have an annual dinner—before the port of London got too much for them altogether. The old facade of the Hospital was just warming to the sunset as we went by, and after that, right and left, the river opened, the sense of the sea increased and prevailed reach after reach from Northfleet to the Nore.

And out you come at last with the sun behind you into the eastern sea. You speed up and tear the oily water louder and faster, sirroo, sirroo—swish—sirroo, and the hills of Kent—over which I once fled from the Christian teachings of Nicodemus Frapp—fall away on the right hand and Essex on the left. They fall away and vanish into blue haze; and the tall slow ships behind the tugs, scarce moving ships and wallowing sturdy tugs, are all wrought of wet gold as one goes frothing by. They stand out bound on strange missions of life and death, to the killing of men in unfamiliar lands. And now behind us is blue mystery and the phantom flash of unseen lights, and presently even these are gone, and I and my destroyer tear out to the unknown across a great grey space. We tear into the great spaces of the future and the turbines fall to talking in unfamiliar tongues. Out to the open we go, to windy freedom and trackless ways. Light after light goes down. England and the Kingdom, Britain and the Empire, the old prides and the old devotions, glide abeam, astern, sink down upon the horizon, pass—pass. The river passes—London passes, England passes. . . .

### 3

This is the note I have tried to emphasise, the note that sounds clear in my mind when I think of anything beyond the purely personal aspects of my story.

It is a note of crumbling and confusion, of change and seemingly aimless swelling, of a bubbling up and medley of futile loves and sorrows. But through the confusion sounds another note. Through the confusion something drives, something that is at once human achievement and the most inhuman of all existing things. Something comes out of it. . . . How can I express the values of a thing at once so essential and so immaterial? It is something that calls upon such men as I with an irresistible appeal.

I have figured it in my last section by the symbol of my destroyer, stark and swift, irrelevant to most human interests. Sometimes I call this reality Science, sometimes I call it Truth. But it is something we draw by pain and effort out of the heart of life, that we disentangle and make clear. Other men serve it, I know, in art, in literature, in social invention, and see it in a thousand different figures, under a hundred names. I see it always as austerity, as beauty. This thing we make clear is the heart of life. It is the one enduring thing. Men and nations, epochs and civilisations pass, each making its contribution. I do not know what it is, this something, except that it is supreme. It is a something, a quality, an element, one may find now in colours, now in forms, now in sounds, now in thoughts. It emerges from life with each year one lives and feels, and generation by generation and age by age, but the how and why of it are all beyond the compass of my mind. . . .

Yet the full sense of it was with me all that night as I drove, lonely above the rush and murmur of my engines, out upon the weltering circle of the sea. . . .

Far out to the north-east there came the flicker of a squadron of war-ships waving white swords of light about the sky. I kept them hull-down, and presently they were mere summer lightning over the watery edge of the globe. . . . I fell into thought that was nearly formless, into doubts and dreams that have no words, and it seemed good to me to drive ahead and on and on through the windy starlight, over the long black waves.

### 4

It was morning and day before I returned with the four sick and starving journalists who had got permission to come with me, up the shining river, and past the old grey Tower. . . .

I recall the back views of those journalists very distinctly, going with a certain damp weariness of movement along a side street away from the river. They were good men and bore me no malice, and they served me up to the public in turgid degenerate Kiplingese, as a modest button on the complacent stomach of the empire. Though as a matter of fact, X2 isn't intended for the empire, or indeed for the hands of any European power. We offered it to our own people first, but they would have nothing to do with me, and I have long since ceased to trouble much about such questions. I have come to see myself from the outside, my country from the outside— without illusions. We make and pass.

We are all things that make and pass, striving upon a hidden mission, out to the open sea.

END OF BOOK IV

# The History of Mr. Polly
## (1910)

*Wells's comic genius, his eye for society's petty oppressions, and his acute ear for the language of a dead marriage come together in this vigorous and intelligent novel. Mr. Polly's inventive, irritated, but always alert mind that finds in language, especially in its ability to make itself new, a secret revenge against the indignities and disappointments of life, is rendered with realism and extraordinary ingenuity. The class and gender meditation visible beginning in* The Wheels of Chance *gives way in* The History of Mr. Polly *to a psychological idea that seems to have much interested Wells. Mr. Hoopdriver goes back to his job, but Mr. Polly attempts suicide. Although foolish and incompetent, the gesture of revolt is itself restorative, much like that gesture Wells himself made at a much earlier age when he ran away from his apprenticeship. Throughout Wells's work we find such moves—when men despair revolt and in so doing change themselves. The structure of* The History of Mr. Polly *parallels that of such earlier novels as* In the Days of the Comet *and* The Food of the Gods, *in that a crisis gives birth to a utopian resolution. In Mr. Polly's case, personal salvation entails escape from suburban routine and a restoration of an almost lost English landscape. Wells appreciated this dimension of the world: a year or two later he and Rebecca West would find refuge in a similar inn. Rebecca herself, in her first novel,* The Return of the Soldier, *written when she was sharing her work with Wells, envisions just such an idyll.*

CHAPTER THE FIRST
BEGINNINGS, AND THE BAZAAR
I

HOLE!" said Mr. Polly, and then for a change, and with greatly increased emphasis: "Ole!" He paused, and then broke out with one of his private and peculiar idioms. "Oh! Beastly Silly Wheeze of a Hole!"

He was sitting on a stile between two threadbare looking fields, and suffering acutely from indigestion.

He suffered from indigestion now nearly every afternoon in his life, but as he lacked introspection he projected the associated discomfort upon the world. Every afternoon he discovered afresh that life as a whole and every aspect of life that presented itself was "beastly." And this afternoon, lured by the delusive blueness of a sky that was blue because the wind was in the east, he had come out in the hope of snatching something of the joyousness of spring. The mysterious alchemy of mind and body refused, however, to permit any joyousness whatever in the spring.

He had had a little difficulty in finding his cap before he came out. He wanted his cap—the new golf cap—and Mrs. Polly must needs fish out his old soft brown felt hat. "'Ere's your 'at," she said in a tone of insincere encouragement.

He had been routing among the piled newspapers under the kitchen dresser, and had turned quite hopefully and taken the thing. He put it on. But it didn't feel right. Nothing felt right. He put a trembling hand upon the crown of the thing and pressed it on his head, and tried it askew to the right and then askew to the left.

Then the full sense of the indignity offered him came home to him. The hat masked the upper sinister quarter of his face, and he spoke with a wrathful eye regarding his wife from under the brim. In a voice thick with fury he said: "I s'pose you'd like me to wear that silly Mud Pie for ever, eh? I tell you I won't. I'm sick of it. I'm pretty near sick of everything, comes to that. . . . Hat!"

He clutched it with quivering fingers. "Hat!" he repeated. Then he flung it to the ground, and kicked it with extraordinary fury across the kitchen. It flew up against the door and dropped to the ground with its ribbon band half off.

"Shan't go out!" he said, and sticking his hands into his jacket pockets discovered the missing cap in the right one.

There was nothing for it but to go straight upstairs without a word, and out, slamming the shop door hard.

"Beauty!" said Mrs. Polly at last to a tremendous silence, picking up and dusting the rejected headdress. "Tantrums" she added. "I 'aven't patience." And moving with the slow reluctance of a deeply offended woman, she began to pile together the simple apparatus of their recent meal, for transportation to the scullery sink.

The repast she had prepared for him did not seem to her to justify his ingratitude. There had been the cold pork from Sunday and some nice cold potatoes, and Rashdall's Mixed Pickles, of which he was inordinately fond. He had eaten three gherkins, two onions, a small cauliflower head and several capers with every appearance of appetite, and indeed with avidity; and then there had been cold suet pudding to follow, with treacle, and then a nice bit of cheese. It was the pale, hard sort of cheese he liked; red cheese he declared was indigestible. He had also had three big slices of greyish baker's bread, and had drunk the best part of the jugful of beer. . . . But there seems to be no pleasing some people.

"Tantrums!" said Mrs. Polly at the sink, struggling with the mustard on his plate and expressing the only solution of the problem that occurred to her.

And Mr. Polly sat on the stile and hated the whole scheme of life—which was at once excessive and inadequate as a solution. He hated Foxbourne, he hated Foxbourne High Street, he hated his shop and his wife and his neighbours—every blessed neighbour—and with indescribable bitterness he hated himself.

"Why did I ever get in this silly Hole?" he said. "Why did I ever?"

He sat on the stile, and looked with eyes that seemed blurred with impalpable flaws at a world in which even the spring buds were wilted, the sunlight metallic and the shadows mixed with blue-black ink.

338

To the moralist I know he might have served as a figure of sinful discontent but that is because it is the habit of moralists to ignore material circumstances,—if indeed one may speak of a recent meal as a circumstance,—with Mr. Polly's circumstance. Drink, indeed, our teachers will criticise nowadays both as regards quantity and quality, but neither church nor state nor school will raise a warning finger between a man and his hunger and his wife's catering. So on nearly every day in his life Mr. Polly fell into a violent rage and hatred against the outer world in the afternoon, and never suspected that it was this inner world to which I am with such masterly delicacy alluding, that was thus reflecting its sinister disorder upon the things without. It is a pity that some human beings are not more transparent. If Mr. Polly, for example, had been transparent or even passably translucent, then perhaps he might have realised from the Laocoon struggle he would have glimpsed, that indeed he was not so much a human being as a civil war.

Wonderful things must have been going on inside Mr. Polly. Oh! Wonderful things. It must have been like a badly managed industrial city during a period of depression; agitators, acts of violence, strikes, the forces of law and order doing their best, rushings to and fro, upheavals, the *Marseillaise*, tumbrils, the rumble and the thunder of the tumbrils. . . .

I do not know why the east wind aggravates life to unhealthy people. It made Mr. Polly's teeth seem loose in his head, and his skin feel like a misfit, and his hair a dry, stringy exasperation. . . .

Why cannot doctors give us an antidote to the east wind?

"Never have the sense to get your hair cut till it's too long," said Mr. Polly catching sight of his shadow, "you blighted, degenerated Paintbrush! Ugh!" and he flattened down the projecting tails with an urgent hand.

2

Mr. Polly's age was exactly thirty-five years and a half. He was a short, compact figure, and a little inclined to a localised embonpoint. His face was not unpleasing; the features fine, but a trifle too pointed about the nose to be classically perfect. The corners of his sensitive mouth were depressed. His eyes were ruddy brown and troubled, and the left one was round with more of wonder in it than its fellow. His complexion was dull and yellowish. That, as I have explained, on account of those civil disturbances. He was, in the technical sense of the word, clean shaved, with a small sallow patch under the right ear and a cut on the chin. His brow had the little puckerings of a thoroughly discontented man, little wrinklings and lumps, particularly over his right eye, and he sat with his hands in his pockets, a little askew on the stile and swung one leg.

"Hole!" he repeated presently.

He broke out in a quavering song. "Ro-o-o-tten Be-e-astly Silly Hole!"

His voice thickened with rage, and the rest of his discourse was marred by an unfortunate choice of epithets.

He was dressed in a shabby black morning coat and vest; the braid that bound these garments was a little loose in places; his collar was chosen from stock and with projecting corners, technically a "wing-poke"; that and his tie, which was new and loose and rich in colouring, had been selected to encourage and stimulate customers—for he dealt in gentlemen's outfitting. His golf cap, which was also from stock and aslant over his eye, gave his misery a desperate touch. He wore brown leather boots—because he hated the smell of blacking.

Perhaps after all it was not simply indigestion that troubled him.

Behind the superficialities of Mr. Polly's being, moved a larger and vaguer distress. The elementary education he had acquired had left him with the impression that arithmetic was a fluky science and best avoided in practical affairs, but even the absence of book-keeping and a total inability to distinguish between capital and interest could not blind him for ever to the fact that the little shop in the High Street was not paying. An absence of returns, a constriction of credit, a depleted till, the most valiant resolves to keep smiling, could not prevail for ever against these insistent phenomena. One might bustle about in the morning before dinner, and in the afternoon after tea and forget that huge dark cloud of insolvency that gathered and spread in the background, but it was part of the desolation of these afternoon periods, these grey spaces of time after meals, when all one's courage had descended to the unseen battles of the pit, that life seemed stripped to the bone and one saw with a hopeless clearness.

Let me tell the history of Mr. Polly from the cradle to these present difficulties.

"First the infant, mewling and puking in its nurse's arms."

There had been a time when two people had thought Mr. Polly the most wonderful and adorable thing in the world, had kissed his toe-nails, saying "myum, myum," and marvelled at the exquisite softness and delicacy of his hair, had called to one another to remark the peculiar distinction with which he bubbled, had disputed whether the sound he had made was just da da, or truly and intentionally dadda, had washed him in the utmost detail, and wrapped him up in soft, warm blankets, and smothered him with kisses. A regal time that was, and four and thirty years ago; and a merciful forgetfulness barred Mr. Polly from ever bringing its careless luxury, its autocratic demands and instant obedience, into contrast with his present condition of life. These two people had worshipped him from the crown of his head to the soles of his exquisite feet. And also they had fed him rather unwisely, for no one had ever troubled to teach his mother anything about the mysteries of a child's upbringing—though of course the monthly nurse and her charwoman gave some valuable hints—and by his fifth birthday the perfect rhythms of his nice new interior were already darkened with perplexity. . . .

His mother died when he was seven.

He began only to have distinctive memories of himself in the time when his education had already begun.

I remember seeing a picture of Education—in some place. I think it was Education, but quite conceivably it represented the Empire teaching her Sons, and I have a strong impression that it was a wall painting upon some public building in Manchester or Birmingham or Glasgow, but very possibly I am mistaken about that. It represented a glorious woman with a wise and fearless face stooping over her children and pointing them to far horizons. The sky displayed the pearly warmth of a summer dawn, and all the painting was marvelously bright as if with the youth and hope of the delicately beautiful children in the foreground. She was telling them, one felt, of the great prospect of life that opened before them, of the spectacle of the world, the splendours of sea and mountain they might travel and see, the joys of skill they might acquire, of effort and the pride of effort and the devotions and nobilities it was theirs to achieve. Perhaps even she whispered of the warm triumphant mystery of love that comes at last to those who have patience and unblemished hearts. . . . She was reminding them of their great heritage as English children, rulers of more than one-fifth of mankind, of the obligation to do and be the best that such a pride of empire entails, of their essential nobility and knighthood and the restraints and the charities and the disciplined strength that is becoming in knights and rulers. . . .

The education of Mr. Polly did not follow this picture very closely. He went for some time to a National School, which was run on severely economical lines to keep down the rates by a largely untrained staff, he was set sums to do that he did not understand, and that no one made him understand, he was made to read the catechism and Bible with the utmost industry and an entire disregard of punctuation or significance, and caused to imitate writing copies and drawing copies, and given object lessons upon sealing wax and silk-worms and potato bugs and ginger and iron and such like things, and taught various other subjects his mind refused to entertain, and afterwards, when he was about twelve, he was jerked by his parent to "finish off" in a private school of dingy aspect and still dingier pretensions, where there were no object lessons, and the studies of book-keeping and French were pursued (but never effectually overtaken) under the guidance of an elderly gentleman who wore a nondescript gown and took snuff, wrote copperplate, explained nothing, and used a cane with remarkable dexterity and gusto.

Mr. Polly went into the National School at six and he left the private school at fourteen, and by that time his mind was in much the same state that you would be in, dear reader, if you were operated upon for appendicitis by a well-meaning, boldly enterprising, but rather overworked and under-paid butcher boy, who was superseded towards the climax of the operation by a left-handed clerk of high principles but intemperate habits,—that is to say, it was in a thorough mess. The nice little curiosities and willingnesses of a child were in a jumbled and thwarted condition, hacked and cut about—the operators had left, so to speak, all their sponges and ligatures in the mangled confusion—and Mr. Polly had lost much of his natural confidence, so far as figures and sciences and languages and the possibilities of learning things were concerned. He thought of the present world no longer as a wonderland of experiences, but as geography and history, as the repeating of names that were hard to pronounce, and lists of products and populations and heights and lengths, and as lists and dates—oh! and boredom indescribable. He thought of religion as the recital of more or less incomprehensible words that were hard to remember, and of the Divinity as of a limitless Being having the nature of a schoolmaster and making infinite rules, known and unknown rules, that were always ruthlessly enforced, and with an infinite capacity for punishment and, most horrible of all to think of! limitless powers of espial. (So to the best of his ability he did not think of that unrelenting eye.) He was uncertain about the spelling and pronunciation of most of the words in our beautiful but abundant and perplexing tongue,—that especially was a pity because words attracted him, and under happier conditions he might have used them well—he was always doubtful whether it was eight sevens or nine eighths that was sixty-three—(he knew no method for settling the difficulty) and he thought the merit of a drawing consisted in the care with which it was "lined in." "Lining in" bored him beyond measure.

But the indigestions of mind and body that were to play so large a part in his subsequent career were still only beginning. His liver and his gastric juice, his wonder and imagination kept up a fight against the things that threatened to overwhelm soul and body together. Outside the regions devastated by the school curriculum he was still intensely curious. He had cheerful phases of enterprise, and about thirteen he suddenly discovered reading and its joys. He began to read stories voraciously, and books of travel, provided they were also adventurous. He got these chiefly from the local institute, and he also "took in," irregularly but thoroughly, one of those inspiring weeklies that dull people used to call "penny dreadfuls," admirable weeklies crammed with imagination that the cheap boys' "comics" of to-day have replaced. At fourteen, when he emerged from the valley of the shadow of education, there survived something, indeed it survived still, obscured and thwarted, at five and thirty, that pointed—not with a visible and prevailing finger like the finger of that beautiful woman in the picture, but pointed nevertheless—to the idea that there was interest and happiness in the world. Deep in the being of Mr. Polly, deep in that darkness, like a creature which has been beaten about the head and left for dead but still lives, crawled a persuasion that over and above the things that are jolly and "bits of all right," there was beauty, there was delight, that somewhere—magically inaccessible perhaps, but still somewhere, were pure and easy and joyous states of body and mind.

He would sneak out on moonless winter nights and stare up at the stars, and afterwards find it difficult to tell his father where he had been.

He would read tales about hunters and explorers, and imagine himself riding mustangs as fleet was the wind across the prairies of Western America, or coming as a conquering and adored whiteman into the swarming villages of Central Africa. He shot bears with a revolver—a cigarette in the other hand—and made a necklace of their teeth and claws for the chief's beautiful young daughter. Also he killed a lion with a pointed stake, stabbing through the beast's heart as it stood over him.

He thought it would be splendid to be a diver and go down into the dark green mysteries of the sea.

He led stormers against well-nigh impregnable forts, and died on the ramparts at the moment of victory. (His grave was watered by a nation's tears.)

He rammed and torpedoed ships, one against ten.

He was beloved by queens in barbaric lands, and reconciled whole nations to the Christian faith.

He was martyred, and took it very calmly and beautifully—but only once or twice after the Revivalist week. It did not become a habit with him.

He explored the Amazon, and found, newly exposed by the fall of a great tree, a rock of gold.

Engaged in these pursuits he would neglect the work immediately in hand, sitting somewhat slackly on the form and projecting himself in a manner tempting to a schoolmaster with a cane. . . .And twice he had books confiscated.

Recalled to the realities of life, he would rub himself or sigh deeply as the occasion required, and resume his attempts to write as good as copperplate. He hated writing; the ink always crept up his fingers and the smell of ink offended him. And he was filled with unexpressed doubts. Why should writing slope down from right to left? Why should downstrokes be thick and upstrokes thin? Why should the handle of one's pen point over one's right shoulder?

His copy books towards the end foreshadowed his destiny and took the form of commercial documents. *"Dear Sir,"* they ran, *"Referring to your esteemed order of the 26th ult., we beg to inform you,"* and so on.

The compression of Mr. Polly's mind and soul in the educational institutions of his time, was terminated abruptly by his father between his fourteenth and fifteenth birthday. His father—who had long since forgotten the time when his son's little limbs seemed to have come straight from God's hand, and when he had kissed five minute toe-nails in a rapture of loving tenderness—remarked:

"It's time that dratted boy did something for a living."

And a month or so later Mr. Polly began that career in business that led him at last to the sole proprietorship of a bankrupt outfitter's shop—and to the stile on which he was sitting.

### 3

Mr. Polly was not naturally interested in hosiery and gentlemen's outfitting. At times, indeed, he urged himself to a spurious curiosity about that trade, but presently something more congenial came along and checked the effort. He was apprenticed in one of those large, rather low-class establishments which sell everything, from pianos and furniture to books and millinery, a department store in fact, The Port Burdock Drapery Bazaar at Port Burdock, one of the three townships that are grouped around the Port Burdock naval dockyards. There he remained six years. He spent most of the time inattentive to business, in a sort of uncomfortable happiness, increasing his indigestion.

On the whole he preferred business to school; the hours were longer but the tension was not nearly so great. The place was better aired, you were not kept in for no reason at all, and the cane was not employed. You watched the growth of your moustache with interest and impatience, and mastered the beginnings of social intercourse. You talked, and found there were things amusing to say. Also you had regular pocket money, and a voice in the purchase of your clothes, and presently a small salary. And there were girls. And friendship! In the retrospect Port Burdock sparkled with the facets of quite a cluster of remembered jolly times.

("Didn't save much money though," said Mr. Polly.)

The first apprentices' dormitory was a long bleak room with six beds, six chests of drawers and looking glasses and a number of boxes of wood or tin; it opened into a still longer and bleaker room of eight beds, and this into a third apartment with yellow grained paper and American cloth tables, which was the dining-room by day and the men's sitting- and smoking-room after nine. Here Mr. Polly, who had been an only child, first tasted the joys of social intercourse. At first there were attempts to bully him on account of his refusal to consider face washing a diurnal duty, but two fights with the apprentices next above him established a useful reputation for choler, and the presence of girl apprentices in the shop somehow raised his standard of cleanliness to a more acceptable level. He didn't of course have very much to do with the feminine staff in his department, but he spoke to them casually as he traversed foreign parts of the Bazaar, or got out of their way politely, or helped them to lift down heavy boxes, and on such occasions he felt their scrutiny. Except in the course of business or at meal times the men and women of the establishment had very little opportunity of meeting; the men were in their rooms and the girls in theirs. Yet these feminine creatures, at once so near and so remote, affected him profoundly. He would watch them going to and fro, and marvel secretly at the beauty of their hair or the roundness of their necks or the warm softness of their cheeks or the delicacy of their hands. He would fall into passions for them at dinner time, and try and show devotions by his manner of passing the bread and margarine at tea. There was a very fair-haired, fair-skinned apprentice in the adjacent haberdashery to whom he said "good-morning" every morning, and for a period it seemed to him the most significant event in his day. When she said, "I *do* hope it will be fine to-morrow," he felt it marked an epoch. He had had no sisters, and was innately disposed to worship womenkind. But he did not betray as much to Platt and Parsons.

To Platt and Parsons he affected an attitude of seasoned depravity towards womankind. Platt and Parsons were his contemporary apprentices in departments of the drapery shop, and the three were drawn together into a close friendship by the fact that all their names began with P. They decided they were the Three Ps, and went about together of an evening with the bearing of desperate dogs. Sometimes, when they had money, they went into public houses and had drinks. Then they would become more desperate than ever, and walk along the pavement under the gas lamps arm in arm singing. Platt had a good tenor voice, and had been in a church choir, and so he led the singing; Parsons had a serviceable bellow, which roared and faded and roared again very wonderfully; Mr. Polly's share was an extraordinary lowing noise, a sort of flat recitative which he called "singing seconds." They would have sung catches if they had known how to do it, but as it was they sang melancholy music hall songs about dying soldiers and the old folks far away.

They would sometimes go into the quieter residential quarters of Port Burdock, where policemen and other obstacles were infrequent, and really let their voices soar like hawks and feel very happy. The dogs of the district would be stirred to hopeless emulation, and would keep it up for long after the Three Ps had been swallowed up by the night. One jealous brute of an Irish terrier made a gallant attempt to bite Parsons, but was beaten by numbers and solidarity.

The three Ps took the utmost interest in each other and found no other company so good. They talked about everything in the world, and would go on talking in their dormitory after the gas was out until the other men were reduced to throwing boots; they skulked from their departments in the slack hours of the afternoon to gossip in the packing-room of the warehouse; on Sundays and Bank holidays they went for long walks together, talking.

Platt was white-faced and dark, and disposed to undertones and mystery and a curiosity about society and the demi-monde. He kept himself *au courant* by reading a penny paper of infinite suggestion called *Modern Society*. Parsons was of an ampler build, already promising fatness, with curly hair and a lot of rolling, rollicking, curly features, and a large blob-shaped nose. He had a great memory and a real interest in literature. He knew great portions of Shakespeare and Milton by heart, and would recite them at the slightest provocation. He read everything he could get hold of, and if he liked it he read it aloud. It did not matter who else liked it. At first Mr. Polly was disposed to be suspicious of this literature, but was carried away by Parsons' enthusiasm. The three Ps went to a performance of 'Romeo and Juliet" at the Port Burdock Theatre Royal, and hung over the gallery fascinated. After that they made a sort of password of: "Do you bite your thumbs at us, Sir?"

To which the countersign was: "We bite our thumbs."

For weeks the glory of Shakespeare's Verona lit Mr. Polly's life. He walked as though he carried a sword at his side, and swung a mantle from his shoulders. He went through the grimy streets of Port Burdock with his eye on the first floor windows—looking for balconies. A ladder in the yard flooded his mind with romantic ideas. Then Parsons discovered an Italian writer, whose name Mr. Polly rendered as "Bocashieu," and after some excursions into that author's remains the talk of Parsons became infested with the word "amours," and Mr. Polly would stand in front of his

345

hosiery fixtures trifling with paper and string and thinking of perennial picnics under dark olive trees in the everlasting sunshine of Italy.

And about that time it was that all three Ps adopted turn-down collars and large, loose, artistic silk ties, which they tied very much on one side and wore with an air of defiance. And a certain swashbuckling carriage.

And then came the glorious revelation of that great Frenchman whom Mr. Polly called "Rabooloose." The three Ps thought the birth feast of Gargantua the most glorious piece of writing in the world, and I am not certain they were wrong, and on wet Sunday evenings when there was danger of hymn singing they would get Parsons to read it aloud.

Towards the several members of the Y.M.C.A. who shared the dormity, the three Ps always maintained a sarcastic and defiant attitude.

"We got a perfect right to do what we like in our corner," Platt maintained. "You do what you like in yours."

"But the language!" objected Morrison, the white-faced, earnest-eyed improver, who was leading a profoundly religious life under great difficulties.

"Language, man!" roared Parsons, "why, it's LITERATURE!"

"Sunday isn't the time for Literature."

"It's the only time we've got. And besides—"

The horrors of religious controversy would begin. . . .

Mr. Polly stuck loyally to the Three Ps, but in the secret places of his heart he was torn. A fire of conviction burnt in Morrison's eyes and spoke in his urgent persuasive voice; he lived the better life manifestly, chaste in word and deed, industrious, studiously kindly. When the junior apprentice had sore feet and homesickness Morrison washed the feet and comforted the heart, and he helped other men to get through with their work when he might have gone early, a superhuman thing to do. Polly was secretly a little afraid to be left alone with this man and the power of the spirit that was in him. He felt watched.

Platt, also struggling with things his mind could not contrive to reconcile, said "that confounded hypocrite."

"He's no hypocrite," said Parsons, "he's no hypocrite, O' Man. But he's got no blessed Joy de Vive; that's what's wrong with him. Let's go down to the Harbour Arms and see some of those blessed old captains getting drunk."

"Short of sugar, O' Man," said Mr. Polly, slapping his trowser pocket.

"Oh, *carm* on," said Parsons. "Always do it on tuppence for a bitter."

"Lemme get my pipe on," said Platt, who had recently taken to smoking with great ferocity. "Then I'm with you."

Pause and struggle.

"Don't ram it down, O' Man," said Parsons, watching with knitted brows. "Don't ram it down. Give it Air. Seen my stick, O' Man? Right O."

And leaning on his cane he composed himself in an attitude of sympathetic patience towards Platt's incendiary efforts.

4

Jolly days of companionship they were for the incipient bankrupt on the stile to look back upon.

The interminable working hours of the Bazaar had long since faded from his memory—except for one or two conspicuous rows and one or two larks—but the rare Sundays and holidays shone out like diamonds among pebbles. They shone with the mellow splendour of evening skies reflected in calm water, and athwart them all went old Parsons bellowing an interpretation of life, gesticulating, appreciating and making appreciate, expounding books, talking of that mystery of his, the "Joy de Vive."

There were some particularly splendid walks on Bank holidays. The three Ps would start on Sunday morning early and find a room in some modest inn and talk themselves asleep, and return singing through the night, or having an "argy bargy" about the stars, on Monday evening. They would come over the hills out of the pleasant English country-side in which they had wandered, and see Port Burdock spread out below, a network of interlacing street lamps and shifting tram lights against the black, beacon-gemmed immensity of the harbour waters.

"Back to the collar, O' Man," Parsons would say. There is no satisfactory plural to O' Man, so he always used it in the singular.

"Don't mention it," said Platt.

And once they got a boat for the whole summer day, and rowed up past the moored ironclads and the black old hulks and the various shipping of the harbour, past a white troopship and past the trim front and the ships and interesting vistas of the dockyard to the shallow channels and rocky weedy wildernesses of the upper harbour. And Parsons and Mr. Polly had a great dispute and quarrel that day as to how far a big gun could shoot.

The country over the hills behind Port Burdock is all that an old-fashioned, scarcely disturbed English countryside should be. In those days the bicycle was still rare and costly and the motor car had yet to come and stir up rural serenities. The three P's would take footpaths haphazard across fields, and plunge into unknown winding lanes between high hedges of honeysuckle and dogrose. Greatly daring, they would follow green bridle paths through primrose studded undergrowths, or wander waist deep in the bracken of beech woods. About twenty miles from Port Burdock there came a region of hop gardens and hoast crowned farms, and further on, to be reached only by cheap tickets at Bank Holiday times, was a sterile ridge of very clean roads and red sand pits and pines and gorse and heather. The three Ps could not afford to buy bicycles and they found boots the greatest item of their skimpy expenditure. They threw appearances to the winds at last and got ready-made working-men's hob-nails. There was much discussion and strong feeling over this step in the dormitory.

There is no country-side like the English country-side for those who have learnt to love it; its firm yet gentle lines of hill and dale, its ordered confusion of features, its deer parks and downland, its castles and stately houses, it hamlets and old churches, its farms and ricks and great barns and ancient trees, its pools and ponds and shining threads of rivers; its flower-starred hedgerows, it orchards and woodland patches, it village greens and kindly inns. Other countrysides have their pleasant aspects, but none such variety, none that shine so steadfastly throughout the year. Picardy is pink and white and pleasant in the blossom time, Burgundy goes on with its sunshine and wide hillsides and cramped vineyards, a beautiful tune repeated and repeated, Italy gives salitas and wayside chapels and chestnuts and olive orchards, the Ardennes has its wood and gorges—Touraine and Rhineland, the wide Campagna with its distant Appennines, and the neat prosperities and mountain backgrounds of South Germany, all clamour their special merits at one's memory. And there are the hills and fields of Virginia, like an England grown very big and slovenly, the woods and big river sweeps of Pennsylvania, the trim New England landscape, a little bleak and rather fine like the New England mind, and the wide rough country roads and hills and woodland of New York State. But none of these change scene and character in three miles of walking, nor have so mellow a sunlight nor so diversified a cloudland, nor confess the perpetual refreshment of the strong soft winds that blow from off the sea as our Mother England does.

It was good for the three Ps to walk through such a land and forget for a time that indeed they had no footing in it all, that they were doomed to toil behind counters in such places as Port Burdock for the better part of their lives. They would forget the customers and shopwalkers and department buyers and everything, and become just happy wanderers in a world of pleasant breezes and song birds and shady trees.

The arrival at the inn was a great affair. No one, they were convinced, would take them for drapers, and there might be a pretty serving girl or a jolly old lady, or what Parsons called a "bit of character" drinking in the bar.

There would always be weighty enquiries as to what they could have, and it would work out always at cold beef and pickles, or fried ham and eggs and shandygaff, two pints of beer and two bottles of ginger beer foaming in a huge round-bellied jug.

The glorious moment of standing lordly in the inn doorway, and staring out at the world, the swinging sign, the geese upon the green, the duckpond, a waiting wagon, the church tower, a sleepy cat, the blue heavens, with the sizzle of the frying audible behind one! The keen smell of the bacon! The trotting of feet bearing the repast; the click and clatter as the tableware is finally arranged! A clean white cloth!

"Ready, Sir!" or "Ready, Gentlemen." Better hearing that than "Forward Polly! look sharp!"

The going in! The sitting down! The falling to!

"Bread, O' Man?"

"Right O! Don't bag all the crust, O' Man."

Once a simple mannered girl in a pink print dress stayed and talked with them as they ate; led by the gallant Parsons they professed to be all desperately in love with

348

her, and courted her to say which she preferred of them, it was so manifest she did prefer one and so impossible to say which it was held her there, until a distant maternal voice called her away. Afterwards as they left the inn she waylaid them at the orchard corner and gave them, a little shyly, three keen yellow-green apples—and wished them to come again some day, and vanished, and reappeared looking after them as they turned the corner—waving a white handkerchief. All the rest of that day they disputed over the signs of her favour, and the next Sunday they went there again.

But she had vanished, and a mother of forbidding aspect afforded no explanations.

If Platt and Parsons and Mr. Polly live to be a hundred, they will none of them forget that girl as she stood with a pink flush upon her, faintly smiling and yet earnest, parting the branches of the hedgerows and reaching down apple in hand. Which of them was it, had caught her spirit to attend to them? . . .

And once they went along the coast, following it as closely as possible, and so came at last to Foxbourne, that easternmost suburb of Brayling and Hampstead-on-the-Sea.

Foxbourne seemed a very jolly little place to Mr. Polly that afternoon. It has a clean sandy beach instead of the mud and pebbles and coaly defilements of Port Burdock, a row of six bathing machines, and a shelter on the parade in which the three Ps sat after a satisfying but rather expensive lunch that had included celery. Rows of verandahed villas proffered apartments, they had feasted in an hotel with a porch painted white and gay with geraniums above, and the High Street with the old church at the head had been full of an agreeable afternoon stillness.

"Nice little place for business," said Platt sagely from behind his big pipe.

It stuck in Mr. Polly's memory.

## 5

Mr. Polly was not so picturesque a youth as Parsons. He lacked richness in his voice, and went about in those days with his hands in his pockets looking quietly speculative.

He specialised in slang and the disuse of English, and he played the role of an appreciative stimulant to Parsons. Words attracted him curiously, words rich in suggestion, and he loved a novel and striking phrase. His school training had given him little or no mastery of the mysterious pronunciation of English and no confidence in himself. His schoolmaster indeed had been both unsound and variable. New words had terror and fascination for him; he did not acquire them, he could not avoid them, and so he plunged into them. His only rule was not to be misled by the spelling. That was no guide anyhow. He avoided every recognised phrase in the language and mispronounced everything in order that he shouldn't be suspected of ignorance, but whim.

"Sesquippledan," he would say. "Sesquippledan verboojuice."

"Eh?" said Platt.

"Eloquent Rapsodooce."

"Where?" asked Platt.

"In the warehouse, O' Man. All among the tablecloths and blankets. Carlyle. He's reading aloud. Doing the High Froth. Spuming! Windmilling! Waw, waw! It's a sight worth seeing. He'll bark his blessed knuckles one of these days on the fixtures, O' Man."

He held an imaginary book in one hand and waved an eloquent gesture. "So too shall every Hero inasmuch as notwithstanding for evermore come back to reality," He parodied the enthusiastic Parsons, "so that in fashion and thereby, upon things and not *under* things articulariously He stands."

"I should laugh if the Governor dropped on him," said Platt. "He'd never hear him coming."

"The O' Man's drunk with it—fair drunk," said Polly. "I never did. It's worse than when he got on to Raboloose."

CHAPTER THE SECOND

THE DISMISSAL OF PARSONS

1

Suddenly Parsons got himself dismissed.

He got himself dismissed under circumstances of peculiar violence, that left a deep impression on Mr. Polly's mind. He wondered about it for years afterwards, trying to get the rights of the case.

Parsons apprenticeship was over; he had reached the status of an Improver, and he dressed the window of the Manchester department. By all the standards available he dressed it very well. By his own standards he dressed it wonderfully. "Well, O' Man," he used to say, "there's one thing about my position here,—I can dress a window."

And when trouble was under discussion he would hold that "little Fluffums"—which was the apprentices' name for Mr. Garvace, the senior partner and managing director of the Bazaar—would think twice before he got rid of the only man in the place who could make a windowful of Manchester goods *tell*.

Then like many a fellow artist he fell a prey to theories.

"The art of window dressing is in its infancy, O' Man—in its blooming Infancy. All balance and stiffness like a blessed Egyptian picture. No Joy in it, no blooming Joy! Conventional. A shop window ought to get hold of people, grip 'em as they go along. It stands to reason. Grip!"

His voice would sink to a kind of quiet bellow. "*Do* they grip?"

Then after a pause, a savage roar; "*Naw!*"

"He's got a Heavy on," said Mr. Polly. "Go it, O' Man; let's have some more of it."

"Look at old Morrison's dress-stuff windows! Tidy, tasteful, correct, I grant you, but Bleak!" He let out the word reinforced to a shout; "Bleak!"

"Bleak!" echoed Mr. Polly.

"Just pieces of stuff in rows, rows of tidy little puffs, perhaps one bit just unrolled, quiet tickets."

"Might as well be in church, O' Man," said Mr. Polly.

"A window ought to be exciting," said Parsons; "it ought to make you say: El-*lo*! *when* you see it."

He paused, and Platt watched him over a snorting pipe.

"Rockcockyo," said Mr. Polly.

"We want a new school of window dressing," said Parsons, regardless of the comment. "A New School! The Port Burdock school. Day after to-morrow I change the Fitzallan Street stuff. This time, it's going to be a change. I mean to have a crowd or bust!"

And as a matter of fact he did both.

His voice dropped to a note of self-reproach. "I've been timid, O' Man. I've been holding myself in. I haven't done myself Justice. I've kept down the simmering, seething, teeming ideas. . . . All that's over now."

"Over," gulped Polly.

"Over for good and all, O' Man."

2

Platt came to Polly, who was sorting up collar boxes. "O' Man's doing his Blooming Window."

"What window?"

"What he said."

Polly remembered.

He went on with his collar boxes with his eye on his senior, Mansfield. Mansfield was presently called away to the counting house, and instantly Polly shot out by the street door, and made a rapid transit along the street front past the Manchester window, and so into the silkroom door. He could not linger long, but he gathered joy, a swift and fearful joy, from his brief inspection of Parsons' unconscious back. Parsons had his tail coat off and was working with vigour; his habit of pulling his waistcoat straps to the utmost brought out all the agreeable promise of corpulence in his youthful frame. He was blowing excitedly and running his fingers through his hair, and then moving with all the swift eagerness of a man inspired. All about his feet and knees were scarlet blankets, not folded, not formally unfolded, but—the only phrase is—shied about. And a great bar sinister of roller towelling stretched across the front of the window on which was a ticket, and the ticket said in bold black letters: "LOOK!"

So soon as Mr. Polly got into the silk department and met Platte he knew he had not lingered nearly long enough outside. "Did you see the boards at the back?" said Platt.

351

He hadn't. "The High Egrugious is fairly On," he said, and dived down to return by devious subterranean routes to the outfitting department.

Presently the street door opened and Platt, with an air of intense devotion to business assumed to cover his adoption of that unusual route, came in and made for the staircase down to the warehouse. He rolled up his eyes at Polly. "Oh Lord!" he said and vanished.

Irresistible curiosity seized Polly. Should he go through the shop to the Manchester department, or risk a second transit outside?

He was impelled to make a dive at the street door.

"Where are you going?" asked Mansfield.

"Lill Dog," said Polly with an air of lucid explanation, and left him to get any meaning he could from it.

Parsons was worth the subsequent trouble. Parsons really was extremely rich. This time Polly stopped to take it in.

Parsons had made a huge symmetrical pile of thick white and red blankets twisted and rolled to accentuate their woolly richness, heaped up in a warm disorder, with large window tickets inscribed in blazing red letters: "Cosy Comfort at Cut Prices," and "Curl up and Cuddle below Cost." Regardless of the daylight he had turned up the electric light on that side of the window to reflect a warm glow upon the heap, and behind, in pursuit of contrasted bleakness, he was now hanging long strips of grey silesia and chilly coloured linen dusterings.

It was wonderful, but—

Mr. Polly decided that it was time he went in. He found Platt in the silk department, apparently on the verge of another plunge into the exterior world. "Cosy Comfort at Cut Prices," said Polly. "Allittritions Artful Aid."

He did not dare go into the street for the third time, and he was hovering feverishly near the window when he saw the governor, Mr. Garvace, that is to say, the managing director of the Bazaar, walking along the pavement after this manner to assure himself all was well with the establishment he guided.

Mr. Garvace was a short stout man, with that air of modest pride that so often goes with corpulence, choleric and decisive in manner, and with hands that looked like bunches of fingers. He was red-haired and ruddy, and after the custom of such complexions, hairs sprang from the tip of his nose. When he wished to bring the power of the human eye to bear upon an assistant, he projected his chest, knitted one brow and partially closed the left eyelid.

An expression of speculative wonder overspread the countenance of Mr. Polly. He felt he must see. Yes, whatever happened he must see.

"Want to speak to Parsons, Sir," he said to Mr. Mansfield, and deserted his post hastily, dashed through the intervening departments and was in position behind a pile of Bolton sheeting as the governor came in out of the street.

"What on Earth do you think you are doing with that window, Parsons?" began Mr. Garvace.

Only the legs of Parsons and the lower part of his waistcoat and an intervening inch of shirt were visible. He was standing inside the window on the steps, hanging up the last strip of his background from the brass rail along the ceiling. Within, the Manchester shop window was cut off by a partition rather like the partition of an old-fashioned church pew from the general space of the shop. There was a panelled barrier, that is to say, with a little door like a pew door in it. Parsons' face appeared, staring with round eyes at his employer.

Mr. Garvace had to repeat his question.

"Dressing it, Sir—on new lines."

"Come out of it," said Mr. Garvace.

Parsons stared, and Mr. Garvace had to repeat his command.

Parsons, with a dazed expression, began to descend the steps slowly.

Mr. Garvace turned about. "Where's Morrison? Morrison!"

Morrison appeared.

"Take this window over," said Mr. Garvace pointing his bunch of fingers at Parsons. "Take all this muddle out and dress it properly."

Morrison advanced and hesitated.

"I beg your pardon, Sir," said Parsons with an immense politeness, "but this is my window."

"Take it all out," said Mr. Garvace, turning away.

Morrison advanced. Parsons shut the door with a click that arrested Mr. Garvace.

"Come out of that window," he said. "You can't dress it. If you want to play the fool with a window—"

"This window's All Right," said the genius in window dressing, and there was a little pause.

"Open the door and go right in," said Mr. Garvace to Morrison.

"You leave that door alone, Morrison," said Parsons.

Polly was no longer even trying to hide behind the stack of Bolton sheetings. He realised he was in the presence of forces too stupendous to heed him.

"Get him out," said Mr. Garvace.

Morrison seemed to be thinking out the ethics of his position. The idea of loyalty to his employer prevailed with him. He laid his hand on the door to open it; Parsons tried to disengage his hand. Mr. Garvace joined his effort to Morrison's. Then the heart of Polly leapt and the world blazed up to wonder and splendour. Parsons disappeared behind the partition for a moment and reappeared instantly, gripping a thin cylinder of rolled huckaback. With this he smote at Morrison's head. Morrison's head ducked under the resounding impact, but he clung on and so did Mr. Garvace. The door came open, and then Mr. Garvace was staggering back, hand to head; his autocratic, his sacred baldness, smitten. Parsons was beyond all control—a strangeness, a marvel. Heaven knows how the artistic struggle had strained that richly endowed temperament. "Say I can't dress a window, you thundering old Humbug," he said, and hurled the huckaback at his master. He followed this up by

353

hurling first a blanket, then an armful of silesia, then a window support out of the window into the shop. It leapt into Polly's mind that Parsons hated his own effort and was glad to demolish it. For a crowded second Polly's mind was concentrated upon Parsons, infuriated, active, like a figure of earthquake with its coat off, shying things headlong.

Then he perceived the back of Mr. Garvace and heard his gubernatorial voice crying to no one in particular and everybody in general: "Get him out of the window. He's mad. He's dangerous. Get him out of the window."

Then a crimson blanket was for a moment over the head of Mr. Garvace, and his voice, muffled for an instant, broke out into unwonted expletive.

Then people had arrived from all parts of the Bazaar. Luck, the ledger clerk, blundered against Polly and said, "Help him!" Somerville from the silks vaulted the counter, and seized a chair by the back. Polly lost his head. He clawed at the Bolton sheeting before him, and if he could have detached a piece he would certainly have hit somebody with it. As it was he simply upset the pile. It fell away from Polly, and he had an impression of somebody squeaking as it went down. It was the sort of impression one disregards. The collapse of the pile of goods just sufficed to end his subconscious efforts to get something to hit somebody with, and his whole attention focused itself upon the struggle in the window. For a splendid instant Parsons towered up over the active backs that clustered about the shop window door, an active whirl of gesture, tearing things down and throwing them, and then he went under. There was an instant's furious struggle, a crash, a second crash and the crack of broken plate glass. Then a stillness and heavy breathing.

Parsons was overpowered. . . .

Polly, stepping over scattered pieces of Bolton sheeting, saw his transfigured friend with a dark cut, that was now at present bleeding, on the forehead, one arm held by Somerville and the other by Morrison.

"You—you—you—you annoyed me," said Parsons, sobbing for breath.

### 3

There are events that detach themselves from the general stream of occurrences and seem to partake of the nature of revelations. Such was this Parsons affair. It began by seeming grotesque; it ended disconcertingly. The fabric of Mr. Polly's daily life was torn, and beneath it he discovered depths and terrors.

Life was not altogether a lark.

The calling in of a policeman seemed at the moment a pantomime touch. But when it became manifest that Mr. Garvace was in a fury of vindictiveness, the affair took on a different complexion. The way in which the policeman made a note of everything and aspirated nothing impressed the sensitive mind of Polly profoundly. Polly presently found himself straightening up ties to the refrain of "'E then 'It you on the 'Ed and—"

In the dormitory that night Parsons had become heroic. He sat on the edge of the bed with his head bandaged, packing very slowly and insisting over and again: "He ought to have left my window alone, O' Man. He didn't ought to have touched my window."

Polly was to go to the police court in the morning as a witness. The terror of that ordeal almost overshadowed the tragic fact that Parsons was not only summoned for assault, but "swapped," and packing his box. Polly knew himself well enough to know he would make a bad witness. He felt sure of one fact only, namely, that "'E then 'It 'Im on the 'Ed and—" All the rest danced about in his mind now, and how it would dance about on the morrow Heaven only knew. Would there be a cross-examination? Is it perjoocery to make a slip? People did sometimes perjuice themselves. Serious offence.

Platt was doing his best to help Parsons, and inciting public opinion against Morrison. But Parsons would not hear of anything against Morrison. "He was all right, O' Man—according to his lights," said Parsons. "It isn't him I complain of."

He speculated on the morrow. "I shall 'ave to pay a fine," he said. "No good trying to get out of it. It's true I hit him. I hit him"—he paused and seemed to be seeking an exquisite accuracy. His voice sank to a confidential note;—"On the head—about here."

He answered the suggestion of a bright junior apprentice in a corner of the dormitory. "What's the Good of a Cross summons?" he replied; "with old Corks, the chemist, and Mottishead, the house agent, and all that lot on the Bench? Humble Pie, that's my meal to-morrow, O' Man. Humble Pie."

Packing went on for a time.

"But Lord! What a Life it is!" said Parsons, giving his deep notes scope. "Ten-thirty-five a man trying to do his Duty, mistaken perhaps, but trying his best; ten-forty—Ruined! Ruined!" He lifted his voice to a shout. "Ruined!" and dropped it to "Like an earthquake."

"Heated altaclation," said Polly.

"Like a blooming earthquake!" said Parsons, with the notes of a rising wind.

He mediated gloomily upon his future and a colder chill invaded Polly's mind. "Likely to get another crib, ain't I—with assaulted the guvnor on my reference. I suppose, though, he won't give me refs. Hard enough to get a crib at the best of times," said Parsons.

"You ought to go round with a show, O' Man," said Mr. Polly.

Things were not so dreadful in the police court as Mr. Polly had expected. He was given a seat with other witnesses against the wall of the court, and after an interesting larceny case Parsons appeared and stood, not in the dock, but at the table. By that time Mr. Polly's legs, which had been tucked up at first under his chair out of respect to the court, were extended straight before him and his hands were in his trouser pockets. He was inventing names for the four magistrates on the bench, and had got to "the Grave and Reverend Signor with the palatial Boko," when his thoughts were recalled to gravity by the sound of his name. He rose with alacrity and was fielded by an expert policeman from a brisk attempt to get into the vacant dock. The clerk to the Justices repeated the oath with incredible rapidity.

"Right O," said Mr. Polly, but quite respectfully, and kissed the book.

His evidence was simple and quite audible after one warning from the superintendent of police to "speak up." He tried to put in a good word for Parsons by saying he was "naturally of a choleraic disposition," but the start and the slow grin of enjoyment upon the face of the grave and Reverend Signor with the palatial Boko suggested that the word was not so good as he had thought it. The rest of the bench was frankly puzzled and there were hasty consultations.

"You mean 'E 'As a 'Ot temper," said the presiding magistrate.

"I mean 'E 'As a 'Ot temper," replied Polly, magically incapable of aspirates for the moment.

'You don't mean 'E ketches cholera."

"I mean—he's easily put out."

"Then why can't you say so?" said the presiding magistrate.

Parsons was bound over.

He came for his luggage while every one was in the shop, and Garvace would not let him invade the business to say good-by. When Mr. Polly went upstairs for margarine and bread and tea, he slipped on into the dormitory at once to see what was happening further in the Parsons case. But Parsons had vanished. There was no Parsons, no trace of Parsons. His cubicle was swept and garnished. For the first time in his life Polly had a sense of irreparable loss.

A minute or so after Platt dashed in.

"Ugh!" he said, and then discovered Polly. Polly was leaning out of the window and did not look around. Platt went up to him.

"He's gone already," said Platt. "Might have stopped to say good-by to a chap."

There was a little pause before Polly replied. He thrust his finger into his mouth and gulped.

"Bit on that beastly tooth of mine," he said, still not looking at Platt. "It's made my eyes water, something chronic. Any one might think I'd been doing a looming Pipe, by the look of me."

### CHAPTER THE THIRD
### CRIBS
### 1

Port Burdock was never the same place for Mr. Polly after Parsons had left it. There were no jest notes in his occasional letters, and little of the "Joy de Vive" got through by them. Parsons had gone, he said, to London, and found a place as warehouseman in a cheap outfitting shop near St. Paul's Churchyard, where references were not required. It became apparent as time passed that new interests were absorbing him. He wrote of socialism and the rights of man, things that had no appeal for Mr. Polly. He felt strangers had got hold of his Parsons, were at work upon him, making him into someone else, something less picturesque. . . . Port Burdock became a dreariness full of faded memories of Parsons and work a bore. Platt revealed himself alone as a tiresome companion, obsessed by romantic ideas about intrigues and vices and "society women."

Mr. Polly's depression manifested itself in a general slackness. A certain impatience in the manner of Mr. Garvace presently got upon his nerves. Relations were becoming strained. He asked for a rise of salary to test his position, and gave notice to leave when it was refused.

It took him two months to place himself in another situation, and during that time he had quite a disagreeable amount of loneliness, disappointment, anxiety and humiliation.

He went at first to stay with a married cousin who had a house at Easewood. His widowed father had recently given up the music and bicycle shop (with the post of organist at the parish church) that had sustained his home, and was living upon a small annuity as a guest with this cousin, and growing a little tiresome on account of some mysterious internal discomfort that the local practitioner diagnosed as imagination. He had aged with mysterious rapidity and become excessively irritable, but the cousin's wife was a born manager, and contrived to get along with him. Our Mr. Polly's status was that of a guest pure and simple, but after a fortnight of congested hospitality in which he wrote nearly a hundred letters beginning:

Sir:
Referring to your advt. In the "Christian World" for an improver in Gents' outfitting I beg to submit myself for the situation. Have had six years' experience. . . .

and upset a bottle of ink over a toilet cover and the bedroom carpet, his cousin took him for a walk and pointed out the superior advantages of apartments in London from which to swoop upon the briefly yawning vacancy.

"Helpful," said Mr. Polly; "very helpful, O' Man indeed. I might have gone on there for weeks," and packed.

He got a room in an institution that was partly a benevolent hostel for men in his circumstances and partly a high minded but forbidding coffee house and a centre for pleasant Sunday afternoons. Mr. Polly spent a critical but pleasant Sunday afternoon in a back seat, inventing such phrases as:

"Soulful Owner of the Exorbiant Largenial Development."—An Adam's Apple being in question.

"Earnest Joy."

"Exultant, urgent Loogoobuosity."

A manly young curate, marking and misunderstanding his preoccupied face and moving lips, came and sat by him and entered into conversation with the idea of making him feel more at home. The conversation was awkward and disconnected for a minute or so, and then suddenly a memory of the Port Burdock Bazaar occurred to Mr. Polly, and with a baffling whisper of "Lill' dog," and a reassuring nod, he rose up and escaped, to wander out relieved and observant into the varied London streets.

He found the collection of men he found waiting about in wholesale establishments in Wood Street and St. Paul's Churchyard (where they interview the buyers who have come up from the country) interesting and stimulating, but far too strongly charged with the suggestion of his own fate to be really joyful. There were men in all degrees between confidence and distress, and in every stage between extravagant smartness and the last stages of decay. There were sunny young men full of an abounding and elbowing energy, before whom the soul of Polly sank in hate and dismay. "Smart Juniors," said Polly to himself, "full of Smart Juniosity. The Shoveacious Cult." There were hungry looking individuals of thirty-five or so that he decided must be "Proletelerians"—he had often wanted to find someone who fitted that attractive word. Middle-aged men, "too Old at Forty," discoursed in the waiting-rooms on the outlook in the trade; it had never been so bad, they said, while Mr. Polly wondered if "De-juiced" was a permissible epithet. There were men with an overweening sense of their importance, manifestly annoyed and angry to find themselves still disengaged, and inclined to suspect a plot, and men so faint-hearted one was terrified to imagine their behaviour when it came to an interview. There was a fresh-faced young man with an unintelligent face who seemed to think himself equipped against the world beyond all misadventure by a collar of exceptional height, and another who introduced a note of gaiety by wearing a flannel shirt and a check suit of remarkable virulence. Every day Mr. Polly looked round to mark how many of the familiar faces had gone, and the deepening anxiety (reflecting his own) on the faces that remained, and every day some new type joined the drifting shoal. He realised how small a chance his poor letter from Easewood ran against this hungry cluster of competitors at the fountainhead.

At the back of Mr. Polly's mind while he made his observations was a disagreeable flavour of dentist's parlour. At any moment his name might be shouted, and he might have to haul himself into the presence of some fresh specimen of employer, and to repeat once more his passionate protestation of interest in the business, his possession of a capacity for zeal—zeal on behalf of anyone who would pay him a yearly salary of twenty-six pounds a year.

The prospective employer would unfold his ideals of the employee. "I want a smart, willing young man, thoroughly willing—who won't object to take trouble. I don't want a slacker, the sort of fellow who has to be pushed up to his work and held there. I've got no use for him."

At the back of Mr. Polly's mind, and quite beyond his control, the insubordinate phrasemaker would be proffering such combinations as "Chubby Chops," or "Chubby Charmer," as suitable for the gentleman, very much as a hat salesman proffers hats.

"I don't think you'd find much slackness about me, sir," said Mr. Polly brightly, trying to disregard his deeper self.

"I want a young man who means getting on."

"Exactly, sir. Excelsior."

"I beg your pardon?"

"I said Excelsior, sir. It's a sort of motto of mine. From Longfellow. Would you want me to serve through?"

The chubby gentleman explained and reverted to his ideals, with a faint air of suspicion. "Do *you* mean getting on?" he asked.

"I hope so, sir," said Mr. Polly.

"Get on or get out, eh?"

Mr. Polly made a rapturous noise, nodded appreciation, and said indistinctly: "*Quite* my style."

"Some of my people have been with me twenty years," said the employer. "My Manchester buyer came to me as a boy of twelve. You're a Christian?"

"Church of England," said Mr. Polly.

"H'm," said the employer a little checked. "For good all round business work I should have preferred a Baptist. Still—"

He studied Mr. Polly's tie, which was severely neat and businesslike, as became an aspiring outfitter. Mr. Polly's conception of his own pose and expression was rendered by that uncontrollable phrasemonger at the back as "Obsequies Deference."

"I am inclined," said the prospective employer in a conclusive manner, "to look up your reference."

Mr. Polly stood up abruptly.

"Thank you," said the employer and dismissed him.

"Chump chops! How about chump chops?" said the phrasemonger with an air of inspiration.

"I hope then to hear from you, sir," said Mr. Polly in his best salesman manner.

"If everything is satisfactory," said the prospective employer.

## 2

A man whose brain devotes its hinterland to making odd phrases and nicknames out of ill-conceived words, whose conception of life is a lump of auriferous rock to which all the value is given by rare veins of unbusiness-like joy, who reads Boccacio and Rabelais and Shakespeare with gusto, and uses "Stertoraneous Shover" and "Smart Junior" as terms of bitterest opprobrium, is not likely to make a great success under modern business conditions. Mr. Polly dreamt always of picturesque and mellow things, and had an instinctive hatred of the strenuous life. He would have resisted the spell of ex-President Roosevelt, or General Baden Powell, or Mr. Peter Keary, or the late Dr. Samuel Smiles, quite easily; and he loved Falstaff and Hudibras and coarse laughter, and the old England of Washington Irving and the memory of Charles the

Second's courtly days. His progress was necessarily slow. He did not get rises; he lost situations; there was something in his eye employers did not like; he would have lost his places oftener if he had not been at times an exceptionally brilliant salesman, rather carefully neat, and a slow but very fair window-dresser.

He went from situation to situation, he invented a great wealth of nicknames, he conceived enmities and made friends—but none so richly satisfying as Parsons. He was frequently but mildly and discursively in love, and sometimes he thought of that girl who had given him a yellow-green apple. He had an idea, amounting to a flattering certainty, whose youthful freshness it was had stirred her to self-forgetfulness. And sometimes he thought of Foxbourne sleeping prosperously in the sun. And he began to have moods of discomfort and lassitude and ill-temper due to the beginnings of indigestion.

Various forces and suggestions came into his life and swayed him for longer and shorter periods.

He went to Canterbury and came under the influence of Gothic architecture. There was a blood affinity between Mr. Polly and the Gothic; in the Middle Ages he would no doubt have sat upon a scaffolding and carved out penetrating and none too flattering portraits of church dignitaries upon the capitals, and when he strolled, with his hands behind his back, along the cloisters behind the cathedral, and looked at the rich grass plot in the centre, he had the strangest sense of being at home—far more than he had ever been at home before. "Portly capons," he used to murmur to himself, under the impression that he was naming a characteristic type of medieval churchman.

He liked to sit in the nave during the service, and look through the great gates at the candles and choristers, and listen to the organ-sustained voices, but the transepts he never penetrated because of the charge for admission. The music and the long vista of the fretted roof filled him with a vague and mystical happiness that he had no words, even mispronounceable words, to express. But some of the smug monuments in the aisles got a wreath of epithets; "Metrorious urnfuls," "funererial claims," "dejected angelosity," for example. He wandered about the precincts and speculated about the people who lived in the ripe and cosy houses of grey stone that cluster there so comfortably. Through green doors in high stone walls he caught glimpses of level lawns and blazing flower beds; mullioned windows revealed shaded reading lamps and disciplined shelves of brown bound books. Now and then a dignitary in gaiters would pass him, "Portly capon," or a drift of white-robed choir boys cross a distant arcade and vanish in a doorway, or the pink and cream of some girlish dress flit like a butterfly across the cool still spaces of the place. Particularly he responded to the ruined arches of the Benedictine's Infirmary and the view of Bell Harry tower from the school buildings. He was stirred to read the Canterbury Tales, but he could not get on with Chaucer's old-fashioned English; it fatigued his attention, and he would have given all the story telling very readily for a few adventures on the road. He wanted these nice people to live more and yarn less. He liked the Wife of Bath very much. He would have liked to have known that woman.

At Canterbury, too, he first to his knowledge saw Americans.

His shop did a good class trade in Westgate Street, and he would see them go by on the way to stare at Chaucer's "Chequers," and then turn down Mercery Lane to Prior Goldstone's gate. It impressed him that they were always in a kind of quiet hurry, and very determined and methodical people,—much more so than any English he knew.

"Cultured Rapacidity," he tried.

"Vorocious Return to the Heritage."

He would expound them incidentally to his attendant apprentices. He had overheard a little lady putting her view to a friend near the Christchurch gate. The accent and intonation had hung in his memory, and he would reproduce them more or less accurately. "Now does this Marlowe monument really and truly matter?" he had heard the little lady enquire. "We've no time for side shows and second rate stunts, Mamie. We want just the Big Simple Things of the place, just the Broad Elemental Canterbury praposition. What is it saying to us? I want to get right hold of that, and then have tea in the very room that Chaucer did, and hustle to get that four-eighteen train back to London."

He would go over these precious phrases, finding them full of an indescribable flavour. "Just the Broad Elemental Canterbury praposition," he would repeat. . . .

He would try to imagine Parsons confronted with Americans. For his own part he knew himself to be altogether inadequate. . . .

Canterbury was the most congenial situation Mr. Polly ever found during these wander years, albeit a very desert so far as companionship went.

### 3

It was after Canterbury that the universe became really disagreeable to Mr. Polly. It was brought home to him, not so much vividly as with a harsh and ungainly insistence, that he was a failure in his trade. It was not the trade he ought to have chosen, though what trade he ought to have chosen was by no means clear.

He made great but irregular efforts and produced a forced smartness that, like a cheap dye, refused to stand sunshine. He acquired a sort of parsimony also, in which acquisition he was helped by one or two phases of absolute impecuniosity. But he was hopeless in competition against the naturally gifted, the born hustlers, the young men who meant to get on.

He left the Canterbury place very regretfully. He and another commercial gentleman took a boat one Sunday afternoon at Sturry-on-the-Stour, when the wind was in the west, and sailed it very happily eastward for an hour. They had never sailed a boat before and it seemed simple and wonderful. When they turned they found the river too narrow for tacking and the tide running out like a sluice. They battled back to Sturry in the course of six hours (at a shilling the first hour and sixpence for each hour afterwards) rowing a mile in an hour and a half or so, until the turn of the tide came to help them, and then they had a night walk to Canterbury, and found themselves remorselessly locked out.

The Canterbury employer was an amiable, religious-spirited man and he would probably not have dismissed Mr. Polly if that unfortunate tendency to phrase things had not shocked him. "A Tide's a Tide, Sir," said Mr. Polly, feeling that things were not so bad. "I've no lune-attic power to alter that."

It proved impossible to explain to the Canterbury employer that this was not a highly disrespectful and blasphemous remark.

"And besides, what good are you to me this morning, do you think?" said the Canterbury employer, "with your arms pulled out of their sockets?"

So Mr. Polly resumed his observations in the Wood Street warehouse once more, and had some dismal times. The shoal of fish waiting for the crumbs of employment seemed larger than ever.

He took counsel with himself. Should he "chuck" the outfitting? It wasn't any good for him now, and presently when he was older and his youthful smartness had passed into the dulness of middle age it would be worse. What else could he do?

He could think of nothing. He went one night to a music hall and developed a vague idea of a comic performance; the comic men seemed violent rowdies and not at all funny; but when he thought of the great pit of the audience yawning before him he realised that his was an altogether too delicate talent for such a use. He was impressed by the charm of selling vegetables by auction in one of those open shops near London Bridge, but admitted upon reflection his general want of technical knowledge. He made some enquiries about emigration, but none of the colonies were in want of shop assistants without capital. He kept up his attendance in Wood Street.

He subdued his ideal of salary by the sum of five pounds a year, and was taken at that into a driving establishment in Clapham, which dealt chiefly in ready-made suits, fed its assistants in an underground dining-room and kept them until twelve on Saturdays. He found it hard to be cheerful there. His fits of indigestion became worse, and he began to lie awake at night and think. Sunshine and laughter seemed things lost for ever; picnics and shouting in the moonlight.

The chief shopwalker took a dislike to him and nagged him. "Nar then Polly!" "Look alive Polly!" became the burthen of his days. "As smart a chap as you could have," said the chief shopwalker, "but no Zest. No Zest! No Vim! What's the matter with you?"

During his night vigils Mr. Polly had a feeling—A young rabbit must have very much the feeling, when after a youth of gambolling in sunny woods and furtive jolly raids upon the growing wheat and exciting triumphant bolts before ineffectual casual dogs, it finds itself at last for a long night of floundering effort and perplexity, in a net—for the rest of its life.

He could not grasp what was wrong with him. He made enormous efforts to diagnose his case. Was he really just a "lazy slacker" who ought to "buck up"? He couldn't find it in him to believe it. He blamed his father a good deal—it is what fathers are for—in putting him to a trade he wasn't happy to follow, but he found it impossible to say what he ought to have followed. He felt there had been something stupid about his school, but just where that came in he couldn't say. He made some perfectly sincere efforts to "buck up" and "shove" ruthlessly. But that was infernal—impossible. He had to admit himself miserable with all the misery of a social misfit, and with no clear prospect of more than the most incidental happiness ahead of him. And for all his attempts at self-reproach or self-discipline he felt at bottom that he wasn't at fault.

As a matter of fact all the elements of his troubles had been adequately diagnosed by a certain high-browed, spectacled gentleman living at Highbury, wearing a gold prince-nez, and writing for the most part in the beautiful library of the Reform Club. This gentleman did not know Mr. Polly personally, but he had dealt with him generally as "one of those ill-adjusted units that abound in a society that has failed to develop a collective intelligence and a collective will for order, commensurate with its complexities."

But phrases of that sort had no appeal for Mr. Polly.

CHAPTER THE FOURTH
MR. POLLY AN ORPHAN
1

Then a great change was brought about in the life of Mr. Polly by the death of his father. His father had died suddenly—the local practitioner still clung to his theory that it was imagination he suffered from, but compromised in the certificate with the appendicitis that was then so fashionable—and Mr. Polly found himself heir to a debatable number of pieces of furniture in the house of his cousin near Easewood Junction, a family Bible, an engraved portrait of Garibaldi and a bust of Mr. Gladstone, an invalid gold watch, a gold locket formerly belonging to his mother, some minor jewelry and bric-a-brac, a quantity of nearly valueless old clothes and an insurance policy and money in the bank amounting altogether to the sum of three hundred and ninety-five pounds.

Mr. Polly had always regarded his father as an immortal, as an eternal fact, and his father being of a reserved nature in his declining years had said nothing about the insurance policy. Both wealth and bereavement therefore took Mr. Polly by surprise and found him a little inadequate. His mother's death had been a childish grief and long forgotten, and the strongest affection in his life had been for Parsons. An only child of sociable tendencies necessarily turns his back a good deal upon home, and the aunt who had succeeded his mother was an economist and furniture polisher, a knuckle rapper and sharp silence, no friend for a slovenly little boy. He had loved other little boys and girls transitorily, none had been frequent and familiar enough to strike deep roots in his heart, and he had grown up with a tattered and dissipated affectionateness that was becoming wildly shy. His father had always been a stranger,

363

an irritable stranger with exceptional powers of intervention and comment, and an air of being disappointed about his offspring. It was shocking to lose him; it was like an unexpected hole in the universe, and the writing of "Death" upon the sky, but it did not tear Mr. Polly's heartstrings at first so much as rouse him to a pitch of vivid attention.

He came down to the cottage at Easewood in response to an urgent telegram, and found his father already dead. His cousin Johnson received him with much solemnity and ushered him upstairs, to look at a stiff, straight, shrouded form, with a face unwontedly quiet and, as it seemed, with its pinched nostrils, scornful.

"Looks peaceful," said Mr. Polly, disregarding the scorn to the best of his ability.

"It was a merciful relief," said Mr. Johnson.

There was a pause.

"Second—Second Departed I've ever seen. Not counting mummies," said Mr. Polly, feeling it necessary to say something.

"We did all we could."

"No doubt of it, O' Man," said Mr. Polly.

A second long pause followed, and then, much to Mr. Polly's great relief, Johnson moved towards the door.

Afterwards Mr. Polly went for a solitary walk in the evening light, and as he walked, suddenly his dead father became real to him. He thought of things far away down the perspective of memory, of jolly moments when his father had skylarked with a wildly excited little boy, of a certain annual visit to the Crystal Palace pantomime, full of trivial glittering incidents and wonders, of his father's dread back while customers were in the old, minutely known shop. It is curious that the memory which seemed to link him nearest to the dead man was the memory of a fit of passion. His father had wanted to get a small sofa up the narrow winding staircase from the little room behind the shop to the bedroom above, and it had jammed. For a time his father had coaxed, and then groaned like a soul in torment and given way to blind fury, had sworn, kicked and struck at the offending piece of furniture and finally wrenched it upstairs, with considerable incidental damage to lath and plaster and one of the castors. That moment when self-control was altogether torn aside, the shocked discovery of his father's perfect humanity, had left a singular impression on Mr. Polly's queer mind. It was as if something extravagantly vital had come out of his father and laid a warmly passionate hand upon his heart. He remembered that now very vividly, and it became a clue to endless other memories that had else been dispersed and confusing.

A weakly willful being struggling to get obdurate things round impossible corners—in that symbol Mr. Polly could recognise himself and all the trouble of humanity.

He hadn't had a particularly good time, poor old chap, and now it was all over. Finished. . . .

Johnson was the sort of man who derives great satisfaction from a funeral, a melancholy, serious, practical-minded man of five and thirty, with great powers of advice. He was the up-line ticket clerk at Easewood Junction, and felt the responsibilities of his position. He was naturally thoughtful and reserved, and greatly sustained in that by an innate rectitude of body and an overhanging and forward inclination of the upper part of his face and head. He was pale but freckled, and his dark grey eyes were deeply set. His lightest interest was cricket, but he did not take that lightly. His chief holiday was to go to a cricket match, which he did as if he was going to church, and he watched critically, applauded sparingly, and was darkly offended by any unorthodox play. His convictions upon all subjects were taciturnly inflexible. He was an obstinate player of draughts and chess, and an earnest and persistent reader of the *British Weekly*. His wife was a pink, short, willfully smiling, managing, ingratiating, talkative woman, who was determined to be pleasant, and take a bright hopeful view of everything, even when it was not really bright and hopeful. She had large blue expressive eyes and a round face, and she always spoke of her husband as Harold. She addressed sympathetic and considerate remarks about the deceased to Mr. Polly in notes of brisk encouragement. "He was really quite cheerful at the end," she said several times, with congratulatory gusto, "quite cheerful."

She made dying seem almost agreeable.

Both these people were resolved to treat Mr. Polly very well, and to help his exceptional incompetence in every possible way, and after a simple supper of ham and bread and cheese and pickles and cold apple tart and small beer had been cleared away, they put him into the armchair almost as though he was an invalid, and sat on chairs that made them look down on him, and opened a directive discussion of the arrangements for the funeral. After all a funeral is a distinct social opportunity, and rare when you have no family and few relations, and they did not want to see it spoilt and wasted.

"You'll have a hearse of course," said Mrs. Johnson. "Not one of them combinations with the driver sitting on the coffin. Disrespectful I think they are. I can't fancy how people can bring themselves to be buried in combinations." She flattened her voice in a manner she used to intimate aesthetic feeling. "I do like them glass hearses," she said. "So refined and nice they are."

"Podger's hearse you'll have," said Johnson conclusively. "It's the best in Easewood."

"Everything that's right and proper," said Mr. Polly.

"Podger's ready to come and measure at any time," said Johnson.

"Then you'll want a mourner's carriage or two, according as to whom you're going to invite," said Mr. Johnson.

"Didn't think of inviting any one," said Polly.

"Oh! you'll have to ask a few friends," said Mr. Johnson. "You can't let your father go to his grave without asking a few friends."

"Funerial baked meats like," said Mr. Polly.

"Not baked, but of course you'll have to give them something. Ham and chicken's very suitable. You don't want a lot of cooking with the ceremony coming into the middle of it. I wonder who Alfred ought to invite, Harold. Just the immediate relations; one doesn't want a great crowd of people and one doesn't want not to show respect."

"But he hated our relations—most of them."

"He's not hating them *now*," said Mrs. Johnson, "you may be sure of that. It's just because of that I think they ought to come—all of them—even your Aunt Mildred."

"Bit vulturial, isn't it?" said Mr. Polly unheeded.

"Wouldn't be more than twelve or thirteen people if they *all* came," said Mr. Johnson.

"We could have everything put out ready in the back room and the gloves and whiskey in the front room, and while we were all at the ceremony, Bessie could bring it all into the front room on a tray and put it out nice and proper. There'd have to be whisky and sherry or port for the ladies. . . ."

"Where'll you get your mourning?" asked Johnson abruptly.

Mr. Polly had not yet considered this by-product of sorrow. "Haven't thought of it yet, O' Man."

A disagreeable feeling spread over his body as though he was blackening as he sat. He hated black garments.

"I suppose I must have mourning," he said.

"*Well!*" said Johnson with a solemn smile.

"Got to see it through," said Mr. Polly indistinctly.

"If I were you," said Johnson, "I should get ready-made trousers. That's all you really want. And a black satin tie and a top hat with a deep mourning band. And gloves."

"Jet cuff links he ought to have—as chief mourner," said Mrs. Johnson.

"Not obligatory," said Johnson.

"It shows respect," said Mrs. Johnson.

"It shows respect of course," said Johnson.

And then Mrs. Johnson went on with the utmost gusto to the details of the "casket," while Mr. Polly sat more and more deeply and droopingly into the armchair, assenting with a note of protest to all they said. After he had retired for the night he remained for a long time perched on the edge of the sofa which was his bed, staring at the prospect before him. "Chasing the O' Man about up to the last," he said.

He hated the thought and elaboration of death as a healthy animal must hate it. His mind struggled with unwonted social problems.

"Got to put 'em away somehow, I suppose," said Mr. Polly.

"Wish I'd looked him up a bit more while he was alive," said Mr. Polly.


2


Bereavement came to Mr. Polly before the realisation of opulence and its anxieties and responsibilities. That only dawned upon him on the morrow—which chanced to be Sunday—as he walked with Johnson before church time about the tangle of struggling building enterprise that constituted the rising urban district of Easewood. Johnson was off duty that morning, and devoted the time very generously to the admonitory discussion of Mr. Polly's worldly outlook.

"Don't seem to get the hang of the business somehow," said Mr. Polly. "Too much blooming humbug in it for my way of thinking."

"If I were you," said Mr. Johnson, "I should push for a first-class place in London—take almost nothing and live on my reserves. That's what I should do."

"Come the Heavy," said Mr. Polly.

"Get a better class reference."

There was a pause. "Think of investing your money?" asked Johnson.

"Hardly got used to the idea of having it yet, O' Man."

"You'll have to do something with it. Give you nearly twenty pounds a year if you invest it properly."

"Haven't seen it yet in that light," said Mr. Polly defensively.

"There's no end of things you could put it into."

"It's getting it out again I shouldn't feel sure of. I'm no sort of Fiancianier. Sooner back horses."

"I wouldn't do that if I were you."

"Not my style, O' Man."

"It's a nest egg," said Johnson.

Mr. Polly made an indeterminate noise.

"There's building societies," Johnson threw out in a speculative tone. Mr. Polly, with detached brevity, admitted there were.

"You might lend it on mortgage," said Johnson. "Very safe form of investment."

"Shan't think anything about it—not till the O' Man's underground," said Mr. Polly with an inspiration.

They turned a corner that led towards the junction.

"Might do worse," said Johnson, "than put it into a small shop."

At the moment this remark made very little appeal to Mr. Polly. But afterwards it developed. It fell into his mind like some small obscure seed, and germinated.

"These shops aren't in a bad position," said Johnson.

The row he referred to gaped in the late painful stage in building before the healing touch of the plasterer assuages the roughness of the brickwork. The space for the shop yawned an oblong gap below, framed above by an iron girder; "windows and fittings to suit tenant," a board at the end of the row promised; and behind was the door space and a glimpse of stairs going up to the living rooms above. "Not a bad position," said Johnson, and led the way into the establishment. "Room for fixtures there," he said, pointing to the blank wall.

The two men went upstairs to the little sitting-room or best bedroom (it would have to be) above the shop. Then they descended to the kitchen below.

"Rooms in a new house always look a bit small," said Johnson.

They came out of the house again by the prospective back-door, and picked their way through builder's litter across the yard space to the road again. They drew nearer the junction to where a pavement and shops already open and active formed the commercial centre of Easewood. On the opposite side of the way the side door of a flourishing little establishment opened, and a man and his wife and a little boy in a sailor suit came into the street. The wife was a pretty woman in brown with a floriferous straw hat, and the group was altogether very Sundayfied and shiny and spick and span. The shop itself had a large plate-glass window whose contents were now veiled by a buff blind on which was inscribed in scrolly letters: "Rymer, Pork Butcher and Provision Merchant," and then with voluptuous elaboration: "The World-Famed Easewood Sausage."

Greetings were exchanged between Mr. Johnson and this distinguished comestible.

"Off to church already?" said Johnson.

"Walking across the fields to Little Dorington," said Mr. Rymer.

"Very pleasant walk," said Johnson.

"Very," said Mr. Rymer.

"Hope you'll enjoy it," said Mr. Johnson.

"That chap's done well," said Johnson sotto voce as they went on. "Came here with nothing—practically, four years ago. And as thin as a lath. Look at him now!"

"He's worked hard of course," said Johnson, improving the occasion.

Thought fell between the cousins for a space.

"Some men can do one thing," said Johnson, "and some another. . . . For a man who sticks to it there's a lot to be done in a shop."

3

All the preparations for the funeral ran easily and happily under Mrs. Johnson's skillful hands. On the eve of the sad event she produced a reserve of black sateen, the kitchen steps and a box of tintacks, and decorated the house with festoons and bows of black in the best possible taste. She tied up the knocker with black crape, and put a large bow over the corner of the steel engraving of Garibaldi, and swathed the bust of Mr. Gladstone, that had belonged to the deceased, with inky swathings. She turned the two vases that had views of Tivoli and the Bay of Naples round, so that these rather brilliant landscapes were hidden and only the plain blue enamel showed, and she anticipated the long-contemplated purchase of a tablecloth for the front room, and substituted a violet purple cover for the now very worn and faded raptures and roses in plushette that had hitherto done duty there. Everything that loving consideration could do to impart a dignified solemnity to her little home was done.

She had released Mr. Polly from the irksome duty of issuing invitations, and as the moment of assembly drew near she sent him and Mr. Johnson out into the narrow long strip of garden at the back of the house, to be free to put a finishing touch or so to her preparations. She sent them out together because she had a queer little persuasion at the back of her mind that Mr. Polly wanted to bolt from his sacred duties, and there was no way out of the garden except through the house.

Mr. Johnson was a steady, successful gardner, and particularly good with celery and peas. He walked slowly along the narrow path down the centre pointing out to Mr. Polly a number of interesting points in the management of peas, wrinkles neatly applied and difficulties wisely overcome, and all that he did for the comfort and propitation of that fitful but rewarding vegetable. Presently a sound of nervous laughter and raised voices from the house proclaimed the arrival of the earlier guests, and the worst of that anticipatory tension was over.

When Mr. Polly re-entered the house he found three entirely strange young women with pink faces, demonstrative manners and emphatic mourning, engaged in an incoherent conversation with Mrs. Johnson. All three kissed him with great gusto after the ancient English fashion. "These are your cousins Larkins," said Mrs. Johnson; "that's Annie (unexpected hug and smack), that's Miriam (resolute hug and smack), and that's Minnie (prolonged hug and smack).

"Right-O," said Mr. Polly, emerging a little crumpled and breathless from the hearty introduction. "I see."

"Here's Aunt Larkins," said Mrs. Johnson, as an elderly and stouter edition of the three young women appeared in the doorway.

Mr. Polly backed rather faint-heartedly, but Aunt Larkins was not to be denied. Having hugged and kissed her nephew resoundingly she gripped him by the wrists and scanned his features. She had a round, sentimental, freckled face. "I should 'ave known 'im anywhere," she said with fervour.

"Hark at mother!" said the cousin called Annie. "Why, she's never set eyes on him before!"

"I should 'ave known 'im anywhere," said Mrs. Larkins, "for Lizzie's child. You've got her eyes! It's a Resemblance! And as for never seeing 'im—I've dandled him, Miss Imperence. I've dandled him."

"You couldn't dandle him now, Ma!" Miss Annie remarked with a shriek of laughter.

All the sisters laughed at that. "The things you say, Annie!" said Miriam, and for a time the room was full of mirth.

Mr. Polly felt it incumbent upon him to say something. "My dandling days are over," he said.

The reception of this remark would have convinced a far more modest character than Mr. Polly that it was extremely witty.

Mr. Polly followed it up by another one almost equally good. "My turn to dandle," he said, with a sly look at his aunt, and convulsed everyone.

"Not me," said Mrs. Larkins, taking his point, "thank you," and achieved a climax.

It was queer, but they seemed to be easy people to get on with anyhow. They were still picking little ripples and giggles of mirth from the idea of Mr. Polly dandling Aunt

369

Larkins when Mr. Johnson, who had answered the door, ushered in a stooping figure, who was at once hailed by Mrs. Johnson as "Why! Uncle Pentstemon!" Uncle Pentstemon was rather a shock. His was an aged rather than venerable figure; Time had removed the hair from the top of his head and distributed a small dividend of the plunder in little bunches carelessly and impartially over the rest of his features; he was dressed in a very big old frock coat and a long cylindrical top hat, which he had kept on; he was very much bent, and he carried a rush basket from which protruded coy intimations of the lettuces and onions he had brought to grace the occasion. He hobbled into the room, resisting the efforts of Johnson to divest him of his various encumbrances, halted and surveyed the company with an expression of profound hostility, breathing hard. Recognition quickened in his eyes.

"You here," he said to Aunt Larkins and then; "You would be. . . . These your gals?"

"They are," said Aunt Larkins, "and better gals—"

"That Annie?" asked Uncle Pentstemon, pointing a horny thumb-nail.

"Fancy your remembering her name!"

"She mucked up my mushroom bed, the baggage!" said Uncle Pentstemon ungenially, "and I give it to her to rights. Trounced her I did—fairly. I remember her. Here's some green stuff for you, Grace. Fresh it is and wholesome. I shall be wanting the basket back and mind you let me have it. . . . Have you nailed him down yet? You always was a bit in front of what was needful."

His attention was drawn inward by a troublesome tooth, and he sucked at it spitefully. There was something potent about this old man that silenced everyone for a moment or so. He seemed a fragment from the ruder agricultural past of our race, like a lump of soil among things of paper. He put his basket of vegetables very deliberately on the new violet tablecloth, removed his hat carefully and dabbled his brow, and wiped out his hat brim with a crimson and yellow pocket handkerchief.

"I'm glad you were able to come, Uncle," said Mrs. Johnson.

"Oh, I came," said Uncle Pentstemon. "I came."

He turned on Mrs. Larkins. "Gals in service?" he asked.

"They aren't and they won't be," said Mrs. Larkins.

"No," he said with infinite meaning and turned his eye on Mr. Polly.

"You Lizzie's boy?" he said.

Mr. Polly was spared much self-exposition by the tumult occasioned by further arrivals.

"Ah! Here's May Punt!" said Mrs. Johnson, and a small woman dressed in the borrowed mourning of a large woman and leading a very small long-haired observant little boy—it was his first funeral—appeared, closely followed by several friends of Mrs. Johnson who had come to swell the display of respect and made only vague, confused impressions upon Mr. Polly's mind. (Aunt Mildred, who was an unexplained family scandal, had declined Mrs. Johnson's hospitality.)

Everybody was in profound mourning, of course, mourning in the modern English style, with the dyer's handiwork only too apparent, and hats and jackets of the current cut. There was very little crape, and the costumes had none of the goodness and specialisation and genuine enjoyment of mourning for mourning's sake that a similar continental gathering would have displayed. Still that congestion of strangers in black sufficed to stun and confuse Mr. Polly's impressionable mind. It seemed to him much more extraordinary than anything he had expected.

"Now, gals," said Mrs. Larkins, "see if you can help," and their three daughters became confusingly active between the front room and the back.

"I hope everyone'll take a glass of sherry and a biscuit," said Mrs. Johnson. "We don't stand on ceremony," and a decanter appeared in the place of Uncle Pentstemon's vegetables.

Uncle Pentstemon had refused to be relieved of his hat; he sat stiffly down on a chair against the wall with that venerable headdress between his feet, watching the approach of anyone jealously. "Don't you go squashing my hat," he said. Conversation became confused and general. Uncle Pentstemon addressed himself to Mr. Polly. "You're a little chap," he said, "a puny little chap. I never did agree to Lizzie marrying him, but I suppose bygones must be bygones now. I suppose they made you a clerk or something."

"Outfitter," said Mr. Polly.

"I remember. Them girls pretend to be dressmakers."

"They are dressmakers," said Mrs. Larkins across the room.

"I will take a glass of sherry. They 'old to it, you see."

He took the glass Mrs. Johnson handed him, and poised it critically between a horny finger and thumb. "You'll be paying for this," he said to Mr. Polly. "Here's *to* you. . . . Don't you go treading on my hat, young woman. You brush your skirts against it and you take a shillin' off its value. It ain't the sort of 'at you see nowadays."

He drank noisily.

The sherry presently loosened everybody's tongue, and the early coldness passed.

"There ought to have been a *post-mortem*," Polly heard Mrs. Punt remarking to one of Mrs. Johnson's friends, and Miriam and another were lost in admiration of Mrs. Johnson's decorations. "So very nice and refined," they were both repeating at intervals.

The sherry and biscuits were still being discussed when Mr. Podger, the undertaker, arrived, a broad, cheerfully sorrowful, clean-shaven little man, accompanied by a melancholy-faced assistant. He conversed for a time with Johnston in the passage outside; the sense of his business stilled the rising waves of chatter and carried off everyone's attention in the wake of his heavy footsteps to the room above.

### 4

Things crowded upon Mr. Polly. Everyone, he noticed, took sherry with a solemn avidity, and a small portion even was administered sacramentally to the Punt boy.

There followed a distribution of black kid gloves, and much trying on and humouring of fingers. "Good gloves," said one of Mrs. Johnson's friends. "There's a little pair there for Willie," said Mrs. Johnson triumphantly. Everyone seemed gravely content with the amazing procedure of the occasion. Presently Mr. Podger was picking Mr. Polly out as Chief Mourner to go with Mrs. Johnson, Mrs. Larkins and Annie in the first mourning carriage.

"Right O," said Mr. Polly, and repented instantly of the alacrity of the phrase.

"There'll have to be a walking party," said Mrs. Johnson cheerfully. "There's only two coaches. I dare say we can put in six in each, but that leaves three over."

There was a generous struggle to be pedestrian, and the two other Larkins girls, confessing coyly to tight new boots and displaying a certain eagerness, were added to the contents of the first carriage.

"It'll be a squeeze," said Annie.

"I don't mind a squeeze," said Mr. Polly.

He decided privately that the proper phrase for the result of that remark was "Hysterial catechunations."

Mr. Podger re-entered the room from a momentary supervision of the bumping business that was now proceeding down the staircase.

"Bearing up," he said cheerfully, rubbing his hands together. "Bearing up!"

That stuck very vividly in Mr. Polly's mind, and so did the close-wedged drive to the churchyard, bunched in between two young women in confused dull and shiny black, and the fact that the wind was bleak and that the officiating clergyman had a cold, and sniffed between his sentences. The wonder of life! The wonder of everything! What had he expected that this should all be so astoundingly different.

He found his attention converging more and more upon the Larkins cousins. The interest was reciprocal. They watched him with a kind of suppressed excitement and became risible with his every word and gesture. He was more and more aware of their personal quality. Annie had blue eyes and a red, attractive mouth, a harsh voice and a habit of extreme liveliness that even this occasion could not suppress; Minnie was fond, extremely free about the touching of hands and suchlike endearments; Miriam was quieter and regarded him earnestly. Mrs. Larkins was very happy in her daughters, and they had the naïve affectionateness of those who see few people and find a strange cousin a wonderful outlet. Mr. Polly had never been very much kissed, and it made his mind swim. He did not know for the life of him whether he liked or disliked all or any of the Larkins cousins. It was rather attractive to make them laugh; they laughed at anything.

There they were tugging at his mind, and the funeral tugging at his mind, too, and the sense of himself as Chief Mourner in a brand new silk hat with a broad mourning band. He watched the ceremony and missed his responses, and strange feelings twisted at his heart-strings.

## 5

Mr. Polly walked back to the house because he wanted to be alone. Miriam and Minnie would have accompanied him, but finding Uncle Pentstermon beside the Chief Mourner they went on in front.

"You're wise," said Uncle Pentstemon.

"Glad you think so," said Mr. Polly, rousing himself to talk.

"I likes a bit of walking before a meal," said Uncle Pentstemon, and made a kind of large hiccup. "That sherry rises," he remarked. "Grocer's stuff, I expect."

He went on to ask how much the funeral might be costing, and seemed pleased to find Mr. Polly didn't know.

"In that case," he said impressively, "it's pretty certain to cost more'n you expect, my boy."

He mediated for a time. "I've seen a mort of undertakers," he declared; "a mort of undertakers."

The Larkins girls attracted his attention.

"Let's lodgin's and chars," he commented. "Least-ways she goes out to cook dinners. And look at 'em!

"Dressed up to the nines. If it ain't borryd clothes, that is. And they goes out to work at a factory!"

"Did you know my father much, Uncle Pentstemon?" asked Mr. Polly.

"Couldn't stand Lizzie throwin' herself away like that," said Uncle Pentstemon, and repeated his hiccup on a larger scale.

"That *weren't* good sherry," said Uncle Pentstemon with the first note of pathos Mr. Polly had detected in his quavering voice.

The funeral in the rather cold wind had proved wonderfully appetising, and every eye brightened at the sight of the cold collation that was now spread in the front room. Mrs. Johnson was very brisk, and Mr. Polly, when he re-entered the house found everybody sitting down. "Come along, Alfred," cried the host cheerfully. "We can't very well begin without you. Have you got the bottled beer ready to open, Betsy? Uncle, you'll have a drop of whiskey, I expect."

"Put it where I can mix for myself," said Uncle Pentstemon, placing his hat very carefully out of harm's way on the bookcase.

There were two cold boiled chickens, which Johnson carved with great care and justice, and a nice piece of ham, some brawn and a steak and kidney pie, a large bowl of salad and several sorts of pickles, and afterwards came cold apple tart, jam roll and a good piece of Stilton cheese, lots of bottled beer, some lemonade for the ladies and milk for the Master Punt; a very bright and satisfying meal. Mr. Polly found himself seated between Mrs. Punt, who was much preoccupied with Master Punt's table manners, and one of Mrs. Johnson's school friends, who was exchanging reminiscences of school days and news of how various common friends had changed and married with Mrs. Johnson. Opposite him was Miriam and another of the Johnson circle, and also he had brawn to carve and there was hardly room for the helpful Betsy to pass behind his chair, so that altogether his mind would have been amply distracted from any mortuary broodings, even if a wordy warfare about the education of the modern young woman had not sprung up between Uncle Pentstemon and Mrs. Larkins and threatened for a time, in spite of a word or so in season from Johnson, to wreck all the harmony of the sad occasion.

The general effect was after this fashion:

First an impression of Mrs. Punt on the right speaking in a refined undertone: "You didn't, I suppose, Mr. Polly, think to 'ave your poor dear father post-mortemed—"

Lady on the left side breaking in: "I was just reminding Grace of the dear dead days beyond recall—"

Attempted replay to Mrs. Punt: "Didn't think of it for a moment. Can't give you a piece of this brawn, can I?"

Fragment from the left: "Grace and Beauty they used to call us and we used to sit at the same desk—"

Mrs. Punt, breaking out suddenly: "Don't swaller your fork, Willy. You see, Mr. Polly, I used to 'ave a young gentleman, a medical student, lodging with me—"

Voice from down the table: "'Am, Alfred? I didn't give you very much."

Bessie became evident at the back of Mr. Polly's chair, struggling wildly to get past. Mr. Polly did his best to be helpful. "Can you get past? Lemme sit forward a bit. Urr-oo! Right O."

Lady to the left going on valiantly and speaking to everyone who cares to listen, while Mrs. Johnson beams beside her: "There she used to sit as bold as brass, and the fun she used to make of things no one could believe—knowing her now. She used to make faces at the mistress through the—"

Mrs. Punt keeping steadily on: "The contents of the stummik at any rate ought to be examined."

Voice of Mr. Johnson. "Elfrid, pass the mustid down."

Miriam leaning across the table: "Elfrid!"

"Once she got us all kept in. The whole school!"

Miriam, more insistently: "Elfrid!"

Uncle Pentstemon, raising his voice defiantly: "Trounce 'er again I would if she did as much now. That I would! Dratted mischief!"

Miriam, catching Mr. Polly's eye: "Elfrid! This lady knows Canterbury. I been telling her you been there."

Mr. Polly: "Glad you know it."

The lady shouting: "I like it."

Mrs. Larkins, raising her voice: "I won't 'ave my girls spoken of, not by nobody, old or young."

POP! imperfectly located.

Mr. Johnson at large: "*Ain't* the beer up! It's the 'eated room."

Bessie: "Scuse me, sir, passing so soon again, but—" Rest inaudible. Mr. Polly, accommodating himself: "Urr-oo! Right? Right O."

The knives and forks, probably by some secret common agreement, clash and clatter together and drown every other sound.

"Nobody 'ad the least idea 'ow 'E died,—nobody. . . . Willie, don't *golp* so. You ain't in a 'urry, are you? You don't want to ketch a train or anything,—golping like that!"

"D'you remember, Grace, 'ow one day we 'ad writing lesson. . . . "

"Nicer girls no one ever 'ad—though I say it who shouldn't."

Mrs. Johnson in a shrill clear hospitable voice: "Harold, won't Mrs. Larkins 'ave a teeny bit more fowl?"

Mr. Polly rising to the situation. "Or some brawn, Mrs. Larkins?" Catching Uncle Pentstemon's eye: "Can't send you some brawn, sir?"

"Elfrid!"

Loud hiccup from Uncle Pentstemon, momentary consternation followed by giggle from Annie.

The narration at Mr. Polly's elbow pursued a quiet but relentless course. "Directly the new doctor came in he said: 'Everything must be took out and put in spirits—everything.'"

Willie,—audible ingurgitation.

The narration on the left was flourishing up to a climax. "Ladies," she sez, "dip their pens in their ink and keep their noses out of it!"

"Elfrid!"—persuasively.

"Certain people may cast snacks at other people's daughters, never having had any of their own, though two poor souls of wives dead and buried through their goings on—"

Johnson ruling the storm: "We don't want old scores dug up on such a day as this—"

"Old scores you may call them, but worth a dozen of them that put them to their rest, poor dears."

"Elfrid!"—with a note of remonstrance.

"If you choke yourself, my lord, not another mouthful do you 'ave. No nice puddin'! Nothing!"

"And kept us in, she did, every afternoon for a week!"

It seemed to be the end, and Mr. Polly replied with an air or being profoundly impressed: "Really!"

"Elfrid!"—a little disheartened.

"And then they 'ad it! They found he'd swallowed the very key to unlock the drawer—"

"Then don't let people go casting snacks!"

"*Who's* casting snacks!"

"Elfrid! This lady wants to know, 'ave the Prossers left Canterbury?"

"No wish to make myself disagreeable, not to God's 'umblest worm—"

"Alf, you aren't very busy with that brawn up there!"

And so on for the hour.

The general effect upon Mr. Polly at the time was at once confusing and exhilarating; but it led him to eat copiously and carelessly, and long before the end, when after an hour and a quarter a movement took the party, and it pushed away its cheese plates and rose sighing and stretching from the remains of the repast, little streaks and bands of dyspeptic irritation and melancholy were darkening the serenity of his mind.

He stood between the mantel shelf and the window—the blinds were up now—and the Larkins sisters clustered about him. He battled with the oncoming depression and forced himself to be extremely facetious about two noticeable rings on Annie's hand. "They ain't real," said Annie coquettishly. "Got 'em out of a prize packet."

"Prize packet in trousers, I expect," said Mr. Polly, and awakened inextinguishable laughter.

"Oh! the things you say!" said Minnie, slapping his shoulder.

Suddenly something he had quite extraordinarily forgotten came into his head.

"Bless my heart!"" he cried, suddenly serious.

"What's the matter?" asked Johnson.

"Ought to have gone back to shop—three days ago. They'll make no end of a row!"

"Lor, you are a Treat!" said cousin Annie, and screamed with laughter at a delicious idea. "You'll get the Chuck," she said.

Mr. Polly made a convulsing grimace at her.

"I'll die!" she said. "I don't believe you care a bit!"

Feeling a little disorganized by her hilarity and a shocked expression that had come to the face of cousin Miriam, he made some indistinct excuse and went out through the back room and scullery into the little garden. The cool air and a very slight drizzle of rain was a relief—anyhow. But the black mood of the replete dyspeptic had come upon him. His soul darkened hopelessly. He walked with his hands in his pockets down the path between the rows of exceptionally cultured peas and unreasonably, overwhelmingly, he was smitten by sorrow for his father. The heady noise and muddle and confused excitement of the feast passed from him like a curtain drawn away. He thought of that hot and angry and struggling creature who had tugged and sworn so foolishly at the sofa upon the twisted staircase, and who was now lying still and hidden, at the bottom of a wall-sided oblong pit beside the heaped gravel that would presently cover him. The stillness of it! the wonder of it! the infinite reproach! Hatred for all these people—all of them—possessed Mr. Polly's soul.

"Hen-witted gigglers," said Mr. Polly.

He went down to the fence, and stood with his hands on it staring away at nothing. He stayed there for what seemed a long time. From the house came a sound of raised voices that subsided, and then Mrs. Johnson calling for Bessie.

"Gowlish gusto," said Mr. Polly. "Jumping it in. Funererial Games. Don't hurt him of course. Doesn't matter to *him.* . . ."

Nobody missed Mr. Polly for a long time.

When at last he reappeared among them his eye was almost grim, but nobody noticed his eye. They were looking at watches, and Johnson was being omniscient about trains. They seemed to discover Mr. Polly afresh just as the moment of parting, and said a number of more or less appropriate things. But Uncle Pentstemon was far too worried about his rush basket, which had been carelessly mislaid, he seemed to think with larcenous intentions, to remember Mr. Polly at all. Mrs. Johnson had tried to fob him off with a similar but inferior basket,—his own had one handle mended with string according to a method of peculiar virtue and inimitable distinction known only to himself—and the old gentleman had taken her attempt as the gravest reflection upon his years and intelligence. Mr. Polly was left very largely to the Larkins trio. Cousin Minnie became shameless and kept kissing him good-by—and then finding out it wasn't time to go. Cousin Miriam seemed to think her silly, and caught Mr. Polly's eye sympathetically. Cousin Annie ceased to giggle and lapsed into a nearly sentimental state. She said with real feeling that she had enjoyed the funeral more than words could tell.

CHAPTER THE FIFTH<br>MR. POLLY TAKES A VACATION<br>1

Mr. Polly returned to Clapham from the funeral celebration prepared for trouble, and took his dismissal in a manly spirit.

"You've merely anti-*separated* me by a hair," he said politely.

And he told them in the dormitory that he meant to take a little holiday before his next crib, though a certain inherited reticence suppressed the fact of the legacy.

"You'll do that all right," said Ascough, the head of the boot shop. "It's quite the fashion just at present. Six Weeks in Wonderful Wood Street. They're running excursions. . . ."

"A little holiday"; that was the form his sense of wealth took first, that it made a little holiday possible. Holidays were his life, and the rest merely adulterated living. And now he might take a little holiday and have money for railway fares and money for meals and money for inns. But—he wanted someone to take the holiday with.

For a time he cherished a design of hunting up Parsons, getting him to throw up his situation, and going with him to Stratford-on-Avon and Shrewsbury and the Welsh mountains and the Wye and a lot of places like that, for a really gorgeous, careless, illimitable old holiday of a month. But alas! Parsons had gone from the St. Paul's Churchyard outfitter's long ago, and left no address.

Mr. Polly tried to think he would be almost as happy wandering alone, but he knew better. He had dreamt of casual encounters with delightfully interesting people

377

by the wayside—even romantic encounters. Such things happened in Chaucer and "Bocashiew," they happened with extreme facility in Mr. Richard Le Gallienne's very detrimental book, *The Quest of the Golden Girl*, which he had read at Canterbury, but he had no confidence they would happen in England—to him.

When, a month later, he came out of the Clapham side door at last into the bright sunshine of a fine London day, with a dazzling sense of limitless freedom upon him, he did nothing more adventurous than order the cabman to drive to Waterloo, and there take a ticket for Easewood.

He wanted—what did he want most in life? I think his distinctive craving is best expressed as fun—fun in companionship. He had already spent a pound or two upon three select feasts to his fellow assistants, sprat suppers they were, and there had been a great and very successful Sunday pilgrimage to Richmond, by Wandsworth and Wimbledon's open common, a trailing garrulous company walking about a solemnly happy host, to wonderful cold meat and salad at the Roebuck, a bowl of punch, punch! and a bill to correspond; but now it was a week-day, and he went down to Easewood with his bag and portmanteau in a solitary compartment, and looked out of the window upon a world in which every possible congeniality seemed either toiling in a situation or else looking for one with a gnawing and hopelessly preoccupying anxiety. He stared out of the window at the exploitation roads of suburbs, and rows of houses all very much alike, either emphatically and impatiently to LET or full of rather busy unsocial people. Near Wimbledon he had a glimpse of golf links, and saw two elderly gentlemen who, had they chosen, might have been gentleman of grace and leisure, addressing themselves to smite little hunted white balls great distances with the utmost bitterness and dexterity. Mr. Polly could not understand them.

Every road he remarked, as freshly as though he had never observed it before, was bordered by inflexible palings or iron fences or severely disciplined hedges. He wondered if perhaps abroad there might be beautifully careless, unenclosed high roads. Perhaps after all the best way of taking a holiday is to go abroad.

He was haunted by the memory of what was either a half-forgotten picture or a dream; a carriage was drawn up by the wayside and four beautiful people, two men and two women graciously dressed, were dancing a formal ceremonious dance full of bows and curtseys, to the music of a wandering fiddler they had encountered. They had been driving one way and he walking another—a happy encounter with this obvious result. They might have come straight out of happy Theleme, whose motto is: "Do what thou wilt." The driver had taken his two sleek horses out; they grazed unchallenged; and he sat on a stone clapping time with his hands while the fiddler played. The shade of the trees did not altogether shut out the sunshine, the grass in the wood was lush and full of still daffodils, the turf they danced on was starred with daisies.

Mr. Polly, dear heart! firmly believed that things like that could and did happen— somewhere. Only it puzzled him that morning that he never saw them happening. Perhaps they happened south of Guilford. Perhaps they happened in Italy. Perhaps they ceased to happen a hundred years ago. Perhaps they happened just round the corner—on weekdays when all good Mr. Pollys are safely shut up in shops. And so dreaming of delightful impossibilities until his heart ached for them, he was rattled along in the suburban train to Johnson's discreet home and the briskly stimulating welcome of Mrs. Johnson.

## 2

Mr. Polly translated his restless craving for joy and leisure into Harold-Johnsonese by saying that he meant to look about him for a bit before going into another situation. It was a decision Johnson very warmly approved. It was arranged that Mr. Polly should occupy his former room and board with the Johnsons in consideration of a weekly payment of eighteen shillings. And the next morning Mr. Polly went out early and reappeared with a purchase, a safety bicycle, which he proposed to study and master in the sandy lane below the Johnson's house. But over the struggles that preceded his mastery it is humane to draw a veil.

And also Mr. Polly bought a number of books, Rabelais for his own, and "The Arabian Nights," the works of Sterne, a pile of "Tales from Blackwood," cheap in a second-hand bookshop, the plays of William Shakespeare, a second-hand copy of Belloc's "Road to Rome," an odd volume of "Purchas his Pilgrimes" and "The Life and Death of Jason."

"Better get yourself a good book on bookkeeping," said Johnson, turning over perplexing pages.

A belated spring was now advancing with great strides to make up for lost time. Sunshine and a stirring wind were poured out over the land, fleets of towering clouds sailed upon urgent tremendous missions across the blue seas of heaven, and presently Mr. Polly was riding a little unstably along unfamiliar Surrey roads, wondering always what was round the next corner, and marking the blackthorn and looking out for the first white flowerbuds of the May. He was perplexed and distressed, as indeed are all right thinking souls, that there is no may in early May.

He did not ride at the even pace sensible people use who have marked out a journey from one place to another, and settled what time it will take them. He rode at variable speeds, and always as though he was looking for something that, missing, left life attractive still, but a little wanting in significance. And sometime, he was so unreasonably happy he had to whistle and sing, and sometimes he was incredibly, but not at all painfully, sad. His indigestion vanished with air and exercise, and it was quite pleasant in the evening to stroll about the garden with Johnson and discuss plans for the future. Johnson was full of ideas. Moreover, Mr. Polly had marked the road that led to Stamton, that rising populous suburb; and as his bicycle legs grew strong his wheel with a sort of inevitableness carried him towards the row of houses in a back street in which his Larkins cousins made their home together.

He was received with great enthusiasm.

379

The street was a dingy little street, a *cul-de-sac* of very small houses in a row, each with an almost flattened bow window and a blistered brown door with a black knocker. He poised his bright new bicycle against the window, and knocked and stood waiting, and felt himself in his straw hat and black serge suit a very pleasant and prosperous-looking figure. The door was opened by cousin Miriam. She was wearing a bluish print dress that brought out a kind of sallow warmth in her skin, and although it was nearly four o'clock in the afternoon, her sleeves were tucked up, as if for some domestic work, above the elbows, showing her rather slender but very shapely yellowish arms. The loosely pinned bodice confessed a delicately rounded neck.

For a moment she regarded him with suspicion and a faint hostility, and then recognition dawned in her eyes.

"Why!" she said, "it's cousin Elfrid!"

"Thought I'd look you up," he said.

"Fancy! you coming to see us like this!" she answered.

They stood confronting one another for a moment, while Miriam collected herself for the unexpected emergency.

"Exploratious meanderings," said Mr. Polly, indicating the bicycle.

Miriam's face betrayed no appreciation of the remark.

"Wait a moment," she said, coming to a rapid decision, "and I'll tell Ma."

She closed the door on him abruptly, leaving him a little surprised in the street. "Ma!" he heard her calling, and swift speech followed, the import of which he didn't catch. Then she reappeared. It seemed but an instant, but she was changed; the arms had vanished into sleeves, the apron had gone, a certain pleasing disorder of the hair had been at least reproved.

"I didn't mean to shut you out," she said, coming out upon the step. "I just told Ma. How are you, Elfrid? You are looking well. I didn't know you rode a bicycle. Is it a new one?"

She leaned upon his bicycle. "Bright it is!" she said. "What a trouble you must have to keep it clean!"

Mr. Polly was aware of a rustling transit along the passage, and of the house suddenly full of hushed but strenuous movement.

"It's plated mostly," said Mr. Polly.

"What do you carry in that little bag thing?" she asked, and then branched off to: "We're all in a mess to-day you know. It's my cleaning up day to-day. I'm not a bit tidy I know, but I do like to 'ave a go in at things now and then. You got to take us as you find us, Elfrid. Mercy we wasn't all out." She paused. She was talking against time. "I am glad to see you again," she repeated.

"Couldn't keep away," said Mr. Polly gallantly. "Had to come over and see my pretty cousins again."

Miriam did not answer for a moment. She coloured deeply. "You do say things!" she said.

She stared at Mr. Polly, and his unfortunate sense of fitness made him nod his head toward her, regard her firmly with a round brown eye, and add impressively: "I don't say which of them."

Her answering expression made him realise for an instant the terrible dangers he trifled with. Avidity flared up in her eyes. Minnie's voice came happily to dissolve the situation.

"'Ello, Elfrid!" she said from the doorstep.

Her hair was just passably tidy, and she was a little effaced by a red blouse, but there was no mistaking the genuine brightness of her welcome.

He was to come in to tea, and Mrs. Larkins, exuberantly genial in a floriferous but dingy flannel dressing gown, appeared to confirm that. He brought in his bicycle and put it in the narrow, empty passage, and everyone crowded into a small untidy kitchen, whose table had been hastily cleared of the debris of the midday repast.

"You must come in 'ere," said Mrs. Larkins, "for Miriam's turning out the front room. I never did see such a girl for cleanin' up. Miriam's 'oliday's a scrub. You've caught us on the 'Op as the sayin' is, but Welcome all the same. Pity Annie's at work to-day; she won't be 'ome till seven."

Miriam put chairs and attended to the fire, Minnie edged up to Mr. Polly and said: "I am glad to see you again, Elfrid," with a warm contiguous intimacy that betrayed a broken tooth. Mrs. Larkins got out tea things, and descanted on the noble simplicity of their lives, and how he "mustn't mind our simple ways." They enveloped Mr. Polly with a geniality that intoxicated his amiable nature; he insisted upon helping lay the things, and created enormous laughter by pretending not to know where plates and knives and cups ought to go. "Who'm I going to sit next?" he said, and developed voluminous amusement by attempts to arrange the plates so that he could rub elbows with all three. Mrs. Larkins had to sit down in the windsor chair by the grandfather clock (which was dark with dirt and not going) to laugh at her ease at his well-acted perplexity.

They got seated at last, and Mr. Polly struck a vein of humour in telling them how he learnt to ride the bicycle. He found the mere repetition of the word "wabble" sufficient to produce almost inextinguishable mirth.

"No foreseeing little accidentulous misadventures," he said, "none whatever."

(Giggle from Minnie.)

"Stout elderly gentleman—shirt sleeves—large straw wastepaper basket sort of hat—starts to cross the road—going to the oil shop—prodic refreshment of oil can—"

"Don't say you run 'im down," said Mrs. Larkins, gasping. "Don't say you run 'im down, Elfrid!"

"Run 'im down! Not me, Madam. I never run anything down. Wabble. Ring the bell. Wabble, wabble—"

(Laughter and tears.)

"No one's going to run him down. Hears the bell! Wabble. Gust of wind. Off comes the hat smack into the wheel. Wabble. Lord! *What's going* to happen? Hat across the road, old gentleman after it, bell, shriek. He ran into me. Didn't ring his bell, hadn't got a bell—just ran into me. Over I went clinging to his venerable head. Down he went with me clinging to him. Oil can blump, blump into the road."

(Interlude while Minnie is attended to for crumb in the windpipe.)

"Well, what happened to the old man with the oil can?" said Mrs. Larkins.

"We sat about among the debreece and had a bit of an argument. I told him he oughtn't to come out wearing such a dangerous hat—flying at things. Said if he couldn't control his hat he ought to leave it at home. High old jawbacious argument we had, I tell you. 'I tell you, sir—' "I tell *you*, sir.' Waw-waw-waw. Infuriacious. But that's the sort of thing that's constantly happening you know—on a bicycle. People run into you, hens and cats and dogs and things. Everything seems to have its mark on you; everything."

"*You* never run into anything."

"Never. Swelpme," said Mr. Polly very solemnly.

"Never, 'E say!" squealed Minnie. "Hark at 'im!" and relapsed into a condition that urgently demanded back thumping. "Don't be so silly," said Miriam, thumping hard.

Mr. Polly had never been such a social success before. They hung upon his every word—and laughed. What a family they were for laughter! And he loved laughter. The background he apprehended dimly; it was very much the sort of background his life had always had. There was a threadbare tablecloth on the table, and the slop basin and teapot did not go with the cups and saucers, the plates were different again, the knives worn down, the butter lived in a greenish glass dish of its own. Behind was a dresser hung with spare and miscellaneous crockery, with a workbox and an untidy work-basket, there was an ailing musk plant in the window, and the tattered and blotched wallpaper was covered by bright-coloured grocer's almanacs. Feminine wrappings hung from pegs upon the door, and the floor was covered with a varied collection of fragments of oilcloth. The windsor chair he sat in was unstable—which presently afforded material for humour. "Steady, old nag," he said; "whoa, my friskiacious palfry!"

"The things he says! You never know what he won't say next!"

### 3

"You ain't talkin' of goin'!" cried Mrs. Larkins.

"Supper at eight."

"Stay to supper with us, now you 'ave come over," said Mrs. Larkins, with corroborating cries from Minnie. "'Ave a bit of a walk with the gals, and then come back to supper. You might all go and meet Annie while I straighten up, and lay things out."

"You're not to go touching the front room mind," said Miriam.

"Who's going to touch yer front room?" said Mrs. Larkins, apparently forgetful for a moment of Mr. Polly.

Both girls dressed with some care while Mrs. Larkins sketched the better side of their characters, and then the three young people went out to see something of Stamton. In the streets their risible mood gave way to a self-conscious propriety that was particularly evident in Miriam's bearing. They took Mr. Polly to the Stamton Wreckery-ation ground—that at least was what they called it—with its handsome custodian's cottage, its asphalt paths, its Jubilee drinking fountain, its clumps of wallflower and daffodils, and so to the new cemetery and a distant view of the Surrey hills, and round by the gasworks to the canal to the factory, that presently disgorged a surprised and radiant Annie.

"El-*lo!*" said Annie.

It is very pleasant to every properly constituted mind to be a centre of amiable interest for one's fellow creatures, and when one is a young man conscious of becoming mourning and a certain wit, and the fellow creatures are three young and ardent and sufficiently expressive young women who dispute for the honour of walking by one's side, one may be excused a secret exaltation. They did dispute.

"I'm going to 'ave 'im now," said Annie. "You two've been 'aving 'im all the afternoon. Besides, I've got something to say to him."

She had something to say to him. It came presently. "I say," she said abruptly. "I *did* get them rings out of a prize packet."

"What rings?" asked Mr. Polly.

"What you saw at your poor father's funeral. You made out they meant something. They didn't—straight."

"Then some people have been very remiss about their chances," said Mr. Polly, understanding.

"They haven't had any chances," said Annie. "I don't believe in making oneself too free with people."

"Nor me," said Mr. Polly.

"I may be a bit larky and cheerful in my manner," Annie admitted. "But it don't *mean* anything. I ain't that sort."

"Right O," said Mr. Polly.

<br>

### 4

It was past ten when Mr. Polly found himself riding back towards Easewood in a broad moonlight with a little Japanese lantern dangling from his handle bar and making a fiery circle of pinkish light on and round about his front wheel. He was mightily please with himself and the day. There had been four-ale to drink at supper mixed with gingerbeer, very free and jolly in a jug. No shadow fell upon the agreeable excitement of his mind until he faced the anxious and reproachful face of Johnson, who had been sitting up for him, smoking and trying to read the odd volume of "Purchas his Pilgrimes,"—about the monk who went into Sarmatia and saw the Tartar carts.

"Not had an accident, Elfrid?" said Johnson.

The weakness of Mr. Polly's character came out in his reply. "Not much," he said. "Pedal got a bit loose in Stamton, O' Man. Couldn't ride it. So I looked up the cousins while I waited."

"Not the Larkins lot?"

"Yes."

Johnson yawned hugely and asked for and was given friendly particulars. "Well," he said, "better get to bed. I have been reading that book of yours—rum stuff. Can't make it out quite. Quite out of date I should say if you asked me."

"That's all right, O' Man," said Mr. Polly.

"Not a bit of use for anything I can see.'

"Not a bit."

"See any shops in Stamton?"

"Nothing to speak of," said Mr. Polly. "Goo-night, O' Man."

Before and after this brief conversation his mind ran on his cousins very warmly and prettily in the vein of high spring. Mr. Polly had been drinking at the poisoned fountains of English literature, fountains so unsuited to the needs of a decent clerk or shopman, fountains charged with the dangerous suggestion that it becomes a man of gaiety and spirit to make love, gallantly and rather carelessly. It seemed to him that evening to be handsome and humorous and practicable to make love to all his cousins. It wasn't that he liked any of them particularly, but he liked something about them. He liked their youth and femininity, their resolute high spirits and their interest in him.

They laughed at nothing and knew nothing, and Minnie had lost a tooth and Annie screamed and shouted, but they were interesting, intensely interesting.

And Miriam wasn't so bad as the others. He had kissed them all and had been kissed in addition several times by Minnie,—"scoolatory exercise."

He buried his nose in his pillow and went to sleep—to dream of anything rather than getting on in the world, as a sensible young man in his position ought to have done.

## 5

And now Mr. Polly began to lead a divided life. With the Johnsons he professed to be inclined, but not so conclusively inclined as to be inconvenient, to get a shop for himself, to be, to use the phrase he preferred, "looking for an opening." He would ride off in the afternoon upon that research, remarking that he was going to "cast a strategitical eye" on Chertsey or Weybridge. But if not all roads, still a great majority of them, led by however devious ways to Stamton, and to laughter and increasing familiarity. Relations developed with Annie and Minnie and Miriam. Their various characters were increasingly interesting. The laughter became perceptibly less abundant, something of the fizz had gone from the first opening, still these visits remained wonderfully friendly and upholding. Then back he would come to grave but evasive discussions with Johnson.

Johnson was really anxious to get Mr. Polly "into something." His was a reserved honest character, and he would really have preferred to see his lodger doing things for himself than receive his money for housekeeping. He hated waste, anybody's waste, much more than he desired profit. But Mrs. Johnson was all for Mr. Polly's loitering. She seemed much the more human and likeable of the two to Mr. Polly.

He tried at times to work up enthusiasm for the various avenues to well-being his discussion with Johnson opened. But they remained disheartening prospects. He imagined himself wonderfully smartened up, acquiring style and value in a London shop, but the picture was stiff and unconvincing. He tried to rouse himself to enthusiasm by the idea of his property increasing by leaps and bounds, by twenty pounds a year or so, let us say, each year, in a well-placed little shop, the corner shop Johnson favoured. There was a certain picturesque interest in imagining cut-throat economies, but his heart told him there would be little in practising them.

And then it happened to Mr. Polly that real Romance came out of dreamland into life, and intoxicated and gladdened him with sweetly beautiful suggestions—and left him. She came and left him as that dear lady leaves so many of us, alas! not sparing him one jot or one tittle of the hollowness of her retreating aspect.

It was all the more to Mr. Polly's taste that the thing should happen as things happen in books.

In a resolute attempt not to get to Stamton that day, he had turned due southward from Easewood towards a country where the abundance of bracken jungles, lady's smock, stitchwork, bluebells and grassy stretches by the wayside under shady trees does much to compensate the lighter type of mind for the absence of promising "openings." He turned aside from the road, wheeled his machine along a faintly marked attractive trail through bracken until he came to a heap of logs against a high old stone wall with a damaged coping and wallflower plants already gone to seed. He sat down, balanced the straw hat on a convenient lump of wood, lit a cigarette, and abandoned himself to agreeable musings and the friendly observation of a cheerful little brown and grey bird his stillness presently encouraged to approach him. "This is All Right," said Mr. Polly softly to the little brown and grey bird. "Business—later."

He reflected that he might go on this way for four or five years, and then be scarcely worse off than he had been in his father's lifetime.

"Vile Business," said Mr. Polly.

Then Romance appeared. Or to be exact, Romance became audible.

Romance began as a series of small but increasingly vigorous movements on the other side of the wall, then as a voice murmuring, then as a falling of little fragments on the hither side and as ten pink finger tips, scarcely apprehended before Romance became startling and emphatically a leg, remained for a time a fine, slender, actively struggling limb, brown stockinged and wearing a brown toe-worn shoe, and then—. A handsome red-haired girl wearing a short dress of blue linen was sitting astride the wall, panting, considerably disarranged by her climbing, and as yet unaware of Mr. Polly. . . .

His fine instincts made him turn his head away and assume an attitude of negligent contemplation, with his ears and mind alive to every sound behind him.

"Goodness!" said a voice with a sharp note of surprise.

Mr. Polly was on his feet in an instant. "Dear me! Can I be of any assistance?" he said with deferential gallantry.

"I don't know," said the young lady, and regarded him calmly with clear blue eyes.

"I didn't know there was anyone here," she added.

"Sorry," said Mr. Polly, "if I am intrudaceous. I didn't know you didn't want me to be here."

She reflected for a moment on the word.

"It isn't that," she said, surveying him.

"I oughtn't to get over the wall," she explained. "It's out of bounds. At least in term time. But this being holidays—"

Her manner placed the matter before him.

"Holidays is different," said Mr. Polly.

"I don't want to actually break the rules," she said.

"Leave them behind you," said Mr. Polly with a catch of the breath, "where they are safe," and marvelling at his own wit and daring, and indeed trembling within himself, he held out a hand for her.

She brought another brown leg from the unknown, and arranged her skirt with a dexterity altogether feminine. "I think I'll stay on the wall," she decided. "So long as some of me's in bounds—"

She continued to regard him with eyes that presently joined dancing in an irresistible smile of satisfaction. Mr. Polly smiled in return.

"You bicycle?" she said.

Mr. Polly admitted the fact, and she said she did too.

"All *my* people are in India," she explained. "It's beastly rot—I mean it's frightfully dull being left here alone."

"All my people," said Mr. Polly, "are in Heaven!"

"I say!"

"Fact!" said Mr. Polly. "Got nobody."

"And that's why—" she checked her artless comment on his mourning. "I say," she said in a sympathetic voice, "I am sorry. I really am. Was it a fire or a ship—or something?"

Her sympathy was very delightful. He shook his head. "The ordinary table of mortality," he said. "First one and then another."

Behind his outward melancholy, delight was dancing wildly. "Are you lonely?" asked the girl.

Mr. Polly nodded.

"I was just sitting there in melancholy rectrospectitiousness," he said, indicating the logs, and again a swift thoughtfulness swept across her face.

"There's no harm in our talking," she reflected.

"It's a kindness. Won't you get down?"

She reflected, and surveyed the turf below and the scene around him.

"I'll stay on the wall," she said. "If only for bounds' sake."

She certainly looked quite adorable on the wall. She had a fine neck and pointed chin that was particularly admirable from below, and pretty eyes and fine eyebrows are never so pretty as when they look down upon one. But no calculation of that sort, thank Heaven, was going on beneath her ruddy shock of hair.

## 6

"Let's talk," she said, and for a time they were both tongue-tied.

Mr. Polly's literary proclivities had taught him that under such circumstances a strain of gallantry was demanded. And something in his blood repeated that lesson.

"You make me feel like one of those old knights," he said. "Who rode about the country looking for dragons and beautiful maidens and chivalresque adventures."

"Oh!" she said. "Why?"

"Beautiful maiden," he said.

She flushed under her freckles with a quick bright flush those pretty red-haired people have. "Nonsense!" she said.

"You are. I'm not the first to tell you that. A beautiful maiden imprisoned in an enchanted school."

"You wouldn't think it enchanted!"

"And here am I—clad in steel. Well, not exactly, but my fiery war horse is anyhow. Ready to absquatulate all the dragons and rescue you."

She laughed, a jolly laugh that showed delightfully gleaming teeth. "I wish you could *see* the dragons," she said with great enjoyment. Mr. Polly felt they were a sun's distance from the world of everyday.

"Fly with me!" he dared.

She stared for a moment, and then went off into peals of laughter. "You *are* funny!" she said. 'Why, I haven't known you five minutes."

"One doesn't—in this medieval world. My mind is made up, anyhow."

He was proud and pleased with his joke, and quick to change his key neatly. "I wish one could," he said.

"I wonder if people ever did!"

"If there were people like you."

"We don't even know each other's names," she remarked with a descent to matters of fact.

"Yours is the prettiest name in the world."

"How do you know?"

"It must be—anyhow."

"It is rather pretty you know—it's Christabel."

387

"What did I tell you?"

"And yours?"

"Poorer than I deserve. It's Alfred."

"I can't call you Alfred."

"Well, Polly."

"It's a girl's name!"

For a moment he was out of tune. "I wish it was!" he said, and could have bitten out his tongue at the Larkins sound of it.

"I shan't forget it," she remarked consolingly.

"I say," she said in the pause that followed. "Why are you riding about the country on a bicycle?"

"I'm doing it because I like it."

She sought to estimate his social status on her limited basis of experience. He stood leaning with one hand against the wall, looking up at her and tingling with daring thoughts. He was a littlish man, you must remember, but neither mean-looking nor unhandsome in those days, sunburnt by his holiday and now warmly flushed. He had an inspiration to simple speech that no practised trifler with love could have bettered. "There is love at first sight," he said, and said it sincerely.

She stared at him with eyes round and big with excitement.

"I think," she said slowly, and without any signs of fear or retreat, "I ought to get back over the wall."

"It needn't matter to you," he said. "I'm just a nobody. But I know you are the best and most beautiful thing I've ever spoken to." His breath caught against something. "No harm in telling you that," he said.

"I should have to go back if I thought you were serious," she said after a pause, and they both smiled together.

After that they talked in a fragmentary way for some time. The blue eyes surveyed Mr. Polly with kindly curiosity from under a broad, finely modelled brow, much as an exceptionally intelligent cat might survey a new sort of dog. She meant to find out all about him. She asked questions that riddled the honest knight in armour below, and probed ever nearer to the hateful secret of the shop and his normal servitude. And when he made a flourish and mispronounced a word a thoughtful shade passed like the shadow of a cloud across her face.

"Boom!" came the sound of a gong.

"Lordy!" cried the girl and flashed a pair of brown legs at him and was gone.

Then her pink finger tips reappeared, and the top of her red hair. "Knight!" she cried from the other side of the wall. "Knight there!"

"Lady!" he answered.

"Come again to-morrow!"

"At your command. But—"

"Yes?"

"Just one finger."

"What do you mean?"

"To kiss."

The rustle of retreating footsteps and silence. . . .

But after he had waited next day for twenty minutes she reappeared, a little out of breath with the effort to surmount the wall—and head first this time. And it seemed to him she was lighter and more daring and altogether prettier than the dreams and enchanged memories that had filled the interval.

## 7

From first to last their acquaintance lasted ten days, but into that time Mr. Polly packed ten years of dreams.

"He don't seem," said Johnson, "to take a serious interest in anything. That shop at the corner's bound to be snapped up if he don't look out."

The girl and Mr. Polly did not meet on every one of those ten days; one was Sunday and she could not come, and on the eighth the school reassembled and she made vague excuses. All their meetings amounted to this, that she sat on the wall, more or less in bounds as she expressed it, and let Mr. Polly fall in love with her and try to express it below. She sat in a state of irresponsible exaltation, watching him and at intervals prodding a vivisecting point of encouragement into him—with that strange passive cruelty which is natural to her sex and age.

And Mr. Polly fell in love, as though the world had given way beneath him and he had dropped through into another, into a world of luminous clouds and of desolate hopeless wildernesses of desiring and of wild valleys of unreasonable ecstasies, a world whose infinite miseries were finer and in some inexplicable way sweeter than the purest gold of the daily life, whose joys—they were indeed but the merest remote glimpses of joy—were brighter than a dying martyr's vision of heaven. Her smiling face looked down upon him out of heaven, her careless pose was the living body of life. It was senseless, it was utterly foolish, but all that was best and richest in Mr. Polly's nature broke like a wave and foamed up at that girl's feet, and died, and never touched her. And she sat on the wall and marvelled at him and was amused, and once, suddenly moved and wrung by his pleading, she bent down rather shamefacedly and gave him a freckled, tennis-blistered little paw to kiss. And she looked into his eyes and suddenly felt a perplexity, a curious swimming of the mind that made her recoil and stiffen, and wonder afterwards and dream. . . .

And then with some dim instinct of self-protection, she went and told her three best friends, great students of character all, of this remarkable phenomenon she had discovered on the other side of the wall.

"Look here," said Mr. Polly, "I'm wild for the love of you! I can't keep up this gesticulatious game any more! I'm not a Knight. Treat me as a human man. You may sit up there smiling, but I'd die in torments to have you mine for an hour. I'm nobody

389

and nothing. But look here! Will you wait for me for five years? You're just a girl yet, and it wouldn't be hard."

"Shut up!" said Christabel in an aside he did not hear, and something he did not see touched her hand.

"I've always been just dilletentytating about till now, but I could work. I've just woke up. Wait till I've got a chance with the money I've got."

"But you haven't got much money!"

"I've got enough to take a chance with, some sort of a chance. I'd find a chance. I'll do that anyhow. I'll go away. I mean what I say—I'll stop trifling and shirking. If I don't come back it won't matter. If I do—"

Her expression had become uneasy. Suddenly she bent down towards him.

"Don't!" she said in an undertone.

"Don't—what?"

"Don't go on like this! You're different! Go on being the knight who wants to kiss my hand as his—what did you call it?" The ghost of a smile curved her face. "Gurdrum!"

"But—!"

Then through a pause they both stared at each other, listening.

A muffled tumult on the other side of the wall asserted itself.

"Shut up, Rosie!" said a voice.

"I tell you I will see! I can't half hear. Give me a leg up!"

"You Idiot! He'll see you. You're spoiling everything."

The bottom dropped out of Mr. Polly's world. He felt as people must feel who are going to faint.

"You've got someone—" he said aghast.

She found life inexpressible to Mr. Polly. She addressed some unseen hearers. "You filthy little Beasts!" she cried with a sharp note of agony in her voice, and swung herself back over the wall and vanished. There was a squeal of pain and fear, and a swift, fierce altercation.

For a couple of second he stood agape.

Then a wild resolve to confirm his worst senses of what was on the other side of the wall made him seize a log, put it against the stones, clutch the parapet with insecure fingers, and lug himself to a momentary balance on the wall.

Romance and his goddess had vanished.

A red-haired girl with a pigtail was wringing the wrist of a schoolfellow who shrieked with pain and cried: "Mercy! mercy! Ooo! Christable!"

"You idiot!" cried Christabel. "You giggling Idiot!"

Two other young ladies made off through the beech trees from this outburst of savagery.

Then the grip of Mr. Polly's fingers gave, and he hit his chin against the stones and slipped clumsily to the ground again, scraping his cheek against the wall and hurting his shin against the log by which he had reached the top. Just for a moment he crouched against the wall.

390

He swore, staggered to the pile of logs and sat down.

He remained very still for some time, with his lips pressed together.

"Fool." He said at last,' "you Blithering Fool!" and began to rub his shin as though he had just discovered its bruises.

Afterwards he found his face was wet with blood—which was none the less red stuff from the heart because it came from slight abrasions.

## CHAPTER THE SIXTH
## MIRIAM
### 1

It is an illogical consequence of one human being's ill-treatment that we should fly immediately to another, but that is the way with us. It seemed to Mr. Polly that only a human touch could assuage the smart of his humiliation. Moreover it had for some undefined reason to be a feminine touch, and the number of women in his world was limited.

He thought of the Larkins family—the Larkins whom he had not been near now for ten long days. Healing people they seemed to him now—healing, simple people. They had good hearts, and he had neglected them for a mirage. If he rode over to them he would be able to talk nonsense and laugh and forget the whirl of memories and thoughts that was spinning round and round so unendurably in his brain.

"Law!" said Mrs. Larkins, "come in! You're quite a stranger, Elfrid!'"

"Been seeing to business," said the unveracious Polly.

"None of 'em ain't at 'ome, but Miriam's just out to do a bit of shopping. Won't let me shop, she won't, because I'm so keerless. She's a wonderful manager, that girl. Minnie's got some work at the carpet place. 'Ope it won't make 'er ill again. She's a loving deliket sort, is Minnie. . . . Come into the front parlour. It's a bit untidy, but you got to take us as you find us. Wot you been doing to your face?"

"Bit of a scrase with the bicycle," said Mr. Polly.

"'Ow?"

"Trying to pass a carriage on the wrong side, and he drew up and ran me against a wall."

Mrs. Larkins scrutinised it. "You ought to 'ave someone look after your scrases," she said. "That's all red and rough. It ought to be cold-creamed. Bring your bicycle into the passage and come in."

She "straightened up a bit," that is to say she increased the dislocation of a number of scattered articles, put a workbasket on the top of several books, swept two or three dogs'-eared numbers of the *Lady's Own Novelist* from the table into the broken armchair, and proceeded to sketch together the tea-things with various such interpolations as: "Law, if I ain't forgot the butter!" All the while she talked of Annie's good spirits and cleverness with her millinery, and of Minnie's affection and Miriam's relative love of order and management. Mr. Polly stood by the window uneasily and thought how good and sincere was the Larkins tone. It was well to be back again.

"You're a long time finding that shop of yours," said Mrs. Larkins.

"Don't do to be precipitous," said Mr. Polly.

"No," said Mrs. Larkins, "once you got it you got it. Like choosing a 'usband. You better see you got it good. I kept Larkins 'esitating two years I did, until I felt sure of him. A 'ansom man 'e was as you can see by the looks of the girls, but 'ansom does. You'd like a bit of jam to your tea, I expect? I 'ope they'll keep their men waiting when the time comes. I tell them if they think of marrying it only shows they don't know when they're well off. Here's Miriam!"

Miriam entered with several parcels in a net, and a peevish expression. "Mother," she said, "you might 'ave prevented my going out with the net with the broken handle. I've been cutting my fingers with the string all the way 'ome." Then she discovered Mr. Polly and her face brightened.

"Ello, Elfrid!" she said. "Where you been all this time?"

"Looking round," said Mr. Polly.

"Found a shop?"

"One or two likely ones. But it takes time."

"You've got the wrong cups, Mother."

She went into the kitchen, disposed of her purchases, and returned with the right cups. "What you done to your face, Elfrid?" she asked, and came and scrutinised his scratches. "All rough it is."

He repeated his story of the accident, and she was sympathetic in a pleasant homely way.

"You are quiet to-day," she said as they sat down to tea.

"Mediatious," said Mr. Polly.

Quite by accident he touched her hand on the table, and she answered his touch.

"Why not?" thought Mr. Polly, and looking up, caught Mrs. Larkins' eye and flushed guiltily. But Mrs. Larkins, with unusual restraint, said nothing. She merely made a grimace, enigmatical, but in its essence friendly.

Presently Minnie came in with some vague grievance against the manger of the carpet-making place about his method of estimating piece work. Her account was redundant, defective and highly technical, but redeemed by a certain earnestness. "I'm never within sixpence of what I reckon to be," she said. "It's a bit too 'ot." Then Mr. Polly, feeling that he was being conspicuously dull, launched into a description of the shop he was looking for and the shops he had seen. His mind warmed up as he talked.

"Found your tongue again," said Mrs. Larkins.

He had. He began to embroider the subject and work upon it. For the first time it assumed picturesque and desirable qualities in his mind. It stimulated him to see how readily and willingly they accepted his sketches. Bright ideas appeared in his mind from nowhere. He was suddenly enthusiastic.

"When I get this shop of mine I shall have a cat. Must make a home for a cat, you know."

"What, to catch the mice?' said Mrs. Larkins.

"No—sleep in the window. A venerable signor of a cat. Tabby. Cat's no good if it isn't tabby. Cat I'm going to have, and a canary! Didn't think of that before, but a cat and a canary seem to go, you know. Summer weather I shall sit at breakfast in the little room behind the shop, sun streaming in the window to rights, cat on a chair, canary singing and—Mrs. Polly. . . ."

"Ello!" said Mrs. Larkins.

"Mrs. Polly frying an extra bit of bacon. Bacon singing, cat singing, canary singing. Kettle singing. Mrs. Polly—"

"But who's Mrs. Polly going to be?" said Mrs. Larkins.

"Figment of the imagination, ma'am," said Mr. Polly. "Put in to fill up picture. No face to figure as yet. Still, that's how it will be, I can assure you. I think I must have a bit of garden. Johnson's the man for a garden of course," he said, going off at a tangent, "but I don't mean a fierce sort of garden. Earnest industry. Anxious moments. Fervious digging. Shan't go in for that sort of garden, ma'am. No! Too much backache for me. My garden will be just a patch of 'sturtiums and sweet pea. Red brick yard, clothes' line. Trellis put up in odd time. Humorous wind vane. Creeper up the back of the house."

"Virginia creeper?" asked Miriam.

"Canary creeper," said Mr. Polly.

"You *will* 'ave it nice," said Miriam, desirously.

"Rather," said Mr. Polly. "Ting-a-ling-a-ling. *Shop!*"

He straightened himself up and then they all laughed.

"Smart little shop," he said. "Counter. Desk. All complete. Umbrella stand. Carpet on the floor. Cat asleep on the counter. Ties and hose on a rail over the counter. All right."

"I wonder you don't set about it right off," said Miriam.

"Mean to get it exactly right, m'am," said Mr. Polly.

"Have to have a tomcat," said Mr. Polly, and paused for an expectant moment. "Wouldn't do to open shop one morning, you know, and find the window full of kittens. Can't sell kittens. . . ."

When tea was over he was left alone with Minnie for a few minutes, and an odd intimation of an incident occurred that left Mr. Polly rather scared and shaken. A silence fell between them—an uneasy silence. He sat with his elbows on the table looking at her. All the way from Easewood to Stamton his erratic imagination had been running upon neat ways of proposing marriage. I don't know why it should have done, but it had. It was a kind of secret exercise that had not had any definite aim at the time, but which now recurred to him with extraordinary force. He couldn't think of anything in the world that wasn't the gambit to a proposal. It was almost irresistibly fascinating to think how immensely a few words from him would excite and revolutionise Minnie. She was sitting at the table with a workbasket among the tea things, mending a glove in order to avoid her share of clearing away.

"I like cats," said Minnie after a thoughtful pause. "I'm always saying to mother, 'I wish we 'ad a cat.' But we couldn't 'ave a cat 'ere—not with no yard."

"Never had a cat myself," said Mr. Polly. "No!"

"I'm fond of them," said Minnie.

"I like the look of them," said Mr. Polly. "Can't exactly call myself fond."

"I expect I shall get one some day. When about you get your shop."

"I shall have my shop all right before long," said Mr. Polly. "Trust me. Canary bird and all."

She shook her head. "I shall get a cat first," she said. "You never mean anything you say."

"Might get 'em together," said Mr. Polly, with his sense of a neat thing outrunning his discretion.

"Why! 'ow d'you mean?" said Minnie, suddenly alert.

"Shop and cat thrown in," said Mr. Polly in spite of himself, and his head swam and he broke out into a cold sweat as he said it.

He found her eyes fixed on him with an eager expression. "Mean to say—" she began as if for verification. He sprang to his feet, and turned to the window. "Little dog!" he said, and moved forward hastily. "Eating my bicycle tire, I believe," he explained. And so escaped.

He saw his bicycle in the hall and cut it dead.

He heard Mrs. Larkins in the passage behind him as he opened the front door.

He turned to her. "Thought my bicycle was on fire," he said. "Outside. Funny fancy! All right, reely. Little dog outside. . . . Miriam ready?"

"What for?"

"To go and meet Annie."

Mrs. Larkins stared at him. "You're stopping for a bit of supper?"

"If I may," said Mr. Polly.

"You're a rum un," said Mrs. Larkins, and called: "Miriam!"

Minnie appeared at the door of the room looking infinitely perplexed. "There ain't a little dog anywhere, Elfrid," she said.

Mr. Polly passed his hand over his brow. "I had a most curious sensation. Felt exactly as though something was up somewhere. That's why I said Little Dog. All right now."

He bent down and pinched his bicycle tire.

"You was saying something about a cat, Elfrid," said Minnie.

"Give you one," he answered without looking up. "The very day my shop is opened."

He straightened himself up and smiled reassuringly. "Trust me," he said.

## 2

When, after imperceptible manaeuvers by Mrs. Larkins, he found himself starting circuitously through the inevitable recreation ground with Miriam to meet Annie, he found himself quite unable to avoid the topic of the shop that had now taken such a grip upon him. A sense of danger only increased the attraction. Minnie's persistent disposition to accompany them had been crushed by a novel and violent and urgently expressed desire on the part of Mrs. Larkins to see her do something in the house sometimes. . . .

"You really think you'll open a shop?" asked Miriam.

"I hate cribs," said Mr. Polly, adopting a moderate tone. "In a shop there's this drawback and that, but one is one's own master."

"That wasn't all talk?"

"Not a bit of it."

"After all," he went on, "a little shop needn't be so bad."

"It's a 'ome," said Miriam.

"It's a home."

Pause.

"There's no need to keep accounts and that sort of thing if there's no assistant. I dare say I could run a shop all right if I wasn't interfered with."

"I should like to see you in your shop," said Miriam. "I expect you'd keep everything tremendously neat."

The conversation flagged.

"Let's sit down on one of those seats over there," said Miriam. "Where we can see those blue flowers."

They did as she suggested, and sat down in a corner where a triangular bed of stock and delphinium brightened the asphalted traceries of the Recreation Ground.

"I wonder what they call those flowers," she said. "I always like them. They're handsome."

"Delphicums and larkspurs," said Mr. Polly. "They used to be in the park at Port Burdock."

"Floriferous corner," he added approvingly.

He put an arm over the back of the seat, and assumed a more comfortable attitude. He glanced at Miriam, who was sitting in a lax, thoughtful pose with her eyes on the flowers. She was wearing her old dress, she had not had time to change, and the blue tones of her old dress brought out a certain warmth in her skin, and her pose exaggerated whatever was feminine in her rather lean and insufficient body, and rounded her flat chest delusively. A little line of light lay along her profile. The afternoon was full of transfiguring sunshine, children were playing noisily in the adjacent sandpit, some Judas trees were brightly abloom in the villa gardens that bordered the Recreation Ground, and all the place was bright with touches of young summer colour. It all merged with the effect of Miriam in Mr. Polly's mind.

Her thoughts found speech. "One did ought to be happy in a shop," she said with a note of unusual softness in her voice.

It seemed to him that she was right. One did ought to be happy in a shop. Folly not to banish dreams that made one ache of townless woods and bracken tangles and red-haired linen-clad figures sitting in dappled sunshine upon grey and crumbling

395

walls and looking queenly down on one with clear blue eyes. Cruel and foolish dreams they were, that ended in one's being laughed at and made a mock of. There was no mockery here.

"A shop's such a respectable thing to be," said Miriam thoughtfully.

"I could be happy in a shop," he said.

His sense of effect made him pause.

"If I had the right company," he added.

She became very still.

Mr. Polly swerved a little from the conversational ice-run upon which he had embarked.

"I'm not such a blooming Geezer," he said, "as not to be able to sell goods a bit. One has to be nosy over one's buying of course. But I shall do all right."

He stopped, and felt falling, falling through the aching silence that followed.

"If you get the right company," said Miriam.

"I shall get that all right."

"You don't mean you've got someone—"

He found himself plunging.

"I've got someone in my eye, this minute," he said.

"Elfrid!" she said, turning on him. "You don't mean—"

Well, did he mean? "I do!" he said.

"Not reely!" She clenched her hands to keep still.

He took the conclusive step.

"Well, you and me, Miriam, in a little shop—with a cat and a canary—." He tried too late to get back to a hypothetical note. "Just suppose it!"

"You mean," said Miriam, "you're in love with me, Elfrid?"

What possible answer can a man give to such a question but "Yes!"

Regardless of the public park, the children in the sandpit and everyone, she bent forward and seized his shoulder and kissed him on the lips. Something lit up in Mr. Polly at the touch. He put an arm about her and kissed her back, and felt an irrevocable act was sealed. He had a curious feeling that it would be very satisfying to marry and have a wife—only somehow he wished it wasn't Miriam. Her lips were very pleasant to him, and the feel of her in his arm.

They recoiled a little from each other and sat for a moment, flushed and awkwardly silent. His mind was altogether incapable of controlling its confusion.

"I didn't dream," said Miriam, "you cared—. Sometimes I thought it was Annie, sometimes Minnie—"

"Always liked you better than them," said Mr. Polly.

"I loved you, Elfrid," said Miriam, "since ever we met at your poor father's funeral. Leastways I would have done, if I had thought. You didn't seem to mean anything you said.

"I can't believe it!" she added.

"Nor I," said Mr. Polly.

"You mean to marry me and start that little shop—"

"Soon as ever I find it," said Mr. Polly.

"I had no more idea when I came out with you—"

"Nor me!"

"It's like a dream."

They said no more for a little while.

"I got to pinch myself to think it's real," said Miriam. "What they'll do without me at 'ome I can't imagine. When I tell them—"

For the life of him Mr. Polly could not tell whether he was fullest of tender anticipations or regretful panic.

"Mother's no good at managing—not a bit. Annie don't care for 'ouse work and Minnie's got no 'ed for it. What they'll do without me I can't imagine."

"They'll have to do without you," said Mr. Polly, sticking to his guns.

A clock in the town began striking.

"Lor'!" said Miriam, "we shall miss Annie—sitting 'ere and love-making!"

She rose and made as if to take Mr. Polly's arm. But Mr. Polly felt that their condition must be nakedly exposed to the ridicule of the world by such a linking, and evaded her movement.

Annie was already in sight before a flood of hesitation and terrors assailed Mr. Polly.

"Don't tell anyone yet a bit," he said.

"Only mother," said Miriam firmly.

### 3

Figures are the most shocking things in the world. The pettiest little squiggles of black—looked at in the right light, and yet consider the blow they can give you upon the heart. You return from a little careless holiday abroad, and turn over the page of a newspaper, and against the name of that distant, vague-conceived railway in mortgages upon which you have embarked the bulk of your capital, you see instead of the familiar, persistent 95-6 (varying at most to 93 ex. *div.*) this slightly richer arrangement of makers: 76½–78½.

It is like the opening of a pit just under your feet!

So, too, Mr. Polly's happy sense of limitless resources was obliterated suddenly by a vision of this tracery:

"298"

instead of the

"350"

he had come to regard as the fixed symbol of his affluence.

It gave him a disagreeable feeling about the diaphragm, akin in a remote degree to the sensation he had when the perfidy of the red-haired schoolgirl became plain to him. It made his brow moist.

"Going down a vortex!" he whispered.

By a characteristic feat of subtraction he decided that he must have spent sixty-two pounds.

"Funererial baked meats," he said, recalling possible items.

The happy dream in which he had been living of long warm days, of open roads, of limitless unchecked hours, of infinite time to look about him, vanished like a thing enchanted. He was suddenly back in the hard old economic world, that exacts work, that limits range, that discourages phrasing and dispels laughter. He saw Wood Street and its fearful suspenses yawning beneath his feet.

And also he had promised to marry Miriam, and on the whole rather wanted to.

He was distraught at supper. Afterwards, when Mrs. Johnson had gone to bed with a slight headache, he opened a conversation with Johnson.

"It's about time, O' Man, I saw about doing something," he said. "Riding about and looking at shops, all very debonnairious, O' Man, but it's time I took one for keeps."

"What did I tell you?" said Johnson.

"How do you think that corner shop of yours will figure out?" Mr. Polly asked.

"You're really meaning it?"

"If it's a practicable proposition, O' Man. Assuming it's practicable. What's your idea of the figures?"

Johnson went to the chiffonier, got out a letter and tore off the back sheet. "Let's figure it out," he said with solemn satisfaction. "Let's see the lowest you could do it on."

He squared himself to the task, and Mr. Polly sat beside him like a pupil, watching the evolution of the grey, distasteful figures that were to dispose of his little hoard.

"What running expenses have we got to provide for?" said Johnson, wetting his pencil. "Let's have them first. Rent? . . ."

At the end of an hour of hideous speculations, Johnson decided: "It's close. But you'll have a chance."

"M'm," said Mr. Polly. "What more does a brave man want?"

"One thing you can do quite easily. I've asked about it."

"What's that, O' Man?" said Mr. Polly.

"Take the shop without the house above it."

"I suppose I might put my head in to mind it," said Mr. Polly, "and get a job with my body.

"Not exactly that. But I thought you'd save a lot if you stayed on here—being all alone as you are."

"Never thought of that, O' Man," said Mr. Polly, and reflected silently upon the needlessness of Miriam.

"We were talking of eighty pounds for stock," said Johnson. "Of course seventy-five is five pounds less, isn't it? Not much else we can cut."

"No," said Mr. Polly.

"It's very interesting, all this," said Johnson, folding up the half sheet of paper and unfolding it. "I wish sometimes I had a business of my own instead of a fixed salary. You'll have to keep books of course."

"One wants to know where one is."

"I should do it all by double entry." Said Johnson. "A little troublesome at first, but far the best in the end."

"Lemme see that paper," said Mr. Polly, and took it with the feeling of a man who takes a nauseating medicine, and scrutinised his cousin's neat figures with listless eyes.

"Well," said Johnson, rising and stretching. "Bed! Better sleep on it, O' Man."

"Right O," said Mr. Polly without moving, but indeed he could as well have slept upon a bed of thorns.

He had a dreadful night. It was like the end of the annual holiday, only infinitely worse. It was like a newly arrived prisoner's backward glance at the trees and heather through the prison gates. He had to go back to harness, and he was as fitted to go in harness as the ordinary domestic cat. All night, Fate, with the quiet complacency, and indeed at times the very face and gestures of Johnson, guided him towards that undesired establishment at the corner near the station. "Oh Lord!" he cried, "I'd rather go back to cribs. I should keep my money anyhow." Fate never winced.

"Run away to sea," whispered Mr. Polly, but he knew he wasn't man enough.

"Cut my blooming throat."

Some braver strain urged him to think of Miriam, and for a little while he lay still. . . .

"Well, O' Man?" said Johnson, when Mr. Polly came down to breakfast, and Mrs. Johnson looked up brightly. Mr. Polly had never felt breakfast so unattractive before.

"Just a day or so more, O' Man—to turn it over in my mind," he said.

"You'll get the place snapped up," said Johnson.

There were times in those last few days of coyness with his destiny when his engagement seemed the most negligible of circumstances, and times—and these happened for the most part at nights after Mrs. Johnson had indulged everybody in a Welsh rarebit—when it assumed so sinister and portentous an appearance as to make him think of suicide. And there were times too when he very distinctly desired to be married, now that the idea had got into his head, at any cost. Also he tried to recall all the circumstances of his proposal, time after time, and never quite succeeded in recalling what had brought the thing off. He went over to Stamton with a becoming frequency, and kissed all his cousins, and Miriam especially, a great deal, and found it very stirring and refreshing. They all appeared to know; and Minnie was tearful, but resigned. Mrs. Larkins met him, and indeed enveloped him, with unwonted warmth, and there was a big pot of household jam for tea. And he could not make up his mind to sign his name to anything about the shop, though it crawled nearer and nearer to him, though the project had materialised now to the extent of a draft agreement with the place for his signature indicated in pencil.

One morning, just after Mr. Johnson had gone to the station, Mr. Polly wheeled his bicycle out into the road, went up to his bedroom, packed his long white night-dress, a comb, and a toothbrush in a manner that was as offhand as he could make it, informed Mrs. Johnson, who was manifestly curious, that he was "off for a day or two to clear his head," and fled forthright into the road, and mounting turned his wheel towards the tropics and the equator and the south coast of England, and indeed more particularly to where the little village of Fishbourne slumbers and sleeps.

When he returned four days later, he astonished Johnson beyond measure by re-marking so soon as the shop project was reopened:

"I've took a little contraption at Fishbourne, O' Man, that I fancy suits me better."

He paused, and then added in a manner, if possible, even more offhand:

"Oh! and I'm going to have a bit of a nuptial over at Stamton with one of the Larkins cousins."

"Nuptial!" said Johnson.

"Wedding bells, O' Man. Benedictine collapse."

On the whole Johnson showed great self-control. "It's your own affair, O' Man," he said, when things had been more clearly explained, "and I hope you won't feel sorry when it's too late."

But Mrs. Johnson was first of all angrily silent, and then reproachful. "I don't see what we've done to be made fools of like this," she said. "After all the trouble we've 'ad to make you comfortable and see after you. Out late and sitting up and everything. And then you go off as sly as sly without a word, and get a shop be-hind our backs as though you thought we meant to steal your money. I 'aven't pa-tience with such deceitfulness, and I didn't think it of you, Elfred. And now the let-ting season's 'arf gone by, and what I shall do with that room of yours I've no idea. Frank is frank, and fair play fair play; so I was told any'ow when I was a girl. Just as long as it suits you to stay 'ere you stay 'ere, and then it's off and no thank you whether we like it or not. Johnson's too easy with you. 'E sits there and doesn't say a word, and night after night 'e's been addin' and thinkin' for you, instead of see-ing to his own affairs—"

She paused for breath.

"Unfortunate amoor," said Mr. Polly, apologetically and indistinctly. "Didn't ex-pect it myself."

## 4

Mr. Polly's marriage followed with a certain inevitableness.

He tried to assure himself that the was acting upon his own forceful initiative, but at the back of his mind was the completest realisation of his powerlessness to resist the gigantic social forces he had set in motion. He had got to marry under the will of society, even as in times past it has been appointed for other sunny souls under the will of society that they should be led out by serious and unavoidable fellow-creatures and ceremoniously drowned or burnt or hung. He would have preferred infinitely a more observant and less conspicuous role, but the choice was no longer open to him. He did his best to play his part, and he procured some particularly neat check trousers to do it in. The rest of his costume, except for some bright yellow gloves, a grey and blue mixture tie, and that the broad crepe hat-band was changed for a livelier piece of silk, were the things he had worn at the funeral of his father. So nearly akin are human joy and sorrow.

The Larkins sisters had done wonders with grey sateen. The idea of orange blossom and white veils had been abandoned reluctantly on account of the expense of cabs. A novelette in which the heroine had stood at the altar in "a modest going-away dress" had materially assisted this decision. Miriam was frankly tearful, and so indeed was Annie, but with laughter as well to carry it off. Mr. Polly heard Annie say something vague about never getting a chance because of Miriam always sticking about at home like a cat at a mouse-hole, that became, as people say, food for thought. Mrs. Larkins was from the first flushed, garrulous, and wet and smeared by copious weeping; an incredibly soaked and crumpled and used-up pocket handkerchief never left the clutch of her plump red hand. "Goo' girls, all of them," she kept on saying in a tremulous voice; "such-goo-goo-goo-girls!" She wetted Mr. Polly dreadfully when she kissed him. Her emotion affected the buttons down the back of her bodice, and almost the last filial duty Miriam did before entering on her new life was to close that gaping orifice for the eleventh time. Her bonnet was small and ill-balanced, black adorned with red roses, and first it got over her right eye until Annie told her of it, and then she pushed it over her left eye and looked ferocious for a space, and after that baptismal kissing of Mr. Polly the delicate millinery took fright and climbed right up to the back part of her head and hung on there by a pin, and flapped piteously at all the larger waves of emotion that filled the gathering. Mr. Polly became more and more aware of that bonnet as time went on, until he felt for it like a thing alive. Towards the end it had yawning fits.

The company did not include Mrs. Johnson, but Johnson came with a manifest surreptitiousness and backed against walls and watched Mr. Polly with doubt and speculation in his large grey eyes and whistled noiselessly and doubtful on the edge of things. He was, so to speak, to be best man, *sotto voce*. A sprinkling of girls in gay hats from Miriam's place of business appeared in church, great nudgers all of them, but only two came on afterwards to the house. Mrs. Punt brought her son with his ever-widening mind, it was his first wedding, and a Larkins uncle, a Mr. Voules, a licensed victualler, very kindly drove over in a gig from Sommershill with a plump, well-dressed wife to give the bride away. One or two total strangers drifted into the church and sat down observantly far away.

This sprinkling of people seemed only to enhance the cool brown emptiness of the church, the rows and rows of empty pews, disengaged prayer-books and abandoned hassocks. It had the effect of a preposterous misfit. Johnson consulted with a thin-legged, short-skirted verger about the disposition of the party. The officiating clergy appeared distantly in the doorway of the vestry, putting on his surplice, and relapsed into a contemplative cheek-scratching that was manifestly habitual. Before the bride arrived Mr. Polly's sense of the church found an outlet in whispered criticism of ecclesiastical architecture with Johnson. "Early Norman arches, eh?" he said, "or Perpendicular."

"Can't say." Said Johnson.

"Telessated pavement, all right."

"It's well laid anyhow."

"Can't say I admire the altar. Scrappy rather with those flowers."

He coughed behind his hand and cleared his throat. At the back of his mind he was speculating whether flight at this eleventh hour would be criminal or merely reprehensible bad taste. A murmur from the nudgers announced the arrival of the bridal party.

The little procession from a remote door became one of the enduring memories of Mr. Polly's life. The little verger had bustled to meet it, and arrange it according to tradition and morality. In spite of Mrs. Larkins' "Don't take her from me yet!" he made Miriam go first with Mr. Voules, the bridesmaids followed and then himself hopelessly unable to disentangle himself from the whispering maternal anguish of Mrs. Larkins. Mrs. Voules, a compact, rounded woman with a square, expressionless face, imperturbable dignity, and a dress of considerable fashion, completed the procession.

Mr. Polly's eye fell first upon the bride; the sight of her filled him with a curious stir of emotion. Alarm, desire, affection, respect—and a queer element of reluctant dislike all played their part in that complex eddy. The grey dress made her a stranger to him, made her stiff and commonplace, she was not even the rather drooping form that had caught his facile sense of beauty when he had proposed to her in the Recreation Ground. There was something too that did not please him in the angle of her hat, it was indeed an ill-conceived hat with large aimless rosettes of pink and grey. Then his mind passed to Mrs. Larkins and the bonnet that was to gain such a hold upon him; it seemed to be flag-signalling as she advanced, and to the two eager, unrefined sisters he was acquiring.

A freak of fancy set him wondering where and when in the future a beautiful girl with red hair might march along some splendid aisle. Never mind! He became aware of Mr. Voules.

He became aware of Mr. Voules as a watchful, blue eye of intense forcefulness. It was the eye of a man who has got hold of a situation. He was a fat, short, red-faced man clad in a tight-fitting tail coat of black and white check with a coquettish bow tie under the lowest of a number of crisp little red chins. He held the bride under his arm with an air of invincible championship, and his free arm flourished a grey top hat of an equestrian type. Mr. Polly instantly learnt from the eye that

Mr. Voules knew all about his longing for flight. Its azure pupil glowed with disciplined resolution. It said: "I've come to give this girl away, and give her away I will. I'm here now and things have to go on all right. So don't think of it any more"—and Mr. Polly didn't. A faint phantom of a certain "lill' dog" that had hovered just beneath the threshold of consciousness vanished into black impossibility. Until the conclusive moment of the service was attained the eye of Mr. Voules watched Mr. Polly relentlessly, and then instantly he relieved guard, and blew his nose into a voluminous and richly patterned handkerchief, and sighed and looked round for the approval and sympathy of Mrs. Voules, and nodded to her brightly like one who has always foretold a successful issue to things. Mr. Polly felt then like a marionette that has just dropped off its wire. But it was long before that release arrived.

He became aware of Miriam breathing close to him.

"Hullo!" he said, and feeling that was clumsy and would meet the eye's disapproval; "Grey dress-suits you no end."

Miriam's eyes shone under her hat-brim.

"Not reely!" she whispered.

"You're all right," he said with the feeling of observation and criticism stiffening his lips. He cleared his throat.

The verger's hand pushed at him from behind. Someone was driving Miriam towards the altar rail and the clergyman. "We're in for it," said Mr. Polly to her sympathetically. "Where? Here? Right O."

He was interested for a moment or so in something indescribably habitual in the clergyman's pose. What a lot of weddings he must have seen! Sick he must be of them!

"Don't let your attention wander," said the eye.

"Got the ring?" whispered Johnson.

"Pawned it yesterday," answered Mr. Polly and then had a dreadful moment under that pitiless scrutiny while he felt in the wrong waistcoat pocket. . . .

The officiating clergy sighed deeply, began, and married them wearily and without any hitch.

"D'b'loved, we gath'd 'gether sight o' Gard 'n face this con'gation join 'gather Man, Wom' Holy Mat'my which is on'bl state stooted by Gard in times man's innocency. . . .'"

Mr. Polly's thoughts wandered wide and far, and once again something like a cold hand touched his heart, and he saw a sweet face in sunshine under the shadow of trees.

Someone was nudging him. It was Johnson's finger diverted his eyes to the crucial place in the prayer-book to which they had come.

"Wiltou lover, cumiler, oner, keeper sickness and health . . ."

"Say 'I will.'"

Mr. Polly moistened his lips. "I will," he said hoarsely.

Miriam, nearly inaudible, answered some similar demand.

Then the clergyman said: "Who gifs Wom married to this man?"

"Well, I'm doing that," said Mr. Voules in a refreshingly full voice and looking round the church. "You see, me and Martha Larkins being cousins—"

He was silenced by the clergyman's rapid grip directing the exchange of hands. "Pete arf me," said the clergyman to Mr. Polly. "Take thee Mirum wed wife—"

"Take thee Mirum wed' wife," said Mr. Polly.

"Have hold this day ford."

"Have hold this day ford."

"Betworse, richpoo'—"

"Bet worsh, richpoo'. . . . "

Then came Miriam's turn.

"Lego hands," said the clergyman; "got the ring? No! On the book. So! Here! Pete arf me, 'withis ring Ivy wed.'"

"Withis ring Ivy wed—"

So it went on, blurred and hurried, like the momentary vision of an utterly beautiful thing seen through the smoke of a passing train. . . .

"Now, my boy," said Mr. Voules at last, gripping Mr. Polly's elbow tightly, "you've got to sign the registry, and there you are! Done!"

Before him stood Miriam, a little stiffly, the hat with a slight rake across her forehead, and a kind of questioning hesitation in her face. Mr. Voules urged him past her.

It was astounding. She was his wife!

And for some reason Miriam and Mrs. Larkins were sobbing, and Annie was looking grave. Hadn't they after all wanted him to marry her? Because if that was the case—!

He became aware for the first time of the presence of Uncle Pentstemon in the background, but approaching, wearing a tie of a light mineral blue colour, and grinning and sucking enigmatically and judiciously round his principal tooth.

## 5

It was in the vestry that the force of Mr. Voules' personality began to show at its true value. He seemed to open out and spread over things directly the restraints of the ceremony were at an end.

"Everything," he said to the clergyman, "excellent." He also shook hands with Mrs. Larkins, who clung to him for a space, and kissed Miriam on the cheek. "First kiss for me," he said, "anyhow."

He led Mr. Polly to the register by the arm, and then got chairs for Mrs. Larkins and his wife. He then turned on Miriam. "Now, young people," he said. "One! or I shall again."

"That's right!" said Mr. Voules. "Same again, Miss."

Mr. Polly was overcome with modest confusion, and turning, found a refuge from this publicity in the arms of Mrs. Larkins. Then in a state of profuse moisture he was assaulted and kissed by Annie and Minnie, who were immediately kissed upon some indistinctly stated grounds by Mr. Voules, who then kissed the entirely impassive Mrs. Voules and smacked his lips and remarked: "Home again safe and sound!" Then with a strange harrowing cry Mrs. Larkins seized upon and be-dewed Miriam with kisses, Annie and Minnie kissed each other, and Johnson went abruptly to the door of the vestry and stared into the church—no doubt with ideas of sanctuary in his mind. "Like a bit of a kiss round sometimes," said Mr. Voules, and made a kind of hissing noise with his teeth, and suddenly smacked his hands together with great *éclat* several times. Meanwhile the clergyman scratched his cheek with one hand and fiddled the pen with the other and the verger coughed protestingly.

"The dog cart's just outside," said Mr. Voules. "No walking home to-day for the bride, Mam."

"Not going to drive us?" cried Annie.

"The happy pair, Miss. *Your* turn soon."

"Get out!" said Annie. "I shan't marry—ever."

"You won't be able to help it. You'll have to do it—just to disperse the crowd." Mr. Voules laid his hand on Mr. Polly's shoulder. "The bridegroom gives his arm to the bride. Hands across and down the middle. Prump. Prump, Perump-pump-pump-pump."

Mr. Polly found himself and the bride leading the way towards the western door.

Mrs. Larkins passed close to Uncle Pentstemon, sobbing too earnestly to be aware of him. "Such a goo-goo-goo-girl!" she sobbed.

"Didn't think *I'd* come, did you?" said Uncle Pentstemon, but she swept past him, too busy with the expression of her feelings to observe him.

"She didn't think I'd come, I lay," said Uncle Pentstemon, a little foiled, but ef-fecting an auditory lodgment upon Johnson.

"I don't know," said Johnson uncomfortably. "I suppose you were asked. How are you getting on?"

"I was *arst*," said Uncle Pentstemon, and brooded for a moment.

"I goes about seeing wonders," he added, and then in a sort of enhanced under-tone: "One of 'er girls gettin' married. That's what I mean by wonders. Lord's good-ness! Wow!"

"Nothing the matter?" asked Johnson.

"Got it in the back for a moment. Going to be a change of weather I suppose," said Uncle Pentstemon. "I brought 'er a nice present, too, what I got in this passel. Vallyble old tea caddy that uset' be my mother's. What I kep' my baccy in for years and years—till the hinge at the back got broke. It ain't been no use to me particular since, so thinks I, drat it! I may as well give it 'er as not. . . ."

Mr. Polly found himself emerging from the western door.

Outside, a crowd of half-a-dozen adults and about fifty children had collected, and hailed the approach of the newly wedded couple with a faint, indeterminate cheer. All the children were holding something in little bags, and his attention was caught by the expression of vindictive concentration upon the face of a small big-eared boy in the foreground. He didn't for the moment realise what these things might import. Then he received a stinging handful of rice in the ear, and great light shone.

"Not yet, you young fool!" he heard Mr. Voules saying behind him, and then a second handful spoke against his hat.

"Not yet," said Mr. Voules with increasing emphasis, and Mr. Polly became aware that he and Miriam were the focus of two crescents of small boys, each with the light of massacre in his eyes and a grubby fist clutching into a paper bag for rice; and that Mr. Voules was warding off probable discharges with a large red hand.

The dog cart was in charge of a loafer, and the horse and the whip were adorned with white favours, and the back seat was confused but not untenable with hampers. "Up we go," said Mr. Voules, "old birds in front and young ones behind." An ominous group of ill-restrained rice-throwers followed them up as they mounted.

"Get your handkerchief for your face," said Mr. Polly to his bride, and took the place next the pavement with considerable heroism, held on, gripped his hat, shut his eyes and prepared for the worst. "Off!" said Mr. Voules, and a concentrated fire came stinging Mr. Polly's face.

The horse shied, and when the bridegroom could look at the world again it was manifest the dog cart had just missed an electric tram by a hairsbreadth, and far away outside the church railings the verger and Johnson were battling with an active crowd of small boys for the life of the rest of the Larkins family. Mrs. Punt and her son had escaped across the road, the son trailing and stumbling at the end of a remorseless arm, but Uncle Pentstemon, encumbered by the tea-caddy, was the centre of a little circle of his own, and appeared to be dratting them all very heartily. Remoter, a policeman approached with an air of tranquil unconsciousness.

"Steady, you idiot. Stead-y!" cried Mr. Voules, and then over his shoulder: "I brought that rice! I like old customs! Whoa! Stead-y."

The dog cart swerved violently, and then, evoking a shout of groundless alarm from a cyclist, took a corner, and the rest of the wedding party was hidden from Mr. Polly's eyes.


6

"We'll get the stuff into the house before the old gal comes along," said Mr. Voules, "if you'll hold the hoss."

"How about the key?" asked Mr. Polly.

"I got the key, coming."

And while Mr. Polly held the sweating horse and dodged the foam that dripped from its bit, the house absorbed Miriam and Mr. Voules altogether. Mr. Voules carried in the various hampers he had brought with him, and finally closed the door behind him.

For some time Mr. Polly remained alone with his charge in the little blind alley outside the Larkins' house, while the neighbours scrutinised him from behind their blinds. He reflected that he was a married man, that he must look very like a fool, that the head of a horse is a silly shape and its eye a bulger; he wondered what the horse thought of him, and whether it really liked being held and patted on the neck or whether it only submitted out of contempt. Did it know he was married? Then he wondered if the clergyman had thought him much of an ass, and then whether the individual lurking behind the lace curtains of the front room next door was a man or a woman. A door opened over the way, and an elderly gentleman in a kind of embroidered fez appeared smoking a pipe with a quite satisfied expression. He regarded Mr. Polly for some time with mild but sustained curiosity. Finally he called: "Hi!"

"Hullo!" said Mr. Polly.

"You needn't 'old that 'orse," said the old gentleman.

"Spirited beast," said Mr. Polly. "And,"—with some faint analogy to ginger beer in his mind—"he's up to-day."

"'E won't turn 'isself round," said the old gentleman, "anyhow. And there ain't no way through for 'im to go."

"Verbum sap," said Mr. Polly, and abandoned the horse and turned to the door. It opened to him just as Mrs. Larkins on the arm of Johnson, followed by Annie, Minnie, two friends, Mrs. Punt and her son and at a slight distance Uncle Pentstemon, appeared round the corner.

"They're coming," he said to Miriam, and put an arm about her and gave her a kiss.

She was kissing him back when they were startled violently by the shying of two empty hampers into the passage. Then Mr. Voules appeared holding a third.

"Here! you'll 'ave plenty of time for that presently," he said, "get these hampers away before the old girl comes. I got a cold collation here to make her sit up. My eye!"

Miriam took the hampers, and Mr. Polly under compulsion from Mr. Voules went into the little front room. A profuse pie and a large ham had been added to the modest provision of Mrs. Larkins, and a number of select-looking bottles shouldered the bottle of sherry and the bottle of port she had got to grace the feast. They certainly went better with the iced wedding cake in the middle. Mrs. Voules, still impassive, stood by the window regarding these things with a faint approval.

"Makes it look a bit thicker, eh?" said Mr. Voules, and blew out both his cheeks and smacked his hands together violently several times. "Surprise the old girl no end."

He stood back and smiled and bowed with arms extended as the others came clustering at the door.

"Why, Un-cle Voules!" cried Annie, with a rising note.

It was his reward.

And then came a great wedging and squeezing and crowding into the little room. Nearly everyone was hungry, and eyes brightened at the sight of the pie and the ham and the convivial array of bottles. "Sit down everyone," cried Mr. Voules, "leaning against anything counts as sitting, and makes it easier to shake down the grub!"

The two friends from Miriam's place of business came into the room among the first, and then wedged themselves so hopelessly against Johnson in an attempt to get out again and take off their things upstairs that they abandoned the attempt. Amid the struggle, Mr. Polly saw Uncle Pentstemon relieve himself of his parcel by giving it to the bride. "Here!" he said and handed it to her. "Weddin' present," he explained, and added with a confidential chuckle, "I never thought I'd 'ave to give you one— ever."

"Who says steak and kidney pie?" bawled Mr. Voules. "Who says steak and kidney pie? You 'ave a drop of old Tommy, Martha. That's what you want to steady you. . . . Sit down everyone and don't all speak at once. Who says steak and kidney pie? . . ."

"Vocificeratious," whispered Mr. Polly. "Convivial vociferations."

"Bit of 'am with it," shouted Mr. Voules, poising a slice of ham on his knife. "Anyone 'ave a bit of 'am with it? Won't that little man of yours, Mrs. Punt—won't 'e 'ave a bit of 'am? . . ."

"And now ladies and gentlemen," said Mr. Voules, still standing and dominating the crammed roomful, "now you got your plates filled and something I can warrant you good in your glasses, wot about drinking the 'ealth of the bride?"

"Eat a bit fust," said Uncle Pentstemon, speaking with his mouth full, amidst murmurs of applause. "Eat a bit fust."

So they did, and the plates clattered and the glasses chinked.

Mr. Polly stood shoulder to shoulder with Johnson for a moment.

"In for it," said Mr. Polly cheeringly. "Cheer up, O' Man, and peck a bit. No reason why you shouldn't eat, you know."

The Punt boy stood on Mr. Polly's boots for a minute, struggling violently against the compunction of Mrs. Punt's grip.

"Pie," said the Punt boy, "Pie!"

"You sit 'ere and 'ave 'am, my lord!" said Mrs. Punt, prevailing. "Pie you can't 'ave and you won't."

"Lor bless my heart, Mrs. Punt!" protested Mr. Voules, "let the boy 'ave a bit if he wants it—wedding and all!"

"You 'aven't 'ad 'im 'sick 'on 'your 'ands, Uncle Voules," said Mrs. Punt. "Else you wouldn't want to humour his fancies as you do. . . ."

"I can't help feeling it's a mistake, O' Man," said Johnson, in a confidential undertone. "I can't help feeling you've been Rash. Let's hope for the best."

"Always glad of good wishes, O' man," said Mr. Polly. "You'd better have a drink of something. Anyhow, sit down to it."

Johnson subsided gloomily, and Mr. Polly secured some ham and carried it off and sat himself down on the sewing machine on the floor in the corner to devour it. He was hungry, and a little cut off from the rest of the company by Mrs. Voules' hat and back, and he occupied himself for a time with ham and his own thoughts. He became aware of a series of jangling concussions on the table. He craned his neck and discovered that Mr. Voules was standing up and leaning forward over the table in the manner distinctive of after-dinner speeches, tapping upon the table with a black bottle. "Ladies and gentlemen," said Mr. Voules, raising his glass solemnly in the empty desert of sound he had made, and paused for a second or so. "Ladies and gentlemen,—The Bride." He searched his mind for some suitable wreath of speech, and brightened at last with discovery. "Here's Luck to her!" he said at last.

"Here's Luck!" said Johnson hopelessly but resolutely, and raised his glass. Everybody murmured: "Here's luck."

"Luck!" said Mr. Polly, unseen in his corner, lifting a forkful of ham.

"That's all right," said Mr. Voules with a sigh of relief at having brought off a difficult operation. "And now, who's for a bit more pie?"

For a time conversation was fragmentary again. But presently Mr. Voules rose from his chair again; he had subsided with a contented smile after his first oratorical effort, and produced a silence by renewed hammering. "Ladies and gents," he said, "fill up for the second toast:—the happy Bridegroom!" He stood for half a minute searching his mind for the apt phrase that came at last in a rush. "Here's (hic) luck to him," said Mr. Voules.

"Luck to him!" said everyone, and Mr. Polly, standing up behind Mrs. Voules, bowed amiably, amidst enthusiasm.

"He may say what he likes," said Mrs. Larkins, "he's got luck. That girl's a treasure of treasures, and always has been ever since she tried to nurse her own little sister, being but three at the time, and fell the full flight of stairs from top to bottom, no hurt that any outward eye 'as even seen, but always ready and helpful, always tidying and busy. A treasure, I must say, and a treasure I will say, giving no more than her due. . . ."

She was silenced altogether by a rapping sound that would not be denied. Mr. Voules had been struck by a fresh idea and was standing up and hammering with the bottle again.

"The third Toast, ladies and gentlemen," he said; "fill up, please. The Mother of the bride. I—er. . . . Uoo. . . . Ere! . . . Ladies and gem, 'Ere's Luck to 'er! . . ."

## 7

The dingy little room was stuffy and crowded to its utmost limit, and Mr. Polly's skies were dark with the sense of irreparable acts. Everybody seemed noisy and greedy and doing foolish things. Miriam, still in that unbecoming hat—for presently they had to start off to the station together—sat just beyond Mrs. Punt and her son, doing her share in the hospitalities, and ever and again glancing at him with a deliberately encouraging smile. Once she leant over the back of the chair to him and whispered cheeringly: "Soon be together now. " Next to her sat Johnson, profoundly silent, and then Annie, talking vigorously to a friend. Uncle Pentstemon was eating voraciously opposite, but with a kindling eye for Annie. Mrs. Larkins sat next to Mr. Voules. She was unable to eat a mouthful, she declared, it would choke her, but ever and again Mr. Voules wooed her to swallow a little drop of liquid refreshment.

There seemed a lot of rice upon everybody, in their hats and hair and the folds of their garments.

Presently Mr. Voules was hammering the table for the fourth time in the interest of the Best Man. . . .

All feasts come to an end at last, and the break-up of things was precipitated by alarming symptoms on the part of Master Punt. He was taken out hastily after a whispered consultation, and since he had got into the corner between the fireplace and the cupboard, that meant everyone moving to make way for him. Johnson took the opportunity to say, "Well—so long," to anyone who might be listening, and disappear. Mr. Polly found himself smoking a cigarette and walking up and down outside in the company of Uncle Pentstemon, while Mr. Voules replaced bottles in hampers and prepared for departure, and the womenkind of the party crowded upstairs with the bride. Mr. Polly felt taciturn, but the events of the day had stirred the mind of Uncle Pentstemon to speech. And so he spoke, discursively and disconnectedly, a little heedless of his listener as wise old men will.

"They do say," said Uncle Pentstemon, "one funeral makes many. This time it's a wedding. But it's all very much of a muchness," said Uncle Pentstemon. . . .

"'Am do get in my teeth nowadays," said Uncle Pentstemon, "I can't understand it. 'Tisn't like there was nubbicks or strings or such in 'am. It's a plain food.

"That's better," he said at last.

"You *got* to get married," said Uncle Pentstemon. "Some has. Some hain't. I done it long before I was your age. It hain't for me to blame you. You can't 'elp being the marrying sort any more than me. It's nat'ral—like poaching or drinking or wind on the stummick. You can't 'elp it and there you are! As for the good of it, there ain't no particular good in it as I can see. It's a toss up. The hotter come, the sooner cold, but they all gets tired of it sooner or later. . . . I hain't no grounds to complain. Two I've 'ad and berried, and might 'ave 'ad a third, and never no worrit with kids—never. . . ."

"You done well not to 'ave the big gal. I will say that for ye. She's a gad-about grinny, she is, if ever was. A gad-about grinny. Mucked up my mushroom bed to rights, she did, and I 'aven't forgot it. Got the feet of a centipede, she 'as—all over everything and neither with your leave nor by your leave. Like a stray 'en in a pea patch. Cluck! cluck! Trying to laugh it off. I laughed 'er off, I did. Dratted lumpin baggage! . . ."

410

For a while he mused malevolently upon Annie, and routed out a reluctant crumb from some coy sitting-out place in his tooth.

"Wimmin's a toss up," said Uncle Pentstemon. "Prize packets they are, and you can't tell what's in 'em till you took 'em 'ome and undone 'em. Never was a bachelor married yet that didn't buy a pig in a poke. Never. Marriage seems to change the very natures in 'em through and through. You can't tell what they won't turn into—no-how.

"I seen the nicest girls go wrong," said Uncle Pentstemon, and added with un- usual thoughtfulness, "Not that I mean you got one of the sort."

He sent another crumb on to its long home with a sucking, encouraging noise.

"The wust sort's the grizzler," Uncle Pentstemon resumed. "If ever I'd ad a griz- zler I'd up and 'it 'er on the 'ed with sumpthin' pretty quick. I don't think I *could* abide a grizzler," said Uncle Pentstemon. "I'd leifer 'ave a lump-about like that other gal. I would indeed. I lay I'd make 'er stop laughing after a bit for all 'er airs. And mind where her clumsy great feet went. . . .

"A man's got to tackle 'em, whatever they be," said Uncle Pentstemon, summing up the shrewd observation of an old-world life time. "Good or bad," said Uncle Pentstemon raising his voice fearlessly, "a man's got to tackle 'em."

8

At last it was time for the two young people to catch the train for Waterloo en route for Fishbourne. They had to hurry, and as a concluding glory of matrimony they trav- elled second-class, and were seen off by all the rest of the party except the Punts, Mas- ter Punt being now beyond any question unwell.

"Off!" The train moved out of the station.

Mr. Polly remained waving his hat and Mrs. Polly her handkerchief until they were hidden under the bridge. The dominating figure to the last was Mr. Voules. He had followed them along the platform waving the equestrian grey hat and kissing his hand to the bride.

They subsided into their seats.

"Got a compartment to ourselves anyhow," said Mrs. Polly after a pause.

Silence for a moment.

"The rice 'e must 'ave bought. Pounds and pounds!"

Mr. Polly felt round his collar at the thought.

"Ain't you going to kiss me, Elfrid, now we're alone together?"

He roused himself to sit forward hands on knees, cocked his hat over one eye, and assumed an expression of avidity becoming to the occasion.

"Never!" he said. "Ever!" and feigned to be selecting a place to kiss with great discrimination.

"Come here," he said, and drew her to him.

"Be careful of my 'at," said Mrs. Polly, yielding awkwardly.

411

CHAPTER THE SEVENTH
THE LITTLE SHOP AT FISHBOURNE
1

For fifteen years Mr. Polly was a respectable shopkeeper in Fishbourne.

Years they were in which every day was tedious, and when they were gone it was as if they had gone in a flash. But now Mr. Polly had good looks no more, he was as I have described him in the beginning of this story, thirty-seven and fattish in a not very healthy way, dull and yellowish about the complexion, and with discontented wrinklings round his eyes. He sat on the stile above Fishbourne and cried to the Heavens above him: "Oh! Roo-o-o-tten Be-e-astly Silly Hole!" And he wore a rather shabby black morning coat and vest, and his tie was richly splendid, being from stock, and his golf cap aslant over one eye.

Fifteen years ago, and it might have seemed to you that the queer little flower of Mr. Polly's imagination must be altogether withered and dead, and with no living seed left in any part of him. But indeed it still lived as an insatiable hunger for bright and delightful experiences, for the gracious aspects of things, for beauty. He still read books when he had a chance, books that told of glorious places abroad and glorious times, that wrung a rich humour from life and contained the delight of words freshly and expressively grouped. But alas! there are not many such books, and for the newspapers and the cheap fiction that abounded more and more in the world Mr. Polly had little taste. There was no epithet in them. And there was no one to talk to, as he loved to talk. And he had to mind his shop.

It was a reluctant little shop from the beginning.

He had taken it to escape the doom of Johnson's choice and because Fishbourne had a hold upon his imagination. He had disregarded the ill-built cramped rooms behind it in which he would have to lurk and live, the relentless limitations of its dimensions, the inconvenience of an underground kitchen that must necessarily be the living-room in winter, the narrow yard behind giving upon the yard of the Royal Fishbourne Hotel, the tiresome sitting and waiting for custom, the restricted prospects of trade. He had visualised himself and Miriam first as at breakfast on a clear bright winter morning amidst a tremendous smell of bacon, and then as having muffins for tea. He had also thought of sitting on the beach on Sunday afternoons and of going for a walk in the country behind the town and picking marguerites and poppies. But, in fact, Miriam and he were extremely cross at breakfast, and it didn't run to muffins at tea. And she didn't think it looked well, she said, to go trapesing about the country on Sundays.

It was unfortunate that Miriam never took to the house from the first. She did not like it when she saw it, and liked it less as she explored it. "There's too many stairs," she said, "and the coal being indoors will make a lot of work."

"Didn't think of that," said Mr. Polly, following her round.

"It'll be a hard house to keep clean," said Miriam.

412

"White paint's all very well in its way," said Miriam, "but it shows the dirt something fearful. Better 'ave 'ad it nicely grained."

"There's a kind of place here," said Mr. Polly, "where we might have some flowers in pots."

"Not me," said Miriam. "I've 'ad trouble enough with Minnie and 'er musk. . . ."

They stayed for a week in a cheap boarding house before they moved in. They had bought some furniture in Stamton, mostly second-hand, but with new cheap cutlery and china and linen, and they had supplemented this from the Fishbourne shops. Miriam, relieved from the hilarious associations of home, developed a meagre and serious quality of her own, and went about with knitted brows pursuing some ideal of "'aving everything right." Mr. Polly gave himself to the arrangement of the shop with a certain zest, and whistled a good deal until Miriam appeared and said that it went through her head. So soon as he had taken the shop he had filled the window with aggressive posters announcing in no measured terms that he was going to open, and now he was getting his stuff put out he was resolved to show Fishbourne what window dressing could do. He meant to give them boater straws, imitation Panamas, bathing dresses with novelties in stripes, light flannel shirts, summer ties, and ready-made flannel trousers for men, youths and boys. Incidentally he watched the small fishmonger over the way, and had a glimpse of the china dealer next door, and wondered if a friendly nod would be out of place. And on the first Sunday in this new life he and Miriam arrayed themselves with great care, he in his wedding-funeral hat and coat and she in her going-away dress, and went processionally to church, a more respectable looking couple you could hardly imagine, and looked about them.

Things began to settle down next week into their places. A few customers came, chiefly for bathing suits and hat guards, and on Saturday night the cheapest straw hats and ties, and Mr. Polly found himself more and more drawn towards the shop door and the social charm of the street. He found the china dealer unpacking a crate at the edge of the pavement, and remarked that it was a fine day. The china dealer gave a reluctant assent, and plunged into the crate in a manner that presented no encouragement to a loquacious neighbour.

"Zealacious commerciality," whispered Mr. Polly to that unfriendly back view. . . .

### 2

Miriam combined earnestness of spirit with great practical incapacity. The house was never clean nor tidy, but always being frightfully disarranged for cleaning or tidying up, and she cooked because food had to be cooked and with a sound moralist's entire disregard of the quality of the consequences. The food came from her hands done rather than improved, and looking as uncomfortable as savages clothed under duress by a missionary with a stock of out-sizes. Such food is too apt to behave resentfully, rebel and work Obi. She ceased to listen to her husband's talk from the day she married him, and ceased to unwrinkle the kink in her brow at his presence, giving herself up to mental states that had a quality of secret preoccupation. And she developed an idea for which perhaps there was legitimate excuse, that he was lazy. He seemed to stand about in the shop a great deal, to read—an indolent habit—and presently to seek company for talking. He began to attend the bar parlour of the God's Providence Inn with some frequency, and would have done so regularly in the evening if cards, which bored him to death, had not arrested conversation. But the perpetual foolish variation of the permutations and combinations of two and fifty cards taken five at a time, and the meagre surprises and excitements that ensue had no charms for Mr. Polly's mind, which was at once too vivid in its impressions and too easily fatigued.

It was soon manifest the shop paid only in the least exacting sense, and Miriam did not conceal her opinion that he ought to bestir himself and "do things," though what he was to do was hard to say. You see, when you have once sunken your capital in a shop you do not very easily get it out again. If customers will not come to you cheerfully and freely the law sets limits upon the compulsion you may exercise. You cannot pursue people about the streets of a watering place, compelling them either by threats or importunity to buy flannel trousers. Additional sources of income for a tradesman are not always easy to find. Wintershed at the bicycle and gramaphone shop to the right, played the organ in the church, and Clamp of the toy shop was pew opener and so forth, Gambell, the greengrocer, waited at table and his wife cooked, and Carter, the watchmaker left things to his wife while he went about the world winding clocks, but Mr. Polly had none of these arts, and wouldn't, in spite of Miriam's quietly persistent protests, get any other. And on summer evenings he would ride his bicycle about the country, and if he discovered a sale where there were books he would as often as not waste half the next day in going again to acquire a job lot of them haphazard, and bring them home tied about with a string, and hide them from Miriam under the counter in the shop. That is a heartbreaking thing for any wife with a serious investigatory turn of mind to discover. She was always thinking of burning these finds, but her natural turn for economy prevailed with her.

The books he read during those fifteen years! He read everything he got except theology, and as he read his little unsuccessful circumstances vanished and the wonder of life returned to him, the routine of reluctant getting up, opening shop, pretending to dust it with zest, breakfasting with a shop egg underdone or overdone or a herring raw or charred, and coffee made Miriam's way and full of little particles, the return to the shop, the morning paper, the standing, standing at the door saying "How do!" to passers-by, or getting a bit of gossip or watching unusual visitors, all these things vanished as the auditorium of a theatre vanishes when the stage is lit. He acquired hundreds of books at last, old dusty books, books with torn covers and broken covers, fat books whose backs were naked string and glue, an inimical litter to Miriam.

There was, for example, the voyages of La Perouse, with many careful, explicit woodcuts and the frankest revelations of the ways of the eighteenth century sailorman, homely, adventurous, drunken, incontinent and delightful, until he floated, smooth and slow, with all sails set and mirrored in the glassy water, until his head was full of the thought of shining kindly brown-skinned women, who smiled at him and wreathed his head with unfamiliar flowers. He had, too, a piece of book about the lost palaces of Yucatan, those vast terraces buried in primordial forest, of whose makers there is now no human memory. With La Perouse he linked "The Island Nights Entertainments," and it never paled upon him that in the dusky stabbing of the "Island of Voices": something poured over the stabber's hands "like warm tea." Queer incommunicable joy it is, the joy of the vivid phrase that turns the statement of the horridest fact to beauty!

And another book which had no beginning for him was the second volume of the Travels of the Abbés Huc and Gabet. He followed those two sweet souls from their lessons in Thibetan under Sandura the Bearded (who called them donkeys to their infinite benefit and stole their store of butter) through a hundred misadventures to the very heart of Lhassa, and it was a thirst in him that was never quenched to find the other volume and whence they came, and who in fact they were. He read Fenimore Cooper and "Tom Cringle's Log" side by side with Joseph Conrad, and dreamt of the many-hued humanity of the East and West Indies until his heart ached to see those sun-soaked lands before he died. Conrad's prose had a pleasure for him that he was never able to define, a peculiar deep coloured effect. He found too one day among a pile of soiled sixpenny books at Port Burdock, to which place he sometimes rode on his aging bicycle, Bart Kennedy's "A Sailor Tramp," all written in livid jerks, and had forever after a kindlier and more understanding eye for every burly rough who slouched through Fishbourne High Street. Sterne he read with a wavering appreciation and some perplexity, but except for the Pickwick papers, for some reason that I do not understand he never took at all kindly to Dickens. Yet he liked Lever and Thackeray's "Catherine," and all Dumas until he got to the Viconte de Bragelonne. I am puzzled by his insensibility to Dickens, and I record it as a good historian should, with an admission of my perplexity. It is much more understandable that he had no love for Scott. And I suppose it was because of his ignorance of the proper pronunciation of words that he infinitely preferred any prose to any metrical writing.

A book he browsed over with a recurrent pleasure was Waterton's *Wanderings in South America.* He would even amuse himself by inventing descriptions of other birds in the Watertonian manner, new birds that he invented, birds with peculiarities that made him chuckle when they occurred to him. He tried to make Rusper, the ironmonger, share this joy with him. He read Bates, too, about the Amazon but when he discovered that you could not see one bank from the other, he lost, through some mysterious action of the soul that again I cannot understand, at least a tithe of the pleasure he had taken in that river. But he read all sorts of things; a book of old Keltic stories collected by Joyce charmed him, and Mitford's *Tales of Old Japan,* and a number of paper-covered volumes, *Tales from Blackwood,* he had acquired at Easewood, remained a stand-by. He developed a quite considerable acquaintance with the plays of William Shakespeare, and in his dreams he wore cinque cento or Elizabethan clothes,

415

and walked about a stormy, ruffling, taverning, teeming world. Great land of sublimated things, thou World of Books, happy asylum, refreshment and refuge from the world of everyday! . . .

The essential thing of those fifteen long years of shopkeeping is Mr. Polly, well athwart the counter of his rather ill-lit shop, lost in a book, or rousing himself with a sigh to attend to business.

Meanwhile he got little exercise, indigestion grew with him until it ruled all his moods, he fattened and deteriorated physically, moods of distress invaded and darkened his skies, little things irritated him more and more, and casual laughter ceased in him. His hair began to come off until he had a large bald space at the back of his head. Suddenly one day it came to him—forgetful of those books and all he had lived and seen through them—that he had been in his shop for exactly fifteen years, that he would soon be forty, and that his life during that time had not been worth living, that it had been in apathetic and feebly hostile and critical company, ugly in detail and mean in scope—and that it had brought him at last to an outlook utterly hopeless and grey.

<h2 style="text-align:center">3</h2>

I have already had occasion to mention, indeed I have quoted, a certain high-browed gentleman living at Highbury, wearing a golden pince-nez and writing for the most part in that beautiful room, the library of the Reform Club. There he wrestles with what he calls "social problems" in a bloodless but at times, I think one must admit, an extremely illuminating manner. He has a fixed idea that something called a "collective intelligence" is wanted in the world, which means in practice that you and I and everyone have to think about things frightfully hard and pool the results, and oblige ourselves to be shamelessly and persistently clear and truthful and support and respect (I suppose) a perfect horde of professors and writers and artists and ill-groomed difficult people, instead of using our brains in a moderate, sensible manner to play golf and bridge (pretending a sense of humour prevents our doing anything else with them) and generally taking life in a nice, easy, gentlemanly way, confound him! Well, this dome-headed monster of intellect alleges that Mr. Polly was unhappy entirely through that.

"A rapidly complicating society," he writes, "which as a whole declines to contemplate its future or face the intricate problems of its organisation, is in exactly the position of a man who takes no thought of dietary or regimen, who abstains from baths and exercise and gives his appetites free play. It accumulates useless and aimless lives as a man accumulates fat and morbid products in his blood, it declines in its collective efficiency and vigour and secretes discomfort and misery. Every phase of its evolution is accompanied by a maximum of avoidable distress and inconvenience and human waste. . . .

"Nothing can better demonstrate the collective dullness of our community, the crying need for a strenuous intellectual renewal than the consideration of that vast mass of useless, uncomfortable, under-educated, under-trained and altogether pitiable people we contemplate when we use that inaccurate and misleading term, the Lower Middle Class. A great proportion of the lower middle class should properly be assigned to the unemployed and the unemployable. They are only not that, because the possession of some small hoard of money, savings during a period of wage earning, an insurance policy or suchlike capital, prevents a direct appeal to the rates. But they are doing little or nothing for the community in return for what they consume; they have no understanding of any relation of service to the community, they have never been trained nor their imagination touched to any social purpose. A great proportion of small shopkeepers, for example, are people who have, through the inefficiency that comes from inadequate training and sheer aimlessness, or improvements in machinery or the drift of trade, been thrown out of employment, and who set up in needless shops as a method of eking out the savings upon which they count. They contrive to make sixty or seventy per cent. Of their expenditure, the rest is drawn from the shrinking capital. Essentially their lives are failures, not the sharp and tragic failure of the labourer who gets out of work and starves, but a slow, chronic process of consecutive small losses which may end if the individual is exceptionally fortunate in an impoverished death bed before actual bankruptcy or destitution supervenes. Their chances of ascendant means are less in their shops than in any lottery that was ever planned. The secular development of transit and communications has made the organisation of distributing businesses upon large and economical lines, inevitable; except in the chaotic confusions of newly opened countries, the day when a man might earn an independent living by unskilled or practically unskilled retailing has gone for ever. Yet every year sees the melancholy procession towards petty bankruptcy and imprisonment for debt go on, and there is no statesmanship in us to avert it. Every issue of every trade journal has its four or five columns of abridged bankruptcy proceedings, nearly every item in which means the final collapse of another struggling family upon the resources of the community, and continually a fresh supply of superfluous artisans and shop assistants, coming out of employment with savings or 'help' from relations, of widows with a husband's insurance money, of the ill-trained sons of parsimonious fathers, replaces the fallen in the ill-equipped, jerry-built shops that everywhere abound. . . ."

I quote these fragments from a gifted, if unpleasant, contemporary for what they are worth. I feel this had to come in here as the broad aspect of this History. I come back to Mr. Polly sitting upon his gate and swearing in the east wind, and in so returning have a sense of floating across unabridged abysses between the General and the Particular. There, on the one hand, is the man of understanding, seeing clearly—I suppose he sees clearly—the big process that dooms millions of lives to thwarting and discomfort and unhappy circumstances, and giving us no help, no hint, by which we may get that better "collective will and intelligence" which would dam the stream of human failure, and, on the other hand, Mr. Polly sitting

417

on his gate, untrained, unwarned, confused, distressed, angry, seeing nothing except that he is, as it were, nettled in greyness and discomfort—with life dancing all about him; Mr. Polly with a capacity for joy and beauty at least as keen and subtle as yours or mine.

## 4

I have hinted that our Mother England had equipped Mr. Polly for the management of his internal concerns no whit better than she had for the direction of his external affairs. With a careless generosity she affords her children a variety of foods unparalleled in the world's history, and including many condiments and preserved preparations novel to the human economy. And Miriam did the cooking. Mr. Polly's system, like a confused and ill-governed democracy, had been brought to a state of perpetual clamour and disorder, demanding now evil and unsuitable internal satisfactions, such as pickles and vinegar and the crackling on pork, and now vindictive external expression, war and bloodshed throughout the world. So that Mr. Polly had been led into hatred and a series of disagreeable quarrels with his landlord, his wholesalers, and most of his neighbours.

Rumbold, the china dealer next door, seemed hostile from the first for no apparent reason, and always unpacked his crates with a full back to his new neighbour, and from the first Mr. Polly resented and hated that uncivil breadth of expressionless humanity, wanted to prod it, kick it, satirise it. But you cannot satirise a back, if you have no friend to nudge while you do it.

At last Mr. Polly could stand it no longer. He approached and prodded Rumbold.

"Ello!" said Rumbold, suddenly erect and turned about.

"Can't we have some other point of view?" said Mr. Polly. "I'm tired of the end elevation."

"Eh?" said Mr. Rumbold, frankly puzzled.

"Of all the vertebracious animals man alone raises his face to the sky, O' Man. Well,—why invert it?"

Rumbold shook his head with a helpless expression.

"Don't like so much Arreary Pensy."

Rumbold distressed in utter obscurity.

"In fact, I'm sick of your turning your back on me, see?"

A great light shone on Rumbold. "That's what you're talking about!" he said.

"That's it," said Polly.

Rumbold scratched his ear with the three strawy jampots he held in his hand. "Way the wind blows, I expect," he said. "But what's the fuss?"

"No fuss!" said Mr. Polly. "Passing Remark. I don't like it, O' Man, that's all."

"Can't help it, if the wind blows my stror," said Mr. Rumbold, still far from clear about it. . . .

"It isn't ordinary civility," said Mr. Polly.

"Got to unpack 'ow it suits me. Can't unpack with the stror blowing into one's eyes."

"Needn't unpack like a pig rooting for truffles, need you?"

"Truffles?"

"Needn't unpack like a pig."

Mr. Rumbold apprehended something.

"Pig!" he said, impressed. "You calling me a pig?"

"It's the side I seem to get of you."

"'Ere," said Mr. Rumbold, suddenly fierce and shouting and marking his point with gesticulated jampots, "you go indoors. I don't want no row with you, and I don't want you to row with me. I don't know what you're after, but I'm a peaceable man—teetotaller, too, and a good thing if you was. See? You go indoors!"

"You mean to say—I'm asking you civilly to stop unpacking—with your back to me."

"Pig ain't civil, and you ain't sober. You go indoors and lemme go on unpacking. You—you're excited."

"D'you mean—!" Mr. Polly was foiled.

He perceived an immense solidity about Rumbold.

"Get back to your shop and lemme get on with my business," said Mr. Rumbold. "Stop calling me pigs. See? Sweep your pavemint."

"I came here to make a civil request."

"You came 'ere to make a row. I don't want no truck with you. See? I don't like the looks of you. See? And I can't stand 'ere all day arguing, See?"

Pause of mutual inspection.

It occurred to Mr. Polly that probably he was to some extent in the wrong.

Mr. Rumbold, blowing heavily, walked past him, deposited the jampots in his shop with a immense affectation that there was no Mr. Polly in the world, returned, turned a scornful back on Mr. Polly and dived to the interior of the crate. Mr. Polly stood baffled. Should he kick this solid mass before him? Should he administer a restounding kick?

No!

He plunged his hands deeply into his trowser pockets, began to whistle and returned to his own doorstep with an air of profound unconcern. There for a time, to the tune of "Men of Harlech," he contemplated the receding possibility of kicking Mr. Rumbold hard. It would be splendid—and for the moment satisfying. But he decided not to do it. For indefinable reasons he could not do it. He went indoors and straightened up his dress ties very slowly and thoughtfully. Presently he went to the window and regarded Mr. Rumbold obliquely. Mr. Rumbold was still unpacking. . . .

Mr. Polly had no human intercourse thereafter with Rumbold for fifteen years. He kept up a Hate.

There was a time when it seemed as if Rumbold might go, but he had a meeting of his creditors and then went on unpacking as obtusely as ever.

419

## V

Hinks, the saddler, two shops further down the street, was a different case. Hinks was the aggressor—practically.

Hinks was a sporting man in his way, with that taste for checks in costume and tight trousers which is, under Providence, so mysteriously and invariably associated with equestrian proclivities. At first Mr. Polly took to him as a character, became frequent in the God's Providence Inn under his guidance, stood and was stood drinks and concealed a great ignorance of horses until Hinks became urgent for him to play billiards or bet.

Then Mr. Polly took to evading him, and Hinks ceased to conceal his opinion that Mr. Polly was in reality a softish sort of flat.

He did not, however, discontinue conversation with Mr. Polly; he would come along to him whenever he appeared at his door, and converse about sport and women and fisticuffs and the pride of life with an air of extreme initiation, until Mr. Polly felt himself the faintest underdeveloped intimation of a man that had ever hovered on the verge of non-existence.

So he invented phrases for Hinks' clothes and took Rusper, the ironmonger, into his confidence upon the weaknesses of Hinks. He called him the "Chequered Careerist," and spoke of his patterned legs as "shivery shakys." Good things of this sort are apt to get round to people.

He was standing at his door one day, feeling bored, when Hinks appeared down the street, stood still and regarded him with a strange malignant expression for a space.

Mr. Polly waved a hand in a rather belated salutation.

Mr. Hinks spat on the pavement and appeared to reflect. Then he came towards Mr. Polly portentously and paused, and spoke between his teeth in an earnest confidential tone.

"You been flapping your mouth about me, I'm told," he said.

Mr. Polly felt suddenly spiritless. "Not that I know of," he answered.

"Not that you know of, be blowed! You been flapping your mouth."

"Don't see it," said Mr. Polly.

"Don't see it, be blowed! You go flapping your silly mouth about me and I'll give you a poke in the eye. See?"

Mr. Hinks regarded the effect of this coldly but firmly, and spat again.

"Understand me?" he enquired.

"Don't recollect," began Mr. Polly.

"Don't recollect, be blowed! You flap your mouth a damn sight too much. This place gets more of your mouth than it wants. . . . Seen this?'"

And Mr. Hinks, having displayed a freckled fist of extraordinary size and pugginess in an ostentatiously familiar manner to Mr. Polly's close inspection by sight and smell, turned it about this way and that and shaken it gently for a moment or so, replaced it carefully in his pocket as if for future use, receded slowly and watchfully for a pace, and then turned away as if to other matters, and ceased to be even in outward seeming a friend. . . .

## 6

Mr. Polly's intercourse with all his fellow tradesmen was tarnished sooner or later by some such adverse incident, until not a friend remained to him, and loneliness made even the shop door terrible. Shops bankrupted all about him and fresh people came and new acquaintances sprang up, but sooner or later a discord was inevitable, the tension under which these badly fed, poorly housed, bored and bothered neighbours lived, made it inevitable. The mere fact that Mr. Polly had to see them every day, that there was no getting away from them, was in itself sufficient to make them almost unendurable to his frettingly active mind.

Among other shopkeepers in the High Street there was Chuffles, the grocer, a small, hairy, silently intent polygamist, who was given rough music by the youth of the neighbourhood because of a scandal about his wife's sister, and who was nevertheless totally uninteresting, and Tonks, the second grocer, an old man with an older, very enfeebled wife, both submerged by piety. Tonks went bankrupt, and was succeeded by a branch of the National Provision Company, with a young manager exactly like a fox, except that he barked. The toy and sweetstuff shop was kept by an old woman of repellent manners, and so was the little fish shop at the end of the street. The Berlin-wool shop having gone bankrupt, became a newspaper shop, then fell to a haberdasher in consumption, and finally to a stationer; the three shops at the end of the street wallowed in and out of insolvency in the hands of a bicycle repairer and dealer, a gramaphone dealer, a tobacconist, a sixpenny-halfpenny bazaar-keeper, a shoemaker, a greengrocer, and the exploiter of a cinematography peep-show—but none of them supplied friendship to Mr. Polly. These adventurers in commerce were all more or less distraught souls, driving without intelligible comment before the gale of fate. The two milkmen of Fairbourne were brothers who had quarrelled about their father's will, and started in opposition to each other; one was stone deaf and no use to Mr. Polly, and the other was a sporting man with a natural dread of epithet who sided with Hinks. So it was all about him, on every hand it seemed were uncongenial people, uninteresting people, or people who conceived the deepest distrust and hostility towards him, a magic circle of suspicious, preoccupied and dehumanised humanity. So the poison in his system poisoned the world without.

(But Boomer, the wine merchant, and Tashingford, the chemist, be it noted, were fraught with pride, and held themselves to be a cut above Mr. Polly. They never quarrelled with him, preferring to bear themselves from the outset as though they had already done so.)

As his internal malady grew upon Mr. Polly and he became more and more a battle-ground of fermenting foods and warring juices, he came to hate the very sight, as people say, of every one of these neighbours. There they were, every day and all the days, just the same, echoing his own stagnation. They pained him all round the top and back of his head; they made his legs and arms weary and spiritless. The air was tasteless by reason of them. He lost his human kindliness.

In the afternoons he would hover in the shop bored to death with his business and his home and Miriam, and yet afraid to go out because of his inflamed and magnified dislike and dread of these neighbours. He could not bring himself to go out and run the gauntlet of the observant windows and the cold estranged eyes.

One of his last friendships was with Rusper, the ironmonger. Rusper took over Worthinton's shop about three years after Mr. Polly opened. He was a tall, lean, nervous, convulsive man with an upturned, back-thrown, oval head, who read newspapers and the *Review of Reviews* assiduously, had belonged to a Literary Society somewhere once, and had some defect of the palate that at first gave his lightest word a charm and interest for Mr. Polly. It caused a peculiar clicking sound, as though he had something between a giggle and gas-meter at work in his neck.

His literary admirations were not precisely Mr. Polly's literary admirations; he thought books were written to enshrine Great Thoughts, and that art was pedagogy in fancy dress, he had no sense of phrase or epithet or richness of texture, but still he knew there were books, he did know there were books and he was full of large windy ideas of the sort he called "Modern (kik) Thought," and seemed needlessly and helplessly concerned about "(kik) the Welfare of the Race."

Mr. Polly would dream about that (kik) at nights.

It seemed to that undesirable mind of his that Rusper's head was the most egg-shaped head he had ever seen; the similarity weighted upon him; and when he found an argument growing warm with Rusper he would say: "Boil it some more, O' Man; boil it harder!" or "Six minutes at least," allusions Rusper could never make head or tail of, and got at last to disregard as a part of Mr. Polly's general eccentricity. For a long time that little tendency threw no shadow over their intercourse, but it contained within it the seeds of an ultimate disruption.

Often during the days of this friendship Mr. Polly would leave his shop and walk over to Mr. Rusper's establishment, and stand in his doorway and enquire: "Well, O' Man, how's the Mind of the Age working?" and get quite an hour of it, and sometimes Mr. Rusper would come into the outfitter's shop with "Heard the (kik) latest?" and spend the rest of the morning.

Then Mr. Rusper married, and he married very inconsiderately a woman who was totally uninteresting to Mr. Polly. A coolness grew between them from the first intimation of her advent. Mr. Polly couldn't help thinking when he saw her that she drew her hair back from her forehead a great deal too tightly, and that her elbows were angular. His desire not to mention these things in the apt terms that welled up so richly in his mind, made him awkward in her presence, and that gave her an impression that he was hiding some guilty secret from her. She decided he must have a bad influence upon her husband, and she made it a point to appear whenever she heard him talking to Rusper.

One day they became a little heated about the German peril.

"I lay (kik) they'll invade us," said Rusper.

"Not a bit of it. William's not the Zerxiacious sort."

"You'll see, O' Man."

"Just what I shan't do."

"Before (kik) five years are out."

"Not it."

"Yes."

"No."

"Yes."

"Oh! *Boil* it hard!" said Mr. Polly.

Then he looked up and saw Mrs. Rusper standing behind the counter half hidden by a trophy of spades and garden shears and a knife-cleaning machine, and by her expression he knew instantly that she understood.

The conversation paled and presently Mr. Polly withdrew.

After that, estrangement increased steadily.

Mr. Rusper ceased altogether to come over to the outfitters, and Mr. Polly called upon the ironmonger only with the completest air of casuality. And everything they said to each other led now to flat contradiction and raised voices. Rusper had been warned in vague and alarming terms that Mr. Polly insulted and made game of him; he couldn't discover exactly where; and so it appeared to him now that every word of Mr. Polly's might be an insult meriting his resentment, meriting it none the less because it was masked and cloaked.

Soon Mr. Polly's calls upon Mr. Rusper ceased also, and then Mr. Rusper, pursuing incomprehensible lines of thought, became afflicted with a specialised shortsightedness that applied only to Mr. Polly. He would look in other directions when Mr. Polly appeared, and his large oval face assumed an expression of conscious serenity and deliberate happy unawareness that would have maddened a far less irritable person than Mr. Polly. It evoked a strong desire to mock and ape, and produced in his throat a cough of singular scornfulness, more particularly when Mr. Rusper also assisted, with an assumed unconsciousness that was all his own.

Then one day Mr. Polly had a bicycle accident.

His bicycle was now very old, and it is one of the concomitants of a bicycle's senility that its free wheel should one day obstinately cease to be free. It corresponds to that epoch in human decay when an old gentleman loses an incisor tooth. It happened just as Mr. Polly was approaching Mr. Rusper's shop, and the untoward chance of a motor car trying to pass a waggon on the wrong side gave Mr. Polly no choice but to get on to the pavement and dismount. He was always accustomed to take his time and step off his left pedal at its lowest point, but the jamming of the free wheel gear made that lowest moment a transitory one, and the pedal was lifting his foot for another revolution before he realised what had happened. Before he could dismount according to his habit the pedal had to make a revolution, and before it could make a revolution Mr. Polly found himself among the various sonorous things with which Mr. Rusper adorned the front of his shop, zinc dustbins, household pails, lawn mowers, rakes, spades and all manner of clattering things. Before he got among them he had one of those agonising moments of helpless wrath and suspense that seem to last ages, in which one seems to perceive everything and think of nothing but words that are better forgotten. He sent a column of pails thundering across the doorway and dismounted with one foot in a sanitary dustbin amidst an enormous uproar of falling ironmongery.

"Put all over the place!" he cried, and found Mr. Rusper emerging from his shop with the large tranquillities of his countenance puckered to anger, like the frowns in the brow of a reefing sail. He gesticulated speechlessly for a moment.

"Kik—jer doing?" he said at last.

"Tin mantraps!" said Mr. Polly.

"Jer (kik) doing?"

"Dressing all over the pavement as though the blessed town belonged to you! Ugh!"

And Mr. Polly in attempting a dignified movement realised his entanglement with the dustbin for the first time. With a low embittering expression he kicked his foot about in it for a moment very noisily, and finally sent it thundering to the curb. On its way it struck a pail or so. Then Mr. Polly picked up his bicycle and proposed to resume his homeward way. But the hand of Mr. Rusper arrested him.

"Put it (kik) all (kik kik) back (kik)."

"Put it (kik) back yourself."

"You got (kik) put it back."

"Get out of the (kik) way."

Mr. Rusper laid one hand on the bicycle handle, and the other gripped Mr. Polly's collar urgently. Whereupon Mr. Polly said: "Leggo!" and again, "D'you hear! Leggo!" and then drove his elbow with considerable force into the region of Mr. Rusper's midriff. Whereupon Mr. Rusper, with a loud impassioned cry, resembling "Woo kik" more than any other combination of letters, released the bicycle handle, seized Mr. Polly by the cap and hair and bore his head and shoulders downward. Thereat Mr. Polly, emitting such words as everyone knows and nobody prints, butted his utmost into the concavity of Mr. Rusper, entwined a leg about him and after terrific moments of swaying instability, fell headlong beneath him amidst the bicycles and pails. There on the pavement these inexpert children of a pacific age, untrained in arms and uninured to violence, abandoned themselves to amateurish and absurd efforts to hurt and injure one another—of which the most palpable consequences were dusty backs, ruffled hair and torn and twisted collars. Mr. Polly, by accident, got his finger into Mr. Rusper's mouth, and strove earnestly for some time to prolong that aperture in the direction of Mr. Rusper's ear before it occurred to Mr. Rusper to bite him (and even then he didn't bite very hard), while Mr. Rusper concentrated his mind almost entirely on an effort to rub Mr. Polly's face on the pavement. (And their positions bristled with chances of the deadliest sort!) They didn't from first to last draw blood.

Then it seemed to each of them that the other had become endowed with many hands and several voices and great accessions of strength. They submitted to fate and ceased to struggle. They found themselves torn apart and held up by outwardly scandalised and inwardly delighted neighbours, and invited to explain what it was all about.

"Got to (kik) puttem all back!" panted Mr. Rusper in the expert grasp of Hinks. "Merely asked him to (kik) puttem all back."

Mr. Polly was under restraint of little Clamp, of the toy shop, who was holding his hands in a complex and uncomfortable manner that he afterwards explained to Wintershed was a combination of something romantic called "Ju-jitsu" and something else still more romantic called the "Police Grip."

"Pails," explained Mr. Polly in breathless fragments. "All over the road. Pails. Bungs up the street with his pails. Look at them!"

"Deliber (kik) lib (kik) liberately rode into my goods (kik). Constantly (kik) annoying me (kik)!" said Mr. Rusper. . . .

They were both tremendously earnest and reasonable in their manner. They wished everyone to regard them as responsible and intellectual men acting for the love of right and the enduring good of the world. They felt they must treat this business as a profound and publicly significant affair. They wanted to explain and orate and show the entire necessity of everything they had done. Mr. Polly was convinced he had never been so absolutely correct in all his life as when he planted his foot in the sanitary dustbin, and Mr. Rusper considered his clutch at Mr. Polly's hair as the one faultless impulse in an otherwise undistinguished career. But it was clear in their minds they might easily become ridiculous if they were not careful, if for a second they stepped over the edge of the high spirit and pitiless dignity they had hitherto maintained. At any cost they perceived they must not become ridiculous.

Mr. Chuffles, the scandalous grocer, joined the throng about the principal combatants, mutely as became an outcast, and with a sad, distressed helpful expression picked up Mr. Polly's bicycle. Gambell's summer errand boy, moved by example, restored the dustbin and pails to their self-respect.

"'E ought—'E ought (kik) pick them up," protested Mr. Rusper.

"What's it all about?"; said Mr. Hinks for the third time, shaking Mr. Rusper gently. "'As 'e been calling you names?"

"Simply ran into his pails—as anyone might," said Mr. Polly, "and out he comes and scrags me!"

"(Kik) Assault!" said Mr. Rusper.

"He assaulted *me*," said Mr. Polly.

"Jumped (kik) into my dus'bin!" said Mr. Rusper. "That assault? Or isn't it?"

"You better drop it," said Mr. Hinks.

"Great pity they can't be'ave better, both of 'em," said Mr. Chuffles, glad for once to find himself morally unassailable.

"Anyone see it begin?" said Mr. Wintershed.

425

"*I* was in the shop," said Mrs. Rusper suddenly from the doorstep, piercing the little group of men and boys with the sharp horror of an unexpected woman's voice. "If a witness is wanted I suppose I've got a tongue. I suppose I got a voice in seeing my own 'usband injured. My husband went out and spoke to Mr. Polly, who was jumping off his bicycle all among our pails and things, and immediately 'E butted him in the stomach—immediately—most savagely—butted him. Just after his dinner too and him far from strong. I could have screamed. But Rusper caught hold of him right away, I will say that for Rusper. . . ."

"I'm going," said Mr. Polly suddenly, releasing himself from the Anglo-Japanese grip and holding out his hands for his bicycle.

"Teach you (kik) to leave things alone," said Mr. Rusper with an air of one who has given a lesson.

The testimony of Mrs. Rusper continued relentlessly in the background.

"You'll hear of me through a summons," said Mr. Polly, preparing to wheel his bicycle.

"(Kik) Me too," said Mr. Rusper.

Someone handed Mr. Polly a collar. "This yours?"

Mr. Polly investigated his neck. "I suppose it is. Anyone seen a tie?"

A small boy produced a grimy strip of spotted blue silk.

"Human life isn't safe with you," said Mr. Polly as a parting shot.

"(Kik) Yours isn't," said Mr. Rusper. . . .

And they got small satisfaction out of the Bench, which refused altogether to perceive the relentless correctitude of the behaviour of either party, and reproved the eagerness of Mrs. Rusper—speaking to her gently, firmly but exasperatingly as "My Good Woman" and telling her to "Answer the Question! Answer the Question!"

"Seems a Pity," said the chairman, when binding them over to keep the peace, "you can't behave like Respectable Tradesmen. Seems a Great Pity. Bad Example to the Young and all that. Don't do any Good to the town, don't do any Good to yourselves, don't do any manner of Good, to have all the Tradesmen in the Place scrapping about the Pavement of an Afternoon. Think we're letting you off very easily this time, and hope it will be a Warning to you. Don't expect Men of your Position to come up before us. Very Regrettable Affair. Eh?"

He addressed the latter enquiry to his two colleagues.

"Exactly, exactly," said the colleague to the right.

"Er—(kik)," said Mr. Rusper.

## 7

But the disgust that overshadowed Mr. Polly's being as he sat upon the stile, had other and profounder justification than his quarrel with Rusper and the indignity of appearing before the county bench. He was for the first time in his business career short with his rent for the approaching quarter day, and so far as he could trust his own handling of figures he was sixty or seventy pounds on the wrong side of solvency. And that was the outcome of fifteen years of passive endurance of dullness throughout the best years of his life! What would Miriam say when she learnt this, and was invited to face the prospect of exile—heaven knows what sort of exile!— from their present home? She would grumble and scold and become limply unhelpful, he knew, and none the less so because he could not help things. She would say he ought to have worked harder, and a hundred such exasperating pointless things. Such thoughts as these require no aid from undigested cold pork and cold potatoes and pickles to darken the soul, and with these aids his soul was black indeed.

"May as well have a bit of a walk," said Mr. Polly at last, after nearly intolerable mediations, and sat round and put a leg over the stile.

He remained still for some time before he brought over the other leg.

"Kill myself," he murmured at last.

It was an idea that came back to his mind nowadays with a continually increasing attractiveness—more particularly after meals. Life he felt had no further happiness to offer him. He hated Miriam, and there was no getting away from her whatever might betide. And for the rest there was toil and struggle, toil and struggle with a failing heart and dwindling courage, to sustain that dreary duologue. "Life's insured," said Mr. Polly; "place is insured. I don't see it does any harm to her or anyone."

He stuck his hands in his pockets. "Needn't hurt much," he said. He began to elaborate a plan.

He found it quite interesting elaborating his plan. His countenance became less miserable and his pace quickened.

There is nothing so good in all the world for melancholia as walking, and the exercise of the imagination in planning something presently to be done, and soon the wrathful wretchedness had vanished from Mr. Polly's face. He would have to do the thing secretly and elaborately, because otherwise there might be difficulties about the life insurance. He began to scheme how he could circumvent that difficulty. . . .

He took a long walk, for after all what is the good of hurrying back to shop when you are not only insolvent but very soon to die? His dinner and the east wind lost their sinister hold upon his soul, and when at last he came back along the Fishbourne High Street, his face was unusually bright and the craving hunger of the dyspeptic was returning. So he went into the grocer's and bought a ruddily decorated tin of a brightly pink fishlike substance known as "Deep Sea Salmon." This he was resolved to consume regardless of cost with vinegar and salt and pepper as a relish to his supper.

He did, and since he and Miriam rarely talked and Miriam thought honour and his recent behaviour demanded a hostile silence, he ate fast, and copiously and soon gloomily. He ate alone, for she refrained, to mark her sense of his extravagance. Then he prowled into the High Street for a time, thought it an infernal place, tried his pipe and found it foul and bitter, and retired wearily to bed.

He slept for an hour or so and then woke up to the contemplation of Miriam's hunched back and the riddle of life, and this bright attractive idea of ending for ever and ever and ever all the things that were locking him in, this bright idea that shone like a baleful star above all the reek and darkness of his misery. . . .

CHAPTER THE EIGHTH
MAKING AN END TO THINGS
1

Mr. Polly designed his suicide with considerable care, and a quite remarkable altruism. His passionate hatred for Miriam vanished directly the idea of getting away from her for ever became clear in his mind. He found himself full of solicitude then for her welfare. He did not want to buy his release at her expense. He had not the remotest intention of leaving her unprotected with a painfully dead husband and a bankrupt shop on her hands. It seemed to him that he could contrive to secure for her the full benefit of both his life insurance and his fire insurance if he managed things in a tactful manner. He felt happier than he had done for years scheming out this undertaking, albeit it was perhaps a larger and somberer kind of happiness than had fallen to his lot before. It amazed him to think he had endured his monotony of misery and failure for so long.

But there were some queer doubts and questions in the dim, half-lit background of his mind that he had very resolutely to ignore.

"Sick of it," he had to repeat to himself aloud, to keep his determination clear and firm. His life was a failure, there was nothing more to hope for but unhappiness. Why shouldn't he?

His project was to begin the fire with the stairs that led from the ground floor to the underground kitchen and scullery. This he would soak with paraffine, and assist with firewood and paper, and a brisk fire in the coal cellar underneath. He would smash a hole or so in the stairs to ventilate the blaze, and have a good pile of boxes and paper, and a convenient chair or so in the shop above. He would have the paraffine can upset and the shop lamp, as if awaiting refilling, at a convenient distance in the scullery ready to catch. Then he would smash the house lamp on the staircase, a fall with that in his hand was to be the onstensible cause of the blaze, and then he would cut his throat at the top of the kitchen stairs, which would then become his funeral pyre. He would do all this on Sunday evening while Miriam was at church, and it would appear that he had fallen downstairs with the lamp, and been burnt to death. There was really no flaw whatever that he could see in the scheme. He was quite sure he knew how to cut his throat, deep at the side and not to saw at the windpipe, and he was reasonably sure it wouldn't hurt him very much. And then everything would be at an end.

There was no particular hurry to get the thing done, of course, and meanwhile he occupied his mind with possible variations of the scheme. . . .

428

It needed a particularly dry and dusty east wind, a Sunday dinner of exceptional virulence, a conclusive letter from Konk, Maybrick, Ghool and Gabbitas, his principal and most urgent creditor, and a conversation with Miriam arising out of arrears of rent and leading on to mutual character sketching, before Mr. Polly could be brought to the necessary pitch of despair to carry out his plans. He went for an embittering walk, and came back to find Miriam in a bad temper over the tea things, with the brewings of three-quarters of an hour in the pot, and hot buttered muffin gone leathery. He sat eating in silence with his resolution made.

"Coming to church?" said Miriam after she had cleared away.

"Rather. I got a lot to be grateful for," said Mr. Polly.

"You got what you deserve," said Miriam.

"Suppose I have," said Mr. Polly, and went and stared out of the back window at a despondent horse in the hotel yard.

He was still standing there when Miriam came downstairs dressed for church. Something in his immobility struck home to her. "You'd better come to church than mope," he said.

"I shan't mope," he answered.

She remained still for a moment. Her presence irritated him. he felt that in another moment he should say something absurd to her, make some last appeal for that understanding she had never been able to give. "Oh! *go* to church!" he said.

In another moment the outer door slammed upon her. "Good riddance!" said Mr. Polly.

He turned about. "I've had my whack," he said.

He reflected. "I don't see she'll have any cause to holler," he said. "Beastly Home! Beastly Life!"

For a space he remained thoughtful. "Here goes!" he said at last.

## 2

For twenty minutes Mr. Polly busied himself about the house, making his preparations very neatly and methodically.

He opened the attic windows in order to make sure of a good draught through the house, and drew down the blinds at the back and shut the kitchen door to conceal his arrangements from casual observation. At the end he would open the door on the yard and so make a clean clear draught right through the house. He hacked at, and wedged off, the tread of a stair. He cleared out the coals from under the staircase, and built a neat fire of firewood and paper there, he splashed about paraffine and arranged the lamps and can even as he had designed, and made a fine inflammable pile of things in the little parlour behind the shop. "Looks pretty arsonical," he said as he surveyed it all. "Wouldn't do to have a caller now. Now for the stairs!"

"Plenty of time," he assured himself, and took the lamp which was to explain the whole affair, and went to the head of the staircase between the scullery and the parlour.

He sat down in the twilight with the unlit lamp beside him and surveyed things. He must light the fire in the coal cellar under the stairs, open the back door, then come up them very quickly and light the paraffine puddles on each step, the sit down here again and cut his throat.

He drew his razor from his pocket and felt the edge. It wouldn't hurt much, and in ten minutes he would be indistinguishable ashes in the blaze.

And this was the end of life for him!

The end! And it seemed to him now that life had never begun for him, never! It was as if his soul had been cramped and his eyes bandaged from the hour of his birth. Why had he lived such a life? Why had he submitted to things, blundered into things? Why had he never insisted on the things he thought beautiful and the things he desired, never sought them, fought for them, taken any risk for them, died rather than abandon them? They were the things that mattered. Safety did not matter. A living did not matter unless there were things to live for. . . .

He had been a fool, a coward and a fool, he had been fooled too, for no one had ever warned him to take a firm hold upon life, no one had ever told him of the littleness of fear, or pain, or death; but what was the good of going through it now again? It was over and done with.

The clock in the pack parlour pinged the half hour.

"Time!" said Mr. Polly, and stood up.

For an instant he battled with an impulse to put it all back, hastily, guiltily, and abandon this desperate plan of suicide for ever.

But Miriam would smell the paraffine!

"No way out this time, O' Man," said Mr. Polly; and he went slowly downstairs, match box in hand.

He paused for five seconds, perhaps, to listen to noises in the yard of the Royal Fishbourne Hotel before he struck his match. It trembled a little in his hand. The paper blackened, and an edge of blue flame ran outward and spread. The fire burnt up readily, and in an instant the wood was crackling cheerfully.

Someone might hear. He must hurry.

He lit a pool of paraffine on the scullery floor, and instantly a nest of snaky, wavering blue flame became agog for prey. He went up the stairs three steps at a time with one eager blue flicker in pursuit of him. He seized the lamp at the top. "Now!" he said and flung it smashing. The chimney broke, but the glass receiver stood the shock and rolled to the bottom, a potential bomb. Old Rumbold would hear that and wonder what it was! . . . He'd know soon enough!

Then Mr. Polly stood hesitating, razor in hand, and then sat down. He was trembling violently, but quite unafraid.

He drew the blade lightly under one ear. "Lord!" but it stung like a nettle!

Then he perceived a little blue thread of flame running up his leg. It arrested his attention, and for a moment he sat, razor in hand, staring at it. It must be paraffine on his trousers that had caught fire on the stairs. Of course his legs were wet with paraffine! He smacked the flicker with this hand to put it out, and felt his leg burn as he did so. But his trousers still charred and glowed. It seemed to him necessary that he must put this out before he cut his throat. He put down the razor beside him to smack with both hands very eagerly. And as he did so a thin tall red flame came up through the hole in the stairs he had made and stood still, quite still as it seemed, and looked at him. It was a strange-looking flame, a flattish salmon colour, redly streaked. It was so queer and quiet mannered that the sight of it held Mr. Polly agape.

"Whuff!" went the can of paraffine below, and boiled over with stinking white fire. At the outbreak the salmon-coloured flames shivered and ducked and then doubled and vanished, and instantly all the staircase was noisily ablaze.

Mr. Polly sprang up and backwards, as though the uprushing in tongues of fire were a pack of eager wolves.

"Good Lord!" he cried like a man who wakes up from a dream.

He swore sharply and slapped again at a recrudescent flame upon his leg.

"What the Deuce shall I do? I'm soaked with the confounded stuff!"

He had nerved himself for throat-cutting, but this was fire!

He wanted to delay things, to put them out for a moment while he did his business. The idea of arresting all this hurry with water occurred to him.

There was no water in the little parlour and none in the shop. He hesitated for a moment whether he should not run upstairs to the bedrooms and get a ewer of water to throw on the flames. At this rate Rumbold's would be ablaze in five minutes! Things were going all too fast for Mr. Polly. He ran towards the staircase door, and its hot breath pulled him up sharply. Then he dashed out through his shop. The catch of the front door was sometimes obstinate; it was now, and instantly he became frantic. He rattled and stormed and felt the parlour already ablaze behind him. In another moment he was in the High Street with the door wide open.

The staircase behind him was crackling now like horsewhips and pistol shots.

He had a vague sense that he wasn't doing as he had proposed, but the chief thing was his sense of that uncontrolled fire within. What was he going to do? There was the fire brigade station next door but one.

The Fishbourne High Street had never seemed so empty.

Far off at the corner by the God's Providence Inn a group of three stiff hobbledehoys in the black, best clothes, conversed intermittently with Taplow, the policeman.

"Hi!" bawled Mr. Polly to them. "Fire! Fire!" and struck by a horrible thought, the thought of Rumbold's deaf mother-in-law upstairs, began to bang and kick and rattle with the utmost fury to Rumbold's shop door.

"Hi!" he repeated, "*Fire!*"

### 3

That was the beginning of the great Fishbourne fire, which burnt its way sideways into Mr. Rusper's piles of crates and straw, and backwards to the petrol and stabling of the Royal Fishbourne Hotel, and spread from that basis until it seemed half Fishbourne would be ablaze. The east wind, which had been gathering in strength all that day, fanned the flame; everything was dry and ready, and the little shed beyond Rumbold's in which the local Fire Brigade kept its manual, was alight before the Fishbourne fire hose could be saved from disaster. In marvellously little time a great column of black smoke, shot with red streamers, rose out of the middle of the High Street, and all Fishbourne was alive with excitement.

Much of the more respectable elements of Fishbourne society was in church or chapel; many, however, had been tempted by the blue sky and the hard freshness of spring to take walks inland, and there had been the usual disappearance of loungers and conversationalists from the beach and the back streets when at the hour of six the shooting of bolts and the turning of keys had ended the British Ramadan, that weekly interlude of drought our law imposes. The youth of the place were scattered on the beach or playing in back yards, under threat if their clothes were dirtied, and the adolescent were disposed in pairs among the more secluded corners to be found upon the outskirts of the place. Several godless youth, seasick but fishing steadily, were tossing upon the sea in old Tarbold's, the infidel's, boat, and the Clamps were entertaining cousins from Port Burdock. Such few visitors as Fishbourne could boast in the spring were at church or on the beach. To all these that column of smoke did in a manner address itself. "Look here!" it said, "this, within limits, is your affair; what are you going to do?"

The three hobbledehoys, had it been a weekday and they in working clothes, might have felt free to act, but the stiffness of black was upon them and they simply moved to the corner of Rusper's to take a better view of Mr. Polly beating at the door. The policeman was a young, inexpert constable with far too lively a sense of the public house. He put his head inside the Private Bar to the horror of everyone there. But there was no breach of the law, thank Heaven! "Polly's and Rumbold's on fire!" he said, and vanished again. A window in the top story over Boomer's shop opened, and Boomer, captain of the Fire Brigade, appeared, staring out with a blank expression. Still staring, he began to fumble with his collar and tie; manifestly he had to put on his uniform. Hinks' dog, which had been lying on the pavement outside Wintershed's, woke up, and having regarded Mr. Polly suspiciously for some time, growled nervously and went round the corner into Granville Alley. Mr. Polly continued to beat and kick at Rumbold's door.

Then the public houses began to vomit forth the less desirable elements of Fishbourne society, boys and men were moved to run and shout, and more windows went up as the stir increased. Tashingford, the chemist, appeared at his door, in shirt sleeves and an apron, with his photographic plate holders in his hand. And then like a vision of purpose came Mr. Gambell, the greengrocer, running out of Clayford's Alley and buttoning on his jacket as he ran. His great brass fireman's helmet was on his head, hiding it all but the sharp nose, the firm mouth, the intrepid chin. He ran straight to the fire station and tried the door, and turned about and met the eye of Boomer still at his upper window. "The key!" cried Mr. Gambell, "the key!"

432

Mr. Boomer made some inaudible explanation about his trousers and half a minute.

"Seen old Rumbold?" cried Mr. Polly, approaching Mr. Gambell.

"Gone over Downford for a walk," said Mr. Gambell. "He told me! But look 'ere! We 'aven't got the key!"

"Lord!" said Mr. Polly, and regarded the china shop with open eyes. He *knew* the old woman must be there alone. He went back to the shop front and stood surveying it in infinite perplexity. The other activities in the street did not interest him. A deaf old lady somewhere upstairs there! Precious moments passing! Suddenly he was struck by an idea and vanished from public vision into the open door of the Royal Fishbourne Tap.

And now the street was getting crowded and people were laying their hands to this and that.

Mr. Rusper had been at home reading a number of tracts upon Tariff Reform during the quiet of his wife's absence in church, and trying to work out the application of the whole question to ironmongery. He heard a clattering in the street and for a time disregarded it, until a cry of Fire! drew him to the window. He pencilled-marked the tract of Chiozza Money's that he was reading side by side with one by Mr. Holt Schooling, made a hasty note "Bal. Of Trade say 12,000,000" and went to look out. Instantly he opened the window and ceased to believe the Fiscal Question the most urgent of human affairs.

"Good (kik) Gud!" said Mr. Rusper.

For now the rapidly spreading blaze had forced the partition into Mr. Rumbold's premises, swept across his cellar, clambered his garden wall by means of his well-tarred mushroom shed, and assailed the engine house. It stayed not to consume, but ran as a thing that seeks a quarry. Polly's shop and upper parts were already a furnace, and black smoke was coming out of Rumbold's cellar gratings. The fires in the engine house showed only as a sudden rush of smoke from the back, like something suddenly blown up. The fire brigade, still much under strength, were now hard at work in the front of the latter building; they had got the door open all too late, they had rescued the fire escape and some buckets, and were now lugging out their manual, with the hose already a dripping mass of molten, flaring, stinking rubber. Boomer was dancing about and swearing and shouting; this direct attack upon his apparatus outraged his sense of chivalry. The rest of the brigade hovered in a disheartened state about the rescued fire escape, and tried to piece Boomer's comments into some tangible instructions.

"Hi!" said Rusper from the window. "Kik! What's up?"

Gambell answered him out of his helmet. "Hose!" he cried. "Hose gone!"

"I (kik) got hose!" cried Rusper.

He had. He had stock of several thousand feet of garden hose, of various qualities and calibres, and now he felt was the time to use it. In another moment his shop door was open and he was hurling pails, garden syringes, and rolls of garden hose out upon the pavement. "(Kik)," he cried, "undo it!" to the gathering crowd in the roadway.

They did. Presently a hundred ready hands were unrolling and spreading and tangling up and twisting and hopelessly involving Mr. Rusper's stock of hose, sustained by an unquenchable assurance that presently it would in some manner contain and convey water, and Mr. Rusper, on his knees, kicking violently, became incredibly busy with wire and brass junctions and all sorts of mysteries.

"Fix it to the (kik) bathroom tap!" said Mr. Rusper.

Next door to the fire station was Mantell and Throbson's, the little Fishbourne branch of that celebrated firm, and Mr. Boomer, seeking in a teeming mind for a plan of action, had determined to save this building. "Someone telephone to the Port Burdock and Hampstead-on-Sea fire brigades," he cried to the crowd and then to his fellows: "Cut away the wood work of the fire station!" and so led the way into the blaze with a whirling hatchet that effected wonders in no time in ventilation.

But it was not, after all, such a bad idea of his. Mantell and Throbsons was separated from the fire station in front by a covered glass passage, and at the back the roof of a big outhouse sloped down to the fire station leads. The sturdy longshoremen, who made up the bulk of the fire brigade, assailed the glass roof of the passage with extraordinary gusto, and made a smashing of glass that drowned for a time the rising uproar of the flames.

A number of willing volunteers started off to the new telephone office in obedience to Mr. Boomer's request, only to be told with cold official politeness by the young lady at the exchange that all that had been done on her own initiative ten minutes ago. She parleyed with these heated enthusiasts for a space, and then returned to the window.

And indeed the spectacle was well worth looking at. The dusk was falling, and the flames were showing brilliantly at half a dozen points. The Royal Fishbourne Hotel Tap, which adjoined Mr. Polly to the west, was being kept wet by the enthusiastic efforts of a string of volunteers with buckets of water, and above at a bathroom window the little German waiter was busy with the garden hose. But Mr. Polly's establishment looked more like a house afire than most houses on fire contrive to look from start to finish. Every window showed eager flickering flames, and flames like serpents' tongues were licking out of three large holes in the roof, which was already beginning to fall in. Behind, larger and abundantly spark-shot gusts of fire rose from the fodder that was now getting alight in the Royal Fishbourne Hotel stables. Next door to Mr. Polly, Mr. Rumbold's house was disgorging black smoke from the gratings that protected its underground windows, and smoke and occasional shivers of flame were also coming out of its first-floor windows. The fire station was better alight at the back than in front, and its woodwork burnt pretty briskly with peculiar greenish flickerings, and a pungent flavour. In the street an inaggressively disorderly crowd clambered over the rescued fire escape and resisted the attempts of the three local constables to get it away from the danger of Mr. Polly's tottering façade, a cluster of busy forms danced and shouted and advised on the noisy and smashing attempt to cut off Mantell and Throbson's from the first station that was still in ineffectual progress. Further, a number of people appeared to be destroying interminable red and grey snakes under the heated direction of Mr. Rusper; it was as if the High Street had a plague of worms, and beyond again the more timid and less active crowded in front of an accumulation of arrested traffic. Most of the men were in Sabbatical black, and this and the white and starched quality of the women and children in their best clothes gave a note of ceremony to the whole affair.

For a moment the attention of the telephone clerk was held by the activities of Mr. Tashingford, the chemist, who, regardless of everyone else, was rushing across the road hurling fire grenades into the first station and running back for more, and then her eyes lifted to the slanting outhouse roof that went up to a ridge behind the parapet of Mantell and Throbson's. An expression of incredulity came into the telephone operator's eyes and gave place to hard activity. She flung up the window and screamed out," "Two people on the roof up there! Two people on the roof!"

### 4

Her eyes had not deceived her. Two figures which had emerged from the upper staircase window of Mr. Rumbold's and had got, after a perilous paddle in his cistern, on to the first station, were now slowly but resolutely clambering up the outhouse roof towards the back of the main premises of Messrs. Mantell and Throbson's. They clambered slowly and one urged and helped the other, slipping and pausing ever and again, amidst a constant trickle of fragments of broken tile.

One was Mr. Polly, with is hair wildly disordered, his face covered with black smudges and streaked with perspiration, and his trouser legs scorched and blackened; the other was an elderly lady, quietly but becomingly dressed in black, with small white frills at her neck and wrists and a Sunday cap of ecru lace enlivened with a black velvet bow. Her hair was brushed back from her wrinkled brow and plastered down tightly, meeting in a small knob behind; her wrinkled mouth bore that expression of supreme resolution common with the toothless aged. She was shaky, not with fear, but with the vibrations natural to her years, and she spoke with the slow quavering firmness of the very aged.

"I don't mind scrambling," she said with piping inflexibility, "but I can't jump and I *wunt* jump."

"Scramble, old lady, then—scramble!" said Mr. Polly, pulling her arm. "It's one up and two down on these blessed tiles."

"It's not what I'm used to," she said.

"Stick to it!" said Mr. Polly. "Live and learn," and got to the ridge and grasped at her arm to pull her after him.

"I can't jump, mind ye," she repeated, pressing her lips together. "And old ladies like me mustn't be hurried."

"Well, let's get as high as possible anyhow!" said Mr. Polly, urging her gently upward. "Shinning up a water-spout in your line? Near as you'll get to Heaven."

"I *can't* jump," she said. "I can do anything but jump."

"Hold on!" said Mr. Polly, "while I give you a boost. That's—wonderful."

"So long as it isn't jumping. . . ."

The old lady grasped the parapet above, and there was a moment of intense struggle.

"Urup!" said Mr. Polly. "hold on! Gollys! where's she gone to? . . ."

Then an ill-mended, wavering, yet very reassuring spring side boot appeared for an instant.

"Thought perhaps there wasn't any roof there!" he explained, scrambling up over the parapet beside her.

"I've never been out on a roof before, " said the old lady. "I'm all disconnected. It's very bumpy. Especially that last bit. Can't we sit here for a bit and rest? I'm not the girl I use to be."

"You sit here ten minutes, "shouted Mr. Polly, "and you'll pop like a roast chestnut. Don't understand me? *Roast chestnut!* ROAST CHESTNUT! POP! There ought to be a limit to deafness. Come on round to the front and see if we can find an attic window. Look at this smoke!"

"Nasty!" said the old lady, her eyes following his gesture, puckering her face into an expression of great distaste.

"Come on!"

"Can't hear a word you say."

He pulled her arm. "Come on!"

She paused for a moment to relieve herself of a series of entirely unexpected chuckles. "Sich goings on!" she said, "I never did! Where's he going now?" and came along behind the parapet to the front of the drapery establishment.

Below, the street was now fully alive to their presence, and encouraged the appearance of their heads by shouts and cheers. A sort of free fight was going on round the fire escape, order represented by Mr. Boomer and the very young policeman, and disorder by some partially intoxicated volunteers with views of their own about the manipulation of the apparatus. Two or three lengths of Mr. Rusper's garden hose appeared to have twined themselves round the ladder. Mr. Polly watched the struggle with a certain impatience, and glanced ever and again over his shoulder at the increasing volume of smoke and steam that was pouring up from the burning fire station. He decided to break an attic window and get in, and so try and get down through the shop. He found himself in a little bedroom, and returned to fetch his charge. For some time he could not make her understand his purpose.

"Got to come at once!" he shouted.

"I hain't 'ad sich a time for years!" said the old lady.

"We'll have to get down through the house!"

"Can't do no jumpin'," said the old lady. "No!"

She yielded reluctantly to his grasp.

She stared over the parapet. "Runnin' and scurrying about like black beetles in a kitchin," she said.

"We've got to hurry."

"Mr. Rumbold 'e's a very Quiet man. 'E likes everything Quiet. He'll be surprised to see me 'ere! Why!—there 'e is!" She fumbled in her garments mysteriously and at last produced a wrinkled pocket handkerchief and began to wave it.

"Oh, come ON!" cried Mr. Polly, and seized her.

He got her into the attic, but the staircase, he found, was full of suffocating smoke, and he dared not venture below the next floor. He took her into a long dormitory, shut the door on those pungent and pervasive fumes, and opened the window to discover the fire escape was now against the house, and all Fishbourne boiling with excitement as on immensely helmeted and active and resolute little figure ascended. In another moment the rescuer stared over the windowsill, heroic, but just a trifle self-conscious and grotesque.

"Lawks a mussy!" said the old lady. "Wonders and Wonders! Why! it's Mr. Gambell! 'Iding 'is 'ed in that thing! I *never* did!"

"Can we get her out?" said Mr. Gambell. "There's not much time."

"He might git stuck in it."

"*You'll* get stuck in it," said Mr. Polly, "come along!"

"Not for jumpin' I don't," said the old lady, understanding his gestures rather than his words. "Not a bit of it. I bain't no good at jumping and I *wunt.*"

They urged her gently but firmly towards the window.

"You lemme do it my own way," said the old lady at the sill. . . .

"I could do it better if 'e'd take it off."

"Oh! *carm* on!"

"It's wuss than Carter's stile," she said, "before they mended it. With a cow a-looking at you."

Mr. Gambell hovered protectingly below. Mr. Polly steered her aged limbs from above. An anxious crowd below babbled advice and did its best to upset the fire escape. Within, streamers of black smoke were pouring up through the cracks in the floor. For some seconds the world waited while the old lady gave herself up to reckless mirth again. "Sich times!" she said, and "*Poor* Rumbold!"

Slowly they descended, and Mr. Polly remained at the post of danger steadying the long ladder until the old lady was in safety below and sheltered by Mr. Rumbold (who was in tears) and the young policeman from the urgent congratulations of the crowd. The crowd was full of an impotent passion to participate. Those nearest wanted to shake her hand, those remoter cheered.

"The fust fire I was ever in and likely to be my last. It's a scurryin', 'urryin' business, but I'm real glad I haven't missed it," said the old lady as she was borne rather than led towards the refuge of the Temperance Hotel.

Also she was heard to remark" "'E was saying something about 'ot chestnuts. I 'aven't 'ad no 'ot chestnuts."

Then the crowd became aware of Mr. Polly awkwardly negotiating the top rungs of the fire escape. "'Ere 'e comes!" cried a voice, and Mr. Polly descended into the world again out of the conflagration he had lit to be his funeral pyre, moist, excited, and tremendously alive, amidst a tempest of applause. As he got lower and lower the crowd howled like a pack of dogs at him. Impatient men unable to wait for him seized and shook his descending boots, and so brought him to earth with a run. He was rescued with difficulty from an enthusiast who wished to slake at his own expense and to his own accompaniment a thirst altogether heroic. He was hauled into the Temperance Hotel and flung like a sack, breathless and helpless, into the tear-wet embrace of Miriam.

## 5

With the dusk and the arrival of some county constabulary, and first one and presently two other fire engines from Port Burdock and Hampstead-on-Sea, the local talent of Fishbourne found itself forced back into a secondary, less responsible and more observant role. I will not pursue the story of the fire to its ashes, nor will I do more than glance at the unfortunate Mr. Rusper, a modern Laocoon, vainly trying to retrieve his scattered hose amidst the tramplings and rushings of the Port Burdock experts.

In a small sitting-room of the Fishbourne Temperance Hotel a little group of Fishbourne tradesmen sat and conversed in fragments and anon went to the window and looked out upon the smoking desolation of their homes across the way, and anon sat down again. They and their families were the guests of old Lady Bargrave, who had displayed the utmost sympathy and interest in their misfortunes. She had taken several people into her own house at Everdean, had engaged the Temperance Hotel as a temporary refuge, and personally superintended the housing of Mantell and Throbson's homeless assistants. The Temperance Hotel became and remained extremely noisy and congested, with people sitting about anywhere, conversing in fragments and totally unable to get themselves to bed. The manager was an old soldier, and following the best traditions of the service saw that everyone had hot cocoa. Hot cocoa seemed to be about everywhere, and it was no doubt very heartening and sustaining to everyone. When the manager detected anyone disposed to be drooping or pensive he exhorted that person at once to drink further hot cocoa and maintain a stout heart.

The hero of the occasion, the centre of interest, was Mr. Polly. For he had not only caused the fire by upsetting a lighted lamp, scorching his trousers and narrowly escaping death, as indeed he had now explained in detail about twenty times, but he had further thought at once of that amiable but helpless old lady next door, had shown the utmost decision in making his way to her over the yard wall of the Royal Fishbourne Hotel, and had rescued her with persistence and vigour in spite of the levity natural to her years. Everyone thought well of him and was anxious to show it, more especially by shaking his hand painfully and repeatedly. Mr. Rumbold, breaking a silence of nearly fifteen years, thanked him profusely, said he had never understood him properly and declared he ought to have a medal. There seemed to be a widely diffused idea that Mr. Polly ought to have a medal. Hinks thought so. He declared, moreover, and with the utmost emphasis, that Mr. Polly had a crowded and richly decorated interior—or words to that effect. There was something apologetic in this persistence; it was as if he regretted past intimations that Mr. Polly was internally defective and hollow. He also said that Mr. Polly was a "white man," albeit, as he developed it, with a liver of the deepest chromatic satisfactions.

Mr. Polly wandered centrally through it all, with his face washed and his hair carefully brushed and parted, looking modest and more than a little absent-minded, and wearing a pair of black dress trowsers belonging to the manager of the Temperance Hotel,—a larger man than himself in every way.

He drifted upstairs to his fellow-tradesmen, and stood for a time staring into the littered street, with its pools of water and extinguished gas lamps. His companions in misfortune resumed a fragmentary disconnected conversation. They touched now on one aspect of the disaster and now on another, and there were intervals of silence. More or less empty cocoa cups were distributed over the table, mantelshelf and piano, and in the middle of the table was a tin of biscuits, into which Mr. Rumbold, sitting round-shoulderedly, dipped ever and again in an absent-minded way, and munched like a distant shooting of coals. It added to the solemnity of the affair that nearly all of them were in their black Sunday clothes; little Clamp was particularly impressive and dignified in a wide open frock coat, a Gladstone-shaped paper collar, and a large white and blue tie. They felt that they were in the presence of a great disaster, the sort of disaster that gets into the papers, and is even illustrated by blurred photographs of the crumbling ruins. In the presence of that sort of disaster all honourable men are lugubrious and sententious.

And yet it is impossible to deny a certain element of elation. Not one of those excellent men but was already realising that a great door had opened, as it were, in the opaque fabric of destiny, that they were to get their money again that had seemed sunken for ever beyond any hope in the deeps of retail trade. Life was already in their imagination rising like a Phoenix from the flames.

"I suppose there'll be a public subscription," said Mr. Clamp.

"Not for those who're insured," said Mr. Wintershed.

"I was thinking of them assistants from Mantell and Throbson's. They just have lost nearly everything."

"They'll be looked after all right," said Mr. Rumbold. "Never fear."

Pause.

"*I'm* insured," said Mr. Clamp, with unconcealed satisfaction. "Royal Salamander."

"Same here," said Mr. Wintershed.

439

"Mine's the Glasgow Sun," Mr. Hinks remarked. "Very good company."

"You insured, Mr. Polly?"

"He deserves to be," said Rumbold.

"Ra-ther," said Hinks. "Blowed if he don't. Hard lines it *would* be—if there wasn't something for him."

"Commercial and General," answered Mr. Polly over his shoulder, still staring out of the window. "Oh! I'm all right."

The topic dropped for a time, though manifestly it continued to exercise their minds.

"It's cleared me out of a lot of old stock," said Mr. Wintershed; "that's one good thing."

The remark was felt to be in rather questionable taste, and still more so was the next comment.

"Rusper's a bit sick it didn't reach 'im."

Everyone looked uncomfortable, and no one was willing to point to the reason why Rusper should be a bit sick.

"Rusper's been playing a game of his own," said Hinks. "Wonder what he thought he was up to! Sittin' in the middle of the road with a pair of tweezers he was, and about a yard of wire—mending somethin'. Wonder he warn't run over by the Port Burdock engine."

Presently a little chat sprang up upon the causes of fires, and Mr. Polly was moved to tell how it had happened for the one and twentieth time. His story had now become as circumstantial and exact as the evidence of a police witness. "Upset the lamp," he said. "I'd just lighted it, I was going upstairs, and my foot slipped against where one of the treads was a bit rotten, and down I went. Thing was a flare in a moment! . . ."

He yawned at the end of the discussion, and moved doorward.

"So long," said Mr. Polly.

"Good night," said Mr. Rumbold. "You played a brave man's part! If you don't get a medal—"

He left an eloquent pause.

"'Ear, 'ear!" said Mr. Wintershed and Mr. Clamp. "Goo'night, O' Man," said Mr. Hinks.

"Goo'night All," said Mr. Polly. . . .

He went slowly upstairs. The vague perplexity common to popular heroes pervaded his mind. He entered the bedroom and turned up the electric light. It was quite a pleasant room, one of the best in the Temperance Hotel, with a nice clean flowered wallpaper, and a very large looking-glass. Miriam appeared to be asleep, and her shoulders were humped up under the clothes in a shapeless, forbidding lump that Mr. Polly had found utterly loathsome for fifteen years. He went softly over to the dressing-table and surveyed himself thoughtful. Presently he hitched up the trowsers. "Miles too big for me," he remarked. "Funny not to have a pair of breeches of one's own. . . . Like being born again. Naked came I into the world. . . ."

Miriam stirred and rolled over, and stared at him.

"Hello!" she said.

"Hello."

"Come to bed?"

"It's three."

Pause, while Mr. Polly disrobed slowly.

"I been thinking," said Miriam. "It isn't going to be so bad after all. We shall get your insurance. We can easy begin all over again."

"H'm," said Mr. Polly.

She turned her face away from him and reflected.

"Get a better house," said Miriam, regarding the wallpaper pattern. "I've always 'ated them stairs."

Mr. Polly removed a boot.

"Choose a better position where there's more doing," murmured Miriam. . . .

"Not half so bad," she whispered. . . .

"You *wanted* stirring up," she said, half asleep. . . .

It dawned upon Mr. Polly for the first time that he had forgotten something.

He ought to have cut his throat!

The fact struck him as remarkable, but as now no longer of any particular urgency. It seemed a thing far off in the past, and he wondered why he had not thought of it before. Odd thing life is! If he had done it he would never have seen this clean and agreeable apartment with the electric light. . . . His thoughts wandered into a question of detail. Where could he have put the razor down? Somewhere in the little room behind the shop, he supposed, but he could not think where more precisely. Anyhow it didn't matter now.

He undressed himself calmly, got into bed, and fell asleep almost immediately.

CHAPTER THE NINTH

THE POTWELL INN

1

But when a man has once broken through the paper walls of everyday circumstance, those unsubstantial walls that hold so many of us securely prisoned from the cradle to the grave, he has made a discovery. If the world does not please you you can change it. Determine to alter it at any price, and you can change it altogether. You may change it to something sinister and angry, to something appalling, but it may be you will change it to something brighter, something more agreeable, and at the worst something much more interesting. There is only one sort of man who is absolutely to blame for his own misery, and that is the man who finds life dull and dreary. There are no circumstances in the world that determined action cannot alter, unless perhaps they are the walls of a prison cell, and even those will dissolve and change, I am told, into the infirmary compartment at any rate, for the man who can fast with resolution.

441

I give these things as facts and information, and with no moral intimations. And Mr. Polly lying awake at nights, with a renewed indigestion, with Miriam sleeping sonorously beside him and a general air of inevitableness about his situation, saw through it, understood there was no inevitable any more, and escaped his former despair.

He could, for example, "clear out."

It became a wonderful and alluring phrase to him: "clear out!"

Why had he never thought of clearing out before?

He was amazed and a little shocked at the unimaginative and superfluous criminality in him that had turned old cramped and stagnant Fishbourne into a blaze and new beginnings. (I wish from the bottom of my heart I could add that he was properly sorry.) But something constricting and restrained seemed to have been destroyed by that flare. *Fishbourne wasn't the world*. That was the new, the essential fact of which he had lived so lamentably in ignorance. Fishbourne as he had known it and hated it, so that he wanted to kill himself to get out of it, *wasn't the world*.

The insurance money he was to receive made everything humane and kindly and practicable. He would "clear out," with justice and humanity. He would take exactly twenty-one pounds, and all the rest he would leave to Miriam. That seemed to him absolutely fair. Without him, she could do all sorts of things—all the sorts of things she was constantly urging him to do.

And he would go off along the white road that led to Garchester, and on to Crogate and so to Tunbridge Wells, where there was a Toad Rock he had heard of, but never seen. (It seemed to him this must needs be a marvel. ) And so to other towns and cities. He would walk and loiter by the way, and sleep in inns at night, and get an odd job here and there and talk to strange people. Perhaps he would get quite a lot of work and prosper, and if he did not do so he would lie down in front of a train, or wait for a warm night, and then fall into some smooth, broad river. Not so bad as sitting down to a dentist, not nearly so bad. And he would never open a shop any more. Never!

So the possibilities of the future presented themselves to Mr. Polly as he lay awake at nights.

It was springtime, and in the woods so soon as one got out of reach of the sea wind there would be anemones and primroses.

2

A month later a leisurely and dusty tramp, plump equatorially and slightly bald, with his hands in his pockets and his lips puckered to a contemplative whistle, strolled along the river bank between Uppingdon and Potwell. It was a profusely budding spring day and greens such as God had never permitted in the world before in human memory (though indeed they come every year), were mirrored vividly in a mirror of equally unprecedented brown. For a time the wanderer stopped and stood still, and even the thin whistle died away from his lips as he watched a water vole run to and fro upon a little headland across the stream. The vole plopped into the water and swam and dived and only when the last ring of its disturbance had vanished did Mr. Polly resume his thoughtful course to nowhere in particular.

For the first time in many years he had been leading a healthy human life, living constantly in the open air, walking every day for eight or nine hours, eating sparingly, accepting every conversational opportunity, not even disdaining the discussion of possible work. And beyond mending a hole in his coat that he had made while negotiating barbed wire, with a borrowed needle and thread in a lodging house, he had done no work at all. Neither had he worried about business nor about time and seasons. And for the first time in his life he had seen the Aurora Borealis.

So far the holiday had cost him very little. He had arranged it on a plan that was entirely his own. He had started with four five-pound notes and a pound divided into silver, and he had gone by train from Fishbourne to Ashington. At Ashington he had gone to the post-office, obtained a registered letter, and sent his four five-pound notes with a short brotherly note addressed to himself at Gilhampton Post-office. He sent this letter to Gilhampton for no other reason in the world than that he liked the name of Gilhampton and the rural suggestion of its containing county, which was Sussex, and having so dispatched it, he set himself to discover, mark down and walk to Gilhampton, and so recover his resources. And having got to Gilhampton at last, he changed his five-pound note, bought four pound postal orders, and repeated his maneuver with nineteen pounds.

After a lapse of fifteen years he rediscovered this interesting world, about which so many people go incredibly blind and bored. He went along country roads while all the birds were piping and chirruping and cheeping and singing, and looked at fresh new things, and felt as happy and irresponsible as a boy with an unexpected half-holiday. And if ever the thought of Miriam returned to him he controlled his mind. He came to country inns and sat for unmeasured hours talking of this and that to those sage carters who rest for ever in the taps of country inns, while the big sleek brass jingling horses wait patiently outside with their waggons; he got a job with some van people who were wandering about the country with swings and a steam roundabout and remained with them for three days, until one of their dogs took a violent dislike to him and made his duties unpleasant; he talked to tramps and wayside labourers, he snoozed under hedges by day and in outhouses and hayricks at night, and once, but only once, he slept in a casual ward. He felt as the etiolated grass and daisies must do when you move the garden roller away to a new place.

He gathered a quantity of strange and interesting memories.

He crossed some misty meadows by moonlight and the mist lay low on the grass, so low that it scarcely reached above his waist, and houses and clumps of trees stood out like islands in a milky sea, so sharply defined was the upper surface of the mist-bank. He came nearer and nearer to a strange thing that floated like a boat upon this magic lake, and behold! something moved at the stern and a rope was whisked at the prow, and it had changed into a pensive cow, drowsy-eyed, regarding him.

He saw a remarkable sunset in a new valley near Maidstone, a very red and clear sunset, a wide redness under a pale cloudless heaven, and with the hills all round the edge of the sky a deep purple blue and clear and flat, looking exactly as he had seen mountains painted in pictures. He seemed transported to some strange country, and would have felt no surprise if the old labourer he came upon leaning silently over a gate had addressed him in an unfamiliar tongue. . . .

Then one night, just towards dawn, his sleep upon a pile of brushwood was broken by the distant rattle of a racing motor car breaking all the speed regulations, and as he could not sleep again, he got up and walked into Maidstone as the day came. He had never been abroad in a town at half-past two in his life before, and the stillness of everything in the bright sunrise impressed him profoundly. At one corner was a startling policeman, standing in a doorway quite motionless, like a waxen image. Mr. Polly wished him "good morning" unanswered, and went down to the bridge over the Medway and sat on the parapet very still and thoughtful, watching the town awaken, and wondering what he should do if it didn't, if the world of men never woke again. . . .

One day he found himself going along a road, with a wide space of sprouting bracken and occasional trees on either side, and suddenly this road became strangely, perplexingly familiar. "Lord!" he said, and turned about and stood. "It can't be."

He was incredulous, then left the road and walked along a scarcely perceptible track to the left, and came in half a minute to an old lichenous stone wall. It seemed exactly the bit of wall he had known so well. It might have been but yesterday he was in that place; there remained even a little pile of wood. It became absurdly the same wood. The bracken perhaps was not so high, and most of its fronds still uncoiled; that was all. Here he had stood, it seemed, and there she had sat and looked down upon him. Where was she now, and what had become of her? He counted the years back and marvelled that beauty should have called to him with so imperious a voice—and signified nothing.

He hoisted himself with some little difficulty to the top of the wall, and saw off under the beech trees two schoolgirls—small, insignificant, pig-tailed creatures, with heads of blond and black, with their arms twined about each other's necks, no doubt telling each other the silliest secrets.

But that girl with the red hair—was she a countess? was she a queen? Children perhaps? Had sorrow dared to touch her?

Had she forgotten altogether? . . .

A tramp sat by the roadside thinking, and it seemed to the man in the passing motor car he must needs be plotting for another pot of beer. But as a matter of fact what the tramp was saying to himself over and over again was a variant upon a well-known Hebrew word.

"Itchabod," the tramp was saying in the voice of one who reasons on the side of the inevitable. "It's Fair Itchabod, O' Man. There's no going back to it."

3

It was about two o'clock in the afternoon one hot day in high May when Mr. Polly, unhurrying and serene, came to that broad bend of the river to which the little lawn and garden of the Potwell Inn run down. He stopped at the sight of the place with its deep tiled roof, nestling under big trees—you never get a decently big, decently shaped tree by the seaside—its sign towards the roadway, its sun-blistered green bench and tables, its shapely white windows and its row of unshooting hollyhock plants in the garden. A hedge separated it from a buttercup-yellow meadow, and beyond stood three poplars in a group against the sky, three exceptionally tall, graceful and harmonious poplars. It is hard to say what there was about them that made them so beautiful to Mr. Polly; but they seemed to him to touch a pleasant scene to a distinction almost divine. He remained admiring them for a long time. At last the need for coarser aesthetic satisfactions arose in him.

"Provinder," he whispered, drawing near to the Inn. "Cold sirloin for choice. And nut-brown brew and wheaten bread."

The nearer he came to the place the more he liked it. The windows on the ground floor were long and low, and they had pleasing red blinds. The green tables outside were agreeably ringed with memories of former drinks and an extensive grape vine spread level branches across the whole front of the place. Against the wall was a broken oar, two boat-hooks and the stained and faded red cushions of a pleasure boat. One went up three steps to the glass-panelled door and peeped into a broad, low room with a bar and beer engine, behind which were many bright and helpful looking bottles against mirrors, and great and little pewter measures, and bottles fastened in brass wire upside down with their corks replaced by taps, and a white china cask labelled "Shrub," and cigar boxes and boxes of cigarettes, and a couple of Toby jugs and a beautifully coloured hunting scene framed and glazed, showing the most elegant and beautiful people taking Piper's Cherry Brandy, and cards such as the law requires about the dilution of spirits and the illegality of bringing children into bars, and satirical verses about swearing and asking for credit, and three very bright redcheeked wax apples and a round-shaped clock.

But these were the mere background to the really pleasant thing in the spectacle, which was quite the plumpest woman Mr. Polly had ever seen, seated in an armchair in the midst of all these bottles and glasses and glittering things, peacefully and tranquilly and without the slightest loss of dignity, asleep. Many people would have called her a fat woman, but Mr. Polly's innate sense of epithet told him from the outset that plump was the word. She had shapely brows and a straight, well-shaped nose, kind lines and contentment about her mouth, and beneath it the jolly chins clustered like chubby little cherubim about the feet of an Assumptioning-Madonna. Her plumpness was firm and pink and wholesome, and her hands, dimpled at every joint, were clasped in front of her; she seemed as it were to embrace herself with infinite confidence and kindliness as one who knew herself good in substance, good in

445

essence, and would show her gratitude to God by that ready acceptance of all that he had given her. Her head was a little on one side, not much, but just enough to speak of trustfulness, and rob her of the stiff effect of self-reliance. And she slept.

"*My* sort," said Mr. Polly, and opened the door very softly, divided between the desire to enter and come nearer and an instinctive indisposition to break slumbers so manifestly sweet and satisfying.

She awoke with the start, and it amazed Mr. Polly to see swift terror flash into her eyes. Instantly it had gone again.

"Law!" she said, her face softening with relief, "I thought you were Jim."

"I'm never Jim," said Mr. Polly.

"You've got his sort of hat."

"Ah!" said Mr. Polly, and leant over the bar.

"It just came into my head you was Jim," said the plump lady, dismissed the optic and stood up. "I believe I was having forty winks," she said, "if all the truth was told. What can I do for you?"

"Cold meat?" said Mr. Polly.

"There is cold meat," the plump woman admitted.

"And room for it."

The plump woman came and leant over the bar and regarded him judicially, but kindly. "There's some cold boiled beef," she said, and added: "A bit of crisp lettuce?"

"New mustard," said Mr. Polly.

"And a tankard!"

"A tankard."

They understood each other perfectly.

"Looking for work?" asked the plump woman.

"In a way," said Mr. Polly.

They smiled like old friends.

Whatever the truth may be about love, there is certainly such a thing as friendship at first sight. They liked each other's voices, they liked each other's way of smiling and speaking.

"It's such beautiful weather this spring," said Mr. Polly, explaining everything.

"What sort of work do you want?" she asked.

"I've never properly thought that out," said Mr. Polly. "I've been looking round—for Ideas."

"Will you have your beef in the tap or outside? That's the tap."

Mr. Polly had a glimpse of an oaken settle. "In the tap will be handier for you," he said.

"Hear that?" said the plump lady.

"Hear what?"

"Listen."

Presently the silence was broken by a distant howl. "Ooooooo-ver!" "Eh?" she said.

He nodded.

"That's the ferry. And there isn't a ferryman."

"Could I?"

"Can you punt?"

"Never tried."

"Well—pull the pole out before you reach the end of the punt, that's all. Try."

Mr. Polly went out again into the sunshine.

At times one can tell so much briefly. Here are the facts then—bare. He found a punt and a pole, got across to the steps on the opposite side, picked up an elderly gentleman in an alpaca jacket and a pith helmet, cruised with him vaguely for twenty minutes, conveyed him tortuously into the midst of a thicket of forget-me-not spangled sedges, splashed some water-weed over him, hit him twice with the punt pole, and finally landed him, alarmed but abusive, in treacherous soil at the edge of a hay meadow about forty yards down stream, where he immediately got into difficulties with a noisy, aggressive little white dog, which was guardian of a jacket.

Mr. Polly returned in a complicated manner to his moorings.

He found the plump woman rather flushed and tearful, and seated at one of the green tables outside.

"I been laughing at you," she said.

"What for?" asked Mr. Polly.

"I ain't 'ad such a laugh since Jim come 'ome. When you 'it 'is 'ed, it 'urt my side."

"It didn't hurt his head—not particularly."

She waved her head. "Did you charge him anything?"

"Gratis," said Mr. Polly. "I never thought of it."

The plump woman pressed her hands to her side and laughed silently for a space. "You ought to have charged him sumpthing," she said. "You better come and have your cold meat, before you do any more puntin'. You and me'll get on together."

Presently she came and stood watching him eat. "You eat better than you punt," she said, and then, "I dessay you could learn to punt."

"Wax to receive and marble to retain," said Mr. Polly. "This beef is a Bit of All Right, Ma'm. I could have done differently if I hadn't been punting on an empty stomach. There's a lear feeling as the pole goes in—"

"I've never held with fasting," said the plump woman.

"You want a ferryman?"

"I want an odd man about the place."

"I'm odd, all right. What's your wages?"

"Not much, but you get tips and pickings. I've a sort of feeling it would suit you."

"I've a sort of feeling it would. What's the duties? Fetch and carry? Ferry? Garden? Wash bottles? *Ceteris paribus?*"

"That's about it," said the fat woman.

"Give me a trial."

447

"I've more than half a mind. Or I wouldn't have said anything about it. I suppose you're all right. You've got a sort of half-respectable look about you. I suppose you 'aven't *done* anything."

"Bit of Arson," said Mr. Polly, as if he jested.

"So long as you haven't the habit," said the plump woman.

"My first time, M'am," said Mr. Polly, munching his way through an excellent big leaf of lettuce. "And my last."

"It's all right if you haven't been to prison," said the plump woman. "It isn't what a man's happened to do makes 'im bad. We all happen to do things at times. It's bringing it home to him, and spoiling his self-respect does the mischief. You don't look a wrong 'un. 'Ave you been to prison?

"Never."

"Nor a reformatory? Nor any institution?"

"Not me. Do I *look* reformed?"

"Can you paint and carpenter a bit?"

"Well, I'm ripe for it."

"Have a bit of cheese?"

"If I might."

And the way she brought the cheese showed Mr. Polly that the business was settled in her mind.

He spent the afternoon exploring the premises of the Potwell Inn and learning the duties that might be expected of him, such as tarring fences, digging potatoes, swabbing out boats, helping people land, embarking, landing and time-keeping for the hirers of two rowing boats and one Canadian canoe, baling out the said vessels and concealing their leaks and defects from prospective hirers, persuading inexperienced hirers to start down stream rather than up, repairing rowlocks and taking inventories of returning boats with a view to supplementary charges, cleaning boots, sweeping chimneys, house-painting, cleaning windows, sweeping out and sanding the tap and bar, cleaning pewter, washing glasses, turpentining woodwork, whitewashing generally, plumbing and engineering, repairing locks and clocks, waiting and tapster's work generally, beating carpets and mats, cleaning bottles and saving corks, taking into the cellar, moving, tapping and connecting beer casks with their engines, blocking and destroying wasps' nests, doing forestry with several trees, drowning superfluous kittens, and dog-fancying as required, assisting in the rearing of ducklings and the care of various poultry, bee-keeping, stabling, baiting and grooming horses and asses, cleaning and "garing" motor cars and bicycles, inflating tires and repairing punctures, recovering the bodies of drowned persons from the river as required, and assisting people in trouble in the water, first-aid and sympathy, improvising and superintending a bathing station for visitors, attending inquest and funerals in the interests of the establishment, scrubbing floors and all the ordinary duties of a scullion, the ferry, chasing hens and goats from the adjacent cottages out of the garden, making up paths and superintending drainage, gardening generally, delivering bottled beer and soda water syphons in the neighbourhood, running miscellaneous errands, removing drunken and offensive persons from the premises by tact or muscle as occasion required, keeping in with the local policemen, defending the premises in general and the orchard in particular from predators. . . .

"Can but try it," said Mr. Polly towards tea time. "When there's nothing else on hand I suppose I might do a bit of fishing."

### 3

Mr. Polly was particularly charmed by the ducklings.

They were piping about among the vegetables in the company of their foster mother, and as he and the plump woman came down the garden path the little creatures mobbed them, and ran over their boots and in between Mr. Polly's legs, and did their best to be trodden upon and killed after the manner of ducklings all the world over. Mr. Polly had never been near young ducklings before, and their extreme blondness and the delicate completeness of their feet and beaks filled him with admiration. It is open to question whether there is anything more friendly in the world than a very young duckling. It was with the utmost difficulty that he tore himself away to practise punting, with the plump woman coaching from the bank. Punting he found was difficult, but not impossible, and towards four o'clock he succeeded in conveying a second passenger across the sundering flood from the inn into the unknown.

As he returned, slowly indeed, but now one might almost say surely, to the peg to which the punt was moored, he became aware of a singularly delightful human being awaiting him on the bank. She stood with her legs very wide apart, her hands behind her back, and her head a little on one side, watching his gestures with an expression of disdainful interest. She had black hair and brown legs and a buff short frock and very intelligent eyes. And when he had reached a sufficient proximity she remarked: "Hello!"

"Hello," said Mr. Polly, and saved himself in the nick of time from disaster.

"Silly," said the young lady, and Mr. Polly lunged nearer.

"What are you called?"

"Polly."

"Liar!"

"Why?"

"I'm Polly."

"Then I'm Alfred. But I meant to be Polly."

"I was first."

"All right. I'm going to be the ferryman."

"I see. You'll have to punt better."

"You should have seen me early in the afternoon."

"I can imagine it. . . . I've seen the others."

"What others?" Mr. Polly had landed now and was fastening up the punt.

"What Uncle Jim has scooted."

449

"Scooted?"

"He comes and scoots them. He'll scoot you too, I expect."

A mysterious shadow seemed to fall athwart the sunshine and pleasantness of the Potwell Inn.

"I'm not a scooter," said Mr. Polly.

"Uncle Jim is."

She whistled a little flatly for a moment, and threw small stones at a clump of meadow-sweet that sprang from the bank. The she remarked:

"When Uncle Jim comes back he'll cut your insides out. . . . P'raps, very likely, he'll let me see."

There was a pause.

"*Who's* Uncle Jim?" Mr. Polly asked in a faded voice.

"Don't you know who Uncle Jim is? He'll show you. He's a scorcher, is Uncle Jim. He only came back just a little time ago, and he's scooted three men. He don't like strangers about, don't Uncle Jim. He can swear. He's going to teach me, soon as I can whissle properly."

"Teach you to wear!" cried Mr. Polly, horrified.

"And spit," said the little girl proudly. "He says I'm the gamest little beast he ever came across—ever."

For the first time in his life it seemed to Mr. Polly that he had come across something sheerly dreadful. He stared at the pretty thing of flesh and spirit in front of him, lightly balanced on its stout little legs and looking at him with eyes that had still to learn the expression of either disgust or fear.

"I say," said Mr. Polly, "how old are you?"

"Nine," said the little girl.

She turned away and reflected. Truth compelled her to add one other statement.

"He's not what I should call handsome, not Uncle Jim," she said. "But he's a scorcher and no mistake. . . . Gramma don't like him."

### 4

Mr. Polly found the plump woman in the big bricked kitchen lighting a fire for tea. He went to the root of the mater at once.

"I say," he asked, "who's Uncle Jim?"

The plump woman blanched and stood still for moment. A stick fell out of the bundle in her hand unheeded.

"That little granddaughter of mine been saying things?" she asked faintly.

"Bits of things," said Mr. Polly.

"Well, I suppose I must tell you sooner or later. He's—. It's Jim. He's the Drorback to this place, that's what he is. The Drorback. I hoped you mightn't hear so soon. . . . Very likely he's gone."

"*She* don't seem to think so."

"'E 'asn't been near the place these two weeks and more," said the plump woman.

"But who is he?"

"I suppose I got to tell you," said the plump woman.

"She says he scoots people," Mr. Polly remarked after a pause.

"He's my own sister's son." The plump woman watched the crackling fire for a space. "I suppose I got to tell you," she repeated.

She softened towards tears. "I try not to think of it, and night and day he's haunting me. I try not to think of it. I've been for easy-going all my life. But I'm that worried and afraid, with death and ruin threatened and evil all about me! I don't know what to do! My own sister's son, and me a widow woman and 'elpless against his doin's!"

She put down the sticks she held upon the fender, and felt for her handkerchief. She began to sob and talk quickly.

"I wouldn't mind nothing else half so much if he'd leave that child alone. But he goes talking to her—if I leave her a moment he's talking to her, teaching her words and giving her ideas!"

"That's a Bit Thick," said Mr. Polly.

"Thick!" cried the plump woman; "it's 'orrible! And what am I to do? He's been here three times now, six days and a week and a part of a week, and I pray to God night and day he may never come again. Praying! Back he's come sure as fate. He takes my money and he takes my things. He won't let no man stay here to protect me or do the boats or work the ferry. The ferry's getting a scandal. They stand and shout and scream and use language. . . . If I complain they'll say I'm helpless to manage here, they'll take away my license, out I shall go—and it's all the living I can get—and he knows it, and he plays on it, and he don't care. And here I am. I'd send the child away, but I got nowhere to send the child. I buys him off when it comes to that, and back he comes, worse than ever, prowling round and doing evil. And not a soul to help me. Not a soul! I just hoped there might be a day or so. Before he comes back again. I was just hoping—I'm the sort that hopes."

Mr. Polly was reflecting on the flaws and drawbacks that seem to be inseparable from all the more agreeable things in life.

"Biggish sort of man, I expect?" asked Mr. Polly, trying to get the situation in all its bearings.

But the plump woman did not heed him. She was going on with her tire-making, and retailing in disconnected fragments the fearfulness of Uncle Jim.

"There was always something a bit wrong with him," she said, "but nothing you mightn't have hoped for, not till they took him and carried him off and re-formed him. . . .

"He was cruel to the hens and chickings, it's true, and stuck a knife into another boy, but then I've seen him that nice to a cat, nobody could have been kinder. I'm sure he didn't do no 'arm to that cat whatever anyone tries to make out of it. I'd

451

never listen to that. . . . It was that reformatory ruined him. They put him along of a lot of London boys full of ideas of wickedness, and because he didn't mind pain—and he don't, I will admit, try as I would—they made him think himself a hero. Them boys laughed at the teachers they set over them, laughed and mocked at them—and I don't suppose they was the best teachers in the world; I don't suppose, and I don't suppose anyone sensible does suppose that everyone who goes to be a teacher or a chapl'in or a warder in a Reformatory Home goes and changes right away into an Angel of Grace from Heaven—and Oh, Lord! where was I?"

"What did they send him to the Reformatory for?"

"Playing truant and stealing. He stole right enough—stole the money from an old woman, and what was I to do when it came to the trial but say what I knew. And him like a viper a-looking at me—more like a viper than a human boy. He leans on the bar and looks at me. 'All right, Aunt Flo,' he says, just that and nothing more. Time after time, I've dreamt of it, and now he's come. 'They've Reformed me,' he says, 'and made me a devil, and devil I mean to be to you. So out with it,' he says."

"What did you give him last time?" asked Mr. Polly.

"Three golden pounds," said the plump woman. "'That won't last very long,' he says. 'But there ain't no hurry. I'll be back in a week about.' If I wasn't one of the hoping sort—"

She left the sentence unfinished.

Mr. Polly reflected. "What sort of a size is he?" he asked. "I'm not one of your Herculaceous sort, if you mean that. Nothing very wonderful bicepitally."

"You'll scoot," said the plump woman with conviction rather than bitterness. "You'd better scoot now, and I'll try and find some money for him to go away again when he comes. It ain't reasonable to expect you to do anything but scoot. But I suppose it's the way of a woman in trouble to try and get help from a man, and hope and hope. I'm the hoping sort."

"How long's he been about?" asked Mr. Polly, ignoring his own outlook.

"Three months it is come the seventh since he come in by that very back door—and I hadn't set eyes on him for seven long years. He stood in the door watchin' me, and suddenly he let off a yelp—like a dog, and there he was grinning at the fright he'd given me. 'Good old Aunty Flo,' he says, 'ain't you dee-lighted to see me?' he says, 'now I'm Reformed.'"

The plump lady went to the sink and filled the kettle.

"I never did like 'im," she said, standing at the sink. "And seeing him there, with his teeth all black and broken—. P'raps I didn't give him much of a welcome at first. Not what would have been kind to him. 'Lord!' I said, 'it's Jim.'"

"'It's Jim,' he said. 'Like a bad shilling'—like a damned bad shilling. Jim and trouble. You all of you wanted me Reformed and now you got me Reformed. I'm a Reformatory Reformed Character, warranted all right and turned out as such. Ain't you going to ask me in, Aunty dear?'

"'Come in,' I said, 'I won't have it said I wasn't ready to be kind to you!'

"He comes in and shuts the door. Down he sits in that chair. 'I come to torment you!' he says, 'you Old Sumpthing!' and begins at me. . . . no human being could ever had been called such things before. It made me cry out. 'And now,' he says, 'just to show I ain't afraid of 'urting you,' he says, and ups and twists my wrist."

Mr. Polly gasped.

"I could stand even his vi'lence," said the plump woman, "if it wasn't for the child."

Mr. Polly went to the kitchen window and surveyed his namesake, who was away up the garden path with her hands behind her back, and whisps of black hair in disorder about her little face, thinking, thinking profoundly, about ducklings.

"You two oughtn't to be left," he said.

The plump woman stared at his back with hard hope in her eyes.

"I don't see that it's my affair," said Mr. Polly.

The plump woman resumed her business wit the kettle.

"I'd like to have a look at him before I go," said Mr. Polly, thinking aloud. And added, "Somehow. Not my business, of course."

"Lord!" he cried with a start at a noise in the bar, "who's that?"

"Only a customer," said the plump woman.

## 5

Mr. Polly made no rash promises, and thought a great deal.

"It seems a good sort of crib," he said, and added, "for a chap who's looking for trouble."

But he stayed on and did various things out of the list I have already given, and worked the ferry, and it was four days before he saw anything of Uncle Jim. And so resistent is the human mind to things not yet experienced that he could easily have believed in that time that there was no such person in the world as Uncle Jim. The plump woman, after her one outbreak of confidence, ignored the subject, and little Polly seemed to have exhausted her impressions in her first communication, and engaged her mind now with a simple directness in the study and subjugation of the new human being Heaven had sent into her world. The first unfavourable impression of his punting was soon effaced; he could nickname ducklings very amusingly, create boats out of wooden splinters, and stalk and fly from imaginary tigers in the orchard with a convincing earnestness that was surely beyond the power of any other human being She conceded at last that he should be called Mr. Polly, in honour of her, Miss Polly, even as he desired.

Uncle Jim turned up in the twilight.

Uncle Jim appeared with none of the disruptive violence Mr. Polly had dreaded. He came quite softly. Mr. Polly was going down the lane behind the church that led to the Potwell Inn after posting a letter to the lime-juice people at the post-office. He was walking slowly, after his habit, and thinking discursively. With a sudden tightening of the muscles he became aware of a figure walking noiselessly beside him. His first impression was of a face singularly broad above and with a wide empty grin as its chief feature below, of a slouching body and dragging feet.

"Arf a mo'," said the figure, as if in response to his start, and speaking in a hoarse whisper. "Arf a mo', mister. You the noo bloke at the Potwell Inn?"

Mr. Polly felt evasive. "'Spose I am," he replied hoarsely, and quickend his pace.

"Arf a mo'," said Uncle Jim, taking his arm. "we ain't doing a (sanguinary) Marathon. It ain't a (decorated) cinder track. I want a word with you, mister. See?"

Mr. Polly wriggled his arm free and stopped. "What is it?" he asked, and faced the terror.

"I jest want a (decorated) word wiv you. See?—just a friendly word or two. Just to clear up any blooming errors. That's all I want. No need to be so (richly decorated) proud, if you are the noo bloke at Potwell Inn. Not a bit of it. See?"

Uncle Jim was certainly not a handsome person. He was short, shorter than Mr. Polly, with long arms and lean big hands, a thin and wiry neck stuck out of his grey flannel shirt and supported a big head that had something of the snake in the convergent lines of its broad knotty brow, meanly proportioned face and pointed chin. His almost toothless mouth seemed a cavern in the twilight. Some accident had left him with one small and active and one large and expressionless reddish eye, and wisps of straight hair sprayed from under the blue cricket cap he wore pulled down obliquely over the latter. He spat between his teeth and wiped his mouth untidily with the soft side of his fist.

"You got to blurry well shift," he said. "See?"

"Shift!" said Mr. Polly. "How?"

"'Cos the Potwell Inn's my beat. See?"

Mr. Polly had never felt less witty. "How's it your beat?" he asked.

Uncle Jim thrust his face forward and shook his open hand, bent like a claw, under Mr. Polly's nose. "Not your blooming business," he said. "You got to shift."

"S'pose I don't," said Mr. Polly.

"You got to shift."

The tone of Uncle Jim's voice became urgent and confidential.

"You don't know who you're up against," he said. "It's a kindness I'm doing to warn you. See? I'm just one of those blokes who don't stick at things, see? I don't stick at nuffin'"

Mr. Polly's manner became detached and confidential—as though the matter and the speaker interested him greatly, but didn't concern him overmuch. "What do you think you'll do?" he asked.

"If you don't clear out?"

"Yes."

"*Gaw!*" said Uncle Jim. "You'd better. '*Ere!*"

He gripped Mr. Polly's wrist with a grip of steel, and in an instant Mr. Polly understood the relative quality of their muscles. He breathed, an uninspiring breath, into Mr. Polly's face.

"What *won't* I do?" he said. "Once I start in on you."

He paused, and the night about them seemed to be listening. "I'll make a mess of you," he said in his hoarse whisper. "I'll do you—injuries. I'll 'urt you. I'll kick you ugly, see? I'll 'urt you in 'orrible ways—'orrible, ugly ways. . . ."

He scrutinised Mr. Polly's face.

"You'll cry," he said, "to see yourself. See? Cry you will."

"You got no right," began Mr. Polly.

"Right!" His note was fierce. "Ain't the old woman me aunt?"

He spoke still closer. "I'll make a gory mess of you. I'll cut bits orf you—"

He receded a little. "I got no quarrel with you," he said.

"It's too late to go to-night," said Mr. Polly.

"I'll be round to-morrer—'bout eleven. See? And if I finds you—"

He produced a blood-curdling oath.

"H'm," said Mr. Polly, trying to keep things light. "We'll consider your suggestions."

"You better," said Uncle Jim, and suddenly, noiselessly, was going.

His whispering voice sank until Mr. Polly could hear only the dim fragments of sentences. "'Orrible things to you—'orrible things. . . . Kick yer ugly. . . . Cut yer—liver out . . . spread it all about, I will. . . . Outing doos. See? I don't care a dead rat one way or the uvver."

And with a curious twisting gesture of the arm Uncle Jim receded until his face was a still, dim thing that watched, and the black shadows of the hedge seemed to have swallowed up his body altogether.


### 6

Next morning about half-past ten Mr. Polly found himself seated under a clump of fir trees by the roadside and about three miles and a half from the Potwell Inn. He was by no means sure whether he was taking a walk to clear his mind or leaving that threat-marred Paradise for good and all. His reason pointed a lean, unhesitating finger along the latter course.

For after all, the thing was not *his* quarrel.

That agreeable plump woman, agreeable, motherly, comfortable as she might be, wasn't his affair; that child with the mop of black hair who combined so magically the charm of mouse and butterfly and flitting bird, who was daintier than a flower and softer than a peach, was no concern of his. Good heavens! what were they to him? Nothing! . . . .

Uncle Jim, of course, had a claim, a sort of claim.

If it came to duty and chucking up this attractive, indolent, observant, humorous, tramping life, there were those who had a right to him, a legitimate right, a prior claim on his protection and chivalry.

Why not listen to the call of duty and go back to Miriam now? . . .

He had had a very agreeable holiday. . . .

And while Mr. Polly sat thinking these things as well as he could, he knew that if only he dared to look up the heavens had opened and the clear judgment on his case was written across the sky.

He knew—he knew now as much as a man can know of life. He knew he had to fight or perish.

Life had never been so clear to him before. It had always been a confused, entertaining spectacle, he had responded to this impulse and that, seeking agreeable and entertaining things, evading difficult and painful things. Such is the way of those who grow up to a life that has neither danger nor honour in its texture. He had been muddled and wrapped about and entangled like a creature born in the jungle who has never seen sea or sky. Now he had come out of it suddenly into a great exposed place. It was as if God and Heaven waited over him and all the earth was expectation.

"Not my business," said Mr. Polly, speaking aloud. "Where the devil do I come in?"

And again, with something between a whine and snarl in his voice, "not my blasted business!"

His mind seemed to have divided itself into several compartments, each with its own particular discussion busily in progress, and quite regardless of the others. One was busy with the detailed interpretation of the phrase "Kick you ugly." There's a sort of French wrestling in which you use and guard against feet. Watch the man's eye, and as his foot comes up, grip and over he goes—at your mercy if you use the advantage right. But how do you use the advantage rightly?

When he thought of Uncle Jim the inside feeling of his body faded away rapidly to a blank discomfort. . . .

"Old cadger! She hadn't no business to drag me into her quarrels. Ought to go to the police and ask for help! Dragging me into a quarrel that don't concern me.

"Wish I'd never set eyes on the rotten inn!"

The reality of the case arched over him like the vault of the sky, as plain as the sweet blue heavens above and the wide spread of hill and valley about him. Man comes into life to seek and find his sufficient beauty, to serve it, to win and increase it, to fight for it, to face anything and dare anything for it, counting death as nothing so long as the dying eyes still turn to it. And fear, and dullness and indolence and appetite, which indeed are no more than fear's three crippled brothers who make ambushes and creep by night, are against him, to delay him, to hold him off, to hamper and beguile and kill him in that quest. He had but to lift his eyes to see all that, as much a part of his world as the driving clouds and the bending grass, but he kept himself downcast, a grumbling, inglorious, dirty, fattish little tramp, full of dreads and quivering excuses.

"Why the hell was I ever born?" he said, with the truth almost winning him.

What do you do when a dirty man who smells, gets you down and under in the dirt and dust with a knee below your diaphragm and a large hairy hand squeezing your windpipe tighter and tighter in a quarrel that isn't, properly speaking, yours?

"If I had a chance against him—" protested Mr. Polly.

"It's no Good, you see," said Mr. Polly.

He stood up as though his decision was made, and was for an instant struck still by doubt.

There lay the road before him going this way to the east and that to the west.

Westward, one hour away now, was the Potwell Inn. Already things might be happening there. . . .

Eastward was the wise man's course, a road dipping between hedges to a hop garden and a wood and presently no doubt reaching an inn, a picturesque church, perhaps, a village and fresh company. The wise man's course. Mr. Polly saw himself going along it, and tried to see himself going along it with all the self-applause a wise man feels. But somehow it wouldn't come like that. The wise man fell short of happiness for all his wisdom. The wise man had a paunch and round shoulders and red ears and excuses. It was a pleasant road, and why the wise man should not go along it merry and singing, full of summer happiness, was a miracle to Mr. Polly's mind, but confound it! the fact remained, the figure went slinking—slinking was the only word for it—and would not go otherwise than slinking. He turned his eyes westward as if for an explanation, and if the figure was no longer ignoble, the prospect was appalling.

"One kick in the stummick would settle a chap like me," said Mr. Polly.

"Oh, God!" cried Mr. Polly, and lifted his eyes to heaven, and said for the last time in that struggle, "It isn't my affair!"

And so saying he turned his face towards the Potwell Inn.

He went back neither halting nor hastening in his pace after this last decision, but with a mind feverishly busy.

"If I get killed, I get killed, and if he gets killed I get hung. Don't seem just somehow.

"Don't suppose I shall frighten him off."

## 7

The private war between Mr. Polly and Uncle Jim for the possession of the Potwell Inn fell naturally into three chief campaigns. There was first of all the great campaign which ended in the triumphant eviction of Uncle Jim from the inn premises, there came next after a brief interval the futile invasions of the premises by Uncle Jim that culminated in the Battle of the Dead Eel, and after some months of involuntary truce there was the last supreme conflict of the Night Surprise. Each of these campaigns merits a section to itself.

Mr. Polly re-entered the inn discreetly. He found the plump woman seated in her bar, her eyes a-stare, her face white and wet with tears. "O God!" she was saying over and over again. "O God!" The air was full of a spirituous reek, and on the sanded boards in front of the bar were the fragments of a broken bottle and an overturned glass.

She turned her despair at the sound of his entry, and despair gave place to astonishment.

"You come back!" she said.

"Ra-ther," said Mr. Polly.

"He's—he's mad drunk and looking for her."

"Where is she?"

"Locked upstairs."

"Haven't you sent to the police?"

"No one to send."

"I'll see to it," said Mr. Polly. "Out this way?"

She nodded.

He went to the crinkly paned window and peered out. Uncle Jim was coming down the garden path towards the house, his hands in his pockets and singing hoarsely. Mr. Polly remembered afterwards with pride and amazement that he felt neither faint nor rigid. He glanced round him, seized a bottle of beer by the neck as an improvised club, and went out by the garden door. Uncle Jim stopped amazed. His brain did not instantly rise to the new posture of things. "You!" he cried, and stopped for a moment. "You—*scoot!*"

"*Your* job," said Mr. Polly, and advanced some paces.

Uncle Jim stood swaying with wrathful astonishment and then darted forward with clutching hands. Mr. Polly felt that if this antagonist closed he was lost, and smote with all his force at the ugly head before him. Smash went the bottle, and Uncle Jim staggered, half-stunned by the blow and blinded with beer.

The lapses and leaps of the human mind are for ever mysterious. Mr. Polly had never expected that bottle to break. In the instant he felt disarmed and helpless. Before him was Uncle Jim, infuriated and evidently still coming on, and for defence was nothing but the neck of a bottle.

For a time our Mr. Polly has figured heroic. Now comes the fall again; he sounded abject terror; he dropped that ineffectual scrap of glass and turned and fled round the corner of the house.

"Bolls!" came the thick voice of the enemy behind him as one who accepts a challenge, and bleeding, but indomitable, Uncle Jim entered the house.

"Bolls!" he said, surveying the bar. "Fightin' with bolls! I'll show 'im fightin' with bolls!"

Uncle Jim had learnt all about fighting with bottles in the Reformatory Home. Regardless of his terror-stricken aunt he ranged among the bottled beer and succeeded after one or two failures in preparing two bottles to his satisfaction by knocking off the bottoms, and gripping them dagger-wise by the necks. So prepared, he went forth again to destroy Mr. Polly.

Mr. Polly, freed from the sense of urgent pursuit, had halted beyond the raspberry canes and rallied his courage. The sense of Uncle Jim victorious in the house restored his manhood. He went round by the outhouses to the riverside, seeking a weapon, and found an old paddle boat hook. With this he smote Uncle Jim as he emerged by the door of the tap. Uncle Jim, blaspheming dreadfully and with dire stabbing intimations in either hand, came through the splintering paddle like a circus rider through a paper hoop, and once more Mr. Polly dropped his weapon and fled.

A careless observer watching him sprint round and round the inn in front of the lumbering and reproachful pursuit of Uncle Jim might have formed an altogether erroneous estimate of the issue of the campaign. Certain compensating qualities of the very greatest military value were appearing in Mr. Polly even as he ran; if Uncle Jim had strength and brute courage and the rich toughening experience a Reformatory Home affords, Mr. Polly was nevertheless sober, more mobile and with a mind now stimulated to an almost incredible nimbleness. So that he not only gained on Uncle Jim, but thought what use he might make of this advantage. The word "strategious" flamed red across the tumult of his mind. As he came round the house for the third time, he darted suddenly into the yard, swung the door to behind himself and bolted it, seized the zinc pig's pail that stood by the entrance to the kitchen and had it neatly and resonantly over Uncle Jim's head as he came belatedly in round the outhouse on the other side. One of the splintered bottles jabbed Mr. Polly's ear—at the time it seemed of no importance—and then Uncle Jim was down and writhing dangerously and noisily upon the yard tiles, with his head still in the pig pail and his bottles gone to splinters, and Mr. Polly was fastening the kitchen door against him.

"Can't go on like this for ever," said Mr. Polly, whooping for breath, and selecting a weapon from among the brooms that stood behind the kitchen door.

Uncle Jim was losing his head. He was up and kicking the door and bellowing unamiable proposals and invitations, so that a strategist emerging silently by the tap door could locate him without difficulty, steal upon him unawares and—!

But before that felling blow could be delivered Uncle Jim's ear had caught a footfall, and he turned. Mr. Polly quailed and lowered his broom,—a fatal hesitation.

"Now I got you!" cried Uncle Jim, dancing forward in a disconcerting zigzag.

He rushed to close, and Mr. Polly stopped him neatly, as it were a miracle, with the head of the broom across his chest. Uncle Jim seized the broom with both hands. "Lea-go!" he said, and tugged. Mr. Polly shook his head, tugged, and showed pale, compressed lips. Both tugged. Then Uncle Jim tried to get round the end of the broom; Mr. Polly circled away. They began to circle about one another, both tugging hard, both intensely watchful of the slightest initiative on the part of the other. Mr. Polly wished brooms were longer, twelve or thirteen feet, for example; Uncle Jim was clearly for shortness in brooms. He wasted breath in saying what was to happen shortly, sanguinary, oriental soul-blenching things, when the broom no longer separated then. Mr. Polly thought he had never seen an uglier person. Suddenly Uncle Jim flashed into violent activity, but alcohol slows movement, and Mr. Polly was equal to him. Then Uncle Jim tried jerks, and for a terrible instant seemed to have the broom out of Mr. Polly's hands. But Mr. Polly recovered it with the clutch of a drowning man. Then Uncle Jim drove suddenly at Mr. Polly's midriff, but again Mr. Polly was ready and swept him round in a circle. Then suddenly a wild hope filled Mr. Polly. He saw the river was very near, the post to which the punt was tied not three yards away. With a wild yell, he sent the broom home into his antagonist's ribs.

"Woosh!" he cried, as the resistance gave.

"Oh! *Gaw!*" said Uncle Jim, going backward helplessly, and Mr. Polly thrust hard and abandoned the broom to the enemy's despairing clutch.

Splash! Uncle Jim was in the water and Mr. Polly had leapt like a cat aboard the ferry punt and grasped the pole.

Up came Uncle Jim spluttering and dripping. "You (unprofitable matter, and printing it would lead to a censorship of novels)! You know I got a weak *chess!*"

The pole took him in the throat and drove him backward and downwards.

"Lea go!" cried Uncle Jim, staggering and with real terror in his once awful eyes.

Splash! Down he fell backwards into a frothing mass of water with Mr. Polly jabbing at him. Under water he turned round and came up again as if in flight towards the middle of the river. Directly his head reappeared Mr. Polly had him between the shoulders and under again, bubbling thickly. A hand clutched and disappeared.

It was stupendous! Mr. Polly had discovered the heel of Achilles. Uncle Jim had no stomach for cold water. The broom floated away, pitching gently on the swell. Mr. Polly, infuriated with victory, thrust Uncle Jim under again, and drove the punt round on its chain in such a manner that when Uncle Jim came up for the fourth time—and now he was nearly out of his depth, too buoyed up to walk and apparently nearly helpless,—Mr. Polly, fortunately for them both, could not reach him.

Uncle Jim made the clumsy gestures of those who struggle insecurely in the water. "Keep out," said Mr. Polly. Uncle Jim with a great effort got a footing, emerged until his arm-pits were out of water, until his waistcoat buttons showed, one by one, till scarcely two remained, and made for the camp sheeting.

"Keep out!" cried Mr. Polly, and leapt off the punt and followed the movements of his victim along the shore.

"I tell you I got a weak chess," said Uncle Jim, moistly. "This ain't fair fightin'."

"Keep out!" said Mr. Polly.

"This ain't fair fightin'," said Uncle Jim, almost weeping, and all his terrors had gone.

"Keep out!" said Mr. Polly, with an accurately poised pole.

"I tell you I got to land, you Fool," said Uncle Jim, with a sort of despairing wrathfulness, and began moving down-stream.

"You keep out," said Mr. Polly in parallel movement. "Don't you ever land on this place again! . . ."

Slowly, argumentatively, and reluctantly, Uncle Jim waded down-stream. He tried threats, he tried persuasion, he even tried a belated note of pathos; Mr. Polly remained inexorable, if in secret a little perplexed as to the outcome of the situation. "This cold's getting to my marrer!" said Uncle Jim.

"You want cooling. You keep out in it," said Mr. Polly.

They came round the bend into sight of Nicholson's gate, where the backwater runs down to the Potwell Mill. And there, after much parley and several feints, Uncle Jim made a desperate effort and struggled into clutch of the overhanging osiers on the island, and so got out of the water with the millstream between them. He emerged dripping and muddy and vindictive. "By *Gaw!*" he said. "I'll skin you for this!"

"You keep off or I'll do worse to you," said Mr. Polly.

The spirit was out of Uncle Jim for the time, and he turned away to struggle through the osiers towards the mill, leaving a shining trail of water among the green-grey stems.

Mr. Polly returned slowly and thoughtfully to the inn, and suddenly his mind began to bubble with phrases. The plump woman stood at the top of the steps that led up to the inn door to greet him.

"Law!" she cried as he drew near, "'asn't 'e killed you?"

"Do I look like it?" said Mr. Polly.

"But where's Jim?"

"Gone off."

"'E was mad drunk and dangerous!"

"I put him in the river," said Mr. Polly. "That toned down his alcolaceous frenzy! I gave him a bit of a doing altogether."

"Hain't he 'urt you?"

"Not a bit of it!"

"Then what's all that blood beside your ear?"

Mr. Polly felt. "Quite a cut! Funny how one overlooks things! Heated moments! He must have done that when he jabbed about with those bottles. Hullo, Kiddy! You venturing downstairs again?"

"Ain't he killed you?" asked the little girl.

"Well!"

"I wish I'd seen more of the fighting."

"Didn't you?"

"All I saw was you running round the house an Uncle Jim after you."

There was a little pause. "I was leading him on," said Mr. Polly.

"Someone's shouting at the ferry," she said.

"Right O. But you won't see any more of Uncle Jim for a bit. We've been having a conversazione about that."

"I believe it *is* Uncle Jim," said the little girl.

"Then he can wait," said Mr. Polly shortly.

He turned round and listened for the words that drifted across from the little figure on the opposite bank. So far as he could judge, Uncle Jim was making an appointment for the morrow. He replied with a defiant movement of the punt pole. The little figure was convulsed for a moment and then went on its way upstream—fiercely.

So it was the first campaign ended in an insecure victory.

461

8

The next day was Wednesday and a slack day for the Potwell Inn. It was a hot, close day, full of the murmuring of bees. One or two people crossed by the ferry, an elaborately equipped fisherman stopped for cold meat and dry ginger ale in the bar parlour, some haymakers came and drank beer for an hour, and afterwards sent jars and jugs by a boy to be replenished; that was all. Mr. Polly had risen early and was busy about the place meditating upon the probable tactics of Uncle Jim. He was no longer strung up to the desperate pitch of the first encounter. But he was grave and anxious. Uncle Jim had shrunken, as all antagonists that are boldly faced shrink, after the first battle, to the negotiable, the vulnerable. Formidable he was no doubt, but not invincible. He had, under Providence, been defeated once, and he might be defeated altogether.

Mr. Polly went about the place considering the militant possibilities of pacific things, pokers, copper sticks, garden implements, kitchen knives, garden nets, barbed wire, oars, clothes lines, blankets, pewter pots, stockings and broken bottles. He prepared a club with a stocking and a bottle inside upon the best East End model. He swung it round his head once, broke an outhouse window with a flying fragment of glass, and ruined the stocking beyond all darning. He developed a subtle scheme with the cellar flap as a sort of pitfall, but he rejected it finally because (A) it might entrap the plump woman, and (B) he had no use whatever for Uncle Jim in the cellar. He determined to wire the garden that evening, burglar fashion, against the possibilities of a night attack.

Towards two o'clock in the afternoon three young men arrived in a capacious boat from the direction of Lammam, and asked permission to camp in the paddock. It was given all the more readily by Mr. Polly because he perceived in their proximity a possible check upon the self-expression of Uncle Jim. But he did not foresee and no one could have foreseen that Uncle Jim, stealing unawares upon the Potwell Inn in the late afternoon, armed with a large rough-hewn stake, should have mistaken the bending form of one of those campers—who was pulling a few onions by permission in the garden—for Mr. Polly's, and crept upon it swiftly and silently and smitten its wide invitation unforgettably and unforgivably. It was an error impossible to explain; the resounding whack went up to heaven, the cry of amazement, and Mr. Polly emerged from the inn armed with the frying-pan he was cleaning, to take this reckless assailant in the rear. Uncle Jim, realising his error, fled blaspheming into the arms of the other two campers, who were returning from the village with butcher's meat and groceries. They caught him, they smacked his face with steak and punched him with a bursting parcel of lump sugar, they held him though he bit them, and their idea of punishment was to duck him. They were hilarious, strong young stockbrokers' clerks, Territorials and seasoned boating men; they ducked him as though it was romping, and all that Mr. Polly had to do was to pick up lumps of sugar for them and wipe them on his sleeve and put them on a plate, and explain that Uncle Jim was a notorious bad character and not quite right in his head.

"Got a regular obsession that the Missis is his Aunt," said Mr. Polly, expanding it. "Perfect noosance he is."

But he caught a glance of Uncle Jim's eye as he receded before the campers' urgency that boded ill for him, and in the night he had a disagreeable idea that perhaps his luck might not hold for the third occasion.

That came soon enough. So soon, indeed, as the campers had gone.

Thursday was the early closing day at Lammam, and next to Sunday the busiest part of the week at the Potwell Inn. Sometimes as many as six boats all at once would be moored against the ferry punt and hiring rowboats. People could either have a complete tea, a complete tea with jam, cake and eggs, a kettle of boiling water and find the rest, or refreshments *à la carte*, as they chose. They sat about, but usually the boiling water-ers had a delicacy about using the tables and grouped themselves humbly on the ground. The complete tea-ers with jam and eggs got the best tablecloth on the table nearest the steps that led up to the glass-panelled door. The groups about the lawn were very satisfying to Mr. Polly's sense of amenity. To the right were the complete tea-ers with everything heart could desire, then a small group of three young men in remarkable green and violet and pale-blue shirts, and two girls in mauve and yellow blouses with common teas and gooseberry jam at the green clothless table, then on the grass down by the pollard willow a small family of hot water-ers with a hamper, a little troubled by wasps in their jam from the nest in the tree and all in mourning, but happy otherwise, and on the lawn to the right a ginger beer lot of 'prentices without their collars and very jocular and happy. The young people in the rainbow shirts and blouses formed the centre of interest; they were under the leadership of a gold-spectacled senior with a fluting voice and an air of mystery; he ordered everything, and showed a peculiar knowledge of the qualities of the Potwell jams, preferring gooseberry with much insistence. Mr. Polly watched him, christened him the "benifluous influence," glanced at the 'prentices and went inside and down into the cellar in order to replenish the stock of stone ginger beer which the plump woman had allowed to run low during the preoccupations of the campaign. It was in the cellar that he first became aware of the return of Uncle Jim. He became aware of him as a voice, a voice not only hoarse, but thick, as voices thicken under the influence of alcohol.

"Where's that muddy-faced mongrel?" cried Uncle Jim. "Let 'im come out to me! Where's that blighted whisp with the punt pole—I got a word to say to 'im. Come out of it, you pot-bellied chunk of dirtiness, you! Come out and 'ave your ugly face wiped. I got a Thing for you. . . . 'Ear me?

"'E's 'iding, that's what 'e's doing," said the voice of Uncle Jim, dropping for a moment to sorrow, and then with a great increment of wrathfulness: "Come out of my nest, you blinking cuckoo, you, or I'll cut your silly insides out! Come out of it— you pock-marked rat! Stealing another man's 'ome away from 'im! Come out and look me in the face, you squinting son of a Skunk! . . ."

Mr. Polly took the ginger beer and went thoughtfully upstairs to the bar.

"'E's back," said the plump woman as he appeared. "I knew 'e'd come back."

"I heard him," said Mr. Polly, and looked about. "Just gimme the old poker handle that's under the beer engine."

The door opened softly and Mr. Polly turned quickly. But it was only the pointed nose and intelligent face of the young man with the gilt spectacles and discreet manner. He coughed and the spectacles fixed Mr. Polly.

"I say," he said with quiet earnestness. "There's a chap out here seems to want someone."

"Why don't he come in?" said Mr. Polly.

"He seems to want you out there."

"What's he want?"

"I *think*," said the spectacled young man after a thoughtful moment, "he appears to have brought you a present of fish."

"Isn't he shouting?"

"He is a little boisterous."

"He'd better come in."

The manner of the spectacled young man intensified. "I wish you'd come out and persuade him to go away," he said. "His language—isn't quite the thing—ladies."

"It never was," said the plump woman, her voice charged with sorrow.

Mr. Polly moved towards the door and stood with his hand on the handle. The gold-spectacled face disappeared.

"Now, my man," came his voice from outside, "be careful what you're saying—"

"Oo in all the World and Hereafter are you to call me, me man?" cried Uncle Jim in the voice of one astonished and pained beyond endurance, and added scornfully: "You gold-eyed Geezer, you!"

"Tut, tut!" said the gentleman in gilt glasses. "Restrain yourself!"

Mr. Polly emerged, poker in hand, just in time to see what followed. Uncle Jim in his shirtsleeves and a state of ferocious decolletage, was holding something—yes!—a dead eel by means of a piece of newspaper about its tail, holding it down and back and a little sideways in such a way as to smite with it upward and hard. It struck the spectacled gentleman under the jaw with a peculiar dead thud, and a cry of horror came from the two seated parties at the sight. One of the girls shrieked piercingly, "Horace!" and everyone sprang up. The sense of helping numbers came to Mr. Polly's aid.

"Drop it!" he cried, and came down the steps waving his poker and thrusting the spectacled gentleman before him as once heroes were wont to wield the ox-hide shield.

Uncle Jim gave ground suddenly, and trod upon the foot of a young man in a blue shirt, who immediately thrust at him violently with both hands.

"Lea go!" howled Uncle Jim. "That's the chap I'm looking for!" and pressing the head of the spectacled gentleman aside, smote hard at Mr. Polly.

But at the sight of this indignity inflicted upon the spectacled gentleman a woman's heart was stirred, and a pink parasol drove hard and true at Uncle Jim's wiry neck, and at the same moment the young man in the blue shirt sought to collar him and lost his grip again.

"Suffragettes," gasped Uncle Jim with the ferule at his throat. "Everywhere!" and aimed a second more successful blow at Mr. Polly.

"Wup!" said Mr. Polly.

But now the jam and egg party was joining in the fray. A stout yet still fairly able-bodied gentleman in white and black checks enquired: "What's the fellow up to? Ain't there no police here?" and it was evident that once more public opinion was rallying to the support of Mr. Polly.

"Oh, come on then all the LOT of you!" cried Uncle Jim, and backing dexterously whirled the eel round in a destructive circle. The pink sunshade was torn from the hand that gripped it and whirled athwart the complete, but unadorned, tea things on the green table.

"Collar him! Someone get hold of his collar!" cried the gold-spectacled gentleman, coming out of the scrimmage, retreating up the steps to the inn door as if to rally his forces.

"Stand clear, you blessed mantel ornaments!" cried Uncle Jim, "stand clear!" and retired backing, staving off attack by means of the whirling eel.

Mr. Polly, undeterred by a sense of grave damage done to his nose, pressed the attack in front, the two young men in violet and blue skirmished on Uncle Jim's flanks, the man in white and black checks sought still further outflanking possibilities, and two of the apprentice boys ran for oars. The gold-spectacled gentleman, as if inspired, came down the wooden steps again, seized the tablecloth of the jam and egg party, lugged it from under the crockery with inadequate precautions against breakage, and advanced with compressed lips, curious lateral crouching movements, swift flashings of his glasses, and a general suggestion of bull-fighting in his pose and gestures. Uncle Jim was kept busy, and unable to plan his retreat with any strategic soundness. He was moreover manifestly a little nervous about the river in his rear. He gave ground in a curve, and so came right across the rapidly abandoned camp of the family in mourning, crunching a teacup under his heel, oversetting the teapot, and finally tripping backwards over the hamper. The eel flew out at a tangent from his hand and became a mere looping relic on the sward.

"Hold him!" cried the gentleman in spectacles. "Collar him!" and moving forward with extraordinary promptitude wrapped the best tablecloth about Uncle Jim's arms and head. Mr. Polly grasped his purpose instantly, the man in checks was scarcely slower, and in another moment Uncle Jim was no more than a bundle of smothered blasphemy and a pair of wildly active legs.

"Duck him!" panted Mr. Polly, holding on to the earthquake. "Bes' thing—duck him."

The bundle was convulsed by paroxysms of anger and protest. One boot got the hamper and sent it ten yards.

465

"Go in the house for a clothes line someone!" said the gentleman in gold spectacles. "He'll get out of this in a moment."

One of the apprentices ran.

"Bird nets in the garden," shouted Mr. Polly. "In the garden!"

The apprentice was divided in his purpose.

And then suddenly Uncle Jim collapsed and became a limp, dead seeming thing under their hands. His arms were drawn inward, his legs bent up under his person, and so he lay.

"Fainted!" said the man in checks, relaxing his grip.

"A fit, perhaps," said the man in spectacles.

"Keep hold!" said Mr. Polly, too late.

For suddenly Uncle Jim's arms and legs flew out like springs released. Mr. Polly was tumbled backwards and fell over the broken teapot and into the arms of the father in mourning. Something struck his head—dazzlingly. In another second Uncle Jim was on his feet and the tablecloth enshrouded the head of the man in checks. Uncle Jim manifestly considered he had done all that honour required of him, and against overwhelming numbers and the possibility of reiterated duckings, flight is no disgrace.

Uncle Jim fled.

Mr. Polly sat up after an interval of an indeterminate length among the ruins of an idyllic afternoon. Quite a lot of things seemed scattered and broken, but it was difficult to grasp it all at once. He stared between the legs of people. He became aware of a voice, speaking slowly and complainingly.

"Someone ought to pay for those tea things," said the father in mourning. "We didn't bring them 'ere to be danced on, not by no manner of means."

## 9

There followed an anxious peace for three days, and then a rough man in a blue jersey, in the intervals of trying to choke himself with bread and cheese and pickled onions, broke out abruptly into information.

"Jim's lagged again, Missus," he said.

"What!" said the landlady. "Our Jim?"

"Your Jim" said the man, and after an absolutely necessary pause for swallowing, added: "Stealin' a 'atchet."

He did not speak for some moments, and then he replied to Mr. Polly's enquiries: "Yes, a 'atchet. Down Lammam way—night before last."

"What'd 'e steal a 'atchet for?" asked the plump woman.

"'E said 'e wanted a 'atchet."

"I wonder what he wanted a hatchet for?" said Mr. Polly, thoughtfully.

"I dessay 'e 'ad a use for it," said the gentleman in the blue jersey, and he took a mouthful that amounted to conversational suicide. There was a prolonged pause in the little bar, and Mr. Polly did some rapid thinking.

He went to the window and whistled. "I shall stick it," he whispered at last. "'Atchets or no 'atchets."

He turned to the man with the blue jersey when he thought him clear for speech again. "How much did you say they'd given him?" he asked.

"Three munce," said the man in the blue jersey, and refilled anxiously, as if alarmed at the momentary clearness of his voice.

## 10

Those three months passed all too quickly; months of sunshine and warmth, of varied novel exertion in the open air, of congenial experiences, of interest and wholesome food and successful digestion, months that browned Mr. Polly and hardened him and saw the beginnings of his beard, months marred only by one anxiety, an anxiety Mr. Polly did his utmost to suppress. The day of reckoning was never mentioned, it is true, by either the plump woman or himself, but the name of Uncle Jim was written in letters of glaring silence across their intercourse. As the term of that respite drew to an end his anxiety increased, until at last it even trenched upon his well-earned sleep. He had some idea of buying a revolver. At last he compromised upon a small and very foul and dirty rook rifle which he purchased in Lammam under a pretext of bird scaring, and loaded carefully and concealed under his bed from the plump woman's eye.

September passed away, October came.

And at last came that night in October whose happenings it is so difficult for a sympathetic historian to drag out of their proper nocturnal indistinctness into the clear, hard light of positive statement. A novelist should present characters, not vivisect them publicly. . . .

The best, the kindliest, if not the justest course is surely to leave untold such things as Mr. Polly would manifestly have preferred untold.

Mr. Polly had declared that when the cyclist discovered him he was seeking a weapon that should make a conclusive end to Uncle Jim. That declaration is placed before the reader without comment.

The gun was certainly in possession of Uncle Jim at that time and no human being but Mr. Polly knows how he got hold of it.

The cyclist was a literary man named Warspite, who suffered from insomnia; he had risen and come out of his house near Lammam just before the dawn, and he discovered Mr. Polly partially concealed in the ditch by the Potwell churchyard wall. It is an ordinary dry ditch, full of nettles and overgrown with elder and dogrose, and in no way suggestive of an arsenal. It is the last place in which you would look for a gun. And he says that when he dismounted to see why Mr. Polly was allowing only the latter part of his person to show (and that it would seem by inadvertency), Mr. Polly merely raised his head and advised him to "Look out!" and added: "He's let fly at me twice already." He came out under persuasion and with gestures of extreme caution.

467

He was wearing a white cotton nightgown of the type that has now been so extensively superseded by pyjama sleeping suits, and his legs and feet were bare and much scratched and torn and very muddy.

Mr. Warspite takes that exceptionally lively interest in his fellow-creatures which constitutes so much of the distinctive and complex charm of your novelist all the world over, and he at once involved himself generously in the case. The two men returned at Mr. Polly's initiative across the churchyard to the Potwell Inn, and came upon the burst and damaged rook rifle near the new monument to Sir Samuel Harpon at the corner by the yew.

"That must have been his third go," said Mr. Polly. "It sounded a bit funny."

The sight inspirited him greatly, and he explained further that he had fled to the churchyard on account of the cover afforded by tombstones from the flight of small shot. He expressed anxiety for the fate of the landlady of the Potwell Inn and her grandchild, and led the way with enhanced alacrity along the lane to that establishment.

They found the doors of the house standing open, the bar in some disorder—several bottles of whisky were afterwards found to be missing—and Blake, the village policeman, rapping patiently at the open door. He entered with them. The glass in the bar had suffered severely, and one of the mirrors was starred from a blow from a pewter pot. The till had been forced and ransacked, and so had the bureau in the minute room behind the bar. An upper window was opened and the voice of the landlady became audible making enquiries. They went out and parleyed with her. She had locked herself upstairs with the little girl, she said, and refused to descend until she was assured that neither Uncle Jim nor Mr. Polly's gun were anywhere on the premises. Mr. Blake and Mr. Warspite proceeded to satisfy themselves with regard to the former condition, and Mr. Polly went to his room in search of garments more suited to the brightening dawn. He returned immediately with a request that Mr. Blake and Mr. Warspite would "just come and look." They found the apartment in a state of extraordinary confusion, the bedclothes in a ball in the corner, the drawers all open and ransacked, the chair broken, the lock of the door forced and broken, one door panel slightly scorched and perforated by shot, and the window wide open. None of Mr. Polly's clothes were to be seen, but some garments which had apparently once formed part of a stoker's workaday outfit, two brownish yellow halves of a shirt, and an unsound pair of boots were scattered on the floor. A faint smell of gunpowder still hung in the air, and two or three books Mr. Polly had recently acquired had been shied with some violence under the bed. Mr. Warspite looked at Mr. Blake, and then both men looked at Mr. Polly. "That's *his* boots," said Mr. Polly.

Blake turned his eye to the window. "Some of these tiles 'ave just got broken," he observed.

"I got out of the window and slid down the scullery tiles," Mr. Polly answered, omitting much, they both felt, from his explanation. . . .

"Well, we better find 'im and 'ave a word with 'im," said Blake. "That's about my business now."

But Uncle Jim had gone altogether. . . .

## 11

He did not return for some days. That perhaps was not very wonderful. But the days lengthened to weeks and the weeks to months and still Uncle Jim did not recur. A year passed, and the anxiety of him became less acute; a second healing year followed the first. One afternoon about thirty months after the Night Surprise the plump woman spoke of him.

"I wonder what's become of Jim," she said.

"I wonder sometimes," said Mr. Polly.

CHAPTER THE TENTH

MIRIAM REVISITED

One summer afternoon about five years after his first coming to the Potwell Inn Mr. Polly found himself sitting under the pollard willow fishing for dace. It was a plumper, browner and healthier Mr. Polly altogether than the miserable bankrupt with whose dyspeptic portrait our novel opened. He was fat, but with a fatness more generally diffused, and the lower part of his face was touched to gravity by a small square beard. Also he was balder.

It was the first time he had found leisure to fish, though from the very outset of his Potwell career he had promised himself abundant indulgence in the pleasures of fishing. Fishing, as the golden page of English literature testifies, is a meditative and retrospective pursuit, and the varied page of memory, disregarded so long for sake of the teeming duties I have already enumerated, began to unfold itself to Mr. Polly's consideration. A speculation about Uncle Jim died for want of material, and gave place to a reckoning of the years and months that had passed since his coming to Potwell, and that to a philosophical review of his life. He began to think about Miriam, remotely and impersonally. He remembered many things that had been neglected by his conscience during the busier times, as, for example, that he had committed arson and deserted a wife. For the first time he looked these long neglected facts in the face.

It is disagreeable to think one has committed Arson, because it is an action that leads to jail. Otherwise I do not think there was a grain of regret for that in Mr. Polly's composition. But deserting Miriam was in a different category. Deserting Miriam was mean.

This is a history and not a glorification of Mr. Polly, and I tell of things as they were with him. Apart from the disagreeable twinge arising from the thought of what might happen if he was found out, he had not the slightest remorse about that fine. Arson, after all, is an artificial crime. Some crimes are crimes in themselves, would be crimes without any law, the cruelties, mockery, the breaches of faith that astonish and wound, but the burning of things is in itself neither good nor bad. A large number of

469

houses deserve to be burnt, most modern furniture, an overwhelming majority of pictures and books—one might go on for some time with the list. If our community was collectively anything more than a feeble idiot, it would burn most of London and Chicago, for example, and build sane and beautiful cities in the place of these pestilential heaps of rotten private property. I have failed in presenting Mr. Polly altogether if I have not made you see that he was in many respects an artless child of Nature, far more untrained, undisciplined and spontaneous than an ordinary savage. And he was really glad, for all that little drawback of fear, that he had the courage to set fire to his house and fly and come to the Potwell Inn.

But he was not glad he had left Miriam. He had seen Miriam cry once or twice in his life, and it had always reduced him to abject commiseration. He now imagined her crying. He perceived in a perplexed way that he had made himself responsible for her life. He forgot how she had spoilt his own. He had hitherto rested in the faith that she had over a hundred pounds of insurance money, but now, with his eye meditatively upon his float, he realised a hundred pounds does not last for ever. His conviction of her incompetence was unflinching; she was bound to have fooled it away somehow by this time. And then!

He saw her humping her shoulders and sniffing in a manner he had always regarded as detestable at close quarters, but which now became harrowingly pitiful.

"Damn!" said Mr. Polly, and down went this float and he flicked up a victim to destruction and took it off the hook.

He compared his own comfort and health with Miriam's imagined distress.

"Ought to have done something for herself," said Mr. Polly, rebaiting his hook. "She was always talking of doing things. Why couldn't she?"

He watched the float oscillating gently towards quiescence.

"Silly to begin thinking about her," he said. "Damn silly!"

But once he had begun thinking about her he had to go on.

"Oh blow!" cried Mr. Polly presently, and pulled up his hook to find another fish had just snatched at it in the last instant. His handling must have made the poor thing feel itself unwelcome.

He gathered his things together and turned towards the house.

All the Potwell Inn betrayed his influence now, for here indeed he had found his place in the world. It looked brighter, so bright indeed as to be almost skittish, with the white and green paint he had lavished upon it. Even the garden palings were striped white and green, and so were the boats, for Mr. Polly was one of those who find a positive sensuous pleasure in the laying on of paint. Left and right were two large boards which had done much to enhance the inn's popularity with the lighter-minded variety of pleasure-seekers. Both marked innovations. One bore in large letters the single word "Museum," the other was as plain and laconic with "Omlets!" the spelling of the latter word was Mr. Polly's own, but when he had seen a whole boatload of men, intent on Lammam for lunch, stop open-mouthed, and stare and grin and come in and asked in a marked sarcastic manner for "omlets," he perceived that his inaccuracy had done more for the place than his utmost cunning could have contrived. In a year or so the inn was known both up and down the river by its new name of "Omlets," and Mr. Polly, after some secret irritation, smiled and was content. And the fat woman's omelettes were things to remember.

(You will note I have changed her epithet. Time works upon us all.)

She stood upon the steps as he came towards the house, and smiled at him richly.

"Caught many?" she asked.

"Got an idea," said Mr. Polly. "Would it put you out very much if I went off for a day or two for a bit of a holiday? There won't be much doing now until Thursday."

<h2 style="text-align:center">2</h2>

Feeling recklessly secure behind his beard Mr. Polly surveyed the Fishbourne High Street once again. The north side was much as he had known it except that Rusper had vanished. A row of new shops replaced the destruction of the great fire. Mantell and Throbson's had risen again upon a more flamboyant pattern, and the new fire station was in the Swiss-Teutonic style and with much red paint. Next door in the place of Rumbold's was a branch of the Colonial Tea Company, and then a Salmon and Gluckstein Tobacco Shop, and then a little shop that displayed sweets and professed a "Tea Room Upstairs." He considered this as a possible place in which to prosecute enquiries about his lost wife, wavering a little between it and the God's Providence Inn down the street. Then his eye caught a name over the window, "Polly," he read, "& Larkins! Well, I'm—astonished!"

A momentary faintness came upon him. He walked past and down the street, returned and surveyed the shop again.

He saw a middle-aged, rather untidy woman standing behind the counter, whom for an instant he thought might be Miriam terribly changed, and then recognised as his sister-in-law Annie, filled out and no longer hilarious. She stared at him without a sign of recognition as he entered the shop.

"Can I have tea?" said Mr. Polly.

"Well," said Annie, "you can. But our Tea Room's upstairs. . . . My sister's been cleaning it out—and it's a bit upset."

"It would be," said Mr. Polly softly.

"I beg your pardon?" said Annie.

"I said I didn't mind. Up here?"

"I daresay there'll be a table," said Annie, and followed him up to a room whose conscientious disorder was intensely reminiscent of Miriam.

"Nothing like turning everything upside down when you're cleaning," said Mr. Polly cheerfully.

"It's my sister's way," said Annie impartially. "She's gone out for a bit of air, but I daresay she'll be back soon to finish. It's a nice light room when it's tidy. Can I put you a table over there?"

"Let *me*," said Mr. Polly, and assisted.

He sat down by the open window and drummed on the table and meditated on his next step while Annie vanished to get his tea. After all, things didn't seem so bad with Miriam. He tried over several gambits in imagination.

"Unusual name," he said as Annie laid a cloth before him.

Annie looked interrogation.

"Polly. Polly & Larkins. Real, I suppose?"

"Polly's my sister's name. She married a Mr. Polly."

"Widow I presume?" said Mr. Polly.

"Yes. This five years—come October."

"Lord!" said Mr. Polly in unfeigned surprise.

"Found drowned he was. There was a lot of talk in the place."

"Never heard of it," said Mr. Polly. "I'm a stranger—rather."

"In the Medway near Maidstone. He must have been in the water for days. Wouldn't have known him, my sister wouldn't, if it hadn't been for the name sewn in his clothes. All whitey and eat away he was."

"Bless my heart! Must have been rather a shock for her!"

"It *was* a shock," said Annie, and added darkly: "But sometimes a shock's better than a long agony."

"No doubt," said Mr. Polly.

He gazed with a rapt expression at the preparations before him. "So I'm drowned," something was saying inside him. "Life insured?" he asked.

"We started the tea rooms with it, " said Annie.

Why, if things were like this, had remorse and anxiety for Miriam been implanted in his soul? No shadow of an answer appeared.

"Marriage is a lottery," said Mr. Polly.

"*She* found it so," said Annie. "Would you like some jam?"

"I'd like an egg," said Mr. Polly. "I'll have two. I've got a sort of feeling—. As though I wanted keeping up. . . . Wasn't particularly good sort, this Mr. Polly?"

"He was a *wearing* husband," said Annie. "I've often pitied my sister. He was one of that sort—"

"Dissolute?" suggested Mr. Polly faintly.

"No," said Annie judiciously; "not exactly dissolute. Feeble's more the word. Weak, 'e was. Weak as water. 'Ow long do you like your eggs boiled?"

"Four minutes exactly," said Mr. Polly.

"One gets talking," said Annie.

"One does," said Mr. Polly, and she left him to his thoughts.

What perplexed him was his recent remorse and tenderness for Miriam. Now he was back in her atmosphere all that had vanished, and the old feeling of helpless antagonism returned. He surveyed the piled furniture, the economically managed carpet, the unpleasing pictures on the wall. Why had he felt remorse? Why had he entertained this illusion of a helpless woman crying aloud in the pitiless darkness for him? He peered into the unfathomable mysteries of the heart, and ducked back to a smaller issue. Was he feeble?

The eggs came up. Nothing in Annie's manner invited a resumption of the discussion.

"Business brisk?" He ventured to ask.

Annie reflected. "It is,' she said, "and it isn't. It's like that."

"Ah!" said Mr. Polly, and squared himself to his egg. "Was there an inquest on that chap?"

"What chap?"

"What was his name?—Polly!"

"Of course."

"You're sure it was him?"

"What you mean?"

Annie looked at him hard, and suddenly his soul was black with terror.

"Who else could it have been—in the very clothes 'e wore?"

"Of course," said Mr. Polly, and began his egg. He was so agitated that he only realised its condition when he was half way through it and Annie safely downstairs.

"Lord!" he said, reaching out hastily for the pepper. "One of Miriam's! I haven't tasted such an egg for five years. . . . Wonder where she gets them! Picks them out, I suppose!"

He abandoned it for its fellow.

Except for a slight mustiness the second egg was very palatable indeed. He was getting on to the bottom of it as Miriam came in. He looked up. "Nice afternoon," he said at her stare, and perceived she knew him at once by the gesture and the voice. She went white and shut the door behind her. She looked as though she was going to faint. Mr. Polly sprang up quickly and handed her a chair. "My God!" she whispered, and crumpled up rather than sat down.

"It's *you*," she said.

"No," said Mr. Polly very earnestly. "It isn't. It just looks like me. That's all."

"I *knew* that man wasn't you—all along. I tried to think it was. I tried to think perhaps the water had altered your wrists and feet and the colour of your hair."

"Ah."

"I'd always feared you'd come back."

Mr. Polly sat down by his egg. "I haven't come back," he said very earnestly. "Don't you think it."

"'Ow we'll pay back the insurance now I *don't* know." She was weeping. She produced a handkerchief and covered her face.

"Look here, Miriam," said Mr. Polly. "I haven't come back and I'm not coming back. I'm—I'm a Visitant from Another World. You shut up about me and I'll shut up about myself. I came back because I thought you might be hard up or in trouble or some silly thing like that. Now I see you again—I'm satisfied. I'm satisfied completely. See? I'm going to absquatulate, see? Hey Presto right away."

473

He turned to his tea for a moment, finished his cup noisily, stood up.

"Don't you think you're going to see me again," he said, "for you ain't."

He moved to the door.

"That was a tasty egg," he said, hovered for a second and vanished.

Annie was in the shop.

"The missus has had a bit of a shock," he remarked. "Got some sort of fancy about a ghost. Can't make it out quite. So Long."

And he had gone.

## 3

Mr. Polly sat beside the fat woman at one of the little green tables at the back of the Potwell Inn, and struggled with the mystery of life. It was one of those evenings, serenely luminous, amply and atmospherically still, when the river bend was at its best. A swan floated against the dark green masses of the further bank, the stream flowed broad and shining to its destiny, with scarce a ripple—except where the reeds came out from the headland—the three poplars rose clear and harmonious against a sky of green and yellow. And it was as if it was all securely within a great warm friendly globe of crystal sky. It was as safe and enclosed and fearless as a child that has still to be born. It was an evening full of the quality of tranquil, unqualified assurance. Mr. Polly's mind was filled with the persuasion that indeed all things whatsoever must needs be satisfying and complete. It was incredible that life had ever done more than seemed to jar, that there could be any shadow in life save such velvet softnesses as made the setting for that silent swan, or any murmur but the ripple of the water as it swirled round the chained and gently swaying punt. And the mind of Mr. Polly, exalted and made tender by this atmosphere, sought gently, but sought, to draw together the varied memories that came drifting, half submerged, across the circle of his mind.

He spoke in words that seemed like a bent and broken stick thrust suddenly into water, destroying the mirror of the shapes they sought. "Jim's not coming back again ever," he said. "He got drowned five years ago."

"Where?" asked the fat woman, surprised.

"Miles from her. In the Medway. Away in Kent."

"Lor!" said the fat woman.

"It's right enough," said Mr. Polly.

"How d'you know?"

"I went to my home."

"Where?"

"Don't matter. I went and found out. He'd been in the water some days. He'd got my clothes and they'd said it was me."

"They?"

"It don't matter. I'm not going back to them."

The fat woman regarded him silently for some time. Her expression of scrutiny gave way to a quiet satisfaction. Then her brown eyes went to the river.

"Poor Jim" she said. "'E 'adn't much Tact—ever."

She added mildly: "I can't 'ardly say I'm sorry."

"Nor me," said Mr. Polly, and got a step nearer the thought in him. "But it don't seem much good his having been alive, does it?"

"'E wasn't much good," the fat woman admitted. "Ever."

"I suppose there were things that were good to him," Mr. Polly speculated. "They weren't *our* things."

His hold slipped again. "I often wonder about life," he said weakly.

He tried again. "One seems to start in life," he said, "expecting something. And it doesn't happen. And it doesn't matter. One starts with ideas that things are good and things are bad—and it hasn't much relation to what *is* good and what *is* bad. I've always been the skeptaceous sort, and it's always seemed rot to me to pretend we know good from evil. It's just what I've *never* done. No Adam's apple stuck in *my* throat, ma'am. I don't own to it."

He reflected.

"I set fire to a house—once."

The fat woman started.

"I don't feel sorry for it. I don't believe it was a bad thing to do—any more than burning a toy like I did once when I was a baby. I nearly killed myself with a razor. Who hasn't?—anyhow gone as far as thinking of it? Most of my time I've been half dreaming. I married like a dream almost. I've never really planned my life or set out to live. I happened; things happened to me. It's so with everyone. Jim couldn't help himself. I shot at him and tried to kill him. I dropped the gun and he got it. He very nearly had me. I wasn't a second too soon—ducking. . . . Awkward—that night was. . . . M'mm. . . . But I don't blame him—come to that. Only I don't see what it's all up to. . . .

"Like children playing about in a nursery. Hurt themselves at times. . . .

"There's something that doesn't mind us," he resumed presently. "It isn't what we try to get that we get, it isn't the good we think we do is good. What makes us happy isn't our trying, what makes others happy isn't our trying. There's a sort of character people like and stand up for and a sort they won't. You got to work it out and take the consequences. . . . Miriam was always trying."

"Who was Miriam?" asked the fat woman.

"No one you know. But she used to go about with her brows knit trying not to do whatever she wanted to do—if ever she did want to do anything—"

He lost himself.

"You can't help being fat," said the fat woman after a pause, trying to get up to his thoughts.

"*You* can't," said Mr. Polly.

"It helps and it hinders."

"Like my upside down way of talking."

"The magistrates wouldn't 'ave kept on the license to me if I 'adn't been fat. . . ."

"Then what have we done," said Mr. Polly, "to get an evening like this? Lord! look at it!" He sent his arm round the great curve of the sky.

"If I was a nigger or an Italian I should come out here and sing. I whistle sometimes, but bless you, it's singing I've got in my mind. Sometimes I think I live for sunsets."

"I don't see that it does you any good always looking at sunsets like you do," said the fat woman.

"Nor me. But I do. Sunsets and things I was made to like."

"They don't 'elp you," said the fat woman thoughtfully.

"Who cares?" said Mr. Polly.

A deeper strain had come to the fat woman. "You got to die some day," she said.

"Some things I can't believe," said Mr. Polly suddenly, "and one is your being a skeleton. . . ." He pointed his hand towards the neighbour's hedge. "Look at 'em—against the yellow—and they're just stingin' nettles. Nasty weeds—if you count things by their uses. And no help in the life hereafter. But just look at the look of them!"

"It isn't only looks," said the fat woman.

"Whenever there's signs of a good sunset and I'm not too busy," said Mr. Polly, "I'll come and sit out here."

The fat woman looked at him with eyes in which contentment struggled with some obscure reluctant protest, and at last turned them slowly to the black nettle pagodas against the golden sky.

"I wish we could," she said.

"I will."

The fat woman's voice sank nearly to the inaudible.

"Not always," she said.

Mr. Polly was some time before he replied. "Come here always when I'm a ghost," he replied.

"Spoil the place for others," said the fat woman, abandoning her moral solicitudes for a more congenial point of view.

"Not my sort of ghost wouldn't," said Mr. Polly, emerging from another long pause. "I'd be a sort of diaphalous feeling—just mellowish and warmish like. . . ."

They said no more, but sat on in the warm twilight until at last they could scarcely distinguish each other's faces. They were not so much thinking as lost in a smooth, still quiet of the mind. A bat flitted by.

"Time we was going in, O' Party," said Mr. Polly, standing up. "Supper to get. It's as you say, we can't sit here for ever."

## THE END

# A Note on Sources

Wells's early work has been reprinted with some frequency. In 1924 Wells collected and edited much of what he had published up to that time in *The Atlantic Edition of the Works of H. G. Wells*, 28 Volumes (London: T. Fisher Unwin, 1924). He also collected his short stories in *The Short Stories of H. G. Wells* (London: Ernest Benn, 1926).

SELECTIONS 1–3, "The Stolen Bacillus" (*Pall Mall Budget*, June 1894), "The Triumphs of a Taxidermist" (*Pall Mall Gazette*, 1894), and "Æpornis Island" (*Pall Mall Budget*, December 1894) were collected with a dozen other short stories in *The Stolen Bacillus and Other Incidents* (London: Methuen and Company, 1895).

SELECTION 4, from *The Time Machine*, *The National Review*, January through June, 1895. The first book edition of *The Time Machine* (London: William Heinemann, 1895) does not contain the episode describing the kangaroo-like evolution between the year 802,701 and the dark vision of the end of life on earth.

SELECTION 5, from *The Wheels of Chance* (London: J. M. Dent, 1896)

SELECTION 6, from *The Island of Doctor Moreau* (London: William Heinemann, 1896).

SELECTION 7, from *The Invisible Man* (London: C. Arthur Pearson, 1897)

SELECTION 8, from *The War of the Worlds* (London: William Heinemann, 1898).

SELECTION 9, from *The First Men in the Moon* (London: George Newnes, 1901).

SELECTION 10, from *The Food of the Gods* (London: Macmillan, 1904).

SELECTION 11, "The Country of the Blind," was first published in *The Strand Magazine*, April 1904, and later included in *The Country of the Blind and Other Stories* (London: Thomas Nelson and Sons, 1911).

SELECTION 12, from *In The Days of the Comet* (London: Macmillan, 1906).

SELECTION 13, from *Tono-Bungay* (London: Macmillan, 1909).

SELECTION 14, *The History of Mr. Polly* (London: Thomas Nelson and Sons, 1910).

# Bibliography

Anderson, Linda R. *Bennett, Wells, and Conrad: Narrative in Transition*. New York: St. Martins Press, 1988.

Batchelor, John. *H. G. Wells*. Cambridge: Cambridge University Press, 1985.

Bergonzi, Bernard. *The Early H. G. Wells: A Study of the Scientific Romances*. Manchester: Manchester University Press, 1961.

———, ed. *H. G. Wells: A Collection of Critical Essays*. Englewood Cliffs, N.J.: Prentice Hall, 1976.

Crossley, Robert. *H. G. Wells*. Mercer Island, Wash.: Starmont House, 1986.

Draper, Michael. *H. G. Wells*. London: Macmillan Publishers, 1987.

Hammond, John, ed. *H. G. Wells: Interviews and Recollections*. Totowa, N.J.: Barnes and Noble, 1980.

Huntington, John. *The Logic of Fantasy: H. G. Wells and Science Fiction*. New York; Columbia University Press, 1982.

———, ed. *Critical Essays on H. G. Wells*. Boston, Mass.: G. K. Hall, 1991.

Kemp, Peter. *H. G. Wells and The Culminating Ape*. New York: St. Martins Press, 1982.

MacKenzie, Norman, and Jeanne Mackenzie. *H. G. Wells*. New York: Simon and Schuster, 1973.

McConnell, Frank. *The Science Fiction of H. G. Wells*. New York: Oxford University Press, 1981.

Parrinder, Patrick. *H. G. Wells*. New York: Capricorn Books, 1970.

———. *H. G. Wells: The Critical Heritage*. London: Routledge & Kegan Paul, 1972.

———. *Shadows of the Future: H. G. Wells, Science Fiction, and Prophesy*. Syracuse, N.Y.: Syracuse University Press, 1995.

Parrinder, Patrick, and Christopher Rolfe, eds. *Wells Under Revision: Proceedings of the International H. G. Wells Symposium, London, July 1986*. Selinsgrove, Pa.: Susquehanna University Press, 1990.

Reed, John. *The Natural History of H. G. Wells*. Athens, Ohio: Ohio University Press, 1982.

Smith, David. *Desperately Mortal*. New Haven: Yale University Press, 1987.

Suvin, Darko, and Robert M. Philmus, eds. *H. G. Wells and Modern Science Fiction*. Lewisberg: Bucknell University Press, 1977.

West, Anthony. *H. G. Wells: Aspects of a Life*. New York: Random House, 1984.